Rick Steves'

Best of
EUROPE

*Make the Most Out of Every Day
and Every Dollar*

John Muir Publications
Santa Fe, New Mexico

Other JMP travel guidebooks by Rick Steves
  Asia Through the Back Door (with Bob Effertz)
  Europe 101: History, Art, and Culture for the
    Traveler (with Gene Openshaw)
  Kidding Around Seattle
  Mona Winks: Self-Guided Tours of Europe's Top Museums
    (with Gene Openshaw)
  Rick Steves' Europe Through the Back Door
  Rick Steves' Best of the Baltics and Russia (with Ian Watson)
  Rick Steves' Best of France, Belgium, and the Netherlands
    (with Steve Smith)
  Rick Steves' Best of Germany, Austria, and Switzerland
  Rick Steves' Best of Great Britain
  Rick Steves' Best of Italy
  Rick Steves' Best of Scandinavia
  Rick Steves' Best of Spain and Portugal
  Rick Steves' Phrase Books for French, German, Italian,
    Spanish/Portuguese, and French/Italian/German

John Muir Publications, P.O. Box 613, Santa Fe, NM 87504
© 1995 by Rick Steves
© 1995 France chapter by Rick Steves and Steve Smith
Cover © 1995 by John Muir Publications
All rights reserved.

Printed in the United States of America
First printing January 1995

ISSN 1078-7992
ISBN 1-56261-195-X

Distributed to the book trade by
Publishers Group West
Emeryville, California

Editor Risa Laib
Editorial Support Elizabeth Wolf, Dianna Delling
Production Kathryn Lloyd-Strongin, Sarah Johansson
Maps Dave Hoerlein
Research Assistance Steve Smith
Cover Design Tony D'Agostino
Interior Design Linda Braun
Typesetting Go West Graphics
Printer Banta Company
Cover Photo Vernazza on the Italian Riveria (see page 372),
          © Rick Steves

EUROPE'S BEST 28 DESTINATIONS

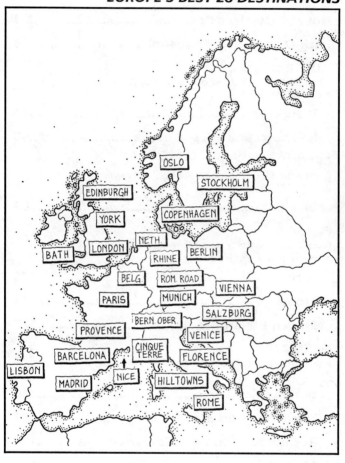

CONTENTS

ITALY
from *Rick Steves' Best of Italy*

THE NETHERLANDS
from *Rick Steves' Best of France, Belgium, and the Netherlands*

PORTUGAL
from *Rick Steves' Best of Spain and Portugal*

SCANDINAVIA
from *Rick Steves' Best of Scandinavia*

SPAIN
from *Rick Steves' Best of Spain and Portugal*

SWITZERLAND
from *Rick Steves' Best of Germany, Austria, and Switzerland*

HOW TO USE THIS BOOK

This book breaks Europe into its 28 top big-city, small-town, and rural destinations. It then gives you all the information and opinions necessary to wring the maximum value out of your limited time and money in each of them. If you plan two months or less in Europe, this lean and mean book is all you need.

Experiencing Europe's culture, people, and natural wonders economically and hassle-free has been my goal during my 20 years of traveling, tour guiding and travel writing. With this book, I pass on to you the lessons I've learned, updated for 1995.

Rick Steves' Best of Europe is the *crème de la crème* of places featured in six of my Country Guides. This book is balanced to include a comfortable mix of exciting big cities and cozy small towns: from Paris, London, and Rome to traffic-free Riviera ports, avalanche-zone Alpine villages, and mom-and-pop châteaus. It covers the predictable biggies and mixes in a healthy dose of Back Door intimacy. Along with Leonardo in the Louvre, you'll enjoy Caterina in her Cantina. I've been very selective. For example, rather than listing the countless castles, hill towns, and Riviera resorts, I recommend the best three or four of each.

I don't recommend anything just to fill a hole. If you find no tips on eating in a town, I've yet to find a restaurant worth recommending above the others. In the interest of smart use of your time, I favor hotels and restaurants handy to your sightseeing activities. Rather than list hotels scattered throughout a city, I describe my favorite two or three neighborhoods and recommend the best accommodations values in each, from $10 bunks to $120 doubles.

The best is, of course, only my opinion. But after two busy decades of travel writing, lecturing, and tour guiding, I've developed a sixth sense for what tickles the traveler's fancy.

This Information Is Accurate and Up-to-Date

Most publishers of guidebooks that cover Europe from top to bottom can afford an update only every two or three years (and even then, it's often by letter). Since this book covers only my favorite places, I am able to personally update it each year. Even with an annual update, things change. But if you're traveling with the current edition of this book, I guarantee you're using the most up-to-date information available. If you're packing an old book, you'll learn the seriousness of your mistake by Day 2. (Your trip costs about $10 per waking hour. Your time is valuable. This guidebook saves lots of time.)

2 to 22 Days Out . . . Modularity In! Europe's Top 28 Destinations

This book used to be called *2 to 22 Days in Europe* and was organized as a proposed 22-day route. It's now expanded to cover much more of Europe and restructured into a more flexible modular system. Each recommended module, or destination, is covered as a mini-vacation on its own, and each is filled with exciting sights; homey, affordable places to stay; and hard opinions on how to best use your limited time. As before, my assumption is that you have limited time and money. My goal remains to help you get the most travel experience out of each day and each dollar. Each destination is broken into these sections:

Planning Your Time, a suggested schedule with thoughts on how to best use your time;

Orientation, including transportation within a destination, tourist information, and a DCH map designed to make the text clear and your entry smooth;

Sights, with ratings: ▲▲▲—Don't miss; ▲▲—Try hard to see; ▲—Worthwhile if you can make it; No rating—Worth knowing about;

Sleeping and **Eating**, with addresses and phone numbers of my favorite budget hotels and restaurants;

Transportation Connections to nearby destinations by train; and

Route Tips for Drivers, with ideas on road-side attractions along the way.

The appendix is a traveler's tool kit with information on climate, exchange rates, telephone numbers, itineraries, and national tourist offices.

Browse through this book, choose your favorite destinations, link them up, and have a great trip. You'll travel like a temporary local, getting the absolute most out of every mile, minute, and dollar. And, as you travel the route I know and love best, you'll be meeting some of my favorite Europeans.

Costs

Five components make up your trip cost: airfare, surface transportation, room and board, sightseeing, and shopping/entertainment/miscellaneous.

Airfare: Don't try to sort through the mess. Get and use a good travel agent. A basic, round-trip U.S.A.-to-Europe flight should cost $600–$1000, depending on where you fly from and when. Consider "open-jaws" (flying into and out of different cities) and understand why the cheapest flights are so cheap.

Surface Transportation: Your best mode depends upon the time you have and the scope of your trip. For many it's a Eurailpass (3 weeks—$648; 2 months—$1,098; 15 days in 2 months—$740). Drivers can figure $200 per person (based on two people sharing car and gas) per week for car rental, tolls, gas, and insurance. Car rental is cheapest from the U.S.A. Leasing, for trips over three weeks, is cheaper.

Room and Board: You can thrive in Europe in 1995 on an overall average of $60 a day plus transportation costs. Students and tightwads will do it on $40. A $50 a day per person budget allows $30 for a double with breakfast, $5 for lunch, and $15 for dinner. Since lousy expensive hotels are major financial pitfalls, I've worked hard to assemble the best accommodations values for each stop. But budget sleeping and eating requires the skills and information covered below (or much more extensively in *Rick Steves' Europe Through the Back Door, 13th Edition*).

Sightseeing: In big cities, figure $5 to $10 per major sight, $2 for minor ones, $25 for splurge experiences (e.g., tours, lifts, gelato binges). An overall average of $15 a day works for most. Don't skimp here. After all, this category directly powers most of the experiences all the other expenses are designed to make possible.

Shopping/Entertainment/Miscellaneous: These costs can vary from nearly nothing to a small fortune. Figure $2 per coffee, beer, and ice cream cone, $1 per post card, $10 to

$20 for evening entertainment. Good budget travelers find that this category has little to do with assembling a trip full of life-long and wonderful memories.

Prices and Discounts

I've priced things in local currencies throughout, with rough exchange rates in each chapter. Prices, hours, and telephone numbers are accurate as of late 1994. Europe is always changing, so expect a few changes. While discounts are not listed in this book, seniors (60 and over), students (with International Student Identity Cards), and youths (under 18) often get discounts—but only by asking.

When to Go

May, June, September, and October are the best travel months. Peak season (July and August) offers the sunniest weather and the most exciting slate of activities—but the worst crowds. During this crowded time, it's best to arrive early in the day or to call your next hotel in advance. (Your receptionist can help you.) As a very general rule of thumb any time of year, the climate north of the Alps is mild (like Seattle) and south of the Alps it's like southern California. For information on weather, check the Climate Chart in the appendix. If you wilt in the heat, avoid the Mediterranean in the summer. If you want blue skies in the Alps, Britain, and Scandinavia, travel in the height of summer. Plan your itinerary to beat the heat (spring trip, start in the south and work north) but also to moderate culture shock (start in mild Britain and work south and east) and minimize crowds. Touristy places in the core of Europe (Germany, the Alps, France, Italy and Greece) suffer most from crowds.

Sample Itineraries

Priority of European Sightseeing Stops (By Train, and Considering Geographical Proximity)

5 days:	London, Paris
7 days, add:	Amsterdam, Haarlem
10 days, add:	Rhine, Rothenburg, Munich
14 days, add:	Salzburg, Swiss Alps
17 days, add:	Venice, Florence
21 days, add:	Rome, Cinque Terre

Europe's Best 70 Days—Whirlwind Tour

24 days, add:	Siena, Bavarian sights
30 days, add:	Arles, Barcelona, Madrid, Toledo
36 days, add:	Vienna, Berlin, Bath/Cotswolds
40 days, add:	Copenhagen, Edinburgh
70 days:	See Whirlwind Tour map below

(The Whirlwind Tour map and suggested 21-days itinerary include everything in the top 24 days except London.)

Europe's Best Three-Week Trip

Day	Plan	Sleep in
1	Arrive in Amsterdam	Haarlem
2	Amsterdam	Haarlem
3	Haarlem, drive to Rhine	Bacharach
4	Cruise Rhine, Rheinfels Castle	Rothenburg
5	Rothenburg	Munich
6	Munich	Munich
7	Castle Day in Bavaria and Tirol	Reutte
8	Drive to Venice	Venice
9	Venice	Venice

10	Drive to Siena	Siena
11	Florence	Siena
12	Rome	Rome
13	Rome	Rome
14	Cività di Bagnoregio	Vernazza
15	Italian Riviera, Cinque Terre	Vernazza
16	Drive into the Alps, Interlaken	Gimmelwald
17	Alps hike, Jungfrau/Schilthorn	Gimmelwald
18	Bern, Beaune in Burgundy	Beaune
19	Versailles, drop car	Paris
20	Paris	Paris
21	Paris	Paris

While this 21-day itinerary is designed to be done by car, with a few small modifications, it works great by train. The gas and tolls for this trip, if you take all the autobahns, will cost around $600 ($75 for tolls in Italy, $25 in France, $25 for your Swiss autobahn sticker, $15 for the Brenner Pass in Austria, 3,000 miles at 28 mpg = 107 gallons of gas at $4 a gallon = $430, plus parking—grand total = $600).

By train, this route would cost about $500 (sample 1995 prices for second-class train tickets: Amsterdam-Frankfurt $70, Frankfurt-Munich $60, Munich-Venice $55, Venice-Rome $45, Rome-Interlaken $90, Interlaken-Paris $110, and Paris-Amsterdam $70). First class is 50 percent more. A 10-days-in-2-months Eurail flexipass ($560), giving you first-class comfort, convenience, and the spontaneity to change your plans, costs only a few dollars more than second class point-to-point tickets.

Travel Smart

Be well-organized. Plan to hit the festivals, markets, and museums on the right day. Anticipate problem days: Mondays are bad in Amsterdam, Munich, Dachau, Florence, and Rome; Tuesdays are bad in Paris.

Sundays have the same pros and cons as they do for travelers in the U.S. City traffic is light, and sightseeing attractions are generally open, but shops and banks are closed. Rowdy evenings are rare on Sundays. Saturdays in Europe are virtually weekdays with earlier closing hours. Hotels in tourist areas are most crowded on Fridays and Saturdays.

Mix intense and relaxed periods—every trip needs a few slack days. Pace yourself. Assume you will return.

Plan ahead for banking, laundry, post office chores, and picnics. Buy and find a way to use up a telephone card in each country. During peak season, call ahead to confirm or reserve your room. Double-check and re-confirm things by phone. See the telephone tips in the appendix.

Upon arrival in a town, lay groundwork for your departure. Keep a list of all the things that should be taken care of, and whenever possible ward off problems *before* they happen. Take full advantage of local tourist offices. Wear your money belt, learn the local currency, and develop a simple formula to quickly estimate rough prices in dollars. If you expect to travel smart, you will.

Tourist Information Offices

Towns with tourism have a tourist information office, usually well-organized and English-speaking. The TI (as I'll call it) should be your first stop in a new city. Try to arrive, or at least telephone, before they close.

While the TI has listings of all the rooms and is eager to book you one, use their room-finding service only as a last resort. Across Europe, room-finding services are charging commissions from hotels, taking fees from travelers, and black-listing establishments that buck their materialistic rules. And TIs are unable to give hard opinions on the relative value of one place over another. The accommodations stakes are too high to go potluck through the TI. By using the listings in this book, you avoid that kind of "help."

Each country's national tourist office in the USA is a wealth of information (addresses are listed in appendix). Before your trip, get their free general information packet and request any specific information you may want such as city maps and schedules of up-coming festivals.

Recommended Guidebooks

Particularly if you'll be traveling beyond the recommended destinations, you may want some supplemental information. When you consider the improvements they'll make in your $3,000 vacation, $25 or $35 for extra maps and books is money well spent. Especially for several people traveling by car, the weight and expense are negligible.

The **Lonely Planet** guides to various European countries are thorough, well researched, and packed with good maps and hotel recommendations for low- to moderate-budget travelers. The hip **Rough Guide** series (British researchers, more insightful), and the highly opinionated **Let's Go** series (by Harvard students, better hotel listings) are great for students and vagabonds. If you're a backpacker with a train pass and interested in the youth and night scene, get Let's Go. The popular, skinny green Michelin guides to most southern countries and French regions are excellent, especially if you're driving. They're known for their city and sightseeing maps, dry but concise and helpful information on all major sights, and good cultural and historical background. English editions are sold locally at tourist shops and gas stations.

Other Rick Steves' Books

Rick Steves' Europe Through the Back Door, 13th Edition (Santa Fe, N.M.: John Muir Publications, 1995) covers all the budget travel skills with chapters on minimizing jet lag, packing light, driving, train travel, finding budget beds without reservations, changing money, theft, terrorism, hurdling the language barrier, health, travel photography, what to do with your bidet, ugly-Americanism, laundry, itinerary strategies, and more. The book also includes chapters on more than 35 of my favorite "Back Doors."

Rick Steves' Country Guides are a series of annually updated guidebooks covering the Baltics and Russia; Germany, Austria, and Switzerland; Great Britain; France; Italy; Scandinavia; and Spain and Portugal, just as this one covers Europe, only with much more extensive coverage (144 to 240 pages each). If you wish this book covered more of any particular country, my Country Guides are for you.

Europe 101: History and Art for the Traveler (co-written with Gene Openshaw, John Muir Publications, 1990) is designed for smart people who were sleeping in their history and art classes before they knew they were going to Europe. It gives you the story of Europe with your sightseeing needs in mind.

Mona Winks: Self-Guided Tours of Europe's Top Museums

(co-written with Gene Openshaw, John Muir Publications, 1993) gives you self-guided tours through Europe's most exhausting and important museums, with one- to three-hour tours of the major museums and historic highlights featured in this book, including Amsterdam's Rijksmuseum and Van Gogh Museum; Venice's St. Mark's, Doge's Palace, and Accademia Gallery; Florence's Uffizi Gallery, Bargello, Michelangelo's *David*, and a Renaissance walk; Rome's Colosseum, Forum, Pantheon, Vatican Museum, and St. Peter's Basilica; and Paris's Louvre, the exciting Orsay Museum, the Pompidou Modern Art Museum, and a tour of Europe's greatest palace, Versailles. If you're planning on touring these sights, *Mona* will be a valued friend.

Rick Steves' Phrase Books: After 20 years as an English-only traveler struggling with other phrase books, I've designed a series of practical, fun, and budget-oriented phrase books to help you ask the gelato man for a free little taste and the hotel receptionist for a room with no street noise. If you want to chat with your cabbie and make hotel reservations over the phone, the new pocket-sized Rick Steves Phrase Books for French; German; Italian; Spanish and Portuguese; and French/German/Italian together (John Muir Publications, 1995) will come in very handy.

Your bookstore should have (or can get) all of these books. Or you can order directly from John Muir Publications using the catalog at the back of this book.

Maps

Don't skimp on maps. Excellent Michelin maps are available throughout Europe (cheaper than in the U.S.A.) at bookstores, newsstands, and gas stations. Train travelers can do fine with a simple rail map (such as the one that comes with your train pass) and free city maps from the TI as you travel. But drivers should invest in good 1:200,000 scale maps. Learn the key to get the most sightseeing value out of your map and your car.

The maps in this book, drawn by Dave Hoerlein, are concise and simple. Dave, who travels in Europe every year as a tour guide, has designed the maps to help you locate recommended places and get to the tourist offices, where you'll find more in-depth maps (usually free) of the cities or regions.

Transportation in Europe

By Car or Train?

Each has pros and cons. Cars are an expensive headache in
big cities but give you more control for delving deep into the
countryside. Groups of three or more go cheaper by car. If
you're packing heavy (with kids), go by car. Trains are best
for city-to-city travel and give you the convenience of doing
long stretches overnight. By train, I arrive relaxed and well-
rested—not so by car. The latest permutation of the train
pass is a popular rail 'n' drive version, which lets you mix
train and car travel. When thoughtfully used, this pass gives
you the best of both transportation worlds economically.

Train Travel

A major mistake Americans make is relating public transportation in Europe to the pathetic public transportation
they're used to at home. By rail you'll have the continent
by the tail. And every year the trains of Europe are getting
speedier and more comfortable. While many simply buy
tickets as they go ("point to point"), the various train passes
give you the simplicity of ticket-free unlimited travel and,
depending on how much travel you do, often a tremendous
savings over regular point-to-point tickets. The Eurailpass
gives you several options (explained in the box on page 12).
For a free 40-page booklet analyzing the rail pass and point-
to-point ticket deals available both in the U.S.A. and in
Europe, call my office at 206/771-8303. The booklet is
updated each January. Regardless of where you get your
train pass, this information will help you know you're getting
the right one for your trip.

Eurailpass and the Europass

The granddaddy of European railpasses, Eurail gives you
unlimited rail travel on the national trains of 17 European
countries. That's 100,000 miles of track through all of western Europe including Ireland, Greece, and Hungary (but
excluding Great Britain and eastern Europe). The pass
includes many bonuses such as boat rides on the Rhine,
Mosel, Danube, and lakes of Switzerland, several international ferries (Ireland–France, Sweden–Finland, Italy–

Greece), and many buses including the Romantic Road bus tour through Germany. The new scaled-down three- to nine-country Europass offers a cheaper, more focused version of the Eurailpass. (Prices listed are good through 1995, kids 4 to 11 pay half fare, those under 4 ride free.)

Eurail Analysis

Break-even point? For an at-a-glance break-even point, remember that a one-month Eurailpass pays for itself if you're traveling from Amsterdam–Rome–Madrid–Paris on first class or Copenhagen–Berlin–Rome–Madrid–Amsterdam–Copenhagen on second class. A one-month Eurail Youthpass saves you money if you're traveling from Amsterdam to Rome to Madrid and back to Amsterdam. Passes pay for themselves quicker in the north where the cost per kilometer is higher. Check the map to follow, Europe by Rail: Time and Cost, to see if your planned travels merit the purchase of a train pass. If it's about even, go with the pass for the convenience of not having to buy tickets as you go and for the fun and freedom to travel "free."

    Using one Eurailpass or a series of country passes: While nearly every country has its own mini-version of the Eurailpass, trips covering several countries are usually cheapest with the budget whirlwind traveler's old standby, the Eurailpass. This is because the more days that are included in a pass, the cheaper your per-day cost is. A group of short country passes will each be high on that curve of diminishing per-day costs, while a Eurailpass (or Europass) with a longer life span offers a better deal overall. While a patchwork of individual country passes is usually more expensive and restrictive than the basic Eurailpass, for traveling in a single country, an individual country railpass (such as Francerail or Germanrail) is a better value.

    EurailDrive Pass analysis: The EurailDrive Pass is a great deal compared to the Eurail Flexipass if two are traveling together and would like three days of car rental. When you back out the cost of a four-day flexi railpass (based on 80 percent of the cost of a five-day pass), the drive option basically gives you three driving days at $14 a day ($7 per person, not including gas or CDW). That's better than the best weekly car rental rate and with the flexibility of a day here

1995 Eurailpasses

FIRST CLASS CONSECUTIVE DAY EURAILPASSES

15-day	$498
21-day	648
1-month	798
2-months	1098
3-months	1398

FIRST CLASS EURAIL SAVERPASSES

15-day Saverpass	$430 per person
21-day Saverpass	$550 per person
1-month Saverpass	$678 per person

Groups of 3 or more people traveling together at any time of year can buy a Saverpass. Two people traveling together can buy the pass only if all their train travel occurs within the months October through March. Just one pass is issued to the entire Saverpass traveling group. All or part of the group may travel with the pass during the period of validity.

Eurail territory

Europe: Countries that honor the Eurailpass.

FIRST CLASS EURAIL FLEXIPASSES

Any 5 days in 2 months	$348
Any 10 days in 2 months	560
Any 15 days in 2 months	740

SECOND CLASS EURAIL YOUTHPASSES

15 consecutive days	$398
1 month of consecutive days	578
2 months of consecutive days	768
Any 5 days out of 2 months	255
Any 10 days out of 2 months	398
Any 15 days out of 2 months	540

EUROPASSES

	1st. class	"Partner"	Youth 2nd.
3 adjacent countries (from France, Ger, Switz, Italy, Spain):			
5 days in 2 months	$280	$140	$198*
6 days in 2 months	318	159	226*
7 days in 2 months	356	178	254*
4 adjacent countries (from France, Ger, Switz, Italy, Spain):			
8 days in 2 months	$394	$197	$282
9 days in 2 months	432	216	310
10 days in 2 months	470	235	338
All 5 countries (France, Germany, Switz, Italy, Spain):			
11 days in 2 months	$508	$254	$366
12 days in 2 months	546	273	394
13 days in 2 months	584	292	422
14 days in 2 months	622	311	450
15 days in 2 months	660	330	478
Extra-cost add-ons available for Europasses:			
Austria:	$35	$35	$25
Belgium & Luxembourg:	22	22	16
Portugal:	22	22	16

Eurail Youthpasses are for travelers under age 26 only.

Europasses are good for use only in the countries shown. Countries of use must be adjacent to one another (for instance, you cannot buy a 3-country pass for Germany, Italy and Spain). Choosing "extra-cost add-ons" does not increase your number of days.

Europass "partner" deal: When one traveler buys a first class Europass at full fare, anyone traveling with that person can buy the same pass for half price. Partners must traveler together at all times. (e.g. Marco Polo pays $280 for a 5-day pass, Mary Polo gets the same pass for $140. If they bring the little Polos, they also go for $140 each.) No "partner" discounts for Youthpasses.
* These Youthpasses include 4 countries, not 3.

EUROPASS DRIVE

5 first class rail days and 3 car days out of 2 months, with extra car and rail days as an option

car categories	2 adults*	1 adult	extra car days
A-Economy	$345	$429	$45
B-Compact	379	475	59
C-Intermediate	399	509	69
Each add'l rail day	38	38	

* Prices per person for two traveling together. Adding more rail days can add more countries, as with regular Europass (see Europasses, above, for details).

FIRST CLASS EURAILDRIVE PASSES

Any 4 days of rail and 3 days of car in a 2 month period.

Car categories (Hertz or Avis)	2 adults	1 adult	extra car day
A-Economy (like Ford Fiesta)	$299	$385	$49 (per car)
B-Compact (like Ford Escort)	339	429	65
C-Intermediate (like Ford Sierra)	359	465	75

* Price per person. Third and fourth persons sharing car get a 4-day out of 2-month railpass for $249. You can add on up to 5 additional days of rail ($49 a day per person) and of car.

---

and a day there. Great areas for a day of joyriding include: the Dutch countryside; the Rhine, Mosel, or Bavaria in Germany; the Loire, Burgundy, Alsace, Provence, and the Pyrenees in France; Tuscany, Umbria, the Dolomites in Italy; the hill towns of Andalusia in Spain; Norway's fjord country; or "car hiking" in the Alps. When considering prices, remember that each day of car rental comes with about $30 of extra expenses (CDW, gas, insurance, parking) which you'll divide by the number in your party.

Car Rental

It's cheaper to arrange European car rentals in the United States, so check rates with your travel agent. Rent by the week, with unlimited mileage. If you'll be renting for three weeks or more, ask your agent about leasing, which is a scheme to save on insurance and taxes. I normally rent the smallest, least expensive model. Explore your drop-off options.

Your car rental price includes minimal insurance with a high deductible. A $10-a-day CDW (Collision Damage Waiver) insurance supplement, sold by car rental agencies, covers you for this deductible (which is as high as the value of the car). Ask your travel agent about money-saving alternatives (such as TravelGuard's insurance package) to this car rental agency rip-off.

Europe by Rail: Time and Cost

This map can help you determine quickly and painlessly whether a railpass is right for **your** trip. Add up the ticket prices for your route. If your total is about the same or more than the cost of a pass, buy the pass.

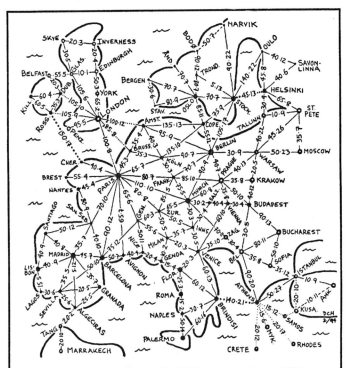

The first number between cities = **cost** in $US for a one-way, 2nd class ticket.
The second number = number of **hours** the trip takes.

- ● = Cities served by Eurailpass.
- ○ = Cities **not** served by Eurailpass (for example, if you want to go from Munich to Prague, you'll need to pay extra for the portion through the Czech Republic).
- ... = Boat crossings covered by Eurailpass.
- .... = Boat crossings **not** covered by Eurailpass.
- - - - = Bus connections **not** covered by Eurailpass.

Important: These fares and times are based on the Eurail Tariff Guide. Actual prices may vary due to currency fluctuations and local promotions. Local competition can cut the actual price of some boat crossings (from Italy to Greece, for example) by 50% or more. For approx. 1st class rail prices, multiply the prices shown by 1.5. In some cases faster trains (like the TGV in France) are available, cutting the hours indicated on the map. Travelers under age 26 can receive up to 1/3 off the 2nd class fares shown. Eurailpasses are **not** honored in the U.K., Turkey or Eastern Europe (except for Hungary).

Driving in Europe

For most of Europe, all you need is your valid U.S. driver's license and a car. Ask your rental company whether an international license is required. While gas is expensive, if you keep an eye on the big picture, paying $4 per gallon is more a psychological trauma than a financial one. I use the freeways whenever possible. They are free in Holland, Germany, and Austria; you'll pay a one-time road fee of about $25 as you enter Switzerland; and the Italian autostradas and French autoroutes are punctuated by toll booths (charging about $1 for every 10 minutes). The alternative to these super-freeways often is being marooned in rural traffic. The autobahn/-strada/-route usually saves enough time, gas, and nausea to justify its expense. Mix scenic country road rambling with high-speed autobahning, but don't forget that in Europe, the shortest distance between two points is the autobahn.

Parking is a costly headache in big cities. You'll pay about $20 a day to park safely. Ask at your hotel for advice. I keep a pile of coins in my ashtray for parking meters, public phones, wishing wells, and Laundromats.

Sleeping in Europe

Now that hotels are so expensive and tourist information offices' room-finding services are so greedy, it's more important than ever for budget travelers to have a good listing of rooms and call directly to make reservations. This book gives you a wide range of budget accommodations to choose from: youth hostels, bed and breakfasts, guest houses, pensions, small hotels, and a smattering of splurges. I like places with firm beds that are clean, small, central, traditional, not in other guidebooks, and friendly. Most places listed are a good value, having at least five of these seven virtues.

The Sleep Code

To save space while giving more specific information for people with special concerns, I've described my recommended hotels with a standard code. When there is a range of prices in one category, the price fluctuates with the season, size of room, or length of stay. Unless otherwise mentioned, room prices include breakfast.

S—single room or price for one person in a double.
D—double or twin-bedded room. Except in France, double beds are usually big enough for non-romantic couples.
T—three-person room (usually a double bed with a small single).
Q—four adult room (adding an extra child's bed to a T is usually cheaper).
B—private shower (most likely) or bath in the room. All rooms have a sink. Rooms with a B are often bigger and renovated, while the cheaper rooms with no B are often on upper floors or yet to be refurbished. Any room with no B has access to a B on the corridor (free unless otherwise noted).
WC—toilet in the room. I add this to distinguish between rooms with only a bath and rooms with a complete bathroom for hotels that offer D, DB, and DBWC rooms. Otherwise, many B rooms have a WC.
CC—accepts credit cards: **V**=Visa, **M**=Mastercard, **A**=American Express. Many also accept Diners Club (which I ignored). With no CC mentioned, assume it accepts only cash.
SE—the likelihood that a staff member speaks English is graded **A** through **F**.

So, a "DB-140 DM, CC-V, SE-A" hotel would offer two-person rooms with a private shower or bath for 140 deutsche marks, accept only Visa cards or cash, and have staff members who speak very good English.

Hotels

While most hotels listed in this book cluster around $60 per double, listings range from about $25 (very simple, toilet and shower down the hall) to $150 (maximum plumbing and more) per double. The cost is higher in big cities and heavily touristed cities and lower when off the beaten track. Three or four people can nearly always save lots of money by requesting one big room. Traveling alone can get expensive: a single room is often only 20 percent cheaper than a double. If you'll accept a room with twin beds and you ask for a double, you may needlessly be turned away. Get in the habit of asking for "a room for two people" if you'll take a twin or a double.

Rooms are generally very safe, but don't leave valuables laying around. More (or different) pillows and blankets are usually in the closet or available on request. Remember, in Europe towels and linen aren't always replaced every day. Drip-dry and conserve.

A very simple continental breakfast is almost always included. (Breakfasts in Europe, like towels and people, get smaller as you go south.) If you like juice and protein for breakfast, supply it yourself. I enjoy a box of juice in my hotel room and often supplement the skimpy breakfast with a piece of fruit and cheese. (A ziplock baggie is handy for petite eaters to grab an extra breakfast roll and slice of cheese, when provided, for a fast and free light lunch.)

To reserve a room from the U.S., write, fax, or call. If you write or fax, state your request (see fax template on page 528), clearly identifying the dates you intend to be there. (A two-night stay in August would be "two nights, 16/8/95 to 18/8/95"—European hotel jargon uses your day of departure.) You will receive a letter or fax back, usually requesting one night's deposit. For a deposit, you can usually send a $50 signed traveler's check, a bank draft in the local currency, or your credit card number. More often now, travelers reserve rooms with a simple phone call, leaving a credit card number as a deposit. You can pay with your card or by cash when you arrive (but if you don't show up, you'll be billed for one night). Ideally, the hotel receptionist will hold a room without a deposit if you promise to arrive by mid-afternoon and call to reconfirm two days before arrival. (Even if you've left a deposit, it's smart to reconfirm.) If you reserve or confirm a room through the local tourist information office, you pay a fee and your hotel loses the 10 percent "deposit." In fact, many hotels will tell the TI they are full when, in actuality, they are waiting for someone to come direct so they can avoid the TI fee. Whenever possible, go direct. Many of the prices in this book are special net prices based on the assumption that you'll book direct.

Except in July or August, I'd travel in Europe without making long-distance hotel reservations. I'd call a day or two ahead, or even the morning of the day I plan to arrive. The most highly recommended hotels in this book get lots of my

likable and reliable readers and will usually hold a room with
a phone call until 18:00 with no deposit. They are usually
accustomed to us English-speaking "monoglots." Use the
telephone! I've listed numbers with area codes. See the
appendix for long-distance dialing instructions.

Bed and Breakfasts

You can stay in private homes throughout Europe and enjoy
double the cultural intimacy for about half the cost of hotels.
You'll find them mainly in smaller towns and in the countryside. In Germany, look for *Zimmer* signs. For Italian *affitta
camere* and French *chambre d'hôte* (CH), ask at local tourist
offices. Doubles cost about $40, and you'll often share a
bathroom with the family. While your European hosts will
rarely speak English (except in Switzerland, the Low
Countries, and Scandinavia), they will almost always be
enthusiastic and a delight to share a home with.

Youth Hostels

For $6 to $15 a night, you can stay at one of Europe's
2,000 youth hostels. While most hostels admit non-
members for an extra fee, it's best to join the club and buy
a youth hostel card before you go. Except in Bavaria, where
you must be under 27, travelers of any age are welcome as
long as they don't mind dorm-style accommodations and
making lots of traveling friends. Cheap meals are sometimes available, and kitchen facilities are usually provided
for do-it-yourselfers. Expect crowds in the summer, snoring, and lots of youth groups giggling and making rude
noises while you try to sleep. Family rooms and doubles are
often available on request, but it's basically boys' dorms and
girls' dorms. Many hostels are locked up from about 10:00
until 17:00, and an 23:00 curfew is often enforced.
Hosteling is ideal for those traveling single: prices are by
the bed, and you'll have an instant circle of friends. More
and more hostels are getting their business acts together,
taking credit card reservations over the phone and leaving
sign-in forms on the door for each available room. In the
north, many hostels have a new telex reservation system
that allows you to reserve and pay for your next hostel from
the one before. If you're serious about traveling cheaply,

have a card, carry your own sheets, and cook in the members' kitchens.

Camping
For $4 to $10 per person per night, you can camp your way through Europe. Camping is an international word, and you'll see signs everywhere. All you need is a tent and a sleeping bag. Good campground guides are published, and camping information is also readily available at local tourist information offices. Europeans love to holiday camp. It's a social rather than a nature experience, and a great way for traveling Americans to make local friends. Many campgrounds will have a small grocery and washing machines, and some even come with discos and mini-golf. Camping is ideal for families traveling by car on a tight budget.

Eating European
Europeans are masters at the art of fine living. That means eating long and eating well. Two-hour lunches, three-hour dinners, and endless hours sitting in outdoor cafés are the norm. Americans eat on their way to an evening event and complain if the check is slow in coming. For Europeans, the meal is an end in itself, and only rude waiters rush you.

Even those of us who liked dorm food will find that the local cafés, cuisine, and wines become a highlight of our European adventure. This is sightseeing for your palate, and even if the rest of you is sleeping in cheap hotels, your taste buds will want an occasional first-class splurge. You can eat well without going broke. But be careful: you're just as likely to blow a small fortune on a mediocre meal as you are to dine wonderfully for $12.

Restaurants
When restaurant hunting, choose a place filled with locals, not the place with the big neon signs boasting "We Speak English and Accept Credit Cards." Look for menus posted outside; if you don't see one, move along. Also look for set-price menus (called the tourist menu, *menu del giorno*, *prix-fixé*, or simply *le menu*) that give you several choices among several courses. Galloping gourmets, bring a menu translator. (The Marling Menu Master, available in French, Italian,

and German editions, is excellent.) These days, tipping is included in the bill in most cafés and restaurants. If it's not, the menu will tell you. Still, it's polite to leave the change if service was good.

When you feel like something halfway between a restaurant and a picnic, look for food stands selling take-out sandwiches and drinks, delis with stools or a table, a department store self-service, or simple little eateries for fast and easy, sit-down restaurant food. Many restaurants offer a good value, three- to five-course "menu" at lunch only. The same menu often costs much more at dinner.

Picnic

So that I can afford the occasional splurge in a nice restaurant, I like to picnic. Besides the savings, picnicking is a great way to sample local specialties. And, in the process of assembling your meal, you get to plunge into local markets like a European.

Gather supplies early. Many shops close for a lunch break. While it's fun to visit the small specialty shops, local *supermarchés* give you the same quality with less color, less cost, and more efficiency.

When driving I organize a backseat pantry in a cardboard box with plastic cups, paper towels, a water bottle (the standard, disposable, European half-liter plastic mineral water bottle works fine), a damp cloth in a ziplock baggie, a Swiss army knife, and a petite tablecloth. To take care of juice once and for all, stow a rack of liter boxes of orange juice in the trunk. (Look for "100%" on the label or you'll get a sickly sweet orange drink.)

Picnics (especially French ones) can be an adventure in high cuisine. Be daring: try the smelly cheeses, midget pickles, ugly pâtés, sissy quiches, and minuscule yogurts. Local shopkeepers are happy to sell small quantities of produce and even slice and stuff a sandwich for you. A typical picnic for two might be fresh bread (half loaves on request), two tomatoes, three carrots, 100 grams of cheese, (about a quarter-pound, called an *etto* in Italy), 100 grams of meat, two apples, a liter box of orange juice, and yogurt. Total cost for two: about $8.

Red Tape, Time, News, and Mail

You currently need a passport but no visa and no shots to travel in Europe. In Europe—and in this book—you'll be using the 24-hour clock. After 12:00 noon, keep going— 13:00, 14:00, and so on. For anything over 12, subtract 12 and add p.m. (14:00 is 2 p.m.).

This book lists in-season hours for sightseeing attractions. Off-season, roughly October through April, expect generally shorter hours, more lunchtime breaks, fewer English guided tours, and fewer activities.

Europeans arrange dates by day/month/year, so Christmas would be 25-12-95. What we Americans call the second floor of a building is the first floor in Europe. Commas and periods are often switched, so there are 5.280 feet in a mile, and your temperature should be 98,6 degrees.

Crossing borders in Europe is easy. Sometimes you won't even realize it's happened. When you do change countries, however, you change money, postage stamps, gas prices, ways to flush a toilet, words for "hello," figurehead monarchs, and breakfast breads. Plan ahead for these changes. Coins and stamps are worthless outside their home countries. Just before crossing a border, I use up my coins on gas, candy, souvenirs, or a telephone call home.

Americans keep in touch with the *International Herald Tribune* (published almost daily via satellite throughout Europe). Every Tuesday, the European editions of *Time* and *Newsweek* hit the stands with articles of particular interest to European travelers. Sports addicts can get their fix from *USA Today*. News in English will only be sold where there's enough demand: in big cities and tourist centers. If you're concerned about how some event might affect your safety as an American traveling abroad, call the U.S. consulate or embassy in the nearest big city for advice.

If you must have mail sent, direct it to a few hotels along your route (reserve in advance) or use the American Express Mail Service (free to those with an AmEx card or checks, get specifics from AmExCo). Allow 10 days for U.S.-to-Europe mail delivery. Federal Express makes two-day deliveries—for a price.

Stranger in a Strange Land

We travel all the way to Europe to enjoy differences—to become temporary locals. Certain truths that we find "God-given" or "self-evident," like cold beer, ice, a bottomless cup of coffee, long, hot showers, body odor smelling bad, and bigger being better, are suddenly not so true. One of the benefits of travel is the eye-opening realization that there are logical, civil, and even better alternatives. Fit in! If the beds are too short, the real problem is that you are too long. Don't look for things American on the other side of the Atlantic and you're sure to enjoy a good dose of local hospitality.

Send Me a Postcard, Drop Me a Line

While I do what I can to keep this book accurate and up-to-date, things are always changing. If you enjoy a successful trip with the help of this book and would like to share your discoveries, please send any tips, recommendations, criticisms, or corrections to me at Europe Through the Back Door, Box 2009, Edmonds, WA 98020. To update the book before your trip or to share tips, tap into our free computer bulletin board travel information service (206/771-1902:1200 or 2400/8/N/1). All correspondents will receive a two-year subscription to *Back Door Travel*, our quarterly newsletter (it's free anyway). Tips actually used will get you a first-class railpass in heaven.

Judging from the positive feedback and happy postcards I receive from travelers using this book, it's safe to assume you're on your way to a great European vacation—independent, inexpensive, and experienced with the finesse of an seasoned traveler. Thanks, and happy travels!

BACK DOOR TRAVEL PHILOSOPHY
As Taught in *Rick Steves' Europe Through The Back Door*

Travel is intensified living—maximum thrills per minute and one of the last great sources of legal adventure. Travel is freedom. It's recess, and we need it.

Experiencing the real Europe requires catching it by surprise, going casual . . . "Through the Back Door."

Affording travel is a matter of priorities. (Make do with the old car.) You can travel—simple, safe, and comfortable—anywhere in Europe for $50 a day plus transportation costs. In many ways, spending more money only builds a thicker wall between you and what you came to see. Europe is a cultural carnival, and time after time, you'll find that its best acts are free and the best seats are the cheap ones.

A tight budget forces you to travel close to the ground, meeting and communicating with the people, not relying on service with a purchased smile. Never sacrifice sleep, nutrition, safety, or cleanliness in the name of budget. Simply enjoy the local-style alternatives to expensive hotels and restaurants.

Extroverts have more fun. If your trip is low on magic moments, kick yourself and make things happen. If you don't enjoy a place, maybe you don't know enough about it. Seek the truth. Recognize tourist traps. Give a culture the benefit of your open mind. See things as different, but not as better or worse. Every culture has much to share.

Of course, travel, like the world, is a series of hills and valleys. Be fanatically positive and militantly optimistic. If something's not to your liking, change your liking. Travel is addicting. It can make you a happier American, as well as a citizen of the world. Our Earth is home to nearly six billion equally important people. It's humbling to travel and find that people don't envy Americans. They like us, but with all due respect, they wouldn't trade passports.

Globe-trotting destroys ethnocentricity. It helps you under-stand and appreciate different cultures. Travel changes people. It broadens perspectives and teaches new ways to measure quality of life. Many travelers toss aside their hometown blinders. Their prized souvenirs are the strands of different cultures they decide to knit into their own character. The world is a cultural yarn shop, and Back Door Travelers are weaving the ultimate tapestry. Come on, join in!

VIENNA

Vienna (Wien) is a head without a body. Built to rule the once-grand Habsburg Empire—Europe's largest—she started and lost World War I, and with it her far-flung holdings. Today, you'll find a grand capital of 1.7 million people (20 percent of Austria's population) ruling a small, relatively insignificant country. Culturally, historically, and from a sightseeing point of view, this city is the sum of its illustrious past. The city of Freud, Kafka, Brahms, a gaggle of Strausses, Maria Theresa's many children, and a dynasty of Holy Roman emperors, is right up there with Paris, London, and Rome.

Planning Your Time

Vienna is worth two days and two nights. It's not only packed with great sights, but it's a joy to kill time in. It seems like it was designed to help people simply meander through a day. To be grand tour efficient, you could sleep in and sleep out on the train (Berlin, Venice, the Swiss Alps, Paris, and the Rhine are each handy night-trains away). But then you'd miss the Danube and Melk. I'd come in from Salzburg via Hallstatt, Melk, and the Danube and spend two days this way:

Day 1:
- 9:00 Orientation tour by tram around the Ring (as explained below).
- 10:00 Stroll Karntnerstrasse (take care of TI and ticket needs).
- 11:00 Tour the Opera.
- 12:00 Browse the Naschmarkt, lunch there.
- 14:00 Kunsthistorisches Museum.
- 17:00 Coffee at the Kursalon for Strauss concert.
- 19:00 Choose classical music, Heuringer wine garden, Prater amusement park, or an Opera performance.

Day 2:
- 9:00 St. Stephen's Cathedral.
- 10:00 Tour Hofburg, Neue Burg, Treasury.
- 13:00 Schonbrunn Palace (possibly, if by car, on way out of town before 5-hour drive to Hall near Innsbruck).

Orientation

(tel. code within Austria: 0222, from outside: 1)
Vienna, or *Wien* ("veen") in German, is bordered on three
sides by the Vienna woods (*Wienerwald*) and the Danube
(*Donau*). To the southeast is industrial sprawl. The Alps,
which arc across Europe from Marseilles, end at Vienna's
wooded hills. These provide a popular playground for walking and new-wine drinking. This greenery's momentum carries on into the city. You'll notice over half of Vienna is park
land, filled with ponds, gardens, trees, and statue memories
of Austria's glory days.

   Think of the city map as a target. The bull's-eye is the
cathedral, the first circle is the Ring and the second is the
Gürtel. The old town snuggles around towering St. Stephan's
Cathedral south of the Donau, bound tightly by the Ringstrasse. The Ring, marking what was the city wall, circles the
first district (or "*Bezirk*"). The Gürtel, a broader ring road,
contains the rest of downtown (Bezirke 2 through 9).

Greater Vienna

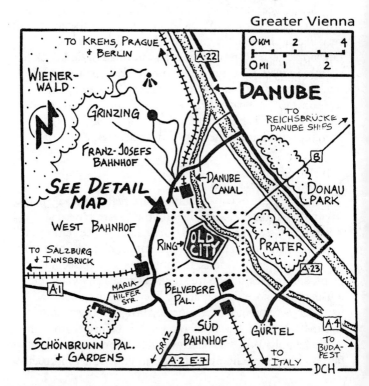

Addresses start with the Bezirk followed by street and street number. Any address higher than the ninth Bezirk is beyond the Gürtel, far from the center. The middle two digits of Vienna postal codes show the district, or Bezirk. The address "7, Lindengasse 4" means in the seventh district, #4 on Linden Street. Its postal code would be 1070. Nearly all your sightseeing will be done in the core first district or along the Ringstrasse. As a tourist, concern yourself only with this small old center, and sprawling Vienna suddenly becomes manageable.

Note that Vienna's telephone code changes: 0222 (from inside Austria) and 1 (from outside Austria).

Arriving by Train at the West Station

Most train travelers arrive at the Westbahnhof. To get situated, walk across the street from the station to the tram/metro station. At a VOR-Fahrkarten machine, push the yellow 24 *stunden* button, the window says 50 AS, put in 50 AS, and get your 24-hour ticket. (The tobacco shop around the corner also has tickets.) To get to the center (and very likely, your hotel), go down the escalator to line U3. Down two levels (on the left) is an information desk. Ask for a free city map. One more level down takes you to the U3 tracks. Catch a train in the direction U3-Erdberg. Ride five stops to "Stephansplatz," escalate in the exit direction "Stephansplatz," and you hit the cathedral. The TI is a 5-minute stroll down the busy Karntnerstrasse pedestrian street.

Tourist Information

The "tourist offices" at the stations are really hotel agencies. Vienna's real tourist office, behind the Opera House at Kärntnerstrasse 38 (daily 9:00-19:00, later in the stations, tel. 0222/513 8892 or 211140) is excellent. Stop here first with a list of needs and questions, to confirm your sightseeing plans, and to pick up the free (and essential) city map, the museum brochure (listing hours, telephone numbers, and handicap accessibility), the monthly program of concerts, and the fact-filled *Youth Scene* magazine. Consider investing in the handy 50-AS *Vienna from A to Z* book. Every important building has a numbered flag banner that keys into this

guidebook. *A to Z* numbers are keyed into the TI's city map.
When lost, find one of the "famous-building flags" and
match its number to your map. If you're at a "famous
building" check the map to see what other key numbers are
nearby, then check the *A to Z* book to see if you want to
drop by. Many of my recommended accommodations keep
enough tourist maps and brochures on hand to make a trip
to the TI unnecessary.

Trains
The Westbahnhof serves most of Europe and the Süd-
bahnhof serves Italy, the former Yugoslavia, and Greece.
Subway line U3 connects the Westbahnhof with the center,
tram D takes you from the Südbahnhof downtown, and tram
#18 connects the two stations. Trains to Krems and the
Wachau Valley leave from a third station, the Franz Josef
Bahnhof. For train information, call 1717.

Getting Around Vienna
To take simple and economical advantage of Vienna's fine
transit system of buses, trams, and sleek, easy subways, buy
the 24-hour (50 AS) or 72-hour (130 AS) subway/bus/tram
pass at a station machine or Tabak shops near any station.
Take a moment to study the eye-friendly city center map on
metro station walls to internalize how the metro and tram
system can help you. I use it mostly to zip along the Ring
(tram #1 or #2). The 15-AS transit map is overkill. The necessary routes are listed on the free tourist city map. Without
a pass, blocks of five tickets for 85 AS are cheaper than the
20-AS individual tickets (each good for one journey with
necessary changes) you can buy from the driver. Eight-strip
8-day, 265-AS transit passes can be shared (for instance, four
people for two days each, a 33% savings over the cheap 24-
hour pass). Stamp your pass as you enter the system or tram
(which puts a time on it). Vienna's comfortable, honest, and
easy-to-flag-down taxis start at 24 AS and mount quickly;
you'll pay about 60 AS for a 5-minute ride.

Sights—Vienna
▲▲▲Ringstrasse Tour—In the 1860s, Emperor Franz
Josef had the city's ingrown medieval wall torn down and

replaced with a grand boulevard 190 feet wide, arcing nearly 3 miles around the city's core. The road pre-dates all the buildings that line it. So what you'll see is neo-Gothic, Neoclassical, and neo-Renaissance. One of Europe's great streets, it's lined with many of the city's top sights. Trams #1 and #2 circle the whole route and so should you.

In fact, start your Vienna visit with this do-it-yourself, 20-AS, circular, 30 minute tour. "Tours" leave every 5 minutes. Tram #1 goes clockwise, tram #2 counterclockwise. Since most of the sights are on the outside of the Ring, tram #2 is best (sit on the right). Ideally, catch it at the Opera house (but anywhere will do). With a 24-hour ticket, you can jump on and off as you go. This is great, since trams come so often. With no ticket, give the driver 20 AS as you board (good for only one ride). All described sights on this tour are on the right unless I say "on left." For more information on many of the sights, see individual descriptions later in the chapter. Let's go:

• Just past the Opera (on left), the city's main pedestrian drag, Karntnerstrasse, leads to the zigzag roof of St. Stephan's Cathedral. This tour makes a 360-degree circle, staying about this far from that spire.

• (At first corner, look towards tall fountain) Schwartzenberg Platz, with its equestrian statue of Prince Charles Schwartzenberg who battled Napoleon, leads to the Russian monument (behind the fountain). This monument was built in 1945 as a forced thanks to the Soviets for liberating Austria from the Nazis. Formerly a sore point, now it's just ignored.

• (Going down Schubertring) The white and yellow concert hall behind the trees is the Kursalon, opened in 1867 by the Strauss brothers who directed many waltzes here. (See below for free concert times.) The huge Stadtpark (city park) honors 20 great Viennese musicians and composers with statues.

• (Immediately after next stop) The gilded statue of Waltz King Johann Strauss shows him holding his violin as he did when he conducted his orchestra.

• (While at next stop at end of park) On the left, a green and white statue of Dr. Karl Lueger honors the popular man who was mayor of Vienna until 1910.

• (At next bend in road) The quaint building with military helmets decorating each window was the Austrian ministry of war, back when that was a serious operation. Field Marshal Radetzky, a military big shot in the 19th century under Franz Joseph, still sits on his high horse.

• (At next corner) The white domed building is the Urania, Franz Joseph's 1910 observatory. Lean forward and look behind it for a peek at the huge red cars of the huge 100-year-old Ferris wheel in Vienna's Prater Park.

• Now you're rolling along the Danube Canal. The actual Danube is father to the right. This was the site of the original Roman town, Vindobona. In three blocks on the left (opposite the Mobile station) you'll see the ivy-covered walls and round romanesque arches of St. Ruprechts, the oldest church in Vienna (built on a bit of Roman ruins). By about 1200 Vienna had grown to fill the area within this ring road.

• (Leaving the canal, turning up Schottenring, at first stop)

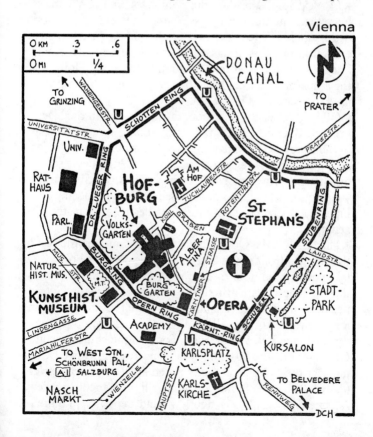

On the left, the pink and white neo-Renaissance temple of money, the Borse, is Vienna's stock exchange.

• (Next stop, at corner) The huge frilly neo-Gothic church is a "votive church" built in 1853 as a thanks to God when an assassination attempt on Emperor Franz Joseph failed. Ahead on the right is the Vienna University building which faces (on the left, behind the gilded angel) a bit of the old city wall.

• (At next stop) The neo-Gothic City Hall, flying the flag of Europe, towers over Rathaus Platz, a festive site of outdoor movies and concerts. Immediately across the street (on left) is the Hofburg Theater.

• (At next stop) The neo-Greek temple of democracy houses the Austrian Parliament. The lady with the golden helmet is Athena, the goddess of wisdom. Across the street (on left) is the Volksgarten.

• (At next stop) Ahead on the right is the first of Vienna's huge twin museums. Empress Maria Theresa sits as a mother of 13 should between the two. On her left is the city's greatest collection of paintings, the Kunsthistorisches Museum. She is facing (on your left) the grand gate to the Hofburg, the emperor's palace. Of the five arches, only the emperor used the center.

• (50 yards after the next stop, through a gate in the black iron fence) On the left is the much-adored statue of Mozart in the Burggarten, which until 1880 was the private garden of the emperor. A few yards later (on the left) Goethe sits in a big thought-provoking chair playing trivia with Schiller (on your right). Behind the statue of Schiller is the Academy of Fine Arts. Vienna had its share of intellectual and creative geniuses.

• Hey, there's the Opera again. Jump out and see the rest of the city. (In front of the Opera, there's a person who'd love to take you on a bus tour of what you just did . . . for 220 AS.)

▲▲St. Stephan's Cathedral—Stephansdom is the Gothic needle around which Vienna spins. Hundreds of years of history are carved in its walls and buried in its crypt (open at various times, tel. 515 52 526). Tours of the church are in German only, the 50-minute daily mass is impressive (schedule near the entry), and the crowded lift to the north tower (daily 9:00-18:00) shows you a big bell but a mediocre view. A great view is only 343 tightly wound steps away, up the spiral staircase to the watchman's lookout, 246 feet above the postcard stand (south tower, daily 9:00-17:30). From the top, figure out the town, using your *Vienna from A to Z* to locate the famous sights. The church is nearly always open. The Cathedral Museum (Dom und Diözesan Museum, 10:00-16:00, Thursday until 18:00, Sunday until 13:00, closed Monday) is at Stephansplatz 6. Downstairs in the Stephansplatz subway stop you can peer into the 13th-century Virgilkapelle.

▲**Stephansplatz**—The atmosphere of the church square is colorful and lively. And at the nearby *Graben* (ditch) street, topnotch street entertainment dances around an exotic plague monument. It was common for cities, when they survived their plague ordeal, to thank God with a monument. Vienna's is one of the grandest plague monuments.

Remains of the Habsburgs—Visiting the remains is not as easy as you might imagine. These original organ donors left their bodies in the Kaisergruft (Capuchin Crypt, a block behind the Opera on Neuer Markt, daily 9:30-16:00, 30 AS, 5-AS map with a Habsburg family tree and a chart locating each coffin), their hearts in St. George Chapel in the church of the Augustinian friars (near the Hofburg, Augustinerstrasse 3, church open daily but to see the goods you'll have to talk to a priest), and their entrails in the crypt below the cathedral. Don't tripe. Rather than chasing down all these body parts, remember that the magnificence of this city is the real remains of the Habsburgs. Pan up. Watch the clouds glide by the ornate gables of Vienna.

▲▲**Hofburg**—The complex, confusing, imposing Imperial Palace with 640 years of architecture, demands your attention (and with so many turnstiles, a lot of your money). The winter residence of the Habsburg rulers until 1918, it's still the home of the Spanish Riding School, the Vienna Boys' Choir, the Austrian president's office, and several important museums. The *A to Z* book sorts out this time-blackened, jewel-stained mess. Or, if overwhelmed, tour the Imperial Apartments first where you can buy a glossy, four-language, 50-AS Hofburg guidebook with a fine map and great photos. While you could lose yourself in its myriad halls and court-yards, I suggest you focus on three things:

▲▲**The Imperial Apartments**—These lavish, Versailles-type "wish I were God" royal rooms are a small, downtown

version of the grander Schönbrunn Palace. Tour one palace
or the other. If rushed, these suffice. (40 AS, 65 AS with a
German tour, Monday-Saturday 8:30-12:00, 12:30-16:00,
Sunday 8:30-12:30, entrance from courtyard under the dome
of St. Michael's Gate, Michaelerplatz, tel. 587 555 4515.) For
any information, you'll have to spring for the 50-AS book.

▲▲**Treasury**—The Weltliche and Geistliche Schatzkammer (secular and religious treasure room) is expensive,
but if you want historic and lavish jewels, these are by far the
best on the Continent. Reflect on the glitter of ten rooms
filled with scepters, swords, crowns, and orbs. Double-
headed eagles, gowns, dangles, and gem-studded bangles.
Remember that these were the Holy Roman Emperor's—
the divine monarch's. The highlight is Room 11 with the
11th-century Reichskrone—the crown of the Holy Roman
Emperor—and two cases of Karls des Grossen (Charlemagne)
riches. (60 AS, 10:00-18:00, closed Tuesday; follow Schatzkammer signs through the Swiss Courtyard; you can rent a
30-minute Walkman tour for 30 AS or 40 AS for two).

▲**The Neue Burg**, or new palace, is the last (from this century, built for Franz Ferdinand but never used) and most
impressive addition to the palace. Its grand facade arches
around Heldenplatz (the horse-and-buggy depot). The
palace houses three museums: an armory, historical musical
instruments, and classical statuary from ancient Ephesus.
The musical instruments are particularly entertaining, with
the free radio headsets which play appropriate music in each
room. Wait at the orange dots for the German description to
finish and you'll often hear the instruments you're seeing.
Stay tuned in, as graceful period music accompanies your
wander through the neighboring halls of medieval
weaponry—a killer collection of crossbows, swords, and
armor. An added bonus is the chance to just wander all alone
among those royal Habsburg halls, stairways, and painted
ceilings (30 AS for all three collections, 10:00-18:00, closed
Tuesday, almost no tourists).

▲▲▲**Opera**—The Staatsoper facing the Ring, just up from
Stephansdom and next to the TI, is a central point for any
visitor. While the critical reception of the building 130 years
ago led the architect to commit suicide, and it's been rebuilt
since the World War II bombings, it's a dazzling place.

(Visits by 40-minute tour only, daily in English, July and August at 10:00, 11:00, 13:00, 14:00, 15:00, and often at 16:00; other months, afternoons only; 40 AS. Tours are often canceled for rehearsals and shows, so check the posted schedule or call 51444-2613.)

The **Vienna State Opera**, with the Vienna Philharmonic Orchestra in the pit, is one of the world's top opera houses. There are performances almost nightly, except in July and August, with expensive seats and shows normally sold out. Unless Pavarotti is in town, it's almost always easy to get one of 500 *Stehplatz* (standing-room spots, which are 20 AS-30 AS; the downstairs spots are best). Join the *Stehplatz* lineup at the Abendkasse side door where the number of available places is posted. The ticket window opens an hour before each performance. Buy your place at the padded leaning rail. If your spot isn't numbered, tie your belt or scarf to it and you can slip out for a snack and return to enjoy the performance. If less than 500 people are in line, don't line up early.

▲▲▲**The Kunsthistorisches Museum**—This exciting museum showcases the great Habsburg collection of work by Dürer, Rubens, Titian, Raphael, and especially Brueghel. There's also a fine display of Egyptian, classical, and applied arts, including a divine golden salt shaker by Cellini. If you forgot to pack the chapter from *Mona Winks*, the museum sells a pamphlet on the top 21 paintings and offers English tours (usually at 11:00 and 15:00) The paintings are hung on one floor, and clear charts guide you (Tuesday-Sunday 10:00-18:00, Thursday until 21:00, closed Monday, tel. 52177-0489; 100 AS, 50 AS for students and seniors over 60).
Natural History Museum—In the twin building facing the art museum, you'll find moon rocks, dinosaur stuff, and the Venus of Willendorf—at 30,000 years old, the world's eldest sex symbol.
▲**Academy of Fine Arts**—This small but exciting collection includes works by Bosch, Botticelli, and Rubens, a Venice series by Guardi, and a self-portrait by 15-year-old Van Dyck (3 minutes from the Opera at Schillerplatz 3, Tuesday, Thursday, and Friday 10:00-14:00, Wednesday 10:00-13:00 and 15:00-18:00, Saturday and Sunday 9:00-13:00, tel. 5881-6225).

▲**Belvedere Palace**—The elegant palace of Prince Eugene
of Savoy (the still-much-appreciated conqueror of the
Turks), and later home of Franz Ferdinand, houses the
Austrian Gallery of 19th- and 20th-century art. Skip the
lower palace and focus on the garden and the top floor of the
upper palace (*Oberes Belvedere*) for a winning view of the city
and a fine collection of Jugendstil art, Klimt, and Kokoschka
(30 AS, Tuesday-Sunday 10:00-17:00, entrance at Prince
Eugen Strasse 27, tel. 784-1580). Your ticket includes the
Austrian baroque and gothic art in the Lower Palace.

▲▲▲**Schönbrunn Palace**—Schloss Schönbrunn, the
Habsburg's summer residence, is second only to Versailles
among Europe's palaces. Located 7 kilometers from the center, it was the Habsburgs' summer residence. It is big—1,441
rooms—but don't worry, only 40 rooms are shown to the
public. (95 AS for 40 rooms with guided tour, 80 AS to romp
unattended through 22 rooms; 8:30-17:00, until 16:30 off-
season, Saturday and Sunday are most crowded; 12:00 to
14:00, and after 16:00 are least crowded, call to confirm
English tour times, tel. 8111-3238.) Nearby is an impressive
coach museum (30 AS, Wagenburg). The sculpted gardens
and Gloriette Park above the palace are open until dusk and
free. The long walk to Gloriette earns you only a fine
city view.

▲**Jugendstil**—Vienna gave birth to its own curvaceous
brand of Art Nouveau around the turn of the century.
Jugendstil art and architecture is popular around Europe
these days, and many come to Vienna solely in search of it.
The TI has a brochure laying out Vienna's 20th-century
architecture. The best of Vienna's scattered Jugendstil sights
are in the Belvedere Palace collection, the Karlsplatz subway
stop, and the clock on Höher Market.

KunstHausWien—This "make yourself at home" modern
art museum, opened in 1990, is a real hit with lovers of modern art. It features the work of local painter/environmentalist
Hundertwasser (daily 10:00-19:00, 3, Weissgerberstrasse 13,
tel. 7120491). Nearby, the one-with-nature
Hundertwasserhaus is a complex of 50 lived-in apartments.
This was built in the 1980s as a breath of architectural fresh
air in a city of blocky, suicidally predictable apartment com-
plexes. It's not open to visitors but worth visiting for its

fun-loving exterior and the Hundertwasser festival of shops across the street, and just to annoy its residents (third district, at Löwengasse and Kegelgasse).

▲**City Park**—Vienna's Stadtpark is a waltzing world of gardens, memorials to local musicians, ponds, peacocks, music in bandstands, and local people escaping the city. Notice the Jugendstil entry at the Stadtpark subway station. The Kursalon orchestra plays Strauss waltzes daily in summer 16:00-18:00 and 19:45-22:35. You can buy an expensive cup of coffee for a front row seat or join the local senior citizens and ants on the grass for free.

▲**Prater**—Vienna's sprawling amusement park tempts any visitor with its huge (220-foot-high, 9:00-23:00 in summer), famous, and lazy Ferris wheel called the Riesenrad; endless food places; and rides like the roller coaster, bumper cars, and Lilliputian Railroad. This is a fun, goofy place to share the evening with thousands of Viennese (subway: Praterstern). For a family local-style dinner, eat at Schweizerhaus or Wieselburger Bierinsel.

▲**Naschmarkt**—Vienna's ye olde produce market bustles daily, near the Opera along Wienzeile Street. It's likeably seedy and surrounded by sausage stands, cafés, and theaters. Each Saturday it's infested by a huge flea market (Monday-Friday 6:00-18:30, Saturday 6:00-13:00). For a picnic park, walk one block down Schleifmuhlgasse.

City Tours—Vienna offers many organized city tours. Of its many guided walks, only a few are in English (90 min, 120 AS, tel. 51450, brochure at TI). The 75-minute "Getting Acquainted" German/English bus tour (220 AS, daily from the Opera at 10:30, 11:45, 15:00, and in summer, 16:30, no reservations necessary, tel. 712 46 830) is essentially what I covered above in the Ring Tour with a detour to and stop at the Upper Belvedere palace. While pricey, it's intensely informative and a good introduction if you're lazy. Cut out at the palace (which is near the end) if you'd like to see its collection of Klimt and Art Nouveau. The TI has a booklet listing all city tours. Eva Prochaska (tel. 513 5294, 1, Weihburggasse 13-15) is an excellent private guide who charges 1,100 AS for a half-day.

Sunbathing—Like most Europeans, the Austrians, worship the sun. Their lavish swimming centers are as much for tanning as for swimming. The Krapfenwaldbad, in the high-class 19th district, is renowned as the gathering point for the best-looking topless locals. For the best man-made island beach scene, head for the "Danube Sea," Vienna's 20 miles of beach along the Danube Island (subway: Donauinsel).

▲▲**Music**—Vienna is Europe's music capital. It's music *con brio* from October through June, with things reaching a symphonic climax during the Vienna Festival each May and June. Sadly, in July and August, the Boys' Choir, the Opera, and many more music companies are—like you—on vacation. But the "Summer of Music" festival (special brochure at TI, tel. 4000-8410 for information, tickets at the Wien Ticket pavilion on Karntnerstrasse next to the Opera House) assures that even in the summer you'll find lots of top-notch classical music.

Music is becoming a tourist trap in Vienna. Powdered, wigged Wolfgang Mozarts are peddling tickets in the streets at all the sights. Every night 400-AS-a-seat Mozart and Strauss concerts are put on for the flash-in-the-pan classical fans. And anything booked in advance or through a box office comes with a stiff 25 percent booking fee. (There's a handy box office next to the TI behind the Opera.)

But you can get great classical music at fair prices (150 AS-250 AS). Get the TI's monthly program. If a show comes to you, be wary. The Summer of Music pavilion (mentioned above) sells tickets to its shows at net prices. If you call a concert hall directly, they can advise you on the availability of (cheaper) tickets at the door. Vienna takes care of its starving artists (and tourists) by offering lots of standing-room places to top-notch music and opera nearly free. And remember, the Philharmonic plays at each opera in a great setting with easy-to-get nearly free standing rooms tickets. But anyone with a yen for classical music can get good tickets virtually any day of the year upon arrival in Vienna. Ask about the free opera films in front of the Opera (festive young atmosphere).

If you opt for the touristy Wiener Mozart Konzerte concert, it is a fun trip back into Vienna's glory days of music. The orchestra, clad in historic costumes and looking better than it sounds, performs Mozart's greatest hits, including his famous opera arias.

The Vienna Boys' Choir—The boys sing (heard but not seen, from a high balcony) at mass in the Imperial Chapel of the Hofburg (entrance at Schweizerhof) at 9:15 Sundays except from July through mid-September. Seats (50 AS-220 AS) must be reserved at least two months in advance but standing room is free and open to the first 60 or 70 who line up. Concerts (on stage in the Vienna Concert Hall) are also given Fridays at 15:30 in May, June, September, and October (320 AS-400 AS, fax 011-43-1-5871268 from U.S.A.). They're nice kids, but for my taste, not worth all the commotion.

Spanish Riding School—Performances are usually sold out in advance, but training sessions in a chandeliered baroque hall are open to the public (February-June and September-October, Tuesday-Saturday 10:00-12:00, 70 AS at the door; Josefsplatz in the Hofburg; long line; if you don't like horses, not worth the trouble).

▲**Wine Gardens**—The Heurige is a uniquely Viennese institution celebrating the *Heuriger*, or new wine. It all started when the Habsburgs let Vienna's vintners sell their own wine tax-free for 300 days a year. Several hundred families opened up Heurigen wine-garden restaurants clustering around the edge of Vienna, and a tradition was born. Today they do their best to maintain their old village atmosphere, serving the homemade new wine (the last vintage, until November 11th) with light meals and strolling musicians. For the whole story and a complete listing with maps and descriptions of each district, get the TI's *Heurige in Wien* brochure.

Of the many Heurigen suburbs, Grinzing is the most famous and touristy. **Neustift am Walde** (bus #35A) is a local favorite with plenty of tourists but much of its original charm intact. **Weinbau Wolff** (on the main street at Rathstrasse 46, tel. 442335) has a great buffet spread, hundreds of outdoor tables, and the right ambience. **Haus Zimmermann** (bus #35A to Mitterwurzergasse 20, tel. 441207) is a local favorite, more remote, low key, and without music. For more crowds and music with your meal, visit Beethoven's home in Heiligenstadt (tel. 371287, tram #37 to last stop and walk 10 minutes to Pfarrplatz). At any of these places you'll fill your plate at a self-serve cold-cut buffet. Waitresses will then take your wine order (30 AS per quarter-liter). Many locals claim it takes several years of practice to distinguish between Heuriger and vinegar. For a near-Heurigen experience right downtown, drop by **Gigerl Stadtheuriger** (see Eating, below).

▲**The Viennese Coffeehouse**—In Vienna, the living room is the coffeehouse down the street. This tradition is just another example of the Viennese expertise in good living. Each of Vienna's many long-established (and sometimes even legendary) coffeehouses has its individual character. They offer newspapers, pastries, sofas, elegance, and a "take all the time you want" charm, for the price of a cup of coffee. You may want to order *brauner* (with a little milk) rather than *schwarzer* (black).

Some of my favorites are: **Café Hawelka** (1, Doro-theergasse 6, closed Tuesday, just off the Graben) with a rumpled "brooding Trotsky" atmosphere, paintings on the walls by struggling artists who couldn't pay, a saloon wood flavor, chalkboard menu, smoked velvet couches, international selection of newspapers, and a phone that rings for regulars; the **Central** (1, Herrengasse 14, Jugendstil decor, great *topfen strudel*); the Jugendstil **Café Sperl** (6, Gumpen-dorfer 11, just off Naschmarkt); and the basic, untouristy **Café Ritter** (6, Mariahilferstrasse 73, near several of my recommended hotels).

Honorable Mention—There's much, much more. The city museum brochure lists everything. If you're into Esperanto, undertakers, tobacco, clowns, firefighting, or the homes of dead composers, you'll find them all in Vienna. Several good museums that try very hard but are submerged in the greatness of Vienna include: Historical Museum of the City of Vienna (Karlsplatz, Tuesday-Sunday 9:00-16:30); Folkloric Museum of Austria (8, Laudongasse 15, tel. 43 89 05); and the Museum of Military History (Heeresgeschichtliches Museum, at 3, Arsenal, Objekt 18, 10:00-16:00, closed Friday, one of Europe's best if you like swords and shields). The Jesuit Church (9 on your city map, on Dr. Ignaz Seipel Platz) has a fascinating false dome painted on its ceiling. Mariahilferstrasse, with over 2,000 shops, is the best-value shopping street. For a walk in the Vienna Woods, catch the U-4 subway to Heiligenstadt, then bus #38A to Kahlenberg for great city views, woodsy restaurants, and plenty of trails.

Nightlife
If old music or new wine isn't your thing, Vienna has plenty of alternatives. For an up-to-date rundown on fun after dark, get the TI's free *Youth Scene* magazine. An area known as the Bermuda *Dreieck* (Triangle), north of the cathedral between Rotenturmstrasse and Judengasse, is the hot local night-spot with lots of classy pubs or *Beisles* (such as Krah Krah, Salzamt, and Roter Engel) and popular music spots (such as the disco P1 at Rotgasse 3, tel. 535 9995, and Jazzland at Franz Josefs-Kai 29, tel. 533 2575). **Tunnel**, popular with local students, features live music and cheap meals (daily 11:00-02:00, a 10-minute walk behind the Rathaus at 8, Florianigasse 39, tel. 423465). Most lively on a balmy summer evening is the scene at the Danube Island.

Sleeping in Vienna
(11 AS = about $1, tel. code within Austria: 0222, from outside: 1)
Plan to spend 150 AS for a hostel bed or 550 AS for the cheapest pension or hotel double with breakfast. I list two places well worth the 1,200-AS splurge. Beds in central private homes are cozier but no cheaper than simple pensions. In the summer, call a few days in advance. All places listed speak some English. Most will hold a room without a deposit if you promise to arrive before 17:00. I've chosen two handy and central locations. Unless otherwise noted, prices include a sparse continental breakfast. (Street addresses start with the district. Postal code is 1XX0 with XX being the district.)

Sleep code: **S**=Single, **D**=Double/Twin, **T**=Triple, **Q**=Quad, **B**=Bath/Shower and usually a toilet, **WC**=Toilet (used only when some rooms are bath only), **CC**=Credit Card (Visa, Mastercard, Amex), **SE**=Speaks English (graded **A** through **F**).

Sleeping Between the Westbahnhof and the Opera
Lively Mariahilferstrasse connects the West Station with the center. The U3 subway line goes from the Westbahnhof, down Mariahilferstrasse to the Cathedral. (For the step-by-step, see Orientation, above.) The first three listings are near the train station. The next five are about halfway

between the station and the opera (two stops from the station down subway U3 to Neubaugasse). The rest are scattered mostly north of Mariahilferstrasse and equally close to the center. Mariahilferstrasse is an attraction in itself for east Europeans who come to shop. While most places are on stern and quiet no-nonsense side roads, the nearby Mariahilferstrasse is a comfortable and vibrant area filled with local shops, cafés, and Viennese being very Viennese.

Pension Funfhaus (D-540 AS, DB-620 AS, T-810 AS, TB-900 AS; 2-bedroom apartments-1,080 AS; Frau Susi Tersch promises these prices through 1995 if you book direct with this book; no elevator, free and easy street parking, closed mid-November through February; Sperrgasse 12, tel. 892-3545 or 892-0286) is big, clean, stark, and quiet with 100 beds split between the main building and an annex. Just a 7-minute walk behind the station (leaving, turn right, and right again on Mariahilferstrasse, go 7 blocks to Sperrgasse), this place is an exciting value, especially the spacious, bright DB rooms.

Hotel Stiegelbrau (DB-1,200 AS, with buffet breakfast, CC:VMA, free parking, 5 minutes' walk behind the station following directions for Funfhaus, at Mariahilferstrasse 156, tel. 892-3335, fax 892-3221-495), for my rich and lazy readers, is a fine value with all the comforts and a restaurant that spills into its breezy, laid-back garden.

Hospiz CVJM (S-360 AS, SB-400 AS, D-640 AS, DB-700 AS, T-900 AS, TB-1,020 AS, Q-1,160 AS, QB-1,320 AS, CC:VM; WC always on the hall, no elevator, free parking; leaving the Westbahnhof, walk 2 blocks left and 1 block right to 7, Kenyongasse 15, tel. 523-1304, fax 523-1304-13) is 47 beds big, sterile, quiet, old-institutional and well-run, as you'd expect a YMCA to be.

Privatzimmer F. Kaled (D-500 AS, DB-600 AS, T-750 AS, 150 AS for extra bed, optional 50-AS breakfast in bed, prices promised through 1995 if you book direct, stay two nights, and have this book; 7, Lindengasse 42, tel. 523-9013, fax 526-2513, credit-card number secures reservation, try to arrive before 14:00), is lovingly run by Tina, Fred, and Freddie. It's bright, airy, homey, quiet, and has TVs (with CNN) in each of the four rooms. Hardworking Tina is a mini tourist information service. (Being Hungarian, she has good contacts for people visiting Budapest.)

Pension Lindenhof (S-350 AS, SBWC-450 AS, D-580 AS, DB-800 AS, showers 20 AS; 7, Lindengasse 4, tel. 523-0498, fax 523-7362) is well-worn but clean, filled with plants, and run with Bulgarian strictness.

Pension Hargita (S-400 AS, SB-450 AS, D-550 AS, DB-650 AS, DBWC-800 AS, TBWC-1,000 AS, QBWC-1,100 AS, breakfast-40 AS, cheaper in winter, corner of Mariahilferstrasse and Andreasgasse, 7, Andreasgasse 1, tel. 526-1928, fax 526-0492), with 19 generally small, bright, and tidy rooms, is a bit overpriced but very handy (right at the Neubaugasse U3 stop).

Pension Quisisana (S-300 AS, SB-370 AS, D-500 AS, DB-600 AS, DBWC-700 AS, third person-270 AS, prices promised through 1995 with book; simple doubles are small with head-to-toe twin beds—it's worth going DB; no elevator; a block south of Mariahilferstrasse at Windmuhlgasse 6, 1060 Vienna, tel. 587-7155, fax 587-7156-33), whose name is Latin for "Don't Worry, Be Happy," is old and ramshackle, but with comfortable rooms and a great value.

Privatzimmer Hilde Wolf (S-395 AS, D-540 AS, T-790 AS, Q-1,025 AS, with a big, friendly, family-style breakfast; 20-AS showers; prices promised through 1995; 4, Schleifmühlgasse 7, A-1040 Vienna, tel. 586 5103, reserve by telephone and credit-card number), 3 blocks off Naschmarkt near U2-Karlsplatz, is a homey place one floor above an ugly entry, with four huge rooms like old libraries. Hilde loves her work, offers free use of her washing machine, and even offers to babysit if traveling parents need a break. Her helpful husband, Otto, speaks English. From West Station: tram # four stops to Eichenstr, tram #62 six stops to Paulinergasse. For a real home in Vienna, this is my best listing.

Jugendherberg Myrthengasse/Neustiftgasse (IYHF hostel, 150 AS with sheets and breakfast in 4- or 6-bed rooms, plus 40 AS for non-members; 7, Myrthengasse 7, tel. 523-6316, fax 523-5849) is actually two hostels side by side. Both are new, cheery, and well-run, have a 1:00 curfew, will hold a rooms until 16:00, and offer 60-AS meals. June and September are the tightest because of visiting school groups.

Across the street is **Believe It Or Not** (160 AS per bed, 110 AS November-April; Myrthengasse 10, no sign, ring apt #14, tel. 526 4658), a friendly and basic place with one big coed dorm for ten travelers. Run by an entrepreneurial and charming Pole named Gosha. Locked up 10:30-12:30; kitchen facilities; no curfew; snorers sleep here at their own risk.

Pension Wild (D-560 AS, T-790 AS, Q-1,000 AS, with plenty of showers and WCs on the floor, CC:VMA, near U2: Rathaus, at Langegasse 10, 1080 Vienna, tel. 406-5174, fax 402-2168) has 14 fine rooms and a good, "keep it simple and affordable" attitude. There are plenty of handy extras, like full kitchen facilities on each floor and cheap passes to health club downstairs.

Pension Andreas (SB-600 AS, DB-820 AS, DBWC-890 AS, big DBWC-990 AS, CC:MA, elevator; near U2: Rathaus, at 8, Schlösselgasse 11, tel. 405-3488, fax 405-3488-50) is run by a gracious woman named Sevil; this well-located, classy, quiet place is a worthwhile splurge.

Turmherberge "Don Bosco" (65-AS dorm beds, 25 AS for sheets, 40 AS extra for those without IYHF cards; 3, Lechnerstrasse 12, tel. 713 1494) is far away but I stayed there in 1973 and it's still the cheapest place in Vienna (with some of the same staff)—Catholic-run, closed 12:00-17:00, open to people of any sex from March-November. Take tram #18 to Stadionbrucke from south station, and U3 to Kardinal Nagl Platz from the west station.

Sleeping Within the Ring, in the Old City Center

These places offer less room per schilling but are comfortable, right in the town center, with elevators and a straight shot by subway from the west station. (For the step-by-step, see Orientation, above.) All are popular and take easy telephone reservations, so call well ahead. The first three are in the shadow of St. Stephan's Cathedral, on or near the Graben where the elegance of Old Vienna strums happily over the cobbles. The last two listings are near the Opera (Subway: Karlsplatz) just off the famous Kärntnerstrasse, near the tourist office and 5 minutes from the cathedral.

At **Pension Nossek** (SB-600 AS, SBWC-770 AS, DBWC-950 AS to 1,050 AS; 1, Graben 17, tel. 533 7041, fax 535 3646) an elevator takes you above any street noise into a

Frau Bernad's world where the dog and children seem to be placed among the lace and flowers by an interior designer. Street musicians, a pedestrian mall filled with cafés, and the plague monument are just outside your door. This is the best value of these first three.

Pension Aclon (S-450 AS, SB-500 AS, SBWC-700 AS, D-800 AS, DB-1,060 AS, T-1,130 AS, TB-1,460, Q-1,430, QB-1,810; CC:VMA, elevator only goes up; 1, Dorotheergasse 6-8, tel. 512 79 400, fax 513 8751) is quiet, elegant, sternly-run, a block off the Graben, above a classic Vienna café.

Pension Pertschy (DB-1,080 AS-1,280 AS depending on the size, third person-300 AS, CC:VM; 1, Habsburger-gasse 5, tel. 53449, fax 5344949) is more hotelesque than the others, with more energy put into the lobby than its rooms. Its big rooms are huge (ask to see a few); those on the court-yard are most quiet.

Pension Suzanne (SB-750 AS, DB-930 AS-1,130 AS, third person-300 AS; push doorbell with caution; 1, Walfischgasse 4, tel. 513 2507, fax 5132500), as baroque and doily as you'll find in this price range, is wonderfully located a few yards from the Opera. Suzanne is professional and quiet, with pink elegance bouncing on every bed.

Hotel zur Wiener Staatsoper (SB-900 AS, DB-1,200 AS, TB-1,450 AS, buffet breakfast, CC:VMA; 1, Kruger-strasse 11, tel. 513 1274, fax 513 1274-15) is quiet, rich, and hotelesque. Its rooms come with high ceilings, chandeliers, and fancy carpets on parquet floors, a great value for this locale and ideal for people whose hotel taste is a cut above mine.

Eating in Vienna

The Viennese appreciate the fine points of life, and right up there with the waltz is eating. The city has many atmos-pheric restaurants. As you ponder the menus, remember that Vienna's diverse empire may be gone but its flavor lingers. You'll find Slavic and Eastern European specialties here along with wonderful desserts and local wine.

On nearly every corner you can find a colorful *Beisl* (Viennese tavern) filled with poetry teachers and their stu-dents, couples loving without touching, housewives on their way home from cello lessons, and waiters who thoroughly enjoy serving hearty food and good drink at an affordable price. All my recommended eateries are within a 5-minute walk of the cathedral.

These **Wine Cellars** are fun, touristic but typical, in the old center of town with painless prices and lots of smoke. **Esterhazykeller** is an inexpensive, rowdy, smoky, self-service cellar (16:00-21:00, at Haarhof near Am Hof, off Naglergasse). **Augustinerkeller** is fun, inexpensive, and, like the Esterhazykeller, touristy (10:00-24:00, next to the Opera under the Albertina Museum on Augustinerstrasse). **Figlmüller** is a popular Beisl famous for its giant schnitzels (one can easily feed two) near St. Stephan's Cathedral (just down the 6 Stephansplatz alley at Wollzeile 5). **Zu den Drei Hacken** is famous for its local specialties (indoor/outdoor, 1, Singerstrasse 28, closed Saturday and Sunday). The less touristy **Pürstner** restaurant (indoor/outdoor, 150-AS meals, a block away at Riemergasse 10, tel. 512-6357, nightly) is pleasantly drenched in Old World atmosphere. **Melker Stiftskeller,** the least touristy, is a deep and rustic cellar with hearty, inexpensive meals and new wine (17:00-24:00, closed Sunday and Monday, halfway between Am Hof and the Schottentor subway stop at Schottengasse 3, tel. 5335530).

For a near "Heuriger" experience (a la Grinzing, see above) without leaving the center, eat at **Gigerl Stadtheuriger** (indoor/outdoor, near the cathedral, a block off Kärntner-strasse, a few cobbles off Rauhensteingasse on Blumenstock, tel. 5134431). Just point to what looks good (cold cuts, spinach strudel, good salads, all sold by the weight, around 150 AS/plate) and choose from many local wines.

Brezel-Gwölb, a wonderfully atmospheric wine cellar with outdoor dining on a quiet square, serves delicious, moderately priced light meals, fine Krautsuppe, and local dishes. It's ideal for a romantic late glass of wine (daily 11:30-1:00, Ledererhof 9, off Am Hof). Around the corner, **Zum Scherer Sitz u. Stehbeisl** (Judenplatz 7, near Am Hof, Monday-Saturday 11:00-1:00, Sunday 17:00-24:00) is just as untouristy, with indoor or outdoor seating, a soothing woody atmosphere, intriguing decor, and local specialties.

For a fast, light and central lunch: **Rosenberger Markt Restaurant** is a popular highway chain that opened an elegant super branch a block toward the cathedral from the

Opera. This place, while not cheap, is brilliant: friendly and efficient, with special theme rooms to dine in, offering a fresh and healthy cornucopia of food and drink and a cheery break from the heavy, smoky, traditional eateries (lots of fruits and vegetables, 11:00-23:00, Maysedergasse 2, just off Kärntner Strasse). The Billa supermarket (2 blocks down Walfischgasse from the Opera) is picnic-friendly.

Buffet Trzesniewski is justly famous for its elegant and cheap finger sandwiches (8 AS) and small beers (9 AS). Three sandwiches and a *kleines Bier* (Pfiff) make a fun, light lunch (just off the Graben, across from the brooding Café Hawelka, on Dorotheergasse, Monday-Friday 9:00-19:30, Saturday 9:00-13:00).

Naschmarkt, 5 minutes beyond the Opera, is Vienna's best Old World market (6:30-18:00, Saturday until 13:00, closed Sunday), with very fresh produce, plenty of cheap eateries, cafés, and sausage stands. For about the cheapest hot meal in town, lunch at the nearby **Technical University's Mensa** (cafeteria) in the huge, modern, light-green building just past Karlsplatz at Wiedner Hauptstrasse 8-19, second floor (Monday-Friday 12:00-14:00). Anyone is welcome to eat here with a world of students. The snack bar is less crowded but the bigger mensa on the same floor has a more interesting selection.

Wherever you're eating, some vocabulary will help. Three interesting drinks to try are *Grüner Veltliner* (dry, white wine, any time), *Traubenmost* (a heavenly grape juice on the verge of wine, autumn only, sometimes just called *Most*), and *Sturm* (barely fermented most, autumn only). The local red wine (called "Portuguese") is pretty good. Since the Austrian wine is often very sweet, remember the word *Trocken* (German for dry). You can order your wine in a quarter-liter (*viertel*) and an eighth-liter (*achtel*). Beer comes in a *Krugel* (.5 liter) or *Seidel* (.3 liter).

SALZBURG AND WEST AUSTRIA

Enjoy the sights and sounds of Salzburg, Mozart's hometown, then commune with nature in the Salzkammergut, Austria's *Sound of Music* Country. Amid hills alive with the *S.O.M.*, you'll find the tiny town of Hallstatt, as pretty as a postcard (and about the same size). On the far western border of Austria, the Golden Roof of Innsbruck glitters, but you'll strike it rich in neighboring Hall, which has twice the charm and none of the tourist crowds.

Salzburg

With a well-preserved old town, gardens, churches, and lush surroundings, set under Europe's biggest intact medieval castle, its river adding an almost seaside ambiance, Salzburg is forever smiling to the tunes of Mozart and *The Sound of Music*. This town knows how to be popular. Eight million tourists crawl its cobbles each year. That's a lot of Mozart balls.

Planning Your Time

Salzburg is the best single stop in Austria. While Vienna measures much higher on the Richter scale of sightseeing thrills, Salzburg is simply a joy. A touristy joy, but a joy nevertheless. If you're going into the nearby Salzkammergut lake country, you don't need to take the *Sound of Music* tour. But this tour kills a nest of sightseeing birds with one ticket (city overview, *S.O.M.* sights, a luge ride, and a fine drive through the lakes). If you're not planning a detour through the lakes, allow half a day for this tour. That means a minimum of two nights and a busy day for Salzburg. Of course, the nights are important for concerts and swilling beer in atmospheric local gardens. The actual town sights are mediocre—it's the town itself that you should enjoy, like the first sight of your lover naked. If you like things slow, bike down the river or hike across the Monchsberg.

Orientation (tel. code: 0662)

Salzburg, a city of 150,000 (Austria's fourth largest) is divided into old and new. The old town, sitting between the Salzach

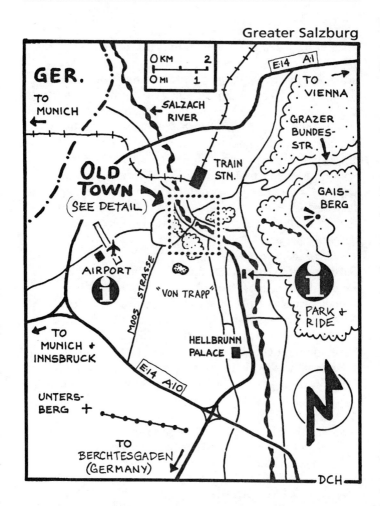

Greater Salzburg

GER.

TO MUNICH

0 KM   2
0 MI   1

SALZACH RIVER

E14 A1

TO VIENNA

GRAZER BUNDES-STR

TRAIN STN.

OLD TOWN (SEE DETAIL)

GAIS-BERG

AIRPORT

MOOS STRASSE

"VON TRAPP"

PARK + RIDE

TO MUNICH + INNSBRUCK

HELLBRUNN PALACE

E14 A10

UNTERS-BERG

N

TO BERCHTESGADEN (GERMANY)

DCH

River and the 1,600-foot-high hill called Mönchsberg, is a bundle of Baroque holding all the charm and most of the tourists.

Tourist Information
Salzburg's helpful tourist offices (at the train station, on Mozartplatz in the old center, and on the freeway entrance to the city, tel. 847568 or 88987) know who butters the local bread. Each is equally helpful. Ask for a city map, the "hotel plan" map, a transit map, a list of sights with current hours, and a schedule of events. Book a concert upon arrival.

The Salzburg Station makes getting set up easy. The TI is at track 2A. Downstairs is the place to leave bags, rent bikes, buy tickets, and get train information. This lower street level faces the bus station (where buses numbers 1, 2, 5, 6, 51, and 55 go to the old center). To walk downtown (15 minutes), leave the station ticket hall near window #8 through the door marked "*Zentrum*" and walk absolutely straight down Rainerstrasse, which leads you under the tracks past Mirabellplatz, changes its name to Dreitaltig-keitsgasse, and takes you to the *Staatsbrucke* (bridge) which deposits you in the old town. For a more dramatic approach, leave the same way but follow the tracks to the river, turn left, and walk the riverside path toward the castle.

Getting Around
Salzburg is served by a fine bus system (info tel. 87 21 45) Single-ride tickets are sold on the bus for 21 AS. Twenty-four-hour passes (sold at TIs and Tobacco shops) cost 30 AS. Salzburg is very bike-friendly and the train station rents good bikes all day until midnight for 50 AS (double if you have no train ticket or pass; no deposit required; go to counter #3 to pay, then pick it up at "left luggage"). I intensified my last visit by having a bike the entire time.

Helpful Hints
The American Express office (Mozartplatz 5, A-5020 Salzburg, open Monday-Friday 9:00-17:30, Saturday 9:00-12:00, tel. 842501) will hold mail for their check- or card-users.

Sights—Salzburg
▲**Salzburg Cathedral** (free, daily 8:00-17:00) claims to be the first Baroque building north of the Alps. Built around 1630, it's modeled after St. Peter's in Rome. Back then, the Bishop of Salzburg was number-two man in the Church hierarchy and Salzburg fancied itself as the "Northern Rome." Check out its 4,000-pipe organ. Sunday Mass (10:00) is famous for its music. For a fee you can tour the excavation site under the church and the Dom Museum in the church.
Residenz—It was Archbishop Wolf Dietrich (not Mozart, or even Julie Andrews) who had the greatest impact on Salzburg. His grandiose vision of Salzburg shaped the city

into the Baroque beauty you'll see today. His palace, the Residenz, next to the cathedral, is impressive—unless you've seen any others. Admission is by tour only (hourly 10:00-15:00, except 13:00; 40 minutes of German only except in July and August; confirm you'll get English before paying the 40 AS).

▲**Carillon**—The bell tower on Mozartplatz chimes throughout the day. The man behind the bells gives fascinating 20-minute tours weekdays at 10:45 and 17:45 but unfortunately only from November through mid-March (in decent weather). You'll actually be up on top among 35 bells as the big barrel turns and the music flies. Buy your 20-AS ticket 10 minutes early. Let the TI know how disappointed you are in the schedule.

▲**Getreidegasse**—Old Salzburg's lively and colorful main drag, famous for its many old wrought-iron signs, still looks much as it did in Mozart's day. *"Schmuck"* means jewelry.

▲**Mozart's Birthplace (Geburtshaus, 1756)**—This best Mozart sight in town, filled with scores, portraits, and old keyboard instruments and violins, is almost a pilgrimage. If you're a fan, you'll have to check it out. It's right in the old town on colorful Getreidegasse #9 (60 AS, daily 9:00-19:00, shorter hours off-season).

▲**Hohensalzburg Fortress**—This castle, one of Europe's mightiest, dominates Salzburg's skyline. The interior is so-so unless you catch a tour (30 AS, confirm that it will be in English as well as German). The basic entry fee (30 AS) gives you only the view and the courtyard. The museum has the noisiest floorboards in Europe. Even so, the prince had a chastity belt. You can see it next to other gruesome torture devices that need no explanation. Upstairs is a mediocre military museum offering a chance to see photos of nice-looking young Nazi officers whose government convinced them that their operation was a just cause. The funicular zips you effortlessly to the castle (32 AS round-trip, every 10 minutes). The castle is open daily 8:00-19:00, until 18:00 in off-season.

▲**Mirabell Gardens and Palace (Schloss)**—The bubbly gardens are always open and free, but to properly enjoy the lavish Mirabell Palace, get a ticket to a *Schlosskonzerte*. Baroque music flying around a Baroque hall is a happy bird

Salzburg

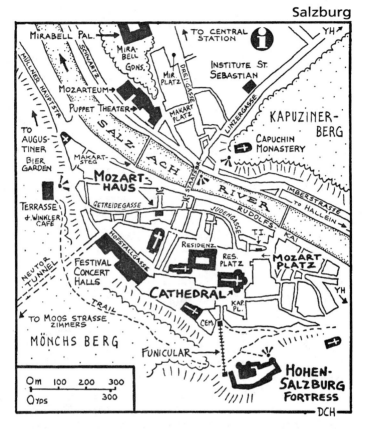

in the right cage. Tickets are around 320 AS (cheaper at the palace and for students) and rarely sold out (tel. 872788).
City Walking Tour—Mediocre two-language 1-hour guided walks of the old town leave from the TI at Mozartplatz (80 AS, 12:15, Monday-Saturday, May-October, tel. 847568).

While walking on your own, be sure to browse through St. Peter's Cemetery, a collection of lovingly tended mini-gardens (at the base of the castle lift). This was where the Trapp family hid out in the *S.O.M.* Tours of the early Christian catacombs leave nearly hourly (tel. 8445780). The nearby open-air market on Universitätsplatz is Salzburg at its liveliest (daily except Sunday).

And for a most enjoyable approach to the castle, consider riding the elevator to the Café Winkler and walking 20

minutes through the woods high above the city to Festung
Hohensalzburg (stay on the high paved paths or you'll have a
needless climb back up to the castle).

▲▲**Bike Ride to Hallein**—The Salzach River has smooth,
flat, and scenic bike paths along each side. On a sunny day, I
can think of no more shout-worthy escape from the city.
Hallein (with its salt-mine tour, about 12 kilometers away,
north or new-town side of river is most scenic, 1 hour each
way) is a pleasant destination. Even a quickie ride just from
one end of town to the other gives you the best possible
views of Salzburg. In the evening, it's a hand-in-hand, flood-
lit-spires world.

▲▲*Sound of Music* **Tour**—I took this tour skeptically (as
part of my research chores) and liked it. It includes a quick
but good general city tour, stops for a luge ride (in season,
fair weather, 30 AS extra), hits all the *S.O.M.* spots (including the stately home, gazebo, and the wedding church), and
shows you a lovely stretch of the Salzkammergut. The Salzburg Panorama Tours Company charges 300 AS for the 4-
hour, English-only tour (from Mirabellplatz daily at 9:30 and
14:00, tel. 874029 for a reservation and a free hotel pickup if
you like; travelers with this book who buy their ticket at the
Mirabellplatz ticket booth get a 10% discount on this and
any other tour they do). This is worthwhile for *S.O.M.* fans
without a car or who won't otherwise be going into the Salzkammergut. Warning: Many think rolling through the Austrian country with 30 Americans singing "Do, a Deer" is
pretty schmaltzy. There are several similar and very competitive tour companies which offer every conceivable tour from
Salzburg. Hotels have their brochures and push them for a
healthy commission. The only minibus tours going are
Bob's Tours.

▲**Hellbrunn Castle**—The attraction here is a garden full of
clever trick fountains and the sadistic joy the tour guide gets
from soaking his tourists. The archbishop's 17th-century
palace is closed through 1995 (and not worth a look anyway).
His Baroque garden, one of the oldest in Europe, is pretty
enough, and now features the "I Am 16, Going on 17" gazebo. The burned-out trilingual tour guides sound like every
night their wives have to remind them "one language is
enough" (daily 9:00-18:00, fewer hours off-season, tel.

82 03 72, 50 AS for the 40-minute tour and admission). The castle is 3 miles south of Salzburg (bus #55 from downtown, twice hourly, 20-minute ride). It's a lot of trouble for a few water tricks.

▲▲**Salzburg Festival**—Each summer from late July to the end of August, Salzburg hosts its famous Salzburger Festspiele, founded in 1920 to employ Vienna musicians in the summer. This fun and festive time is crowded but (except for a few August weekends) there are plenty of beds, and tickets (except for the big shows) are normally available the day of the concert.

Salzburg is busy throughout the year with 1,600 classical performances in its palaces and churches annually (ticket office on Mozartplatz; contact the Austrian National Tourist Office in the U.S.A. for specifics on this year's festival schedule and tickets). I have never planned in advance and have enjoyed great concerts with every visit. While you may find folk evenings twice a week in the summer, Innsbruck is better for these.

Sights—Near Salzburg
▲**Bad Dürnberg Salzbergwerke**—Like its neighbors, this salt-mine tour above the town of Hallein, 8 miles from Salzburg, respects only the German-speakers. You'll get information sheets or headphones but none of the jokes. Still, it's a fun experience—wearing white overalls, sliding down the sleek wooden chutes, and crossing underground from Austria into Germany (daily 9:00-17:00, easy bus and train connections from Salzburg or a great riverside bike ride).
▲**Berchtesgaden**—This Alpine resort just across the German border (20 km from Salzburg) flaunts its attractions very effectively, and you may find yourself in a traffic jam of desperate tourists looking for ways to turn their money into fun. From the station and the TI (tel. 08652/9670), buses go to the idyllic Königsee (19 DM, 2-hour scenic cruises, 4 per hour, stopovers anywhere, tel. 08652/963618) and the salt mines (a 30-minute walk otherwise).

At the salt mines (16 DM, daily 8:30-17:00, winter Monday-Friday, 12:30-15:30, tel. 08652/60020) you put on the traditional miners' outfits, get on funny little trains, and zip deep into the mountain. For 60 minutes you'll cruise subterranean lakes; slide speedily down two long, slick wooden banisters; and learn how they mined salt so long ago. Call for crowd avoidance advice. You can buy a ticket early and browse through the town until your tour time.

Hitler's famous (but overrated) "Eagle's Nest" towered high above Obersalzberg near Berchtesgaden. The site is open to visitors, but little remains of Hitler's Alpine retreat, which he visited only five times. The bus ride up the private road and the lift to the top (a 2,000-foot altitude gain) cost 25 DM from the station, 19 DM from the parking lot. If the weather's cloudy, as it often is in the morning, you'll Nazi a thing.

Berchtesgaden is a train ride from Munich (hrly, one change, 2½ hrs). From Salzburg, ride the scenic and more-direct-than-train bus connection (2/hr, 50 min). Berchtesgaden caters to long-term German guests. During peak season, it's not worth the headaches for the speedy tourist.

Sleeping in Salzburg
(11 AS = about $1, zip code: 5020, tel. code: 0662)
Finding a room in Salzburg, even during the Music Festival, is usually easy. The tourist offices have pamphlets listing all the pensions, hostels, and private rooms in town. Or, for a couple of dollars, they'll find you an inexpensive bed in a private home in the area of your choice. If you want dorm-style budget alternatives, ask for their list of ten youth hostels and student dorms. Some English is spoken and breakfast is included at all my listings. Most will hold a room with a phone call and more expensive places charge more during the music festival (late July and August).

Sleep code: **S**=Single, **D**=Double/Twin, **T**=Triple, **Q**=Quad, **B**=Bath/Shower and toilet, **CC**=Credit Card (**V**isa, **M**astercard, **A**mex), **SE**=Speaks English (graded **A** through **F**).

Sleeping on Linzergasse
The first three listings are on lower Linzergasse, directly across the bridge from Mozart-ville and a 15-minute walk from the station. Its bustling crowds of shoppers overwhelm the few shy cars that venture onto it.

Institute St. Sebastian plans to open after major renovation in July of 1995 (expected rates: 170-AS dorm beds,

450-AS doubles, breakfast is 35 AS extra, guests with sheets save 25 AS; Linzergasse 41, enter through arch at #37, tel. 871386 or 882606, fax 87138685, reception open 8:00-12:00, 15:00-22:00). This is a friendly, clean, historic convent. Mozart's mom is buried in the courtyard and they usually have rooms available.

Troglodytes love **Hotel zum Jungen Fuchs** (S-220 AS, D-380 AS, T-480 As, 15 AS showers down hall; across from Institute St. Sebastian at Linzergasse 54, tel. 875496). It's wonderfully located in a funky, dumpy old building, very plain but clean, with a tired, elderly management that serves no breakfast and little else.

Hotel Pension Goldene Krone (D-700 AS-750 AS, DB-800 AS-970 AS, TB-1,100 AS-1,200 AS, elevator; Linzergasse 48, tel. 872300) is big, quiet, creaky-traditional but modern, with comforts rare in this price range.

Gasthaus Ganslhof (DB-780 AS, 900 AS during the festival, elevator and lots of ground floor rooms; Vogel-weiderstr. 6, a 10-minute walk up Linzergasse from the old town, tel. 873853, fax 87385323) is clean, central, and comfortable. It's back in the real world, with Motel 6 ambience and a parking lot.

Two plain and decent old places two blocks in front of the train station but a 15-minute walk from the sightseeing action on a slightly sleazy street: **Gasthof Jahn** (D-520 AS-570 AS, spacious DB-640 AS-700 AS, TB-800 AS- 900 AS; CC:VM, Elisabethstrasse 31, tel. 871405, fax 875535) is better than the **Pension Adlerhof** (D-490 AS-570 AS, DB-650 AS-720 AS, T-740 AS-790 AS, TB-890 AS-950 AS, public shower is a hike away; Elisabethstrasse 25, tel. 875236, fax 8736636, quirky staff).

Sleeping in or above the Old Town
Gasthaus "Zur Goldenen Ente" (DB-900 AS-980 AS, 100 AS more in August, CC:VMA; Goldgasse 10 in the old center, tel. 845622, fax 8456229), run by the Family Steinwender, is a great splurge if you'd like to sleep in a 600-year-old building above a fine restaurant as central as you can be on a pedestrian street in old Salzburg. Somehow the 15 modern and comfortable doubles fit into this building's medieval-style stone arches and narrow stairs. The breakfast

is buffet-big, they have a 70-AS/day deal on the nearby parking lot, and they'll hold a room if you leave your credit-card number. For dinner, try their roast *Ente* (duck). Robert, the cook, also specializes in fish.

Gasthof Hinterbrühl (S-370 AS, D-470 AS, T-540 AS, plus optional 50-AS breakfast; on a village-like square just under the castle at Schanzlgasse 12, tel. 846798) is a smoky, ramshackle old place with spacious rooms, a handy location, and not a tourist in sight.

Naturfreundehaus (D-250 AS, 110 AS per person in 4- to 6-bed dorms, 45-AS breakfast, 70-AS dinner with city view; Mönchsberg 19, 2 minutes from the top of the 25-AS round-trip Mönchsberg elevator, tel. 841729, 01:00 curfew, open May-October) is a local version of a mountaineer's hut It's a great budget alternative guarded by singing birds and snuggled in the remains of a 15th-century castle wall overlooking Salzburg with magnificent old-town and mountain views. High above the old town, it's the stone house to the left of the glass Café Winkler.

Bed and Breakfasts

These are generally roomy, modern, very comfortable, and come with a good breakfast. Off-season, competition is tough and you can consider it a buyer's market. Most are a bus ride from town, but with the cheap 24-hour pass and the frequent service, this shouldn't keep you away. Unsavory *Zimmer* skimmers lurk at the station. If you have a reservation, ignore them. If you need a place . . . they need a customer.

Brigitte Lenglachner (S-270 AS, bunk bed D-390 AS, D-450 AS, DB-500 AS, T-650 AS, 2 nights minimum; breakfast served in your room; in a chirpy neighborhood a 10-minute walk from the station, cross the pedestrian Pioneer bridge, turn right past park and second left to Scheibenweg 8, tel. 43 80 44) fills her big traditional house with a warm welcome, lots of tourist information, and American tourists.

Moosstrasse, south of Mönchsberg, is lined with *Zimmer*. Those farther out are farmhouses. From the station, catch bus #1 and change to bus #60 immediately after crossing the river. From the old town, ride bus #60. If you're driving from the center, go through the tunnel, straight

on Neutorstrasse, and take the fourth left onto Moosstrasse.
Maria Gassner (SB-300 AS, DB-440 AS, 500 AS, and 600
AS, family deals; 60-AS coin-op laundry; first bus #60 stop
after American High School at Moosstrasse 126-B, tel.
824990) rents 10 sparkling clean, comfortable rooms in her
modern house. She can often pick you up at the station.
Frau Ballwein rents seven charming and comfortable rooms
in an old farmhouse (S-250 AS, D-400 AS, DBWC-480 AS,
Moosstrasse 69A, tel. 824029). Her family operates one of
the touristic old horse-buggies. For the cost of a bus ticket,
guests can hitch a ride in the buggy downtown as it goes to
work at 9:30. **The Ziller Family Farm** rents three huge
rooms with kitchenettes in a kid-friendly, horse-filled environment (DB-550 AS, minimum two nights, Moosstrasse 76,
tel. 824940). **Gästehaus Blobergerhof** (Hammerauerstrasse
4, Querstrasse zur **Moosstrasse**, tel. 830227) and **Helga
Bankhammer** (D-400 AS minimum two nights, Moosstrasse
77, tel. 830067) are also rural, warm, and reasonable.

Youth Hostels
Salzburg has more than its share of hostels (and tourists).
The TI has a complete listing (with directions from the station) and there are nearly always beds available. The most
fun, handy, and American is **Gottfried's International
Youth Hotel** (4 D-320 AS, 3 Q-140 AS per bed, or 6- to
8-bed dorm-120 AS, sheets not required but rentable-
20 AS; 5 blocks from the station towards the center at
Paracelsusstr. 9, tel. 87 96 49). This easygoing but impressively run place speaks English first, has cheap meals, lockers,
a laundry, tour discounts, no curfew, plays *The Sound of Music*
free daily at 13:30, runs a lively bar, and welcomes anyone.

Eating in Salzburg
Salzburg boasts many inexpensive, fun, and atmospheric
places to eat. I'm a sucker for the big cellars with their
smoky Old World atmosphere, heavy medieval arches, time-
darkened paintings, many antlers, and hearty meals to match.
These places are famous with visitors but also enjoyed by
the locals.
   Gasthaus "Zum Wilder Mann" (enter from
Getreidegasse 20 or Griesgasse 17, tel. 841787, food served

11:00-21:00) is the place if the weather's bad and you're in the mood for Hofbräu atmosphere in one small well-antlered room and a hearty cheap meal at a shared table, 2 minutes from Mozart's place. For a quick 100-AS lunch, get the Bauernschmaus, a mountain of dumpling, *kraut*, and peasant's meats.

Stieglkeller (50 yards uphill from the lift to the castle, tel. 84 26 81), a huge, atmospheric institution with several rustic rooms and outdoor garden seating offering a great rooftop view of the old town, is an inexpensive way to get really schnitzeled.

Krimplestätter (Müllner Hauptstrasse 31, 10 minutes north of the old town near the river) employs 500 years of experience serving authentic old-Austrian food in its authentic old-Austrian interior or in its cheery garden. For fine food with a wild finale, eat here and drink at the nearby Augustiner Bräustübl.

Augustiner Bräustübl (Augustinergasse 4, walk through the Mirabellgarten, over the Müllnersteg bridge and ask for "Müllnerbräu," its local nickname; don't be fooled by second-rate gardens serving the same beer nearby—this huge 1,000-seat place is in the huge Augustiner brewery; open daily 15:00-23:00, order carefully, prices can sting; great beer, pick up a 25-AS half-liter or a 50-AS full-liter mug, pay the lady and give Mr. Keg your empty mug). This monk-run brewery is so rustic and crude that I hesitate to show my true colors by recommending it, but I must. On busy nights, it's like a Munich beer-hall with no music but the volume turned up. When its cool you'll enjoy a historic setting with beer-sloshed smoke-stained halls. On balmy evenings you'll eat under trees in a pleasant outdoor beer-garden. Local students mix with tourists eating hearty slabs of *schnitzel* with their fingers or cold meals from the self-serve picnic counter. It'll bring out the barbarian in you. For dessert (after a visit to the *strudel* kiosk), enjoy the incomparable floodlit view of old Salzburg from the nearby pedestrian bridge and then stroll home along the river. Delicious memories.

Stiftskeller St. Peter (next to St. Peter's church at the foot of Mönchsberg, outdoor and indoor seating, daily until midnight, meals 100 AS-200 AS, tel. 8412680) has been in business for over a thousand years. It's classier, with strolling musicians, more central, not too expensive, and your best splurge for traditional Austrian cuisine in medieval sauce. The "Monastery Pot" (hearty soup in a bowl made of dark bread) takes away your munchies. If you start singing "The hills are alive . . ." they'll throw you out.

Café Haydn Stube (1 Mirabellplatz at the entry to the Aicherpassage, Monday-Friday 9:30-20:00), run by the local music school, is cheap and very popular with students. The **Mensa Aicherpassage** (hiding in the basement, Monday-Friday 11:30-14:00) serves even cheaper meals.

Picnics: Classy Salzburg delis serve good, cheap, sit-down lunches on weekdays. Have them make you a sandwich or something hot, toss in a carrot, a piece of fruit, yogurt, and a box of milk and sit at a small table with the local lunch crowd. **Frauenberger** (8:00-14:00, 15:00-18:00, closed Monday and Saturday afternoon and Sunday; it's little hot-dog stand is open until 24:00, across from 16 Linzergasse) is friendly, picnic-ready, cheap and offers indoor or outdoor seating. The University Square, just behind Mozart's house, hosts a bustling produce market daily (except Sunday).

You'll see a mountainous sweet souffle served all over town. The memorable "Salzberger Nockerl" is worth a try (if you have someone to split it with). It's really big enough for four.

Train Connections
Salzburg to: Innsbruck (every 2 hrs, 2 hrs), **Munich** (hrly, 2 hrs), **Vienna** (hrly, 3½ hrs), **Hallstatt** (hrly, 50 min to Attnang Puchheim, 20 minutes wait, 1½ hrs to Hallstatt), **Reutte** (change in Innsbruck, 4 hrs).

Salzkammergut Lake District
Commune with nature in Austria's Lake District. "The hills are alive," and you're surrounded by the loveliness that has turned on everyone from Emperor Franz Josef to Julie Andrews. This is *The Sound of Music* country. Idyllic, majestic, but not rugged, it's a gentle land of lakes, forested mountains, and storybook villages, rich in hiking opportunities and inexpensive lodging. Settle down in the postcard-pretty, fjord-cuddling town of Hallstatt.

Planning Your Time

While there are plenty of lakes, Hallstatt is really the only one that matters. One night and two hours to browse is all you need to fall in love with it. To relax or take a hike in the surroundings, give it two nights and a day. It's a good stop between Salzburg and Vienna. And a visit here (with a bike ride along the Danube) balances out your Austrian itinerary.

While the Salzkammergut is well-served by trains and buses, Eurailers in a hurry can see it from the window of the half-day *Sound of Music* bus tour (see Salzburg for description).

Hallstatt

Lovable Hallstatt is a tiny town bullied onto a ledge between a selfish mountain and a swan-ruled lake with a waterfall ripping furiously through its middle. It can be toured on foot in about 10 minutes. The town is one of Europe's oldest, going back centuries before Christ. The charm of Hallstatt is the village and its lakeside setting. Go there to relax, nibble, wander, and paddle. (In August, tourist crowds trample much of Hallstatt's charm.)

Tourist Information

The TI (tel. 06134/8208, open daily in summer, often closed for lunch) can find you a room. Its hotel "guest card" gives you free parking and sightseeing discounts.

Trains

Hallstatt's train station is a wide spot on the tracks across the lake. *Stefanie* (a boat) meets you at the station and glides across the lake into town (20 AS, with each train). The ride is gorgeous.

Sights—Hallstatt

Prehistory Museum—The humble Prehistory Museum adjacent to the TI is interesting since little Hallstatt was the important salt-mining hub of a culture which spread from France to the Balkans during what archaeologists call the "Hallstatt Period" (800-400 B.C.). Back then, Celtic tribes dug for precious salt and Hallstatt was, as its name means, the "salt place." Your 40-AS Prehistory Museum ticket gets you into the Heimat (Folk Culture) Museum around the

Salzkammergut and Hallstatt

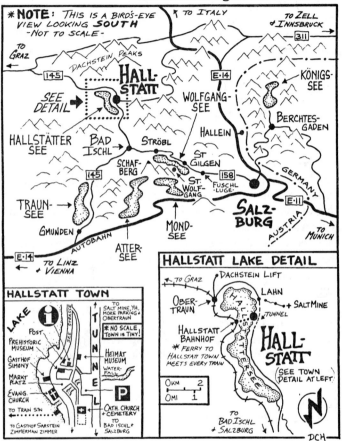

NOTE: THIS IS A BIRD'S-EYE VIEW LOOKING **SOUTH** -NOT TO SCALE-

TO ITALY
TO ZELL & INNSBRUCK
311
TO GRAZ
DACHSTEIN PEAKS
E·14
KÖNIGS-SEE
145
HALL-STATT
WOLFGANG-SEE
BERCHTES-GADEN
SEE DETAIL
HALLEIN
HALLSTÄTTER SEE
BAD ISCHL
STRÖBL
ST GILGEN
158
GERMANY
SCHAF-BERG
FUSCHL-LUGE
145
ST. WOLF-GANG
SALZ-BURG
E·11
TRAUN-SEE
AUSTRIA
TO MUNICH
GMUNDEN
AUTOBAHN
MOND-SEE
ATTER-SEE
E·14
TO LINZ & VIENNA

HALLSTATT TOWN

LAKE
Post
TO SALT MINE, YH, MORE PARKING & OBERTRAUN
SEE STRASSE
TUNNEL
NO SCALE, TOWN IS TINY!
PREHISTORIC MUSEUM
GASTHOF SIMONY
HEIMAT MUSEUM
WATER-FALL
MARKT PLATZ
EVANG. CHURCH
TO TRAIN STN
P
CATH. CHURCH + CEMETERY
TO GASTHOF SARSTEIN ZIMMERMAN ZIMMER
TO BAD ISCHL + SALZBURG

HALLSTATT LAKE DETAIL

TO GRAZ
DACHSTEIN LIFT
OBER-TRAUN
LAHN
SALT MINE
HALLSTATT BAHNHOF
TUNNEL
FERRY TO HALLSTATT TOWN MEETS EVERY TRAIN
HALL-STATT
(SEE TOWN DETAIL AT LEFT)
0 KM 2
0 MI 1
TO BAD ISCHL & SALZBURG
N
DCH

corner (10:00-18:00 in summer). It's cute but barely worth
the trouble. The Janu sport shop across from the TI
recently dug into a prehistoric site and now its basement
is another small museum.

Hallstatt Church and Cemetery—From near the boat
dock, hike up the covered wooden stairway to the church.
The church is lovely (500-year-old altars and frescoes) but
the cemetery will rot your flesh. Space is so limited in
Hallstatt that bones got only 12 peaceful buried years before
making way for the freshly dead. The result is a fascinating
chapel of bones (10 AS, 10:00-18:00) in the cemetery. Each

skull is lovingly named, dated, and decorated, with the men getting ivy and the women roses. They stopped this practice in the 1960s, about the same time the Catholic Church began permitting cremation.

Salt-Mine Tour—If you have yet to do a salt mine, Hallstatt's is as good as any. You'll ride a frighteningly steep funicular high above the town (95 AS, round-trip), take a 10-minute hike, put on old miners' clothes, take an underground train, slide down the banisters, and listen to an English tape-recorded tour while your guide speaks German (130 AS, daily 9:30-16:30, closes early off-season; no children under age 4). The well-publicized ancient Celtic graveyard excavation sites, nearby, are really dead. The scenic 50-minute hike back into town is (with strong knees) a joy.

Hiking and Spelunking—Mountain lovers, hikers, and spelunkers can keep busy for days using Hallstatt as their home base. Get information from the TI on the various caves with their ice formations, the thunderous rivers, mountain lifts, nearby walks, and harder hikes. With a car, consider hiking around nearby Altaussee (flat, 3-hour hike) or along Grundlsee to Tolpitzsee. Regular buses connect Hallstatt with Gosausee for a pleasant walk around that lake. The TI can recommend a great 2-day hike with an overnight in a nearby mountain hut.

Sleeping in Hallstatt

(11 AS = about $1, zip code: A-4830, tel. code: 06134)
Hallstatt's TI can almost always find you a room. July and August can be tight. Early August is worst. A bed in a private home costs about 180 AS with breakfast. It's hard to get a one-night reservation. But if you drop in and they have a spot, they're happy to have you. All prices include breakfast, lots of stairs, and a silent night. "*Zimmer mit Aussicht?*" means "Room with view?" . . . worth asking for.

Gasthof Simony (500 AS-800 AS doubles depending upon the plumbing, view, season, and length of stay; 250 AS for third person, cheaper for families; tel. 8231, SE-B) is my stocking-feet-tidy 500-year-old favorite, right on the square with a lake view, balconies, creaky wood floors, slip-slidey rag rugs, antique furniture, lakefront garden, and a huge breakfast. Call friendly Susan Scheutz for a reservation.

Pension Seethaler (200 AS per person, 180 AS if you stay more than one night, in S, D, T, or Q, no extra for great views; Dr Morton weg 22, tel. 8421, SE-D) is a simple old lodge with 45 beds, perched a little above the lake on the parking-lot side of town.

Pension Sarstein (D-400 AS, DB-500 AS-600 AS; for people with this book, one-night stays are okay; Gosaumühlstr. 83, tel. 8217) has 25 beds in a charming building a few minutes walk along the lake from the center, with a view, run by friendly Frau Fisher. You can swim from her lakeside garden. Her sister, friendly **Frau Zimmermann** (180 AS per person B&B in a double or triple, can be musty; Gosaumühlstr. 69, tel. 8309), runs a small *Zimmer* (as her name implies) in a 500-year-old ramshackle house with low beams, time-polished wood, and fine lake views just down the street. These elderly ladies speak almost no English, but you'll find yourself caught up in their charm and laughing together like old friends.

Helga Lenz (160 AS per person in 2-, 3-, or 4-bed rooms, gives family discounts, welcomes one-nighters; high above the paddleboat dock at Hallberg 17, tel. 8508, SE-B) has a big, sprawling, woodsy house on top of the town with great lake and town views and a neat garden perch. Ideal for those who sleep well in tree houses.

Gasthaus Zauner (DB-1100 AS; Marktplatz 51, tel. 8246, fax 82468) is a business machine offering more normal hotel rooms on the main square, with a restaurant specializing in grilled food. You'll eat better at Gasthaus Weisses Lamm.

The **Gasthaus Mühle Naturfreunde-Herberge** (135 AS per bed with sheets in 2- to 20-bed coed dorms, 35-AS breakfast, cheaper if you BYO hostel sheet, run by Ferdinand; Kirchenweg 36 just below the tunnel car park, tel. 8318) has the best cheap beds in town and is clearly the place to eat well on a budget. Their wonderful pizzas are big enough for two. Closed in November. Restaurant closed on Wednesdays. ("Nature's friends' houses" are found throughout the Alps. Like mountaineers' huts, they're a good, fun, and basic bargain.)

BRUGES

With Renoir canals, pointy guilded architecture, time tunnel art, and stay-awhile
cafés, Bruges is a heavy weight sightseeing
destination, as well as a joy. Where else can
you ride a bike along a canal, munch mussels
washed down with the world's best beer, savor heavenly
chocolate, and see Flemish Primatives and a Michelangelo, all
within 300 yards of a belltower that rings out "don't worry,
be happy" jingles every 15 minutes? And there's no language
barrier.

The town is Brugge in Flemish (broo-gha). It's Bruges
in French and English (broozh). Before it was Flemish or
French, it was a Viking word for "wharf" or "embarkment."
Right from the start, it was a trading center. By the 14th
century, Bruges' population was 35,000, in a league with
London, and the city was the most important cloth market
in northern Europe. By the 16th century, the harbor had
silted up and the economy had collapsed. In the 19th century,
a new port, Zeebrugge, brought renewed vitality to the area.
But today, Bruges prospers mainly because it is now being
rediscovered in an age of tourism: a uniquely well-preserved
Gothic city and a handy gateway to Europe. It's no secret,
but even with the crowds, it's the kind of city where you
don't mind being a tourist.

Planning Your Time

Bruges needs at least two nights and a full, well-organized
day. Even non-shoppers enjoy browsing here and the Belgian
love of life makes a hectic itinerary seem a little senseless.

With one day, spend it like this: 9:30 climb the belfry;
10:00 catch the minibus orientation town tour; 11:00 tour
the Burg sights (visit the TI if necessary); 12:15 walk to the
brewery, have lunch there and catch the 13:00 tour; 14:30
walk throught the Beguinage; 15:00 tour the Memling
Museum (six paintings); 15:45 see the Michelangelo in the
church; and 16:00 tour the Groeninge Museum (closes at
17:00). Rent a bike for a evening ride through the quiet back
streets. Lose the tourists and find a dinner.

Orientation

The tourists' Bruges (you'll be sharing it) is contained within a 1-km square canal or moat. Nearly everything of interest and importance is within a cobbled and convenient swath between the train station and the Market Square (a 15-minute walk).

Bruges

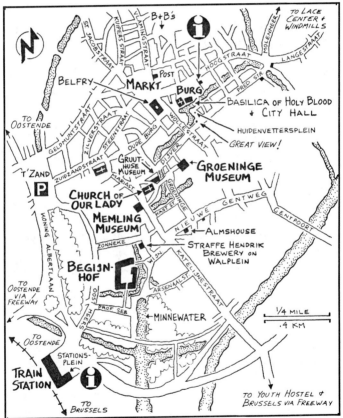

Tourist Information

The main office (on the Burg Square, daily 9:30-18:30; Saturday and Sunday 10:00-12:00, 14:00-18:30, closed at 17:00 and Sunday off season, tel. 050/448686) and the train station office (10:30-18:30, closed Sunday, tel. 050/381842) sell a great 20BF all-inclusive Bruges visitors' guide with a map and listing of all sights, hours, and services. The free monthly "Agenda Bruges," lists the many events the town put on to keep its hoardes of tourists entertained. Skip their "combo" museum ticket. They also have specifics on the various kinds of tours available.

Arrival

By Train: Upon arrival, pick up the city info booklet/map at the station TI. Most buses (#1, #3, #4, #6, #8, #11, #13, #16) go right to the Market Square (40BF ticket, buy from driver, good for an hour). Taxi fare to most hotels is 180BF. It's a scenic 15-minute walk to the center: cross the busy street and canal in front of the station and have people direct you to the Market Square via the Beguinage. You could rent a bike at the station for the duration of your stay (130BF/day with a train ticket). Drivers should park in the underground t'Zand parking garage near the station and pretend they arrived by train.

Helpful Hints

Shops are open 9:00-18:00; a little later on Friday. Market day is Wednesday (Burg) and Saturday (t'Zand). Saturday and Sunday there is a flea market along Dijver (in front of Groeninge Museum). There's a botanical garden in the center at Astrid Park. Brussel Lambert Bank (on the Market) is a decent place to change travelers checks.

Sights—Bruges

An Orientation Tour on Foot—Bruges' sights are listed in walking order: from the Market Square to the Burg to the cluster of museums around the Church of Our Lady to the Beguinage (a 10-minute walk from begining to end). Like Venice, the ultimate sight is the town itself, and the best way to enjoy that is to get lost on the back streets away from the lace shops and ice cream stands.

    The Market Square or "Market" ringed by banks, the post office, lots of restaurant terraces, great gabled old buildings, and the belltower or belfry is the modern heart of the city. Most city buses go from there to the station. Under the belfry are two great Belgian "french fry" stands and a quadralingual Braille description and model of the tower. In its day, a canal went right up to the central square of this formerly great trading center.

▲▲**The Belfry** (belfort) has towered mightily over Market since 1300. In 1486, the octagonal lantern was added making it 83 meters high—that's 366 steps which you can pay 100BF to climb (daily 9:30-17:00, October-March closed 12:30-13:30). The view is worth the climb. Survey the town. On the horizon you can see the towns along the coast. Just before you reach the top, peek into the carillon room. The 47 bells can be played mechanically with the giant barrel and movable tabs (as it does on each quarter hour) or with a manual keyboard (as it does for regular concerts) with fists and feet rather than fingers. Be there on the quarter hour when things ring. It's *bellissimo* on the top of the hour. Carillon concert times are listed at the base of the belfry (usually Monday, Wednesday, and Saturday 21:00-22:00, Sunday at 14:15). From Market and the belfry, Breidelstraat leads to Burg Square.

▲▲**Burg Square**—The opulant square called Burg is Bruges' civic center, historically the birthplace of Bruges and the site of the 9th-century castle of the first Count of Flanders. Today, it's the scene of outdoor concerts, a parking place for horse buggies, home of the TI (with a public WC), and surrounded by six centuries of architecture. Sweeping 360 degrees from Romanesque (the round arches and thick walls of the basilica in the corner, best seen inside the lower chapel) to the pointed Gothic arches of the Town Hall (with its "Gothic Room") to the well-proportioned Renaissance windows of the Old Recorder's House (next door, under the guilded statues) past the TI and the park to the elaborate 17th-century Baroque of the Provost's House.

▲**The Basilica of the Holy Blood**, originally the Chapel of Saint Basil, is famous for its relic of the blood of Christ which, according to tradition, was brought to Bruges in 1150, after the Second Crusade. The lower chapel is dark, solid, and a fine expample of Romanesque (with some beautiful statues). The upper chapel is decorated Gothic and often filled with appropriately contemplative music. An English flier tells about the relic, art, and history. The **Basilica Museum** (next to the upper chapel, 40BF, open 9:30-12:00, 14:00-18:00, less off-season) is small but sumptuous containing the gem-studded hexagonal reliquary that carries the relic on its yearly Ascension Day trip through the streets of Bruges.

▲**The City Hall's Gothic Room**—Built around 1400, this is the oldest in the Low Countries. Your ticket gives you a room full of old town maps and paintings, and a grand "Gothic Hall" beautifully restored with a painted and carved wooden ceiling featuring "hanging arches" (explained by an English flier). The free ground-level lobby is a picture gallery of Belgium's colonial history, from the Spanish Bourbon king to Napoleon (60BF, open 9:30-17:00, closed 12:30-14:00 off-season).

Provincial Museum "Brugse Vrije"—This just one ornate room with one giant impressive Renaissance chimney. If you're into heraldry, the symbolism, well-explained on the free English flier, makes this a worthwhile 5-minute stop. If you're not, you'll wonder where the rest of the museum is (20BF, open 10:00-12:00, 13:30-17:00, closed Monday).

Fish Market—From Burg walk under the guilded statues down Blinde Ezel straat to the persistent little fish market and Huidevettersplein, a tiny picturesque and restaurant-filled square, to Roezenhoedkaai, from where you can get a great photo of the Belfry reflected in the canal. Can you see its tilt? It leans about 4 feet. Down the canal (past a flea market on weekends) looms the huge brick spire of the church of our lady (tallest spire in the low countries). Between you and that are the next three museums.

▲▲▲**The Groeninge Museum** (130BF, open 9:30-17:00, October-March, closed 12:30-14:00 and Tuesday) is a diverse and classy collection of mostly Flemish art from Memling to Magritte. While it has plenty of worthwhile modern art, the highlights are its vivid and pristine Flemish Primitives. ("Primitive" meaning before the Renaissance.) Flemish art is shaped by its playful love of detail, the egos of its merchant patrons, and the power of the Church. Lose yourself in the halls of Groeninge: gazing across 15th-century canals, into the eyes of reassuring Marys, and through town squares littered with leotards, lace, and lopped-off heads.

The **Brangwyn Museum**, next door, is only interesting if you are into lace or the early 20th-century art of Brangwyn (80BF, open 9:30-17:00, less off-season).

▲**The Gruuthuse Museum**—A wealthy brewer's home, this is a sprawling smattering of everything from medieval bed pans to a guillotine. There's no information inside, so to understand the crossbows, dark old paintings, and what a beer merchant's doing with box seats peeking down on the altar of the Church of Our Lady next door, you'll have to buy or browse through the 600BF guidebook (130BF, open 9:30-17:00, less off-season).

▲▲**The St. Jans Hospital/Memling Museum** (130BF, open October-March 9:30-17:00, closed 12:30-14:00 and Wednesday), just beyond the Church of Our Lady, is a medieval hospital with six much-loved paintings by the greatest of the Flemish Primitives, Hans Memling. The fascinating medieval hospital is closed until at least 1996, but the Memling art is wide open. His "Mystical Wedding of St. Catherine" triptych deserves a close look. Catherine and her "mystical groom," the baby Jesus, are flanked by a headless John the Baptist and a pensive John the Evangelist. The chairs are there so you can study it. If you understand the Book of Revelations, you'll understand St. John's wild and intricate vision. The Reliquary of St. Ursula, an ornate little mini-church in the same room, is filled with impressive detail.

▲▲**Church of Our Lady** stands as a memorial to the power and wealth of Bruges in its heyday. Just inside the door is a delicate Madonna and Child by Michelangelo. It's said to be the only Michelangelo statue to leave Italy in his lifetime (cloth money). If you like tombs and church art, pay to wander through the apse (Michelangelo free, art-filled apse 60BF, open 10:00-11:30, 14:30-17:00, closed Sunday morning and Saturday at 16:00; off-season until 16:30).

▲▲**Straffe Hendrik Brewery Tour**—Belgian's are Europe's beer connoisseurs. This fun and handy tour is a great way to pay your respects. The happy gang at this working family brewery gives entertaining and informative 45-minute 3-language tours (piles of very steep steps, a great rooftop panorama, 120BF including a beer, daily on the hour 10:00-17:00, occassionally skipping 14:00, October-March 11:00 and 15:00 only, bordering the Begihnhof towards the center on the square called Walplein, #26, tel. 332697). Originally "Henri Maes," this delicious brew is now known as Straffe

Hendrik (strong Henry). Their bistro, where you'll be given your included-with-the-tour beer, serves a quick and hearty lunch plate (the 110BF "bread with paste" is the best value, although the 250BF "meat selection and vegetables" is a beer-drinker's picnic for two) indoors with the smell of hops or outdoors with the smell of hops. This is a great place to wait for your tour or linger afterwards.

▲▲**Beguinage**—For military (and various) reasons there were more women than men in the medieval low countries. Town's provided Beguinages, a dignified place in which these "beguines" could live a life of piety and service (without having to take the same vows a nun would). You'll find Beguinages all over Belgium and Holland. Bruges' Beguinage almost makes you want to don a habit and fold your hands as you walk under its whispy trees and whisper past its frugle little homes. For a thin slice of Beguinage life, walk through the simple museum (free, Beguine's House 60BF with English flier, open daily 10:00-12:00, 13:45-17:30; Sunday 10:45-12:00, 13:45-18:00; much less off-season).

Minnewater—Beyond the Beguinage is Minnewater, an idyllic, clip-clop world of flower boxes, canals, swans, and tour boats packed like happy egg cartons. Beyond that is the train station.

Almshouses—Walking from the Beguinage back to the center you might detour along Nieuwe Gentweg to visit one of about 20 almshouses in the city. At #8, go through the door into the peaceful courtyard. This was a medieval form of housing the poor. The rich would pay for someone's tiny room here in return for lots of prayers.

Lace and Windmills by the Moat—A 10-minute walk from the center to the northeast end of town by the "big moat" canal are three windmills in a pleasant grassy canalside setting. One windmill is open as a museum. Bruges used to have 27 windmills. To actually see lace being made, drop by the nearby **Lace Centre** where ladies toss bobbins madly as their eyes go bad (40BF includes demonstration and a small lace museum, Kantcentrum adjacent the Jerusalem church, open weekdays 14:00-18:00; Saturday 14:00-17:00, closed Sunday). The **Folklore Museum** (80BF, open 9:30-17:00, less off-season, Rolweg 40), in the same neighborhood, is cute but forgettable.

▲▲**Rent a Bike**—While the sights are close enough for easy walking, the town is a treat to bike through, and you'll be able to get away from the tourist center. Consider a peaceful evening ride through the back streets and around the outer canal. Rental shops have maps and ideas. The TI sells a handy "5X On The Bike Around Bruges" map/guide, narrating five different bike routes through the idyllic nearby countryside. The best basic trip is 30 minutes along the canal out to Damme and back. The Netherlands/Belgium border is a 40-minute pedal beyond Damme. The cheapest rentals are at the station (130BF/day with a train ticket). Two shops rent bikes under the belfry on Hallestraat (250BF/day, 150BF/4 hours, fast and easy, no security deposit required, tel. 343262). At Popelier Eric's you can pick up a bike at 18:00 and drop it back the next morning for the 4-hour rate.

Tours of Bruges

Bruges by Boat—The most relaxing and scenic (if not informative) way to see this city of canals is by boat with the captain narrating. Boats leave from all over town (copycat 35-minute rides, 150BF, 10:00-18:00).

City Minibus Tours—"City Tour Bruges" gives 50-minute 330BF rolling overviews of the town in a 13-seat, 3-skylight minibus with dail-a-language headsets and earphones. The tour leaves hourly (on the hour, 10:00-19:00 in summer, 18:00 spring and fall) from the Market Square. The audio is clean and the narration gives a good history as you tour the town the lazy way.

Walking Tours—Local guides walk small groups through the core of town daily in July and August (120BF, depart from TI, 1,200BF for a private guide). The tours, while earnest, are heavy on history and in two languages so they may be less than peppy. Still, to propel you beyond the pretty gables and canal swans of Bruges, they are good medicine.

Bruges by Bike—"Bruges with Bart" does bike tours of the city (400BF, 105 min, daily, 10:00) and countryside (550BF, daily, 12:30). Prices include guide, bike, and a rain coat. There is also a Bruges-by-night bike tour.

Quasimodo Tours is a hip outfit offering those with extra time two all-day tours through the rarely visited Flemish countryside. Every other day (9:00-16:30) you can do "Flanders

Fields" (WWI battlefields, trenches, memorials, and poppy-splattered fields) and "Triple Treat" (the port of Damme, a castle, monastery, brewery, and chocolate factory and sampling the treats: a waffle, chocolate, and beer). (English-only, 22-seat bus, canceled if 8 don't sign up, lots of walking, pick-up at your hotel, no smoking, 1,300BF, 1,000BF for backpackers, tel. 050/370470 to book, fax 374960).

Eating in Bruges

Local specialties include mussels cooked a variety of ways, fish dishes, grilled meats, and french fries. The city is breaded in bistros. I don't know which are best.

Picnics

Geldmuntstraat is handy when you're hungry. Just off the Market Square at Geldmuntstraat 1, the **Fresh Spegelaere** shop serves salads by the weight. A block further, past the Verbeke chocolate shop mentioned below, the **Napri Supermarket** is great for picnics (push-button produce pricer lets you buy as little as one mushroom, open 9:00-18:00, closed Sunday). There's a small grocery store on the **Market Square** opposite the belfry.

Fritjes

These local french fries are a treat. Two proud and traditional *frituur* serve tubs of fries and various local-style shish kebabs. Belgians dip their fritjes in mayonnaise, but ketchup is there for the Yankees (along with spicier sauces). For a quick, cheap, and scenic meal, hit a *frituur* and sit on the steps or benches overlooking the Market Square about 50 yards past the post office.

Beer

Belgium boasts over 350 types of beer. Straffe Hendrik (strong Henry), a potent, powerful, local brew is, even to a Bud Lite kind of guy, obviously great beer. Among the more unusual of the others to try: Kriek (a cherry-flavored beer) and Trappist (a dark, monk-made beer). Each beer is served in its own unique glass. Any pub carries the basic beers, but for a selection of 300 types, drink at **t'Brugs Beertje** (5 Kemelstraat, open 16:00-1:00, closed Wednesday). When you've finished those, step next door, where **Dreupel Huisje "1919"** serves over 100 Belgian gins and liquers. Another good place to gain an appreciation of the Belgian beer culture is **"de Garre"** off Breidelstraat between Burg and Market on the tiny Garre alley (open 12:00-24:00, closed Wednesday).

Taste Bud Tours: Chocolate

Bruggians are conoisseurs of fine chocolate. You'll be tempted by chocolate-filled display windows all over town. Godiva is the best big factory/high price/high quality local brand. But for the best small family operation, drop by "Maitre Chocolatier Verbeke." While Mr. Verbeke is downstairs, busy making chocolates, Mrs. Verbeke is in the shop making sure customers get the chocolate of their dreams. Ask her to assemble a small 100-gram bag (80BF, the smallest amount sold) of your favorites. Most are "pralines," which means they're filled. While the "hedgehogs" are popular, be sure to get a "pharoah's head." Pray for cool weather, since it's closed when it's very hot. (Open at least in the mornings, a block off the Market Square at Geldmuntstraat 25, tel. 334198.)

Sleeping in Bruges
(tel. code 050, zip code: 8000)

I've listed these places from most expensive to cheapest (not by value or preference). All are located between the train station and the old center with the most distant (and best) being a few blocks beyond (north and east) the Market. All serve breakfast, speak English, are on quiet streets, and (with one exception) keep the same prices throughout the year.

Hansa Hotel (SBWC-2,700BF-3,200BF, DBWC-3,000BF-3,600BF, extra bed 1,250BF, price varies with size of room, CC:VMA, elevator, a block north of Market, N. Desparsstraat 11, tel. 338444, fax 334205) offers 20 rooms in a completely modernized old building. It's bright, tastefully decorated in elegant pastels, and each of the rooms have all the hotelesque comforts. This is a great splurge.

Hans Memling (SBWC-1,,750BF, DBWC-2300BF, TBWC-2,800BF, QBWC-3,400BF, cheaper in winter, skimpy breakfast, elevator, 2 blocks north of Market, Kiupersstraat 18, tel. 332096, easy phone reservations if arriving before 18:00) gets more interesting as its owner, Gilbert, does. The parrot speaks Flemish, while the first king and queen of an independent Belgium (Leopole I and Louise Marie, 1835) peer down on you through the chandeliers as you breakfast. There's Mozart in the morning (Beethoven in the afternoon) and a huge menagerie out the window. The giant living room/ breakfast room is literally palatial, while the 17 huge bed- rooms upstairs are decorated with a man's touch. Across the street, **Hotel Cavalier** (DBWC-2,300BF, CC:VM, Kuiperstraat 25, tel. 330207, Viviane De Clerck) is tall and skinny with less charm, but serves a hearty buffet breakfast in a royal setting and offers two lofty "backpackers doubles" on the fourth floor for DB-1,600BF.

Hotel St. Christophe (D-1,800BF, DBWC-2,500BF, Nieuwe Gentweg 76, CC:VM, tel. 331176, fax 340938) is like a medieval motel overlooking a garden.

Hotel Rembrandt-Rubens (1 D-1,500BF with no shower access, DB-2,000BF, DBWC-2,200BF, on a quiet square between the Memlings and the brewery at Walplein 38, tel. 336439, locked-up at 24:00) has 18 well-worn rooms in a creaky 500-year-old building with tipsy floors, throw rugs, elephant tusks, a gallery of creapy old paintings, and probably the holy grail in a drawer somewhere. Breakfast in what must have been the knights' hall overlooking a canal (while Rembrandt and Rubens overlook you from an ornately carved and tiled 1648 chimney). There's a little warmth behind Mrs. DeBuyser's crankiness. She's run the place for 44 years.

Hotel t'Keizershof (D-1,250BF, a block in front of the station, Oostmeers 126, easy parking, tel. 338728, run by Stefaan) is a doll house of a hotel which lives by its motto, "spend a night, not a fortune." It's simple and tidy with 8 small, cheery rooms split between two floors with a shower and toilet on each.

Bed and Breakfast Places are really the best value of all. Each of these places are central, run by people who enjoy their work, and offer 3 or 4 doubles you'd pay 2,000BF- 2,200BF for in a hotel. **Yvonne De Vriese** (D-1,500BF, DBWC-1,700BF, breakfast served in your room, all with kitchenettes, TV, stereos, and little libraries, CC:VMA, easy parking, 4 blocks east of Berg, Predikherenstraat 40, tel. 334224) rents 3 B&B rooms on a corner overlooking two canals. The DBWC-room is smaller, on the ground floor, and closer to traffic. The cheaper D-rooms are big and bright; one over-looks both canals and the other is on the quiet backside. **Koen and Annemie Dieltiens** (S-950BF, SBWC-1,300BF, D-1,250BF, DBWC-1,600BF, T-1,750BF, TBWC-2,100BF, QBWC-2,600BF, lots of steep stairs, 3 blocks east of Market at Sint-Walburgastraat 14, tel. 334294) are a young couple who enjoy translating for the guests who eat a hearty breakfast around a big table in their bright, homey, comfortable house. They are a friendly wealth of information on Bruges. **Paul and Roos Gheeraert** (small D-1,350BF, D-1,500BF, T-2,000BF, 4 blocks east of Market at Ridderstraat 9, tel. 335627) live on the first floor, while their guests take the second. Lots of stairs, but with bright, comfy rooms, this is a fine value.

Youth Hostels
Bruges has several good hostels offering beds for around 350BF in 3- to 7-bed rooms. Pick up the hostel info sheet at the station TI. Smallest, loosest, and closest to the center are: **Snuffel Travelellers Inn** (Ezelstraat 47, tel. 333133), **Bauhaus International Youth Hotel** (Langestraat 135, tel. 341093) and Passage (Dweerstraat 26, tel. 340232). Bigger, more modern, and less central are: **International Youth Hostel Europa** (Baron Ruzettelaan 143, tel. 352679), **IYH Herdersbrug** (Louis Coiseaukaai 46, tel. 599321), and the **Merkenveld Scout Center** (Merkenveldweg 15, tel. 277698).

PARIS

Paris offers sweeping boulevards, sleepy parks, world-class art galleries, chatty crêpe stands, Napoleon's body, sleek shopping malls, the Eiffel Tower, and people-watching from outdoor cafés. Climb the Notre Dame and the Eiffel Tower, cruise the Seine and Champs-Elysées, and master the Louvre and Orsay museums. Save some after-dark energy for one of the world's most romantic cities. Many people fall in love with Paris. Some see the essentials and flee, overwhelmed by the huge city. With the proper approach and a good orientation, you'll fall head over heels for Europe's capital city.

Orientation (tel. code: 1)

Paris is split in half by the Seine River, divided into 20 *arrondissements* (proud and independent governmental jurisdictions), and circled by a ring-road freeway (the *périphérique*). You'll find Paris much easier to negotiate if you know which side of the river you're on, which *arrondissement* you're in, and which subway (Métro) stop you're closest to. Remember, if you're north of the river (above on any city map), you're on the right bank (*rive droite*), and if you're south of it, you're on the left bank (*rive gauche*). *Arrondissements* are numbered, starting at ground zero (the Louvre is 1ème) and moving in a clock-wise spiral out to the ring road. The last two digits in a Parisian zip code are the *arrondissement* number, and the notation for the Métro stop is "Mo." In Parisian jargon, Napoleon's tomb is on *la rive gauche* (the left bank) in the 7ème, zip code 75007, Métro: Invalides. Paris Métro stops are a standard aid in giving directions.

Tourist Information

Avoid the Paris TIs—long lines and short information. This book, the *Pariscope* magazine, and one of the freebie maps available at any hotel are all you need for a short visit. The main TI is at 127 avenue des Champs-Élysées (open 9:00-20:00), but the neighborhood TIs (see Sleeping in Paris) are handier.

Paris

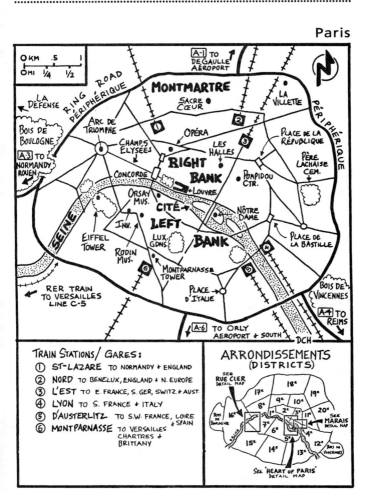

TRAIN STATIONS/ GARES:
① ST-LAZARE TO NORMANDY & ENGLAND
② NORD TO BENELUX, ENGLAND & N. EUROPE
③ L'EST TO E. FRANCE, S. GER, SWITZ. & AUST.
④ LYON TO S. FRANCE & ITALY
⑤ D'AUSTERLITZ TO S.W. FRANCE, LOIRE & SPAIN
⑥ MONTPARNASSE TO VERSAILLES, CHARTRES & BRITTANY

ARRONDISSEMENTS (DISTRICTS)

The *Pariscope* weekly magazine (or one of its clones, 3F, at any newsstand) lists museum hours, concerts and musical festivals, plays, movies, nightclubs, and special art exhibits. For recorded concert and special events information in English, call 47 20 88 98. For a complete list of museum hours and scheduled English museum tours, pick up the free *Musées, Monuments Historiques, et Expositions* booklet from any museum.

While it's easy to pick up free maps of Paris once you've arrived (your hotel has them), they don't show all the streets, and you may want the huge Michelin #10 map of Paris. For an extended stay, consider the excellent *Paris par Arrondisement* map book, as well as two fine guidebooks: *Michelin Green Guide* (somewhat scholarly) and the *Access Guide to Paris*.

There are 11 English-language bookstores in Paris where you can pick up guidebooks: Shakespeare and Co. (with used travel books, 37 rue de la Boucherie, across the river from Notre Dame, 12:00-24:00), W. H. Smith (248 rue de Rivoli), and Brentano (47 avenue de L'Opéra) are three good ones.

The American Church is a nerve center for the American émigré community and publishes and distributes *Free Voice. France*, a handy monthly, and *France—USA Contacts*, an advertisement paper, is full of useful information for those looking for work or long-term housing.

Trains

Paris has six train stations, all connected by Métro and bus, all with luggage storage, banks, and tourist information offices. Here's how they're organized: the Gare de l'Est covers destinations to the east; the Gare du Nord and Gare St. Lazare serve northern and central Europe; the *gares* Austerlitz and Lyon cover southern Europe, and the newly revamped Montparnasse *gare* handles western France and TGV service to France's southwest. Any *gare* can give you schedule information, make reservations and sell tickets for any destination.

Getting Around Paris

A word of caution: Pickpockets are skilled at relieving Americans of their wallets and waist packs on subways and buses. Keep valuables in your money belt.

By Métro: Europe's best subway is divided into two systems: the Métro covers the city and the RER connects suburban destinations. You'll be using the Métro for almost all your trips. In Paris, you're never more than a 10-minute walk from a Métro station. One ticket takes you anywhere in the system with unlimited transfers. Save nearly 50 percent by buying a *carnet* (car-nay) of ten tickets for about 40F at any Métro station. Métro tickets work on city buses, though one ticket cannot be used as a transfer between subway and bus.

If you've only got one day to do Paris, buy the *Formule 1 pass* (30F) which allows unlimited travel for a single day. If you're staying longer, the *Carte d'Orange* pass gives you free run of the bus and Métro system for one week (60F, ask for the *Carte d'Orange Coupon Vert*) or a month (*290F, ask for the Carte d'Orange Coupon Orange*). The weekly pass begins Monday and ends Sunday, and the monthly pass begins the first day of the month and ends the last day of that month, so mid-week or mid-month purchases are generally not worthwhile. You'll also need a photo of yourself to buy a *Carte d'Orange* (many Métro stations have self-serve photo booths). All passes can be purchased at any Métro station.

Before entering the station, find the "Mo" stop closest to your destination and which line(s) will get you there. The lines have numbers, but they're best known by their *direction* or end-of-the-line stop. (For example, the Saint-Denis/Châtillon line runs between Saint-Denis in the north and Châtillon in the south.)

Once in the Métro station, you'll see blue on white signs directing you to the train going in your direction (e.g., direction: Saint-Denis). Insert your ticket in the automatic turnstile, pass through, reclaim and *keep your ticket until you exit the system* (fare inspectors accept no excuses from anyone). Transfers are free and can be made wherever lines cross. When you transfer, look for the orange *correspondance* (connections) signs when you exit your first train, then follow the proper "direction" sign.

Before you *sortie* (exit), check the helpful *plan du quartier* (map of the neighborhood) to get your bearings and decide which sortie you want. At stops with several *sorties*, you can save lots of walking by choosing the best exit. Remember your essential Métro words: *direction* (direction), *correspondance* (connections), *sortie* (exit), *carnet* (cheap set of ten tickets), and *donnez-moi mon porte-monnaie!* (Give me back my wallet!). Thieves thrive in the Métro.

The RER suburban train system (thick lines on your subway map identified by letters A, B, C etc.) works like the Métro—but is much speedier because it makes only a few stops within the city. One Métro ticket is all you need for RER rides within Paris. You can transfer between the Métro and RER systems with the same ticket and, unlike the Métro, you need your ticket to exit the RER system. To travel outside the city (to Versailles or the airport, for example), you'll need to buy another ticket at the station window before boarding, and make sure your stop is served by checking the signs over the train platform.

By City Buses: The trickier bus system is worth using, though you'll need to spend some time to understand it. The same yellow tickets are good on both bus and Métro, though you can't use the same ticket to transfer between the two systems, and longer rides require more than one ticket. While the Métro shuts down about 00:45, some buses continue much later. Schedules are posted at bus stops.

To ride the bus, study the big system maps at each stop to figure out which route(s) you need. Then look at the individual route diagrams, showing the exact route of the lines serving that stop to verify your route. Major stops are also painted on the side of each bus. Enter through the front doors. Punch your yellow Métro ticket(s) in the machine behind the driver, or pay the higher cash fare. Get off the bus using the rear door. Even if you're not certain you've figured it out, do some joyriding (outside of rush hour). Lines #24, #63, and #69 are Paris' most scenic routes and make a great introduction to this city.

By Taxi: Parisian taxis are almost reasonable. A 10-minute ride costs about 50F (versus 4F to get anywhere in town on the Métro), and luggage will cost you more. You can try waving one down, but it's easier to ask for the nearest taxi stand (*"oo-ay la tet de stah-see-oh taxi"*). Sunday and night rates are higher, and if you call from your hotel, the meter starts as soon as the call is received. Taxis are tough to find on Friday and Saturday night, especially after the Métro closes.

Helpful Hints

Museums: Most museums are closed on Monday or Tuesday. Most offer reduced prices and shorter hours on Sunday. Many begin closing rooms 30 minutes before the actual closing time. For the fewest crowds, visit very early, at lunch, or very late. Most museums have shorter hours October-March, and holidays are usually 1/1, 5/1, 5/8, 7/14, 11/1, 11/11, and 12/25.

Youth and Senior Discounts: Those under age 26 and over 60 get big discounts on some sights.

Restaurants: Check price lists before ordering at any café or restaurant. Rude surprises await sloppy tourists.

Toilets: Carry small change for pay toilets, or walk into any outdoor café like you own the place and find the toilet in the back.

Walking: Pedestrians don't have the right of way—drivers do and they know it.

Theft Alert: Use your money belt, and never carry a wallet in your back pocket or a purse over your shoulder.

Telephone Cards: Pick up the essential France telecarte at any *tabac*, post office, or tourist office (*une petite carte* is 40F, *une grande* is 90F). You'll need it for most calls.

Useful Telephone Numbers: American Hospital, 46 41 25 25; American pharmacy, 47 42 49 40 (Opéra); Police, 17; U.S. Embassy, 42 96 12 02; Paris and France directory assistance, 12; AT&T operator, 19 00 11; MCI operator, 19 00 19.

Sightseeing in Paris

The price of Parisian sights continues to climb. To control these costs, know if you qualify for an age discount (under 18, 26, or over 60), visit the more expensive museums on Sunday when they're all half off, and consider purchasing the "monuments/museum pass" if you plan to do some serious sightseeing and don't qualify for age discounts. It's sold at museums, main Métro stations, and tourist offices, and gets you into all major sights (including Versailles) with no lining up. (One day-60F, 3 consecutive days-120F, 5 consecutive days-170F.) With average sights running at 30F or more this card can pay for itself quickly.

Bonjour, Paris

Your first goal is to get comfortably set up in your hotel, learn the subway system, and take a Paris orientation walk through the city's old core. I've outlined three interesting full-day sightseeing walks and a shorter welcome-to-Paris orientation stroll.

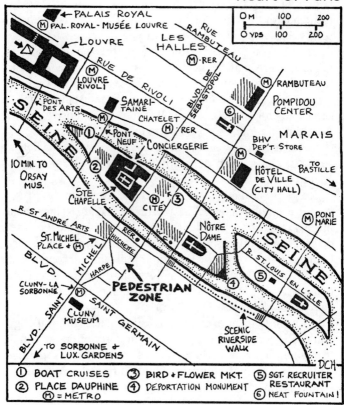

Heart of Paris

PALAIS ROYAL
Ⓜ PAL. ROYAL - MUSÉE LOUVRE
LOUVRE
LES HALLES
RUE RAMBUTEAU
Ⓜ · RER
RUE DE RIVOLI
Ⓜ LOUVRE RIVOLI
SAMARI-TAINE
CHATELET
BLVD. DE SEBASTOPOL
⑥
Ⓜ RAMBUTEAU
POMPIDOU CENTER
SEINE
PONT DES ARTS
① PONT NEUF
Ⓜ
CHATELET
RER
CONCIERGERIE
MARAIS
BHV DEP'T. STORE
Ⓜ
HÔTEL DE VILLE (CITY HALL)
TO BASTILLE
10 MIN. TO ORSAY MUS.
② STE. CHAPELLE
Ⓜ CITÉ
③
NÔTRE DAME
Ⓜ PONT MARIE
R. ST ANDRÉ ARTS
RER
HUCHETTE
SEINE
ST. MICHEL PLACE Ⓜ
BLVD. SAINT MICHEL
HARPE
PEDESTRIAN ZONE
R. ST. LOUIS EN L'ILE
④ ⑤
CLUNY-LA SORBONNE Ⓜ
CLUNY MUSEUM
SAINT GERMAIN
SCENIC RIVERSIDE WALK
BLVD. TO SORBONNE & LUX. GARDENS
DCH

0 M   100   200
0 YDS   100   200

① BOAT CRUISES   ③ BIRD & FLOWER MKT.   ⑤ SGT. RECRUITER RESTAURANT
② PLACE DAUPHINE   ④ DEPORTATION MONUMENT   ⑥ NEAT FOUNTAIN !
Ⓜ = METRO

First Evening Orientation Walk

(This is ideal for *les laggards du jet*.) Once you've set up in your hotel, introduce yourself to Paris. If you just landed in Europe, an evening walk will show you some of Paris' delights and keep your jet-laggy body moving until a reasonable European bedtime. Bring a map and whenever you run out of steam, just find the nearest Métro and head back home.

Start with a Métro ride to the Louvre stop. (Note: This is no longer the Louvre museum stop.) Study the Métro lesson above and use this ride to put each of those tips into action. Exit the station, walk to the river, jog right, and cross the pedestrian-only bridge (Pont des Arts).

Here, take your time, snap lots of photos, and grab a
bench. On the Left Bank, find your way around to the
right side of the Palais de l'Institut de France (that domed
semi-circular building in front of you), part of which is
Académie Français, then angle left up the rue de Seine.
Consider a stop at the very Parisian La Palette café, then
take a brief right on rue de Buci. Take a left onto the
famous boulevard St. Germain, the heart and soul of Paris
cafés and shopping. Look for Paris' most expensive café,
Au Deux Magots, as soon as you enter St. Germain.
(Ernest Hemingway hung out here while writing *The Sun
Also Rises,* back when they didn't charge $9 for a glass of
champagne.)

Check out Paris' oldest church, St. Germain des Pres,
then cruise the boulevard St. Germain, making a right at the
place de l'Odéon. Meander around the temple-like Theatre
de l'Odéon into Paris' most beautiful park, the Luxembourg
Gardens. Grab a chair by the center fountain and contemplate
where you are—as Hemingway loved to do, right here. (The
handiest Métro stop from here is Luxembourg or Odéon,
back on boulevard St. Germain.)

Our busy plan of attack is outlined here, with walking
guides for each day. Refer to the sight descriptions as you
plan your days and do these walks. Train travelers should go
to any Paris train station information office to verify train
schedules for the first few days of their trip.

Latin Quarter/Louvre/
Arc de Triomphe Walk

Last night we oriented; today we attack. Start at the St.
Michel Métro stop, where you'll find the heart of an
uncharacteristically sleepy Latin Quarter. This is a street-
hoppin' place at night. It uses mornings to recover. Walk
down rue de la Huchette (past the popular jazz cellar at
#5—check the schedule) and over the bridge to Notre
Dame cathedral. It took 200 years to build this church.
Walk around to its impressive back side and visit the moving memorial to the 200,000 French people deported by
Hitler in World War II.

Across the bridge is the Île (island) of St. Louis (we'll
tour it later). Walking back through the center of the Île de

la Cité, you'll come to the Ste. Chapelle church, a Gothic gem. After touring it, continue to the tip of the island (lovely park) through the peaceful, triangular place Dauphine. Next, cross the oldest bridge in town, the Pont Neuf, to the Right Bank. Drop into the Samaritaine department store across the bridge—don't miss the remarkable interior of this French JC Penney. Lunch on the fifth floor (cafeteria open 11:30-15:00, 15:30-18:30).

Then tackle the Louvre, at one time Europe's grandest palace, today, its most grueling and overwhelming museum. The new Louvre entry is a magnificent glass pyramid in the central courtyard. After mastering the Louvre, unwind with a stroll through the Tuilleries to the place de la Concorde, where over 1,300 heads rolled during the French Revolution, and bop up the world's most famous street, the Champs-Élysées. From the majestic Arc de Triomphe, you can take the Métro home.

Eiffel Tower/rue Cler/Rodin Museum/Orsay Museum Walk

Métro to Trocadéro. Exit the subway, following the *Sortie Tour Eiffel* signs to one of Europe's great views (come back at night for a real thrill). From here, the tower seems to straddle the military school (École Militaire). Napoleon lies powerfully dead under the golden dome of Les Invalides to the left. Take the elevator up to the second level of the tower, then walk away from the river through the park. Follow the third cross street left into the classy area around rue de Grenelle. Turn right on rue Cler for a rare bit of village Paris (shops closed 13:00-16:00 and on Monday).

Assemble a picnic and follow avenue de la Motte Piquet left to the grand esplanade des Invalides, a fine picnic spot. The Hôtel des Invalides, with Napoleon's tomb and the army museum, is on your right. Cross the square, turn right on avenue des Invalides, and look for the Rodin Museum (Hôtel Biron) on the left. Tour the great sculpture museum. You can picnic or eat in the cafeteria surrounded by Rodin's works in the elegant backyard.

Now it's on to the dazzling Musée d'Orsay. Make a right when you come out of the Rodin Museum and a quick

left on rue de Bourgogne, follow it to the Assemblée
Nationale, where you'll turn right on rue de l'Université,
cross boulevard St. Germain, and follow signs to the Musée
d'Orsay. If you still have energy, walk away from the river
and hook up with Paris' best people-watching, shopping, and
café street, the boulevard St. Germain.

Ile St. Louis/Marais/Beaubourg Walk

Start in front of the Hôtel de Ville, the old city hall
(Métro: Hôtel de Ville). Admire the superb restoration,
then follow the river down to the Pont Louis Phillipe.
Cross it into the charm and tranquillity of the Île St. Louis.
Bisect the island along rue St. Louis (good place for dinner
tonight), admiring the doorway at #51 and the minuscule
travel bookstore at #35, then take the last left across the
Pont de Sully and angle up the rue du Petit Musc to the
rue St Antoine. A left on the rue St. Antoine and a right
on the rue Biraque takes you into the most beautiful
square in Paris, the place des Vosges.

Now it's decision time: Are you a Picasso fan or
more curious about Parisian history? Tour either the
Picasso Museum or the Carnavalet Museum, then drop
down to the rue Rosiers (the heart of Paris' Jewish community) for some character and lunch or grab a falafel
sandwich to go. Resume your stroll down rue Rosiers and
turn right when it ends. A left on rue des Francs Bourgeois
brings you back to the 20th century with the bizarre architecture of the Pompidou Center. Join the fray around the
center and take in a street show or two. Ride the escalators
through the Star Wars tubes of the Pompidou to the top
for the view and consider seeing its excellent modern art
collection on the fourth floor. (See Beaubourg listing
below for more information.)

Sights—Paris

▲▲▲**Latin Quarter**—This area, which gets its name from
the language used here when it was an exclusive medieval
university district, lies between the Luxembourg Gardens
and the Seine, centering around the Sorbonne University
and boulevards St. Germain and St. Michel. This is the core

of the Left Bank—the artsy, liberal, hippy, Bohemian district
of poets, philosophers, and winos. It's full of international
eateries, far-out bookshops, street singers, pale girls in black
berets, and jazz clubs. For colorful wandering and café-
sitting, afternoons and evenings are best.

▲▲**Notre Dame Cathedral**—The cathedral is 700 years
old and packed with history and tourists. Climb to the top
for a great gargoyle's-eye view of the city (entrance on outside left, open 9:30-17:30, closed at lunch and earlier off-
season), you get over 400 stairs for only 33F. Study its
sculpture (Notre Dame's forte) and windows, take in a mass
(or the free Sunday 17:30 recital on the 6,000-pipe organ,
France's largest), eavesdrop on guides, and walk all around
the outside. (Open 8:00-18:45, treasury open 9:30-18:00,
admission free. Ask about the free English tours, normally
Wednesday at noon June-September, tel. 43 26 07 39. Clean
2.50F toilets in front of the church near Charlemagne's statue.
Sunday Mass at 8:00, 8:45, 10:00, 11:30, 12:30, and 18:30).

Back outside, the archaeological crypt offers a fascinating
look at the remains of the earlier city and church (enter 100
yards in front of church, 26F, daily 10:00-18:00). Drop into
the Hôtel Dieu, on the square opposite the river, for a pleasant
courtyard and a look at a modern hospice, offering many a
pleasant last stop before heaven. If you're hungry near Notre
Dame, the only grocery store on the Île de la Cité is tucked
away on a small street running parallel to the church, one
block north.

▲▲**Deportation Memorial**—The architecture of this
memorial to the French victims of the Nazi concentration
camps is a powerful blend of water, sky, bars, confinement,
concrete, eternal flame, the names of many concentration
camps, and a crystal for each of the 200,000 victims. (Free,
open 10:00-12:00, 14:00-19:00, closes off-season at 17:00,
east tip of the island near Île St. Louis, behind Notre
Dame.)

▲▲▲**Sainte-Chapelle**—The triumph of Gothic church
architecture, a cathedral of glass, like none other. It was built
in just five years to house the supposed Crown of Thorns
(which cost the king more than the church). Downstairs was
for commoners, upstairs for royal Christians. Hang out at
the top of the spiral stairs and watch the room's beauty suck

the breath from emerging tourists. There's a good little book on sale (with color photos) that explains the stained glass in English. There are concerts almost every summer evening (120F). Anything going on tonight? Even a beginning violin class would sound lovely here. (Open 9:30-18:00; off-season 10:00-16:30, 27F. Stop at the ticket booth outside the church, or call 43 54 30 09 for concert information. Handy free public toilets just outside).

▲▲▲The Louvre—This is Europe's oldest, biggest, greatest, and maybe most crowded museum. The newly rennovated Richelieu wing and underground shopping mall extension add the finishing touches to *Le Grand Louvre Project* (that started in 1989 with the pyramid entrance) and make extremely helpful and dazzling additions to the museum. Once inside, walk toward the inverted pyramid and uncover a post office, a Virgin Megastore, a dizzying assortment of eateries, and the Palais Royal Métro entrance. A new pricing policy allows you to save 50 percent by entering the musuem after 15:00.

Don't try to cover the museum thoroughly. The 90-minute English-language tours leave nearly every half hour except Sunday and Monday and are the best way to enjoy this huge museum (find Accueil des Groupes desk at entry, information tel. 40 20 50 50, usually almost hourly, 30F). My book, *Mona Winks*, (buy in U.S.A.) includes a self-guided tour of the Louvre, as well as of the Orsay, the Pompidou, and Versailles.

If you're unable to get a guide, a good do-it-yourself tour of the museum's highlights would include (in this order, starting in the Denon wing): Ancient Greek (Parthenon frieze, *Venus de Milo*, Nike of Samothrace); Apollo Gallery (jewels); French and Italian paintings in the Grande Galerie (a quarter-mile long and worth the hike); the *Mona Lisa* and her Italian Renaissance roommates; the nearby neoclassical collection (*Coronation of Napoleon*); and the romantic collection with works by Delacroix and Gericault. You can enter the pyramid for free until 21:30. Go in at night to see it glow. (Open daily 9:00-18:00; Wednesday until 21:45; Monday until 21:30. Note: Not all of the collection is on view on Monday evening. Closed Tuesday. 40F until 15:00, 20F after 15:00, on Sunday and for the younger and older, and free if you're under 18. Use the handy ticket dispensing machines to save time if lines are long. Tel. 40 20 53 17 or 40 20 51 51 for recorded information. Métro: Palais-Royale/Musée du Louvre—not the Louvre stop.)

Best Impressionist Art Museums—The following three museums offer the best look at Impressionist art in Paris:

▲**The Marmottan**—In this intimate, lesser-visited museum you'll find over 100 paintings by Claude Monet (thanks to his son Michel) and a variety of other famous Impressionist works. (Open 10:00-17:30, closed Monday, 36F, 2 rue Louis Boilly, tel. 42 24 07 02, Métro: La Muette.)

▲▲▲**Orsay Museum**—This is Paris' 19th-century art museum (actually, art from 1848-1914), including Europe's greatest collection of Impressionist works (call for 30F English tour schedule). Start on the ground floor. The "pretty" conservative establishment art is on the right, then cross left into the brutally truthful, and at that time, very shocking art of the realist rebels and Manet. Then go way up the escalator at the far end to the series of Impressionist rooms (Monet, Renoir, Degas, et al) and van Gogh. Don't miss the Art Nouveau on the mezzanine level. The museum is housed in a former train station (Gare d'Orsay) across the river and 10 minutes downstream from the Louvre. (Open July and August and all Sundays 9:00-18:00; other days 10:00-18:00; Thursday until 21:45, closed Monday, most crowded around 11:00 and 14:00, 36F, 24F for the young and old, tel. 40 49 48 14, 3, rue Bellechasse, Métro: Solferino, or better the RER: Musee d'Orsay.)

▲▲**L'Orangerie**—This small, quiet, and often overlooked museum houses Monet's water lilies, many famous Renoirs, and a scattering of other Impressionist works. (Open 9:45-17:15, closed Tuesday, 27F, located in the Tuileries Gardens near the place de la Concorde.)

▲▲**Napoleon's Tomb and the Army Museum**—The emperor lies majestically dead inside several coffins under a grand dome—a goose-bumping pilgrimage for historians—surrounded by the tombs of other French war heroes and Europe's greatest military museum, in the Hôtel des Invalides. (Open daily 10:00-18:00, 34F, tel. 44 42 37 67, Métro: La Tour Maubourg.)

▲▲**Rodin Museum**—This user-friendly museum is filled with surprisingly entertaining work by the greatest sculptor since Michelangelo. See *The Kiss, The Thinker*, and many more. Near Napoleon's Tomb. (Open 9:30-17:45, closed Monday and at 17:00 off-season. 27F, 17F on Sunsay, 5F for gardens only, which may be Paris' best deal as many works are well displayed in the gardens, tel. 47 05 01 34. 77, rue de Varennes, Métro: Varennes, 75007.) Good self-serve cafeteria and idyllic picnic spots in back garden.

▲▲**Pompidou Center**—Europe's greatest collection of far-out modern art, the Musée National d'Art Moderne is housed in this colorfully exoskeletal building. After so many Madonnas and Children, a piano smashed to bits and glued to the wall is refreshing. It's a social center with lots of people, street theater, and activity inside and out—a perpetual street fair. Ride the escalator for a free city view from the café terrace on top and don't miss the free exhibits on the ground floor. (Open Monday-Friday 12:00-22:00; Saturday, Sunday, and most holidays 10:00-22:00, closed Tuesday, 30F, 20F for the young and old, free Sunday 10:00-14:00, tel. 44 78 12 33, Métro: Rambuteau.)

Jeu de Paume—Modern art fans should not miss this one-time home to the impressionist art collection now located in the Musee d'Orsay. Completely rennovated, this museum hosts rotating exhibits of top contemporary artists, brilliantly displaying their works. (Open 12:00-19:00; weekends 10:00-19:00, ciosed Monday, 35F. Located on the place de la Concorde, just inside the Tuileries gardens on the rue de Rivoli side. Métro Concorde.)

▲**Beaubourg**—This was a separate village until the 12th century, and today it includes the area from the Pompidou Center to the Forum des Halles shopping center. Most of Paris' renovation energy over the past 20 years seems to have been directed here—before then it was a slum. Don't miss the new wave fountains (the *Homage to Stravinsky*) on the river side of the Pompidou Center, or the eerie clock you'll find through the *Quartier d'Horloge* passage on the other side. A colorful stroll down rue Rambuteau takes you to the space age Forum des Halles, Paris' largest shopping mall, on the site of what was a wonderful outdoor food market. As you tour this shopping mecca, peek into the huge 350-year-old St. Eustache Church. The striking round building at the end of the esplanade is Paris' old Bourse, or Commercial Exchange. For an oasis of peace, continue to the interior gardens of the Palais-Royal. (Métro: Les Halles or Rambuteau.)

▲▲**Eiffel Tower**—Crowded and expensive but worth the trouble. The higher you go, the more you pay. I think the view from the 400-foot-high second level is plenty. Pilier Nord (the north pillar) has the biggest elevator—with the fastest moving line. The Restaurant Belle France serves decent 90F meals (first level). Don't miss the entertaining free movie on the history of the tower on the first level. Heck of a view. (Open daily 9:00-24:00, 20F to first level, 36F to second, 52F to go all the way for the 1,000-foot view. On a budget? You can climb the stairs to the second level for only 10F, tel. 45 50 34 56. Métro: Trocadero. RER: Champs de Mars.) Arrive early for less crowds. For another great view, especially at night, cross the river and enjoy the tower from Trocadero, or have a picnic in front of the tower after the grass guards have left.

▲**Montparnasse Tower**—A 59-floor superscraper, cheaper and easier to get to the top of than the Eiffel Tower. Possibly Paris' best view, since the Eiffel Tower is in it and the Montparnasse tower isn't. Buy the photo-guide to the city, go to the rooftop and orient yourself. This is a fine way to understand the lay of this magnificent land. It's a good place to be as the sun goes down on your first day in Paris. Find your hotel, retrace your day's steps, locate the famous buildings. (Open summer 9:30-23:00; off-season 10:00-22:00, 40F, Métro Montparnasse.)

▲**Samaritaine Department Store View Point**—Enter the store, go to the rooftop (ride the elevator from near the Pont Neuf entrance, then find the spiral staircase; watch your head). Quiz yourself. Working counterclockwise, find the Eiffel Tower, Invalides/Napoleon's Tomb, Montparnasse Tower, Henry IV statue on the tip of the island, Sorbonne University, the dome of the Panthéon, Sainte-Chapelle, Hôtel de Ville (city hall), the wild and colorful Pompidou Center, Sacré-Coeur, Opéra, and Louvre. Light meals on the breezy terrace and a moderately priced restaurant on the fifth floor with fine views and dull food. (Rooftop view is free. tel. 40 41 20 20, Métro: Pont Neuf.)

▲▲**Sacré-Coeur and Montmartre**—This Byzantine-looking church is only 100 years old, but it's very impressive. It was built as a "praise the Lord anyway" gesture after the French were humiliated by the Germans in a brief war in 1871. The place du Tertre was the haunt of Toulouse-Lautrec and the original Bohemians. Today it's mobbed by tourists and unoriginal Bohemians—but still fun. Watch the artists, tip the street singers, have a dessert crêpe, and wander down the rue Lepic to the two remaining windmills (there were once 30) and down the rue des Saules to see Paris' only vineyard. The church is open daily and evenings. (Plaster of Paris comes from the gypsum found on this *mont*. Place Blanche is the white place nearby where they used to load it, sloppily.) Métros: Anvers (use the funicular to avoid stairs, one Métro ticket) or closer, but less scenic Abbesses.

Pigalle—Paris' red-light district, the infamous "Pig Alley," is at the foot of Butte Montmartre. Ooh la la. More shocking than dangerous. Stick to the bigger streets, hang onto your wallet, and exercise good judgment. Can-can can cost a fortune as can con artists in topless bars. (Métro: Pigalle.)

Best Shopping—Forum des Halles is a grand new subterranean center, a sight in itself. Fun, mod, colorful, and very Parisian. (Métro: Halles). The Lafayette Galleries behind the Opera House is your best elegant, Old World, one-stop, Parisian department store/shopping center. Also, visit the Printemps store and the historic Samaritaine department store near Pont Neuf.

Good Browsing

Rue Rambuteau from the Halles to the Pompidou Center, the Marais/Jewish Quarter/place des Vosges area, the Champs-Élysées, and the Latin Quarter. Window-shop along the rue de Rivoli, which borders the Louvre. The rue de Rivoli is also the city's souvenir row, especially for fun T-shirts. Ritzy shops are around the Ritz Hotel at place Vendôme. (Métro: Tuileries.)

▲▲▲**Place de la Concorde and the Champs-Élysées**—This is Paris' backbone and greatest concentration of traffic.

All of France seems to converge on the place de la Concorde, Paris' largest square. It was here that the guillotine made hundreds "a foot shorter at the top"—including King Louis XVI. Back then it was called the place de la Revolution.

Catherine de Medici wanted a place to drive her carriage, so she started draining the swamp that would become the Champs-Élysées. Napoleon put on the final touches, and it's been the place to be seen ever since. The Tour de France bicycle race ends here, as do all French parades of any significance. (Métro: FDR, Etoile, or George V.)

▲▲▲**Arc de Triomphe**—Napoleon had the magnificent Arc de Triomphe constructed to commemorate his victory at the Battle of Austerlitz. There's no arch bigger in the world—or a crazier traffic circle. Eleven major boulevards feed into the place Charles de Gaulle (Étoile) that surrounds the arch. Watch the traffic tangle, and pray you don't end up here in a car. Take the underpass to visit the eternal flame and tomb of the unknown soldier. There's a cute museum of the arch (open daily 10:00-17:30, 26F) and a great view from the top.

▲▲**Luxembourg Gardens**—Paris' most beautiful, interesting, and enjoyable garden/park/recreational area is a great place to watch Parisians at rest and play. Check out the card players (near the tennis courts), find a free chair near the main pond, and take a breather. Notice any pigeons? A poor Ernest Hemingway used to hand-hunt (strangle) them here. The grand Neoclassical domed Panthéon is a block away. (The park is open until dusk, Métro: Odéon.)

▲**Other Parisian Parks**—If you enjoy the Luxembourg Gardens and want to see more, try these central parks: **Parc Monceau** (Métro: Monceau), **Le Buttes Chaumont** (Métro: Buttes Chaumont), and the **Jardin des Plantes** (Métro: Jussieu).

▲▲**Le Marais**—This once smelly swamp (*marais*) was drained in the 12th century and soon became a fashionable place to live, at least until the Revolution. It's Paris at its medieval best. This is how much of the city looked until, in the mid-1800s, Napoleon III had Baron Haussmann blast through the boulevards (open and wide enough for the guns and marching ranks of the army, too wide for revolutionary barricades), creating modern Paris. Here you'll find a tiny but thriving Jewish neighborhood; Paris' most striking and oldest square, *place des Vosges*; a monument to the revolutionary storming of the Bastille at place de la Bastille (nothing but memorial marks on the street is left of the actual Bastille prison); the new controversial Opera House; the largest collection of Picassos in the world; Paris' great history museum (see below); and endless interesting streets to wander. (Métro: St. Paul.)

▲**Carnavalet (History of Paris) Museum**—Inside this fine example of a Marais mansion, complete with classy courtyards and statues, are paintings of Parisian scenes, French Revolution paraphernalia, old Parisian store signs, a guillotine, a superb model of 16th-century Île de la Cité (notice the bridge houses) and rooms full of 15th-century Parisian furniture. (Open 10:00-17:30, closed Monday, 26F, 23 rue du Sévigné, tel. 42 72 21 13, Métro: St. Paul.)

▲**Picasso Museum (Hôtel de Sale)**—The largest collection in the world of Pablo Picasso's paintings, sculpture, sketches, and ceramics, as well as his personal collection of Impressionist art. It's well explained in English and worth ▲▲▲ if you're a fan. (Open daily except Tuesday 9:30-18:00; until 22:00 on Wednesday, 26F, tel. 42 71 25 21, Métro: St. Paul or Rambuteau, 5 rue Thorigny.)

▲**Père Lachaise Cemetery**—Littered with the tombstones of many of the city's most illustrious dead, this is your best one-stop look at the fascinating and romantic world of the "permanent Parisians." The place is confusing, but maps (from the guardhouse or the cemetery flower shops) will direct you to the graves of Chopin, Molière, and even Jim Morrison. In section 92, a series of statues memorializing the war makes the French war experience a bit more real. (10F maps at flower store near entry, closes at dusk.)

St.-Germain-des-Prés—A church was first built on this site in A.D. 452. The church you see today was constructed in 1163, and has been recently restored. The area around the church hops at night, with fire eaters, mimes, and scads of artists. (Métro: St.-Germain-des-Prés.)

Grande Arche, La Defense—A new Paris attraction is a modern architectural wonder and the pride of modern Paris. Take the Métro or RER to La Defense, then follow signs to Grande Arche. Great city views from the Arche elevator (40F

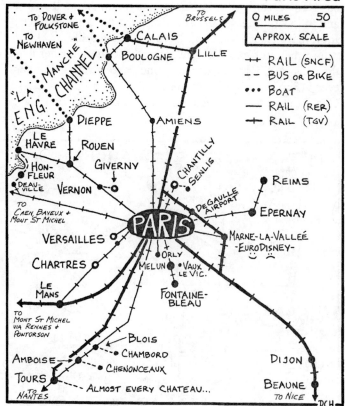

Paris Area

includes a film on its construction) and a huge shopping mall for comparison shoppers. (Open daily 9:00-19:00, weekends 9:00-20:00.)

Side Trips from Paris

▲▲▲Versailles—Every king's dream, Versailles was the residence of the French king and the cultural heartbeat of Europe for about 100 years—until the Revolution of 1789 ended the notion that God deputized some people to rule for Him on earth. Louis XIV spent half a year's income of Europe's richest country to build this palace fit for the ultimate divine monarch. Europe's next best palaces are, to a certain degree, Versailles wanna-be's.

Versailles is 12 miles from downtown Paris. Subway to
any RER-C station (the RER paralleling the Seine River)
and follow the RER signs to the train bound for Versailles
R.G. (Rive Gauche station). Do not ride Versailles C.H.
trains; they stop at a different Versailles station, farther from
the palace. (27F round-trip, 25 minutes each way; trains run
every 15 minutes, most but not all trains go to Versailles.
Check the stops listed on signs over the platform, or ask a

Versailles

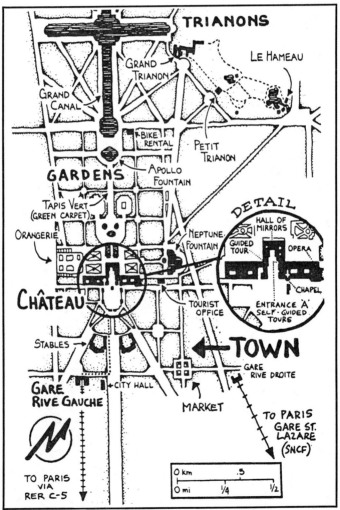

local for help. From the Versailles R.G. station, it's a 10-minute walk to the palace.)

There's a helpful tourist information office across the street from Versaille's R.G. station, and two info desks on the approach to the palace. Ask questions and read the useful brochure, *Versaille Orientation Guide*, to help you understand your sightseeing options.

The palace recently inaugurated an entirely new tour and pricing system. The base price of 40F gets you into the main palace for a self-guided tour. (The base price is only 26F for those under 26, over 60, and anyone visiting on Sunday or arriving 1½ hours before closing time on other days.) To the base price, add 22F for a guided tour, 22F for a Walkman-cassette tour, or 20F for admission to both Trianon châteaus in the garden. Read on before purchasing your ticket. (The main palace is open Tuesday-Sunday 9:00-18:30; October-April 9:00-17:30, last entry 30 minutes before closing, closed Monday, information tel. 30 84 76 18 or 30 84 74 00. Peak visitation is 9:00-15:00, Tuesday and Sunday are most crowded. If you dislike crowds, arrive at 16:00 and pay a reduced admission charge, tour the main palace and then the gardens after the palace closes.

If you are interested only in the base-price self-guided tour, join the line at entrance A (to the right as you face the palace). Enter the palace and take a one-way walk through the state apartments and the magnificent Hall of Mirrors. Before going downstairs at the end, take a historic stroll clockwise around the long room filled with the great battles of France murals. If you don't have *Mona Winks*, the guide-book called *The Châteaux, The Gardens, and Trianon* gives a room-by-room rundown.

If you are interested in a private tour, pay the base-price admission at the same time you pay for your tour (and avoid entrance A). The tours, led by an English-speaking art historian, take you through sections of Versailles not included in the base-price visit. Tours last 60 minutes, and groups are limited to less than 30. There are six different English-speaking tours possible; each costs 22F. If you've never been to Versailles, I strongly recommend the tour of the Opera and church or the tour of Louis XV apartments. (Some people do both.) Register for your tour(s) and times at entrance D (to the left and front as you face the palace). The tours leave from entrance F, straight across the courtyard from entrance D. Another option is the self-guided Walkman-cassette tour of the King's Chamber (22F, entrance C, to the left and front as you face the palace, 30 yards from entrance D). If the guided-tour line pushes your patience, this is a good option.

Many enjoy the gardens as much if not more than the palace. This is a divine picnic spot. Food is not allowed into the palace, but you can check your bag (and picnic) at the palace entrance, pick up your bag after your tour, and head off for your picnic. Or try the decent restaurant on the canal in the gardens. Every Sunday, May-October, when music fills the king's backyard and the garden's fountains are in full squirt (at 11:15 and 15:30), there's a 19F admission charge for the gardens—well worth it. (Free except Sunday, May-October, open 7:00-sunset.)

In the gardens, you'll find the Grand Trianon and the more intimate Petit Trianon, châteaus built for the king as private refuges from the palace. (Open May-September 10:00-18:00; off-season 10:00-17:00; with lunch break, except Saturday and Sunday, open all day; closed Monday; Grand Trianon-20F, Petit Trianon-12F. For 60F, payable at the main palace, you can get a combination ticket to the palace and both Trianons.)

Walk 45 minutes from the palace, take the 28F tourist train, or pedal a bike (rented in the garden) to visit the Little Hamlet where Marie Antoinette played peasant girl, tending her perfumed sheep and manicured garden, in her almost understandable retreat from reality.

The town of Versailles is quiet and pleasant. The central market is a great place to pick up a picnic, and the cozy *crêperie* on rue de la Deux Portes has a crêpe selection that would impress Louis himself. If you want to stay here, try the **Hotel Le Cheval Rouge** (DB-255F, DBWC-300F-390F, PD-30F, CC:VM), 18 rue Andre Chenier, tel. (1) 39 50 03 03, fax (1) 39 50 61 27).

▲▲**Chartres**—This is one of Europe's most important Gothic cathedrals. Malcolm Miller, or his impressive assistant, gives great "Appreciation of Gothic" tours daily (except Sunday and off-season) usually at noon and 14:45 (verify in advance, call the TI at (16) 37 21 50 00). Each tour is different, and costs 30F. Just show up at the church (open 7:00-19:00). Find time to explore Chartres pleasant center city and discover the picnic-perfect park behind the cathedral. The TI is next to the cathedral and has a map with a self-guided tour of Chartres (open 9:30-18:45). Chartres is a 1-hour train trip from Paris (hourly departures from the Gare Montparnasse, about 130F round-trip) and is a delightful overnight stop. The **Hotel St. Jean** is a fine value (D-160F, 6 rue Faubourg St. Jean, tel. 37 21 35 69).

▲▲**Château of Chantilly** (shan-tee-yee)—One of France's best château experiences is just 30 minutes and 30F by RER train from Paris's Gare du Nord station and then a 20-minute walk. Moat, drawbridge, sculpted gardens, little hamlet (the prototype for the more famous *hameau* at Versailles), lavish interior that rivals Versailles, world-class art collection (including two Raphaels), and reasonable crowds. (Open daily except Tuesday 10:00-18:00; off-season 10:00-13:00, 14:00-17:00, required French language tour included in admission price of 35F, 15F for gardens only.) Horse lovers will enjoy the nearby stables (expensive) built for a prince who believed he'd be reincarnated as a horse. The quaint and impressively preserved medieval town of Senlis is a 30-minute bus ride from the Chantilly station.

▲**Giverny**—Monet's gardens and home are very popular with his fans—so popular that you should count on a long wait to get in and serious crowds once inside. Still, the ponds, water lilies, and lovely gardens are pleasant and provide a more personal look at this very popular artist's life. The new American Impressionist Art Museum in Giverny, devoted to American artists who followed Claude to Giverny (worth the time if you've made the effort to get here, same price and hours as Monet's home), and the growing popularity of Monet's garden have made this sight a headache, even to devout fans. (Open April 1-October 31 10:00-18:00; closed off-season and Monday, 30F, 20F for gardens only, tel. 32 51 28 21. Nice restaurant next door has pricey but good lunches.) Take the Rouen train from Paris' Gare St. Lazare station to Vernon, a pleasant Normandy city (erratic schedule, very little service between 8:00-noon, check ahead). To get from the Vernon train station to Monet's garden (4 km away), take the

Vernon-Giverny bus (summer only), walk, hitch, taxi, or rent a bike at the station.

▲▲**Vaux-le-Vicomte**—This château is considered the prototype for Versailles. In fact, when its owner, Nicolas Fouquet, gave a grand party, Louis XIV was so jealous that he arrested the host and proceeded with the construction of the bigger and costlier, but not necessarily more splendid, palace of Versailles. Vaux-le-Vicomte is a joy to tour, elegantly furnished, and surrounded by royal gardens. It's not crowded, but it's difficult to get to without a car. Take the 65F (one-way) train ride from Paris' Gare de Lyon to Melun. Rent a bike (crummy ride on a busy road) or taxi (about 70F) the 6 km to the château. (Open daily 10:00-18:00, a steep 56F, gardens only 30F. Special candle-lit visits cost 68F and are on Saturday May-September 20:30-23:00; and Friday and Saturday in July and August. The fountains run April-October on the last two Saturdays of each month 15:00-18:00, tel. 64 14 41 90.)

▲▲**Disneyland Paris**—Europe's Disneyland is basically a modern remake of the one in California—with most of the same rides, smiles, and a French-speaking Mickey Mouse. My kids went ducky. Locals love it, except for the fact that the weather is gray and wine is hard to find. It's worth a day if Paris is handier than Florida or California. Crowds are a problem. Avoid Saturday, Sunday, Wednesday, school holidays, and July and August, if possible. The park is occasionally so crowded that they close the gates at 60,000 people (tel. 64 74 30 00 for the latest). After dinner the crowds are gone. Food service is fun, but expensive. Save money with a picnic. Disney brochures are in every Paris hotel. Ride the RER, about 30F each way, for 30 minutes direct from downtown Paris to Station Marne-la-Vallee, which takes you right to the park's gate. The last train to Paris leaves shortly after midnight. (Open daily 9:00-23:00 in summer, and Saturday and Sunday off-season; weekdays off-season 9:00-19:00, 250F adults, 150F for kids 3-11, 25F less in spring and fall, 50F less in winter, tel. 49 41 49 41 for park and hotel information.) To sleep cheaply at the huge Disney complex, try Hotel Sante Fe (550F family rooms for 2-4, 450F off-season).

▲▲▲**Reims and Verdun**—Both are daytripable from Paris (90 minutes by train to Reims, 3 hours to Verdun, both use the Gare de l'Est), but not on the same day.

Sleeping in Paris
(tel. code: 1 from outside France, 16-1 from within; 5.5F = about $1)

Paris is a huge city with a huge selection of hotels. To keep things manageable, I've focused on three safe, handy, and colorful neighborhoods, listing good hotels and helpful hints for each, to help make you a temporary resident. Good restaurants and cafés for each area are listed below, under Restaurants.

Choose your price range and neighborhood. French hotels come with a star classification. One star is simple, two has most of the basic comforts, and three is, for this book, plush (stars are indicated here by an *). Old, characteristic, budget Parisian hotels have always been cramped. Now they've added elevators, WC's, and private showers, and are even more cramped. Almost every hotel accepts Visa and Mastercard.

While you can save up to 100F by finding the increasingly rare room without a shower, these rooms are often smaller, and many places charge around 20F for each shower you take down the hall. Remember, baths and twin beds cost more than showers and double beds. And a toilet in the room costs even more. Breakfasts are usually optional and 20F-40F (prices listed are without breakfast). You can save about 10F each by eating in a nearby café, more by picnicking. Singles (unless the hotel has a few closet-type rooms that fit only one twin bed) are simply doubles inhabited by one person, renting for only a little, if any, less than a double.

Assume Paris will be tight. Look early, or better, have a reservation. Conventions clog the city in September (worst), October, May, and June. July and August are easier. Most hotels accept telephone reservations only for the same day or the next day. Most will have and hold a room for you if you call just after breakfast. Most require prepayment for a reservation far in advance (call first, and if they won't take a credit card number, follow up with a $50 traveler's check or a bank check in francs for the first night). Some, usually the very cheapest places, take no reservations at all.

Paris, Rue Cler Neighborhood

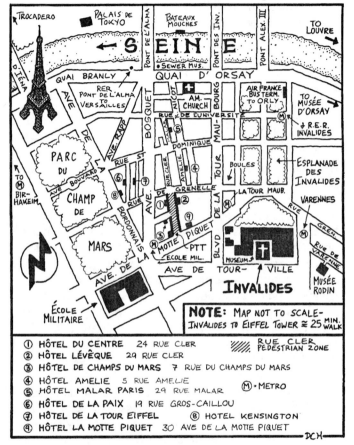

① HÔTEL DU CENTRE   24 RUE CLER   ▨▨ RUE CLER
② HÔTEL LÉVÊQUE   29 RUE CLER   PEDESTRIAN ZONE
③ HÔTEL DE CHAMPS DU MARS   7 RUE DU CHAMPS DU MARS
④ HÔTEL AMELIE   5 RUE AMELIE
⑤ HÔTEL MALAR PARIS   29 RUE MALAR   Ⓜ=METRO
⑥ HÔTEL DE LA PAIX   19 RUE GROS-CAILLOU
⑦ HÔTEL DE LA TOUR EIFFEL   ⑧ HÔTEL KENSINGTON
⑨ HÔTEL LA MOTTE PIQUET   30 AVE DE LA MOTTE PIQUET

Sleep code: **S**=Single, **D**=Double/Twin, **T**=Triple,
Q=Quad, **B**=Bath/Shower, **WC**=Toilet, **PD**=Breakfast,
CC=Credit Card (**V**isa, **M**astercard, **A**mex). Note: Quad
rooms are usually two double beds.

Sleeping in the Rue Cler Neighborhood (7th district, Métro: École Militaire, zip code: 75007)

Rue Cler, a village-like pedestrian street, is safe, tidy, and
makes me feel like I must have been a poodle in a previous
life. How such coziness lodged itself between the high-

powered government/business district and the expensive Eiffel Tower and Invalides areas, I'll never know. This is the ideal place to call home in Paris. Living here ranks with the top museums as one of the city's great experiences.

On rue Cler, you can step outside your hotel to eat and browse your way through a street full of tart shops, colorful outdoor produce stalls, cheeseries, and fish vendors. And you're within an easy walk of the Eiffel Tower, Les Invalides, and the Seine, as well as the Orsay and Rodin museums.

Hôtel Leveque* (S/D-195F-220F, DB-285F, DBWC-310F-345F, TBWC-420F, CC:VM, 29 rue Cler, tel. 47 05 49 15, fax 45 50 49 36 for reservation confirmations, English normally spoken, except by friendly Michele, who is very creative at communicating) is simple, clean, and well run, with a helpful staff, a singing maid, and the cheapest breakfast (25F) on the block. Reserve by phone; leave Visa number. No elevator, right in the traffic-free rue Cler thick of things. The newly renovated rooms on the street are well worth the few extra francs.

The **Hôtel du Centre*** (D-220F-240F, DBWC-350F-380F, TBWC-450F, all with TV, showers 10F, 30F-breakfast, CC:VMA, 24 rue Cler, tel. 47 05 52 33, fax 40 62 95 66), across the street from Leveque, is funkier, Edith-Bunker-esque, and a bit less free flowing than the Leveque.

The **Hôtel du Champs de Mars**** (DBWC-370F-400F, TBWC-500F, 35F breakfast, CC:VM, 7 rue du Champs de Mars, tel. 45 51 52 30), with its fine rooms and a helpful English-speaking staff, is a top "normal hotel" rue Cler option.

Hôtel la Motte Piquet** (DBWC-330F-430F, third person-100F, 33F-breakfast, CC:VM, 30 avenue de la Motte Piquet, on the corner of rue Cler, tel. 47 05 09 57, fax 47 05 74 36), with a plush lobby and basic comfortable rooms, is high on gadgets and low on charm.

Hôtel Rustic (DBWC-240F, T-300F, tel. 47 05 89 27) around the corner from the rue Cler on 2 rue Duvivier, with no breakfast room, no public area, skinny dark halls, sleep-able rooms, and miniscule bathrooms, should be avoided if you tend toward depression.

Hôtel de la Paix** (S-145F, DB-270F, 19 rue du Gros-Caillou, tel. 45 51 86 17) is a well-worn, spartan place, with springy twin beds, bright bed lights, easy telephone reservations, no elevator, peeling plaster and filthy hallways, run very agreeably by English-speaking Noél.

Hôtel de la Tour Eiffel** (DBWC-370F, 25F-breakfast, CC:VM, 17 rue des Expositions, tel. 47 05 14 75, fax 47 53 99 46), with petite but wicker-pleasant rooms, all with private facilities and TV, is like a small salad with lots of dressing.

Hôtel Eiffel Rive Gauche** (DWC-250F, DBWC-350F, 410F, and 450F, CC:VMA, with TV and phone, 6 rue du Gros-Caillou, tel. 45 51 24 56, fax 45 51 11 77) is a decent value on a quiet street, with a tiny, leafy courtyard giving the place a little more brightness than average.

Hôtel Malar Paris* (DB-300F, DBWC-360F, 24F-breakfast, CC:VM, 29 rue Malar, tel. 45 51 38 46, fax 45 55 20 19), run by friendly Mylene Caill and her husband, is cozy, quiet, and a great value if you don't mind stairs.

Hôtel Amelie** (DBWC-420F-460F, 35F-breakfast, CC:VM, 5 rue Amelie, tel. 45 51 74 75, fax 45 56 93 55) is pleasant and quiet.

Hotel Kensington** (DWC-310F, DBWC 370F-470F, 28F-breakfast, extra bed 80F, CC:VMA, 79 Avenue de La Bourdonnais, tel. 47 05 74 00, fax 47 05 25 81), in a stately neighborhood closer to the Eiffel Tower, is bigger, more professional, and a decent value.

Rue Cler Helpful Hints

Become a local at a rue Cler café for breakfast, or join the afternoon crowd for *une bière pression* (a draft beer). Cute shops and bakeries line the rue Cler, and there's a self-serve laundry at 16 rue Cler and another (more expensive) just off rue Cler on rue de la Grenelle. The Métro station and a post office with phone booths are at the end of rue Cler, on avenue de la Motte Piquet. Your neighborhood TI is at the Eiffel Tower (open May-September 11:00-18:00, tel. 45 51 22 15). There's a small late night grocery on rue de Grenelle near the Champ de Mars. You can change money at the Credit du Nord on rue Grenelle near rue Cler. Free curbside parking is sometimes available near the Champs de Mars. Park here if you're feeling lucky, or you can pay to park at the underground lot at École Militaire. Remember, metered parking is free in August.

At 65 quai d'Orsay, you'll find the American Church and College, the community center for Americans living in Paris. The interdenominational service at 11:00 on Sunday and coffee-fellowship and 50F lunch feast that follow are a great way to make some friends and get a taste of émigré life in Paris. Stop by and pick up copies of the *Free Voice* and *France-U.S.A.* Contacts newspapers (tel. 47 05 07 99). Information is available for those in need of housing or work through the community of 30,000 Americans living in Paris.

Afternoon *boules* (lawn bowling) on the esplanade des Invalides is competitive and a relaxing spectator sport. Look for the dirt area to the upper right as you face the Invalides.

For a magical picnic dinner, assemble it in no fewer than six shops on rue Cler and lounge on the best grass in Paris (the police don't mind after dark) with the dogs, Frisbees, a floodlit Eiffel Tower, and a cool breeze in the Parc du Champs de Mars. For an after-dinner cruise on the Seine, it's just a short walk across the river over the bridge (Pont d'Alma) to the Bâteaux Mouches. For corn flakes, baked beans, and Cracker Jacks, The Real McCoy (194 rue de Grenelle) is an "authentic" American grocery store. Also, don't miss the chocolate Eiffel Towers at La Maison du Petit Four on 187 rue de Grenelle.

Sleeping in the Marais Neighborhood
(4th district, Métro: St. Paul, zip code: 75004)

Those interested in a more Soho/Greenwich, gentrified, urban jungle locale would enjoy making the Marais/Jewish Quarter/St. Paul/Vosges area their Parisian home. The Marais is a cheaper and definitely more-happening locale than rue Cler. Narrow medieval Paris at its finest, only 15 years ago was a forgotten Parisian backwater. Now the Marais is one of Paris's most popular residential areas. It's a short walk to Notre Dame, Île St. Louis, and the Latin Quarter. The Métro stop St. Paul puts you right in the heart of the Marais.

Castex Hôtel** (SB-215F, SBWC-235F, DB-280F-310F, DBWC-300F-340F, TBWC-440F triple, extra bed 75F, 25F-breakfast, CC:VM, 5 rue Castex, just off place de la Bastille and rue Saint Antoine, Métro: Bastille, tel. 42 72 31 52, fax 42 72 57 91) is newly renovated, clean, cheery,

Paris, Marais Neighborhood

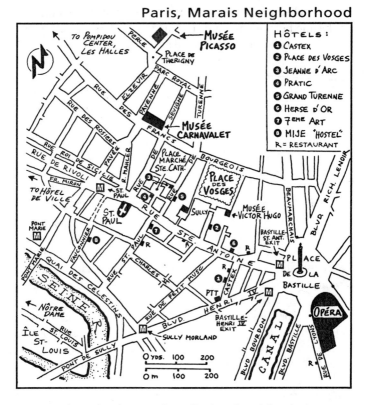

quiet, and run by the very friendly Bouchand family (son Blaise [blaze], speaks English). This place is a great value, with the distinctly un-Parisian characteristic of seeming like it wants your business. Reserve by phone and leave your Visa number.

Hôtel de la Place des Vosges** (DBWC-400F-425F, 40F-breakfast, CC:VMA, 12 rue de Biraque, just off the elegant place des Vosges, and just as snooty, tel. 42 72 60 46, fax 42 72 02 64, English spoken), classy with a freshly made, antique feel, rents 16 rooms on a quiet street.

Grand Hôtel Jeanne d'Arc** (DBWC-370F, TBWC-450F-510F triples, QBWC-570F, extra bed 75F, 35F-breakfast, 3 rue Jarente, tel. 48 87 62 11, fax 48 87 37 31), a plush and friendly place, elegant breakfast room, on a quiet street just off a cozy square, is the best normal hotel option in the Marais.

Hotel St. Louis Marais** is a delightful, wood-beamed ceiling and antiques everywhere mini-splurge in a great location (SBWC-490F, DBWC-590F-690F, 39F-breakfast, CC: VM, 1, rue Charles V, tel. 48 87 87 04, fax 48 87 33 26).

Hôtel Pratic* (D-230F, DB-275F, DBWC-340F, showers 10F, 25F-breakfast, 9 rue d'Ormesson, 75004 Paris, tel. 48 87 80 47, fax 48 87 40 04) has a slightly Arabic feel in its cramped lobby. The rooms are clean and bright, stairs are many, and it's right on a great people-friendly square.

Hôtel du Grand Turenne*** (DBWC-750F, 60F-breakfast, CC:VMA, 6 rue de Turenne, tel. 42 78 43 25, fax 42 74 10 72, SE-A) is newly renovated, very comfortable, offers a rare no-smoking floor, and is well situated.

Hôtel de 7ème Art** (DWBC-400F-450F, 35F-breakfast, all with shower, WC, TV, 20 rue St. Paul, tel. 42 77 04 03, fax 42 77 69 10) is a Hollywood nostalgia place run by young hip Marais types with a full service café/bar and Charlie Chaplin murals.

Hôtel de la Herse d'Or* (190F-250F, 25F-breakfast, Métro: St. Paul, 20 rue St. Antoine, tel. 48 87 84 09) is basic with a Middle Eastern flavor. Get a room off the busy street. The similar but even dumpier Hotel Moderne (D-190F, DB-220F, next to Hotel Practic at 3 rue Caron, tel. 48 87 97 05) is better than the youth hostel if you want privacy.

MIJE "Youth Hostels"

The Maison Internationale de la Jeunesse des Etudiants (MIJE) runs three classy old residences for travelers under age 30. Each offers simple, clean, single sex, mostly two- and four-bed rooms for 110F per bed, including shower and breakfast. Rooms are locked 12:00-16:00. MIJE Forcey (6 rue de Fourcey, just south of the rue Rivoli), MIJE Fauconnier (11 rue Fauconnier), and the best, MIJE Moubisson (12 rue des Barres) share one telephone number (42 74 23 45) and Métro stop (St. Paul).

Marais Helpful Hints

Place des Vosges is Paris' oldest square, built for Henry IV. Victor Hugo lived at #6 (small museum). Rue des Rosiers is the teeming main street Paris for the Orthodox Jewish community. The new opera house is just to the east, and a short wander west takes you into the hopping Beaubourg/Les Halles area. Paris' biggest and best budget department store is BHV, next to the Hôtel de Ville. Marais post offices are on rue Castex at boulevard Henri IV, and on the corner of rue Pavée and Franc Bourgois.

The nearest TI is in the Gare de Lyon (tel. 43 43 33 24). Neighborhood laundromats are at 40 rue de Roi de Sicile and 23 rue de Petit Musc. Most banks, shops, and other services are on the rue St. Antoine between Métro stops St. Paul and Bastille.

Sleeping in the Contrescarpe Neighborhood (5th district, Métro: Monge, zip code: 75005)

This neighborhood is over the hill from the Latin Quarter, 5 minutes from the Panthéon and an easy walk to Notre Dame, Île de la Cité, Île St. Louis, and boulevards St. Germain and St. Michel. Stay here if you like to be close to the action, which in the summer will be mostly that of tourists. The rue Mouffetard and place Contrescarpe are the thriving heart and soul of the neighborhood, a market street by day and restaurant row by night. Listed here are one elegant, hard-to-get-into gem and three rock-bottom dives.

The Hôtel des Grandes Écoles** (SWC-300F, DWC-320F-350F, DBWC-450F-600F, TWC-480F, TBWC-630F, QBWC-650F, 37F-breakfast, 75 rue de Cardinal Lemoine, tel. 43 26 79 23, fax 43 25 28 15) is a pricey but peaceful oasis with three buildings protecting its own garden courtyard. This place is deservedly popular, so call far in advance or try your luck in the morning. Their cheapest rooms are basic, but their top rooms are elegant.

Hôtel Central* (SB-150F-200F, DB-210F-240F, toilets in hall and no breakfast, 6 rue Descartes, tel. 46 33 57 93) has a romantic location, a steep and slippery, castlelike stairway, and stark rooms with saggy beds and meek showers. Nothing fancy, but very Parisian.

The low-key and bare bones **Hôtel du Commerce** (no stars, S-120F, SB-150F, D-130F, DB-160F, TB-200F, QB-240F, toilets down the hall, showers 15F if not in room, no breakfast, 14 rue de La Montagne Sainte-Geneviève, Métro: Place Maubert, tel. 43 54 89 69, takes no reservations, call at 10:00 and he'll say "*oui*" or "*non*") is run by Monsieur Mattuzzi, who must be a pirate gone good. He brags that the place is 300 years old. Judging by the vinyl in the halls, I believe him. It's a great rock-bottom deal and as safe as any dive next to the police station can be. In the morning, the landlady will knock and chirp "*Restez-vous?*" ("Are you staying for one more night?")

Y&H (Young and Happy) Hostel
Great location, easygoing, hip management, but depressing showers and generally crowded and filthy conditions. (4- to 8-bed rooms, closed 11:00-17:00, no reservations but call to see what's open, 80F per bed, plus 10F for sheets, 80 rue Mouffetard, tel. 45 35 09 53.)

Contrescarpe Helpful Hints
The neighborhood TI is in the gare Austerlitz (open Monday-Saturday 8:00-15:00), and the best post office (PTT) is between rue Mouffetard and rue Monge at 10 rue de l'Épée du Bois. Place Monge hosts a colorful outdoor market on Wednesday, Friday, and Sunday until 13:00. The street market at the bottom of rue Mouffetard bustles daily (8:00-12:00, 15:30-19:00), and the heart of this neighborhood, the place Contrescarpe bustles after dark.

The Jardin des Plantes is close by and great for evening walks. But those in the know will head through the doorway at 49 rue Monge and into the surprising Roman Arena de Lutèce. Today, boules players occupy the stage, while couples cuddle on the stone bleachers. Walk over to the Panthéon, admire it from the outside, but go into the wildly beautiful St. Étienne-du-Mont church.

Eating in Paris
Everything goes here. Paris is France's wine and cuisine melting pot. While it lacks a distinctive style of its own, it draws from the best of all French provinces.

Paris could hold a gourmet's Olympics—and import nothing. Picnic or go to snack bars for quick lunches and linger longer over dinner. You can eat very well, restaurant-style, for 120F. Ask your hotel to recommend a small nearby restaurant in the 80F-100F range. Famous places are often overpriced, overcrowded, and overrated. Find a quiet neighborhood and wander, or follow a local recommendation, but don't arrive before 19:00.

Cafeterias and Picnics
Many Parisian department stores have top-floor restaurants offering not really cheap but low-risk, low-stress, what-you-see-is-what-you-get, quick budget meals. Try **Samaritaine** (Pont-Neuf near the Louvre, fifth floor) or **Mélodine** (Métro: Rambuteau, next to the Pompidou Center, open daily 11:00-22:00).

For picnics, you'll find handy little groceries (*épiceries*) and delis (*charcuteries*) all over town (but rarely near famous sights). Good picnic fixings include roasted chicken, half-liter boxes of demi-crème (2%) milk, drinkable yogurt, fresh bakery goods, melons, and exotic pâtés and cheeses. Great take-out deli-type foods like gourmet salads and quiches abound. Although wine is taboo in public places in the U.S., this is *pas de problème* (no problem) in France. Most shops close 12:30-14:00.

The ultimate classy picnic shopping place is Fauchon, the famous "best gourmet grocery in France." It's fast and expensive but worth the detour to window shop alone. Try the new "inexpensive" bistro/cafeteria next to the bakery (26 place de la Madeleine, behind the Madeleine church, Métro: Madeleine, open 9:30-19:00, closed Sunday).

Good Picnic Spots
The pedestrian bridge, Pont des Arts, with unmatched views and plentiful benches, is great. Bring your own dinner feast and watch the riverboats light up the city for you. The Palais Royal (across the street from the Louvre) is a good spot for a peaceful and royal lunchtime picnic. Also try the little triangular Henry IV Park on the west tip of the Île de la Cité, people-watching at the Pompidou Center, the elegant place des Vosges (closes at dusk), the Rodin Museum, the Luxembourg Gardens, or (after dark) in the Eiffel Tower park (Champs de Mars).

Restaurants (by Neighborhood)

The Parisian eating scene is kept at a rolling boil, and entire books are written and lives are spent on the subject. If you are traveling outside Paris, save your splurges for the countryside, where restaurants are far less expensive and the quality of cuisine generally better. Here are a few places to consider working into your busy sightseeing strategy. If you'd like to visit a district specifically to eat, consider the many romantic restaurants that line the cozy Ile St. Louis' main street; the colorful, touristic but fun string of eateries along rue Mouffetard behind the Panthéon; Montmartre, which is very touristy around the place du Tetre but hides some vampy values in the side streets (try rue Lepic); and the well-worn Latin Quarter (see below).

Restaurants in Rue Cler and Invalides Neighborhoods

The rue Cler neighborhood isn't famous for its restaurants. That's why I eat here. **Restaurant La Serre** (29, rue de l'Exposition) is friendly, good, and reasonable. **Au Petit Paname** (across the street) serves a good traditional 88F menu (tel. 45 56 98 98, closed Saturday). **Au Café de Mars**, on the corner of rue Augerau and Gros-Caillou (tel. 47 05 05 91), is a contemporary Parisian café/restaurant with Franco-Californian cuisine, fair prices, and an English-speaking staff. **L'Ami de Jean** (near Hôtel Malar at 29 rue Malar) is a lively place to sample Basque cuisine. The **Ambassade du Sud-Ouest** is a locally popular wine store cum restaurant specializing in French Southwest cuisine. Try the *daubes de canard* and toast your own bread (46 ave. de la Bourdonnais, tel. 45 55 59 59). Two good traditional French brasserie in the area are **le Bosquet** (plat du jour 60F-80F, indoor/outdoor, on big street, 46 avenue Bosquet, tel. 45 51 38 13, closed Sunday) and the dressy **Thoumieux** (79 rue St. Dominique, tel. 47 05 49 75). For a take-out meal, try **Tarte Julie's** (28 rue Cler) or classy take-out at Flo's, on la Motte Piquet near the École Militaire Métro stop (open until 22:00).

Restaurants in the Marais Neighborhood

The candlelit windows of the Marais are filled with munching sophisticates. The epicenter of all this charm is the tiny square where rue Caron and rue d'Ormesson intersect, midway between the St. Paul Métro stop and the place des Vosges. For more conspicuous and atmospheric elegance, a coffee or dinner on the place des Vosges is good (Ma Bourgogne restaurant is worth the splurge). Hoboes with taste have a picnic on the place des Vosges itself, trying not to make the local mothers with children nervous (closes at dusk). For a memorable picnic dinner, 10 minutes from the Marais, cross the river to Île St. Louis and find a river-level bench on the tip facing Île de la Cité. A variety of take-away delis can be found on the rue St. Antoine, including the excellent Chinese **Delice House** (#81, open until 21:00). Try the **Le Paradis de Fruit** (salads and organic foods mix with a young crowd on the small square at rues Turenne and St. Antoine). The restaurant next door, **La Perle**, is good and cheap. I dine locally at Les Temps Cerises at the corner of rue du Petit Musc and rue Cerisaie for about 80F. **L'Énoteca** (across from Hôtel du 7ème Art at 20 rue St. Paul) has lively Italian cuisine in a relaxed, open setting. **Auberge de Jarente** (7 rue Jarente) is well respected, popular, atmospheric, and reasonable. Near the Hôtel Castex, the restaurant **La Poste** and the **Crêperie** across the street (13 rue Castex) are both inexpensive and good values.

Restaurants in the Latin Quarter
La Petite Bouclerie is a cozy place with classy family cooking (moderate, 33 rue de la Harpe, center of touristy Latin Quarter). Friendly Monsieur Millon runs **Restaurant Polidor**, an old turn-of-the-century-style place, with great *cuisine bourgeois*, a vigorous local crowd, and a historic toilet. Arrive at 19:00 to get a seat—in the restaurant, that is (moderate, 41 rue Monsieur le Prince, midway between Odéon and Luxembourg Métro stops, tel. 43 26 95 34).

Restaurants on the Île St. Louis
Cruise the island's main street for a variety of good options. For crazy (but touristy and expensive) cellar atmosphere and hearty fun food, feast at **La Taverne du Sergeant Recruiter**. The "Sergeant Recruiter" used to get young Parisians drunk and stuffed here, then sign them into the army. It's all-you-can-eat, including wine and service, for 200F (41 rue St.

Louis, in the center of Île St. Louis, 3 minutes from Notre
Dame, open Monday-Saturday from 19:00, tel. 43 54 75 42).
There's a just-this-side-of-a-food-fight clone next door at
Nos Ancêtres Les Gaulois ("Our Ancestors the Gauls," 39
rue St. Louis-en-l'Île, tel. 46 33 66 07, open daily at 19:00).

Restaurants in Pompidou Center
The popular and very French **Café de la Cité** has long
wooden tables and great lunch specials (inexpensive, 22 rue
Rambuteau, Métro: Rambuteau, open daily except Sunday).
The **Mélodine** self-service is right at the Rambuteau Métro
stop. **Dame Tartine** overlooks the Homage to Stravinsky
fountain and serves a young clientele and offers excellent,
cheap, lively meals.

Restaurants in Other Paris Locations
For an elegant splurge surrounded by lavish Art Nouveau
decor, dine at **Julien** (200F meals with wine, 16 rue du
Faubourg St. Denis, Métro: Strasbourg-St. Denis, tel. 47 70
12 06, make reservations). On Momartre, try the excellent
and cozy Le Montagnarde and say bonsoir to Didier, 2
blocks down rue Lepic from the place du Tetre.
    Three gourmet working-class fixtures in Paris are
Le Chartier (7 rue du Faubourge Montmartre, Métro:
Montmartre), **Le Commerce** (51 rue du Commerce, Métro:
Commerce) and **Le Drouot** (103 rue de Richelieu, Métro:
Richelieu-Drouot). Each wraps very cheap and basic food
in a bustling, unpretentious atmosphere.

Parisian Nightlife
Paris nightlife thrives in three areas: the Latin Quarter and
Boulevard St. Germain; the Pompidou Center-Les Halles
area; and the very touristy but fun Momartre area. Café
lurking and sidewalk strolling are the chief pastimes.

Jazz Clubs
The Caveau de la Huchette is the handiest characteristic
old jazz club for visitors. Filling an ancient Latin Quarter
cellar with live jazz and frenzied dancing every night (open
21:30-2:30 or later, 70F admission, 30F drinks, 5 rue de la
Huchette, 75005 Paris, tel. 43 26 65 05). You'll also find

several well reputed clubs bordering the Forum shopping center in Les Halles area on the rue Berger.

Transportation Connections

France's rail system radiates from Paris making almost any destination easily accessible.

Paris and Nice: 10 TGVs/day, 7 hrs.

Paris and London: 4/day, 8 hrs, night boat-train, inquire about "chunnel" service.

Paris and Amsterdam: 9/day, 6½ hrs, night train.

Airports

Charles de Gaulle Airport

There are two main terminals, 1 and 2. Air France uses terminal 2, all others use terminal 1. This information is for terminal 1 (the terminals are connected every few minutes by a free shuttle bus, *navette*). A helpful tourist office is located at the "Meeting Point," where you can get free Paris city maps and up-to-date sightseeing information. Buy a *télécarte* at the Relais H next to the tourist office and pick up French currency if you need it at the bank near gate 16 (acceptable rates). Car rental offices are found on the arrival level at gates 18-24 and a handy SNCF (train) office is at gate 22. Tel. 48 62 22 80.

Transportation Between Paris and Charles de Gaulle Airport

The transporation services listed below leave from terminal 1. Three efficient public transportation routes link the airport and central Paris. A free shuttle bus (navette) runs between the airport's gate 28 and the **RER Roissy Rail** station, where a train zips you into Paris' subway system in 30 minutes (40F, stops at Gare du Nord, Chatelet, St. Michel, and Luxembourg Gardens). The **Roissy Bus** runs between the airport (near gate 32F) and the old Paris Opera (stop is on the rue Scribe, in front of the American Express), costs 30F and takes 40 minutes but is often jammed. The **Air France Bus** leaves every 15 minutes from gate 34 and serves the Arc de Triomphe and the Porte Maillot in about 40 minutes for 48F, and the Montparnasse Tower in 60 minutes for 64F

Your best option will depend on where your hotel is; for most the RER Roissy Rail works best. A taxi ride with luggage costs about 250F, gate 16.

Sleeping at Charles de Gaulle Airport

If you have an early flight, consider sleeping in Terminal 1 at **Cocoon** (60 "cabins," S-250F, D-300F). Take the elevator down to "boutique level" (it's near the Burger King, tel: 48 62 06 16, fax 48 62 03 21). You get 16 hours of silence buried under the check-in level with TV and WC. **The Hotel IBIS** (at the Roissy Rail station; free shuttle bus to either terminal takes 2 minutes) offers more normal accommodations (D-380F with full bath, tel. 48 62 49 49, fax 48 62 54 22).

Sleeping near Charles de Gaulle Airport

If you've rented a car and want to stay near but not at the airport, consider staying in the charming city of Senlis, about 15 minutes by car. **The Hostellerie de la Porte Bellon** is very comfortable (D-160F, DBWC-300F-410F, CC:VM, 51 rue Bellon, tel.44 53 03 05, fax 44 53 29 94).

Orly Airport

Unless you're using a French carrier, you'll arrive at **Terminal Sud.** En route to the baggage claim at terminal Sud you'll pass the ADP counter, a quasi tourist office where you can get free city maps and current sightseeing information. Ask where you can buy a *télécarte*, then cash checks at the bank if you need to (acceptable rates), near the baggage claim (tel. 49 75 15 15).

Transportation Between Paris and Orly Airport

The **Air France Bus**, which runs between gate F and Paris's Invalides Métro stop (every 15 min, 30-min trip, 32F), is a good choice if you're staying in my recommended hotels in the rue Cler neighborhood. For the Marais neighborhood and other Paris destinations, take the **Jetbus** (20F, every 10 minutes) from near gate F to the the Villejuif Métro stop, buy a carnet of 10 Métro tickets and you're in the Métro system. Get off at the Sully Morland stop for Marais area hotels. Figure on 175F for a taxi into central Paris.

PROVENCE

This magnificent region is shaped like an upside down funnel, stretching along the Mediterranean east from Nimes to Nice and north along the Rhone Valley to Orange. The Romans were here in force and left tons of ruins—some of the best in Europe. Seven popes and great artists like van Gogh, Cézanne, and Picasso called Provence home. Provence offers a splendid recipe of arid climate (but brutal winds, known as the *mistral*), captivating cities, remarkably varied landscapes (from the marshy Camargue to the jutting cliffs of the Alpilles hills), and a spicy cuisine. The locals have a contagious *esprit de vivre* (spirit of living).

Wander through the ghost town of ancient Les Baux and clamber over France's greatest Roman ruin, the Pont du Gard. Spend your starry, starry nights where van Gogh did, in Arles. Explore its surprising number of sights and find the light, ambience, and colorful corners that inspired Vincent. Just north of Arles, Avignon's superb center city bustles in the shadow of its gleaming popes palace. It's a short hop from Arles and Avignon into the splendid scenery and hill towns that make Provence so popular today.

Planning Your Time

Make Arles or Avignon your base and daytrip from here (I prefer Arles). Most area sights are connected by buses or trains with one of these cities. You'll want a full day for Arles sightseeing (Arle's fantastic outdoor market rages on Wednesday and Saturday mornings), a half day for Avignon, and at the very least, one full day for the villages and sights in the countryside. If you bring your swimsuit, you can float under the 2,000-year-old Pont du Gard in cool comfort. If you have a car, or patience with bus schedules, get out of the city and spend at least one night in a *provencale* village (see Sights—Provence).

Arles

"The stranger who succeeds in threading its labyrinth of dirty, narrow streets will be duly rewarded." Since these words w120ere written of Arles in the 18th century, most of

the dirty streets have disappeared, though Arles remains neither slick nor aloof. A thriving river port city in Roman
times, Arles (arl) remained so until the 18th century, when it
all but disappeared from the map. After taking a beating from
Amer-ican bombers in World War II, Arles has made a
remarkable comeback. Today, this compact city is alive with
great Roman ruins, an eclectic assortment of museums,
pedestrian streets for meandering, and squares that play
hide-and-seek with visitors. It makes an ideal base for your
Provence explorations.

Tourist Information
Arles has two TIs. The one at the train station is relaxed and
easy by car. (Open 9:00-19:00 in summer; closed 13:00-14:00
otherwise, and at 17:00 in winter. Open Sunday 9:00-13:00.
The main TI on esplanade Charles de Gaulle is a high-pow-
ered mega-information site. Ask about bullfights. (Open year
round 9:00-19:00, Sunday 9:00-13:00, tel. 90 96 29 35.) Pick
up the free handy *Guide Touristique*.

Arrival
By Car: Follow signs to *Centre-ville*, then be on the lookout
for signs to the gare SNCF (go there if you need the TI).
Just before the *gar*, you'll come to a huge roundabout, place
Lamartine, with a Monoprix to the right. The best parking is
on the left, along the base of the wall. Pay attention to no-
parking signs on Wednesday and Saturday until 13:00—they
mean it. Take everything out of your car for safety. Walk
into the city through the two stumpy towers.
By Train and Bus: Both are located on the river about a 10-
minute walk from the city center (TI in *gare*). Simply walk to
the river and turn left to reach the city.

Helpful Hint
There is a laundromat on the rue Cavalarie between the
place Voltaire and place Lamartine, or at #12 rue Portagnel,
just up from the place Voltaire.

Sights—Arles
If you plan to visit most of Arles' sights, buy the "global billet."
The ticket, sold at all sights (44F, 31F for students), gets you

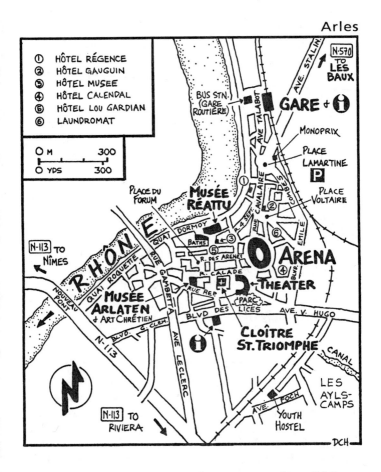

Arles

①	HÔTEL RÉGENCE
②	HÔTEL GAUGUIN
③	HÔTEL MUSÉE
④	HÔTEL CALENDAL
⑤	HÔTEL LOU GARDIAN
⑥	LAUNDROMAT

into all of Arles' monuments and museums, and is valid for as many days as you need it. Otherwise, it's 15F per sight and museum. All sights keep the same hours: 9:00-12:30, 14:00-19:00 April-September, and 9:00-12:15, 14:00-17:45 October-March (sights close at 17:15 December-February).

▲**Place du Forum**—This café-crammed square is full of life, particularly at night. This was the center of Roman Arles; find the few remains of the Roman Forum. Don't let yourself out of Arles without hanging out here. (Always open, free entry.)

▲▲▲**Wednesday and Saturday Market**—Until around noon, on the ring road (best near the main TI), Arles erupts into an outdoor market of fish, flowers, produce, and you-name-it. Join in, buy some flowers, sample the wine, and watch your wallet.

▲▲▲**Roman Arena (Amphithéâtre)**—Here, 2,000 years ago, gladiators fought all kinds of wild animals to the delight of 20,000 screaming fans. Today, modern gladiators only fight bulls, and if you don't mind the gore, it's an exciting show. Be sure to climb the tower. These were the cheap seats in Roman times. Walk through the inner corridors and notice the similarity to 20th-century stadium floor plans.

▲▲**Bullfights (Courses Camarguaise)**—Occupy the same seats fans have been sitting in for 2,000 years and take in one of Arles' greatest treats—a bullfight *à la Provençal.* Three classes of bullfights take place here. The *course protection* is for aspiring matadors, and not a bloody, dodge-bull game of scraping hair off the angry bull's nose for money. The *trophée de l'avenir* is the next class, with amateur matadors. The *trophée des as excellence* is the real thing à la Spain: outfits, swords, spikes, and the whole gory shabang. (Mid-March to early October is the season. Check with the TI for dates and times—frequent in summer, less in shoulder seasons.) Skip their "rodeo" spectacle.

▲**Classical Theater (Théâtre Antique)**—Where the high-brow Romans went for entertainment, this theater, built about 2,000 years ago, held over 7,000 people. Take a seat. Imagine sitting through a long play on the rock-hard seats. There's cool shade on the grassy side.

▲**St. Trophime Cloisters and Church**—A cool, shady, two-story pool of peace and tranquillity fills this perfect square of delicate arches. Admire the church's Romanesque facade and exquisite sculpture. View the cloisters from upstairs.

▲**Musée Réattu**—Here is an interesting collection of 70 Picasso drawings, some two-sided, all done in a flurry of creativity. I enjoyed the room with Henri Rousseau's Camargue watercolors and the magnetic balls display. (15F.)

▲▲**Musee Arlaten**—This cluttered folklore museum is filled with interesting odds and ends of Provence life. The employees wear the native costumes. You'll also find shoes, hats, wigs, hundreds of old photos of unattractive women, bread cupboards, and a beetle-dragon monster. If you like folklore museums, this is a must.

Museum of Christian Art—The Musée du l'Art Chretien has the best tomb sculpture outside Rome. Its creepy basement gallery was once a Roman forum. It's worth a quick diversion if you've got the global billet. Be sure to go downstairs.

Sleeping in Arles
(5.5 F = about $1, zip code: 13200)

Inexpensive accommodations are a snap in Arles, though July is crowded; blame the annual photography festival. Take everything out of your car, and ask your hotelier for the best place to park. The hotels below are identified from place Lamartine on rue Cavalerie.

Sleep code: **S**=Single, **D**=Double/Twin, **T**=Triple, **Q**=Quad, **B**=Bath/Shower, **WC**=Toilet, **PD**=Breakfast, **CC**=Credit Card (Visa, Mastercard, Amex).

Hôtel Régence** is immaculate, comfortable, and homey, with good beds and a fine breakfast featuring homemade jams and fruit. It is family-run by Marriette and Réné, who almost trip over themselves being helpful and friendly. Their daughter, Sylvie, speaks English. (DBWC-260F, TBWC-340F, safe, free parking in back, 5 rue Marius Jouveau; take a right on the first street after passing through the towers and you'll see it, tel. 90 96 39 85, fax 90 96 67 64.)

Hôtel du Musée** is a quiet, delightfully restored manor house hideaway with spacious rooms and a terrific courtyard terrace. Its very friendly owners speak some English (D-160F, DBWC-270F, TBWC-360F, CC:VM), 11 rue de la Grande Prieure, follow signs to Musée Réattu, tel. 90 93 88 88, fax 90 49 98 15).

The **Hôtel Calendal**** is in other guidebooks and deservedly popular. Old World character and an outdoor garden make this a pleasant, peaceful refuge (DWC-190F-220F, DBWC-290F-320F, TBWC-320F, QBWC-460F, located above the arena at 22 place Pomme, tel. 90 96 11 89, fax 90 96 05 84).

Hôtel Le d'Arlatan*** is one of France's more affordable classy hotels, with a beautiful lobby, courtyard terrace, and antique-filled rooms (DBWC-500F-1,300F, CC:VMA, 26 rue du Savage, tel. 90 93 56 66; fax 90 49 68 45). Reserve ahead.

Two bare bones budget hotels even Vincent could have afforded are: **Hotel La Gallia** (D-120F, DWC-140F, above a friendly cafe at 22 rue de l'Hotel de Ville, tel. 90 96 00 63) and **Le Studio's** more spacious rooms (D-90F, DB-130F, TB/QB-160F, located above a fine Pizzeria on 6 rue Reattu, tel. 90 96 33 25). Look on the place Voltaire for more budget rooms, or try the sterile from the outside but acceptable from within **Hôtel Voltaire*** (get a room with a balcony, D-120F-140F, add 40F per person for 3 or 4, PD-20F, CC:VM, place Voltaire, tel. 90 96 13 58).

Cuisine Scene—Provence

The almost extravagant use of garlic, olive oil, herbs, and tomatoes makes Provence cuisine France's liveliest. To sample it, order anything *à la Provençal*. Among the area's spicy specialties are *ratatouille* (a thick mixture of vegetables in herb-flavored tomato sauce), *brandade* (a salt cod, garlic, and cream mousse), *aïoli* (a garlicky mayonnaise often served atop fresh vegetables), *tapenade* (a sauce of puréed olives, anchovies, tuna fish, and herbs), *soupe au pistou* (vegetable soup with basil, garlic, and cheese), and *soupe à l'ail* (garlic soup). Banon (wrapped in chestnut leaves) and Picodon (nutty taste) are the native cheeses. Provence also produces some of France's great wines at relatively reasonable prices. Look for Châteauneuf-du-Pape (not always so reasonable), Gigondas, Hermitage, Cornas, Côte du Rhône, and Côte de Provence. If you like rosé, try the Tavel.

Eating in Arles

The restaurants and cafés, such as **L'Estaminet** on place du Forum, serve basic food with great atmosphere. **Les Saveurs Provencale** is *the* place to enjoy regional specialties at moderate prices, a block below the arena. For good food at bargain prices, try **Le Cote d'Adam** (just off the place du Forum on 12 rue de la Liberte). **Lou Caleu** is fine for a semi-splurge place (27 rue porte de Laure, tel. 90 49 71 77, reserve here).

Picnics

Stock up at the ugly Monoprix on place Lamertine, or try the snack counter on place Voltaire, where you can take away quiches, pizzas, and spinach-stuffed croissants. Ask for them to be *chauffé* (heated). The riverfront walk is a good spot for a picnic dinner.

Transportation Connections
Arles and Nimes: 14 daily trains, 25-minute trip.
Arles and Carcassonne: Six daily trains, about 3 hours.
Arles and Beaune: Several daily trips, transfer in Lyon, allow about 5 hours.
Arles and Nice: Regular service connects Arles with Nice and other Cote d'Azur destinations in about 3 hours. A transfer (easy) may be necessary in Marseille.

Provence

Getting Around Provence
The Michelin map to this region is essential for navigation by car or bike. Public transit is surprisingly good in this region. Very frequent trains link Avignon and Arles in half

an hour, Les Baux is easily accessible by bus (hilly but close by bike) from Arles, and the Pont du Gard and Uzès are accessible by bus, from Avignon. To thoroughly explore the hill town-crowned region of Provence, get on a bike or rent a car. The Camargue makes a good, flat biking destination unless it's windy.

Trains: There is frequent service between Arles and Avignon—every 20 minutes—but check for afternoon gaps.

Buses: Four daily buses to Les Baux (30 minutes) and St. Remy leave from Arles bus station and from #16 boulevard Clemenceau in downtown Arles, tel. 90 49 38 01. Service is reduced November-March, and on Sunday and holidays.

Bike Rental: You can rent bikes at the *gare* or better, at the Peugeot store at #15 rue du Pont, tel. 90 96 03 77.

Car Rental: Avis is at the *gare*, tel. 90 96 82 42; Europcar is in the city at 15 Bd. Victor Hugo, tel. 90 93 23 24.

Sights—Provence

▲▲▲**Les Baux**—This rocktop ghost town is worth visiting for the lunar landscape alone. Arrive early or late to avoid the crowds. A 12th-century regional powerhouse with 6,000 fierce residents, Les Baux was razed in 1632 by a paranoid Louis XIII, afraid of these troublemaking upstarts. What remains are a reconstructed "live city" of tourist shops and snack stands, and the "dead city" ruins carved into, out of, and on top of a 600-foot-high rock. Spend most of your time in the dead city—scenery is spectacular in the morning or early evening light. In the tourist-trampled live city, you'll find artsy shops, several interesting Rennaissance homes, and a simple church on place St. Vincent. (The dead city is open Easter-October 8:30-dusk; otherwise 19:00-20:00, 9:30-17:30, 30F, tickets include entry to all the town's sights, don't rush past the small museum at the entry to the dead city, TI tel. 90 54 34 39.) Four daily buses serve Les Baux from Arles *gare*, and two daily buses leave from Avignon, summers only. Les Baux is only 20 minutes northest of Arles, just past Fontvielle.

St. Rémy—This *tres provencale* town is a scenic ride just over the hill from Les Baux. Here you'll find the crumbled ruins of **Glanum**, a once-thriving Roman city located at the cross-roads of two ancient trade routes between Italy and Spain, and the mental ward in Arles where Vincent van Gogh was sent after cutting off his ear. Glanum is just outside St. Remy on the road to Les Baux (D-5). Walk to the gate and peek in to get a feel for its scale. The ruins are worth the effort if you have the time and haven't been to Pompeii or Epheses recently (24F, open 9:00-12:00, 14:00 -18:00, closes at 17:00 October-April). Backtrack across the street to the free Roman arch and tower. The arch marked the entry into Glanum. The tower is a memorial to the grandsons of Emperor Augustus, located there to remind folks of them when entering or leaving Glanum.

Across the street from Glanum is **Van Gogh Hospital**. While it's still a functioning mental hospital, you don't have to cut anything off to be allowed to enter. Wander into the small chapel and peaceful cloisters. Vincent's favorite walks outside the hospital are clearly sign-posted.

▲**The Camargue**—One of the few truly "wild areas" of France, where pink flamingos, wild bulls, and the famous white horses wander freely amid rice fields and lagoons. If you don't have a car, and wild horses won't drag you to the Camargue, rent a bike—it's as flat as flat gets (but skip it if it's windy). Pick up the local Michelin map and leave Arles toward St. Maries-de-la-Mer and take a left onto the D-36 toward Le Sambuc and Salins, then veer right onto the D-36A to Villeneuve, and the Etang de Vaccarès. Head all the way out to the digue (dike) for the best flamingo watching.

▲▲▲**Pont du Gard**—One of Europe's great treats, this remarkably well-preserved Roman aqueduct was built before Christ. It was the missing link of a 35-mile canal that supplied 44 million gallons of water to Nîmes daily. Dare to walk across the towering 160-foot-high aqueduct. If acrophobia is a cross you bear, carry it inside the aqueduct where the water used to run, and peek through the roof's occasional holes. Walk up the steps at the base of the aqueduct and follow the panorama signs to a great picnic site. The best view of the aqueduct is from the cool of the river below, floating flat on your back (bring a swimsuit, always open and free.) Buses run from Nimes, Uzes, or Avignon. By car, the Pont du Gard is an easy 30-minute drive due west of Avignon (follow Nimes) and 45 minutes northwest of Arles (via Tarascon).

Uzès—A very pleasant, less trammeled town near the Pont du Gard, Uzès is best seen slowly on foot, with a long coffee break in its mellow main square (place aux Herbes). Check out the Tour Fenestrelle and the Duché de Uzès. Uzès is a short hop west of the Pont du Gard by bus and is well served from Nimes (9 daily trips) and Avignon (3 daily trips).

Hill Towns of Luberon—The Luberon region east of Avignon hides what may be France's most appealing hill towns. Bonnieux, Menerbes, Oppède le Vieux, and the very discovered (and overpriced) Gordes, to mention a few, are quintessential Provençal hill towns. Discover your own, then head to **Roussillon.** Walk up to the end of the village and into the dazzling ocher cliffs. Keep going high into the caves. You'll find several reasonable outdoor restaurants on Roussillon's delightful main square, and one very comfortable hotel, the **Hotel Residence des Ocres**, (DBWC-270F-340F, TBWC-315F-360F, QBWC-360F, tel. 90 05 60 50, zip code 84220).

There are no trains in this region and it's difficult by bus though you can reach some hill towns through Cavaillon (bus here from Avignon). By car, get on the N-100 toward Apt, east of Avignon. Veer left onto the D-2, where you'll see signs to Gordes. Roussillon is signed from Gordes.

Loop Trip for Wine Lovers—If you have a car (or lots of time and a bike; ideal riding here) and a fondness for fine wine, take a loop trip of Provence's wine country. From Avignon, head to Carpentras (a fine city itself, worthy of exploration) to Vaqueryas to Gigondas to Ste. Cecile. This is France's most hospitable and relaxed wine-tasting region. Generous free samples and no pressure to buy—highlight the servive by merchants wearing shorts and thongs. This a long way from haughty Bordeaux. Near **Rasteau village**, at **Le Domaine des Girasols**, a friendly couple will take your palate on a tour of some of the area's best wine. It's well marked and worth a stop. The scenery is the best in Provence. Ideally, have lunch in Gigondas at the only outdoor restaurant in town, and end your day with an outdoor coffee under the shady maples of Ste. Cecile. The wine village of Sablet makes a good base to see this area, since it is chock full of chambre d'hôtes (try **Madame Fert's chambres**, look for the signs, tel. 90 46 94 77).

Avignon

Cross the street from the bus or train station to enter Avignon's center city and you'll be on the main drag, the cours Jean Juares. The main TI will be on your right in a few blocks. Drivers should park along the wall close to the Pont St. Benezet (ruined old bridge) and use the TI here. The rue de la République, place de l'Horloge, and Palace of the Popes form Avignon's spine, from which all roads and activity radiate.

Famous for its nursery rhyme, medieval bridge, and brooding Palace of the Popes, contemporary Avignon (a-veen-yohn) bustles and prospers behind its walls. During the 68 years (1309-1377) that Avignon played Franco Vaticano, it grew from an irrelevant speck on the map to the important blob that it still is today. This is the white-collar, sophisticated city of Provence. The slick cafés and smart boutiques should tip you off right away. If you're here in July, try to save evening time for Avignon's wild and woolly theater festival. The streets throng with mimes, skits, singing, and visitors from around the world. Stroll the rue de la République, snag a table and enjoy the performers on the place de l'Horloge, and meander the back streets. Avignon's shopping district is concentrated on the pedestrian streets just off the place de l'Horloge. Take a spin on the double-decker merry-go-round. (A good public W.C. is just behind it.) Walk out on the wall and across the Pont Daladier for a great view back on Avignon.

Tourist Information

The main TI is at 41 cours Jean Juares, which becomes rue de la République, open Monday-Friday 9:00-18:00, Saturday 9:00-12:00, 14:00-18:00, tel. 90 82 65 11. You'll find a smaller TI at the Pont St. Benezet.

Transportation Connections

Trains

To Arles: Service is frequent, 20-minute trip.
To Nimes: Very frequent service, 21 minutes.
To Nice: Regular departures, 4-hour trip with several direct runs, though the Marseille transfer is quik and convenient.
To Carcassonne and Barcelona: A few direct runs are

available in each case, (the night train to Barcelona is handy), otherwise transfer in Narbonne for these trips. Allow 3 hours to Carcassonne (regular service) and 5 hours to reach Barcelona (infrequent service).

To Paris' Gare de Lyon: Regular service on high speed TGVs make this trip in a blurry 4 hours.

Buses

A few daily trips run to **Les Baux** from Avignon, summers only (return via bus to Arles, then train to Avignon often works well. You can reach the **Pont du Gard**, **Uzes**, and **Nimes** by bus from Avignon, then return by train from Nimes. Bus schedules are hopeless for the round-trip solely to the Pont du Gard from Avignon. Be careful of reduced service on all routes Sunday and on holidays. The bus station is adjacent to the train station, tel. 90 93 74 90.

Sights—Avignon

▲**Palais des Papes (Palace of the Popes)**—In 1309, Pope Clement V decided he'd had enough of unruly, aggressive Italians. So he loaded up his carts and moved to Avignon for a steady rule under a friendly king. The Catholic church literally bought Avignon, then a two-bit town, and popes resided here until 1403. From 1377 on, there were twin popes, one in Rome and one in Avignon, causing a split in the Catholic church that wasn't fully resolved until 1449.

The palace is two distinct buildings, one old and one older. You'll see brilliant frescoes, enormous tapestries, remarkable floor tiles, and lots of big, empty rooms. You can tour this massive structure on your own or with a guide. Scheduling your day around the English tour times can be a hassle, but the tours are usually good. If it's a hot day, skip the tour and visit on your own. (32F; 11F more for the guided tour, open mid-March to November 9:00-19:00; otherwise 9:00-12:45, 14:00-18:00. Tours in English twice daily, about 10:00 and 15:00, roughly March-October, tel. 90 27 30 50.)

▲**Petit Palais**—In this palace you'll find a superbly displayed collection of early Italian (14th- and 15th-century) painting and sculpture. All of the 350 paintings portray Christian themes; the Catholic church was the patron of the arts in those days. The new special exposition room is superb for

lovers of medieval art. Tour this museum before going to
the Palace of the Popes to get a sense of art and life during
the Avignon papacy. Notice the improvement in perspective
in the later paintings. In room 8, look for Mary's "neck
breast," and check out baby Jesus' cocky grin. (18F, open
March-September 10:30-18:00, off-season 9:30-12:00,
13:30-17:30, closed Tuesday.)

Notre-Dame-des-Doms—This cozy, 12th-century church
is worth a glance on your way up to the park.

Parc de Rochers des Doms and Pont St. Bénezet—You'll
like this unassuming little park. Located right above the
church, it provides a panoramic view over Avignon, the
Rhône, and the vineyard-strewn countryside. Walk to the far
end for a good view of the Pont St. Bénezet. This is the
famous *"sur le Pont d'Avignon,"* whose construction and location were inspired by a shepherd's religious vision. Imagine
the bridge extending across to the Tower of Philippe the
Fair, far on the other side, which was the tollgate for the
bridge and marks its original length. The island the bridge
spanned is now filled with campgrounds. You can pay 10F
to do your own jig on the bridge, but it's better appreciated
from where you are. The castle you can see to the right, the
St. André Fortress, was once another island in the Rhône.
Cross Daladier Bridge for the best view of the old bridge
and Avignon's skyline. There is a pleasant café in the park.

Sleeping in Avignon
(5.5F = about $1)

Don't miss the very cozy and almost elegant **Hôtel
Blauvac**** (in the pedestrian zone on 11 rue de La Bancasse,
DBWC-280F-350F, TBWC-400F-460F, QBWC-480F,
CC:VMA, tel. 90 86 34 11, fax 90 86 27 41). The compact
Hôtel Mignon is less luxurious but a good value, very
friendly and clean (SB-130F, DB-170F, DBWC-230F, 12
rue Joseph Vernet, tel. 90 82 17 30, fax 90 85 78 46). The
comfortable rooms at the **Hotel Splendid*** (SB-170F, DB-
210F, 17 rue Agricole Perdiguier, tel. 90 86 14 46) are near
the main TI and station and a good value.

THE FRENCH RIVIERA

This longtime resort mecca, a.k.a. the Côte d'Azur, is wedged between the Alpes Maritimes (foothills of the Alps) and the Mediterranean Sea. For over a hundred years, celebrities from central and northern Europe and Russia flocked here to escape the drab, dreary weather at home. Some of Europe's most stunning scenery and superb museums lie along this strip of land. Unfortunately, so do millions of sun-worshiping tourists.

Nice is this region's capital, and in every way an urban experience. Nearby Antibes has fine beaches, Monte Carlo welcomes all with open cash registers, and the hill towns offer a breezy and photogenic alternative to the beach scene. Evenings on the Riviera were made for the promenade.

Planning Your Time

The first tough decision is where to base. Nice is the logical choice for most, with excellent public transportation to most regional sights, world class museums, scads of hotels in all price ranges, and a marvelous beachfront promenade. But the smaller village feel and sandy beaches that Antibes or Villefranche offer lure many their way. I've focused my accommodations listings in Nice, but have provided a few good listings for Villefranche and Antibes. If you choose Nice, remember: it's one of France's largest urban areas and if it's a sandy nap in the sun you need, you won't get it here—Nice beaches are a rock lover's dream.

Once situated, I'd spend at least one full day getting to know my home base, then consider half day trips to Monaco, Antibes and St. Paul, and Vence—in that order. If daytripping into Nice, allow a full day.

Getting Around

By train or bus there's no problem getting around this region, no matter where you base. Pick up transportation schedules at any bus or train station to make your traveling easier. Nice is perfectly located for exploring the Riviera's alluring sights. Villefranche is a 10-minute bus trip from Nice's *gare routiere*, (buses every 15 minutes) on the way to Monaco. Regular

The French Riviera

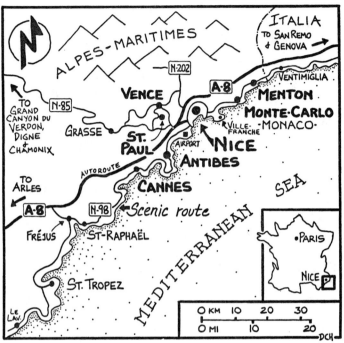

train and bus service link Antibes with all day-trip suggestions in this chapter.

Nice

Nice is a melting pot of thousands of tanning tourists and 340,000 already-tanned residents. Here, you'll see the chicquest of the chic, the cheapest of the cheap, and everyone in between vacationing side by side, each busy relaxing. Nice's superb mountain-to-Mediterranean scenery, its thriving old city, eternally entertaining seafront promenade, and superb museums make settling into this town a joy. Nice is nice—but hot and jammed in overcrowded July and August.

Take only a piece of Nice (that rhymes) and leave the rest to the residents. Outside of a few museums, everything you want is within a small area—near the Old City and along the seafront.

Tourist Information

Nice has three energetic TIs. The main TI, next to the train station on avenue Thiers, is the most crowded, knowledge-able, and helpful. (Open Monday-Saturday, July and August 8:45-18:45; otherwise 8:45-12:15, 14:00-17:40. Summer Sundays, open 8:45-11:45, 14:00-17:45, tel. 93 87 07 07). The best TI for drivers is next to the airport on RN-7; you'll pass it arriving from the west. Ask for parking advice. (Open Monday-Saturday 7:15-18:30, Sunday 8:00-noon, tel. 93 83 32 64.) The most convenient downtown TI is at 5 avenue Gustave V, on place Massena next to Hôtel Méridien. (Open Monday-Saturday 8:45-12:15, 14:00-17:45, closed Saturday November-April; tel. 93 87 60 60.) At any TI, you can pick up a city map, list of museums, and excursion information. The TIs will make hotel reservations for a small fee that will be deducted from your hotel bill.

Arrival

By Car: For some of the Riviera's best scenery, follow the coast road between Cannes and Frejus. As you enter Nice, use the road side TI just past the airport (see Tourist Information) and park at the lot at Nice Etoile on avenue Jean Medecin. Most Nice street parking is metered.

By Train: Trains arrive at the main station on avenue Thiers. To reach the hotels in this book, turn left out of the station, then right on avenue Jean Medecin.

Sights—Nice

▲▲▲**Vieux Nice (Old City)**—This thriving old city is for real, not restored for our tourist eyes. Here Italian and French flavors mix to create a Mediterranean dressing full of life and spice. Sniff the flower market on the cours Saleya, slosh through the fish market, hang out in the place Rossetti, and explore spindly streets of tiny shops. The flower and fish markets close at 12:30 and all day Monday.

▲**Castle Hill**—Climb or elevator here for a 360-degree view of Nice, the Alps, and the Mediterranean. Walk up and up and up rue Rossetti. Pause at the base of the waterfall for a cooling blast of air. The views are better and the souvenirs tackier at the top of the waterfall. The elevator wisks you up

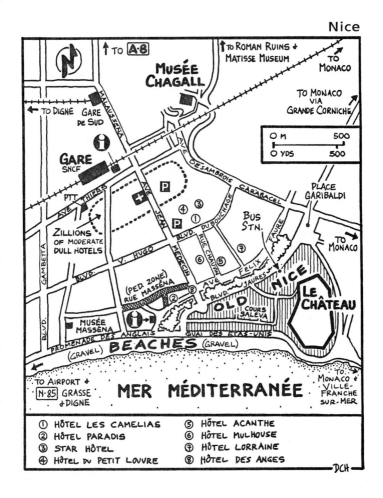

Nice

①	HÔTEL LES CAMELIAS	⑤	HÔTEL ACANTHE
②	HÔTEL PARADIS	⑥	HÔTEL MULHOUSE
③	STAR HÔTEL	⑦	HÔTEL LORRAINE
④	HÔTEL DU PETIT LOUVRE	⑧	HÔTEL DES ANGES

from the Mediterrean side. Go all the way to the cemetery.
There is no castle on Castle Hill.

▲▲▲**Promenade des Anglais**—There's something for
everyone along this seafront circus. Watch the Europeans at
play, admire the azure Mediterranean, anchor yourself in one
of the blue chairs, and prop your feet up on the made-to-order
guardrail. Ahhh, the Riviera! Join the evening parade of tans
along the promenade.

Beaches of Nice—Where the jet set lies on the rocks. After
some time settling into the pebbles, you can play beach volley-
ball, ping-pong, or *boules*, rent paddle boats, jet skis, or wind

surfers, explore ways to use your zoom lens as a telescope, or
snooze on comfy beach-beds with end tables. Before you head
off in search of sandy beaches, try it on the rocks.

▲▲**Musée National Marc Chagall**—Even if you're suspi-
cious of modern art, this museum is a joy (20 minutes from
most hotels listed). A wonderful selection of Chagall's work
is impressively displayed according to the artist's design. The
brilliant blues and reds of his large oil paintings are exhila-
rating, as are the spiritual and folk themes. Don't miss the
stained glass windows of the auditorium. The small guidebook has a great rundown on each meaningful painting. (27F,
open July-September 10:00-19:00; off-season 10:00-12:20,
14:00-17:20, closed Tuesday. To get there from the train
station, turn left along avenue Thiers and walk about 8
blocks, or take bus #15.)

Nice Municipal Museums—The city of Nice has established 12 free, interesting museums with themes ranging
from archaeological to naval and Renaissance to modern art.
Get a Nice museum brochure at the TI for descriptions and
current hours. My favorite is the Nice knickknack Musée
Masséna, housed in a beautiful mansion across from the
promenade des Anglais and full of historical paraphernalia
(65 rue de France).

Modern art fans will enjoy the new Modern Art
Museum's collection of art from the 1960s and 1970s inter-
estingly displayed in this ultra-modern museum. (Free, open
11:00-18:00, Friday evening until 22:00, closed Tuesday.)
Located on the promenade des Arts near the bus station.

▲**Russian Cathedral**—Even if you've been to Russia, this
is worth a detour. Situated between two tennis courts, the
stunning onion domes seem proud, but odd, on the racy
Riviera. (12F, no shorts, open 9:00-12:00, 14:30-17:00; July
and August until 18:00. At 17 boulevard du Tsarevitch.)

Shopping Streets—The pedestrian streets of rue Masséna
are packed with tourists, uninteresting cafés, and overpriced
boutiques. Window-shop the expensive boutiques and sift
through the fascinating crowds. The dime-a-dozen cafés are
well stocked with predictable food.

▲**Matisse Museum**—A three-star sight for his fans, the art
is beautifully displayed in this newly rennovated showpiece
and represents the largest collection of Matisse paintings.

(Free, open 10:00-17:00 Wednesday-Monday. Take bus #15, #17, #20, or #22 to the Arènes stop, or hike 45 minutes to 164 avenue des Arènes de Cimiez.)

Nightlife—Nice's bars play host to a lively late night scene with jazz and rock' n' roll. Most activity focuses on Old Nice, near the place Rosetti. Avoid walking alone if you're out very late. Plan on a cover charge or expensive drinks, and try these places: the **Tam Tam** on the place Massena, or **Chez Wayne** in Old Nice at 15 rue de la Prefecture.

Sleeping in Nice
(5.5 F = about $1, zip code: 06000)

Don't look for charm in Nice. Go for modern and clean with a central location. Reserve early for summer visits. There are virtually no hotels in the Old City, and the many hotels near the station are overrun, overpriced, and loud. The best area is between the Old City and the station, east of avenue Jean Médecin, where our suggested hotels are located. To reach the hotels from the train station, turn left out of the station onto avenue Thiers, then right onto avenue Jean Médecin. This handy location is peaceful and close to the Old City, train station, bus station, and seafront.

Sleep code: **S**=Single, **D**=Double/twin, **T**=Triple, **Q**=Quad, **B**=Bath/shower, **WC**=Toilet, **PD**=breakfast, **CC**=Credit Card (**V**isa, **M**astercard, **A**mex).

Hôtel Star** is very comfortable and popular—and deservedly so. It's quiet, clean, modern, and ideally located (SB-200F, DBWC-290F, TBWC-390F, CC:VMA, 14 rue Biscarra, tel. 93 85 19 03, fax 93 13 04 23).

Hôtel du Petit Louvre* has art-festooned walls, warm owners, pleasant rooms, and is a superb value (DBWC-220F, TBWC-240F-275F, CC:VM, 10 rue Emma Tiranty, tel. 93 80 15 54, fax 93 62 45 08).

The excellent bargain rooms at the small **Hôtel Lorrain***, (S-140F, DB-160F, DBWC-250F, TBWC-260F, CC:none, 6 rue Gubernatis, tel. 93 85 42 90) are like small apartments with kitchenettes. This is a very clean, simple, and friendly hotel that may request longer stays in the high season.

Hôtel les Camelias** is Nice's bargain Old World hotel and one of my favorites, as it reminds me of hotels I stayed in with my parents—simple rooms with the "necessary comforts" and a loyal clientele who gather in the TV lounge after dinner. There's a small courtyard with limited parking; some rooms have balconies and all have meek showers (prices include PD, SB-180F-220F, DBWC-350F, TBWC-400F, CC:VM, 3 rue Spitaleri, tel. 93 62 15 54).

The Hotel Mulhouse** is close to Old Nice, rather plain but comfortable and a fair value (SBWC-230F, DBWC-320F, TBWC-400F, QBWC-480F, 9 rue de Chauvain, CC:VMA, tel. 93 92 36 39, fax 93 13 96 80). **Hôtel Paradis** is quiet, pleasant, and centrally located on a pedestrian street (DB-200F, DBWC-280F, 1 rue de Paradis, tel. 93 87 71 23). **Hôtel des Anges** is located right in the thick of traffic, but it's a cushy place with a spacious lobby, helpful elevator, and breakfast in bed. Get a room off the street or you'll regret it (DBWC-270F-360F, 1 place Massena, tel. 93 82 12 28).

Sleeping in Villefranche sur Mer
(5.5 F = about $1, zip code: 06230)

Nice is nice as a home base, but if you're seeking a smaller, more village-like atmosphere, try nearby Villefranche sur Mer. Villefranche, only 15 minutes from Nice and Monte Carlo, with frequent bus and train service to both, makes an excellent, if somewhat more expensive, Riviera base.

Bargain values don't exist here, and I've only listed two hotels, each fairly expensive. Even if you decide to stay in Nice, drop by for dinner at the beachfront café just below the train station, then wander into the village for an ice cream and find the hidden rue Obscure. The TI is in the small park (Jardin François Binon) just below the main intersection, tel. 93 01 73 68.

Sleep code: **S**=Single, **D**=Double/twin, **T**=Triple, **Q**=Quad, **B**=Bath/shower, **WC**=Toilet, **PD**=breakfast, **CC**=Credit Card (Visa, Mastercard, Amex).

Those with the means should stay at the **Hôtel La Flore*** (DBWC-400F-600F, TBWC/QBWC-750F-850F, substantial reduction November-March, CC:VMA, avenue Princess Grace de Monaco, tel. 93 76 30 30, fax 93 76 99 99). Ask for a room on the bay side if you can afford a splurge for balconies and a million-dollar view over cruise ships and the Cap Ferrat. Private pool. Reserve long in advance for summer season.

The less expensive **Hôtel Provençal**** (prices include PD, DBWC-380F-460F, TBWC-460F-550F, QBWC-550F-640F, CC:VM, just below the main intersection in Villefranche, avenue Maréchal Joffre, tel. 93 01 71 42, fax 93 76 96 00) offers similar views in hotelesque surroundings with a heated pool, sauna, and a costly mandatory half-pension in summer.

Cuisine Scene—Côte d'Azur

The Côte d'Azur (technically a part of Provence) gives Provence's cuisine a Mediterranean flair. *Bouillabaisse* (the spicy seafood stew-soup seems worth the cost only for those with a seafood fetish), *bourride* (a creamy fish soup thickened with aïoli), and *salade niçoise* (nee-swaz) a tasty tomato, potato, olive, anchovy, and tuna salad) are the must-tries around here. You'll also find France's tastiest bread specialties: *pissaladière* (bread dough topped with onions, olives, and anchovies), *fougasse* (a spindly, lacelike bread), *socca* (a thin chick-pea crêpe), and *pan bagna* (a bread shell stuffed with tomatoes, anchovies, olives, onions, and tuna). Bellet is the local wine, both red and white, served chilled.

Eating in Nice

Eat in Nice's old city. It overflows with cheap, moderate, and expensive restaurants, pizza stands, and taverns.

Charcuterie Julien is a terrific deli/restaurant in which to sample the local seafood salads. Walk inside, pick out what looks best, remember its name, then take a seat outside to order. Try the *salade niçoise*. (On rue de la Poissonnerie, at the end of the cours Saleya; open 11:00-19:30.) The **Nissa Socca** café, a block off the place Rossini on the rue Reparate, offers the best cheap Italian cuisine in town in a lively atmosphere. Come early.

Rue Droite has the best pizza stands and most local eateries in Nice. Check out **Acchiardo's** (#37) for flavor, and sample the fish soup. Stop by **Le four à bois** bakery (#38), and watch them make the *fougasse*. For more traditional, more atmospheric, and more expensive eating, try the locally popular **La Cambuse** on the cours Saleya, or to save money, choose a place on the place Rossetti. Near the Hotel les Camelias is the excellent restaurant **Le Blacas**, specializing in seafood and pizza. Relax on the outdoor terrace (moderate, 9 rue Chauvin).

Transportation Connections
Nice and Arles: See Arles connections.
Nice and Chamonix: A handy night train makes this run sans transfer (leaves Nice around 20:30), though a very scencic train leaves Nice to Digne early (around 6:30). From Digne it's a series of scenic bus trips (via St. Auban, Veynes and Grenoble, and St. Gervais) and train trips to get up and over the Alps, arriving in Chamonix at about 17:00.
Nice and Florence: 2 daily trips (morning departures) make this trip in about 8 hours (transfer in Pisa and or Genoa).
Nice and Paris: TGV service makes the 7-hour trip between these cities 7 times daily.

Riviera Connections
Trains: Regular train service connects all beachfront stops.
From Nice: Cannes is 35 minutes, Antibes is 20 minutes, and Monaco is 20 minutes.
Buses: Buses depart frequently from the Gare Routière near the old city (Bd. Jaures, see map) to all daytrip destinations described in this book. Buses parallel train service along the coast amd take longer, but run more frequently and often closer to your desired destination.
Bike and Moped Rental: Cycles Arnaud, 4 place Grimaldi, Nice (just off rue Jean Medecin near pedestrian streets, tel. 93 87 88 55).

French Riviera Towns

Antibes
For sandy beaches, an interesting old town, and a fine Picasso collection, visit Antibes. Antibes' glamorous port glistens with luxurious yachts and quaint fishing boats. You're welcome to browse. The Old City is charming in a sandy-sophisticated way. The daily market bustles until 13:00 except on Monday.

The helpful TI, **Maison de Tourisme**, (11, place de Gaulle tel. 93 33 95 64) and another small TI booth is at the port entrance to the old city. Most of what we're interested in lies near the port within the old city walls. If arriving by train, you'll see the port to your left, the center of Antibes is straight ahead as you exit, 10 minutes on foot. The bus station is dead center on place Guynemer, one block from the TI, about 15 minutes on foot from the port. If driving, park near the old city walls on the port.

Sights—Antibes

▲▲▲The **Musée Picasso** sits serenely where the Old City meets the sea (look for signs from the Old City) in the Chateau Grimali and offers an enjoyable collection of this artists work. You'll understand why Picasso liked working here, and several photos of the artist make this already intimate museum more so. Don't miss the Joie de Vivre painting. (20F, open July-September 10:00-12:00, 15:00-19:00; October-June 10:00-12:00, 14:00-18:00, closed Tuesday.)
Beaches—The best beaches stretch between Antibe's port and the Cap d'Antibes and offer long stretches of fine sand. Only in the summer are the main beaches (near the Cap d'Antibes) jammed, though the smaller plage (beach) de la Gravette at the port remains calm in any season.

Sleeping in Antibes
(zip code: 06600)

Rooms fill quickly here. Without question, the best moderate priced hotel in Antibes (and maybe the entire Riviera) is the ideal **Hotel Ponteil**** (S-220F, D-250F, DBWC-310-340F, CC:VMA, 11 Imapsse Jean-Mesnier, tel. 93 34 67 92, fax 93 34 49 47), has a variety of good value rooms located in and around a delightful manor house with private parking, a garden terrace, tranquility, quick beach access, and friendly owners. Reserve early. A fair half-pension required in summer, and it's long walk from the station. The more central **Relais du Postillon**** offers pleasant, comfortable rooms on a central square and helpful owners (DBWC-300F-385F, TBWC-385F, CC:VMA, 8 rue Championnet, tel. 93 34 20 77, fax 93 34 61 24). **The Auberge Provencale*** (S-150F, D-200F, DBWC-280F-400F, TBWC-320F-450F, QBWC-

500F, CC:VMA) is right in the thick of things (61 place Nationale) and has character and pleasant rooms (noisy if on the square).

Monaco

Still dazzling (particularly at night) despite overdevelopment and crass commercialization, Monaco will disappoint those who look for something below the surface. The 30-minute ride alone may make you glad you came. (It's slower but cheaper by bus, 18F, round-trip with same company. Tell the driver you want the Place d'Armes stop—Monaco's old city and palace.) This 2-square-kilometer country is a tax haven for its fewer than 5,000 residents. The TI is near the Casino (2 boulevard des Moulins, tel. 92 16 61 66). Small buses shuttle tourists and locals through Monaco effortlessly.

Monaco (the principality) is best understood when separated into two distinct areas: Monaco Ville, the old city housing Prince Rainier's palace; and the area around the Casino, Monte Carlo. The harbor divides the two. A short bus ride or long walk (30 min) links each area to the bus and train stations. Start with a look at Monaco Ville for a magnifique view (particularly at night) over the harbor and the Casino. If you arrive in the morning, you can watch the uninspiring changing of the guard (11:55), then wander over to the beautiful Cathedrale de Monaco where Princess Grace is buried, and picnic in the immaculate and scenic gardens overlooking the blue Mediterranean. (Pick up a *pan bagna* sandwich in the old city.)

The nearby and costly (60F) Musée de l'Océanographique (Cousteau Aquarium) is the largest of its kind. It can be jammed and disappoints some, though the aquarium lovers leave impressed. The *Monte Carlo Story* (40F) film gives an interesting account (in English) of this city's history (next to the aquarium, down the steps into the parking garage).

Leave Monaco Ville and ride the shuttle bus or stroll the harborfront up to the Casino. Count the counts and Rolls Royces in front of the Hôtel de Paris. Strut inside the lavish Casino (opens at 12:00)—anyone can get as far as the one-armed bandits, but only adults (21 and older) can pay the 50F or 100F charge (depending on how serious you take this) to get into the private game rooms where you can rub shoulders with the richest of the rich (some rooms open at 15:00, others not until 21:00). Entrance is free to all games in the new, plebeian Loews American-style Casino, adjacent to the Casino.

Menton
Just a few minutes by train from Monte Carlo or Nice, Menton is a relatively quiet and relaxing spa and beach town (TI tel. 93 57 57 00).

Cannes
Its sister city is Beverly Hills.

St. Paul (de-Vence) and Vence
If you prefer hill towns to beaches, head for St. Paul and Vence (the same bus from Nice's Gare Routière serves both towns, 45-min ride, 20F one-way every 30 min). Unless you go early, you'll escape only some of the heat and none of the crowds. **St. Paul** is part cozy medieval hill town and part local artist shopping mall. It's pleasantly artsy but gets swamped with tour buses. Meander into St. Paul's quieter streets and wander far to enjoy the panoramic views. (TI tel. 93 32 86 95.)

The prestigious, far-out, and high-priced **Fondation Maeght** art gallery is a 10-minute steep walk uphill from St. Paul. If ever modern art could appeal to you, this would be the place. Its world-class contemporary art collection is thoughtfully arranged between pleasant gardens and well lit rooms. (45F, open daily July-September 10:00-18:30; October-June 10:00-12:30, 14:30-17:30, tel. 93 32 81 63.)

The enjoyable hill town of **Vence** (10 minutes from St. Paul by bus) disperses St. Paul's crowds over a larger and more interesting city. Vence bubbles with workaday and tourist activity. Catch the daily market (ends at 12:30), and don't miss the small church with its Chagall mosaic and moving Chapelle St. Sacrament. The Vence TI is on place du Grand Jardin, tel. 93 58 06 38. Matisse's much raved about **Chapelle du Rosaire** (1 mile from Vence toward St. Jeannet, taxi or walk) may disappoint all but Matisse fans for whom this is a necessary pilgrimage: the yellow, blue, and green filtered sunlight does a cheery dance in stark contrast to the gloomy tile sketches. (Donation requested. Open only Tuesday and Thursday 10:00-11:30, 14:30-17:30, most days in summer same hours, closed November-December 15, tel. 93 58 03 26.)

Best Sandy Beaches

Villefranche sur Mer and Cap d'Ail to the east of Nice, and Antibes and Cannes to the west, all have fine, sandy beaches and many competing sun-seekers in the summer. Beaches seem less crowded east of Nice. Buses and trains serve each beach.

France

BERLIN

No tour of Germany is complete without a look at its historic and newly united capital, Berlin. Enjoy the thrill of walking over what was The Wall and through Brandenburg Gate. Crossing "into the East" is now like stepping on a dead dragon, no longer mysterious and foreboding—just ugly. That thrill is gone.

Berlin has shut the door on a tumultuous 50-year chapter in its 750-year history. It was flattened in World War II, then divided by the Allied powers, with the American, British, and French sectors being West Berlin and the Russian sector, East Berlin. The division was set in stone when the East built the Berlin Wall in 1961. In 1989 the Wall fell, and in 1990 Germany was formally reunited. Today the city is like a man who had a terrible accident and half the body was given the best of care and the other was denied therapy. But Dr. Capitalism has arrived and the east is healing quickly.

The new right-wing city government is eager to charge forward with little nostalgia for anything that was "eastern." Big corporations and the national government have moved in and the dreary swath of land that was the Wall will soon again be the city center. The entire area is a construction zone, its skyline a nest of cranes as city planners are boldly taking the reunification of the city and the return of the national government (in the year 2000) as a good opportunity to make Berlin a great capital once again.

Planning Your Time

Because of its location, on a quick trip I'd spend either one or two days in Berlin and sleep in and out on the train. On a three-week trip through Germany, Austria and Switzerland, I'd give Berlin two days and spend them this way:

Day 1: Arrive early on the overnight train, visit TI and check into hotel, visit memorial church and KaDeWe, do the complete Bus #100 orientation tour with a visit to the Reichstag and Brandenburg Gate (or take the Guide Friday tour). After lunch near Alexanderplatz, tour the Pergamon Museum, spend the afternoon strolling Kurfurstendamm.

Day 2: Check out of hotel, leave bags there. Subway to Hermannplatz and ride bus #129 through Kreuzberg to Haus am Checkpoint Charlie. Tour the museum, see remains of the Wall, tour the Topography of Terror exhibit. Divide rest of day between the paintings of the Gemaldegalerie, the Egyptian museum, and Charlottenburg Palace. Depart on an overnight train.

Orientation (tel. code: 030)

The tourist's Berlin can be broken into chunks: (1) The area around the Bahnhof Zoo and the grand Kurfürstendamm boulevard (transportation, information, hotel, shopping, and nightlife hub), (2) former downtown East Berlin (Brandenburg Gate, Unter den Linden boulevard, Pergamon Museum, Wall-related sights), (3) the museums and palace at Charlottenburg, and (4) the museums at Dahlem. Chunks 1 and 2 can be done on foot or with bus #100. Catch the U-Bahn to chunks 3 and 4.

Arriving by Train

Berlin's central station is called Bahnhof Zoo because it's near Berlin's famous zoo. Berlin has three stations. "Zoo" is for most of Western Europe. Hauptbahnhof is for most eastbound and southbound trains. And Lichtenberg is for eastbound and northbound trains. All trains are connected by subway. Train info: tel. 19419.

Most travelers arrive at the "Zoo Bahnhof." There's no clear front of the station, but eventually you'll end up on Hardenbergplatz (filled with city buses). Tip-toe through the riff-raff to the big intersection on the right. Looking down Hardenbergstrasse, past the close skyscraper with the giraffe on it, you'll see the black bombed-out hulk of the Kaiser-Wilhelm Memorial Church. The TI is behind that, in the Europa Center (with the Mercedes symbol spinning on its roof). Facing the church, most of the hotels I recommend are to your right. Just ahead amidst the traffic is the BVG transport information kiosk. (Buy the 24-hour 13-DM pass here, pick up a free subway map and maybe the 2-DM transit map.) From here, walk to the TI, descend into the subway system, and catch bus #100 for the intro tour.

Tourist Information

The main TI office is 5 minutes from the Berlin Zoo train station, in the Europa Center (with Mercedes symbol on top, enter outside to the left, on Budapesterstrasse, 8:00-22:30, 9:00-21:00 on Sunday, tel. 030/262-6031). Their free *Berlin Berlin* magazine has good reading on Berlin and lists the latest location and hours of major sights. The *Berlin Program*, a 3-DM German language monthly, lists upcoming events. The transit map is worth 2 DM only if you'll be riding a lot of buses. Get the free metro map. Smaller TIs: Zoo Bahnhof (8:00-23:00, closed Sunday, tel. 313-9063), Hauptbahnhof (daily 8:00-20:00, tel. 279-5209), and Brandenburg Gate (may be in business in 1995).

Getting Around Berlin

Berlin is miserable on foot. Use Berlin's fine public-transit system. The U-Bahn, S-Bahn, and all buses are now one "BVG" system operating conveniently on the same tickets. (The S-Bahn is free with a Eurailpass.) A basic buy-as-you-board or buy-from-machines (Erwachsene Normaltarif) 3.50 DM ticket gives you 2 hours of travel on buses or subways. For a single short ride (a distance of six bus stops or three subway stations, with one transfer) get the "Einzelfahrschein" ticket (2.30 DM). A "Sammelkarte" gives you four of either of these tickets at a small discount. The 13-DM "Berlin Ticket" is a great deal, giving you the works for 24 hours. The many police escorting cheaters out of the subway make you happy you're not taking advantage of this honor system. The double-decker buses are a joy to ride, and the subway is a snap. Right from the start, commit yourself to public transit in Berlin. Taxis are expensive.

Bus #100 Do-It-Yourself Orientation Tour

Berlin's bus #100 is made to order for sightseers (Bahnhof Zoo, Europa Center/Hotel Palace, Siegessäule, Reichstag, Brandenburg Gate, Unter den Linden, Pergamon Museum, to Alexanderplatz). If you have the 30 DM and 90 minutes for a Guide Friday tour, take that. But this 3.50-DM, 30-minute tour is a winning intro to the city. Buses leave from Hardenbergplatz in front of the Zoo station (or near the Europa Center TI, in front of the Hotel Palace). Get out when you like. Buses come every 10 minutes and tickets are good for 2 hours. Climb aboard, stamp your ticket (giving it a time) and grab a front seat on top. If you have the TI's fun free pictorial "Kurfurstendamm to Alexanderplatz" map, use it to follow the route (and tell me the giraffe's not doing what I think he's doing). Major sights are mentioned here and described in more depth below (listed in the order bus #100 hits them).

• (On right, before descending into the tunnel) The bombed-out hulk of the Kaiser-Wilhelm Memorial Church, with its new sister church (described below).

• (Stop: in front of the Hotel Palace) On the left, the Berlin Zoo entrance and its aquarium (described below).

• (Driving down Kurfurstenstrasse, turning left into Tiergarten) The 60-meter-tall Victory Column or Siegessaüle (described below).

• (On the left immediately after leaving the Siegessaüle) The 18th-century late-rococo Bellevue Palace is the new German "White House," the residence of the federal president. If the flag's flying, he's home.

• (Driving along the Spree River) This park area was a residential district before WWII. Soon it will be filled with the buildings of the new national government. Construction has already started. Floating in front of the slope-roofed "House of World Cultures" (left side) is a Henry Moore sculpture. The modern tower (next on left) is a Carillon with 68 bells (1987).

• (Big, black, flag-waving building on left) The Reichstag building is as full of history as its bullet-riddled and patched up complexion suggests (described below).

• (Immediately around the corner, on left) Brandenburg Gate (described below) was the center of old Berlin. As you drive under it look left and right. That was all important government buildings, bombed to smithereens, and later the Wall. Behind you on the right is the Siegessaüle and a grand 10-mile-long boulevard leading from Charlottenburg, through the Brandenburg Gate, up Unter den Linden, to the heart of old imperial Berlin and what was the palace of the Prussian emperor, Frederick the Great.

• (Driving up Unter den Linden straight toward the TV tower in the distance) In the 15th century this was a horse-way leading from the palace to the hunting lodge. In the 17th century, Hohenzollern princes and princesses moved in, building their palaces here to be near the Prussian emperor. Linden trees still give it a pleasant strolling ambiance. This was the most elegant street of Prussian Berlin, and the main drag of East Berlin.

• (First big building on right) The Russian embassy is not quite as important now as it was a few years ago. It flies the Russian white, blue, and red. Next to it is the Russian airline, Aeroflot.

• (The large equestrian statue in the street ahead) On the horse is Frederick II ("the Great"). Most of the buildings around you were from his governmental center. His palace would have been just ahead. Behind the statue is the Humboldt University (formerly one of Europe's greatest, Marx and Lenin—not the brothers or the sisters—studied here). The Greek temple-like building next on the left is

West Berlin

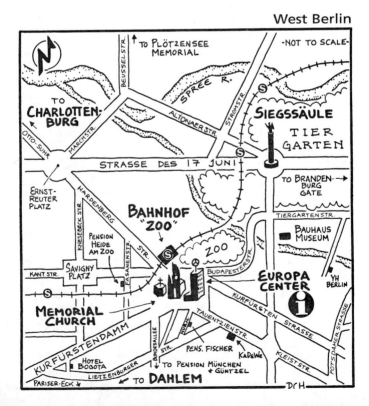

the "New Watch" (from the early 1800s) which is now a
national memorial for the German dead of both great wars.

• (Crossing the bridge) You're now on the "Museum
Island," home of Germany's first museums and today
famous for its Pergamon Museum (described below). The
museum complex starts with the Neoclassical facade on the
left. The huge church is the 100-year-old Berlin Cathedral,
or "Dom" (inside, the great reformers stand around the
dome like stern saints guarding their theology).

Immediately across the street (right) is the "Palace of the
People," the grand center and international showcase of
East Berlin. Debate rages over whether or not to tear it
down. It sits on the spot of the original palace of the
Prussian emperor.

• (Crossing another bridge, you leave the Museum Island) On
your right are the pointy twin spires of the Nikolai church.
This was medieval Berlin (not worth a visit). The huge red-

East Berlin

brick building is the city hall, built after the revolution of 1848 and arguably the first democratic building in the city. Next to this were the DDR presidential palace and head-quarters of the Communist party. The much closer church, the Marien church, dates back to 1270.

• (Under the TV tower) Alexanderplatz, under the tracks on the right, was the commercial heart of East Berlin (described below).

• This is the end of the tourist's bus #100 route. There are plenty of handy eateries and a subway station here. Stay on the bus to ride through workaday eastern Berlin, with its Lego-hell apartments (30 minutes round-trip). Are the people different? They are politically free. Are they economically free? How's the future? (At the end of the line, get out. At the same stop, in a few minutes, another bus will take you back to Alexanderplatz, or even back to the start at Zoo.)

Sights—Near Bahnhof Zoo

▲Kurfürstendamm—In the 1850s, when Berlin became a wealthy and important capital, Berlin's new rich chose Kurfurstendamm as their street. Bismarck made it Berlin's Champs-Elysees. In the 1920s it became a chic and fashionable drag of cafés and boutiques. During the Third Reich, as home to the international community of diplomats and journalists, it enjoyed more freedom than the rest of Berlin. Throughout the Cold War, economic subsidies from the West made sure that capitalism thrived on Ku'damm, as west Berlin's main drag is popularly called. And today, while much of the old charm has been hamburgerized, Ku'damm is still the place to feel the pulse of the city and enjoy its most elegant shops (around Fasanenstrasse) and department stores. Ku'damm, starting at Kaiser Wilhelm Memorial Church, does its commercial can-can for over 2 miles.

Europa Center—This shiny high-rise shopping center, where you'll find the city Tourist Information and lots of shops and restaurants, was built as a showcase of Western capitalism during the cold war. If you arrive in Berlin before the TI opens, the Deli French (ground floor, open at 7:00, 8:00 Sunday) is a more pleasant place to brush your teeth and start your day than the seedy Bahnhof Zoo.

▲**Kaiser Wilhelm Memorial Church
(Gedächtniskirche)**—Originally a memorial to the first
emperor of Germany, who died in 1888, this is now a
memorial to the destruction of Berlin in WWII. The
charred and gutted ruins of this bombed-out church (free,
Tuesday-Saturday 10:00-16:00) have great ceiling mosaics
and an interesting photo exhibit about the bombing. Next to
it, a new church (1961) offers a world of 11,000 little blue
glass windows.

▲**Kaufhaus des Westens (KaDeWe)**—The "department
store of the West" is the biggest department store in Europe.
It takes a staff of more than 3,000 to help you find and purchase what you need from the vast selection of more than
200,000 items. You can get everything from a haircut and
train ticket to souvenirs (fourth floor). The sixth floor is a
world of taste treats. This biggest selection of deli and exotic
food in Germany offers plenty of free samples and classy
opportunities to sit down and eat. Or, better, ride the glass
elevator to the seventh floor's glass-domed Le Buffet
self-service cafeteria (9:30-18:30, Saturday until 14:00,
Thursday until 20:30, closed Sunday, tel. 21210, U-Bahn:
Wittenbergplatz).

The Berlin Zoo—1,500 different kinds of animals call
Berlin's famous zoo home (or so the zookeepers like to think,
10 DM, 9:00-18:30, feeding times posted at entry, morning
is the best visiting time, enter near TI in front of Hotel
Palace, tel. 254010).

Tiergarten/Siegessaüle—Berlin's "Central Park" stretches
about 2 miles from the Zoo train station to the Brandenburg
Gate. Its centerpiece, the Siegessaüle (Victory Column), was
built to commemorate the Prussian defeat of France in 1870.
The pointy-helmeted Germans rubbed it in, decorating the
tower with French cannon and paying for it all with francs
received as war reparations. Statues of Moltke and other
German military greats goose-step around the angel at night.
You can climb its 285 steps for a fine Berlin-wide view
(1.50 DM, 9:00-18:00, Monday 13:00-18:00, bus #100).
From the tower the grand Strasse des 17 Juni leads to the
Brandenburg Gate (via a thriving flea-market each Saturday
and Sunday).

Sights—East Berlin

▲▲**Brandenburg Gate**—The historic Brandenburg Gate was the symbol of Berlin and then the symbol of divided Berlin. It sat, part of a sad circle dance called the Wall, for over 25 years. Now a free little photo exhibit in the gate and postcards all over town show the ecstatic day—December 23, 1989—when the world enjoyed the sight of happy Berliners jamming the gate like flowers on a parade float. A carnival atmosphere continues as tourists stroll, past hawkers with "authentic" pieces of the wall, DDR flags and military paraphernalia, to the traditional rhythm of an organ-grinder. Step aside for a minute, and think about struggles for freedom—past and present. Ebertstrasse leads from Brandenburg Gate to Potsdamer Platz, formerly the busiest square in all of Europe, then for decades a vacant lot. Sony and Mercedes are busy making Potsdamer Platz once more a vibrant center of commerce.

▲**The Reichstag**—It was from this old Parliament building that the German republic was proclaimed in 1918. Hitler burned this symbol of democracy to frame the Communists in 1933. And it was in here that the last 1,500 Nazis made their last stand, extending WWII in Europe by four days. For its 101st birthday, in 1995, the Bulgarian artist Cristo will wrap it up. The Reichstag houses a modern German history exhibit, "Questions on German History" (free, 10:00-17:00 Tuesday-Sunday, enter from side opposite the bus #100 stop, cheap cafeteria, lots of free literature on the German government). Nothing is explained in English but you can follow a good, socio-economico-meaty and exhausting 45-minute tape-recorded tour for 2 DM. In a few years this collection will move, as the Reichstag resumes its real function as Germany's Parliament building. On the Brandenburg Gate side of the building, the garden of crosses is a memorial to those killed trying to cross The Wall.

▲▲**Under den Linden and Alexanderplatz, the heart of East Berlin**—In Berlin's good old days, Unter den Linden was one of Europe's grand boulevards. Walk or catch bus #100 from Brandenburg Gate to Alexanderplatz. The "Bus #100 tour" above describes the sights along the way. The 1,200-foot-tall Fernsehturm TV tower (built 1969, 6 DM, 9:00-24:00) offers a fine view from 600 feet at the deck and café. Farther east, pass under the train tracks into Alexanderplatz, formerly the DDR's consumer paradise.

▲▲▲**The Museum of the Wall (Haus am Checkpoint Charlie) and a surviving chunk of The Wall**—The 100-mile "Anti-Fascist Protective Rampart," as it was called by the DDR, was erected almost overnight in 1961. It was 13 feet high with a 16-foot tank ditch, 160 feet of no-man's-land, and 300 sentry towers. In its 28 years there were 1,693 cases when border guards fired, 3,221 arrests, 5,043 documented successful escapes (565 of these were DDR guards), and 80 deaths.

The fascinating **Haus am Checkpoint Charlie** museum tells the gripping history of The Wall and the many ingenious escape attempts. A visit includes plenty of video and film coverage of those heady days when people-power tore it down (U-Bahn to Kochstrasse, 7.50 DM daily, 9:00-22:00). Formerly up against the wall and on nearly worthless land, the rent here has skyrocketed and the museum may have to move.

The gate of **Checkpoint Charlie**, the famous American military border crossing, stands permanently raised as a memorial. When the Wall fell, it was literally carried away by the euphoria. Little remains. From Checkpoint Charlie, Zimmerstrasse leads to a small surviving stretch. Walk the length of this bit. Then look left to see the "Topography of Terror" exhibit.

The **Topography of Terror**, built atop the recently excavated air-raid shelter next to what was the Gestapo headquarters, shows the story of Nazism in Germany (English translation 1 DM, free, 10:00-18:00, closed Monday). Between this building and Checkpoint Charlie is a park with English descriptions of this once-formidable center of tyranny.

The German Resistance Memorial Centre—This center tells the story of the German resistance to Hitler. "The Benderblock" was a military headquarters where an ill-fated conspiracy to assassinate Hitler was plotted and its instigators executed. There is a memorial and rooms explaining Germany's struggles against its Fuhrer (9:00-18:00, Saturday and Sunday 9:00-13:00, just south of the Tiergarten at Stauffenbergstrasse 11, tel. 2654 2202).

▲▲**Pergamon Museum**—Many of Berlin's top museums cluster on the Museuminsel (Museum Island), just off Unter den Linden, in East Berlin. Only the Pergamon Museum, with the fantastic Pergamon Altar, the Babylonian Ishtar Gate, and many ancient Greek and Mesopotamian treasures, is of interest to the normal tourist. (Walk along the canal, passing the first bulky Neoclassical building on your right, to a bridge that leads to a second bulky Neoclassical building, 4 DM, 9:00-17:00, closed Monday, free Sunday). Take advantage of the free 30-minute tape-recorder tours of the museum's highlights.

Sights—Around Charlottenburg Palace
Schloss Charlottenburg—This only surviving Hohen-zollern Palace is Berlin's top baroque palace (8 DM, Tuesday-Friday 9:00-17:00, Saturday and Sunday 10:00-17:00, U-1 to Sophie-Charlotte Platz and a 10-minute walk, or bus #121, bus #145, or bus #204 direct from Bahnhof Zoo). If you've seen the great palaces of Europe, this one comes in at about tenth place, especially since its center is tourable only with a German guide. For a quick look, the Knöbelsdorff Wing (3 DM) is set up to let you wander on your own, a substantial hike through restored-since-the-war, gold-crusted white rooms filled with Frederick the Great's not-so-great collection of baroque paintings. Ahhh, skip it all together.

▲▲The Egyptian Museum—Across the street from the palace is a fine little museum filled with Egyptian treasures. It offers one of the great thrills in art appreciation—gazing into the still-young and beautiful face of 3,000-year-old Queen Nefertiti, the wife of King Akhenaton (4 DM, Monday-Thursday 9:00-17:00, Saturday and Sunday 10:00-17:00, Schlossstrasse 70).

▲The Bröhan Museum is like walking through a dozen beautifully furnished Art Nouveau (Jugendstil) and Art Deco living rooms. If you're tired, the final rooms are not worth the six flights of stairs (6 DM, 10:00-18:00, closed Monday, next to the Egyptian Museum, across the street from the Charlottenburg Palace).

Other Berlin Sights
▲▲Dahlem Gemälde-galerie—Dahlem is actually a cluster of important museums that, one by one over the next

decade, will be moved to the new museum complex in the Tiergarten. The *Gemälde-galerie* (picture gallery), Dahlem's essential stop, may be moved as early as 1995. Check at the TI before heading out. It has more than 600 canvases by the likes of Dürer, Titian, Botticelli, Rubens, Vermeer, and Bruegel, and one of the world's greatest collection of Rembrandts. The *Man with the Golden Helmet*, recently determined not to have been painted by Rembrandt, still shines (4 DM, free on Sunday, Tuesday-Friday 9:00-17:00, Saturday and Sunday 10:00-17:00, closed Monday, U-Bahn to Dahlem-Dorf).

Kreuzberg—This poorer district along the Wall, with old restored and unrestored buildings and plenty of student and Turkish street life, offers the best look at melting-pot Berlin in a city where original Berliners are as rare as old buildings. Berlin is the fourth-largest Turkish city and this is its "downtown." But to call it a little Istanbul insults the big one. You'll see mothers wearing scarves, *doner kebap* stands, and spray-paint decorated shops. For a dose of Kreuzberg without getting your fingers dirty, you can joyride on bus #129. (Take U8 to Hermannplatz, you'll ascend through the Karstadt department store's great cafeteria, #129 buses wait immediately outside its door, leaving every 5 minutes. After leaving Kreuzberg, they stop right at the Checkpoint Charlie Museum and go all the way to KaDeWe and Ku'damm.) For a walk, wander the area between the Kottbusser Tor and Schlesisches Tor subway stops, ideally on Tuesday and Friday afternoons when a Turkish Market sprawls along the bank of the Maybachufer River (U-Bahn: Kottbusser Tor, 12:00-18:00).

East Side Gallery—The biggest remaining stretch of the Wall is now "the world's longest art gallery," stretching for about a mile and completely covered with murals painted by artists from around the world, mostly in celebration of the Wall's demise. While not overly impressive, and in dire need of restoration, it does make for a thought-provoking walk. From Schlesisches Tor (end of Kreuzberg) walk across the river on the pedestrian bridge, turn left, follow the Wall to the Berlin Hauptbahnhof (a train station two stops from Alexanderplatz).

Käthe-Kollwitz Museum—This local artist (1867-1945), who experienced much of Berlin's most tumultuous century, conveys some powerful and mostly sad feelings through the black-and-white faces of her art (6 DM, 11:00-18:00, closed Tuesday; off Ku'damm at Fasanenstrasse 24).

Museum of Natural History (Museum für Naturkunde)— Worth a visit just to see the largest dinosaur skeleton ever assembled. While you're there meet "Bobby," the stuffed ape. (3 DM, open 9:30-17:00, closed Monday; U-6 to Zinnowitzer Strasse, at Invalidenstrasse 43).

City Bus Tours—Several companies do quick, 1- to-2-hour, 15- to-30-DM orientation bus tours. I'm a Guide Friday bus-tour fan. They are established throughout Britain and now have hop-on-and-hop-off, 90-minute, fast-talking tours of Berlin (30 DM, buses every half-hour, in German and English). These do the basic predictable circle (east, west, and out to Charlottenburg) and, on a sunny day when the double-decker buses go topless, they are a photographer's delight. They're fairly competitive with several companies doing short and long tours, mostly departing from the Ku'damm (Severin & Kühn, Ku'damm 216, tel. 883 1015, BVB buses, doing quicker tours, from Ku'damm 225). The TI has all the brochures.

City Walking Tours—Walking tours give a more intimate glimpse of the city. Several companies do short, inexpensive, English-only walks: a general walk (2½ hrs, 10 DM, tel. 611-7425) and more specialized Third Reich and Wall Nostalgia walks (2 hrs, around 20 DM, tel. 211-6663). Both give student discounts. Since Nazi sights are so hard to find and really understand, the Third Reich walk is the best way to cover this slice of Berlin. Raymond Huygelen is a good freelance city guide (tel. 261-6625).

Late-Night Berlin

Zitty and *Tip* (sold at kiosks) are the top guides to youth and alternative culture. The TI's *Berlin Program* lists the nonstop parade of concerts, plays, exhibits, and cultural events. Berlin's top night spots are near Ku'damm. If you just wander around Savignyplatz, Olivaerplatz, Leninerplatz, and Ludwigskirchplatz, you'll find plenty of action. Contributing to Berlin's wild late-night scene is the fact that while the rest of Germany must close down at midnight or 1:00, Berlin night spots must close for only one hour a day.

Sleeping in Berlin
(1.6 DM = about $1, tel. code: 030)

Since reunification, costs in Berlin have skyrocketed: 32-DM hostel beds; 70-DM dumpy hotel doubles; 100-DM pleasant, small, pension doubles; 200-DM "normal" hotel doubles. Because of the cost of lodging and the distance necessary to travel to Berlin, I sleep on the train in and sleep on the train out.

Discount Business Hotels

For the most comforts at the least cost, arrive without a reservation (ideally in the morning) and let the TI book you a room in a fancy hotel on their push list. As in so many cities, business hotels over-built and when there are no conventions or fairs, rather than go empty, they rent rooms through the TI to lowly tourists for around half price. June, July, and August are dead for business travel. During these months hotels are empty and you can expect to land a modern, all-the-comforts, 200-DM business hotel double with a buffet breakfast within walking distance of the TI for around 100 DM. That's the price you'll pay for a tattered but comfortable room in the struggling little pensions recommended below. (They can't afford to play the discount game.)

My listings are a 5- to 15-minute walk from the Zoo Bahnhof, near the Ku'damm, in decent and comfortable neighborhoods. Most cluster conveniently around subway stops. Nearly all are a couple of flights up in big, run-down buildings. But inside they are clean, quiet, and big enough so that their well-worn character is actually charming. Most rooms are thoughtfully appointed, big with high ceilings, and on relatively quiet streets. Rooms in the back are on quiet courtyards. Unless otherwise noted, hallway showers are free, breakfast is included, they speak English, and take no credit cards.

Sleep code: **S**=Single, **D**=Double/Twin, **T**=Triple, **Q**=Quad, **B**=Bath/Shower, **WC**=Toilet, **CC**=Credit Card (Visa, Mastercard, Amex), **SE**=Speaks English (graded **A** through **F**).

Sleeping Between Zoo Station and Savingyplatz
Pension Heide am Zoo (S-85 DM, SB-110 DM, D-130 DM, DB-150 DM; Fasanenstr. 12, from Zoo Bahnhof walk

down Kant Strasse, left on Fasanenstrasse, 10623 Berlin, tel.
3130496, fax 3130497), run by friendly Frau Bäumer, is styl-
ish but homey on a quiet street a 5-minute walk from the
station. Call first; no rooms are given to drop-ins. Farther
down the same street, **Hotel-Pension Funk** (S-60 DM to 70
DM, SB-75, D-100, DB-120, DBWC-135 DM; Fasanenstrasse
69, tel. 8827193, fax 8833329) is the former home of a
1920s silent-movie star, offering 14 elegant, richly furnished
old rooms for a great price. **Alpenland Hotel** (D-110 DM,
DBWC-180 DM, CC:VM, their prices may be soft in summer, just off colorful Savignyplatz on a quiet street, Carmerstrasse 8, D-10623 Berlin, tel. 312-3970, fax 313-8444) is
a classy hotel with a fine restaurant which has a handful
of great value shower-less doubles. Many are on the fourth
floor and there's no elevator. But the rooms are big, bright
and clean and there are plenty of showers on the hall. Down
the same street, **Hotel-Pension Bialas** (S-70 DM, SB-100
DM, D-100 DM, DB-155 DM, T-140 DM, TB-210 DM,
Carmerstrasse 16, tel. 312 5025, fax 312 4396) feels a bit
like a hostel with 30 big, bright, airy rooms.

Sleeping at Augsburgerstrasse U-Bahn Stop
Hotel-Pension Nürnberger Eck (SB-75 DM, DB-120
DM, extra bed 45 DM, Nürnberger Strasse 24a, D-10789
Berlin, tel. 2185371, fax 2141540) has 8 big, plush rooms.
Just upstairs, **Pension Fischer** (S-50 DM, D-70 DM-80 DM,
DB-90 DM, 35 DM for third or fourth person, breakfast
7 DM, tel. 218 6808, fax 2134225) is run-down, simple,
and the best I found in its price range.

Sleeping at Güntzelstrasse U-Bahn Stop (three stops from Zoo on U9)
Hotel Pension München (S-56 DM-60 DM, D-75 DM-
95 DM, DBWC-115 DM-130 DM, 35 DM extra for third
or fourth person, breakfast 9 DM, elevator; Güntzelstrasse
62, 10717 Berlin, tel. 857-9120, fax 853 2744) is bright,
cheery, and filled with modern art. At the same address,
Pension Güntzel (SB-90 DM, DB-110 DM-130 DM,
DBWC-130 DM-150 DM, 35 DM for third person, tel. 857
9020, fax 853 1108) rents 8 fine rooms. **Pension Finck** (D-
100 DM, DB-110 DM, 50 DM for third person, elevator,

Guntzelstrasse 54, tel. 861-2940, fax 861-8158) has 12 big,
bright rooms in a more traditional building.

   Hotel Bogota (S-68 DM, SB-95 DM, D-110 DM,
DB-140 DM, DBWC-180 DM, 45 DM for third person,
CC:VMA, elevator, Schlüterstr. 45, 10707 Berlin, tel. 881
5001, fax 883 5887) has big, bright, modern rooms in a
spacious old building half a block off Ku'damm. The service
is brisk and hotelesque. This is the best no-nonsense hotel-
type listing.

   Youth hostels feature small rooms and are open to
all. While many are often packed with West German school
groups field-tripping to Berlin, the TI has a long list of
places renting dorm beds. **Jugendgastehaus Berlin** (35-
DM beds with sheets and breakfast in 4- to 6-bed rooms;
Kluckstrasse 3, take bus #129 from the Europa Center or the
Ku'damm U-Bahn stop, tel. 261 1097 or 261 1098; over 400
beds but often filled with groups, so call up to two weeks in
advance and leave your name; non-members pay 6 DM extra,
9 DM lunches and dinners) is most central. The **Studenten
Hotel Berlin** (35-39 DM per bed in doubles and quads with
sheets and breakfast; Meiningerstrasse 10, tel. 784 6720,
near the City Hall on JFK Platz or U-Bahn to Rathaus
Schoneberg) is also decent.

Eating in Berlin

Berlin has plenty of fun food places, both German and
imported. If the *kraut* is getting *wurst*, try one of the many
Turkish, Italian, or Balkan restaurants. **Wertheim** department store (at Ku'damm U-Bahn) has cheap basement food
counters and a fine self-service cafeteria up six banks of escalators with a view. **KaDeWe's** sixth-floor deli food department is a picnicker's nirvana. Drool your way through more
than 1,000 kinds of sausage and 1,500 types of cheese. You
can even get peanut-butter here! Put together a picnic and
grab a sunny bench. For cheap and substantial *kebabs*, eat
Turkish in Kreuzberg.

   The local pubs, called *Kneipe*, are colorful places to get
a light meal and to try out the local beer, Berliner Weiss.
Ask for it *mit Schuss* and you'll get a shot of syrup in your
suds.

Train Connections

Berlin to: Amsterdam (8/day, 9 hrs), **Budapest** (5/day, 13 hrs), **Frankfurt** (8/day, 5 hrs), **Copenhagen** (4/day, 8 hrs), **Köln** (hrly, 6½ hrs), **London** (4/day, 15 hrs), **Munich** (8/day, 8½ hrs), **Paris** (6/day, 13 hrs), **Prague** (10/day, 4½ hrs), **Warsaw** (4/day, 8 hrs), **Vienna** (5/day, 12 hrs), **Zurich** (12/day, 10 hrs). Berlin is connected by easy overnight trains from **Bonn, Köln, Frankfurt, Munich, Vienna,** and **Copenhagen.** A *Liege-platz*, or bunk bed, on the train is money well spent (26 DM for a place in a six-bed cabin, 40 DM in the same cabin with two beds left empty). The beds are the same for first- and second-class tickets. Trains are rarely full, but get your bed reserved a few days in advance from any travel agency or train station.

Germany

THE RHINE AND MOSEL VALLEYS

These valleys are storybook Germany, a fairy-tale world of Rhine legends and robber-baron castles. Cruise the most castle-studded stretch of the romantic Rhine as you listen for the song of the treacherous Loreley. For hands-on castle thrills, climb through the Rhineland's greatest castle, Rheinfels, above the town of St. Goar. Then for a sleepy and laid-back alternative, mosey through the neighboring Mosel Valley.

In the north, you'll find powerhouse cities of Köln and Bonn on an industrial stretch of the unromantic Rhine. Bonn is Germany's easy-going capital (until Berlin takes over) and Köln has Germany's greatest Gothic cathedral, best collection of Roman artifacts, a world-class art museum, and a good dose of German urban playfulness. These bustling cities merit a visit, but spend your nights in a castle-crowned village. On the Rhine, stay in St. Goar or Bacharach. On the Mosel, choose Zell.

Planning Your Time

The Rhineland does not take much time. The blitziest tour is 1 hour on the train. For a better look, cruise in, tour a castle, sleep in a medieval town, and train out. With limited time, cruise less and be sure to get into a castle. Ideally, spend two nights here, sleep in Bacharach, cruise the best hour of the river (from Bacharach to St Goar) and tour the Rhinefels castle. Those with more time could bike the riverside bike path. With two days, split your time between the Rhine and Mosel, seeing Berg Eltz and Cochem. With three days, add Bonn and/or Koln. Four days: add Trier and a sleepy night on the Mosel river valley.

The Rhine

Ever since Roman times, when this was the Empire's northern boundary, the Rhine has been one of the world's busiest shipping rivers. You'll see a steady flow of barges with 1,000- to 2,000-ton loads. Buses packed with tourists, hot train tracks, and highways line both banks.

Best of the Rhine

Many of the castles were "robber-baron" castles, put there by petty rulers (there were 300 independent little countries in medieval Germany) to levy tolls on all the passing river traffic. A robber baron would put his castle on, or even in, the river. Then, often with the help of chains and a tower on the opposite side of the river, he'd stop each ship and get his toll. There were ten customs stops between Mainz and Koblenz alone (no wonder merchants were early proponents of the creation of larger nation-states).

Some castles were built to control and protect settlements, and others were the residences of kings. As times changed, so did the lifestyles of the rich and feudal. Many castles were abandoned for more comfortable mansions in the towns.

Most of the Rhine castles were originally built in the 11th, 12th, and 13th centuries. When the pope successfully asserted his power over the German emperor in 1076, local princes ran wild over the rule of their emperor. The castles saw military action in the 1300s and 1400s as emperors began reasserting their control over Germany's many silly kingdoms.

The castles were also involved in the Reformation wars that saw Europe's Catholic and "protesting" dynasties fight it out using a fragmented Germany as their battleground. The Thirty Years War (1618–1648) devastated Germany. The outcome: each ruler got the freedom to decide if his people would be Catholic or Protestant, and one-third of Germany was dead.

The French destroyed most of the castles prophylacti-cally (Louis XIV in the 1680s, the Revolutionary army in the 1790s, and Napoleon in 1806). They were often rebuilt in neo-Gothic style in the Romantic Age—the late 1800s—and today are enjoyed as restaurants, hotels, youth hostels, and museums.

Getting Around the Rhine

While the Rhine flows from Switzerland to Holland, the stretch from Mainz to Koblenz is by far the most interesting. Studded with the crenelated cream of Germany's castles, it bustles with boats, trains, and highway traffic. Have fun exploring with a mix of big steamers, tiny ferries, bikes, and trains.

While many travelers do the whole trip by boat, the most scenic hour is from St. Goar to Bacharach. Sit on the top deck with your handy Rhine map-guide and enjoy the parade of castles, towns, boats, and vineyards. Rhine boats cruise only from Easter through October. Off-season is so quiet that many hotels close down.

There are several boat companies, but most travelers sail on the bigger, more expensive and romantic Köln—Düsseldorf line (free with Eurail, otherwise about 15 DM per hour, tel. 0221/2088). Boats run daily in both direc-tions (no express boat on Monday) from May through September with fewer boats off-season. Complete, up-to-date, and more complicated schedules are posted in any station, Rhineland hotel, TI, or current Thomas Cook Timetable. Purchase tickets at the dock 5 minutes before departure.

The boat is never full. (Confirm times at your hotel the night before.)

The smaller Bingen–Rüdesheimer line (tel. 06721/ 14140, Eurail not valid, buy tickets on the boat) is 25 percent cheaper than K-D with three 2-hour St. Goar–Bacharach trips daily in summer (departing St. Goar at 11:00, 14:10, and 16:10; departing Bacharach at 10:10, 12:30, 15:00; 11 DM one way, 14 DM round-trip).

Drivers have these options: (1) skip the boat; (2) take a round-trip cruise from St. Goar or Bacharach on the Bingen–Rüdesheimer line; (3) draw pretzels and let the loser drive, prepare the picnic, and meet the boat; (4) rent a bike, bring it on the boat (free), and bike back; or (5) take the boat one way and return by train (hourly milk-run trains down the Rhine hit every town: St. Goar–Bacharach, 12 min; Bacharach–Mainz, 30 min; Mainz–Frankfurt, 30 min).

You can rent bikes at the St. Goar TI or at Bacharach's Hotel Gelber Hof (10-speeds, 15 DM per day, 5 DM for child's seat). The best riverside bike path is from Bacharach to Bingen. The path is also good but closer to the highway

Lower Rhine

from St. Goar to Bacharach. Consider sailing to Bingen and biking back, visiting Rheinstein Castle (you're on your own to wander the well-furnished castle) and Reichenstein Castle (admittance with groups) and maybe even taking a ferry across the river to Kaub (where a tiny boat shuttles sightseers to the better-from-a-distance castle on the island). While there are no bridges between Koblenz and Mainz, several small ferries do their job constantly and cheaply.

Sights—The Romantic Rhine

(These sights are south to north, from Bingen to Koblenz.)
▲▲▲**Der Romantische Rhine Blitz Zug Fahrt**—One of Europe's great train thrills is zipping along the Rhine in this fast train tour. Here's a quick and easy, from-the-train-window tour (also works for car, boat, or bike) that skips the syrupy myths and the life story of Dieter von Katzeneln-bogen that fill normal Rhine guides.

For more information than necessary, buy the handy *Rhine Guide from Mainz to Cologne* (6-DM book with foldout map, at most shops). Sit on the right (river) side of the train going north from Bingen. While nearly all the castles listed are viewed from this side, clear a path to the left window for the times I yell, "Crossover."

You'll notice large black-and-white kilometer markers along the riverbank. I put those up years ago to make this tour easier to follow. They tell the distance from the Rhinefalls where the Rhine leaves Switzerland and becomes navigable. Now the river-barge pilots have accepted these as navigational aids as well. We're tackling just 36 miles of the 820-mile-long Rhine. Your Blitz Rhine tour starts near Mainz, Rüdesheim, and Bingen. If you're going the other direction, it still works. Just follow the kilometer markings.

Km 528: Niederwald monument—Across from the Bingen station on a hilltop is the 120-foot-high Niederwald monument, a memorial built with 32 tons of bronze in 1877 to commemorate "the reestablishment of the German Empire." A lift takes tourists to this statue from the famous and extremely touristic wine town of Rüdesheim.

Km 530: Ehrenfels Castle—Opposite the Bingerbrück station, you'll see the ghostly Ehrenfels Castle (clobbered by the Swedes in 1636 and by the French in 1689). Since it had no view of the river traffic to the north, it built the cute little *Mäuseturm* (Mouse Tower) on an island (the yellow tower you'll see near the train station today). Rebuilt in the 1800s in neo-Gothic style, today it's used as a Rhine navigation signal station.

Km 533: (cross to the other side of train)—**Burg Rheinstein** and (at km 534) **Burg Reichenstein** are some of the first to be rebuilt in the Romantic era (both are privately owned, tourable and connected by a pleasant trail, info at TI).

Km 538: (cross to other side of train)—**Castle Sooneck**, built in the 11th century, was twice destroyed by people sick and tired of robber barons.

Km 540: Lorch—This pathetic stub of a castle is barely visible from the road. Notice the small car ferry, one of several between Mainz and Koblenz, where there are no bridges.

Km 543: (cross to other side of train)—**Bacharach** is a great stop (see Sleeping, below) with 14th-century fortifications preserved throughout the town. One of the old towers is my favorite Rhine hotel. The train screams within 5 yards of Hotel Kranenturm. Perched above the town, the 13th-century Berg Stahleck is now a youth hostel. Bacharach, which once prospered from its wood and wine trade, is just a pleasant medieval town that misses most of the tourist glitz. Next to the K-D dock is a great park for a picnic (TI, Monday-Friday 9:00-12:00 and 14:00-17:00, tel. 06743/1297; look for "i" on the main street, then go through nearby door and follow signs to "Verkehrsamt" up the stairs, and down the squeaky hall). Some of the Rhine's best wine is from this town, whose name means "altar to Bacchus." The huge Jost beer stein "factory outlet," a block north of the church, carries everything a shopper could want (8:30-18:00, till 16:00 on Saturday, 11:00-15:00 on Sunday, 10% discount with this book).

Km 546: Burg Gutenfels (white painted "Hotel" sign) and the ship-shape **Pfalz Castle** (built in the river in the 1300s, notice the overhanging his-and-hers "outhouses") worked very effectively to tax medieval river traffic. The town of Kaub grew rich as Pfalz raised its chains when boats came and lowered them only when the merchants had paid their duty. Those who didn't pay spent time touring its

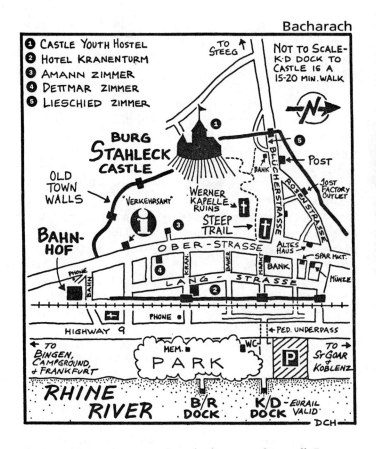

Bacharach

❶ CASTLE YOUTH HOSTEL
❷ HOTEL KRANENTURM
❸ AMANN ZIMMER
❹ DETTMAR ZIMMER
❺ LIESCHIED ZIMMER

TO STEEG

NOT TO SCALE-
K·D DOCK TO
CASTLE IS A
15-20 MIN. WALK

N

BURG STAHLECK CASTLE

OLD TOWN WALLS

VERKEHRSAMT

BANK

POST

BLÜCHERSTRASSE

ROSENSTRASSE

JOST FACTORY OUTLET

WERNER KAPELLE RUINS

STEEP TRAIL

BAHN-HOF

OBER - STRASSE

ALTES HAUS

SPAR MKT.

PHONE

BAHN

KRAN

BAUER

LANG - STRASSE

MARKT

BANK

MÜNZE

PHONE

HIGHWAY 9

← PED. UNDERPASS

← TO BINGEN, CAMPGROUND, & FRANKFURT

MEM.

PARK

WC

P

TO ST GOAR & KOBLENZ

RHINE RIVER

B/R DOCK

K/D DOCK

EURAIL VALID

DCH

fascinating prison, on a raft at the bottom of its well. In 1504, a pope called for the destruction of Pfalz, but a six-week siege failed. Pfalz is tourable but pretty empty, accessible by 3-DM ferry from Kaub on the other side (4 DM, 9:00-13:00, 14:00-18:00, tel. 06774/570).

Km 550: (cross to other side of train)—**Oberwesel** was Celtic town in 400 B.C., then a Roman military station, and has some of the best Roman wall-and-tower remains on the Rhine. Notice how many of the train tunnels have entrances designed like medieval turrets, built in the Romantic 19th century. Okay, back to the riverside.

Km 554: The Loreley—Steep a big slate rock in centuries of legend and it becomes a tourist attraction, the ultimate Rhinestone. The Loreley (two flags on top, name painted near shoreline) rises 450 feet over the narrowest and deepest point of the Rhine. (The fine echoes here were thought to be ghostly voices in the old days, fertilizing the legendary soil.)

Because of the killer reefs just upstream (at km 552, called the "Seven Maidens"), many ships never made it to St. Goar. Sailors (after days on the river) blamed their misfortune on a wunderbar Fräulein whose long blond hair almost covered her body. (You can see her statue at about km 555.) Heinrich Heine's *Song of Loreley* (the *Cliff Notes* version is on local postcards) tells the story of a count who sent his men to kill or capture this siren after his son was killed because of her. When the soldiers cornered the nymph in her cave, she called her father (Father Rhine) for help. Huge waves, the likes of which you'll never see today, rose out of the river and carried her to safety. And she has never been seen since.

But alas, when the moon shines brightly and the tour buses are parked, a soft, playful Rhine whine can still be heard from the Loreley. As you pass, listen carefully ("Sailors . . . sailors . . . over my bounding mane").

Km 556: Burg Katz—From the town of St. Goar, you'll see Burg Katz (Katzenelnbogen) across the river. Look back on your side of the river to see the mighty Rheinfels castle over St. Goar.

Together, Burg Katz (b. 1371) and Rheinfels had a clear view up and down the river and effectively controlled traffic. There was absolutely no duty-free shopping on the medieval Rhine. Katz got Napoleoned in 1806 and rebuilt around 1900; today it's a convalescent home.

Km 557: St. Goar and Rheinfels Castle—The pleasant town of St. Goar was named for a sixth-century hometown monk. It originated in Celtic times (really old) as a place where sailors would stop, catch their breath, send home a postcard, and give thanks after surviving the seductive and treacherous Loreley crossing.

St. Goar is worth a stop (see Sleeping, below) to explore its **Rheinfels Castle**. Sitting like a dead pit-bull above St. Goar, this mightiest of Rhine castles rumbles with ghosts from its hard-fought past. Burg Rheinfels (b. 1245) withstood a siege of 28,000 French troops in 1692, but was creamed by the same team in 1797. It was huge, the biggest

St. Goar

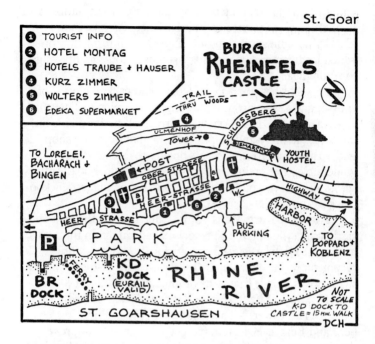

1 TOURIST INFO
2 HOTEL MONTAG
3 HOTELS TRAUBE + HAUSER
4 KURZ ZIMMER
5 WOLTERS ZIMMER
6 EDEKA SUPERMARKET

BURG RHEINFELS CASTLE

TRAIL THRU WOODS

ULMENHOF TOWER

SCHLOSSBERG

BISMARCKWEG

YOUTH HOSTEL

TO LORELEI, BACHARACH + BINGEN

POST

OBER STRASSE

HEER-STRASSE

HIGHWAY 9

WC

HARBOR

HEER-STRASSE

P PARK

BUS PARKING

TO BOPPARD + KOBLENZ

BR DOCK

FERRY

KD DOCK (EURAIL VALID)

RHINE RIVER

ST. GOARSHAUSEN

NOT TO SCALE
K·D DOCK TO CASTLE ≈ 15 MIN. WALK

DCH

on the Rhine, then used as a quarry. Today it's a hollow but interesting shell and offers your best single hands-on castle experience on the river. Follow the castle map with English instructions (.50 DM from the ticket window). If you follow the castle's perimeter, circling counterclockwise and downward, you'll find an easy-to-explore chunk of the several miles of spooky tunnels. Bring your flashlight (and bayonet). These tunnels were used to lure in and entomb enemy troops. You'll be walking over the remains (from 1626) of 300 unfortunate Spanish soldiers. The reconstruction of the castle in the museum shows how much bigger it was before Louis XIV destroyed it. Climb to the top for the Rhine view (5 DM, daily 9:00-18:00, in October until 17:00; winter, Saturday and Sunday only; form a group of ten English-speaking tourists to get a cheaper ticket and a free English tour; tel. 383; a 15-minute steep hike up from St. Goar, you can call a taxi at tel. 430 for a 7-DM lift from the boat dock to the castle, 10 DM for a mini-bus).

The St. Goar TI (daily 8:00-12:30, 14:00-17:00; Saturday 9:30-12:00; closed Sunday and earlier in winter, tel. 06741/383) now functions as the town's train station with free left-luggage service and 10-DM-per-day bike rentals (50 DM or a passport deposit). They have information on which local wineries do English-language tours and tastings for individuals.

St. Goar has good shops (steins and cuckoo clocks, of course) and a waterfront park hungry for a picnic. The small supermarket (EDEKA) on Main Street is fine for picnic fixings. The friendly and helpful Montag family in the shop under the Hotel Montag has Koblenz-to-Mainz Rhine guidebooks, fine steins, and copies of this guidebook. And across the street, you'll see what must be the biggest cuckoo clock in the world.

Km 559: Burg Maus got its name because the next castle was owned by the Katzenelnbogen family. In the 1300s, it was considered a state-of-the-art fortification . . . until Napoleon had it blown up in 1806 with state-of-the-art explosives. It was rebuilt true to its original plans around 1900.

Km 567: The "Hostile Brothers" castles (with the white square tower)—Take the wall between Burg Sterrenberg and Burg Liebenstein (actually designed to improve the defenses of both castles), add two greedy and jealous brothers and a fair maiden, and create your own legend. They are restaurants today.

Km 570: Boppard—Once a Roman town, Boppard has some impressive remains of fourth-century walls. Notice the Roman tower just after the Boppard's train station and the substantial chunk of Roman wall just before.

Boppard is worth a stop. Just above the market square are the remains of the Roman wall. Below the square is a fascinating church. Notice the carved Romanesque crazies at the doorway. Inside, to the right of the entrance, you'll see Christian symbols from Roman times. Also notice the painted arches and vaults. Originally, most Romanesque churches were painted this way. Down by the river, notice the high water (*Hochwasser*) marks on the arches from various flood years. (Throughout the Rhine and Mosel valleys you'll see these flood marks.)

Km 580: Marksburg (with the three modern chimneys behind it) is the best-looking of all the Rhine castles and the only surviving medieval castle on the Rhine. Because of its commanding position, it was never attacked. It's now open as a museum with a medieval interior second only to the Mosel's Burg Eltz (10:00-17:00, by 7-DM tour only, tours generally in German, worth a visit only if you can tag along with a rare English tour, call ahead, tel. 02627/206).

Km 585: Burg Lahneck—This castle (above the modern autobahn bridge over the Lahn river) was built in 1240 to defend local silver mines, ruined by the French in 1688, and rebuilt in the 1850s in neo-Gothic style. Burg Lahneck faces the yellow Schloss Stolzenfels (out of view above the train, open for touring, a 10-minute climb from the tiny car park, closed Monday).

Km 590: Koblenz—The Romantic Rhine thrills and the Blitz Rhine tour ends at Koblenz. Not a nice city, it was really hit hard in World War II, but its place as the historic *Deutsches-Eck* (German corner)—the tip of land where the Mosel joins the Rhine—gives it a certain magnetism. "*Koblenz*," Latin for "confluence," has Roman origins. Walk through the park, noticing the blackened base of what was once a huge memorial to the Kaiser. Across the river, the yellow Ehrenbreitstein Castle is now a youth hostel. It's a 30-minute hike from the station to the Koblenz boat dock.

Sleeping on the Rhine in Bacharach and St. Goar (1.6 DM = about $1)

The Rhine is an easy place for cheap sleeps. *Zimmer* and *Gasthäuser* abound, offering beds for 25 DM-30 DM per person (and *Zimmer* normally discount their prices for longer stays). Several exceptional Rhine-area youth hostels offer even cheaper beds. Each town's helpful TI is eager to set you up, and finding a room should be easy any time of year (except for wine-festy weekends in September and October). St. Goar and Bacharach, the best towns for an overnight stop, are about 10 miles apart, connected by milk-run trains, river boats, and a riverside bike path. Bacharach is less touristic; St. Goar has the famous castle.

Sleep Code: **S**=Single, **D**=Double/Twin, **T**=Triple, **Q**=Quad, **B**=Bath/Shower normally with a WC, **CC**=Credit Card (**V**isa, **M**astercard, **A**mex). Breakfast included unless otherwise noted. All hotels speak some English. Most *Zimmer* do not.

Sleeping in Bacharach (zip code: 55422, tel. code: 06743)

Bacharach's **youth hostel, Jugendherberge Stahleck**, is a 12th-century castle on the hilltop high above Bacharach with a royal Rhine view (IYHF members of all ages welcome, 20 DM dorm beds with breakfast, 5 DM for sheets, normally places available but call and leave your name, they'll hold a bed until 18:00, tel. 1266, English spoken, easy parking). This is a gem but very much a youth hostel—with six to eight beds per room. A 15-minute climb on the trail from the town church, it's warmly and energetically run by Evelyn and Bernhard Falke (FALL-kay), who serve hearty, cheap meals.

Hotel Kranenturm gives you the feeling of a castle without the hostel-ity or the climb. This is my choice for the best combination of comfort and hotel privacy with *Zimmer* warmth, central location, and medieval atmosphere (DB-80 DM with this book, discounts for staying several nights, kid-friendly, family rooms available, Rhine views come with train noise, the back side is quieter, CC:VMA, easy reservations by phone, SE-A; Langstrasse 30, tel. 1308, fax 1021, closed January and February). Run by hardworking Kurt Engel and his intense but friendly wife Fatima, this hotel is actually part of the medieval fortification. Its former *Kranen* (crane) towers are now round rooms. When the riverbank was higher, cranes on this tower loaded barrels of wine onto Rhine boats. Hotel Kranenturm is 5 yards from the train tracks (just under the medieval gate at the Frankfurt end of town), but a combination of medieval sturdiness, triple-pane windows, and included ear plugs make the riverside rooms sleepable. The Kranenturm really stretches it to get toilets and showers in each room. Kurt, a great cook, serves fine inexpensive dinners. His big-enough-for-three Kranenturm ice-cream special may ruin you (9 DM). For a quick trip to Fiji in a medieval German cellar, check out his tropical bar.

Frau Amann (D-50 DM; Oberstrasse 13, in the old center on a side lane a few yards off the main street, tel. 1271) rents two rooms in her quiet, homey, traditional place. Guests get a cushy living room, a self-serve kitchen, and the free use of bikes. You'll laugh right through the language barrier with this lovely woman.

Annelie and Hans Dettmar (DB-50 DM, TB-70 DM, QB-100 DM; Oberstrasse 8, on the main drag in the center, tel. 2661 or 2979, SE-A, kid-friendly) are a young entrepreneurial couple who rent four smoke-free rooms (one is a huge family-of-four room, several have kitchenettes) in a modern house above their craft shop. Breakfast is served in their shop with knickknacks dangling everywhere.

Frau Erna Lieschied (D-60 DM, Blucherstrasse 39, tel. 1510, speaks German fluently) shares her ancient, higgledy-piggledy, half-timbered house, 3 blocks uphill from the church, next to the medieval town gate. The rooms are very comfortable.

Ursula Orth rents out two rooms in her home next to the Dettmars' in the town center (a bit musty, DB-50 DM, Spurgasse 3, tel. 1557).

For inexpensive and atmospheric dining in Bacharach, try the **Hotel Kranenturm** or **Altes Haus** (the oldest building in town). For a little wine tasting, drop in on entertaining Fritz Bastian's **Weingut zum Brunen Baum** winestube (just past the Altes Haus, tel. 1208). He's the president of the local vintners club.

Sleeping in St. Goar (zip code: 56329, tel. code 06741)

Hotel Montag (SB-70 DM, DB-130 DM, price can drop if you arrive late or it's a slow time, CC:VMA; Heerstrasse 128, tel. 1629, fax 2086) is just across the street from the world's largest free-hanging cuckoo clock. Mannfred Montag, his wife Maria, and son Misha speak New Yorkish. Even though Montag gets a lot of bus tours, it's friendly, laid back, and comfortable. Check out their adjacent crafts shop (heavy on beer steins).

Hotel Hauser (S-42 DM, D-84 DM, DB-98 DM, DB with Rhine view balconies-110 DM to 130 DM, show this book and plead poverty and you'll get a view room for the low price if available, cheaper in off-season, CC:VMA, Heerstrasse 77, tel. 333, fax 1464, telephone reservations easy), very central and newly redone with solid beds, is warmly run by Frau Velich.

Hotel am Markt, big, well-run by another Frau Velich, and rustic with all the modern comforts, features a hint of

antler with a pastel flair and bright rooms in the center of
town (DB-100 DM, QB-140 DM, CC:VMA, Am Markt 1,
tel. 1689, fax 1721).

St. Goar's best *Zimmer* deal is the home of **Frau Kurz**,
with a breakfast terrace, fine view, easy parking, and all the
comforts of a hotel (S-34 DM, D-60 DM, DB-70 DM,
showers-5 DM, minimum two nights; Ulmenhof 11, 5401
St. Goar/Rhein, tel. 459, 2-minute walk above the station).

The Germanly run **St. Goar hostel** (18 DM beds with
breakfast, 28 DM if you're over 28, Bismarckweg 17, tel. 388
morning and after 17:00), the big beige building under the
castle, is a good value with cheap dorm beds, a few smaller
rooms, a 22:00 curfew, and hearty 8-DM dinners.

Transportation Connections
Milk-run trains stop at all Rhine towns each hour. **Koblenz,
Boppard, St. Goar, Bacharach, Bingen,** and **Mainz** are
each about 15 minutes apart. From Koblenz to Mainz takes
75 minutes. To get a big train go to Mainz or Koblenz.
From Mainz regular trains go to **Frankfurt** (40 min),
Frankfurt airport (20 min), **Köln** (1½ hrs), **Munich** (4 hrs),
Baden-Baden (2½ hrs, changing in Mannheim), **Cochem**
(1½ hrs, changing in Koblenz).

Mosel Valley
The misty Mosel is what many visitors hoped the Rhine
would be—peaceful, sleepy, romantic villages slipped
between the steep vineyards and the river, fine wine, a sprin-
kling of castles, and lots of friendly *Zimmer*. Boat, train, and
car traffic here is a trickle compared to the roaring Rhine.
While the swan-speckled Mosel moseys from France to
Koblenz, where it dumps into the Rhine, the most scenic
piece of the valley lies between the towns of Bernkastel-Kues
and Cochem. I'd savor only this section.

Getting Around the Mosel
For sightseeing along the Mosel, Eurailers have some interesting transportation options. While the train can take you
along much of the river, the K-D (Köln–Düsseldorf) line
sails once a day in each direction (May through mid-
October, Koblenz to Cochem 10:00-14:30, or Cochem

to Koblenz 15:50-20:10, free with Eurail). You can also rent
bikes at some stations and leave them at others, or rent a
bike in Cochem from the K-D line kiosk at the dock or from
Kreutz at Ravenestrasse 7. If you find yourself stranded,
hitching isn't bad.

Sights—Mosel Valley

Cochem—With a majestic castle and picturesque medieval
streets, Cochem is the touristic hub of this part of the river.
The Cochem TI has a free town history and a walking tour
brochure. The pointy Cochem castle is the work of over-
imaginative 19th-century restorers (March-October, 9:00-
17:00, German language—with written English explanation—tours on the hour, 5 DM). Consider a boat ride from
Cochem to Zell (3 hours, 2 per day) or Beilstein (1 hour,
4 per day, 17 DM round-trip). The Beilstein-Cochem bus
takes 15 minutes (4 DM). The Cochem TI (Monday-Friday
10:00-13:00, 14:00-17:00; summer Saturdays 10:00-15:00;
Sundays 10:00-12:00, tel. 02671/3971) books rooms and
keeps a thorough 24-hour listing in its window. Many train
travelers end up sleeping in Cochem. **Gästezimmer Götz**
(7 big 60-DM doubles, 1 family apartment, CC:MA,
Ravenestrasse 34, next to the station, tel. 02671/8438,
ground floor rooms, speaks some English) is a good and
handy value that welcomes one-night stays.

   Throughout the region on summer weekends and during
the fall harvest time, wine festivals with oompah bands, dancing, and colorful costumes are powered by good food and wine.
▲▲▲**Burg Eltz**—My favorite castle in all of Europe lurks
in a mysterious forest, left intact for 700 years, and furnished

Mosel River Valley

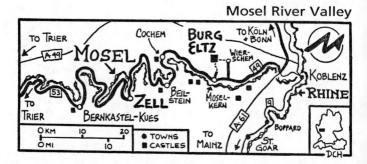

throughout as it was 500 years ago. Burg Eltz is still owned by the aristocratic family Eltz. The countess arranges for new flowers in each room weekly. Unless you happen to visit when an English-speaking group is scheduled, the only way to tour the castle is by hour-long German-only tours (depart every 15 minutes, English fact sheets provided). It's worth a phone call to see if there's an English-language group scheduled that you could tag along with (8 DM, daily April-October 9:30-17:30, tel. 02672/1300, constant 1.50-DM shuttle bus service from car park).

Reaching Burg Eltz by train, walk 1 (steep) hour from Moselkern station (midway between Cochem and Koblenz) through a pine forest where sparrows carry crossbows, and maidens, disguised as falling leaves, whisper "watch out." Driving to Burg Eltz, leave the river at Hatzenport following the white "Burg Eltz P&R" sign. More signs will direct you past Wiersheim to the castle car park, a 10-minute walk from the castle. (It seems like a long way, but I promise it's worth it.) There are three "Burg Eltz" parking lots. Only this one is close enough for an easy walk.

▲**Beilstein**—Farther downstream is the quaintest of all Mosel towns. (For accommodations, see Sleeping, below.) Beilstein is Cinderella land. Check out the narrow lanes, ancient wine cellar, resident (and very territorial) swans, and ruined castle. (TI open daily in summer 7:00-19:00, tel. 02673/1417.)

▲**Zell**—This is the best Mosel town for an overnight stop (see Sleeping, below). It's peaceful, with a fine riverside promenade, a pedestrian bridge over the river, plenty of *Zimmer*, and a long pedestrian zone filled with colorful shops, restaurants, and winestubes. (TI open 8:00-12:30, 13:30-17:00, tel. 06542/4031 or 70122).

▲▲**Trier**—Germany's oldest city lies at the head of the scenic Mosel Valley, near the Luxembourg border. Founded by Augustus in 15 B.C., it was 80,000 strong when Emperor Constantine used the town as the capital of his fading western Roman Empire. A short stop here offers you a look at Germany's oldest Christian church, the *Dom*, or cathedral, which houses the "Holy Robe" of Christ (found by Constantine's mother, St. Helena, and only very rarely on display, next showing in 1996). Connected to the Dom is the

Liebfrau church from 1235, which claims to be the oldest
Gothic church in Germany (7:00-18:00). Communists can
lick their wounds at Karl Marx's house (15-minute film at 20
past each hour, 10:00-18:00, Monday 13:00-18:00).

Trier has some epic Roman ruins. The basilica is the
largest intact Roman building outside of Rome. It's now a
church, but you can still imagine Constantine giving audi-
ences from his altar-like throne. From the basilica a fragrant
garden leads to the remains of a Roman bath and a 25,000-
seat amphitheater. On the other side of town, next to the TI,
is the famous and huge Porta Nigra (best Roman fortifications in Germany, climb-able). Skip the city museum in the
adjacent courtyard.

The Hauptmarkt square is a people-filled swirl of fruit
stands, flowers, painted facades, and fountains—with a handy
public WC. Trier's tourist office, next to the Porta Nigra
(9:00-18:30, Sunday 9:00-15:30, less off-season, tel. 0651/
978080) organizes 2-hour, 9-DM town walks in English
daily at 14:00.

Sleeping on the Mosel
(1.6 DM = about $1)

Sleeping in Zell (zip code: 56856, tel. code: 06542)
If the Mosel charms you into spending the night, do it in
Zell. By car, this is a natural. By train, you'll need to go to
Bullay (from Cochem or Trier) where the hourly 10-minute
bus ride takes you to little Zell. Its hotels are a disappointment, but its private homes are great. The owners speak
almost no English and discount their rates if you stay more
than one night. My favorites are on the south end of town,
a 2-minute walk from the town hall square and the bus
stop.

The comfortable and modern home of **Fritz and
Susanne Mesenich** is quiet, friendly, clean, central, and
across from a good winestube (D-60 DM, 50 DM if you stay
two nights, Oberstrasse 3, tel. 4753). Frau Mesenich can find
you a room if her place is full. Herr Mesenich can take you
into his cellar for a look at the *haus* wine. Notice the flood
marks on the wall across the street and flood photos in her
breakfast room and hope it doesn't rain.

Gästhaus Gertrud Thiesen (S-35 DM, D-60 DM for 1 night, 50 DM for 2 nights; Balduinstrasse 1, tel. 4453) is across the street, just as much fun but classier, with a TV-living-breakfast room and a river view. The Thiesen house has big, bright rooms and is on the town's first corner overlooking the Mosel from a great terrace.

The cheapest beds in town are in the simple but comfortable home of **Natalie Huhn** (D-40 DM for 1 night, 35 DM for 2; near the pedestrian bridge behind the church at Jakobstrasse 32, tel. 41048).

If you're looking for room service, a sauna, pool, and elevator, sleep at **Hotel Grüner Kranz** (DB-140 DM with Mosel views, CC:VMA, elevator, tel. 4549 or 4276, fax 4311).

Weinhaus Mayer, a classy old pension next door, is perfectly central with Mosel-view rooms (13 rooms, DB-120 DM, CC:V, Balduinstrasse 15, tel. and fax 4530).

Sleeping in Beilstein (zip code: 56814, tel. code: 02673)

Cozier and farther north, Beilstein is very small and quiet, with no train nearby but plenty of Cochem bus connections.

Hotel Haus Lipmann (5 rooms, DB-120 DM-150 DM, tel. 1573) is your chance to live in a medieval mansion with hot showers and TVs. A prize-winner for atmosphere, it's been in the Lipmann family for 200 years. The creaky wooden staircase and the elegant dining hall with long wooden tables surrounded by antlers, chandeliers, and feudal weapons will get you in the mood for your castle sightseeing but the riverside terrace may mace your momentum.

The half-timbered, river-front **Altes Zollhaus Gästzimmer** (DB-95 DM, 15 DM more on Friday and Saturday, tel. 1574 or 1850, open March-October) has crammed all the comforts into tight, bright and modern rooms.

Gasthaus Winzerschenke an der Klostertreppe (DB-60 DM, tel. 1354) is comfortable and a great value, right in the tiny heart of town. There are cheaper rooms in Beilstein's gaggle of private homes.

ROTHENBURG AND THE ROMANTIC ROAD

From Munich or Füssen to Frankfurt, the Romantic Road takes you through Bavaria's medieval heartland, a route strewn with picturesque villages, farmhouses, onion-domed churches, Baroque palaces, and walled cities.

Dive into the Middle Ages via Rothenburg, Germany's best-preserved walled town. Countless renowned travelers have searched for the elusive "untouristy Rothenburg." There are many contenders (such as Michelstadt, Miltenberg, Bamberg, Bad Windsheim, and Dinkelsbühl), but none holds a candle to the king of medieval German cuteness. Even with crowds, over-priced souvenirs, Japanese-speaking night watchmen, and yes, even with schneeballs, Rothenburg is best. Save time and mileage, and be satisfied with the winner.

Planning Your Time

The best one-day look at the medieval heartland of Germany is the Romantic Road bus tour. Train travelers go free on the daily bus (Frankfurt to Munich or Füssen, or vice versa). Drivers can follow the route laid out in the tourist brochures. The only stop worth more than a few minutes is Rothenburg. Twenty-four hours is ideal for this town. Two nights and a day is a bit much unless you're actually relaxing on this trip.

Rothenburg in a day is easy. Four essential experiences: the Criminal museum, the wood carving in the church, the city walking tour, and a walk along the wall. With more time there are several mediocre but entertaining museums, walking and biking in the nearby countryside, and lots of cafés and shops. Make a point to spend at least one night. The town is yours after dark when the groups vacate and the town's floodlit cobbles wring some romance out of any travel partner.

Rothenburg

In the Middle Ages, when Frankfurt and Munich were just wide spots on the road, Rothenburg was Germany's second-largest free imperial city with a whopping population of 6,000. Today it's her best-preserved medieval walled town, enjoying tremendous tourist popularity without losing its

Rothenburg

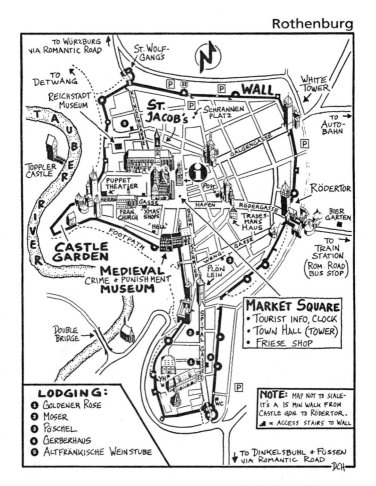

TO WÜRZBURG VIA ROMANTIC ROAD

ST. WOLF-GANGS

N

WHITE TOWER

TO DETWANG

REICHSTADT MUSEUM

WALL

P

P

P

TO AUTO-BAHN

ST. JACOB'S

SCHRANNEN PLATZ

GALGENGASSE

P

TAUBER RIVER

TOPPLER CASTLE

PUPPET THEATER

HERRN GASSE

FRAN. CHURCH

XMAS SHOPS

HELL

POST

HAFEN

RÖDERGASSE

TRADES MANS HAUS

RÖDERTOR

BIER GARTEN

FOOTPATH

CASTLE GARDEN

GASSE

TO TRAIN STATION (ROM. ROAD BUS STOP)

MEDIEVAL CRIME & PUNISHMENT MUSEUM

WENG

PLÖN LEIN

DOUBLE BRIDGE

MARKET SQUARE
• TOURIST INFO, CLOCK
• TOWN HALL (TOWER)
• FRIESE SHOP

YH

P

WC

LODGING:
❶ GOLDENER ROSE
❷ MOSER
❸ PÖSCHEL
❹ GERBERHAUS
❺ ALTFRÄNKISCHE WEINSTUBE

NOTE: MAP NOT TO SCALE-IT'S A 15 MIN WALK FROM CASTLE GDN. TO RÖDERTOR.
▟ = ACCESS STAIRS TO WALL

↓ TO DINKELSBUHL + FÜSSEN VIA ROMANTIC ROAD

DCH

charm. Get medievaled in Rothenburg. Walk the wall, see the exquisitely carved altarpiece and the strangely enjoyable medieval crime-and-punishment museum. Be careful . . . this cobbled mall is Germany's best shopping town.

Orientation (tel. code: 09861)

To orient yourself in Rothenburg (ROE-ten-burg), think of the town map as a human head. Its nose—the castle garden—sticks out to the left, and the neck is the skinny lower part, with the youth hostel and my favorite hotels in the Adam's apple. You can walk across the town in 12 minutes.

During Rothenburg's heyday, from 1150 to 1400, it was the crossing point of two major trade routes: Tashkent-Paris and Hamburg-Venice. Most of the buildings you'll see were built by 1400. The city was born around its long-gone castle (today's castle garden; built in 1142, destroyed in 1356). You can see the shadow of the first town wall, which defines the oldest part of Rothenburg, in its contemporary street plan. A few gates from this wall survive. The richest and therefore biggest houses were in this central part. The commoners built higgledy-piggledy (read: picturesquely) farther from the center near the present walls. Today, the great trade is tourism; two-thirds of the townspeople are employed serving you. Too often, Rothenburg brings out the shopper in visitors before they've had a chance to appreciate the historic city. True, this is a great place to do your German shopping, but first see the town. While 2.5 million people visit each year, a mere 500,000 spend the night. Rothenburg is most enjoyable early and late when the tour groups are gone.

Tourist Information

The TI is on the market square (Monday-Friday 9:00-12:00, 14:00-18:00, Saturday 9:00-12:00, 14:00-16:00, closed Sunday, tel. 40492, after-hours board lists rooms still available). Pick up a map and the "sights worth seeing and knowing" brochure (a virtual walking guide to the town; read it all). The TI's free "Hotels and Pensions of Rothenburg" map has the most detail and names all streets. Confirm sightseeing plans and ask about the daily 13:30 walking tour and evening entertainment. The travel agency in the TI is a handy place to arrange train and couchette reservations. The best town map is available free at the Friese shop, two doors toward the nose. Rothenburg is a joy on foot. No sight or hotel is more than a 12-minute walk from the station or each other. Many hotels and guesthouses will pick desperate heavy packers up at the station.

Sights—Rothenburg

▲▲**Walk the Wall**—Just over a mile around, with great views, and providing a good orientation, this walk can be done by those under six feet tall in less than an hour and requires no special sense of balance. Photographers go through lots of film, especially before breakfast or at sunset when the lighting is best and the crowds are least. The best fortifications are in the Spitaltor (south end). Walk from there counterclockwise to the forehead. Climb the Rödertor in route. The names you see along the way are people who donated money to repair the wall after WWII.

▲**Rödertor**—The wall tower nearest the train station is the only one you can climb. It's worth the hike up for the view and a fascinating rundown on the bombing of Rothenburg in the last weeks of World War II (the northeast corner of the city was destroyed; photos, English translation, 1 DM, 9:00-17:00, closed off-season).

Walking Tours—The TI on the market square offers 90-minute guided tours in English (4 DM, daily May-October at 13:30 from the market square). The equally informative but more dramatic "night watchman's tour" leaves each evening at 20:00 (8 DM, April-October, in English). You can hire a private guide. For 50 DM, a local historian—who's usually an intriguing character as well—will bring the ramparts alive. Eight hundred years of history are packed between the cobbles. (Manfred Baumann, tel. 09861/4146, and Anita Weinzierl, tel. 09868/7993, are good guides.)

▲▲**Climb Town Hall Tower**—The best view of Rothenburg and the surrounding countryside and a closeup look at an old tiled roof from the inside (9:30-12:30, 13:00-17:00; off-season Saturday and Sunday 12:00-15:00 only) are yours for 1 DM and a rigorous (214 steps, 180 feet) but interesting climb. Ladies, beware: some men find the view best from the bottom of the ladder just before the top.

▲▲**Herrengasse and the Castle Garden**—Any town's Herrengasse, where the richest patricians and merchants (the *Herren*) lived, is your chance to see its finest old mansions. Wander from the market square down Herrengasse (past the old Rothenburg official measurement rods on the City Hall wall), drop into the lavish front rooms of a ritzy hotel or two. Pop into the Franciscan Church (from 1285, oldest in town, with a Riemenschneider altarpiece; free, 10:00-12:00, 14:00-16:00), continue on down past the old-fashioned puppet theater, through the old gate (notice the tiny after-curfew door in the big door and the frightening mask mouth from which hot tar was poured onto attackers) and into the garden that used to be the castle. (Great picnic spots and Tauber Riviera views at sunset.)

▲▲**Medieval Crime and Punishment Museum**—It's the best of its kind, full of fascinating old legal bits and *Kriminal* pieces, instruments of punishment and torture, even a special cage—complete with a metal gag—for nags. Exhibits are in English. (Fun cards and posters, 5 DM, daily 9:30-18:00, in winter 14:00-16:00).

▲**Toy Museum**—Two floors of historic *kinder* cuteness is a hit with many (just off the market square, downhill from the fountain, Hofbronneng 13; daily 9:30-18:00, 5 DM, 12 DM per family).

▲▲**St. Jacob's Church**—Here you'll find a glorious 500-year-old wooden altarpiece by Tilman Riemenschneider, located up the stairs and behind the organ. Riemenschneider was the Michelangelo of German wood-carvers. This is the one required art treasure in town (2 DM, daily 9:00-17:30, off-season 10:00-12:00, 14:00-16:00, free helpful English info sheet).

Meistertrunk Show—Be on the main square at 11:00, 12:00, 13:00, 14:00, 15:00, 20:00, 21:00, or 22:00 for the ritual gathering of the tourists to see the less-than-breath-taking reenactment of the Meistertrunk story. In 1631, the Catholic army took the Protestant town and was about to do its rape, pillage, and plunder thing when, as the story goes, the mayor said, "Hey, if I can drink this entire 3-liter tankard of wine in one gulp, will you leave us alone?" The invading commander, sensing he was dealing with an unbalanced people, said, "Sure." Mayor Nusch drank the whole thing, the town was saved, and the mayor slept for three days.

Hint: for the best show, don't watch the clock; watch the open-mouthed tourists gasp as the old windows flip open. At the late shows, the square flickers with flash attachments.

▲**Historical Vaults**—Under the town hall tower is a city history museum that gives a waxy but good look at medieval Rothenburg and a good-enough replica of the famous Meistertrunk tankard (well described in English, 2 DM, 9:00-18:00, closed off-season).

Museum of the Imperial City (Reichsstadt Museum)—This stuffier museum, housed in the former Dominican

Convent, gives a more scholarly look at old Rothenburg with
some fine art and the supposed Meistertrunk tankard, labeled
"*Kürfurstenhumpen*" (3 DM, 10:00-17:00, in winter 13:00-
16:00).

St. Wolfgang's Church—This fortified Gothic church is
built into the medieval wall at Klingentor (near the "forehead"). Explore its dungeon-like passages below and check
out the shepherd's dance exhibit to see where they hot-oiled
the enemy back in the good old days (2 DM, 10:00-13:00,
14:00-17:00, closed off-season).

Alt Rothenburger Handwerkerhaus—This 700-year-old
tradesman's house shows the typical living situation of
Rothenburg in its heyday (Alter Stadtgraben 26, near the
Markus Tower; 3 DM, daily 9:00-18:00, closed off-season).

▲Walk in the Countryside—Just below the Burggarten
(castle garden) in the Tauber Valley is the cute, skinny, 600-
year-old castle/summer home of Mayor Toppler (2 DM,
13:00-16:00 on Friday, Saturday, and Sunday in summer
only). Intimately furnished, it's well worth a look. On the top
floor, notice the photo of bombed-out 1945 Rothenburg.
Then walk on past the covered bridge and huge trout to the
peaceful village of Detwang. **Detwang** is actually older than
Rothenburg, with another Riemenschneider altarpiece in its
church (from 968, the second oldest in Franconia). For a
scenic return, loop back to Rothenburg through the valley
along the river past a café with outdoor tables, great desserts,
and a town view to match.

A Franconian Bike Ride—For a fun, breezy look at the
countryside around Rothenburg, rent a bike from the train
station (12 DM per day, 8 DM with a train pass or ticket,
extra gears available for 1 DM each, 5:00-18:30). For a
pleasant half-day pedal, bike south down to Detwang via
Topplerschloss. Go north along the level bike path to
Tauberscheckenbach, then huff and puff uphill about 20
minutes to Adelshofen and south back to Rothenburg.

Swimming—Rothenburg has a fine modern recreation
center, with an indoor/outdoor pool and a sauna, a few minutes walk down the Dinkelsbühl Road (8:00 or 9:00-20:00,
tel. 4565).

Franconian Open-Air Museum—Twenty minutes drive
from Rothenburg in the undiscovered "Rothenburgy" town

of Bad Windsheim is a small, open-air folk museum that, compared with others in Europe, isn't much. But it's trying very hard and gives you the best look around at traditional rural Franconia (5 DM, 9:00-18:00, closed off-season).

Shopping

Rothenburg is one of Germany's best shopping towns. Do it here, mail it home, and be done with it. Lovely prints, carvings, wineglasses, Christmas-tree ornaments, and beer steins are popular.

The Kathe Wohlfahrt Christmas trinkets phenomenon is spreading across the half-timbered reaches of Europe. In Rothenburg, tourists flock to the Kathe Wohlfahrt Kris Kringle Market and the Christmas Village (on either side of Herrengasse, just off the main square). This Christmas wonderland is filled with enough twinkling lights to require a special electric hookup, instant Christmas spirit mood music (best appreciated on a hot day in July), and American and Japanese tourists hungrily filling little woven shopping baskets with 5- to 10-DM goodies to hang on their trees. (Okay, I admit it, my Christmas tree dangles with a few KW ornaments.) Note: prices have hefty tour-guide kickbacks built into them.

The Friese shop (just off the market square, west of the tourist office on the corner across from the public WC) offers a charming contrast. Cuckoo with friendliness, it gives shoppers with this book tremendous service: a 10 percent discount, 14 percent tax deducted if you have it mailed, and a free Rothenburg map. Anneliese, who runs the place with her sons, Frankie and Berni, charges only her cost to ship things, changes money at the best rates in town with no extra charge, and lets tired travelers leave their bags in her back room for free.

For good prints, etchings, and paintings, 10 percent off marked prices with this book, and a free shot of German brandy, visit the Ernst Geissendörfer print shop where the main square hits Schmiedgasse.

Those who prefer to eat their souvenirs shop the *Bäckerei* (bakeries). Their succulent pastries, pies, and cakes are pleasantly distracting. Skip the good-looking but bad-tasting "Rothenburger Schneeballs."

Evening Fun and Beer Drinking

The best beer garden for balmy summer evenings is just outside the wall at the Rödertor (red gate). If this is dead, as it often is, go a few doors farther out to the alley (left) just before the Sparkasse for two popular bars and the hottest disco in town.

For a rare chance to mix it up with locals who aren't selling anything, bring your favorite slang and tongue-twisters to the English conversation club (Wednesdays, 20:00-24:00) at Mario's Altefränkische Weinstube. This dark and smoky pub is an atmospheric hangout any night but Tuesday, when it's closed (Klosterhof 7, off Klingengasse, behind St. Jacob's church, tel. 6404).

For mellow ambience, try the beautifully restored Alte Keller's Weinstube on Alterkellerstrasse under walls festooned with old toys. Wine lovers enjoy the Glocke Hotel's stube.

Sleeping in Rothenburg

(1.6 DM = about $1, zip code: 91541, tel. code: 09861)
Rothenburg is crowded with visitors, including probably Europe's greatest single concentration of Japanese tourists. But when the sun sets, most retreat to big-city high-rise hotels. Except for the rare Saturday night, room-finding is easy throughout the year. In fact, those who arrive by train may be greeted by the *Zimmer* skimmer trying to waylay those on their way to a reserved room. If you arrive without a reservation, try talking yourself into one of these more desperate B&B rooms for a youth hostel price.

My first five listings are at the south end of town, 15 minutes from station, a 7-minute (without shopping) walk downhill from the market square. Walk downhill on Schmiedgasse (*gasse* means lane) until it becomes Spitalgasse (Hospital Lane). Unless otherwise indicated, room prices include breakfast.

Sleep code: **S**=Single, **D**=Double/Twin, **T**=Triple, **Q**=Quad, **B**=Bath/Shower, **WC**=Toilet, **CC**=Credit Card (**V**isa, **M**astercard, **A**mex), **SE**=Speaks English (graded **A** through **F**).

I stay in **Hotel Goldener Rose** (S-32 DM, D-60 DM, DBWC-80 DM-85 DM in classy annex behind the garden, some triples, SE-B, kid-friendly, EZ in annex, CC:VMA; Spitalgasse 28, tel. 4638, fax 86417, closed in January and

February) where scurrying Karin serves breakfast and stately Henni causes many monoglots to dream in fluent Deutsche. The hotel has only one shower for two floors of rooms and the streetside rooms can be noisy, but the rooms are clean and airy and you're surrounded by cobbles, flowers, and red-tiled roofs. The Favetta family also serves good, reasonably priced meals. Remember to keep your key to get in after they close (at the side gate in the alley).

For the best real, with-a-local-family, comfortable, and homey experience, stay with **Herr und Frau Moser** (30 DM per person, one double and one triple; Spitalgasse 12, tel. 5971). This charming retired couple speak little English but try very hard. Speak slowly, in clear, simple English.

Pension Pöschel (S-30 DM, D-60, T-90 DM, small kids free; Wenggasse 22, tel. 3430, SE-D) is also friendly, has 9 bright rooms, and is a little closer to the market square. Just across the street, the **Gastehaus Raidel** (D-64 DM, DB-84 DM; Wenggasse 3, tel. 3115) offers bright rooms with cramped facilities down the hall. It's run by grim people who make me want to sing the "Addams Family" theme song, but it works in a pinch.

Hotel Gerberhaus, a classy new hotel in a 500-year-old building, is warmly run by Ingra, who mixes modern comforts into bright and airy rooms while keeping the traditional flavor. Great buffet breakfasts, a guest's washer and dryer, and pleasant garden in back (DB-100 DM to 140 DM, no CC but takes personal checks, SE-B; Spitalgasse 25, tel. 3055, fax 86555).

Rothenburg's fine youth hostel, the **Rossmühle** (19 DM beds, 6 DM sheets, 8 DM dinners, tel. 4510, reception open 7:00-9:00, 17:00-20:00, 21:00-22:00, will hold rooms until 18:00 if you call, lockup at 23:30) has three to five double bunks per room and is often filled with school groups on weekdays. This droopy-eyed building is the old town horse-mill (used when the town was under siege and the river-powered mill was inaccessible). Here in Bavaria, hosteling is limited to those under 27, except for families traveling with children under 16. In 1995 Rossmuhle's newly renovated sister hostel will open (same phone number).

Gasthof Greifen is a big, traditional old place with all the comforts. It's family-run and creaks just the way you want it to (S-40 DM, SB-70DM, D-70 DM, DB-110 DM, T-100 DM, TB-150 DM, CC:VMA, half a block downhill from the Markt Platz at Obere Schmiedgasse 5 tel. 2281, fax 86374).

Right on the town square, **Gasthof Marktplatz** (S-35 DM, D-60 DM, DB-75 DM, DBWC-90 DM, T-81 DM, TB-100 DM; Grüner Markt 10, tel. 6722, Herr Rosner SE) has simple rooms and a cozy atmosphere. Its cheap rooms have sinks, but access to absolutely no shower.

Frau Guldemeister rents 2 simple and plain rooms (DB-60 DM-70 DM, breakfast in the room, SE-A; off the market square behind the Christmas shop, Pfaffleinsgasschen 10, tel. 8988).

Bohemians with bucks enjoy the **Hotel Altfränkische Weinstube am Klosterhof** (SB-65 DM, DB-90 DM-100 DM, TB-120 DM, CC:VM, kid-friendly, SE-A; behind St. Jacob's church, just off Klingengasse at Klosterhof 7, tel. 6404). A young couple, Mario and Erika, run this dark and smoky pub in a 600-year-old building. Upstairs they rent *gemütliche* rooms with upscale Monty Python atmosphere, TVs, modern showers, open-beam ceilings, and "*himmel* beds" (canopied four-poster "heaven" beds). Their pub is a candlelit classic, serving hot food until 22:00, closing at 1:00. You're welcome to drop by on Wednesday evenings (20:00-24:00) for the English conversation club.

If money doesn't matter, the **Burg Hotel** (DB-230 DM-300 DM, SE-A, CC:VMA; Klostergasse 1, on the wall near the castle garden, tel. 5037, fax 1487), with elegance almost unimaginable in a medieval building with a Tauber Valley view and a high-heeled receptionist, offers a good way to spend it.

In the modern world, a block from the train station, you'll find **Pension Willi Then,** run by a cool guy (Willi played the sax in a jazz band for seven years after the war and is a regular at the English language club) on a quiet street (D-65 DM, DB-75 DM, SE-A; across from a handy laundro-mat at 8 Johannitergasse, tel. 5177).

The town of Detwang, a 15-minute walk below Rothenburg, is loaded with quiet *Zimmer*. The clean, quiet, and comfortable old **Gasthof zum Schwarzen Lamm** in Detwang (D-80 DM, DB-98 DM, tel. 6727) serves good food, as does the popular and very local-style **Eulenstube** next door. **Gastehaus Alte Schreinerei** (8801 Bettwar,

tel. 1541) offers good food and quiet, comfy, reasonable
rooms a little farther down the road in Bettwar.

Eating in Rothenburg

Finding a reasonable meal (or a place serving late) in the
town center can be tough. Most places serve meals only
from 11:30-13:30 and 18:00-20:00. Galgengasse (Gallows
Lane) has two cheap and popular standbys: **Pizzeria Roma**
(19 Galgengasse, 11:30-24:00, 10-DM pizzas and normal
schnitzel fare) and **Gasthof zum Ochsen** (26 Galgengasse,
11:30-13:30, 18:00-20:00, closed Thursday, decent 10-DM
meals). **Zum Schmolzer** (corner of Stollengasse and
Rosengasse) is a local favorite for its cheap beer and good
food. If you need a break from schnitzel, the **Hong Kong
China Restaurant**, outside the town near the train tracks (1
Bensenstrasse, tel. 7377), serves good Chinese food. There
are two supermarkets near the wall at Rödertor (the one outside the wall to the left is cheaper).

Transportation Connections

A tiny train line from Rothenburg to **Steinach** (hrly, 15 min)
connects Rothenburg to the rest of Germany. From Steinach,
hourly trains go to **Wurzburg** (30 min), **Munich** (2 hrs) and
Frankfurt (2 hrs, change in Wurzburg). Otherwise the
Romantic Road bus tour takes you in and out each afternoon.

Romantic Road

The Romantic Road (Romantische Strasse) winds you past
the most beautiful towns and scenery of Germany's medieval
heartland. Once Germany's medieval trade route, now it's
the best way to connect the dots between Füssen, Munich,
and Frankfurt.

    Wander through quaint hills and rolling villages, and
stop wherever the cows look friendly or a town fountain
beckons. My favorite sections are from Füssen to Landsberg
and Rothenburg to Weikersheim. For ideas on planning
your time see Rothenburg (above).

Getting Around

By car, you can simply follow the green *Romantische
Strasse* signs.

By train . . . take the bus. The Europa Bus Company runs buses daily between Frankfurt and Munich in each direction (April-October). A second route goes between Rothenburg and Füssen daily. Buses leave from train stations in towns served by a train. The 11-hour ride costs about $70 but is free with a Eurailpass. Each bus stops in Rothenburg (75-120 min) and Dinkelsbühl (50-105 min) and briefly at a few other attractions, and has a guide who hands out brochures and narrates the journey in English. While many claim Eva Braun survives as a Romantic Road bus-tour guide, there is no quicker or easier way to travel across Germany and get such a hearty dose of its countryside. Bus reservations are free but rarely necessary (except possibly on summer weekends; call 069/790 3256 one day in advance). You can start, stop, and switch over where you like.

Romantic Road Bus Schedule (Daily, April-October)

Frankfurt	8:15	
Wurzburg	9:45	
Arrive Rothenburg	12:30	
Depart Rothenburg	14:45	14:45
Arrive Dinkelsbuhl	15:30	15:25
Depart Dinkelsbuhl	16:20	16:20
Munich	19:30	—
Füssen		20:15
Füssen	8:00	
Arrive Wieskirche	8:30	
Depart Wieskirche	8:45	
Munich	—	9:00
Arrive Dinklesbuhl	12:20	12:00
Depart Dinklesbuhl	—	13:45
Arrive Rothenburg	—	14:30
Depart Rothenburg	—	16:30
Wurzburg	—	18:15
Frankfurt	—	20:00

MUNICH

Munich (München), Germany's most livable city, is also one of its most historic, artistic, and entertaining. It's big and growing, with a population of over 1.5 million.

Just a little more than a century ago, it was the capital of an independent Bavaria. Its imperial palaces, jewels, and grand boulevards constantly remind visitors that this was once a political as well as a cultural powerhouse. Its recently-bombed-out feeling reminds us that 50 years ago it lost a war.

Orient yourself in Munich's old center with its colorful pedestrian mall. Immerse yourself in Munich's art and history—crown jewels, baroque theater, Wittelsbach palaces, great art, and beautiful parks. Munich evenings are best spent in frothy beer halls—oompah bunny-hopping and belching Bavarian atmosphere. Pry big pretzels from no-nonsense, buxom beer maids.

Planning Your Time

Munich is worth two days, including a half-day side trip to Dachau. If necessary, its essence can be nicely captured in a day (walk the center, tour a palace and a museum, and enjoy a beer-filled evening). Those without a car and in a hurry can do the castles of Ludwig as a daytrip from Munich by tour. Even Salzburg can be done as a daytrip from Munich.

Orientation (tel. code: 089)

The tourist's Munich is circled by a ring road (which was the town wall) marked by four old gates: Karlstor (near the train station), Sendlinger Tor, Isartor (near the river), and Odeonsplatz (near the palace). Marienplatz is the city center. A great pedestrian-only street cuts this circle in half, running nearly from Karlstor and the train station through Marienplatz to Isartor. Orient yourself along this east-west axis. Most sights are within a few blocks of this people-filled walk. Nearly all the sights and hotels I recommend are within about a 20-minute walk of Marienplatz and each other. Most Munich sights are closed on Monday.

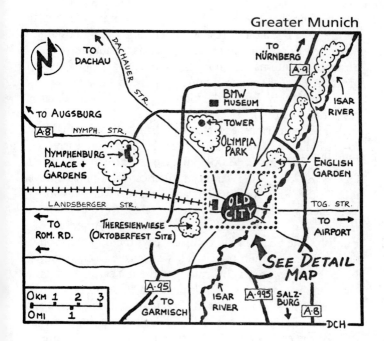

Greater Munich

Tourist Information

Take advantage of the TI in the train station (Monday-
Saturday 8:00-22:00, Sundays 11:00-19:00, tel. 089/2391-256
or 257, near street exit at track 11). Have a list of questions
ready, confirm your sightseeing plans, and pick up brochures, the free and excellent city map, and subway map.
Consider buying the 2.50-DM "Monatsprogram" for a
German-language list of sights and calendar of events or the
"Young People's Guide" (1 DM, in English, good regardless
of your age). They have a room-finding service (5 DM,
you'll save money by contacting my recommended hotels
directly.). If the line is worse than your questions are important, skip your questions and go directly to the cash window
to pick up the map and other brochures (or go to EurAide,
described below).

Trains

Munich's station is a sight in itself, one of those places that
stoke anyone's wanderlust. For a quick orientation in the station, use the big wall maps of the train station, Munich, and

Bavaria (through the center doorway as you leave the tracks on the left). For a quick rest stop, the Burger King upstairs has toilets as pleasant and accessible as its hamburgers. Sussmann's Internationale Presse (across from track 24) is great for English-language books, papers, and magazines including *Munich Found* (the informative English-speaking residents' monthly).

The industrious, eager-to-help **EurAide** office (halfway to the Bahnhof Mission, down track 11, daily May-early October, 7:30-11:30, 13:00-18:00, closes at 16:30 in May, tel. 089/593889, fax 550-3965) is an American whirlpool of travel information ideal for Eurailers and budget travelers. Alan Wissenberg and his staff know your train travel and accommodations questions and have answers in clear American English. The German rail company pays them to help you design your best train travels. They also have Dachau and Neuschwanstein tours (frustrating without a car), advice on cheap money-changing, transit tickets, a "Czech Prague Out" train pass (convenient for Prague-bound Eurailers), and a free newsletter; they can also find you a room, for a fee.

At the other end of the station, near track 30, **Radius Touristik** (daily, 10:00-18:00, May through mid-October, tel. 596113, run by Englishman Patrick Holder) rents three-speed bikes (5 DM/hour, 20 DM/day, 25 DM/24 hours, 40 DM/48 hours) and organizes city bike tours. Patrick dispenses all the necessary tourist information (city map, bike routes).

Getting Around Munich

The great Munich tram, bus, and subway system is a sight in itself. Subways are called U- or S-bahns. Subway lines are numbered (e.g., S3 or U5). Eurail passes are good on the S-bahn (actually an underground-while-in-the-city commuter railway). Regular tickets cost 3.50 DM and are good for 2 hours of changes in one direction. For the shortest rides (one or two stops) get the smallest 2-DM ticket. The 10-DM all-day pass is a great deal. One pass is good for up to two adults and three kids. If more than one adult is using it on a weekday, it's good only after 9:00. Get a pass, validate it in a machine, and you have Munich-by-rail for a day (purchase at tourist offices, subway booths, and in machines at

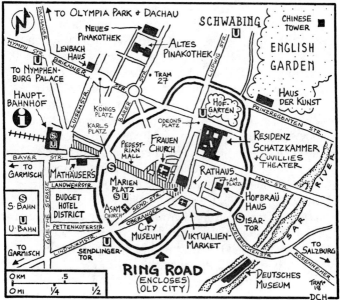

Munich Center

most stops). The entire system (bus/tram/subway) works on the same tickets. You must punch your own ticket before boarding. (Plainclothes ticket-checkers enforce this "honor system," rewarding freeloaders with stiff fines.) I see the town by bike, rentable quick and easy at the train station (see above). Munich—level and compact, with plenty of bike paths—feels good on two wheels. Taxis are expensive and needless.

Sights—Munich
▲▲**Marienplatz and the Pedestrian Zone**—The glory of Munich will slap you in the smile as you ride the escalator out of the subway and into the sunlit Marienplatz (Mary's Place): great buildings bombed flat and rebuilt, the ornate facades of the new and old City Halls (the Neues Rathaus, built in neo-Gothic style from 1867 to 1910, and the Altes Rathaus), outdoor cafés, and people bustling and lingering like the birds and breeze they share this square with. From here the pedestrian mall (Kaufingerstrasse and Neuhauser-strasse) leads you through a great shopping area past carni-

vals of street entertainers, the twin-towering Frauenkirche (built in 1470, rebuilt after World War II), and several fountains, to Karlstor and the train station. The not-very-old Glockenspiel "jousts" on Marienplatz daily through the tourist season at 11:00, 12:00, 17:00, and a shorty at 21:00.

▲▲**City Views**—The highest viewpoint is from a 350-foot-high perch on top of the **Frauenkirche** (elevator, 4 DM, 10:00-17:00, closed Sunday). **Neues Rathaus** (2 DM, elevator from under the Marienplatz Glockenspiel, 9:00-19:00, closed Sunday). For a totally unobstructed view, but with no elevator, climb the **St. Peter's Church** tower just a block away. It's a long climb, much of it with two-way traffic on a one-way staircase, but the view is dynamite (2.50 DM, 9:00-18:00, Sunday 10:00-18:00). Try to be two flights from the top when the bells ring at the top of the hour (and when your friends ask you about your trip, you'll say, "What?"). The church, built upon the hill where the first monks founded the city in the 12th century, has a fine interior with photos of the WWII bomb damage on a column near the entrance.

▲▲**Residenz**—For a long hike through rebuilt corridors of gilded imperial Bavarian grandeur, tour the family palace of the Wittelsbachs, who ruled Bavaria for more than 700 years (4 DM, 10:00-16:30, closed Monday, enter on Max-Joseph Platz, 3 blocks from Marienplatz). The **Schatzkammer** (treasury) shows off a thousand years of Wittelsbach crowns and knickknacks (same hours, another 4 DM from the same window). Vienna's palace and jewels are better, but this is Bavaria's best.

▲**The Cuvillies Theater**—Attached to the Residenz, this National Theater, designed by Cuvillies, is dazzling enough to send you back to the days of divine monarchs (3 DM, Monday-Saturday 14:00-17:00, Sunday 10:00-17:00).

▲▲**Münchner Stadtmuseum**—The underrated Munich city museum is a pleasant surprise. Exhibits include: life in Munich through the centuries (including WWII and Hitler's planned urban fantasy) illustrated in paintings, photos, and models, historic puppets and carnival gadgets; a huge collection of musical instruments from around the world; old photography; and a first-class medieval armory. No crowds, bored and playful guards (5 DM, 7.50 DM for families, Tuesday-Sunday 10:00-17:00, Wednesday until 20:30, closed Monday; 3 blocks off Marienplatz at St. Jakob's Platz 1, a fine children's playground faces the entry).

▲▲**Alte Pinakothek**—Bavaria's best collection of art is closed for renovation at least through 1996. Thankfully, most of its top masterpieces will be displayed in the normally-much-less-interesting neighboring Neue Pinakothek (6 DM, Tuesday-Sunday 10:00-17:00, Tuesday and Thursday 10:00-20:00, closed Monday, tel. 238-05195). The collection's forte is Italian and North European artists, such as Rubens and Dürer. (U-2 to Königsplatz or tram #27).

▲**Haus der Kunst**—Built by Hitler as a temple of Nazi art, this bold and fascist building now houses modern art, much of which the Führer censored. It's a fun collection—Kandinsky, Picasso, Dali, and much more from this century (3.50 DM, 9:00-16:30, Thursday evening 19:00-21:00, closed Monday).

Bayerisches Nationalmuseum—An interesting collection of Riemenschneider carvings, manger scenes, traditional living rooms, and old Bavarian houses (5 DM, free on Sunday, 9:30-17:00, closed Monday; tram #20 or bus 53 or 55 to Prinzregentenstrasse 3).

▲▲**Deutsches Museum**—Germany's answer to our Smithsonian Institution has everything of scientific and technical interest from astronomy to zymurgy but can be disappointing because of its overwhelming size and lack of English descriptions (there is an English guidebook). With 10 miles of exhibits, even those on roller skates will need to be selective. Technical types enjoy lots of hands-on gadgetry, a state-of-the-art planetarium and an IMAX theater (8 DM, self-serve cafeteria, museum open daily 9:00-17:00; S-Bahn to Isartorplatz).

Schwabing—Munich's artsy, bohemian university district or "Greenwich Village" has been called "not a place but a state of mind." All I experienced was a mental lapse. The bohemians run the boutiques. I think the most colorful thing about Schwabing is the road leading back downtown. U3 or U6 will take you to the Münchener-Freiheit Center if you want to wander. Most of the jazz and disco joints are near Occamstrasse. The Haidhausen neighborhood (U-

bahn: Max Weber Platz) is becoming the "new Schwabing."
▲**Englischer Garten**—One of Europe's great parks,
Munich's "Central Park" is the Continent's largest, laid
out in 1789 by an American. There's a huge beer garden
near the Chinese Pagoda. Caution: while a local law
requires sun-worshippers to wear clothes on the tram,
this park is sprinkled with nude sunbathers. A rewarding
respite from the city, it's especially fun on a bike under
the summer sun (rental shop where Veterinar Strasse
hits the park).

Asam Church—Near the Stadtmuseum, this private church
of the Asam brothers is a gooey, drippy masterpiece by
Bavaria's top two rococonuts, showing off their very popular
baroque-concentrate style.

The Centre of Unusual Museums is a collection of
mediocre but occasionally interesting one-room museums
featuring goofy topics such as padlocks, Easter bunnies,
chamber pots, and so on (not worth 8 DM, daily 10:00-
18:00; near Marienplatz and Isartor at Westenriederstr. 26).

▲**Olympic Grounds**—Munich's great 1972 Olympic
stadium and sports complex is now a lush park offering a
tower (5 DM, commanding but so high it's a boring view
from 820 feet, 8:00-24:00), an excellent swimming pool (5
DM 7:00-22:30, Monday from 10:00, Thursday closed at
18:00,), a good look at its striking "cobweb" style of architecture, and plenty of sun, grass, and picnic potential. Take
U3 to Olympiazentrum direct from Marienplatz.

BMW Museum—The BMW headquarters, located in
a striking building across the street from the Olympic
Grounds, offers free factory tours (normally one a day in
English) and a 5-DM museum (daily 9:00-17:00, last ticket
sold at 16:00, tel. 389-53307, closed much of August). The
museum is popular with car buffs.

Bus Tours of the City and Nearby Countryside—
Panorama Tours (at the train station, tel. 591504) offers
all-day tours of Neuschwanstein and Linderhof (75 DM)
and 1-hour city orientation bus tours (at 10:00, 11:30, and
14:30, 15 DM). EurAide does a train/bus Neuschwanstein-
Linderhof-Wies Church day tour twice a week in June and
July (transportation only, 70 DM, 55 DM with a train

pass). Renate Suerbaum (tel. 283374, 130-DM tours) is a good local guide.

▲▲**Nymphenburg Palace**—This royal summer palace is impressive, but if you've already seen the Residenz, it's only mediocre. If you do tour it, don't miss King Ludwig's "Gallery of Beauties"—a room stacked with portraits of Bavaria's loveliest women—according to Ludwig (who had a thing about big noses). The palace park, good for a royal stroll, contains the tiny, more-impressive-than-the-palace Amalienburg hunting lodge, a rococo jewel by Cuvillies. The sleigh and coach collection (Marstallmuseum) is especially interesting for "Mad" Ludwig fans (9:00-12:30 and 13:30-17:00, closed Monday, shorter hours October-March, admission to all 6 DM, less for individual parts, use the little English guidebook, tel. 179080, reasonable cafeteria; U1 to Rotkreuzplatz than tram or bus #12).

Oktoberfest

When King Ludwig the First had a marriage party in 1810 it was such a success that they made it an annual bash. These days the Oktoberfest lasts 16 days, ending with the first full weekend in October. It starts (usually on the third Saturday in September) with an opening parade of more than 6,000 participants and fills eight huge beer tents with about 6,000 people each. A million gallons of beer later, they roast the last ox.

It's crowded, but if you arrive in the morning (except Friday or Saturday), and haven't called ahead for a room, the TI can normally find you a place. The fairground, known as the Wies'n (a few blocks from the train station), erupts in a frenzy of rides, dancing, and strangers strolling arm-in-arm down rows of picnic tables, while the beer god stirs tons of beer, pretzels, and wurst in a bubbling caldron of fun. The "three-loops" roller coaster must be the wildest on earth (best before the beer drinking). During the fair, the city functions even better than normal, and it's a good time to sightsee even if beer-hall rowdiness isn't your cup of tea. The Fasching carnival time (early January to mid-February) is nearly as crazy. And the Oktoberfest grounds are set up for a mini-Oktoberfest to celebrate spring for the two weeks around May Day.

Sights—Near Munich

▲▲**Andechs**—A fine baroque church in a Bavarian setting at a monastery that serves hearty food and the best beer in Germany in a carnival atmosphere full of partying locals? That's the Andechs Monastery, crouching quietly with a big smile between two lakes just south of Munich. Come ready to eat chunks of tender pork chain-sawed especially for you, huge and soft pretzels (best I've had), spiraled white radishes, savory sauerkraut, and Andecher monk-made beer that would almost make celibacy tolerable. Everything is served in medieval proportions; two people can split a meal. Great picnic center, too. Open daily 9:00-21:00, first-class view, second-class prices (TI tel. 08152/5227). To reach Andechs from Munich without a car, take the S5 train to Herrsching and catch a "Rauner" shuttle bus (hourly) or walk 2 miles from there. Don't miss a stroll up to the church where you can sit peacefully and ponder the striking contrasts a trip through Germany offers.

▲▲**Dachau**—Dachau was the first Nazi concentration camp (1933). Today it's the most accessible camp to travelers and a very effective voice from our recent but grisly past, warning and pleading "Never Again," the memorial's theme. This is a valuable experience and, when approached thoughtfully, well worth the trouble. In fact, it may change your life. See it. Feel it. Read and think about it. After this most powerful sightseeing experience, many people gain more respect for history and the dangers of not keeping tabs on their government.

Upon arrival, pick up the mini-guide and note when the next documentary film in English will be shown (25 minutes, normally at 11:30 and 15:30). The museum and the movie are exceptional. Notice the Expressionist fascist-inspired art near the theater, where you'll also find English books, slides, and a WC. Outside, be sure to see the reconstructed barracks and the memorial shrines at the far end (9:00-17:00, closed Monday; 45 minutes from downtown taking S2, direction: Petershausen, to Dachau, then bus 722, Dachau-Ost, from the station to "Gedenkstätte"; the two-zone 6-DM ticket covers the entire trip; with a train pass, just pay for the last leg) If you're driving, follow Dachauerstrasse from downtown Munich. If lost, signs to Augsburg will lead to signs to Dachau. Then follow the KZ-Gedenkstätte signs.

The town of Dachau (TI tel. 08131/84566) is more pleasant than its unfortunate image.

Sleeping in Munich
(1.6 DM = about $1, tel. code: 089)

There are no cheap beds in Munich. Youth hostels strictly enforce their 25-year-old age limit, and side-tripping in is a bad value. But there are plenty of decent, moderately priced rooms, most located within a few blocks of the Haupt-bahnhof (central train station). August, September, and early October are most crowded, but conventions can clog the city on any day. Call ahead and reserve one of my recommenda-tions. Assuming these hotels honor their 1995 prices, you won't get a better value through a TI room service.

Sleep code: **S**=Single, **D**=Double/Twin, **T**=Triple, **Q**=Quad, **B**=Bath/Shower, **WC**=Toilet (if not listed, a WC is normally included with B), **CC**=Credit Card (**V**isa, **M**astercard, **A**mex). English is spoken at nearly all places; prices include breakfast and increase with conventions and festivals. The cheapest rooms with no showers usually charge a few marks for one down the hall.

Hotels

Budget hotels (90-DM doubles, no elevator, shower down the hall) cluster in the area immediately south of the station. It's seedy after dark (erotic cinemas, barnacles with lingerie tongues, men with moustaches in the shadows) but danger-ous only to those in search of trouble. Still, I've listed places in more polite neighborhoods, generally a 5- or 10-minute walk from the station and handy to the center. Those far-thest from the station are most pleasant. The last four list-ings are in the nearly traffic-free old town center. Places are listed in order of closeness to the station.

Jugendhotel Marienherberge (S-35 DM, 30 DM per bed in D and T, 25 DM 4- to 7-bed rooms, open 8:00-24:00; 1 block from the station at Goethestrasse 9, tel. 555805) is a pleasant, friendly convent accepting young women only (loosely enforced 25-year age limit). These are the best cheap beds in town.

Hotel Gebhardt (D-95 DM, DB-120 DM, T-120 DM, TB-160 DM, Q-150 DM, QB-170 DM, CC:VMA;

Goethestrasse 38, Munich, 4 blocks from the station, tel. 539446, fax 53982663) offers a combination of decent neighborhood, comfort, and price surrounded by cold institutional hotel plastic and plaster.

YMCA (CVJM), open to people of all ages and sexes (D-80 DM, T-108 DM, a bed in a shared triple-36 DM; Landwehrstrasse 13, 80336 Munich, elevator, tel. 5521410, fax 5504282), has modern, simple rooms and serves cheap dinners (18:00-21:00, Tuesday-Friday).

Hotel Pension Luna (D-95 DM, DB-110 DM, T-125 DM, TB-135 DM, CC:VMA, lots of stairs; 5 Landwehrstrasse, tel. 597833, fax 550-3761) employs a loving touch to give a dumpy building quiet, bright, and cheery rooms. **Hotel Pension Erika** (D-85 DM, DB-95 DM, DBWC-115 DM, TB-120 DM, showers 3 DM, CC:VMA; Landwehrstrasse 8, tel. 554327), bright as dingy yellow can be, is sleepable.

Hotel Pension Zöllner (small twin-85 DM, big double-95 DM, DB-129 DM; near Karlstor at Sonnenstrasse 10, tel. 554035, fax 550-3714, elevator) is plain, clean, and concrete on the big ring road between the station and the old center.

Hotel Pension Utzelmann (S-50 DM, D-90 DM, DB-110 DM, T-125 DM, TB-150 DM; showers loosely 5 DM each, Pettenkoferstrasse 6, tel. 594889) has huge rooms, especially the curiously cheap Room 6. Each lacy room is richly furnished. It's in an extremely decent neighborhood a 10-minute walk from the station, a block off Sendlinger Tor.

Hotel Uhland (DB-140, TB-180 DM, all with WC, elevator, reserve with CC number, huge breakfast; 1 Uhlandstrasse, 80336 Munich, near the Theresienwiese Oktoberfest grounds, 10-minute walk from the station, tel. 539277, fax 531114), a mansion with sliding glass doors and a garden, is a worthwhile splurge. Easy parking.

Pension Westfalia overlooks the Oktoberfest grounds from the top floor of a quiet and elegant old building. Well-run by Peter Deiritz, this is a great value if you prefer sanity and personal touches to centrality (S-60 DM, SB-80 DM, D-85 DM, DB-110 DM, extra bed 25 DM, showers 3 DM, includes buffet breakfast; Mozartstr 23, 80336 Munich, easy parking, U3 or U6 to Goetheplatz, tel. 53037778, fax 5439120).

Pension Mariandl (D-95 DM, CC:VMA, 41 DM per person in larger rooms, CC:VA; Goethestrasse 51, tel. 534108, fax 543 8471, will hold rooms until 18:00) is an uppity place in an old, formerly elegant mansion with peeling vinyl floors, weak lights, and yellow corridors. The rooms are basic but fine, the neighborhood is peaceful and residential, and the classy dining hall plays free classical music Monday through Friday with dinner.

Hotel Westend, a big group-friendly place on the fifth floor of a nondescript office building on the big road parallel to the tracks a 10-minute walk away from the center from the station, offers affordable comfort rather than character (D-95 DM, DB-130 DM with this book, higher on Fair days, CC:VMA; Landsbergerstr 20, 80339 Munich, S-bahn: Hackerbrucke, tel. 504004, fax 5025896).

Pension Diana (D-98 DM, T-132 DM, Q-172, CC: VA; Altheimer Eck 15, U- or S-bahn to Karlsplatz, tel. 2603107, fax 263934; run by Mr. Geza Szabo, who is from Hungary, and Atilla the son), 70 steps up and no elevator, 17 bright and airy doubles, narrow halls, and two power showers, is my home in Munich. It's in the old center, a block off the pedestrian mall (through the green "Arcade"). 16-DM/day parking garage across the street.

Pension Linder (S-55 DM, D-95 DM, DB-120 DM, DBWC-135 DM; Dultstrasse 1, just off Sendlinger Strasse, 80331 Munich, tel. 263413, Marion Sinzinger) is clean, quiet, and modern, with pastel-bouquet rooms hiding behind a concrete stairway. Along with the Diana, this is the most central of my listings, a few blocks from Marienplatz.

Hotel Herzog Wilhelm is hotelesque with a few simple rooms (S-69 DM, D-99 DM, T-125 DM, DB-150 DM, CC:VMA, elevator; Herzog-Wilhelm Str 23, 80331 Munich, tel. 230360, fax 23036701). Around the corner, the forgettable **Hotel Atlanta** is cheap, beautifully located, and more comfortable than a youth hostel (DB-90 DM, Sendlinger Str 58, tel. 263605).

Hostels and Cheap Beds

Munich's youth hostels charge 25 to 32 DM with sheets and breakfast and strictly limit admission to YH members who are under 26. The **Burg Schwaneck hostel** (30 minutes from the center, S7 to Pullach, then walk 10 minutes to Burgweg 4, tel. 7930643) is a renovated castle. Other hostels are at Miesingstrassse 4 (U-bahn: Thalkirchen, tel. 7236560) and Wendl-Dietrichstrasse 20 (U-bahn to Rothreuzplatz, tel. 131156).

"The Tent," Munich's **International Youth Camp Kapuzinerhölzl**, offers 400 places on the wooden floor of a huge circus tent with a mattress, blankets, good showers, and free tea in the morning for 6 DM to anyone under 25 (flexible). It's a fun experience—kind of a cross between a slumber party and Woodstock (if anyone under 25 knows what that was). Call 1414300 (recorded message before 17:00) before heading out. No curfew. Cool ping-pong-and-frisbee atmosphere throughout the day. Take U1 to Rotkreuzplatz, then tram #12 to Botanischer Garten (direction Amalienburgstrasse), and follow the youthful crowd down Franz-Schrank-strasse to the big tent. This is near the Nymphenburg Palace. Open late June through August. There is a theft problem, so sleep on your bag or leave it at the station.

Eating in Munich

Munich's most memorable budget food is in the beer halls. You have two basic choices: famous touristy places with music or mellower beer gardens with Germans.

The touristy ones have great beer, reasonable food, and live music, and are right downtown. These days Germans go there for the entertainment—to sing "Country Roads," see how Texas girls party, and watch salarymen from Tokyo chug beer. The music-every-night atmosphere is thick; the fat and shiny-leather band has even church mice standing up and conducting three-quarter time with a breadstick. Meals are inexpensive (for a light 10-DM meal, I like the local favorite, *Schweinswurst mit Kraut*); huge, liter beers called *ein Mass* (or "ein pitcher" in English) are 9 DM; white radishes are salted and cut in delicate spirals; and surly beermaids pull mustard packets from their cleavages. You can order your beer *"Helles"* (light, what you'll get if you say "ein beer"), *"Dunkle"* (dark), or *"Radler"* (half lemonade, half light beer). Notice the vomitoriums in the WC.

The most famous beer hall, the **Hofbräuhaus** (Platzl 9, near Marienplatz, tel. 221676, music for lunch and dinner), is most touristy. But check it out; it's fun to see 200 Japanese people drinking beer in a German beer hall. (They have a gimmicky folk evening upstairs in the "Festsaal" nightly at 19:00, 8 DM, tel. 290136-10, food and drinks are sold from the same menu.) My long-time favorite, **Mathäser Bierstadt** (dinner #94 is light, good, typical, and cheap; tel. 592896, Bayerstrasse 5, halfway between the train station and Karlstor, music after 17:00) has joined the Hofbräuhaus as the tour-group beer hall. For typical Bavarian fast food, try the self-serve at Mathäser's entry.

The **Weisses Bräuhaus** (Tal 10, between Marienplatz and Isartor) is more local and features the local fizzy "wheat beer." Hitler met with fellow fascists here in 1920 when his Nazi party had yet to ferment. The **Augustiner Beer Garden** (across from the train tracks, 3 blocks from the station away from the center on Arnulfstrasse) is a sprawling haven for local beer-lovers on a balmy evening. Upstairs in the tiny **Jodlerwirt** (4 Altenhofstrasse, between the Hofbräuhaus and Marienplatz, after 19:00, closed Sunday) is a woodsy, smart-aleck, yodeling kind of pub. For a classier evening stewed in antlers and fiercely Bavarian, eat under a tree or inside at the **Nürnberger Bratwurst Glöckl am Dom** (Frauenplatz 9, under the twin-domed cathedral, tel. 220385, closed Sunday).

For outdoor atmosphere and a cheap meal, spend an evening at the **Englischer Garten's Chinese Pagoda** (*Chinesischer Turm*) **Biergarten**. You're welcome to BYO food and grab a table or buy from the picnic stall (*Brotzeit*) right there. Don't bother to phone ahead: there are six thousand seats! For similar BYOF atmosphere right behind Mairienplatz, eat at Viktualien market's beer garden. Lunch or dinner here taps you into about the best budget eating in town. Countless stalls surround the beer garden selling wurst, sandwiches, produce, and so on. This BYOF tradition goes back to the days when monks were allowed to sell beer but not food. (A tablecloth indicates picnics are *verboten*.)

The crown in its emblem indicates that the royal family assembled its picnics in the historic, elegant, and expensive **Alois Dallmayr** delicatessen at 14 Dienerstrasse just behind the Rathaus (9:00-18:30, Saturday 9:00-14:00, closed Sunday). Wander through this dieter's purgatory, put together a royal

picnic, and eat it in the nearby, adequately royal Hofgarten.
To save money, browse at Dallmayr's, but buy in the basement of the Kaufhof across Marienplatz

Transportation Connections

Munich is a super transportation hub (one reason it was the
focus of so many WWII bombs). Direct trains connect
Munich to: Berlin (6/day, in 8 hrs), **Frankfurt** (14/day, 3½
hrs), **Salzburg** (12/day, 2 hrs), **Vienna** (4/day, 5 hrs), **Venice**
(2/day, 9 hrs), **Paris** (3/day, 9 hrs), **Prague** (2/day, 7-10 hrs),
Füssen (10/day, in 2 hrs, the 8:50 departure is good for a
castles day trip), and just about every other point in western
Europe. By train, Munich is 3 hours from **Reutte** (hrly
departures to Garmish where you connect to Reutte).
Munich's airport is an easy 40-minute ride on the S-bahn
(10 DM or free with train pass).

BAVARIA AND TIROL

Straddling the border, 2 hours south of Munich between Germany's Bavaria and Austria's Tirol, is a timeless land of fairy-tale castles, painted buildings shared by cows and farmers, and locals who still yodel when they're happy.

In Germany's Bavaria, tour "Mad" King Ludwig's ornate Neuschwanstein Castle, Europe's most spectacular. Stop by the Wies Church, a textbook example of Bavarian rococo bursting with curly curlicues, and browse through Oberammergau, Germany's wood-carving capital and home of the famous Passion Play. In Austria's Tirol, hike to the Ehrenberg ruined castle, scream down a nearby ski slope on an oversized skateboard, then catch your breath for an evening of yodeling and slap-dancing.

In this chapter, I'll cover Bavaria first, then Tirol. My favorite home base for exploring Bavaria's castles is actually in Austria, in the town of Reutte. Füssen, in Germany, is a handier home base for train travelers.

Planning Your Time

While locals come here for a week or two, the typical speedy American traveler will find two days worth of sightseeing. With a car and some more time you could enjoy the more remote corners but the basic visit ranges anywhere from a long day-trip from Munich to a three-night, two-day visit. If the weather's good and you're not going to Switzerland, be sure to ride a lift to an Alpine peak.

Getting Around Bavaria and Tirol

This region is ideal by car. All the sights are within an easy 60-mile loop. It's frustrating by train. Local bus service in the region is spotty for sightseeing. Without wheels, Reutte, the luge ride, and the Wies church are probably not worth the trouble. Füssen (with a direct 2-hour train ride to and from Munich every 2 hours) is 3 miles from Neuschwanstein castle with easy bus and bike connections. Oberammergau (hourly 2-hour trains from Munich with one change) has decent bus connections to nearby Linderhof castle. Oberammergau to

Bavaria and Tirol Castle Loop

Füssen is a pain. If you're interested only in Bavarian castles, consider an all-day organized bus tour of the Bavarian biggies as a side trip from Munich (see Munich chapter).

This is great biking country. Most train stations (including Reutte and Füssen) and many hotels rent bikes for 9 DM a day (tandems for 20 DM). Hitchhiking is a slow-but-possible way to connect the public transportation gaps.

Füssen, Germany

Füssen has long been a strategic place. Its main street sits on the Via Claudia Augusta, which crossed the Alps (over Brenner Pass) in Roman times. And the town was the southern terminus of a medieval trade route which happens to be today's Romantic Road. Dramatically situated under a renovated castle on the lively Lech River, that liveliness will spread through the town in 1995 as Füssen celebrates its 700th birthday.

Unfortunately, in the summer it's entirely overrun by tourists. Traffic can be exasperating, but by bike or on foot, it's not bad. Off-season, the town is a jester's delight.

Apart from Füssen's cobbled and arcaded town center, there's little real sightseeing. The striking-from-a-distance castle houses a boring picture gallery. The city museum in the monastery below the castle exhibits lifestyles of 200 years ago, the story of the monastery, and displays on the development of the violin for which Füssen was famous (explanations in German only, 11:00-16:00, closed Monday). Halfway between Füssen and the border (as you drive, or a woodsy walk from the town) is the Lechfall, a thunderous waterfall with a handy potty stop.

The train station is a few minutes' walk from the TI, the town center (a cobbled shopping mall), the youth hostel, and good rooms (listed at the end of this chapter).

Orientation

Tourist Information
The TI, 2 blocks past the train station, has a free room-finding service (look for *Kurverwaltung*, 8:00-12:00, 14:00-18:00, Saturday 10:00-12:00, Sunday 10:00-12:00, closed off-season Sundays, tel. 08362/7077 or 7078, fax 39181).

Trains
Füssen is well connected only to Munich (2-hour trip, almost hourly). The station rents bikes. Buses go twice an hour to Neuschwanstein and four times a day to Reutte. The Romantic Road bus tour leaves at 8:00 and arrives at 20:05 (bus stop: Hotel Hirsch, just past the TI at the Green and Yellow sign). Taxis from Füssen station to Reutte cost 35 DM. Füssen's laundromat, "Self serve Wäsche service," is next to the TI (Sebastianstrasse 3, tel. 4529).

Sights—Bavaria
(These are listed in driving order from Füssen.)
▲▲▲**Neuschwanstein and Hohenschwangau Castles (Königsschlösser)**—The fairy-tale castle, Neuschwanstein,

looks medieval, but it's only about as old as the Eiffel Tower. It was built to suit the whims of Bavaria's King Ludwig II and is a textbook example of the romanticism that was popular in 19th-century Europe.

Beat the crowds. See Neuschwanstein, Germany's most popular castle, early in the morning. The castle is open every morning at 8:30; by 11:00, it's packed. Rushed 25-minute English-language tours are less rushed early. They leave regularly, telling the sad story of Bavaria's "mad" king.

After the tour, climb up to Mary's Bridge to marvel at Ludwig's castle, just as Ludwig did. This bridge was quite an engineering accomplishment a hundred years ago. From the bridge, the frisky can hike even higher to the "Beware— Danger of Death" signs and an even more glorious castle view. For the most interesting (but 15-minute longer and extremely slippery when wet) descent, follow signs to the Pöllat Gorge.

The big yellow Hohenschwangau Castle nearby was Ludwig's boyhood home. It's more lived-in and historic and actually gives a better glimpse of Ludwig's life. (Each castle

Neuschwanstein

NOTE: MAP NOT TO SCALE
BORDER TO ALPSEE PARKING = 5 KM DRIVE
ALPSEE PARKING TO NEUSCH. = 20 MIN. WALK

costs 9 DM and is open daily 8:30-17:30, October-March
10:00-16:00, tel. 08362/81035. If not enough English-
speakers gather, you may have to do Hohenschwangau with
a German group. TI tel. 08362/8198-40)

The "village" at the foot of the castles was created
for and lives off the hungry, shopping tourists who come
in droves to Europe's "Disney" castle. The big yellow
Bräustüberl restaurant by the lakeside parking lot is cheapest,
with food that tastes that way. Next door is a little family-
run, open-daily souvenir/grocery store with the makings for
a skimpy picnic and a microwave fast-food machine. Picnic
in the lakeside park or in one of the old-fashioned rent-
by-the-hour rowboats. The bus stop, the post/telephone
office, and a helpful TI cluster around the main intersection.

It's a steep hike to the castle. (The best and closest
parking lot is the lakeside Schloss Parkplatz am Alpsee—all
lots cost 6 DM.) To reach the castle, you can take a 20-
minute uphill hike or take advantage of the buses (3.50 DM
up, 5 DM round-trip, dropping you at Mary's Bridge, a steep
10 minutes above the castle) or horse carriages (slower than
walking, stops 5 minutes short of the castle, 7 DM up, 3.50
DM down) that go constantly (watch your step). Your work
continues inside the castle as your tour takes you up and
down more than 300 stairs. Signposts and books often refer
to these castles in the German, "*Königsschlösser*."

To give your castle experience a romantic twist, hike or
bike over from Austria (trailhead is at Hotel Schluxenhof in
Pinswang). When the dirt road forks at the top of the hill, go
right (downhill), cross the Austrian/German border (marked
by a sign and deserted hut), and follow the paved road to the
castles. It's an hour's hike with bus connections back to
Füssen and Reutte or a great circular bike trip.

From Reutte, you can bus directly to the castle at
Neuschwanstein (11:25-12:00) and return (15:45-16:10).
Buses from the Füssen station to Neuschwanstein run hourly
(4.40 DM round-trip).

▲**Tegelberg Gondola**—Just north of Neuschwanstein,
you'll see hang gliders hovering like vultures. They jumped
from the top of the Tegelberg gondola. For 23 DM, you can
ride high above the castle to the 5,500-foot summit and back
down (last lift at 17:00, tel. 08362/81018). On a clear day,

you get great views of the Alps and Bavaria and the vicarious thrill of watching hang gliders and parasailers leap into airborne ecstasy. From there, it's a pleasant 2-hour hike down to Ludwig's castle.

▲▲**Wies Church**—Germany's greatest Rococo-style church, *Wieskirche* (the church in the meadow), is newly restored and looking as brilliant as the day it floated down from heaven. With flames of decoration, overripe but bright and bursting with beauty, this church is a divine droplet, a curly curlicue, the final flowering of the Baroque movement. The ceiling depicts the Last Judgment.

This is a pilgrimage church. In the early 1700s, a carving of Christ, too graphic to be accepted by that generation's church, was the focus of worship in a peasant's private chapel. Miraculously, it wept. And pilgrims came from all around. Bavaria's top Rococo architects, the Zimmerman brothers, were then commissioned to build this church, which features the amazing carving above its altar and still attracts countless pilgrims. Take a commune-with-nature-and-smell-the-farm detour back through the meadow to the car park.

Wieskirche (daily 8:00-20:00, admission for a donation) is 30 minutes north of Neuschwanstein. The northbound Romantic Road bus tour stops here for 15 minutes. Füssen-to-Wieskirche buses go twice a day. By car, head north, turn right at Steingaden, and follow the signs. If you can't visit Wies, other churches that came out of the same heavenly spray can are Oberammergau's church, Munich's Asam church, the Würzburg Residenz chapel, or the splendid Ettal Monastery (free and near Oberammergau).

If you're driving from Wies church to Oberammergau you'll cross the Echelsbacher Bridge, arching 250 feet over the Pöllat Gorge. Drivers should let their passengers walk across and meet them at the other side. Any kayakers? Notice the painting of the traditional village woodcarver (who used to walk from town to town with his art on his back) on the first big house on the Oberammergau side, a shop called Almdorf Ammertal. It has a huge selection of overpriced carvings and commission-hungry tour guides.

▲**Oberammergau**—The Shirley Temple of Bavarian villages and exploited to the hilt by the tourist trade, Oberammergau wears way too much makeup. It's worth a wander, only if you're passing through anyway. Browse through the woodcarvers' shops—small art galleries filled with very expensive whittled works—or the local Heimat (folk art) Museum. (TI tel. 08822/1021; off-season, closed Saturday afternoon and Sunday.)

Visit the church, a poor cousin of the one at Wies. This church looks richer than it is. Put your hand on the "marble" columns. If they warm up they're painted fakes. Wander through the graveyard. Ponder the deaths that two wars dealt Germany. Behind the church are the photos of three Schneller brothers, all killed within two years in World War II.

Still making good on a deal the townspeople made with God if they were spared devastation by the Black Plague 350 years ago, once each decade Oberammergau performs the Passion Play. The next show is in the year 2000 when 5,000 people a day for 100 summer days will attend Oberammergau's all-day dramatic story of Christ's cruci-fixion. For the rest of this millenium, you'll have to settle for browsing through the theater's exhibition hall (4 DM, 9:30-12:00 and 13:30-16:00, tel. 32278), seeing Nicodemus tool-ing around town in his VW, or reading the Book.

Gasthaus zum Stern (SB-45 DM, DB-90 DM; Dorfstrasse 33, 8103 Oberammergau, tel. 08822/867) is friendly, serves good food, and for this tourist town, is a fine value (closed Tuesday and November). Oberammergau's modern **youth hostel** (18 DM beds, open all year, tel. 08822/4114) is on the river a short walk from the center.

Driving into town from the north, cross the bridge, take the second right, follow "Polizei" signs, and park by the huge gray Passionsspielhaus. Leaving town, head out past the church and turn toward Ettal on road 23. You're 20 miles from Reutte via the scenic Plansee.

▲▲**Linderhof Castle**—This was Mad Ludwig's "home," his most intimate castle. It's small and comfortably exquisite, good enough for a minor god. Set in the woods, 15 minutes by car or regular bus from Oberammergau, surrounded by fountains and sculpted, Italian-style gardens, it's the only palace I've toured that actually had me feeling envious. Don't miss the grotto (8 DM, April-September 9:00-17:30, off-season 10:00-16:00, fountains often erupt on the hour,

English tours constantly, tel. 08822/3512). Plan for lots of crowds, lots of walking, and a 2-hour stop.

▲▲**Zugspitze**—The tallest point in Germany is a border crossing. Lifts from Austria and Germany go to the 10,000-foot summit of the Zugspitze. Straddle two great nations while enjoying an incredible view. There are restaurants, shops, and telescopes at the summit. The hour-long trip from Garmisch on the German side costs 60 DM (by direct lift or a combo cogwheel train/cable car ride, tel. 08821/7970). On the Austrian side, from the less crowded Talstation Obermoos, above the village of Erwald, the tram zips you to the top in ten minutes (385 AS round-trip, 8:40 to 16:40, tel. 05673/2309). The German ascent is easier for those without a car. But buses do connect the Erwald train station and the Austrian lift nearly twice an hour.

Reutte, Austria

Reutte (pronounced "ROY-teh," rolled "r"), population 5,000, is a relaxed town, far from the international tourist crowd but popular with Germans and Austrians for its climate. Doctors recommend its "grade 1" air. You won't find Reutte in any American guidebook. Its charms are subtle. It never was rich or important. Its castle is ruined, its buildings have paint-on "carvings," its churches are full, its men yodel for each other on birthdays, and lately its energy is spent soaking its Austrian and German guests in *gemütlichkeit*. Because most guests stay for a week, the town's attractions are more time-consuming than thrilling. If the weather's good, hike to the mysterious Ehrenberg ruins or ride the luge. For a slap-dancing bang, enjoy a Tirolean folk evening.

Orientation

Tourist Information

The helpful Reutte TI is a block in front of the train station (weekdays 8:30-12:00 and 13:00-17:00 or 18:00, Saturday 8:00-12:00, and mid-July to mid-August on Saturday and Sunday afternoons from 16:00-18:00; tel. 05672/2336, or direct from Germany, 0043-5672/2336). Go over your sightseeing plans, ask about a folk evening, pick up a city map, ask about discounts with the hotel guest cards. Don't ask about a

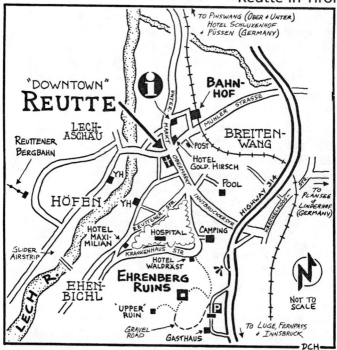

Reutte in Tirol

laundromat. Unless you can infiltrate the local campground, the town has none. (Accommodations are listed at the end of this chapter.)

Getting Around

While Reutte is a short bus ride from Füssen (departures at 8:35, 12:10, 13:50, 16:45; returning from Füssen to Reutte at 9:30, 12:50, 15:20 and 17:10), its train line goes to Garmisch (2/hr, 60 min ride). The station rents bikes cheaply. From Reutte, you can bus directly to the castle at Neuschwanstein (11:25-12:00) and return (15:45-16:10).

Sights—Reutte

▲▲**Ehrenberg Ruins**—The brooding ruins of Ehrenberg (two castle ruins atop two neighboring hills) are a mile outside of Reutte on the road to Lermoos and Innsbruck. These 13th-century rock piles, a great contrast to King Ludwig's "modern" castles, are a great opportunity to let your imagination off its leash. Hike up from the parking lot at the base of the hill; it's a 15-minute walk to the small (*kleine*) castle for a great view from your own private ruins. (Facing the hill from the parking lot, the steeper but more scenic trail is to the right, the easy gravelly road is to the left.) Imagine how proud Count Meinrad II of Tirol (who built the castle in 1290) would be to know that his castle repelled 16,000 Swedish soldiers in the defense of Catholicism in 1632.

You'll find more medieval mystique atop the taller neighboring hill in the big (*gross*) ruins. You can't see anything from below and almost nothing when you get there, but these bigger, more desolate and overgrown ruins are a little more romantic (and a lot harder to get to).

The easiest way down is via the small road from the gully between the two castles. The car park, with a café/guest house (offering a German language flyer about the castle), is just off the Lermoos/Reutte road. Reutte is a pleasant 60-minute walk away. The town museum and many Reutte hotels have sketches of the intact castle.

Folk Museum—Reutte's *Heimatmuseum* (10:00-12:00, 14:00-17:00, closed Monday; in the Green House on Untermarkt, around the corner from Hotel Goldener Hirsch) offers a quick look at the local folk culture and the story of the castle, but so do the walls and mantels of most of the hotels.

▲▲Tiroler Folk Evening—Ask in your hotel if there's a Tirolean folk evening scheduled. About two evenings a week in the summer, Reutte or a nearby town puts on an evening of yodeling, slap-dancing, and Tirolean frolic—usually worth the 70 AS and short drive. Off-season, you'll have to do your own yodeling.

Swimming—Plunge into Reutte's Olympic-sized swimming pool to cool off after your castle hikes (58 AS, 10:00-21:00, off-season 14:00-21:00, closed Monday).

The Reuttener Bergbahn (mountain lift) swoops you high above the tree line to a starting point for several hikes and an Alpine flower park with special paths leading you past countless local varieties.

Flying and Gliding—For a major thrill on a sunny day, drop by the tiny airport in Hofen across the river and fly. A small single-prop plane (three people for 30 minutes, 1,200

AS; 60 minutes for 1,900 AS) can buzz the Zugspitze and Ludwig's castles and give you a bird's-eye peek at Reutte's Ehrenberg ruins (that's about the cost of three lift tickets up the Zugspitze, and a lot easier). Or for something more angelic, how about *Segelfliegen*? For 280 AS, you get 30 minutes in a glider for two (you and the pilot). Just watching the tow rope launch the graceful glider like a giant slow motion rubber-band gun is thrilling (late May-October, 11:00-19:00, in good weather, tel. 05672/3207).

Sights—In Tirol, Near Reutte

▲▲*Sommerrodelbahn*, **the Luge**—Near Lermoos, on the Innsbruck-Lermoos-Reutte road, you'll find two rare and exciting luge courses. In the summer, these ski slopes are used as luge courses, or *Sommerrodelbahn*. To try one of Europe's great $5 thrills, take the lift up, grab a sled-like go-cart, and luge down. The concrete bobsled course banks on the corners, and even a novice can go very, very fast. Most are cautious on their first run and speed demons on their second. (Recently, a woman showed me her journal illustrated with her husband's dried 5-inch-long luge scab. He disobeyed the only essential rule of luging: keep both hands on your stick.) No one emerges from the course without a windblown hairdo and a smile-creased face. Both places charge a steep 70 AS per run, with five-trip or ten-trip discount cards; both are open weekends from late May and daily from about mid-June through September and into October if weather permits, from 9:00 or 10:00 until about 17:00. They're closed in wet weather, so call before going out. Unfortunately, you'll need a car to get to the luge.

The small and steep luge: The first course (100-meter drop over 800-meter course) is 6 kilometers beyond Reutte's castle ruins. Look for a chairlift on the right and exit on the tiny road at the yellow Riesenrutschbahn sign (call ahead, tel. 05674/5350, the local TI at 05674/5354 speaks more English).

The longest luge: The Biberwier Sommerrodelbahn, 15 minutes closer to Innsbruck, just past Lermoos in Biberwier (the first exit after a long tunnel), is a better luge, the longest in Austria—1,300 meters—but has a shorter season. (9:00-16:30, tel. 05673/2111, local TI tel. 05673/

2922.) A block or two down hill from this luge, behind
the Sport und Trachtenstüberl shop, is a wooden church-
dome with a striking Zugspitze backdrop. If you have sun-
shine and a camera, don't miss it.

▲**Fallershein**—A special treat for those who may have been
Kit Carson in a previous life, this extremely remote log-
cabin village is a 4,000-foot-high, flower-speckled world of
serene slopes and cowbells. Thunderstorms roll down the
valley like it's God's bowling alley, but the pint-sized church
on the high ground, blissfully simple in a land of baroque,
seems to promise that this huddle of houses will survive and
the river and breeze will just keep flowing. The couples
sitting on benches are mostly Austrian vacationers who've
rented cabins here. Many of them, appreciating the remote-
ness of Fallershein, are having affairs.

For a rugged chunk of local Alpine peace, spend a night
in the local **Matratzenlager Almwirtschaft Fallershein**,
run by friendly Kerle Erwin (80 AS per person with breakfast; open, weather permitting, May-November; 27 very
cheap beds in a very simple loft dorm, meager plumbing,
good inexpensive meals; 6671 Weissenbach 119a, b/Reutte;
tel. 05678/5142, rarely answered, and then not in English).
It's crowded only on weekends. Fallershein is at the end of a
miserable 2-kilometer fit-for-jeep-or-rental-car-only gravel
road that looks more closed than it is, near Namlos on the
Berwang road southwest of Reutte. To avoid cow damage, park
300 meters below the village at the tiny lot before the bridge.

Sleeping in Bavaria and Tirol
Austria's Tirol is easier and cheaper than touristy Bavaria.
The town of Reutte, just inside the Austrian border, is my
home base for the area. But if you're relying on public transportation, Füssen, with its quicker, easier connections, is
handier.

Sleep code: **S**=Single, **D**=Double/Twin, **T**=Triple,
Q=Quad, **B**=Bath/Shower, **WC**=Toilet, **CC**=Credit Card
(**V**isa, **M**astercard, **A**mex). Breakfast is included, showers
down the hall are free, nearly all speak at least a little
English. Prices listed are for one-night stays. Some places
give a discount for longer stays. Always ask.

Sleeping in Füssen, Germany
(1.6 DM = about $1, zip code: 87629, tel. code: 08362)

Füssen, 2 miles from Ludwig's castles, is a cobbled, cren–
elated, riverside oompah treat but very touristy. It has just
about as many rooms as tourists, though, and the TI has a
free room-finding service. All places I've listed here are an
easy walk from the train station and the town center. They
are used to travelers getting in after the Romantic Road bus
arrives (20:00) and will hold rooms for a telephone promise.

Hotels

Hotel Gasthaus zum Hechten offers all the modern conve-
niences in a traditional shell right under the Füssen castle in
the old-town pedestrian zone (D-90 DM, DB-100 DM-
110 DM; Ritterstrasse 6, tel. 7906, fax 39841). Adjacent this
gasthaus is "Infooday," a clever, modern self-service eatery
that sells its hot meals and salad bar by weight and offers lots
of English newspapers (10:30-18:30, closed Sunday, 7 DM/
filling salad).

    Gasthof Krone is a rare bit of pre-glitz Füssen also
in the pedestrian zone (dumpy halls and stairs but bright,
cheery, comfy rooms: S-50 DM, D-88 DM, T-132 DM,
10% less for 2-night stays, CC:MA; Schrannenplatz 17, tel.
7824, fax 37505, may renovate in '95).

    Bräustüberl (D-90 DM, T-135 DM; Rupprechtstrasse
5, a block from the station, tel. 7843, fax 38781, may renovate in '95) has clean and bright rooms in a musty old beer-
hall-type place.

Zimmer

Haus Peters (DB-70 DM, QB-120 DM; Augustenstrasse
5½, tel. 7171), Füssen's best value, is a comfy, smoke-free
home renting four rooms, 2 blocks from the station (toward
town, second left). Herr and Frau Peters are friendly, speak
English, and know what travelers like: a peaceful garden,
self-serve kitchen, and good prices. The funky old ornately
furnished **Pension Garni Elisabeth** (D-80 DM, DB-100,
showers-5 DM; Augustenstrasse 10, tel. 6275) in a garden
just across the street, exudes a chilling Addams-family friendliness. Floors creak and pianos are never played.

    Inexpensive farmhouse *Zimmer* abound in the Bavarian

countryside around Neuschwanstein and are a good value. Look for *Zimmer Frei* signs. The going rate is about 70 DM per double including breakfast; you'll see plenty of green "Vacancy" signs. For a *Zimmer* in a classic Bavarian home within walking distance of Mad Ludwig's place, try **Haus Magdalena** (SB-45 DM, D-70 DM, DB-81, extra bed-22 DM; free parking, Brumme Family; from the castle intersection, about 2 blocks down the road to Schwangau at Schwangauerstrasse 11, 8959 Schwangau, tel. 08362/81126).

Youth Hostel
The excellent Germanly run **Füssen youth hostel** (4-bed rooms, 18 DM for B&B, 8 DM for dinner, 6 DM for sheets, the Bavarian age limit is not enforced here, laundry facilities; Mariahilferstrasse 5, tel. 7754) is a 10-minute walk from town, backtracking from the train station. You might rent a bike at the station to get there quick and easy.

Sleeping in Reutte, Austria
(11 AS = about $1, zip code: 6600, tel. code: 05672)
For less crowds, easygoing locals with a contagious love of life, and a good dose of Austrian ambience, homebase in Reutte. (To call Reutte from Germany, dial 0043-5672 and the local number.)

Hotels
Reutte is popular with Austrians and Germans who come here year after year foɪ a one- or two-week vacation. The hotels are big and elegant, full of comfy carved furnishings and creative ways to spend so much time in one spot. They take great pride in their restaurants, and the owners send their children away to hotel management schools.

    Hotel Goldener Hirsch, a grand old hotel renovated to the hilt with a mod Tirolean Jugendstil flair, has sliding automatic doors, mini-bars, TV with cable in the room, and one lonely set of antlers. It's located right downtown (2 blocks from the station). For those without a car, this is the most convenient hotel (SB-490 AS, DB-820 AS, CC:VMA, a 3-minute walk from the station; 6600 Reutte-Tirol, tel. 2508 and ask for Helmut or Monika, fax 2508-100).

    Hotel Maximilian, up the river a mile or so in the village of Ehenbichl, is the best splurge. It includes the use of bicycles, ping-pong, a children's playroom, and the friendly service of the Koch family. Daughter Gabi speaks fine English. There always seems to be a special event here, and the Kochs host many Tirolean folk evenings (DB-840 AS, TB-1260 AS, cheaper for families, far from the train station in the next village but they may pick you up; A-6600 Ehenbichl-Reutte, tel. 2585, fax 2585-54).

Gasthof zum Schluxenhof gets the "remote old hotel in an idyllic setting" award (DB-700 AS, modern rustic elegance, A-6600 Pinswang-Reutte, between Reutte and Füssen in the village of Unterpinswang, tel. 05677/8903, fax 890323). **Gasthof Säuling**, also in Pinswang, is less idyllic (DB-600 AS, A-6600 Oberpinswang bei Reutte, tel. 05677/8698, fax 8153).

Gasthof-Pension Waldrast (550-650 AS per double; 6600 Ehenbichl, on Ehrenbergstrasse, a half-mile out of town toward Innsbruck, past the campground, just under the castle, tel. 05672/2443) separates a forest and a meadow and is warmly run by the Huter family. It has big rooms, like living rooms, many with a fine castle view, and it's a good coffee stop if you're hiking into town from the Ehrenberg ruins.

Zimmer

The tourist office has a list of over 50 private homes that rent out generally elegant rooms with facilities down the hall, a pleasant communal living room, and breakfast. Most charge 180 AS per person per night, don't like to rent to people staying less than three nights, and speak little if any English. Reservations are nearly impossible for a one- or two-night stay. But short stops are welcome if you just drop in and fill in available gaps. The TI can always find you a room when you arrive (free service).

The tiny village of Breitenwang is older and quieter than Reutte and has all the best central *Zimmer* (a 10-minute walk from the Reutte train station: at the post office roundabout, follow Plannseestrasse past the onion dome to the pointy straight dome, unmarked Kaiser Lothar strasse is the first right past this church). These four places are comfortable, quiet, and kid-friendly; accept one-nighters, have few stairs, speak some English, and are within 2 blocks of the

Breitenwang church steeple: **Maria Auer** (D-350 AS, minimum stay: 2 nights; Kaiser Lothar Strasse 25, tel. 29195), **Inge Hosp** (a more old-fashioned place with 360-AS doubles, a 190-AS single and antlers over the breakfast table; Kaiser Lothar Strasse 36, tel. 2401), across the street is her cousin **Walter Hosp** (D-350 AS; Kaiser Lothar Strasse 29, tel. 5377), and **Helene Haissl** (D-340 AS, 320 AS for a 2-night stay; Planseestrasse 63, tel. 41504).

Youth Hostels

Reutte has two excellent little youth hostels. If you've never hosteled and are curious, try one of these. They accept non-members of any age. The downtown hostel is clean, rarely full, and lacking in personality. It serves no meals but has a members' kitchen (80 AS per bed; a pleasant 10-minute walk from the town center, follow the Jugendherberge signs to the Kindergarten sign, 6600 Reutte, Prof. Dengelstrasse 20, Tirol, open mid-June to late August, tel. 71479).

The newly renovated **Jugendgastehaus Graben** (130-AS beds with breakfast; A-6600 Reutte-Höfen, Postfach 3, Graben 1; from downtown Reutte, cross the bridge and follow the road left along the river, about 2 miles from the station; tel. 2644, fax 5904) has 2-6 beds per room and includes breakfast, shower, and sheets. Frau Reyman, who keeps the place traditional, homey, clean, and friendly, serves a great dinner. No curfew, open all year, direct bus connection to Neuschwanstein Castle.

Eating in Reutte

Each of the hotels takes great pleasure in serving fine Austrian food at reasonable prices. Rather than go to a cheap restaurant, I'd order low on a hotel menu. For cheap food, the **Prima** self-serve cafeteria near the station (Mühler Strasse 20; Monday-Friday 8:00-18:30) and the **Metzgerei Storf Imbiss** (better but open only Monday-Friday 8:30-15:00), above the deli across from the Heimatmuseum on Untermarkt Street, are the best in town. For a late dinner in Reutte try **zum Mohren** on the main street (across from #31, tel. 2345).

LONDON

London, more than 600 square miles of urban jungle with 7 million struggling people, many of whom speak English, is a world in itself, a barrage on all the senses.

On my first visit, I felt very, very small. London is much more than its museums and famous landmarks. It's a living, breathing organism that manages to thrive.

London has changed dramatically in recent years, and many visitors are surprised to find how "un-English" it is. Whites are now actually a minority in major parts of a city that once symbolized white imperialism. Arabs have nearly bought out the area north of Hyde Park. Chinese take-outs now outnumber fish-and-chips shops (or "fee'n' chee" shops as some locals call them). Many hotels are run by people with foreign accents (who hire English chambermaids), while outlying suburbs are home to huge communities of Indians and Pakistanis. London is learning—sometimes fitfully—to live as a microcosm of its formerly vast empire.

With just a few days here, you'll get no more than a quick splash in this teeming human tidepool. But, with a quick orientation, you'll get a good sampling of its top sights, history, cultural entertainment, and ever-changing human face.

Blow through London on the open deck of a double-decker orientation tour bus, and take a pinch-me-I'm-in-Britain walk through downtown. Ogle the crown jewels at the Tower of London, hear the chimes of Big Ben, and see the Halls of Parliament in action. Hobnob with the tombstones in Westminster Abbey, duck WWII bombs in Churchill's underground Cabinet War Rooms, and brave the earth-shaking Imperial War Museum. Overfeed the pigeons at Trafalgar Square. Visit with Leonardo, Botticelli, and Rembrandt in the National Gallery. Whisper across the dome of St. Paul's Cathedral and rummage through our civilization's attic at the British Museum. Cruise down the Thames River. You'll enjoy some of Europe's best people-watching at Covent Gardens and the Buckingham Palace Changing of the Guard. Just sit in Victoria Station, at a major tube station, at Piccadilly Square, or on Trafalgar Square, and observe. Spend one evening at a theater and the others catching your breath.

Planning Your Time: Three Days in London

The sights of London alone could easily fill a trip to Britain. But on a three-week tour of Britain, I'd give it three busy days. If you're flying in, consider starting your trip in Bath and letting London be your British finale. Especially if you hope to enjoy a play or concert, a night or two of jet lag is bad news. Here's a suggested three-day schedule:

Day 1:

9:00   Tower of London (Beefeater tour, crown jewels).

12:00   Picnic on Thames, cruising from Tower to Westminster Bridge.

13:00   Big Ben, Halls of Parliament, Westminster Abbey, walk up Whitehall, visit the Cabinet War Rooms.

16:00   Trafalgar Square, National Gallery.

17:30   Visit National Tourist Information Centre near Piccadilly, planning ahead for your trip.

18:30   Dinner near Piccadilly. Take in a play?

Day 2:

9:00   Spend 30 minutes in a phone booth getting all essential elements of your trip nailed down. If you know where you'll be and when, call those B&Bs now!

10:00   Take the Round London bus tour. (Consider hopping off for the 11:30 Changing of the Guard at Buckingham Palace.)

12:30   Covent Gardens for lunch and people-watching.

14:00   Tour British Museum.

17:30   Visitor's Gallery in Houses of Parliament (if in session).

19:00   Take in a play, concert, or evening walking tour (if still awake).

Day 3:

9:00   Choose among these activities for the day: some serious shopping at Harrods or open-air markets, Museum of the Moving Image, Imperial War museum, Tate Gallery, cruise to Greenwich or Kew, tour St. Paul's Cathedral, Museum of London, a walking tour, or an early train to Bath.

18:15   Train to Bath.

19:30   Check into Bath B&B.

After considering nearly all of London's tourist sights, I have pruned them down to just the most important (or fun) for a first visit. You won't be able to see all of these, so don't try. You'll keep coming back to London. After 15 visits myself, I still enjoy a healthy list of excuses to return.

Orientation
(downtown tel. code: 0171, suburban: 0181)

To grasp London comfortably, see it as the old town without the modern, congested sprawl. Most of the visitors' London lies between the Tower of London and Hyde Park—about a 3-mile walk.

Tourist Information

London Tourist Information Centres are located at Heathrow Airport (daily 8:30-18:00, most convenient and least crowded), at Victoria Station (daily 8:00-18:00, shorter hours in winter), at Selfridges Department Store on Oxford Street (regular store hours). The handier National Tourist Info Centre (described below) covers London just about as well as the LTICs. Bring your itinerary and a checklist of questions. Buy a ticket to a play, save a pound by buying your orientation bus tour ticket here, and pick up these publications: *London Planner*, walking tour brochures, theater guide, *Quick Guide to London*, a Britain map (£1), and a London map (£1). The £1 London map is as good as the £4 maps sold in newsstands and well worth while (free from BTA in the U.S.A: 551 5th Ave., #701, New York, NY 10176). Smelling a new source of profit, London TIs are pushing a 50p-per-minute telephone information service. Avoid it.

    The National Tourist Information Centre is energetic and impressive (9:00-18:30, Saturday and Sunday 10:00-16:00, a block downhill from Piccadilly Circus at 12 Regent St.). Check out the well-equipped London/England desk, Wales desk (tel. 409-0969), and Ireland desk (tel. 839-8416). At the center's extensive book shop, gather whatever books, maps, and information you'll need for your entire trip. Consider getting the *Michelin Green Guide to Britain* (£7.50). Train travelers can pick up *Let's Go: Britain and Ireland* (£15, 50% over U.S. price) and hostelers may want the *Youth Hostel Association 1995 Guide* (£6). To cover the highlights of Britain, consider the following maps: Cotswolds Wyedean Official Tourist Map (£2.60, Tintern to Coventry); the Lake District Touring Map (£3, entire region or just the NW corner, Ordnance Survey); the Wales Tourist Map (£1.50); and the Leisure Touring Map of Scotland (£3.25). Drivers will need a Britain Road Atlas (£7, AA). Stock up. You're your own guide. Be a good one.

The center has a British Rail information desk and an American Express Bank (no change fee, decent rates, Sundays, too). The Scottish Tourist Centre is a block away (19 Cockspur St., tel. 930-8661).

Trains and Buses

London, a major transportation hub in Britain, has a different train station for each region. For schedule information, call the appropriate station. King's Cross covers northeast England and Scotland (tel. 278-2477). Paddington covers west and southwest England and south Wales (tel. 262-6767). For the others, call 928-5100. Buses are considerably cheaper than trains. Give the National Express bus company a call (tel. 730-0202).

Getting Around London

London's taxis, buses, and subway system make a private car unnecessary. In a city this size, you must get comfortable with its public transportation. Don't be timid.

By Taxi: Big, black, carefully regulated cabs are everywhere. I never met a crabby cabbie in London. They love to talk and know every nook and cranny in town. Rides start at £1 and cost about £1 per tube stop. Often legitimate charges are added on, but for a short ride, three people in a cab travel at tube prices. If a cab's top light is on, just wave it down. If that doesn't work, ask for directions to a nearby taxi stand. Telephoning is unnecessary; taxis are everywhere. Stick with the metered cabs.

By Bus: London's extensive bus system is easy to follow if you have a map listing the routes. Get a free map from a TI or tube station. Signs at stops list routes clearly. Conductors are terse but helpful. Ask to be reminded when it's your stop. Just hop on, tell the driver where you're going, pay what he says, grab a ticket, take a seat, and relax. (Go upstairs for the best view.) Buses and taxis are miserable during rush hours, 8:00-10:00 and 16:00-19:00. Rides start at 90p. Get in the habit of hopping buses for quick little straight shots if you have a transit pass.

By Tube: London's subway is one of this planet's great people-movers. Every city map includes a tube map. Rip one out and keep it in your shirt pocket. Navigate by color-coded lines and north (always up on London maps), south, east, or west. (In fact, think in terms of N, S, E, and W in your general London navigation.) Buy your ticket at the window or from coin-op machines to avoid the line (practice a few fares on the punchboard to see how the system works), then descend to the platform level. You'll need your ticket to leave the system. Many tracks are shared by several lines, and electronic signboards announce which train is next. Each train has its final destination or line name above its windshield. Read the system notices clearly posted on the platforms; they explain the tube's latest flood, construction, or bomb scare. Ask questions of locals and watch your wallet. Bring something to do to pass the waits productively, especially on the notoriously tardy Circle Line. When leaving the tube, save time by choosing the best street exit (look at the maps on the walls). "Tubing" is the fastest long-distance transport in town. Any ride in the Central Zone (on or within the Circle Line, including virtually all my recommended sights and hotels) costs 90p. Remember, "subway" means pedestrian underpass in "English." For tube and bus information, call 222-1234.

London Tube and Bus Passes: There are three handy tube/bus passes to consider: The "Travel Card," covering Zones 1 and 2, gives you unlimited travel for a day starting after 9:30 for £2.80. The "LT Card" offers the same benefits, without the "off peak" restriction, for £4. The "7 Day Travel Card" costs £10.50, covers Zone 1, and requires a passport-type photo (cut one out of any old snapshot and bring it from home). All passes are purchased as easily as a normal ticket from any station, and cover both tube and bus transportation. If you figure you'll take three rides, get the day pass.

Helpful Hints
Theft Alert: Be on guard here more than anywhere in Britain for pickpockets and thieves, particularly on public

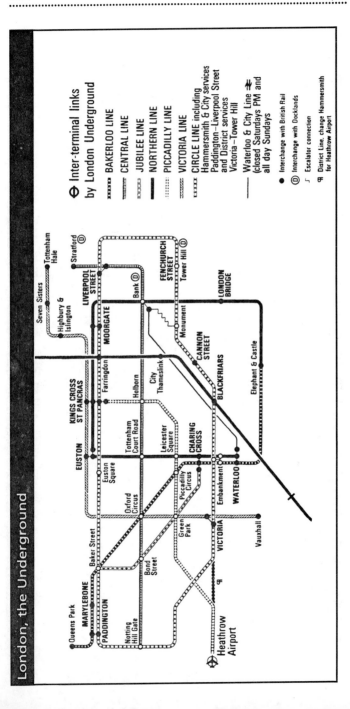

London, the Underground

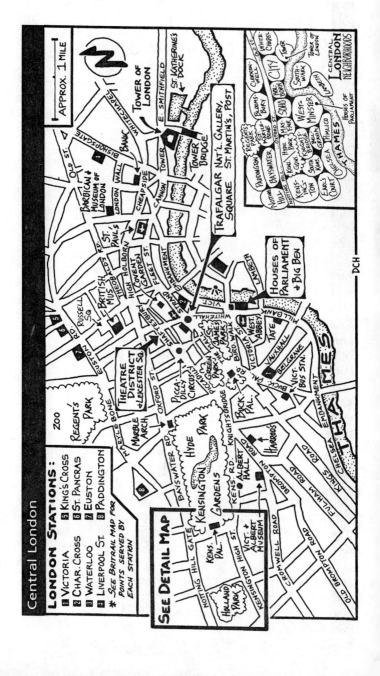

Central London

LONDON STATIONS:

1 VICTORIA   5 KING'S CROSS
2 CHAR. CROSS 6 ST. PANCRAS
3 WATERLOO   7 EUSTON
4 LIVERPOOL ST. 8 PADDINGTON

* SEE BRITRAIL MAP FOR
POINTS SERVED BY
EACH STATION

ZOO

Regent's Park

MARYLEBONE

MARBLE ARCH

THEATRE DISTRICT + LEICESTER SQ.

OXFORD ST.

PICCADILLY

Green Park   St. James's Park

BUCK. PAL.

Hyde Park

BAYSWATER RD.

KENSINGTON GARDENS

Kens. Pal.

NOTTING HILL GATE   KENSINGTON HIGH ST.

HOLLAND PARK

KNIGHTSBRIDGE

Albert Hall

KENS. RD.

VICT. + ALBERT MUSEUM

HARRODS

BROMPTON RD.

CROMWELL ROAD

OLD BROMPTON ROAD

FULHAM ROAD

KING'S ROAD

CHELSEA EMBANKMENT

SEE DETAIL MAP

APPROX. 1 MILE

N

Tower of London

St. Katherine's Dock

E. SMITHFIELD

OLD ST.

BISHOPSGATE

WHITECHAPEL

BARBICAN + MUSEUM OF LONDON

LONDON WALL

BANK

CHEAPSIDE

CANNON TOWER

TOWER BRIDGE

St. Paul's

LUDGATE RD.

FLEET ST.

COVENT GARDEN

HIGH HOLBORN

THEOBALD'S RD.

STRAND

BRITISH MUS.

RUSSELL SQ.

EUSTON RD.

5   6

7

STAFFORD RD.

EMBANKMENT

VICT.

WHITEHALL

TRAFALGAR NAT'L GALLERY, ST. MARTIN'S, POST SQUARE

HOUSES OF PARLIAMENT + BIG BEN

LAMBETH

MILLBANK

TATE

WEST. ABBEY

VICTORIA ST.

BIRD WALK

VAUXHALL

BELGRAVE

VICT. BUS STN.

THAMES

DCH

CENTRAL LONDON NEIGHBORHOODS

PADDINGTON   BAYSWATER

NOTTING HILL   KENSINGTON   KNIGHTSBRIDGE   SOUTH KEN.

EARL'S COURT   CHELSEA   PIMLICO

REGENT'S PARK   MARYLEBONE   MAYFAIR   HYDE PARK   GREEN PARK   ST. JAMES PARK

BLOOMSBURY   SOHO   HOL. BORN   COVENT GARDEN   STRAND

CLERKEN- WELL   CITY   SOUTH- WARK

WHITE- CHAPEL   TOWER   TOWER OF LONDON

WEST- MINSTER   LAMBETH   Houses of Parliament

THAMES

transportation and in places crowded with tourists. Tourists, considered naive and rich, are targeted.

Telephones: In London, dial 999 for emergency help and 142 for directory assistance (both calls are free). The area code for any downtown London phone number is 0171, for suburban London, 0181. Beware of the many area-code-0839 toll numbers. At a TI or post office, buy a handy phone card.

What's Up: For the best listing of what's happening (plays, movies, restaurants, concerts, exhibitions, protests, walking tours, and children's activities), pick up a current copy of *What's On* or *Time Out* (40p more, more theater reviews, more hip) at any newsstand. Call 222-8070 for a taped run-down on "Children's London" (Monday-Friday 16:00-18:00).

Sunday Activities: Few London sights are open on Sunday before 14:00. (Major museums are usually open Sunday afternoons.) Some Sunday morning activities: a church service at St. Paul's, Westminster Abbey, or the Tower of London chapel; Original London Sightseeing Tour by bus; a Thames cruise; Cabinet War Rooms; Imperial War Museum; Museum of the Moving Image; Kew Gardens and Palace; Madame Tussaud's; open-air markets at Petticoat Lane and Campden Market; the Victoria and Albert Museum. Speakers' Corner in Hyde Park gets going at noon.

Sights—London

Hello London Walk—Catch a bus to Westminster Bridge (#12 from Notting Hill Gate or #211 from Victoria Station). Sit on the top deck and relax until the first stop after the bridge. Walk downstream along the Jubilee Promenade for a capital view, then for that "Wow, I'm really in London!" feeling, cross the bridge for a close-up view of the Houses of Parliament and Big Ben (floodlit at night). If you ride the tube (and not the bus), the Westminster stop is right at Big Ben. Walk halfway across the bridge for the great view.

To thrill your loved ones (or bug the envious), call home from a pay phone near Big Ben at about 3 minutes before the hour. (You'll find a phone on Great George Street, across from Parliament Square.) As Big Ben chimes, stick the receiver outside the booth and prove you're in London: Ding dong ding dong . . . dong ding ding dong.

Then cross Whitehall to see the Churchill Statue in the park. (He's electrified to avoid the pigeon problem that stains so many other great statues.) Walk up Whitehall toward Trafalgar Square. Stop at the barricaded and guarded little Downing Street to see #10, home of the British prime minister. Break the bobby's boredom—ask him a question. Just before Trafalgar Square, drop into the Clarence Pub for a reasonable meal or pint of whatever you fancy (cheaper cafeterias and eateries are on the same block or under St. Martin's church on Trafalgar). From Trafalgar, walk to thriving Leicester Square and continue to Piccadilly.

For seediness, walk through Soho (north of Shaftesbury Avenue) up to Oxford Street. From Piccadilly or Oxford Circus you can taxi, bus, or tube home.

▲▲**Original London Sightseeing Tour**—This 90-minute, once-over-lightly, double-decker bus tour drives by all the most famous sights. It comes with a great commentary and provides a stressless way to get your bearings and at least see the biggies. Since you can also "hop on and hop off" at any of the 23 stops and catch a later bus, it's an inexpensive form of transport as well as an informative tour (£10, £9 if you pre-purchase at tourist information offices, daily departures from 9:30 until early evening from Marble Arch, Piccadilly Circus, and Victoria Street, 1 block in front of Victoria Station, reservations unnecessary, ticket good for all the next day if purchased after 14:00, tel. 828-7395.) While every bus leaving from Victoria has a live guide, only every other bus from the other points does. A live guide is worth waiting for. Bring a sweater and extra film. Pick up the wonderful free city map as you board. Note: if you pick up the bus at Victoria (no later than 10:00), you can hop off near the end of the 90-minute loop, a 5-minute walk from Buckingham Palace to catch the changing of the guard. There are several "original" copy-cat tours.

▲▲**Walking Tours**—Several times every day, top-notch local guides lead small groups through specific slices of London's past. While the TI and many hotels have the various flyers, only *Time Out* and *What's On* list all scheduled walks, enabling you to choose according to your schedule and interests. Simply show up at the announced location, pay £4, and enjoy two hours of Dickens, the Plague, Shakespeare,

Legal London, the Beatles, Jack the Ripper, or whatever is on the agenda. Evenings feature organized pub crawls and ghost walks. "London Walks" is the dominant company (for recorded schedule of today's walks, tel. 624-3978).

▲▲**Westminster Abbey** is a crowded collection of England's most famous tombs. Like a stony refugee camp waiting outside St. Peter's gates, this English hall of fame is historic, thought-provoking but a bit over-rated (£4, Monday-Friday 9:00-16:45, Saturday 9:00-14:45 and 15:45-17:45, tel. 222-5152, "super tours" £7, 6/day, 90 min, tel. 222-7110 to book and get times).

▲▲**The Houses of Parliament** (Commons and Lords) are too tempting to terrorists to be opened wide to tourists. But if Parliament is in session, you can view debates in either house at times when most of the building is closed. A light atop Big Ben or a flag flying from the highest tower indicates that Parliament is sitting. (Monday-Thursday 17:15-22:00—long waits until 18:00, Friday 9:30-15:00; use St. Stephens entrance, tel. 219-4272, cloakroom.) The House of Lords has more pageantry, shorter lines, shorter hours, and less-interesting debates (tel. 219-3107). Notice the magnificent hammer-beamed Westminster Hall on the left as you go through security. For the classic view, walk halfway over Westminster Bridge. You won't actually see Big Ben, the 13-ton bell inside the neo-Gothic tower, but you'll hear him. Remember, these old-looking buildings are neo-Gothic—just 19th century, reflecting the Victorian move away from Neoclassicism to a more Christian, medieval style.

▲**Whitehall**, the center-of-government boulevard, runs from Big Ben to Trafalgar past lots of important but mostly boring buildings. Stop by the barricade at #10 Downing Street (the British "White House") and the Horse Guards farther up the street (10:00 -16:00, 11:00 inspection, 16:00 colorful dismounting ceremony, the rest of the day is terrible for camcorders).

▲▲**Cabinet War Rooms**—This is a fascinating walk through the underground headquarters of the British government's fight against the Nazis in the darkest days of the Battle for Britain. Churchill's room, the map room, and so on, are still just as they were in 1945 (£4, daily 10:00-18:00, follow signs, on King Charles St., just off Whitehall).

▲**The Banqueting Hall**, England's first Renaissance building (designed by Inigo Jones in 1625) and one of the few London landmarks to survive the 1666 fire, is notable for its Rubens ceiling which, at Charles I's request, drove home the doctrine of the legitimacy of the divine right of kings. In 1649, divine right ignored, Charles I was beheaded on the balcony of this building by a Cromwellian parliament. Admission includes a fine 20-minute audiovisual history, an interesting-only-to-history-buffs 35-minute tape-recorded tour, and a look at a fancy banqueting hall (£3, Monday-Saturday 10:00-17:00, aristocratic WC, immediately across Whitehall from the Horse Guards, tel. 930-4179).

▲▲**Trafalgar Square**—London's central square is a thrilling place to just hang out. There's Lord Nelson's towering column surrounded by giant lions (part of the memorial is made from the melted-down cannons of his victims at Trafalgar), hordes of people, and even more pigeons. (When bombed, resist the impulse to wipe immediately—it'll smear. Wait for it to dry and flake off gently.) The square is the climax of most marches and demonstrations.

▲▲**National Gallery**—Newly renovated, displaying Britain's top collection of European paintings from 1300 to 1900—works by Leonardo, Botticelli, Velazquez, Rembrandt, Turner, van Gogh, and the Impressionists—this is one of Europe's classiest galleries. Don't miss the "Micro Gallery," a computer room even your dad could have fun in. You can study any artist, style, or topic in the museum and even print out a tailor-made tour map. (Free, Monday-Saturday 10:00-18:00, Sunday 14:00-18:00, on Trafalgar Square. Tube: Charing Cross or Leicester Square, free 1-hour tours weekdays at 11:30 and 14:30, Saturdays at 14:00 and 15:30, tel. 839-3321). **The National Portrait Gallery**, just around the corner, is as exciting as somebody else's yearbook (free, same hours, tel. 306-0055).

▲▲**Piccadilly**—London's touristy "Town Square" is surrounded by fascinating streets and swimming with youth on the rampage. Nearby Shaftesbury Avenue and Leicester Square teem with fun-seekers, theaters, Chinese restaurants, and street singers. The shiny new Trocadero Center (between Coventry and Shaftesbury, just off Piccadilly) has the Guinness World Records Exhibit. Next door, the new

Rock Circus offers a very commercial but serious history of rock music with Madame Tussaud wax stars. It's an entertaining hour under radio earphones for rock 'n' roll romantics (£7, plenty of photo ops, 11:00-22:00).

Soho, to the north of Piccadilly, isn't as sleazy as it used to be, but it's still worth a gawk. This is London's red-light district where "friendly models" wait in tiny rooms up dreary stairways and scantily-clad con artists sell strip shows. Anyone who goes into any one of these shows will be ripped off. Every time. Even a £3 show comes with a £100 cover or minimum (as it's printed on the drink menu). If you object the security man will be called in. The door has no handle until you pay.

▲**Covent Gardens** is a boutique-ish people-watcher's delight with cigarette-eaters, Punch 'n' Judy acts, food that's good for you (but not your wallet), trendy crafts, whiffs of pot, and two-tone (neither natural) hair. For the best lunch deals, walk a block or two away from the eye of this touristic tornado. It's hard to go wrong in a little tea-and-sandwich deli.

▲▲▲**British Museum**—The greatest chronicle of our civilization anywhere, visiting this immense museum is like hiking through Encyclopedia Britannica National Park. After an overview ramble, cover just two or three sections of your choice more thoroughly. The Egyptian, Mesopotamian, Greek (Parthenon), and Manuscripts (Magna Carta, Bibles, Beethoven, and the Beatles) sections are a few of my favorites. (Free, Monday-Saturday 10:00-17:00, Sunday 14:30-18:00, least crowded weekday mornings, tube: Tottenham Court Road, tel. 636-1555.)

▲**Buckingham Palace**—In order to pay for the restoration of fire-damaged Windsor Palace, the royal family is opening their lavish home to the public for the next five summers (£8; August and September only; daily 9:30-17:30; limited to 8,000 a day; come early to get an appointed visit time; tel. 930-5526; if the Queen's not home, leave a message). If the flag is flying, the Queen is home.

▲**Changing of the Guard at Buckingham Palace**—Overrated but almost required. The changing of the guard (most days in summer at 11:30, every other day September-March, no band when wet) is a mob scene. Join the mob at the back side of the palace (the front faces a huge and very private park). The pageantry and parading are colorful and even stirring, but the actual changing of the guard is a non-event. It is interesting to see nearly every tourist in London gathered in one place at the same time. Hop into a big black taxi and say, "To Buckingham Palace, please." For all the color with none of the crowds, see the Inspection of the Guard Ceremony at 11:00 in front of the Wellington Barracks, east of the Palace on Birdcage Walk. Afterwards, stroll through nearby St. James Park.

▲**Hyde Park**—London's "Central Park" has more than 600 acres of lush greenery, a huge man-made lake, a royal palace, and the ornate neo-Gothic Albert Memorial across from the Royal Albert Hall. On Sunday early afternoons, check out Speaker's Corner (tube: Marble Arch). This is soapbox oratory at its best. "The grass roots of democracy" actually is a holdover from when the gallows stood here and the criminal was allowed to say just about anything he wanted to before he swung. I dare you to raise your voice and gather a crowd—it's easy to do.

▲▲**The City of London**—When Londoners say "the City," they mean the 1-square-mile business, banking, and journalism center that 2,000 years ago was Roman Londinium. The outline of the Roman city walls can still be seen in the arc of roads from Blackfriars Bridge to Tower Bridge. Within the City are 24 churches designed by Christopher Wren. It's a fascinating district to wander, but since nobody actually lives there, avoid Saturday and Sunday when it's quiet and empty. Also worth a look is the **Central Criminal Courts**, known as "Old Bailey." An hour in the visitors' gallery is always interesting (at Old Bailey and New-gate St.; Monday-Friday 10:00 -13:00 and 14:00-16:00; quiet in August; tel. 248-3277; no cameras, bags, or cloakroom).

▲▲**St. Paul's Cathedral**—Wren's most famous church is the great St. Paul's, its elaborate interior capped by a 365-foot dome. St. Paul's was Britain's World War II symbol of resistance, as Nazi bombs failed to blow it up. (There's a memorial chapel to the heroic firefighters who kept watch over it with hoses cocked.) The crypt (free with admission) is a world of historic bones and memorials, including Admiral Nelson's tomb. It also has interesting Cathedral models and a worthwhile 15-minute audiovisual story of the church (constant, free). This was the wedding church of Prince Charles and Lady Di. Climb the dome for a great city view and some fun in the whispering gallery. Talk discreetly into the wall and your partner on the far side can hear you. (£3 entry, free on Sunday but restricted viewing due to services, open daily 9:30-16:30, £2.50 to climb the dome, allow an hour to go up and down—good exercise, 90-minute £3 cathedral and crypt tours at 11:00, 11:30, 13:30 and 14:00, tube: St. Paul's, tel. 248-2705.) The **Sir Christopher Wren Pub** (not restaurant) serves good, inexpensive lunches in fun surroundings, just north of the church on Paternoster Square, 11:30-15:00, Monday-Friday.

▲**Museum of London** offers a guided walk through London history—from pre-Roman times to the Blitz (£3, free after 16:30, 10:00-18:00, Sunday 12:00-18:00, closed Monday, tube: Barbican or St. Paul's, tel. 600-3699). This regular stop for the local schoolkids gives the best overview of London history in town.

▲▲▲**Tower of London**—You'll find more bloody history per square inch here than anywhere in Britain. Don't miss the entertaining 50-minute Beefeater tour (free, leaving regularly from inside the gate, last one usually at 15:30) of this historic fortress, palace, prison, and host to more than 3 million visitors a year. Britain's best armory and most lovely Norman chapel are in the White Tower. The crown jewels are the best on earth—and consequently have long midday lines for viewing in July and August. To avoid the crowds, arrive at 9:00 and go straight to the jewels, doing the tour and tower later. (£8, tower hours: Monday-Saturday 9:00-18:30, last entry 17:00, Sunday 10:00-18:30. The long, but fast-moving, line is worst on Sundays. Tube: Tower Hill, tel. 709-0765.) Visitors are welcome on the grounds to worship in the Royal Chapel on Sunday (9:15 communion, 11:00 service with fine choral music, free).

Sights Next to the Tower—The best remaining bit of London's **Roman Wall** is just north of the tower (at the Tower Hill tube station). The **Tower Hill Pageant,** a 15-minute high-tech historical amusement ride takes you through twenty centuries of London history, followed by a small but fine exhibition of Roman and Saxon artifacts

uncovered during the recent riverside development. It's
worthwhile for rich kids with time to kill (£5.50, daily
9:30-17:30, until 16:30 off-season, across the street from
the Tower turnstile, tel. 709-0081). Freshly painted and
restored, **Tower Bridge** has an 1894–1994 history exhibit
(£5, good view, poor value, daily 10:00-18:30, tel. 403-3761).
St. Katherine Yacht Harbor, chic and newly renovated, just
east of the Tower Bridge, has mod shops and the classic old
Dickens Inn, fun for a drink or pub lunch.

▲▲**Cruise the Thames**—Boat tours with an entertaining
commentary sail regularly between Westminster Bridge and
the Tower (£3.50, round-trip £5, 10:20-17:00, 30 minutes,
3 tours hourly, tel. 930-8589). Leaving from Westminster
pier, similar boats also go to Greenwich (£5.60 round-trip,
2 hourly) and Kew Gardens (£7 round-trip, 3/day, 90 min
round-trip, tel. 930-2062).

▲▲**Greenwich**—Salty sightseers should make time for
England's maritime capital, Greenwich. You can crawl
through the *Cutty Sark* (clipper-ship queen of the seas in her
day, £3.50), marvel at the little *Gipsy Moth IV* (the 53-foot
sailboat Sir Francis Chichester used for his solo voyage
around the world in 1967), straddle the zero meridian and
set your wristwatch to Greenwich mean time at the Old
Royal Observatory, and relive four centuries of Britannia-
rules-the-waves history by visiting the National Maritime
Museum (£4, 10:00-18:00, Sundays 14:00-18:00, off-season
until 17:00, tel. 0181/858-4422). Getting there is either a
snap (tube to Island Gardens in Zone 2, free with tube pass,
then walk under pedestrian Thames tunnel) or a joy (cruise
down the Thames from central London).

▲▲**Tate Gallery**—One of Europe's great houses of art, the
Tate specializes in British painting (14th century through
contemporary), pre-Raphaelites, Impressionism, and modern
art (Matisse, van Gogh, Monet, Picasso). Learn about the
mystical watercolorist Blake and the romantic nature-
worship art of Turner (free, Monday-Saturday 10:00-18:00,
Sunday 14:00-18:00, tube: Pimlico, excellent free tours daily,
call for schedule, tel. 887-8000).

▲**Victoria and Albert Museum**—A gangly but surprisingly
interesting collection of costumes, armor, furniture, decorative arts, and much more from Asia, Islam, and mostly the

West. Walk through centuries of aristocratic living rooms and follow the evolution of fashion in England (through 40 fascinating and well-described display cases) from 1600 to today (£5 donation politely requested but not required, daily 10:00-18:00, Monday 12:00-18:00, tube: So. Kensington, pleasant garden cafe, tel. 938-8500.)

▲▲**Imperial War Museum**—This impressive museum covers the wars of this century from heavy weaponry to love notes and Varga Girls to Monty's Africa campaign tank to Schwartzkopf's Desert Storm uniform. You can trace the development of the machine gun, watch footage of the first tank battles, hold your breath through the gruesome WWI trench experience, and buy WWII-era toys in the fun museum shop. Rather than glorify war, the museum does its best to shine a light on the powerful human side of one of mankind's most persistent traits. (£3.70, daily 10:00-18:00, free after 16:30, 90 minutes is enough time for most visitors, tube: Lambeth North, tel. 416-5000.)

▲▲**Museum of the Moving Image**—This high-tech, interactive, hands-on museum traces the story of moving images from a caveman's flickering fire to modern TV. There's great footage of the earliest movies and TV shows. Turn-of-the-century-clad staff speak as if silent films are the latest marvel. You can make your own animated cartoon. Don't miss the speedy 50-year montage of magic MGM moments. (£5.50, daily 10:00-18:00, tube: Embankment, then walk across the Thames pedestrian bridge.)

Honorable Mention—The Thames Barrier, the world's largest movable flood barrier, welcomes visitors with an informative and entertaining exhibition (by tube or boat, £2.50, daily 10:00-17:00, tel. 0181/854-1373). At the **Geffrye Decorative Arts Museum** you can walk through British front rooms from 1600 to 1960 (tel. 739-9893). Architects love the quirky **Sir John Soane's Museum** (free). For a fine park and a palatial greenhouse jungle to swing through, take the tube or the boat to **Kew Gardens** (£4, daily 9:30-18:30, Sunday until 20:00, tel. 0181/940-1171).

Day-Trips—You could fill a book with the many easy and exciting day-trips from London (*Daytrips in Britain by Rail, Bus or Car from London and Edinburgh* by Earl Steinbicker, Hastings House). Several tour companies take London-based travelers out and back every day (call Evan Evans at 930-2377 or National Express at 730-0202 for ideas). Evan Evans has three tours which can be used by those without a car as a "free" way to get to Bath or Stow-on-the-Wold (saving you, for instance, the £27 London-Bath train ticket). Tours leave from behind Victoria Station at 9:00 (with your bag stowed under the bus), include a full day of sightseeing with £5 to £10 worth of admissions, and leave you in Bath or Stow before returning to London (£27 Stonehenge and Bath, £42 Salisbury, Stonehenge, Bath, and £39 Oxford, Blenheim, Burford, Stow). The British rail system uses London as a hub and normally offers round-trip fares (after 9:30) that cost the same as one-way fares (e.g., Cambridge, £13.70 normal fare, is £12.30 "cheap day return."). See BritRail's handy "Day Trips from London" booklet. But given the high cost of big-city living and the charm of small-town England, I wouldn't do much day-tripping.

Shopping in London

▲**Harrods**—One of the few stores in the world that manages to be both big and classy, Harrods is filled with wonderful displays, elegant high teas, and fingernail-ripping riots during its July sales. Harrods has everything from elephants to toothbrushes. Need some peanut butter? The food halls are sights to savor (with reasonable cafeterias, tel. 730-1234). For royal window-shopping, cruise nearby King's Road in Chelsea. Most stores close around 18:00, but stay open until 20:00 on Thursdays.

Street Markets—If you like garage sales and people-watching, hit a London street market. The tourist office has a complete, up-to-date list. Some of the best are: **Berwick Street** (Monday-Saturday 9:00-17:00, produce, tube: Piccadilly), **Jubilee Market** (daily 9:00-17:00, antiques and bric-a-brac on Monday, general miscellany Tuesday-Friday, crafts Saturday-Sunday, tube: Covent Garden), **Kensington Market** (Monday-Saturday 10:00-18:00, a collection of shops with modern and far-out clothing, tube: High Street Kensington), **Petticoat Lane** (Sunday 9:00-13:30, the largest, specializing in general junk, on Middlesex St., tube: Liverpool St.), **Portobello Road** (Saturday 6:00-17:00, flea market, near recommended B&Bs, tube: Notting Hill Gate),

Camden Market (Saturday and Sunday 9:00-17:00; a big, trendy flea market; tube: Camden Town), and **Camden Passage** (Wednesday, Thursday, and Saturday 8:00-15:00, offers a pleasant stroll through lots of expensive antiques on Islington High St., tube: Angel). Warning: street markets attract two kinds of people—tourists and pickpockets.
Famous Auction?—London's famous auctioneers welcome the curious public. For schedules (most weekdays, closed mid-summer), telephone Sotheby's (493-8080, tube: Oxford Circus) or Christie's (839-9060, tube: Green Park).

Entertainment and Theater in London
London bubbles with top-notch entertainment seven nights a week. Everything's listed in the monthly *Time Out* or *What's On* magazines, available at most newsstands. You'll choose from classical, jazz, rock, and far-out music, Gilbert and Sullivan, dance, comedy, Bahai meetings, poetry readings, spectator sports, film, and theater.

London's theater rivals Broadway's in quality and beats it in price. Choose from the Royal Shakespeare Company, top musicals, comedy, thrillers, sex farces, and more. Performances are nightly except Sunday, usually with one matinee a week. Matinees (listed in a box in *What's On*) are cheaper and rarely sold out. Tickets range from about £8 to £25.

Most theaters, marked on tourist maps, are in the Piccadilly-Trafalgar area. Box offices, hotels, and TIs have a handy "Theater Guide" brochure listing everything in town.

The best and cheapest way to book a ticket is simply to call the theater box office directly, ask about seats and dates available, and book by credit card. You can call from the U.S.A. as easily as from England (photocopy your hometown library's London newspaper theater section). Pick up your ticket 15 minutes before the show.

Getting a ticket through a ticket agency (at most tourist offices or scattered throughout London) is quick and easy, but prices are inflated by a standard 20 to 25 percent booking fee. Ticket agencies are scalpers with an address. Agencies are worthwhile only if a show you've got to see is sold out at the box office. They scarf up hot tickets, planning to make a killing after the show is otherwise sold out. U.S.A.

booking agencies get their tickets from another agency, adding even more to your expense by involving yet another middleman.

Cheap theater tricks: Most theaters offer cheap returned tickets, standing room, matinee, and senior or student stand-by deals. Picking up a late return can get you a great seat at a cheap-seat price. Standing room costs only a few pounds. If a show is "sold out," there's usually a way to get a seat. Call and ask how. The famous "half-price booth" in Leicester (pronounced "Lester") Square sells cheap tickets to shows on the push list the day of the show only (14:30-18:30, Monday-Saturday). I usually buy the second-cheapest tickets directly from the theater box office. Many theaters are so small that there's hardly a bad seat. "Scooting up" later on is less than a capital offense. Shakespeare did it.

Royal Shakespeare Company—If you'll ever enjoy Shakespeare, it'll be here. (But lo, I've tried and failed.) The RSC splits its 12-play April-through-January season between the Royal Shakespeare Theatre in Stratford (tel. 01789/295623; recorded information tel. 01789/269191) and the Barbican Centre (open daily 9:00-20:00; credit-card booking, they mail out schedules; tel. 638-8891, tel. for recorded information: 628-2295). Tickets range in price from £8 to £22. For a complete schedule, write to the Royal Shakespeare Theatre, Stratford-upon-Avon, Warwickshire, CV37 6BB. Shakespeare fans stay tuned for the opening of the reconstructed Globe Theater (1996?) which will be doing Shakespeare as it was done in his day.

Music—For a fun classical event, attend a "Prom Concert." This is an annual music festival with almost nightly concerts in the Royal Albert Hall from July through September at give-a-peasant-some-culture prices (£3 standing-room spots sold at the door, tel. 589-8212). Look into the free lunchtime concerts popular in churches (listed at TI, especially Wren's St. Brides' Church, tel. 353-1301, and St. Martin-in-the-Fields, weekdays except Thursday at 13:05, tel. 930-1862).

The Ultimate Round of Beer—The London tube's Circle Line makes 21 stops during each orbit. There just happens to be a pub near the entry of each of these tube stops. A popular game is to race around trying to drink a pint (or a half-pint) at each of the 21 bars between the "old" pub hours (17:30 to 23:00). Twenty-one pints is about 2 gallons of beer. Locals prefer starting at the Farrington stop. A few of the pubs are tough to find—ask at the nearest newsstand for directions. (If you do this, send me a report.)

Sleeping in London
(£1 = about $1.50, tel. code: 0171)

London is expensive but there's no need to spend a fortune or stay in a depressing dump. Plan on spending about £50 (about $75) for a basic, clean, reasonably cheery double in a usually cramped, cracked-plaster building with an English (as opposed to continental) breakfast. Spending £34 gets you a double with breakfast in a safe, clean, tiny, dreary place where the landlords are absentee and service is minimal. (Hang up your towel to dry and reuse). My London splurges, at £70, are places you'd be happy to entertain in. Unless otherwise noted, the prices include a big English breakfast. Those traveling on a shoestring off-season save a few pounds by arriving late without a reservation and calling around.

I reserve my London room in advance with a phone call direct from the States (dial 011/44/171/London phone number). Assure the manager you'll arrive before 16:00, and leave your credit-card number as security. If you must send a deposit, ask if you can send a signed $100 traveler's check. (Leave the "pay to" line blank and include a note explaining that you'll be happy to pay cash upon arrival, so they can avoid bank charges, if they'll just hold your check until you get there.)

Sleep code: **S**=Single, **D**=Double/Twin, **T**=Triple, **Q**=Quad, **B**=Bath/Shower, **WC**=Toilet, **CC**=Credit Card (**V**isa, **M**astercard, **A**mex).

Sleeping in Victoria Station Neighborhood

The streets behind Victoria Station teem with budget B&Bs. It's a safe, surprisingly tidy and decent area without a hint of the trashy touristy glitz of the streets in front of the station. The first two listings are on Ebury street, between the train and coach stations, proudly part of Belgravia. Even with Margaret Thatcher living around the corner (you'll see the policeman standing outside #73 Chester Square), this is a

London, Victoria Neighborhood

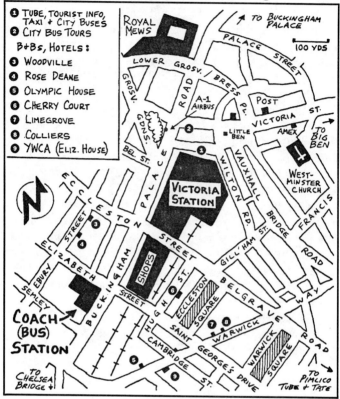

❶ Tube, Tourist Info, Taxi + City Buses
❷ City Bus Tours
B+Bs, Hotels:
❸ Woodville
❹ Rose Deane
❺ Olympic House
❻ Cherry Court
❼ Limegrove
❽ Colliers
❾ YWCA (Eliz. House)

classy and peaceful place to call home in London. Neighboring Elizabeth Street is the center for shops and eateries (#23 for take-out or eat-in fish and chips). The Duke of Wellington pub (63 Eaton Terrace, meals 18:00-22:30, not Sunday) is good, if smoky, for dinner. The cheaper listings are relatively dumpy. Don't expect £50 cheeriness in a £34 room. For the Warwick Way hotels, you might want to request a quiet back room. All are within a 5-minute walk of the Victoria tube and train station.

Woodville House is an oasis of small-town warmth and hospitality in downtown London. As in most budget hotels, the quarters are tight, but you'll get a small garden, homemade müesli, color-coordinated decor, orthopedic beds, showers down the hall, TVs in the room, a library, lots of travel tips, and endless tea, coffee, and friendly chat (especially about the local rich and famous) from the "extremely sociable, even at six in the morning" host Rachel Joplin and her husband Ian. (S-£36, D-£54; bunky family deals for three, four, or five in a room; easy credit-card reservations; 107 Ebury Street, Belgravia, SW1W 9QU, tel. 730-1048, fax 730-2574).

Rosedene Hotel, on the same fine street without the homey flair, is not as cramped as others in this price range. Its breakfast room doubles as a TV lounge (absentee owners but Saleha will take good care of you; S-£26, D-£35, T-£45, Q-£60; only a continental breakfast; CC:VM; 119 Ebury Street, SW1, tel. 730-4872, fax 224-6902).

Cherry Court Hotel is a minimal little place, plain, well-worn and cramped but very close to the station and offering eleven rooms at near-youth-hostel prices on a quiet street (SB-£25, D-£28, DB-£32, TB-35, Mrs. Patel promises these prices through 1995; toilets always down the hall; tea, coffee, and continental breakfast in your room; CC:VMA; 23 Hugh Street, SW1V 1QJ, tel. 828-2840).

Limegrove Hotel (S-£22, small D-£30, D-£32, T-£39, prices promised through 1995; 101 Warwick Way, SW1V 4HT, tel. 828-0458), carefully run by hard-working Joyce, is a little smoky and has only two toilets and two showers for nine rooms but is a fine value with TV and full English breakfast in the room. Back rooms are a bit quieter. **Colliers Hotel** (D-£32, DBWC-34; 97 Warwick Way, tel. 834-6931, fax 834-8439) next door, is a bit bigger with more showers but less personality. **Olympic House Hotel** (S-£30, D-£38; 115 Warwick Way, tel. 828-0757; run by Eddie and Betty) is a tall, skinny, claustrophobic tower of chaos with clean, quiet rooms and lots of steps.

Elizabeth House YWCA offers people of any sex inexpensive beds in a big, well-run, friendly, musty place with narrow yellow halls and stark rooms (S-£21, D-£42, DB-£45, shared T and Q-£15 per bed, with a buffet continental breakfast, request a quiet room off the street; 118 Warwick Way, SW1V 1SD, tel. 630-0741).

"South Kensington," He Said, Loosening His Cummerbund

For a chance to live on a quiet street so classy it doesn't allow hotel signs, surrounded by trendy shops and colorful eateries, 200 yards from the handy South Kensington tube station (on the Circle Line, direct connection to Heathrow, 2 stops from Victoria Station), call South Kensington home in London. Shoppers will enjoy the location, a short walk from Harrods and the designer shops of King's Road and Chelsea. You'll find plenty of ethnic and colorful budget eateries around the corner on Brompton Road (such as **La Bouchee**, daily 9:00-23:00, £8 French entrees). This has got to be the ultimate fairy-tale London home-away-from-home. Of course, you'll pay for it. But these places are a fine value.

Five Sumner Place Hotel is informal but professional, "highly commended" and recently voted "the best small hotel in London." You'll talk softly but not feel like you have to dress up as you wander, with your free daily newspaper, under the chandeliers out to the Victorian-style conservatory, a greenhouse dressed in blue, for breakfast. Each room is tastefully decorated with traditional period furnishings in a 150-year-old building (SBWC-£72, DBWC-£111, TBWC-£135, all with TV and telephone, elevator, CC:VMA, 5 Sumner Place, South Kensington, SW7 3EE, tel. 584-7586, fax 823-9962, if enough of you sleep here, maybe they'll give me a free room).

The Prince Hotel, right next door, is a bit smoky and relatively dumpy (but still nice). It also has an elegant, glass-covered conservatory, period decor throughout, and TVs and telephones in each of its 20 rooms. Its cheaper rooms ("without facilities," meaning with a shower but the toilet down the hall) are an especially good value (S-£42, SB-£48, SBWC-£61, DB-£61, DBWC-£74, TBWC-£92, QBWC-£108; breakfast in fancier hotel next door, 6 Sumner Place, SW7 3AB, CC:VMA, tel. 589-6488, fax 581-0824).

Aster House Hotel also offers you a chance to be elegant in London without going broke. The hotel's brochure reminds guests when they're going out to L'Orangerie (Victorian greenhouse) for breakfast, "To be considerate of your table companions, your neighbors and your hosts, we hope to welcome you in elegant attire, even if relaxed." Each room has a TV, telephone, fridge, and separate bathroom. Their third-floor rooms (no elevator) are the best deal. (SBWC-£61, third floor DBWC-£78, DBWC-£91, deluxe four-poster DBWC-£94 and £99, CC:VM, CC deposits non-refundable if you cancel with less than 2 weeks notice; entirely no smoking, 3 Sumner Place, SW7 3EE, tel. 581-5888, fax 584-4925). The breakfast room is whisper-elegant. Break the silence by asking who was scalded by their shower.

The **Uptown Reservations** B&B service has a line on 50 private homes renting classy rooms with breakfast in the "uptown" Chelsea, Knightsbridge, and Belgravia areas (S-37, D-£63, 50 Christchurch St. SW3 4AR London, tel. 351-3445, fax 351-9383). They also book flats and apartments. Monica and Sara work to match interests, so if you're an archaeologist or a coin collector, let them know.

Sleeping in Notting Hill Gate Neighborhood

Residential Notting Hill Gate is the perfect traveler's neighborhood. It has quick and easy bus or tube access to downtown, on the A2 Airbus line from Heathrow (second stop from airport, after Kensington Hilton), is relatively safe (except for the dangerous, riot-plagued Notting Hill Carnival, the last weekend of August), and, for London, is very "homely." Notting Hill Gate has a late-hours supermarket, self-serve launderette, artsy theater, and lots of fun budget eateries (see below). All recommendations are near the Holland Park or Notting Hill Gate tube station. (Notting Hill Gate is in the central zone and on the Circle Line, handier and 40p cheaper from anywhere in the center than the Holland Park station.)

Vicarage Private Hotel is understandably popular. Family-run and elegantly British in a quiet, classy neighborhood, it has 19 rooms furnished with taste and quality. Martin, Mandy, and Jim maintain a homey and caring atmosphere. Lots of stairs, a TV lounge, TVs in most rooms, and facilities on each floor. Reserve long in advance with a one-night deposit. (S-£32, D-£54, T-£66, Q-£72, a 6-minute walk from the Notting Hill Gate and High Street Kensington tube stations near Kensington Palace at 10 Vicarage Gate, Kensington, W8 4AG, tel. 229-4030).

London, Notting Hill Gate Neighborhood

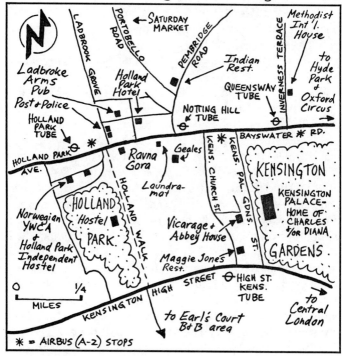

Abbey House Hotel, next door, is similar but has no lounge and is a bit less cozy (S-£32, D-£54, T-£64, Q-£74, Quint-£84; 11 Vicarage Gate, Kensington, W8, tel. 727-2594).

Hotel Ravna Gora—Formerly the mansion of 18th-century architect Henry Holland, now it's a large Yugoslavian-run B&B, eccentric and well-worn but comfortable, spacious, and handy for the price. Manda and Rijko take good care of their guests with a royal TV room and a good English breakfast (but no OJ). Plain, bright rooms; grand old creaky spiral staircase; easy parking (S-£28, D-£46, DB-£56, T-£54, TB-£66, Q-£68, QB-£80, CC:V; 50 yards from Holland Park tube station facing but set back from a busy road, 29 Holland Park Ave., W11, tel. 727-7725, fax 221-4282).

Dean Court Hotel—This wild and crazy Aussie hang-out offers young travelers good basic facilities (£11 beds in 3- to 5-bed rooms, D-£32, Twins-£35; 100 yards from Bayswater Tube, 57 Inverness Terrace, W2, reservations with deposit only, tel. 229-2961, fax 727-1190).

Holland Park Hotel—Professional and "hotelesque," but a fine value. Royal lounge, sleepy garden, TVs in rooms, buffet continental breakfast, a little smoky, quiet, on a pleasant woodsy street, easy credit-card reservations (S-£38, SB-£47, D-£47, DB-£64, extra beds £12, CC:VMA; 6 Ladbrook Terrace, W11 3PG, tel. 792-0216, fax 727-8166).

Westend Hotel is comfortable and convenient but strict and without flavor (DB-£80, £68 in the annex, elevator in main building, all rooms with TV, telephone, hair dryer, coffee maker, and so on; CC:VMA, reserve with a credit-card number; 154 Bayswater Road, W2 4HP, tel. 229-9191, fax 727-1054).

Methodist International House—This Christian residence, filled mostly with Asian and African students, is great if you want a truly worldwide dorm experience at a price that will bolster your faith. Each smoke-free room is studious, with a desk and reading lamp. The atmosphere is friendly, safe, and controlled but well-worn with a silent study room, reading lounge, TV lounge, and laundry facilities (£16 beds in shared doubles or triples, S-£20, D-£34, T-£48, includes breakfast and a cafeteria dinner—no typo; near Bayswater tube, 2 Inverness Terrace, W2 3HY, tel. 229-5101, fax 229-3170.)

Norwegian YWCA (Norsk K.F.U.K.)—For women under 25 only (and men with Norwegian passports), this is an incredible value—smoke-free; Norwegian atmosphere; on quiet, stately street; piano lounge, TV room, study; all rooms with private showers. They have mostly quads, so those willing to share with strangers are most likely to get a place. (July-August: SB-£24, bed in shared double-£21, shared quad-£16, with breakfast. September-June: same prices but with dinner included. Monthly rates-£11 a day in shared quad with breakfast and dinner. 52 Holland Park, W11 3R5, tel. and fax 727-9897). With each visit I wonder which is easier—getting a sex change or a Norwegian passport?

Holland Park Independent Hostel has spacious, ramshackle rooms; a TV lounge; no lockers; members' kitchen; and bugs (S-£13, D-£24, T-£33, bed in small unisex dorm-£9, no breakfast—and that's probably a blessing; 41 Holland Park, tel. 229-4238, 723-6833). On an aristocratic quiet street, it's a lovely alternative to the bushes.

Sleeping in London's Bloomsbury District

These places are between the British Museum and King's Cross Station, all within 3 blocks of the Russell Square tube station. **Cambria House**, an amazing value, is run by the Salvation Army. (Relax. This is a good thing when it comes to cheap big-city hotels.) This smoke-free old building with a narrow maze of halls is all newly painted and super clean— if institutional. The rooms are spacious and perfectly good. There are ample showers and toilets on each floor and a TV lounge (S-£23, D-£36, DBWC-£45, extra bed-£11, CC:VM; north of Russell Square at 37 Hunter Street, WC1N 1BJ, tel. 837-1654, fax 837-1229).

Repton Hotel is the cheapest and most run-down of several hotels on an elegant Georgian Terrace, a 2-minute walk from the British Museum. Prices may be soft and, with luck during slow times, you may get a dorm to yourself—in which case it's a great value. (S-£30, D-£40, DB-£56, 6-bed dorms-£12 per person, with a continental breakfast, TV in each room; 31 Bedford Place, WC1B 5JH, tel. 436-4922, tel. and fax 636-7045). **The Thanet** (D-£50, DBWC-£62, at #8 across the street, tel. 636-2869) is much nicer, but more expensive.

Central University of Iowa Hostel rents to non-Iowans from mid-May through August. It's clean, basic, and reminiscent of elegance with plenty of facilities (TV lounge, washer and dryer). (D-£32, beds in 3- to 4-bed rooms-£14, with continental breakfast; 7 Bedford Place, WC1B 5JA, tel. 580-1121).

Sleeping in Other Neighborhoods

Mary Ward's Guest House—Sleepable but very simple on a quiet street in a well-worn neighborhood south of Victoria near Clapham Common, this beats the hostel. Friendly Mary Ward (Edith Bunker's English aunt) has been renting her five super-cheap rooms to budget travelers for 25 years. (S-£10, D-£20 with English breakfast, 98 Hambalt Rd., Clapham Common, London, tel. 0181/673-1077, 15 minutes by tube to Clapham Common and a 12-minute walk—exit left down Chapham South Road, left on Elms, right on Abbeville Road, left on Hambalt.)

Lynwood Guest House—Outside of London (30 minutes by train) near Gatwick Airport (10 minutes by train), this place offers a cozy, friendly alternative to big-city lodging in Redhill, a normal workaday English town. Easy parking, a 5-minute walk from train station, owner Shanta may pick you up, genuinely caring and gracious (SB-£24, DB-£38, DBWC-£40, TB-£50, QB-£56; discount for 2 nights or more, 50 London Rd., Redhill, Surrey RH1 1LN, tel. 01737/766894).

The peaceful **Crutchfield Inn B&B** offers three comfortable rooms in a 500-year-old renovated farmhouse. Mrs. Blok includes a ride to and from the airport (DB-£45, 2 miles from Gatwick airport, 30 minutes by train from London, at Hookwood, Surrey, RH6OHT, tel. 01293/863110, fax 863233).

Eating in London

If you want to dine (as opposed to eat), check out the extensive listings in *What's On*. The thought of a £25 meal generally ruins my appetite, so my London dining is limited mostly to unremarkable, but inexpensive, alternatives. My listings are chosen mostly for their handy location to your B&B or sightseeing.

Your £5 budget choices are pub grub, a café, fish and chips, pizza, ethnic, or picnic. Pub grub is the most atmospheric budget option. Many of London's 7,000 pubs serve fresh, tasty buffets under ancient timbers, with hearty lunches and dinners priced around £5. Ethnic restaurants from all over the world more than make up for the basically lackluster English cuisine. Eating Indian or Chinese is "going local" in London. It's also going cheap (cheaper if you take out). Pizza places all over town offer £3.50 all-you-can-stomach buffets. Of course, picnicking is the fastest and cheapest way to go. There are plenty of good grocery stores and sandwich shops, fine park benches, and polite pigeons in Britain's most expensive city.

Eating near Trafalgar Square

For a meal on a monk's budget in an ancient crypt sitting on somebody's tomb, climb down into the **St.Martin-in-the-Fields Restaurant** (10:00-19:30, Sunday 12:00-15:00, £5-£7 cafeteria plates, cheaper sandwich bar, profits go to the church; underneath St. Martin-in-the-Fields on Trafalgar Square, tel. 839-4342). Down Whitehall (towards Big Ben), a block from Trafalgar Square, you'll find the atmospheric **Clarence Pub** (decent grub) and several cheaper cafeterias and pizza joints. For a classy lunch, treat your palate to the pricier **Brasserie** (first floor, Sainsbury Wing of the National Gallery).

Eating near Piccadilly

Wren at St. James Church Coffeehouse (8:00-19:00, Sunday 10:00-16:00, not exclusively vegetarian, 2 minutes off Piccadilly, at 35 Jermyn St., tel. 437-9419) is wonderfully green and in a pleasant garden next to one of Wren's best churches (peek in). **Stockpot** is famous and rightly popular for its edible cheap meals (8:00-23:30, Sunday 12:00-22:00, 40 Panton St., off Haymarket near Piccadilly). The palatial **Criterion Restaurant** (tel. 925-0909), serving a two-course dinner for £10 under gilded tiles and chandeliers, is 20 yards and a world away from the punk junk of Piccadilly Circus. **The Carvery** serves a £15 all-you-can-eat meaty buffet with plenty of vegetables and a salad bar, Yorkshire and bread pudding, dessert and coffee included—a carnivore's delight with concessions to vegetarians. Puffy-hatted carvers help you slice. (Regent Palace Hotel on Glasshouse St., a cigarette-butt toss from Piccadilly Circus, 12:00-14:30 and 17:15-21:00, Sunday 12:30-14:30 and 18:00-21:00).

Eating near Recommended Notting Hill Gate B&Bs

Costas has Greek food or eat-in or take-out fish and chips (£5 meals, closed Sunday, near the Coronet Theatre at Hillgate Street #18). Next door, the **Hillgate Pub** has good food and famous hot saltbeef sandwiches (indoor/outdoor, closed Sunday). The not-too-spicy **Modhubon** Indian restaurant is worth the moderate splurge (cheap lunch specials, 29 Pembridge Road, tel. 727-3399). There's a cheap Chinese take-out next door (19 Pembridge Road, 17:30-24:00, closed Sunday). The small, woodsy **Arc** at 122 Palace Gardens Terrace is popular and worth the moderate splurge (indoor-outdoor seating, £10-£15 meals, go early or call ahead, 18:30-23:15 nightly, tel. 229-4024). The **Churchill Arms** pub is a hot local hangout with good beer and decent

£5 Thai plates. The **Ladbroke Arms** serves country-style meals that are one step above pub grub in quality and price, daily from 12:00-14:30 and 19:00-21:30 (indoor/outdoor, 54 Ladbroke Road, behind Holland Park Tube station, tel. 727-6648). The almost-too-popular **Geale's** has long been considered one of London's best fish-and-chips joints (£6 meals, 2 Farmer Street, just off Notting Hill Gate behind the Gate Theatre, 12:00-15:00, 18:00-23:00, closed Sunday and Monday, tel. 727-7969). Get there early for a place to sit and the best selection of fish. The very English **Maggie Jones** (6 Old Court Place, just east of Kensington Church St., near the High Street Kensington tube stop, tel. 937-6462, CC:VM) serves my favorite £20 London dinner. If you eat well once in London, eat here.

Transportation Connections

Flying into London
At Heathrow Airport: Heathrow Airport is user-friendly. Read signs, ask questions. Most flights land at Terminal 3, but British Air flights land at Terminal 4 (same services as Terminal 3, but no tourist information office.) In Terminal 3, you'll find: **Banks** (open 24 hours daily, okay rates), airport terminal information desk (pick up a London map and ask questions, but for the official TI, see below), **car rental agencies** (if you're renting a car, stop by to confirm your plans), and a TI. Heathrow's TI (daily 8:30-18:00) gives you all the help that London's Victoria Station does, with none of the crowds. To reach the TI, walk 5 minutes following signs to the "underground." (If you're riding the Airbus into London, leave your partner at the terminal with your bags.) At the TI, get a free map and brochures, and buy a subway pass if you're riding the tube into London. Then either hop on the London-bound subway or walk back into the airport to catch the Airbus into London. The National Express Central Bus Station offers direct bus connections from the airport to Bath (every 2 hours, 2½-hour ride, tel. 0171/730-0202).
At Gatwick Airport: More and more flights, especially charters, land at Gatwick Airport, halfway between London and the southern coast. Trains shuttle conveniently between

Heathrow and the Four Terminals

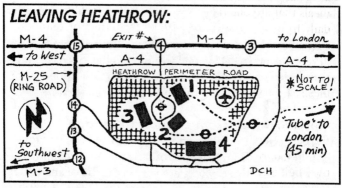

Gatwick and London's Victoria Station 4 times an hour (30-minute ride, £8.60).

When you fly to Europe, you lose a day. If you leave on Friday, you land on Saturday. Most flights from the U.S.A. arrive before noon.

Transportation to London from Heathrow Airport
By Tube (subway): For £3 (free with £4 all-day pass) the tube takes you 14 miles to Victoria Station in 45 minutes (6/hr).
By Airbus: Hop on a convenient Airbus (£5, 2/hr, 6:30-20:00, buy ticket on bus, tel. 0181/897-3305). All my recommended hotel neighborhoods are on one of the two Airbus lines. If you take A1, South Kensington is the third stop, and Victoria Station is the last stop. On A2, the second and third stops cover Notting Hill Gate, or stay on till the last stop, Russell Square, for Bloomsbury. The tube works fine, but with baggage I prefer taking the Airbus—no connections underground and a lovely view from the top of the double-decker bus. Ask the driver to remind you when to get off.
Taxis from the airport are expensive but rides from London to Heathrow can be reasonable. Locals can usually negotiate a £15 ride to Heathrow. Even at £20, for three traveling together this can be a deal.

Train and Bus Connections
Bath: Trains leave London's Paddington Station every hour (at a quarter after) for the 75-minute ride to Bath. The £26 tickets can be bought in advance or on the train from the

conductor. For about the same price, you can take a guided bus tour from London to Stonehenge and Bath, and simply leave the tour in Bath.

Points North: London is the country's transportation hub. All of England is well-served from its capital. Speedy trains run hourly from London's King Cross Station stopping in York (2 hrs), Durham (3 hrs), and Edinburgh (5 hrs).

Transportation from London to Europe

While it's hard to nail down exact prices and options for those traveling from London to Paris or Amsterdam, it's safe to say that these routes are very competitive and you'll get better prices in London than from the U.S.A. Taking the bus is cheapest, and round-trips are a bargain. Flying is more reasonable than you might expect—students get great deals.

London to Paris—By bus: £33 one-way, £55 round-trip within six months, 10 hours, day or overnight, on Eurolines (tel. 0171/730-8235) or CitySprint (tel. 01304/240241). By train: £42 one-way overnight, £57 by day, 7 hours, £65 round-trip within five days, £85 round-trip within 2 months. BritRail Hover Speed crossing in 6 hours for £60. By plane: £90 regular, £40 student stand-by.

London to Amsterdam—By bus: £32 one-way, 12 hours, day or night, £53 round-trip within six months on Eurolines, same price to Brussels. By train: £50 one-way, day or night, 12 hours, £63 round-trip within five days, £83 round-trip within two months. The Jetfoil adds £9 to the ticket but cuts the channel crossing time from 4 to 1½ hours. To fly: £92 regular.

The English Channel Tunnel

Finally, you can take a train under the English Channel—for about what it costs to fly over it. And, when you take into account airport-downtown connections hassles, the "Chunnel" is now the fastest way to get from Big Ben to the Eiffel Tower. Imagine London to Paris in three hours! "Eurostar" Chunnel train tickets are like plane tickets—they require reservations and prices fluctuate according to season, time, and demand.

BATH

Any tour of Britain that skips Bath stinks. Two hundred years ago, this city of 80,000 was the trend-setting Hollywood of Britain. If ever a city enjoyed looking in the mirror, Bath's the one. It has more "government listed" or protected historic buildings per capita than any other town in England. The entire city, built of creamy warm-tone limestone called "Bath stone," beams in its cover-girl complexion. An architectural chorus line, it's the triumph of Georgian style. Proud locals remind visitors that the town is routinely banned from the "Britain in Bloom" contest to give other towns a chance to win. Bath's narcissism is justified.

Promenade through the ages with a tour of Bath's Roman and medieval mineral baths, followed by tea and Vivaldi in the elegant Pump Room.

Planning Your Time

Bath is a two-night town even on a quick trip. There's plenty to do and it's a joy to do it. On a three-week British trip, I'd spend three nights in Bath with one day for the city and one for a side trip to Well, Glastonbury, and Avebury. Bath could easily fill another day. Ideally, use Bath as your jet lag recovery pillow (catching the bus directly from Heathrow airport, departures to "Bath Spa" at 10:30, 12:30, 14:30, 16:30; tel. 081/730-0202) and do London at the end of your trip.

Here's how I'd start a three-week British vacation:
Day 1: Land at Heathrow. Catch the National Express bus to Bath (depart every 2 hrs, 2½-hr trip). While you don't need or want a car in Bath, and most rental companies have an office there, those who pick up their cars at the airport can do Stonehenge (and maybe Salisbury) on their way to Bath on this day.
Day 2: 9:00, tour the Roman Baths; 10:30, catch the free city walking tour; 12:30, munch a picnic lunch on the open deck of a Guide Friday bus tour; 14:30, free time in the shopping center of old Bath; 16:00, take a guided tour through the Costume Museum.

Day 3: Pick up your rental car and tour Avebury, Glastonbury (Abbey and Tower), and Wells (17:15 evensong at the Cathedral). Without a car, consider a one-day Avebury/Stonehenge/cute towns Mad Max minibus tour.

Day 4: 9:00, leave Bath early for South Wales; 10:30, tour St. Fagan's Folk Museum (grounds, lunch, then museum); 15:00, short stop at Tintern Abbey; drive to Cotswolds; 18:00, set up in your Cotswold homebase (Stow or Chipping).

Orientation (tel. code: 01225)

Bath's town square, three blocks in front of the bus and train station, is a bouquet of tourist landmarks including the Abbey, the Roman and medieval baths, and the royal Pump Room.

Tourist Information

Near the Abbey (Monday-Saturday 9:30-18:00, Sunday 10:00-16:00, shorter hours off-season, tel. 462831). Pick up the 25p Bath map/guide and the packed-with-info, free *This Month in Bath*, and browse through scads of fliers.

Trains and Buses

The Bath Station is a pleasure (small-town charm and an international tickets desk). The bus station is immediately in front of the train station. My recommended B&Bs are within a 10- or 15-minute walk or a £2 taxi ride. For my top four listings, consider using the "Guide Friday" city bus tour (described below) as transportation. It leaves every 12 minutes from Lane 1 of the bus station, a block in front of the train station. Start the tour, jump out, check into your B&B, and hop back on to finish the circle.

Sights—Bath

▲▲**The Guide Friday City Bus Tour**—This green-and-cream open-top tour bus makes a 90-minute figure-eight circuit of Bath's main sights with an exhaustingly informative running commentary. For one £5.50 ticket, tourists can stop and go at will for a whole day. The buses cover the city center and the surrounding hills (14 sign-posted pick-up points, departures every 12 minutes in summer, hourly in winter, about 9:25-17:00, tel. 444102, children are often let on for

Bath

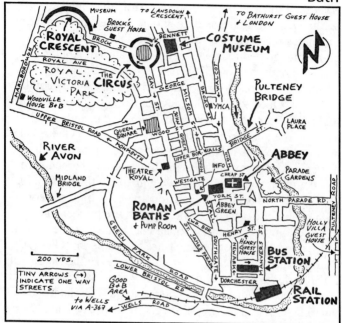

free). This is great in sunny weather, a feast for photographers, and a fine way to work on a tan and sightsee at the same time. The competing red Citytour buses (£4, family of 5 for £10) do basically the same tour without the swing through the countryside and ask the hard-to-answer question, "Why pay more?"

▲▲▲**Walking Tours of Bath**—These 2-hour tours, offered free by trained local volunteers who simply want to share their love of Bath with its many visitors, are a pure, chatty, historical-gossip-filled joy, essential for your understanding of this town's amazing Georgian social scene. How else will you learn that the old "chair ho" call for your sedan chair evolved into today's "cheerio" greeting? Tours leave from in front of the Pump Room daily except Saturday at 10:30 (often at 14:00 or 14:30 and 19:00, May-October). For Ghost Walks and Bizarre Bath Comedy Walks, see below under "Entertainment."

▲▲▲**The Baths (Roman and Medieval)**—Back in ancient Roman times, high society enjoyed the mineral springs at

Bath. Roman Londoners traveled to Aquae Sulis, as the city
was called then, so often to "take a bath" that finally it
became known simply as Bath. Today a fine Roman museum
surrounds the ancient bath. With the help of an excellent
20-minute guided tour, the complex of ancient Roman and
medieval baths and buildings makes sense. (£5; £6.60
"combo" ticket includes Costume Museum, a family combo
costs £16. Open 9:00-18:00 daily, and 20:00-22:00 in August;
slightly shorter hours off-season. Tours are included and
leave on the quarter-hour throughout the day. Tel. 461111)

▲**Pump Room**—After a centuries-long cold spell, Bath was
reheated when previously barren Queen Mary bathed here
and ten months later bore a male heir to the throne (1687).
Once Bath was back on the aristocratic map, high society
soon turned the place into one big pleasure palace. The
Pump Room, an elegant Georgian Hall just above the Roman
baths, offers the visitor's best chance to sample this Old
World elegance. Drop by to sip coffee or tea to the rhythm of
a string trio (tea/coffee and pastry for £2.50, live music all year
10:30-13:00, summers 15:00-17:00). Now's your chance to
have a famous (but not especially good) "Bath bun" and (split
a 35p) drink of the awfully curative water. The Pump Room's
toilets are always nearby and open to the discreet public.

▲**The Abbey**—Bath town wasn't much in the Middle Ages.
As late as 1687, there were only about 3,000 inhabitants
gathered around its great abbey. But an important church
has stood on this spot since Anglo-Saxon times. In 973,
Edgar, the first king of England, was crowned here. Domi-
nating the town center, the present church is 500 years old
and a fine example of Late Perpendicular Gothic, with
breezy fan vaulting and enough stained glass to earn it the
nickname "Lantern of the West" (concert and evensong
schedule is on the door, worth the £1 donation, handy flier
narrates a 19-stop tour). **The Heritage Vaults** (£2, 10:00-
16:00, closed Sunday) is a small but interesting exhibit telling
the story of Christianity in Bath since Roman times.

Pulteney Bridge—Bath is inclined to compare its shop-
lined bridge to Florence's Ponte Vecchio. That's pushing it.
But to best enjoy a sunny Bath kind of day, pay 60p to go
into the garden below the bridge. Tour boats run hour-long
£3.50 cruises from under the bridge.

▲▲**Royal Crescent and The Circus**—Bath is an architectural can-can and these are the kickers. These first elegant Georgian (that's British for "Neoclassical") "condos" by John Wood are well-explained in the city walking tours. The museum at #1 Royal Crescent is your best look into a house from Jane Austen's day. It's worth the £3 admission to get behind all those classy exteriors (10:30-17:00, closed Monday, tel. 428126). Stroll the Crescent after dark. Pretend you're rich. Pretend you're poor. Study the cute little rooms below each entry walk. There're peasants on the lawn.

▲▲▲**Costume Museum**—One of Europe's great museums, displaying 300 years of fashion—from Anne Boleyn to Twiggy—one frilly decade at a time, is housed in Bath's elegant Assembly Rooms. Enthralling 45-minute tours will "knock your spots off." The tours normally leave on the hour or on the half-hour; drop by or call to confirm tour times. Learn why Yankee Doodle "stuck a feather in his cap and called it macaroni," and much more (£3.20, cheaper on combo ticket with Roman Baths, daily 10:00-17:00, from 11:00 on Sunday, last tour often at 16:00, tel. 461111).

▲▲**The Industrial Heritage Centre** is a grand title for Mr. Bowler's Business, a turn-of-the-century engineer's shop, brass foundry, and fizzy-drink factory. It's just a pile of meaningless old gadgets until a volunteer guide resurrects Mr. Bowler's creative genius (£3, plus a few pence for a glass of genuine Victorian lemonade, daily 10:00-17:00, 2 blocks uphill from the Assembly Rooms on Julian Rd., call to be sure a volunteer is available to give a tour, tel. 318348).

Small Special-Interest Museums: Building of Bath Museum offers a fascinating look behind the scenes at how the Georgian city was actually built. This is just one large room of exhibits but anyone interested in construction will find it worth the £2.50 (10:30-17:00, closed Monday, near the Circus on a street called "the Paragon," tel. 333895). **British Folk Art Collection** is also just one large room (next to the Building museum), offering a charming collection of crude but elegant folk art (£2, £3.50 combo ticket with Building Museum, tel. 446020). **Royal Photographic Society**, a hit with shutterbugs, exhibits the earliest cameras and photos and their development, along with temporary contemporary exhibits (£3, daily 9:30-17:30).

▲**American Museum**—I know, you need this in Bath like
you need a Big Mac. But this offers a fascinating look at
colonial and early-American lifestyles. Each of 18 completely
furnished rooms (from the 1600s to the 1800s) is hosted by
an eager guide waiting to fill you in on the candles, maps,
bedpans, and various religious sects that make domestic
Yankee history surprisingly interesting. One room is a quil-
ter's nirvana (£5, Tuesday-Saturday 14:00-17:00, Sunday
11:00-17:00, closed November-March, tel. 460503). The
museum is outside of town and a headache to reach without
a car (15-minute walk from the Guide Friday stop or a
10-minute walk from bus #18).

Shopping—There's great browsing between the Abbey and
the Assembly Rooms. Shops close at 17:30, later on Thursdays.
Interested in antiques? For the best deal, pick up the local
paper (usually out on Fridays) and shop with the dealers at
estate sales and auctions listed in the "What's On" section.

Entertainment—*This Month in Bath* (available at the TI and
many B&Bs) lists events and evening entertainment. There
are almost nightly historical walks (19:15, 2 hrs). For a walking comedy act, the entertainingly off-the-wall Bizarre Bath
walk is a kick (£3, 20:00 nightly, 75 minutes, from the
Huntsman pub near the Abbey, confirm at TI or call
335124). Ghost Walks are another way to pass the after-dark
hours (20:00, 2 hrs, £3, tel. 463618). The Bath Sports and
Leisure Centre (just across the North Parade Bridge, open
until 22:30, tel. 462563) has a swimming pool and more.

Sleeping in Bath
(£1 = about $1.50, tel. code: 01225)

Bath is one of England's busiest tourist towns. To get a good
B&B, make a telephone reservation in advance. Competition
is stiff and it's worth asking any of these places for a non-
weekend, three nights in a row, or off-season deal. Friday
and Saturday nights are tightest (especially if you're staying
only one night, since B&Bs favor those staying longer).

Sleep code: **S**=Single, **D**=Double/Twin, **T**=Triple,
Q=Quad, **B**=Bath/Shower, **WC**=Toilet, **CC**=Credit Card
(**V**isa, **M**astercard, **A**mex).

Brock's Guest House—If you can afford the splurge,
this Georgian townhouse will put bubbles in your Bath expe-

rience. Marion Dodd has redone her place in a way that would make the famous architect John Wood, who built it in 1765, proud. This charming house couldn't be better located, between the prestigious Royal Crescent and the elegant Circus (S-£22, DB-£42 and £44, DBWC-£48 and £52, TB-£55, TBWC-£66; 32 Brock St., BA1 2LN, reserve far in advance, tel. 338374, fax 334245). Marion serves a royal breakfast. You'll find a TV and teapot in your room, and a launderette around the corner. Like most listings in this book, she'll hold telephone reservations with no deposit until 15:00 (call if you'll be a little late). If Marion's place is full, she can set you up in a friend's B&B nearby. If you can't find a sedan chair, Marion is a 15-minute walk, £2.50 taxi, or short bus ride (to Assembly Rooms and short walk) from the station. Guide Friday buses stop on Brock Street.

In the **Woodville House**, Anne and Tom Toalster offer Bath's best cheap beds. This tidy little house has three charming rooms, one shared shower, and a TV lounge. Breakfast is a help-yourself buffet around one big family-style table (D-£27, minimum 2 nights; just off busy Bristol Road below the Royal Crescent at 4 Marlborough Lane, BA1 2NQ, tel. 319335, absolutely no smoking).

Elgin Villa (DB-£30, DBWC-£36 for 2 nights minimum with this book promised through 1995; next door to Woodville House at 6 Marlborough Lane, BA1 2NQ Bath, tel. 424557), run by Rex and Edie Haldenby, has three rooms and serves a big continental breakfast in your bedroom.

Holly Villa Guest House, with a cheery garden and a cozy TV lounge, an 8-minute walk from the station and center, is enthusiastically and thoughtfully run by Jill McGarrigle. (D-£34, DB-£38, DBWC-£46, T-£48, TB-£60, Q-£56, double rooms have double beds only, seven rooms, non-smoking, free parking, cheap rooms get the famous "loo with a view." From city center, walk over North Parade Bridge, take first right, then second left, a block from a Guide Friday bus stop, 14 Pulteney Gardens, BA2 4HG, tel. 310331.)

The **Henry Guest House** is a clean, cheery, and vertical little 8-room family-run place 2 blocks in front of the train station on a quiet side street (S-£16, D-£32, T-£48, TVs in rooms, lots of narrow stairs, one shower and one bath for all; 6 Henry Street, BA1 1JT, tel. 424052, Mrs.

Cox). This kind of decency at this price this central is found nowhere else in Bath. **Harington's of Bath Hotel**, with 12 rooms on a quiet street in the town center, is sleepable in a pinch (D-£40, DB-£46, family room deal, CC:VMA, Queen Street, tel. 461728).

The Bathurst Guest House—Mrs. Elizabeth Tovey runs a fine B&B (S-£16.50, D-£33, DB-£38, extra bed-£8, non-smoking, TVs in rooms, lots of stairs, easy parking, 11 Walcot Parade, London Road, Bath BA1 5NF, tel. 421884) with a great piano/game lounge, 1 block above the A-4 London Road about a 15-minute walk north of the town center. The friendly **Claremont B&B** is farther out of town (D-£32, DB-£40, T-£50; 9 Claremont Rd., Bath, Diane Harding, tel. 428859).

For the cheapest beds, the **Youth Hostel** is in a grand old building, but not central (bus #18 from the station, £8.40 per bed without breakfast, tel. 465674). The **YMCA** is a bit grungy, but friendly and wonderfully central on Broad Street. Doubles are £12 per person; the dorm is cheaper at about £11, with breakfast (tel. 460471).

Eating in Bath

Bath is flooded with cutesy eateries. There's something for every appetite and budget—just stroll around the center of town. A picnic dinner or take-out fish and chips in the Royal Crescent Park is ideal for aristocratic hobos.

Eating on or just off the Abbey Green

Evans Self-Service Fish Restaurant is the best eat-in or take-out fish and chips deal in town (11:30-22:00, closed Sunday, 7 Abbeygate, student discounts, tel. 463981). The **Crystal Palace Pub**, with hearty meals under rustic timbers or in the sunny courtyard, is a good handy standby (meals under £5, daily from 12:00-14:30 and 18:00-20:30, 11 Abbey Green; children welcome on the patio, not indoors; tel. 423944). **Sally Lunn's House** is a cutesy quasi-historic place for expensive doily meals, tea, pink pillows, and lots of lace (4 North Parade Passage). **The Huntsman** (next to Sally Lunn's buns, tel. 460100) offers good, filling meals. Its pub is cheapest, the Cellar Bar is inexpensive and full of young locals, and the restaurant upstairs is a bit classier. For very cheap meals, try **Spike's Fish and Chips** (open very late) and the neighboring café just behind the bus station.

Eating between the Abbey and the Circus
For lunch, try **Lovejoy's Café** upstairs in the Bartlett Street Antique Centre or the **Green Tree Pub**, with a non-smoking room, on Green Street (both serve lunch only, downhill from the Assembly Rooms). The Guildhall Market across from the Pulteney Bridge, fun for browsing and picnic shopping, has a very cheap cafeteria if you'd like to sip tea surrounded by stacks of used books, bananas on the push list, and honest-to-goodness old-time locals. The **Broad Street Bakery** (at 14 Broad St.) is a budgetricious place with great quiches and pizzas to eat in or take away. **Devon Savouries** serves greasy, delicious take-out pasties; sausage rolls; and vegetable pies (on the main walkway between New Bond Street and Upper Borough Walls). **Sam Wellers Pub** serves good £5 dinners (open until 20:00, closed Sunday, 14 Upper Borough Walls, tel. 466627).

Eating near the Circus and Brock's Guesthouse
The **Circus**, on Brock Street, is intimate and a good value with candle-lit prices. The **Cedars Lebanese Restaurant** (on a lane called Margaret's Buildings, just off Brock Street) serves an elegant have-it-all £12 "Cedars Mezze." A block or so away, the **Chequers Inn** (50 Rivers St.) is a smoky dive of a pub with cheap and finger-sticking disgusting grub.

Transportation Connections
Bath to London: Trains to London's Paddington station (hrly, 90 minutes, £26 one-way), National Express buses are cheaper (hrly, 3 hrs, £18 round-trip, £17 one-way, ask about £7 cheap day returns). Consider using an all-day Stonehenge and Bath organized **bus tour** from London as transportation to Bath. For the same cost of the train ticket (£25), you can see Stonehenge, tour Bath, and leave the tour before it returns to London (they'll let you stow your bag underneath). Direct National Express **buses** run between Heathrow airport and Bath (9 daily, 2½ hrs), and Gatwick and Bath (8 daily, 4½ hrs, change at Heathrow). Public transportation is such a snap that it's better to rent a **car**

in Bath than rent a car in London and drive to Bath. Most major car rental companies have offices in Bath and offer free hotel pick-ups.

The Cotswolds: National Express **buses** (tel. 01272/541022) run between Bath and various destinations in the Cotswolds, such as **Cheltenham** (4 daily, 2 hrs), **Stratford** (2 daily, 3 hrs), and nearby **Oxford** (3 daily, 2 hrs).

Birmingham, points north: From Bath, catch a **train** to **Bristol** (twice hourly, 15-minute ride) and from Bristol to **Birmingham** (hrly, 1½ hrs). From Birmingham, a major transportation hub, trains depart for **Blackpool, York, Durham,** and **Scotland,** or use a train and bus combination to reach **Ironbridge Gorge, North Wales,** and the **Lakes District.**

Great Britain

YORK

Historical York has world-class sights and a past that won't quit. Marvel at York's Minster, the finest Gothic church in England, and ramble through the Shambles, York's wonderfully preserved medieval quarter. Enjoy a walking tour led by an old Yorker. Hop a train at Europe's greatest Railway Museum, travel to the 1800s in the York Castle Museum, and head back to the year 994 at Jorvik, the original Viking settlement.

Planning Your Time

York is a great sightseeing city. On a three-week trip through Britain, it deserves two nights and a day. To maximize sightseeing time, catch the city walking tour at 19:00 on the evening of your arrival. The next morning you might walk the medieval wall to the Castle Museum. This museum is actually worth three hours. Have a touristy walk through the Shambles, browse the Newgate Market, lunch in the Golden Fleece pub if you're in the mood for some second-hand smoke. Tour the Minster at 16:00 before catching the 17:00 evensong service. Wander down to the Jorvik exhibit just before it closes at 19:00 to see it without the wait. Still more energy? Take the Ghost walk. This schedule assumes you're there in the summer (evening orientation walk) and that there's an evensong on. Confirm plans with TI first. Major omission/alternate: the National Railway Museum.

Orientation (tel. code: 01904)

York is big only in historical terms. Virtually everything—the sights, train station, tourist information, and B&Bs—is within a few minutes' walk. The farthest walk a visitor would make (from B&B across the old town to the Castle Museum) takes no more than 15 minutes.

Bootham Bar, a gate in the medieval town wall, is the hub of your York visit. At Bootham Bar (and on Exhibition Square facing it), you'll find the TI, the starting points for most walking tours and bus tours, and handy access to the medieval town wall, and Gillygate, lined with good eateries.

Tourist Information

The TI at Bootham Bar has a free *What's On* and can sell you a map and answer your questions (Monday-Saturday 9:00 -19:00, Sunday 10:00-13:00 in July and August, Monday-Saturday 9:00-17:00, closed Sunday the rest of the year, tel. 01904/621756). It sells a £1 "discount card" which gives two adults and two kids substantial discounts on major sights. If a single traveler uses it twice it's worthwhile.

Trains

The station is a 5-minute walk from town (turn left down station Road and follow the crowd toward the gothic towers of the minster which you'll see in the distance. After the bridge a block before the minster, signs to the TI will send you left.

While no one seems to use them, buses #30, #31, and #32 go from the station to my recommended B&Bs. Otherwise it's a £2.30 taxi ride.

In York, a "bar" is a gate and a "gate" is a street (from the Norse, a reminder of the town's Viking heritage).

Sights—York

▲▲▲**Walking Tours**—Charming local volunteer guides give energetic and entertaining free 2-hour walks through York (daily, 10:15 and 14:15 April-October, plus 19:00 June-August, leaving from the TI). These are better than the gimmicky commercial walks. There are many other York walking tours. The Ghost tours, offered after nightfall, are popular (but the evening free walks also throw in a few ghosts). For a walkman tour you can rent one of three entertaining "Yorspeed" audio tours ("The Streets," around "The Walls," or with "The Ghosts," 1 hour each without stops, £4 for one, £6 for two with this book, tel. 652653, from the TI).

▲**Guide Friday Hop-on and Hop-off Bus Tours**—York's Guide Friday offers tour guides on speed who can talk enthusiastically to three sleeping tourists in a gale on a topless double-decker bus for an hour without stopping. Buses make the hour-long circuit, covering much that the city walking tours don't (£5.50 for all day, departures every 10 or 15 minutes from 9:20 until around 18:00, tel. 640896). While you can hop on and off where you like, the York

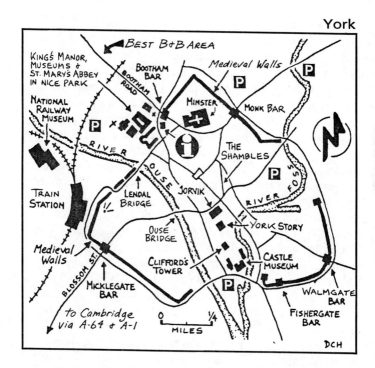

route is of no value from a transportation-to-the-sights point of view. I'd catch it at the TI and ride it all the way around or get off at the Railway Museum, skipping the last 5 minutes.

▲**City Walls**—The historic walls of York provide a fine 2-mile walk. Be sure to walk from Bootham Bar (gate) to Monk Bar for outstanding cathedral views. Open until dusk and free.

▲▲**The National Railway Museum**—This thunderous museum shows 150 fascinating years of British railroad history. Fanning out from a grand roundhouse are an array of historic cars and engines, including Queen Victoria's lavish royal car and the very first "stagecoaches on rails." There's much more, including exhibits on dining cars, post cars, Pullman cars, train posters, and videos. This is the biggest and best railroad museum anywhere (£4.20, Monday-Saturday 10:00-18:00, Sunday 11:00-18:00, tel. 621261).

▲▲▲**The York Minster (cathedral)**—The pride of York, this largest Gothic church in Britain is a brilliant example of how the High Middle Ages were far from dark. Pick up the *Welcome to the York Minster* flyer at the information desk and

ask about a free guided tour. The helpful blue-armbanded
Minster Guides are there to answer your questions. The east
window is the largest medieval glass window in existence. For
most, the chapter room and the crypt are not worth the
admission. But the tower (£2, long climb, great view) and the
undercroft/treasury (£1.80) are. The undercroft gives you a
chance to climb down, archaeologically and physically, through
the centuries to see the roots of the much smaller but still
huge Norman church (Romanesque, 1100) which stood on
this spot, and below that, to the Roman excavations. Constantine
was proclaimed Roman emperor here in 306 A.D. The undercroft also give you a look at the modern concrete save-the-
church foundations. The cathedral is open daily, 7:30-20:30
(tel. 624426). The chapter room, tower, and undercroft have
shorter hours, usually 10:00-17:00. Evensong is a glorious
chance to experience the cathedral in musical and spiritual
action. Evensong services are held daily at 17:00. (16:00 on
Saturday and Sunday, but usually spoken on Wednesday and
when the choir is off). While a donation of £1.50 is reasonably
ably requested, if I'm visiting the undercroft or climbing the
tower, I give it (and more) in the form of those admissions.

▲**The Shambles**—This is the most colorful old York street
in the half-timbered core of town. Ye olde downtown York
is very touristy but a window-shopping, people-watcher's
delight. Wander through the Newgate Market a block over.
The center of York is nearly traffic-free and a busker-filled
joy for walking.

▲▲▲**York Castle Museum**—Truly one of Europe's top
museums, this is a walk with Dickens, the closest thing to a
time-tunnel experience England has to offer. It includes a
magnificent collection of old shops well-stocked exactly as
they were 150 years ago, costumes, armor, an incredible
Anglo-Saxon helmet (from 750 A.D.), and the "every home
needs one" exhibit showing the evolution of vacuum clean-
ers, toilets, TVs, bicycles, stoves, and so on, from their crude
beginnings to now. (£4, 9:30-18:00, Sunday 10:00-18:00,
cafeteria, shop, car park; the £2 guidebook is unnecessary,
but a nice souvenir, tel. 653611.)

▲▲**Jorvik**—The innovative museum of Viking York takes
you back a thousand years—literally backward—in a little
Disney-type train car. Then, still seated, you cruise slowly

for 13 minutes through the sounds, sights, and even smells of the re-created Viking village of Jorvik. Next your little train takes you through the actual excavation sight (best Viking dig I've seen anywhere), then lets you off to browse through a gallery of Viking shoes, combs, locks, and other intimate glimpses of that redheaded culture (£4; daily 9:00-19:00; November-March 9:00-17:30; tel. 643211). Don't be pressured into buying the colorful guidebook with your ticket. To minimize time in line—which can be more than an hour—go very early (at 8:45) or very late. In summer the last entrance is 19:00. Day-trippers make summer midday lines routinely 2 hours long. Jorvik is not worth even a 30-minute wait. Get there at 18:00 and you'll sail right in. Some love this "ride"; others call it a gimmicky rip-off. While it has inspired a chain of copycat historical rides around England, most of which are also gimmicky rip-offs, I like Jorvik.

Honorable Mention—York has a number of other sights and activities (described in TI material) which pale in comparison to the biggies but are worth a look if you have the time. The York Story (£1.60, associated with, across the street from, and pushed by the Castle Museum) is an exhibit displaying the city's past, with a 45-minute video on the history of York. It's good, straight history.

Sleeping in York
(£1 = about $1.50, tel. code: 01904)

I've listed peak-season book-direct prices. If you use the TI, they'll charge you more. Outside of the peak July-August months, York B&B prices get soft and some places may drop by several pounds. Ask for off-season deals. I've limited my recommendations to the handiest B&B neighborhood, just outside the old town wall's Bootham gate, along the road called Bootham. All are within about 5 minutes' walk of the Minster and TI and a 10-minute or £2.30 taxi ride from the station. If you're driving, take A19 into town. It becomes Bootham and you'll find the B&Bs just before Bootham hits York's medieval town gate.

These B&Bs are small, family-run, will generally hold a room with a phone call, work hard to help their guests sightsee and eat smartly, have lots of fairly steep stairs, and are all on quiet, residential side streets. Parking is generally no

York, Our Neighborhood

problem. Most places have their own spots or loaner permits for street parking. The train tracks bordering many places are used by the little Scarborough train that doesn't run at night.

Sleep code: **S**=Single, **D**=Double/Twin, **T**=Triple, **Q**=Quad, **B**=Bath/Shower, **WC**=Toilet, **CC**=Credit Card (**V**isa, **M**astercard, **A**mex).

Airden House—Susan and Keith Burrows keep this snug and traditional place simple and friendly. They are a great source of local travel tips. Airden House, the most central of these Bootham-area listings, has eight rooms, a grandfather-clock-cozy TV lounge, and brightness and warmth throughout. Two of their *en suite* doubles are way up on top (D-£36, DB-£40; 1 St. Mary's, York Y03 7DD, tel. 638915).

The Sycamore, run by Margaret and David Tyce, is a fine value with cozy rooms and plenty of personal touches, at the end of a dead-end right across from a fun-to-watch bowling green (D-£30, DB-£36, family deals, no lounge but TVs in the rooms; 19 Sycamore Place off Bootham Terrace, YO3 7DW, tel. 624712).

Astoria Hotel—Mr. and Mrs. Bradley offer 17 rooms in an old, well-worn, but respectable place (S-£16, SB-£16, D-£30, DB-£35, family deals, CC:V; 6 Grosvenor Terrace, Bootham, York, Y03 7AG, tel. 659558).

Claremont Guest House is a friendly, non-smoking house offering three rooms, thoughtful touches, and solid beds (D-£30, DB-£40; 18 Claremont Terrace off Gillygate, YO3 7EJ, tel. 625158, Gill and Martyn Cornell).

The Hazelwood is my most hotelesque listing. Ian and Carolyn McNabb run this elegant and spacious old 16-room place in a stately, proper way, paying careful attention to details and serving a classy breakfast (S-£22.50, D-£40, DWC-£41, DBWC-£48, DBWC with four-poster-£53, family deals, CC:VM, non-smoking, 1 ground-floor room, reserve by letter; 24 Portland St, Gillygate, YO3 7EH, tel. 626548, fax 628032).

White Doves is a cheery little place with four bright and comfy rooms (DB-£38, 20 Claremont Terrace off Gillygate, YO3 7EJ, tel. 625957, Pauline Pearce).

23 St. Mary's is a rococo riot. Mrs. Hudson has done everything super-correctly, and offers nine rooms with strong beds, modern facilities, a classy lounge and all the doily touches (SB-£30, DB-£56, no smoking; 23 St. Mary's, YO3 7DD, tel. 622738).

Queen Anne's Guest House is compact, clean, and cheery (D-£28, DB-£30 promised through 1995 with this book; 24 Queen Anne's Road, tel. 629389, Judy and David West). For similar prices, you could try **Arron Guest House** (42 Bootham Crescent, tel. 625927). **St. Mary's Hotel** is a decent non-smoking place (D-£32, DB-£44 with book through 1995, CC:V; 17 Longfield Terrace, tel. 626972, Barry Lyons).

The Golden Fleece—For a funky, murky, creaky experience right in the center of the old town, consider this historic 400-year-old pub that rents five rooms upstairs (pub closed at 23:00). The floors aren't level, the beds are four-posters, and the local crowd fills the ground-floor pub with smoke and belly laughs (D-£37, family room with a four-poster and bunks, 1-person jacuzzi in the shared bathroom, private car park; at the bottom end of the Shambles, 16 Pavement, York, YO1 2ND, tel. 625171).

York's Youth Hotel is clean, cheery, and well-run, with lots of extras like a kitchen, laundromat, games, and bar. They take no telephone reservations, but normally have beds until noon (D-£24, £11 in 4- to 6-bed dorms, sheets and breakfast extra, 11 Bishophill Senior Road, York YO1 1EF, tel. 625904 or 630613).

Eating in York

Good Meals Downtown

The old center is slathered with cute eateries. Consider one of several places along the street called Pavement. The **Golden Fleece** pub is a hopping place serving famous Yorkshire Pudding and hearty meals until 22:00. Next door, the **York Pie Shop** does traditional meat pies well. **Kites**, closer to the center, on Grape Lane, serves tasty, fresh, and unusual French and English meals at good prices. **Ye Olde Starre Inn**, the oldest pub in town, has yet to learn the art of cooking.

York is famous for its elegant teahouses. Around four-ish, drop into one for tea and cakes. **Betty's** is most famous, with people lining up to get in, but several others can satisfy your king- or queen-for-a-day desires.

Eating near Bootham Bar and Your B&B

For pub dinners, consider the **Coach House** (18:30-21:30 nightly, 20 Marygate, tel. 652780), **Elliot's Hotel Restaurant and Pub** (dinners nightly, just off Bootham Terrace), or one of several pubs on Gillygate. **Bootham Bistro** (18 Bootham, tel. 630678) is a cheery little no-smoking place serving good English meals for £5. Gillygate, which starts at Bootham Bar, is lined with interesting, cheap, healthy and/or fun eateries: **Mama Mia's** (#20 Gillygate, daily 11:30-14:00 and 17:30-23:00) is great for Italian. A popular extremely vegetarian place, **Miller's Yard Cafe**, is across the street and the **Phoenix** cooks first-class Chinese (eat-in or take-out). There's also a traditional little "chippie" (fish-and-chips joint) at #59 where tattooed people eat in and house-bound mothers take out. Or go with the latest pub-grub advice from the people who run your B&B.

For a reasonable, historic, handy lunch, try the **King's Manor Refectory** on Exhibition Square (through the courtyard on the left, lunch, noon-14:00, Monday-Friday). The tea room at the **Bootham Bar Hotel** (10:00-17:30 daily, 4 High Petergate, near the TI) serves a tasty and reasonable lunch.

Train Connections
York is on the speedy London-Edinburgh rail line. Trains go to: **Durham** (hrly, 1 hr) or **Edinburgh** (hrly, 3 hrs), **London** (hrly, 2 hrs, £44), **Bath** (via Bristol, hrly, 5 hrs), **Cambridge** (nearly hrly, 2 hrs with a change in Petersborough).

Near York: North York Moors
The North York Moors are a vacant lot compared with the Windermere Lakes District. But that's unfair competition. In the lonesome North York Moors, you can wander through the stark beauty of its time-passed villages, bored sheep, and powerful landscapes. Here are the highlights:

Sights—North York Moors
▲**The Moors**—Danby Lodge, the North York Moors Visitors Centre, provides the best orientation for exploring the moors. It's a grand old lodge offering exhibits, shows, and nature walks, an information desk with plenty of books and maps, brass-rubbing, a cheery cafeteria, and brochures on several good walks that start right there (free, daily 10:00-17:00, April-October, tel. 01287/660654).

North Yorkshire Moors Railway—If you're tired of driving (or without wheels), this 18-mile, 50-minute steam-engine ride from Grosmont and Goathland to Pickering goes through some of the best parts of the moors almost hourly. Unfortunately, the windows are small and dirty (wipe off the outside of yours before you roll), and the tracks are in a scenic gully (£10, tel. 01751/72508). Pickering, with its rural-life museum, castle, and Monday market, is worth a stop.

▲**Hutton-le-Hole**—This postcard-pretty town is home of the fine little Ryedale Museum, which illustrates "farm life in the moors" through reconstructed and furnished 18th-century local buildings (daily 10:30-17:30, April-October, tel. 017515/367). Car park and public toilets are nearby.

Castle Howard—Especially popular since the filming of "Brideshead Revisited," this is a fine palatial home but about half as interesting as Cotswolds' Blenheim Palace (late March-October, 2 buses a day from York, 30 minutes).

Rievaulx Abbey—A highlight of the North York Moors, but if you've seen other fine old abbeys, this is a rerun.

EDINBURGH

Edinburgh, the colorful city of Robert Louis Stevenson, Walter Scott, and Robert Burns, is Scotland's showpiece and one of Europe's most entertaining cities. Historical, monumental, fun and well-organized, it's a tourist's delight.

Take a royal hike down the Royal Mile through the old town. Historic, fascinating buildings pack the Royal Mile between the castle (on the top) and Holyrood Palace (on the bottom). Medieval skyscrapers stand shoulder-to-shoulder, hiding peaceful little courtyards connected to High Street by narrow lanes or even tunnels. This colorful jumble, in its day the most crowded city in the world, is the tourist's Edinburgh.

Edinburgh (ED'n-burah) was once two towns divided by a lake. To alleviate crowding, the lake was drained and a magnificent Georgian city, today's New Town, was laid out to the north. Georgian Edinburgh, like the city of Bath, shines with broad boulevards, straight streets, square squares, circular circuses, and elegant mansions decked out in colonnades, pediments, and sphinxes in the proud, Neoclassical style of 200 years ago.

Planning Your Time

While the major sights can be seen in a day, on a 3-week tour of Britain, I'd give Edinburgh 2 days.

Day 1: Orient yourself with a Guide Friday bus tour. Do the whole loop, getting off only to tour the Georgian House. After touring the castle, grab a quick lunch on the Royal Mile. Catch the 14:00 walking tour of the Royal Mile. If you decide to tour Holyrood Palace do it after your walk, at about 16:00.

Day 2: Climb Sir Walter Scott Memorial for a city view; tour the National Gallery. Spend the rest of the day on the Royal Mile museum-going, shopping, or taking the "City, Sea, and Hills" bus tour. Evening: Scottish show, folk pub, or haunted walk.

Orientation (tel. code: 0131)

In the center of Edinburgh are a lovely park and Waverley Bridge where you'll find the TI, Waverley Shopping and Eating Center, train station, bus info office, the starting point for most city bus tours, festival office, the National Gallery, and a covered dance and music pavilion.

Tourist Information

The crowded tourist office (central as can be atop the Waverley Market on Princes Street, 9:00-20:00, Sunday 11:00-20:00, shorter hours and closed Sunday in off-season, tel. 0131/557-1700) has become a profit-seeking business with advice colored by who gives the best commissions. Ideally, skip it and telephone if you have questions. Their misnamed *Essential Guide to Edinburgh* (which costs 25p and shuffles a little information between lots of ads) has a cruddy little map. *The List*, the best monthly entertainment listing, is sold at newsstands. The TI's room-finding service bloats prices to get its cut. "Platform 19," another room-finding service in the station, is a little better—but there's no reason to use either. Call your B&B direct. For real information without the sales push, take advantage of the **Old Town Information Centre** at the Tron Church, where South Bridge hits the Royal Mile. They have a great free map of the Royal Mile. A couple of blocks down the Mile at 5 Blackfriars Street, the Backpackers' Centre is also a good source of information.

Trains and Buses

Arriving by train puts you in the city center a few steps from the TI and bus to my recommended B&Bs. Train info tel. 556-2451. Both National Express (tel. 452-8777) and Scottish Citylink (tel. 557-5717) buses use the bus station a block from the train station in the Georgian town on St. Andrew Square.

The Edinburgh Airport is close to town and well connected by shuttle buses (4/hr, £3.20, flight info: tel. 344-3302).

Getting Around

City buses are handy and inexpensive (LRT information office at the corner of Waverley Bridge and Market Street,

Edinburgh

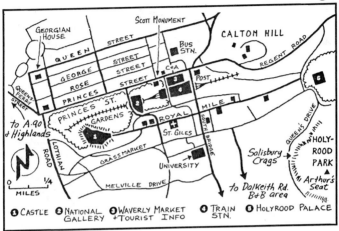

● Castle ❷ National Gallery ❸ Waverly Market + Tourist Info ❹ Train Stn. ❺ Holyrood Palace

info tel. 220-4111, average fare 55p, tell the driver where you're going, drop exact change into box or lose the excess, grab your ticket as you board, and push the stop button so your stop isn't skipped). Taxis are reasonable (easy to flag down, several handy pick-up points, 90p drop charge, 60p extra after 18:00, average ride between downtown and B&B district—£2.50). Nearly all Edinburgh sights are within walking distance.

Banking
Barclays has decent rates and no 2 percent charge if you have Barclays or "interpayment" bank checks (9:30-17:00, 50 meters into new town from TI and station at 18 South Andrew St).

Sights—Along the Royal Mile
(In walking order from top to bottom.)
▲▲▲**Royal Mile**—This is one of Europe's most interesting historic walks. Follow a local guide (daily at 10:00, 11:00 and 14:00, often free during the festival, £4 other times, see below) or do it yourself with a Royal Mile guidebook. Each step of the way is entertaining. Start at the top and loiter down to the palace. I've listed the top sights of the Royal Mile—working downhill.

   The Royal Mile is actually a series of different streets in a straight line. All along, you'll find interesting shops, cafés, and closes (lanes leading to tiny squares), providing the thoughtful visitor a few little rough edges of the old town. See it now. In a few years, it will be a string of tourist gimmicks, woolen shops, and contrived "sights."

▲▲**Edinburgh Castle**—The fortified birthplace of the city 1,300 years ago, this is the imposing symbol of Edinburgh. Start with the free 30-minute guided introduction tour (every 20 minutes from entry, see clock for the next departure). See the Scottish National War Memorial, the Banqueting Hall with fine Scottish Crown Jewels, the room full of Battle of Culloden mementos, St. Margaret's Chapel (oldest building in town), the giant cannon, and the city view from the ramparts (in that order). Allow 90 minutes, including the tour. (£5, 9:30-18:00, until 17:00 in winter and on holidays, tel. 244-3101, cafeteria.)

The Scotch Whiskey Heritage Centre is only for the desperate. Even with little whiskey kegs for train cars and toilets that actually got the "Loo of the Year" award, the Whiskey ride is a rip-off designed to distill £4 out of your pocket. The Camera Obscura across the street is just as rewarding.

▲▲**Gladstone's Land**—Take a good look at this typical 16th- to17th-century house, complete with lived-in furnished interior and guides in each room who love to talk. (£2.50, April-October 10:00-17:00, Sunday 14:00-17:00, good Royal Mile photo from the top-floor window or from the top of its entry stairway through the golden eagle.)

▲**Lady Stair's House/Writers' Museum**—This interesting house, which dates back to 1622, is filled with manuscripts and knickknacks of Scotland's three greatest literary figures:

Royal Mile

Robert Burns, Sir Walter Scott, and Robert Louis Stevenson. Worth a few minutes for anyone, fascinating for fans (free, 10:00-18:00, till 17:00 off-season, closed Sunday).

Deacon Brodies' Tavern—A decent place for a light meal (see below); read the story of its notorious namesake on the wall facing Bank Street.

▲**St. Giles Cathedral**—Don't miss this engaging Gothic church's ornate, medieval thistle chapel (to the right of the altar, 50p) or the Scottish crown steeple on top (daily 9:00-19:00, until 17:00 off-season, fine café downstairs). John Knox, founder of austere Scottish Presbyterianism, is buried out back, austerely, under the parking lot (spot 44).

The Parliament House—Stop in to see the grand hall with its fine hammer-beamed ceiling and stained glass (free, public welcome). For a trip into the 18th century, drop by Tuesday through Friday around 10:00 or 10:30, the best time to see all the wigged and robed legal beagles hard at work. Greater eminence . . . longer wig. You are welcome to observe trials in action (10:00-16:00). The doorman is helpful (entry behind St. Giles Church near parking spot 21, open daily).

Museum of Childhood is a 5-story playground of historical toys and games (free, 10:00-18:00, till 17:00 off-season, closed Sundays).

John Knox's House—Fascinating for Reformation buffs. This fine 16th-century house is filled with things from the life of the Great Reformer. (£1.25, 10:00-16:30, firmly closed on Sunday.)

▲**Scottish Experience and Living Craft Centre**—This commercial venture actually fills a void and, for many, makes an entertaining visit. You'll see several crafts in action (bagpipe-making, weaving, kilt-making) and a computerized study-your-clan center. The tiny theater (£1) continuously runs two videos on Edinburgh or Scotland and is ringed by an exhibit on Highland dress (free, 10:00-18:00, tel. 557-9350, home of recommended Scottish Evening, described below).

People's Story is an interesting exhibition tracing the lot of the working class through the 18th, 19th, and 20th centuries (free, 10:00-18:00, till 17:00 off-season, closed Sundays).

▲**Huntly House**—Another old house full of old stuff, worth a look for its early Edinburgh history and handy ground-floor WC. Don't miss the copy of the National Covenant written on an animal skin or the sketches of pre-Georgian Edinburgh with its lake still wet (free, 10:00-18:00, closed Sunday).

▲**Holyrood Palace**, at the bottom end of the Royal Mile, is where the Queen stays when she's in town. On a mandatory guided tour, see the royal apartments, state apartment, lots of rich furnishings, paintings, and history (£3.50, 9:30-18:00, Sunday 10:30-16:30, closed when the Queen's home, tel. 556-7371).

Bonnie Wee Other Sights

▲**Walter Scott Monument**—Built in 1840, this elaborate, neo-Gothic monument honors the great author, one of Edinburgh's many illustrious sons. Climb 287 steps for a royal view of the Royal Mile (£1, 9:00-18:00, until 17:00 off-season, closed Sunday).

▲▲**Georgian House** is a trip back to 1796. This refurbished Georgian house comes with a volunteer guide in each room trained in the force-feeding of stories and trivia. Start your visit with the interesting video (£3, 10:00-17:00, Sunday 14:00-17:00, at 7 Charlotte Square). From this museum, walk through Georgian Edinburgh. The grand George Street, connecting St. Andrew and Charlotte Squares, was the centerpiece of the elegantly planned New Town.

Princes Street Gardens—This grassy former lake-bed separates Edinburgh's new and old towns with a wonderful escape from the city-ness of it all. There are plenty of concerts and dances in the summer and the oldest floral clock in the world. Join local office workers for a picnic-lunch break.

National Gallery—An elegant Neoclassical building with a small, but impressive, collection of European masterpieces and the best look you'll get at Scottish paintings (free, 10:00-17:00, Sunday 14:00-17:00, tel. 556-8921).

▲▲**Walking Tours**—Several competitive and hard-working little companies do Royal Mile (usually 10:00, 11:00 and 14:00) and Ghost walks (usually 19:00 and 21:00). Tours are about 1½ to 2 hours long and cost £4. Pick up brochures for Robin's (start at TI, tel. 661-0125) and Mercat (meet 30 minutes early at the TI for those who can't find Mercat Cross on the Royal Mile, tel. 661-4541). The Royal Mile tour is most important. These entertaining tours are led by guides who enjoy making a short story long. They ignore the big sights, taking you behind the scenes with piles of barely historic gossip, bully-pulpit Scottish pride, and fun but forgettable trivia. The evening walks, more than a pile of ghost stories, are an entertaining and cheap night out. You can also rent **audio tape tours** (£4, from Tolbooth Church near castle, drop walkman near palace) for an hour-long professional narration-with-music that walks you the length of the Mile and offers little more than the information you already have in your hands. (Audio tours can also be rented at the Tron Church Old Town Information Centre.)

▲**Hop-on and Hop-off City Bus Tours**—Guide Friday (£5.50, tel. 556-2244) and LRT's "Edinburgh Classic Tour" (£4.50, tel. 220-4111) both circle the town center—Waverley Bridge, around the castle, Royal Mile, Calton Hill, Georgian town, and Princes Street—in about an hour with pick-ups about every 15 minutes and an informative narration. You can stop and go all day on one ticket. Overlapping can be interesting, since each guide has her own story to tell. On sunny days they go topless (the buses), but can suffer from traffic noise and congestion.

City Bus Tours—Several all-day bus tours can take you as far as Loch Ness. Tours leave from near the train station. "City, Sea, and Hills" is the best 90-minute tour of greater Edinburgh (£3, information at LRT office, on Waverley Bridge, tel. 220-4111).

Royal Commonwealth Games Swimming Pool—The biggest pool I've ever seen. Open to the public, good Café Aqua overlooking the pool, weights, saunas, and plenty of water rides, including Europe's biggest "flume" or water slide (£1.75, Monday-Friday 9:00-21:00, Saturday and Sunday 8:00-19:00, tel. 667-7211). If you'd rather be skiing, there's an open-all-year hill covered with brush, with a chairlift, T-bar, and rentable skis, boots, and poles, on the edge of town (daily 9:30-21:00, tel. 445-4433).

▲**Arthur's Seat**—A 30-minute hike up the 822-foot volcanic mountain (surrounded by a fine park overlooking Edinburgh), starting from the Holyrood Palace or the Commonwealth Pool, gives you a rewarding view. It's the easiest "I climbed a mountain" feeling I've ever had. You can drive up most of the way from behind; follow the one-way street from the palace (park by the little lake).

Greyhound Races—This is a pretty lowbrow scene. But if you've never seen dog racing, this is a memorable night out combining great dog- and people-watching with a chance to lose some money gambling. Races are held about two nights a week at Powderhall Stadium.

Edinburgh Crystal—Blowing, molding, cutting, polishing, engraving, the Edinburgh Crystal Company glassworks tour smashes anything you'll see in Venice. The 35-minute tours start at regular intervals between 9:15 and 15:30, Monday-Friday (£2, children under age 8 and large dogs are not allowed in for safety reasons). There is a shop full of "bargain" second-quality pieces, a video show, and a good cafeteria. (Free red minibus shuttle service from Waverley Bridge departs 10:00, 11:00, 12:00, 14:00, and 15:00 in summer, or drive 10 miles south of town on A701 to Penicuik. Call first, tel. 01968/675128.)

Stirling Castle—It's popular but currently used as a barracks, and nowhere near as interesting as Edinburgh's castle. The town is pleasantly medieval, however, and many commute (1 hour by train) to the more hectic Edinburgh from here. (TI tel. 01786/475019.)

▲▲▲The Edinburgh Festival—One of Europe's great cultural events, Edinburgh's annual festival turns the city into a carnival of culture. There are enough music, dance, art, drama, and multicultural events to make even the most jaded tourist get frisky and drool with excitement. Every day is jammed with formal and spontaneous fun. The official and fringe festivals rage from mid-August through early September (August 13-September 2 in 1995, August 11-31 in 1996), with the Military Tattoo starting a week earlier. Many city sights run on extended hours, and those that normally close on Sundays, don't. It's a glorious time to be in Edinburgh.

The official festival is more formal and serious, with entertainment by festival invitation only. Although major events sell out well in advance, 50 seats are held to be sold at 8:00 on the day of the show at the show office at 21 Market Street (£4-£35, major credit cards accepted, booking from April on, tel. 225-5756).

The less formal, "on the edge" comedy and theater, Fringe Festival (ticket and info office just below St. Giles Cathedral on the Royal Mile, tel. 226-5259, bookings tel. 226-5138) has hundreds of events and, it seems, more performers than viewers. Tickets are usually available at the door.

The Military Tattoo is a massing of the bands, drums, and bagpipes with groups from all over what was the British Empire. Displaying military finesse with a stirring lone-piper finale, this grand spectacle fills the castle esplanade nightly except Sunday, normally from a week before the festival starts until a week before it finishes (£8-£15, major credit cards accepted, booking starts in January, tel. 225-1188, Friday and Saturday shows sell out, Monday-Thursday shows rarely do). If nothing else, it is a really big show.

If you do manage to hit Edinburgh during the festival, extend your stay by a day or two and book a room far in advance. While fringe tickets and most Tattoo tickets are available the day of the show, you may want to book an official event or two in advance. Do it direct and easy by telephone, leaving your credit-card number. You can pick up your ticket at the office the day of the show. Several publications list and evaluate festival events, including the festival's official schedule, the *Festival Times*, *The List*, *Fringe Program*, and the *Daily Diary*.

Shopping—The best shopping is along Princes Street (don't miss elegant old Jenner's Department Store), Victoria Street (antiques galore), and the Royal Mile (touristy but competitively priced, shops usually open 9:00-17:30, later on Thursday).

Entertainment in Edinburgh

▲**Scottish folk evenings**—These £25 to £30 dinner shows, are generally for tour groups, held in huge halls of expensive hotels. (Prices are bloated to include 20% commissions, without which, the show don't go on.) You get a "traditional" meal followed by a full slate of swirling kilts, blaring bagpipes, and colorful Scottish folk dancing with an "old-time music hall"-type master of ceremonies. **Prince Charlie's Extravaganza** at The Scottish Experience (described above), across from John Knox's house on the Royal Mile, is a fun show. It's too small for a massing of the tour groups (about 60 seats), smoke-free (thank goodness, you're pretty packed in), and serves a decent four-course meal (Scotch broth, haggis with neeps and tatties, and a beef pastry with vegetables, wine, ice cream and coffee, vegetarian alternatives available). The dancing and music (piping, accordion, singing) are good, and if you reserve directly showing this book you get a 20 percent discount off the £25 price (meal at 19:00, show starts at 19:30, and you sing "Auld Lang Syne" by 22:00, shows nearly nightly, tel. 557-9350). The boss, Mike Boyle, promised this special price for 1995.

▲**Folk music in pubs**—For an informal evening of folk music, head on down to Grassmarket (below the castle) and find the right pub. The Fiddlers Arms (tel. 229-2665), White Hart Inn, and Black Bull, among others, regularly feature live folk music. Preservation Hall (a block away on Victoria Street, tel. 226-3816) has live jazz and rock on many Thursday, Friday, and Saturday nights. Just off the Royal Mile on Cockburn Street, the Malt Shovel Pub is a typical Edinburgh pub with impromptu folk and jazz most nights and the best selection of malt whiskey in town (225-6843). My favorite Scottish band, the North Sea Gas, plays every Friday and many Saturdays (20:30-23:00, free) at Platform One in the Caledonian Hotel on Princes Street. The Edinburgh Folk Club, which meets at the Bistro Bar Wednesday evenings (£4, near Princes Street, tel. 557-4792), is a good bet for traditional music and dancing.

Sleeping in Edinburgh
(£1 = about $1.50, tel. code: 0131)

The annual festival fills the city every year in the last half of August (August 13-September 2 in 1995). Conventions, school holidays, and other surprises can make room-finding tough at almost any time. If you don't call in advance you'll probably end up paying 30 percent extra for a relative dump. The good places are a fine value; the rest are depressing. Downtown hotels are overpriced (minimum £70 doubles). For the best prices, book direct and call in advance! Going direct (rather than through the greedy TI), you're likely to get the best price. When a room has no "en suite facilities," they are usually a tissue toss away.

My favorite B&B district, where you'll find all these recommendations, is south of town near the Royal Commonwealth Pool, just off Dalkeith Road. This com-

Edinburgh, Our Neighborhood

fortably safe neighborhood is a 20-minute walk or short bus ride from the Royal Mile. All listings are on quiet streets, a 2-minute walk from a bus stop, and well-served by city buses. Near the B&Bs, you'll find plenty of eateries, easy free parking, and a handy laundromat (Monday-Friday 8:30-17:00, Saturday and Sunday 10:00-14:30, £2.50 for a self-serve load; ask about drop-off-and-pick-up service, 208 Dalkeith Road, tel. 667-0825).

From the station, TI, or Scott Monument cross Princes Street and wait under the C&A sign (buses #21, #33, #82, #C11, or #86, 60p, exact change or pay more, ride 10 minutes to first stop 100 yards after the Pool, push the button). These buses also stop at North Bridge and High Street on the Royal Mile. Prices may vary with the seasonal demand.

Sleep code: **S**=Single, **D**=Double/Twin, **T**=Triple, **Q**=Quad, **B**=Bath/Shower, **WC**=Toilet, **CC**=Credit Card (**V**isa, **M**astercard, **A**mex).

Millfield Guest House, run by Liz and Ed Broomfield, is thoughtfully furnished with antique class, a rare sit-and-chat ambience, and a comfy TV lounge. Since the showers are down the hall, you'll get spacious rooms and great prices (S-£15.50 to £16.50, D-£31 to £33, T-£46 to £49 for direct bookings only; good beds, absolutely no smoking, quiet but friendly, CC:VM, easy reservation with CC which lets you arrive late; 12 Marchhall Road, EH16 5HR, tel. 031/ 667-4428). Decipher the breakfast prayer by Robert Burns. See how many stone (14 lb) you weigh in the elegant throne room. This is worth calling well in advance.

The Belford House is tidy, simple, fresh, bright, friendly, and a fine value (D-£34, T-£51, family deals; 13 Blacket Avenue, tel. 667-2422, Mrs. Borthwick).

Ravensneuk Guest House is also good (D-£34 to £40 depending on room and season, DBWC-£50, family deals, great lounge, solid beds, some non-smoking rooms; 11 Blacket Ave., EH9 1RR, tel. 667-5347). Jeanette and Jim Learmonth rent five rooms in this quiet, comfortable, and very Victorian home.

Dunedin Guest House is bright and pastel, nearly non-smoking, and a good value for those who need a private bathroom (S-£20, DB-£38 to £42 depending on the season, family deals, 7 rooms, solid beds, TVs in rooms, Scotland and Edinburgh videos in lounge; 8 Priestfield Road, EH16 5HH, tel. 668-1949, Annette Preston).

Dorstan Private Hotel is small and personable, but professional and hotelesque with all the comforts. Several of its 14 prim rooms are on the ground floor. (DB-£56, DBWC-£62, family rooms, CC:VM; 7 Priestfield Road, EH16 5HJ, tel. 667-6721, fax 668-4644, Mairae Campbell).

Kenvie Guest House (one small twin-£30, D-£32, DB-£40; prices for direct bookings promised through 1995; family rooms; 16 Kilmaurs Rd., EH16 5DA, tel. 668-1964, easy telephone reservations, Dorothy Vidler) offers no-smoking rooms and lots of personal touches.

Priestville B&B (D-£30, DBWC-£36, priced for direct bookings through 1995, 10 Priestfield Road, tel. 667-2435, Audrey and Jim Christie) is a big old place, a little smoky, with charming rough edges and a friendly welcome.

These places are sleepable in the same fine neighbor-hood: **Highland Park House** (D-£32, 16 Kilmaurs Terrace, tel. 667-9204, Mrs. Cathy Kelly), and **Turret Guest House** (D-£34, DBWC-£42, 8 Kilmaurs Terrace, Mrs. Jackie Cameron, tel. 667-6704).

Sleeping in Dorms and Hostels

Although Edinburgh's youth hostels are well-run, open to all, and provide £8 bunk beds, an £8 savings over B&Bs, they include no breakfast and are comparatively scruffy. They are **The Bruntsfield Hostel** (on a park, 7 Bruntsfield Crescent, buses #11, #15, #16 to and from Princes St., tel. 447-2994); the **Edinburgh Hostel** (4 to 22 beds per room, 18 Eglinton Crescent, tel. 337-1120). The **High Street Independent Hostel** (8- to 10-bed rooms, young, hip, well-run, scruffy, videos, my mom wouldn't sleep a wink here, but my little sister would dig it, 50 yards off the Royal Mile; 8 Blackfriars St., tel. 557-3984, free historic walks many mornings, no mem-bership needed) is perfectly located; bursting with user-friendly services; runs another place up the street; is a grapevine for shoestring, nose-ring travelers; and little old ladies have reportedly enjoyed a stay here. They are certainly welcome.

Eating in Edinburgh

Eating Along the Royal Mile

Historic pubs and doily cafés with reasonable, unremarkable meals abound. **Deacon Brodie's Pub** serves soup, sand-wiches, and snacks on the ground floor and good £5 meals upstairs (daily 12:00-22:00, crowded after 20:00). For a cheap lunch in legal surroundings, try the cafeteria in the **Parliament House** (9:30-15:00, Monday-Friday, entry behind St. Giles church near parking spot 21). Or munch prayerfully in the **Lower Aisle** restaurant under St. Giles church (Monday-Friday 10:00-16:30). **Clarinda's Tea Room**, near the bottom of the Royal Mile, is also good (9:00-16:45 daily). **Dubh Prais Restaurant** serves decent Scottish food in a small, candlelit, stone-walled basement (£15 and up, reserve in advance, lunchtime and 18:30-22:30, closed Sunday and Monday; just below St. Giles Cathedral at 123b High Street, tel. 557-5732; chef/owner James

McWillians). On Victoria Street, consider the very French **Pierre Victoire** (£10 meals, lunch and 18:00-23:00, closed Sunday, #9 Victoria St, tel. 225-1721) or the upstairs café in the Byzantium antique mall, across the street from Pierre Victoire.

Eating in the New Town
The **Waverley Center Food Court**, below the TI and above the station, is a ring of flashy, trendy, fast-food joints (including Scot's Pantry for quick traditional edibles) littered with paper plates and shoppers. Edinburgh seems to be a lunching kind of place. Local office workers pile into **Lanterna** for good Italian food (family-run, fresh and friendly, 83 Hanover St., 2 blocks off Princes St., tel. 226-3090). Rose Street has tons of pubs.

Eating in Dalkeith Road Area, near Your B&B
Within a block of the corner of Newtington and Preston Streets are all kinds of little eateries. For a fun local atmosphere that makes up for the food, the **Wine Glass Pub**, serves filling "basket meals" (Sunday-Thursday, 18:00-20:30, £3.50. **Chinatown**, next to the Wine Glass, is moderate and good. The **Chatterbox** (8:30-20:00, down Preston St. from the big pool) is fine for a light meal with tea. For bad fish-and-chips, **Brattisanis** at 87 Newington Road is good. Skip the milkshakes, but if you need some cheap haggis, they've got it. The huge **Commonwealth Pool** has a noisy cafeteria for hungry swimmers and budget travelers (pass the entry without paying, sit with a poolside view).

Train Connections
Edinburgh to Inverness (7/day, 4 hrs), **York** (hrly, 2½ hrs), **London** (hrly, 5 hrs), **Durham** (hrly, 2 hrs), **Lake District** (train south past Carlisle to Penrith, catch a bus to Keswick; 6/day, 40-min trip).

ROME

Rome (Roma) is magnificent and brutal at the same time. Your ears will ring, your nose will turn your hankie black, the careless will be run down or pickpocketed, you'll be frustrated by chaos that only an Italian can understand. You may even come to believe Mussolini was necessary. But Rome is required. If your hotel provides a comfortable refuge; if you pace yourself, accept and even partake in the siesta plan; if you're well-organized for sightseeing; and if you protect yourself and your valuables with extra caution and discretion, you'll do fine. You'll see the sights and leave satisfied.

Rome at its peak meant civilization itself. Everything was either civilized (part of the Roman Empire, Latin- or Greek-speaking) or barbarian. Today, Rome is Italy's political capital, the capital of Catholicism, and a splendid . . . "junkpile" is not quite the right word . . . of western civilization. As you wander, you'll find its buildings, people, cats, laundry, and traffic endlessly entertaining. And then, of course, there are its magnificent sights.

Tour St. Peter's, the greatest church on earth, and scale Michelangelo's 100-yard-tall dome, the world's largest. Learn something about eternity by touring the huge Vatican Museum. You'll find paradise—bright as the day it was painted—in the Sistine Chapel. Do the "Caesar shuffle" walk from the historic Colosseum through the ancient Forum, and over the Capitoline Hill. Enjoy the sweet life. Take an early evening "Dolce Vita Stroll" down the Via del Corso with Rome's beautiful people.

Planning Your Time

For most, Rome is best done fast. It's great, but exhausting. Time is normally short and Italy is more charming elsewhere.

To "do" Rome in a day, consider it as a side trip from Orvieto or Florence and maybe before the night train to Venice. Crazy as that sounds, if all you have is a day, it's a great one.

If you only have a day, be brutally selective: Vatican (2 hours in museum and Sistine and an hour in St. Peter's), march over river to Pantheon, then over the Capitoline Hill, through the Forum and to the Colosseum. Dinner on Campo di Fiori and evening stroll (Piazza Navona to Spanish Steps).

With two days (the optimal first visit): To maximize open hours do odd sights that close at 13:00 first and finish the day with the "Caesar Shuffle" through the Forum and Colosseum. On the second day do the Vatican (St. Peters, climb the dome, tour the museum). After a siesta, join the locals strolling (Piazza del Popolo to Spanish Steps) or Trastevere to Campo di Fiori to Spanish Steps.

With a third day consider adding a side trip to Ostia and another museum.

Rome Area

Orientation (tel. code: 06)

The modern sprawl of Rome is of no interest to us. Our Rome is the old core—within the triangle formed by the train station, Colosseum, and Vatican. Get a handle on Rome by considering it in these chunks: **The ancient city** had a million people. Tear it down to size by walking through just the core. The best of the classical sights stand in a line from the Colosseum to the Pantheon. In the time of **Medieval Rome**, the population dipped as low as 50,000, and a good part of them were thieves. The medieval city, a colorful tangle of lanes, lies between the Pantheon and the river. **Window-shoppers' Rome** twinkles with nightlife and ritzy shopping near medieval Rome, on or near Rome's main drag, the Via del Corso. **The Vatican City** is a compact world of its own with two great sights: a huge basilica and the museum. And **Trastevere**, the seedy/colorful wrong-side-of-the-river neighborhood-village, is Rome at its crustiest. **Baroque Rome** is an overleaf that embellishes great squares throughout the town with fountains and church facades.

Tourist Information

Rome offers less tourist information per capita than any city in the First World. Most available publications are two years old, and nobody seems to know or care what is actually going on. The Ente Provinciale Per il Turismo (EPT) has three offices (8:15-19:15): at the airport, in the train station (near track #1, very crowded, the only one open on Sunday), and the central office (5 Via Parigi, just a 5-minute walk out the front of the station, near Piazza della Republica's huge fountain, less crowded and more helpful, air-conditioned with comfortable sofas and a desk to plan on—or sit at to overcome your frustration, tel. 06/48899255 or 48899253). Get the free EPT city map (better than the free McDonald's version, ask for one with bus lines) and a monthly periodical guide if there is one. (If all you need is a map, forget the TI. Most hotels carry the EPT map.) Fancy hotels carry a free and helpful English monthly, *Un Ospite a Roma* (A Guest in Rome). All hotels list an inflated rate to cover the hefty commission any room-finding service charges. You'll save money by booking direct.

Enjoy Rome (8:30-13:00, 15:30-18:00, closed Saturday afternoon and on Sunday, 3 blocks northeast of the station at Via Varese 39, tel. 4451843, English-speaking) is a free and friendly new information service providing maps, museum hours, and a room-finding service.

Apart from the normal big bus tours, the ATAC city buses do a 3-hour orientation tour daily. And American

Rome

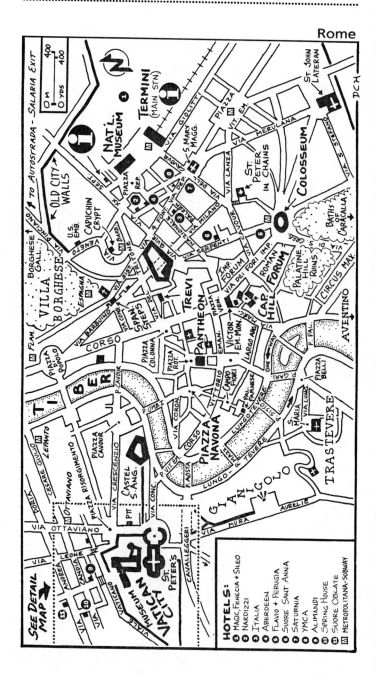

HOTELS:
1. Magic, Fenecia + Sileo
2. Nardizzi
3. Italia
4. Aberdeen
5. Flavio + Perugia
6. Suore Sant'Anna
7. Saturnia
8. YMCA
9. Alimandi
10. Spring House
11. Suore Obl-ate
Ⓜ Metropolitana-Subway

students in Rome lead "Secret Walks" (May-October). Three or four different walks are given daily (L5,000 membership card required plus L12,000 per tour or L9,000 for students, children under 15 go free, tel. 39728728).

Trains and Buses
The Termini train station is a mine field of tourist services: a late-hours bank, a day hotel, luggage lockers, 24-hour thievery, the city bus station, and a subway stop. Handy multilingual charts make locations very clear. La Piazza is a bright and cheery self-service restaurant (open 11:00-22:30).

Getting Around Rome
Sightsee on foot, by city bus, or taxi. I've grouped your sightseeing into walkable neighborhoods. Public transportation is efficient, cheap, and part of your Roman experience.
Buses: Bus routes are clearly listed at the stops. Bus #64 is particularly useful, connecting the station, Victor Emmanuel Monument (near the Forum), and the Vatican. Ride it for a city overview and to watch pickpockets in action. Buy tickets at newsstands, tobacco shops, or at major bus stops but not on board (L1,200, good for 90 minutes, punch them yourself as you board). Buy a bunch so you can hop a bus without searching for an open tobacco shop. (Riding without a ticket, while relatively safe, is still stressful. Inspectors fine even innocent-looking tourists L50,000 if found on a bus or subway without a ticket.) If you hop a bus without a ticket, locals who use tickets rather than a monthly pass can sell you a ticket from their wallet bundle. All-day bus/Metro passes cost L4,000. Learn which buses serve your neighborhood.

Buses, especially the touristic #64, and the subway, are havens for thieves and pickpockets. Assume any commotion is a thief-created distraction. Watch your pack, wear no wallet, and keep your money belt out of sight. When it's crowded, a giggle or a jostle can be expensive. For six trips in a row, I've met a tourist who was pickpocketed. You are a target.
Subway: The Roman subway system (Metropolitana) is simple, with two clean, cheap, fast lines. While much of Rome is not served by its skimpy subway, these stops may be helpful to you: Termini (central train station, several recommended hotels, National Museum), Republica (main tourist office,

Metropolitana: Rome's Subway

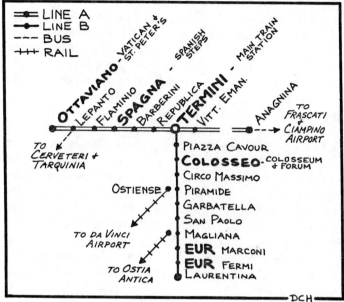

several recommended hotels), Barberini (Cappuccin Crypt, Trevi Fountain), Spagna (Spanish Steps, Villa Borghese, classiest shopping area), Flaminio (Piazza del Popolo, start of the Via del Corso Dolce Vita stroll), Ottaviano (the Vatican, recommended hotels), Colosseo (the Colosseum, Roman Forum, recommended hotels), and EUR (Mussolini's futuristic suburb). Buy your L1,000 subway tickets at subway ticket counters. (Attendants will try to short-change you.)

Taxis: Taxis' big drop-charge (L6,400) covers you for 3 kilometers. (L5,000 surcharge after 22:00.) From the train station to the Colosseo costs about L8,000, to the Vatican about L12,000. Three or four traveling together with more money than time should taxi almost everywhere. Rather than wave and wave, ask in local shops for the nearest taxi stand (*"Dov'e una fermata dei tassi?"*). The meter is fair.

Helpful Hints

General Museum Hours: 9:00-14:00, closed on Monday (except the Vatican) and at 13:00 on Sunday. Outdoor sights like the Colosseum, Forum, and Ostia Antica are open

9:00-19:00 (15:00 in winter), and are often closed one day a week. The Capitoline Hill museums, Rome's only nocturnal museums, are open Tuesday 17:00-20:00, and Saturday 20:00-23:00. There are absolutely no absolutes in Italy. These hours will vary. Confirm sightseeing plans each morning with a quick L200 telephone call asking, "Are you open today?" (*"Aperto oggi?"*) and "What time do you close?" (*"A che ora chiuso?"*). I've included telephone numbers for this purpose. The last pages of the daily "Messaggero" newspaper list current events, exhibits, and hours.

Churches: Churches open early, close for lunch, and reopen for a few hours around 16:00. Modest dress means no bare shoulders, mini-skirts, or shorts (men or women). Kamikaze tourists maximize their sightseeing hours by visiting churches before 9:00, seeing the major sights that don't close for siesta (St. Peter's and the Forum), when all good Romans are taking it cool and easy, and doing the nocturnal museums after dark.

Shop Hours: Usually 9:00-13:00 and 16:00-20:00. In the holiday month of August, many shops and restaurants close up for vacation—*Chiuso per ferie* (and closed for restoration) signs decorate locked doors all over town.

Theft Alert: With sweet-talking con artists, pickpockets on buses and at the station, and thieving gangs at the ancient sights, Rome is a gauntlet of rip-offs. Other than getting run down, there's no great physical risk. But green tourists will be ripped off. Thieves strike when you're distracted. Don't trust kind strangers and keep nothing important in your pockets. Assume you're being stalked.

Buyer Beware: I carefully understand the final price before I order *anything* and I deliberately count my change. Expect the "slow count." Wait for the last bits of your change to straggle over to you. There are legitimate extras (café prices skyrocket when you sit down, taxis get L5,000 extra after 22:00, and so on) to which paranoid tourists wrongly take offense. But the waiter who charges you L70,000 for the pizza and beer assumes you're too polite to involve the police. If you have any problem with a restaurant, hotel, or taxi, get a cop to arbitrate. Rome is trying to civilize itself.

Siesta: The siesta is a key to survival in summertime Rome. Lie down and contemplate the extraordinary power of gravity in the eternal city. I drink lots of cold, refreshing water from

Rome's many drinking fountains (the Forum has three). If you get sick, call the International Medical Center (tel. 4882371).

Sights—Rome
(These sights are in walking order.)

▲**St. Peter-in-Chains Church (San Pietro in Vincoli)**—
The original chains and Michelangelo's able-to-stand-and-toss-those-tablets *Moses* are on exhibit in an otherwise unexceptional church. Just a short walk uphill from the Colosseum (free, 6:30-12:30, 15:30-19:00, modest dress required).

Downtown Ancient Rome

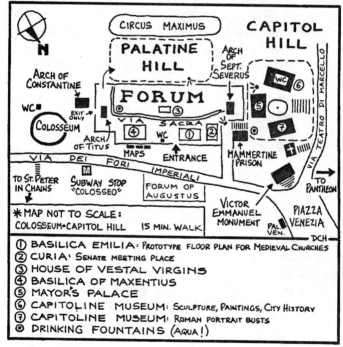

① BASILICA EMILIA: Prototype floor plan for Medieval Churches
② CURIA: Senate meeting place
③ HOUSE OF VESTAL VIRGINS
④ BASILICA OF MAXENTIUS
⑤ MAYOR'S PALACE
⑥ CAPITOLINE MUSEUM: Sculpture, Paintings, City History
⑦ CAPITOLINE MUSEUM: Roman portrait busts
⊙ DRINKING FOUNTAINS (Aqua!)

▲▲▲**Colosseum**—This is the great example of Roman engineering, 2,000 years old. The Romans, using concrete, brick, and their trademark round arches, were able to construct much larger buildings than the Greeks. But in deference to the higher Greek culture, notice how they finished their no-nonsense mega-structure by pasting all three orders (Doric, Ionic, and Corinthian) of Greek columns as decorations on the outside. The Flavian Amphitheater's popular name "Colosseum" comes from the colossal statue of Nero that used to stand in front of it.

Romans were into "big." By putting two theaters together, they created a circular amphitheater. They could fill and empty its 50,000 numbered seats as quickly and efficiently as we do our super-stadiums. They had teams of sailors who could hoist canvas awnings over the stadium to give the fans shade. This was where the ancient Romans, whose taste was nearly as violent as modern America's, enjoyed their Dirty Harry and Terminator. Gladiators, criminals, and wild animals fought to the death in every conceivable scenario. They could even flood the place to wage mock naval battles (free, L6,000 to go upstairs, daily 9:00-19:00, Sunday and Wednesday 9:00-13:00, less off-season, tel. 7004261).

▲▲▲**Roman Forum (Foro Romano)**—Ancient Rome's birthplace and civic center, the Forum was the common ground between Rome's famous seven hills. To help resurrect this confusing pile of rubble, study the before-and-after pictures in the cheap city guidebooks sold on the streets. (Check out the small red *Rome, Past and Present* books with plastic overleafs to un-ruin the ruins. They're priced at L25,000— pay no more than L10,000.)

Start at the Basilica Aemilia, on your right as you walk down the entry ramp. This ancient palace's floor plan shows how medieval churches adopted the "basilica" design. Then walk the Via Sacra, the main street of ancient Rome, running from the Arch of Septimus Severus on the right, past Basilica Aemilia, up to the Arch of Titus and the Colosseum on the left. The plain, intact brick building near the Arch of Septimus Severus was the Curia where the Roman senate sat. (Peek inside.) Only the giant barrel vault remains of the huge Basilica Maxentius, looming crumbly and weed-eaten to the left of Via Sacra as you walk to the Arch of Titus (direction: Colosseum).

As you stand in the shadow of the Bas Max, reconstruct the place in your mind. The huge barrel vaults were just side niches. Extend the broken nub of an arch out over the vacant lot and finish your imaginary Roman basilica with rich marble and fountains. People it with plenty of toga-clad Romans. Yeow.

The Arch of Titus is carved with propaganda celebrating the defeat, in A.D. 70, of the Jews which began the Diaspora that ended only with the creation of Israel in 1947 (find the menorah).

From the Titus drinking fountain, walk up the Palatine Hill to the remains of the Imperial palaces. We get our word "palace" from this hill, where the emperors chose to live. The pleasant garden overlooks the Forum; on the far side, look down on the dusty old Circus Maximus. (L10,000, Forum open 9:00-19:00, Sunday 9:00-13:00, off-season 9:00-15:00, last tickets sold an hour before closing, tel. 6990110). Just past the entry, there's a WC and a handy headless statue for you to pose behind.

▲**Thief Gangs**—If you know what to look out for, the omnipresent groups of children picking the pockets and handbags of naive tourists are no threat but an interesting, albeit sad, spectacle. Gangs of city-stained children, too young to prosecute but old enough to rip you off, troll through the tourist crowds around the Forum, Colosseum, and train and Metro stations. Watch them target tourists distracted with a video camera or overloaded with bags. They look like beggars and use newspapers or cardboard signs to distract their victims. Every year they get bolder, but they'll still scram like stray cats if you're on to them. A fast-fingered mother with a baby is often nearby.

▲**Mammertine Prison**—The 2,500-year-old converted cistern that once imprisoned Saints Peter and Paul is worth a look. On the walls are lists of prisoners (Christian and non-Christian) and how they were executed: Strangolati, Decapitato, Morto di Fame . . . (donation requested, 9:00-12:00, 14:30-18:00). At the top of the stairs leading to the Campidoglio, you'll find a refreshing water fountain. Block the spout with your fingers; it spurts up for drinking.

▲▲**Capitoline Hill (Campidoglio)**—This hill was the religious and political center of ancient Rome. It's still the home of the city's government. Michelangelo's lovely Renaissance square is bounded by two fine museums and the mayoral palace.

The Capitoline Museum (Musei Capitolini) in the Palazzo Nuovo (the building closest to the river) is the world's oldest museum (500 years old) and more important than its sister (opposite). Outside the entrance, notice the marriage announcements (and, very likely, wedding party photo ops). Inside the courtyard, have some photo fun with chunks of a giant statue of Emperor Constantine. (A rare public toilet hides near the museum ticket-taker.) The museum is worthwhile, with lavish rooms housing several great statues including the original (500 B.C.) Etruscan Capitoline wolf and the enchanting Commodus as Hercules. Across the square is a museum full of ancient statues—great if you like portrait busts of forgotten emperors or want to see the restored equestrian statue of Marcus Aurelius that used to sit on the pedestal in the square. (L10,000, Both open Tuesday-Saturday 9:00-13:30, Tuesday 17:00-20:00, Saturday 20:00-23:00, Sunday 9:00-13:00, closed Monday, tel. 67102475.) There's a fine view of the Forum from the terrace just past the mayor's palace on the right.

To approach the great square the way Michelangelo wanted you to, walk halfway down the grand stairway toward Piazza Venezia, spin around, and walk back up. At the bottom of the stairs, look up the long stairway to your right for a good example of the earliest style of Christian church and be thankful it's not worth climbing up to see.

Way down the street on your left, you'll see a modern building actually built around surviving ancient pillars and arches. Farther ahead (toward Piazza Venezia), look into the ditch (on the right), and see how everywhere modern Rome is built on the countless bricks and forgotten mosaics of ancient Rome.

Piazza Venezia—This square is the focal point of modern Rome. The Via del Corso, starting here, is the city's axis, surrounded by the classiest shopping district. From the Palazzo di Venezia's balcony above the square (to your left with back to Victor Emmanuel Monument), Mussolini whipped up the nationalistic fervor of Italy. Fascist masses filled the square screaming, "Four more years!" or something like that. (Fifteen years later, they hung him from a meat hook in Milan.)

Victor Emmanuel Monument—This oversize monument

to an Italian king loved only by his relatives and the ignorant is known to most Romans as "the wedding cake," "the typewriter," or "the dentures." It wouldn't be so bad if it weren't sitting on a priceless acre of Ancient Rome. Soldiers guard Italy's Tomb of the Unknown Soldier as the eternal flame flickers.

▲▲▲**Pantheon**—For the greatest look at the splendor of Rome, antiquity's best-preserved interior is a must (free, normally open 9:00-18:00, Sunday and Monday 9:00-13:00, less in winter, tel. 369831). Walk past its one-piece granite columns and through the original bronze door. Sit inside under the glorious skylight and study it. The dome, 140 feet high and wide, was Europe's biggest until Brunelleschi's dome was built in Florence 1,200 years later. You'll understand why this wonderfully harmonious architecture was so inspirational to the artists of the Renaissance, particularly Raphael; along with Italy's first two kings, he chose to be buried here. As you walk around the outside of the Pantheon, notice the "rise of Rome"—about 15 feet since it was built.

▲**Curiosities near the Pantheon**—The only Gothic church you'll see in Rome is Santa Maria sopra Minerva. On a little square behind the Pantheon to the left, past the Bernini elephant and the Egyptian obelisk statue, it was built *sopra*, or over, a pre-Christian temple of Minerva. Rome was at its low ebb, almost a ghost town through much of the Gothic period, and the little building done from this time was later redone Baroque. This church is a refreshing exception. St. Catherine's body lies under the altar (her head is in Siena) and a little-known Michelangelo statue, *Christ Bearing the Cross*, stands to the left. Fra Angelico's tomb is in the left, or north, transept.

Nearby (head out the church's rear door behind the Michelangelo statue and turn left) you'll find the **Chiesa di St. Ignazio** church, a riot of Baroque illusions. Study the ceiling in the back of the nave. Then stand on the yellow disk on the floor between the two stars. Look at the central (black) dome. Keeping your eyes on the dome, walk under and past it. Church building project runs out of money? Hire a painter to paint a fake (and flat) dome. Turn around and look at the fresco over the entry. Walk left, then right . . . then look at the altar. What would you say if I told you it was a flat painting? (free, churches open until 19:00, take a 12:30-16:00 siesta, and welcome modestly dressed visitors.)

A few blocks away, back across Corso Victor Emmanuel, is the very rich and Baroque **Gesu Church**, headquarters of the Jesuits in Rome. The Jesuits powered the Church's Counter-Reformation. With Protestants teaching that all roads to heaven didn't pass through Rome, the baroque churches of the late 1500s were painted with spiritual road maps that said they did.

▲▲**The Dolce Vita Stroll down Via del Corso**—The city's chic and hip "cruise" from the Piazza del Popolo (Metro: Flaminio) down a wonderfully traffic-free section of the Via del Corso and up Via Condotti to the Spanish Steps each evening around 18:00. Shoppers, take a left on Via Condotti for the Spanish Steps and Gucci (shops open after siesta, 16:30-19:30). Historians, start with a visit to the Baroque Church of Santa Maria del Popolo (with Raphael's Chigi Chapel and two Caravaggio paintings), continue down the Via del Corso to the Victor Emmanuel Monument, climb Michelangelo's stairway to his glorious Campidoglio Square, and visit Rome's Capitoline Museum, open Tuesday and Saturday evenings. Catch the lovely view of the Forum (from past the mayor's palace on right) as the horizon reddens and cats prowl the unclaimed rubble of ancient Rome.

▲**Villa Borghese**—Rome's unkept "Central Park" is great for people-watching (plenty of modern-day Romeos and Juliets). Take a row on the lake, or visit its fine museums. The **Borghese Gallery** has some world-class Baroque art, including the exciting Bernini statue of Apollo chasing Daphne, and paintings by Caravaggio and Rubens (L4,000, 9:00-14:00, Sunday 9:00-13:00, closed Monday, tel. 8548577; for a few years the paintings will be in Trastevere at via de San Michele 22, 10:00-13:00, 16:00-20:00, closed Monday and Sunday afternoon). The nearby Museo di Villa Giulia is a fine Etruscan museum (L8,000, 9:00-19:00, Sunday 9:00-13:00, closed Monday, also often closed, tel. 3201951).

▲**National Museum of Rome (Museo Nazionale Romano delle Terme)**—Directly in front of the station, it houses much of the greatest ancient Roman sculpture

(L3,000, 9:00-14:00, Sunday until 13:00, closed Monday, tel. 4880530). This collection is being moved to the nearby Palazzo Massimo, so call before visiting.

▲▲▲**Floodlit Rome Hike: Trastevere to the Spanish Steps**—Rome can be grueling. But a fine way to enjoy this historian's fertility rite is an evening walk lacing together Rome's flood-lit night spots. Fine urban spaces, real-life theater vignettes, sitting close enough to the Bernini fountain to hear no traffic, water flickering its mirror on the marble, jostling with local teenagers to see all the gelati flavors, enjoying lovers straddling more than the bench, jay-walking past flak-vested *polizia*, marveling at the ramshackle elegance that softens this brutal city for those who were born here and can imagine living nowhere else—these are the flavors of Rome best tasted after dark.

Taxi or ride the bus (#23 from the Vatican area) to Trastevere, the colorful neighborhood across (*tras*) the Tiber (*tevere*). Start your hike at Santa Maria in Trastevere. Trastevere offers the best look at medieval-village Rome. The action all marches to the chime of the church bells. Go there and wander. Wonder. Be a poet. This is Rome's Left Bank.

Santa Maria in Trastevere from the third century (free, 8:00-12:00, 16:00-19:00) is one of Rome's oldest churches. Notice the ancient basilica floor plan and early Christian symbols in the walls near the entry.

From the square, Via del Moro leads to the river and Ponte Sisto, a pedestrian bridge with a good view of St. Peter's dome. Cross the bridge and continue straight ahead for one block. Take the first left, which leads through the scary and narrow darkness to Piazza Farnese with the imposing Palazzo Farnese. The palace's beautiful interior, designed in part by Michelangelo, is closed to the public. One block from there is **Campo di Fiori** (Field of Flowers), which is an affordable outdoor dining room after dark (Trattoria Virgilio is one of several decent restaurants).

If the statue on the square did a hop, step, and a jump forward and turned right, he'd cross the busy Corso Vittorio Emanuele and find Piazza Navona. Rome's most interesting night scene features street music, artists, fire-eaters, local Casanovas, ice cream, outdoor cafés (splurge-worthy if you've got time to sit and enjoy the human river of Italy), and three fountains by Bernini, the father of Baroque art. This oblong square is molded around the long-gone stadium of Domitian, an ancient chariot race track that was often flooded so the masses could enjoy major water games.

Leave Piazza Navona directly across from the Tre Scalini café, go past rose peddlers and palm readers, jog left around the guarded building, and follow the yellow sign to the Pantheon straight down Via del Salvatore (cheap pizza place on left just before the Pantheon). From the obelisk (facing the Pantheon), head left to Casa del Caffe, then left down Via degli Orfani. At the square, pass the church on the left down Via Aquiro. At the obelisk (if it's gelati time, take a detour left behind Albergo Nazionale), turn right, walk between the Italian parliament and the huge Il Tempo newspaper building to the busy Via del Corso. You'll pass the huge second-century column honoring Marcus Aurelius, cross the street, and go into the lofty gallery. Take the right branch of this Y-shaped gallery and exit continuing straight down Via de Crociferi to the roar of the water, light, and people of the Trevi fountain.

The **Trevi fountain** is an example of how Rome took full advantage of the abundance of water brought into the city by its great aqueducts. This watery Baroque avalanche was built in 1762. Romantics toss two coins over their shoulder thinking it will give them a wish and assure their return to Rome. That may sound stupid, but every year I go through this touristic ritual . . . and it seems to work very well.

Take some time to people-watch (whisper a few breathy *bellos* or *bellas*) before leaving. Facing the fountain, go past it on the right down Via delle Stamperia to Via del Triton. Cross the busy street and continue to the Spanish Steps (ask, "*Dové Piazza di Spagna?*") a few short blocks and thousands of dollars of shopping opportunities away.

The **Piazza di Spagna**, with the very popular Spanish Steps, got its name 300 years ago when this was the site of the Spanish Embassy. It's been the hangout of many romantics over the years (Keats, Wagner, Openshaw, Goethe, and others). The Boat Fountain at the foot of the steps was done by Bernini's father, Bernini.

Facing the steps, walk to your right about a block to tour one of the world's biggest and most lavish McDonald's

Vatican City, St. Peter's, and the Museum

About a block on the other side of the steps is the subway, or *Metropolitana*, which (until 23:30) will zip you home.

▲▲**Ostia Antica**—Rome's ancient seaport (80,000 people in the time of Christ, later a ghost town, now excavated), less than an hour from downtown, is the next best thing to Pompeii. Start at the 2,000-year-old theater, buy a map, explore the town, and finish with its fine little museum. To get there, take the subway's B Line to the Magliana stop, catch the Lido train to Ostia Antica (twice an hour), walk over the overpass, go straight to the end of that road, and follow the signs to (or ask for) "scavi" Ostia Antica. Open daily from 9:00 to one hour before sunset. The L8,000 entry fee includes the museum (which closes at 14:00). Just beyond is the filthy beach (Lido), an interesting anthill of Roman sun-worshipers.

▲▲**Vatican City**—This tiny independent country of just over 100 acres is contained entirely within Rome. Politically powerful, the Vatican is the religious capital of 800 million Roman Catholics. If you're not one already, become a Catholic for your visit. Start by dropping by the helpful tourist office just to the left of St. Peter's Basilica (Monday-Saturday, 8:30-19:00, tel. 69884466.) Check out the glossy L5,000 guidebooklet (crowded piazza on cover), which doubles as a classy souvenir. Telephone them if you're interested in the pope's schedule (Sundays at noon for a quick blessing of the crowds in Piazza San Pietro from the window of his study above the square, or Wednesday mornings when a reservation is necessary), or in their sporadic but very good tours of the Vatican grounds or the church interior. If you don't care to see the pope, remember that the times he appears are most crowded. Handy buses shuttle visitors between the church and the museum (L2,000, twice an hour, 8:45 until about 13:00). This is far better than the exhausting walk around the Vatican wall, and it gives you a pleasant peek at the garden-filled Vatican grounds.

▲▲▲**St. Peter's Basilica**—There is no doubt: this is the richest and most impressive church on earth. To call it vast is like calling God smart. Marks on the floor show where the next largest churches would fit if they were put inside. The ornamental cherubs would dwarf a large man. Birds roost

St. Peter's Basilica

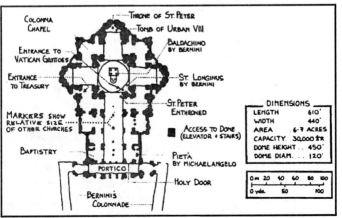

inside, and thousands of people wander about, heads craned heavenward, hardly noticing each other. Don't miss Michelangelo's *Pietà* (behind bullet-proof glass) to the right of the entrance. Bernini's altar work and huge bronze canopy (*baldacchino*) are brilliant.

While for most the treasury (in the sacristy) is not worth the admission, the crypt is free and worth a wander. Directly under the dome, stairs will lead you down to the level of the earlier church and the tombs of many of the popes, including the very first one . . . Peter.

The dome, Michelangelo's last work, is (you guessed it) the biggest anywhere. Taller than a football field is long, it's well worth the sweaty climb (330 steps after the elevator, allow an hour to go up and down) for a great view of Rome, the Vatican grounds, and the inside of the Basilica—particularly heavenly while there is singing. (Last entry is about an hour before closing. Catch the elevator just outside the church to the right as you face it.) The church strictly enforces its dress code. Dress modestly—a dress or long pants, shoulders covered. You are usually required to check any bags at a cloak room near the entry. St. Peter's is open daily 7:00-19:00, 18:00 in winter; ticket booths to the treasury and dome close an hour early. All are welcome to join in the mass (most days at the front altar, 17:00).

The church is particularly moving at 7:00 while tourism is still sleeping. Volunteers who want you to understand and appreciate St. Peter's give free 90-minute "Pilgrim Service" tours in English often at 10:15 and 15:00. Check at the desk just after the dress code check as you're entering for the day's schedule. Seeing the *Pietà* is neat, understanding it is divine.

▲▲▲**The Vatican Museum**—Too often, the immense Vatican Museum is treated as an obstacle course, with four nagging miles of displays, separating the tourist from the Sistine Chapel. Even without the Sistine, this is one of Europe's top three or four houses of art. It can be exhausting, so plan your visit carefully, focusing on a few themes, and allow several hours. The museum uses a nearly-impossible-not-to-follow, one-way system.

Required minimum stops, in this order: Etruscan Gallery (impressive for 500 B.C. and well-explained in English), Egyptian mummies and statues; *Apollo Belvedere* and *Laocoön* in Octagonal Courtyard, *Belvedere Torso* (all three showing the Classical mastery of the body and very influential to Renaissance artists); past the rooms of animals, the giant porphyry hot tub, between the porphyry sarcophagi of Constantine's mother and daughter, then down the hall of broken penises and past the corridor of maps to huge rooms plastered with church propaganda (Constantine's divine vision and his victory at Milvian Bridge which led him to become Christian, and the 19th-century Vatican declaration of the immaculate conception of the Virgin Mary), past a small chapel frescoed by Fra Angelico and into the Raphael rooms.

The masterpiece here is the School of Athens, remarkable for its blatant pre-Christian Classical orientation wallpapering the apartments of Pope Julius II. Raphael honors the great pre-Christian thinkers—Aristotle, Plato, and company—who are portrayed as the leading artists of Raphael's day: the bearded figure of Plato is Leonardo da Vinci, and Michelangelo broods in the foreground—supposedly added late, after Raphael snuck a peek at the Sistine Chapel and decided that his arch-competitor was so good he had to put their personal differences aside and include him in this tribute to the artists of his generation. Today's St. Peter's was under construction as Raphael was working. In this fresco he gives us a sneak preview of the unfinished church. (The School of Athens is likely to be scaffolded up through 1995.)

Next (unless you detour through the refreshing modern Catholic art section) is the newly restored Sistine Chapel. Michelangelo's pictorial culmination of the Renaissance shows the story of Creation with a powerful God weaving in and out of each scene through that busy week. This is an optimistic and positive expression of the high Renaissance. Later, after the Reformation wars had begun and after the Catholic army of Spain had sacked the Vatican, the reeling church began to fight back. As part of its Counter-Reformation, Michelangelo was commissioned to paint the Last Judgment (behind the altar). Newly restored, the message is as brilliant and clear as the day Michelangelo finished it: Christ is returning, some will go to hell and some to heaven, and some will be saved by the power of the rosary.

The Vatican's small but fine collection of paintings, the Pinacoteca (with Raphael's *Transfiguration* and Caravaggio's *Deposition*) is near the entry/exit. Early Christian art is the final possible side trip before exiting via the souvenir shop.

The museum clearly marks out four color-coded visits of different lengths. Rentable headphones (L6,000) give a recorded tour of the Raphael rooms and Michelangelo's Sistine masterpiece. (Easter, July, August, September, and first half of October hours: 8:45-16:30, Saturday 8:45-14:00, closed Sunday, except last Sunday of month when museum is free; the rest of the year it's open 8:45-13:45. Last entry an hour before closing. Many minor rooms close 13:45-14:45 or from 13:30 on. The Sistine Chapel is closed 30 minutes before the rest of the museum. A small door at the rear of the Sistine Chapel is used by speedy tour groups to escape via St. Peter's. If you squirt out here you're done with the museum. The Pinacoteca is the only important part left. Consider doing it at the start. Otherwise, it's a 10-minute heel-to-toe slalom through the tourists from the Sistine to the entry/exit, L13,000, tel. 69883333. The museum is closed on 5/1, 6/29, 8/15, 11/1, 12/8, and on church holidays.)

The museum's excellent book and card shop offers a priceless (L10,000) black-and-white photo book of the *Pietà*— great for gifts. The Vatican post has an office in the museum and one on Piazza San Pietro (comfortable writing rooms, Monday-Friday 8:30-19:00, Saturday 8:30-18:00); the Vatican post is the only reliable mail service in Italy, and the stamps are a collectible bonus (Vatican stamps are good throughout Rome, Italian stamps are not good at the Vatican). The Vatican bank has sinful rates.

▲**Cappuccin Crypt**—If you want bones, this is it: below Santa Maria della Immaculata Concezione on Via Veneto, just off Piazza Barberini, are thousands of skeletons, all artistically arranged for the delight—or disgust—of the always wide-eyed visitor. The monastic message on the wall near the entry explains that this is more than just a macabre exercise. Pick up a few of Rome's most interesting postcards (9:00-12:00, 15:00-18:30). A bank with long hours and good exchange rates is next door and the American Embassy is just up the street.

▲**E.U.R.**—Mussolini's planned suburb of the future (60

years ago) is a 10-minute subway ride from the Colosseum to Metro: Magliana. From the Magliana subway stop, walk through the park uphill to the Palace of the Civilization of Labor (Pal. d. Civilta d. Concordia), the essence of Fascist architecture with its giant, no-questions-asked, patriotic statues and its this-is-the-truth simplicity. On the far side is the Museo della Civilta Romana (history museum, Piazza G. Agnelli; Metro: EUR Fermi; L5,000, 9:00-13:30, Tuesday and Thursday 15:00-18:00, closed Monday, tel. 5926041), including a large-scale model of ancient Rome.

Overrated Sights—The Spanish Steps (with Italy's first, and one of the world's largest, McDonald's—McGrandeur at its greatest—just down the street) and the commercialized Catacombs, which contain no bones, are way out of the city, and are not worth the time or trouble. The venerable old Villa d'Este garden of fountains near Hadrian's Villa outside of town at Tivoli is now run-down, overpriced, and a disappointment.

Entertainment in Rome
Nighttime fun in Rome is found in the piazzas, along the river, and at its outdoor concerts and street fairs. Pick up a local periodical entertainment guide for a rundown on special events.

Sleeping in Rome
(L1,600 = about $1, tel. code: 06)
The absolute cheapest doubles in Rome are L50,000, without shower or breakfast. You'll pay L22,000 in a sleazy dorm or hostel. A nicer hotel (L100,000 doubles), providing an oasis/ refuge, makes it easier to enjoy this intense and grinding city. If you're going door to door, prices are soft—so bargain. Official prices that hotels list assume an agency or room-finding service kick-back which, if you're coming direct, they avoid. Many hotels have high season (mid-March through October) and low season prices. Easter and September are the crowded times. July and August are too hot for crowds. Most of my recommended hotels are small with huge, murky entrances that make you feel like a Q-tip someone dropped. The amount of English spoken drops with the price. Most places speak some and will hold a room with a phone call.

I've listed mostly places with minimal traffic noise. Many prices here are promised only to people who use no credit card, use no room-finding service, and show this book. Prices are generally guaranteed through 1995 (except for a few holiday times).

Sleep code: **S**=Single, **D**=Double/Twin, **T**=Triple, **Q**=Quad, **B**=Bath/Shower, **WC**=Toilet, **CC**=Credit Card (**V**isa, **M**astercard, **A**mex), **SE**=Speaks English (graded **A-F**). Breakfast is normally included only in the expensive places (as noted).

Sleeping near the Train Station

The cheapest hotels in town are near the station. Avoid places on the seedy south (Colosseum) side of the station. The first two bunches of listings are closest in a safe and decent area (which gets a little weird and spooky late at night), two blocks northeast of the station. The next are a 5-minute walk in front of the station near the Via Nazionale.

Via Magenta 39: These odd ducks are about as cheap as the youth hostel and much handier (no breakfast). **Albergo Sileo** is a shiny chandeliered ten-room place with an elegant touch that has a contract to house train conductors who work the night shift, so they offer rooms from 17:00 to 9:00 only. If you can handle this, it's a great value (D-L40,000, cheap breakfasts, elevator, Via Magenta 39, fourth floor, tel. 4450246, Allesandro and Maria Savioli, SE-D). **Pensione Stefanella** is a dark, homey, quiet place with trampoline beds in four very simple rooms run by an elderly lady named Stefanella (S-L35,000, D-L45,000, SE-F, tel. 4451646). **The Faulty Towers** is a backpacker-type place run by the folks from Enjoy Rome. It's young, hip,and English-speaking, with a rooftop terrace and lots of information (shared triples or quads for L22,000-L25,000 per bed, D-L60,000, DB-L80,000, tel. 4450374).

Via Milazzo 20: Hotel Magic is a tiny, simple place run by a friendly mother-daughter team (Carmella and Rosanna). It's clean and high enough off the road to have no traffic problems (S-L50,000, D-L60,000, DB-L70,000, T-L90,000, TB-L105,000, with this book, no breakfast, Via Milazzo 20, third floor, 00185 Roma, tel. 4959880, little English spoken). In the same building these places are about the same price, good values for cheap rooms but mustier: **Hotel Fenicia** (owner Anna promises my readers a discount, tel. 490342), **Hotel Galli** (tel. 4456859), **Soggiorno Spagna** (tel. 4941191). A self-serve Lavanderia is at 8 via Milazzo (daily, 8:00-22:00 6 kilos washed and dried for L12,000).

    Hotel Nardizzi Americana (D-L100,000, DB-L120,000, T-L140,000, TB-L160,000, including breakfast, rates promised through 1995, also 4- and 5-bed rooms, Via Firenze 38, 00184 Roma, elevator, tel. 4880368, fax 4880035, Nik, Fabrizio, and Rugero speak English) is a fine splurge in the station area. Traffic noise in the front rooms is a problem in the summer when you'll want the window open, but it's a tranquil haven, safe, handy, central, and a short walk from the central station and Piazza Barberini on the corner of Via Firenze and Via XX Septembre. (Parking is actually workable here. Double-park below the hotel until a space without yellow lines becomes available and grab it. The defense ministry is across the street, and you've got heavily armed guards all night.

    The nearby **Residence Adler** (D-L100,000, DB-L125,000, T-L120,000, TB-L150,000, including breakfast, CC:VM, elevator, Via Modena 5, 00184 Roma, tel. 484466, fax 4880940), with 16 big, quiet, and elegant rooms in a great locale, is another worthwhile splurge.

    Hotel Pensione Italia (SB-L75,000, DB-L120,000 with this book and cash only, including breakfast, elevator, Via Venezia 18, just off Via Nazionale, tel. 4828355, fax 4745550), in a busy, interesting, handy locale, placed safely next to the Ministry of the Interior, is pleasant, clean, and thoughtfully run by English-speaking Andrea.

    Hotel Aberdeen (DB-L180,000, less off-season, CC:VMA, Via Firenze 48, 00184 Roma, tel. 4819340, fax 4821092, SE-A) with mini-bars, phones, TVs, and showers in its modern rooms, a first-class breakfast buffet, and no traffic noise, is my classiest hotel listing and a good value for Rome.

Sleeping near the Colosseum

A couple of stops on the subway from the train station, these places are out-of-the-station sleaze and buried in a very Roman world of exhaust-stained medieval ambience.

    Hotel Flavio (S-L60,000, D-L85,000, DB-L105,000, CC:VM, no breakfast, hiding almost torch-lit under vines on a tiny street a block toward the Colosseum from Via Cavour at Via Frangipane 34, 00184 Roma, tel. 6797203, fax 6796246, not much English) is a real hotel with a classy TV-lounge/lobby, an elevator, and elegant furnishings throughout in a quiet setting. Its weakness is lousy tub-showers down the hall for the five cheap doubles.

Albergo Perugia (S-L38,000, D-L60,000, DB-L90,000, no breakfast, near the corner of Via Cavour and Via Fori Imperiali at Via del Colosseo 7, tel. 6797200, fax 6784635, only Maria speaks English) is yellow, peely, and filled with furniture not fit for a garage sale, but family-run, friendly, peaceful, and beautifully located. Poor couples might offer to share the large-bedded single (for L50,000).

Suore di Sant Anna (S-L35,000, D-L70,000, including breakfast, monkish lunch or dinner for L18,000 more, off the corner of Via dei Serpenti and Via Baccina at Piazza Madonna dei Monti 3, 00184 Roma, tel. 485778, fax 4873903) was built for Ukrainian pilgrims. The sisters are sweet, but the male staff doesn't seem to want your business. It's clumsy and difficult, but once you're in, you've got a comfortable home in a classic locale.

The **YWCA Casa Per Studentesse** (L26,000 per person in 3- and 4-bed rooms, D-L64,000, breakfast included, Via C. Balbo 4, 00184 Roma, 5 blocks toward the Colosseum from the station, tel. 4880460, fax 4871028) accepts women, couples, and couples with children. It's a grey and institutional place, filled with maids in white, more colorful Third World travelers, and 75 single beds.

In old Rome but nowhere near these others, the **Albergo del Sole** (D-L90,000, DB-L120,000, no breakfast, Via del Biscione 76, 00186 Roma, tel. 68806873, fax 6893787) is just off the colorful Campo dei Fiori, right in the Roman thick of things. It's clean and impersonal; has 65 rooms, a roof garden, and lots of Germans; and is spoiled by its success.

Sleeping Two Blocks from the Vatican Museum

Pension Alimandi (D-L97,000, DB-L113,000, TB-L143,000, 5% discount off these prices with this book and cash, CC:VM, elevator to most rooms, optional hearty L10,000 breakfast, great roof garden; just down the stairs in front of the Vatican Museum, Via Tunisi 8, 00192 Roma, tel. 39726300, fax 39723943, credit card by telephone or fax accepted to secure reservation, SE-A) is a good value, run by friendly and entrepreneurial Paolo and Enrico. From the train station follow Metro line A to last stop, Ottaviano, exit subway station to "V. le G. Cesare," walk straight up that street four or five blocks (it becomes Via Candia), and turn left at Via Tunisi.

Hotel Spring House (D-L110,000, DB-L130,000, including breakfast, CC:VMA, Via Mocenigo 7, a block from Alimandi, tel. 39720948, fax 39721047) offers clean, quiet rooms with balconies, TVs, refrigerators, and a fine sixth-floor breakfast terrace.

Sleeping in Convents near the Vatican

Suore Oblate dell Assunzione (via Andrea Doria 42, 3 blocks in front of the Vatican Museum entrance, tel. 3729540) and a convent across the street from the museum (Viale Vaticano 92, tel. 39723797, fax 39723792) are clean, peaceful, and inexpensive, but no English is spoken and it's hard to get in.

Sleeping in Youth Hostels and Dorms

Rome has only one real youth hostel—big, institutional, not central or worth the trouble. For cheap dorm beds, consider **Pensione Ottaviano** (25 beds in 2- to 6-bed rooms, L23,000 per bed with sheets, depending on the season and their mood, call from the station), free showers, no lockers but a storage room, a fun, laid-back clubhouse feel, close to the Ottaviano Metro stop (near the Vatican) at Via Ottaviano 6, tel. 39737253 (reservations held until noon). The same slum visionaries run the dumpier **Pensione Sandy** (south of station, up a million depressing stairs, Via Cavour 136, tel. 4884585, L20,000 beds).

Eating in Rome

The cheapest meals in town are picnics (from *alimentari* shops or open-air markets), self-serve **Rostisseries**, and stand-up or take-out meals from a **Pizza Rustica** (pizza slices sold by the weight, 100 grams is a hot cheap snack, 200 grams or 2 *etti* make a light meal). Most *alimentari* will slice and stuff your sandwich (*panini*) for you if you buy the stuff there.

Eating in Trastevere or on the Campo di Fiori

My best dinner tip is to go for Rome's Vespa street ambience and find your own place in Trastevere (bus #23 from the Vatican area) or on Campo di Fiori. Guidebooks list Trastevere's famous places, but I'd wander the fascinating maze of streets around the Piazza Santa Maria in Trastevere and find a mom-and-pop place with barely a menu. For the basic meal with lots of tourists, eat amazingly cheaply at **Mario's** (three courses with wine and service for L15,000, near the Sisto bridge at via del Moro 53, tel. 5803809, closed Sunday). For the ultimate romantic square setting, eat at whichever place looks best on Campo di Fiori (**Virgilio's** setting makes up for its service, tel. 68802746, closed Wednesday).

Eating near the Pantheon

Il Delfino is a handy self-service cafeteria on the Largo Argentina square (7:00-21:00, closed Monday, not cheap but fast). The alimentari on the Pantheon square will make you a sandwich for a temple porch picnic.

Eating on Via Firenze,
near Hotel Nardizzi and Hotel Alder

Lon Fon, at #44, serves reasonably priced Chinese food with elegant atmosphere, **Snack Bar Gastronomia** (#34, really cheap hot meals dished up from under glass counter, open until 24:00, closed Sunday), and an *alimentari* (grocery store, at #54). McDonald's on Piazza della Republica has free piazza seating and a great salad bar that no American fast-food joint would recognize.

Eating near the Vatican Museum
and Pension Alimandi

Viale Giulio Cesare is lined with cheap, fun eateries (such as **Cipriani Self-Service Rosticceria** near the Ottaviano subway stop at Via Vespasiano, with pleasant outdoor seating). Don't miss the wonderful **Via Andrea Doria** open-air market in front of the Vatican Museum, two blocks between Via Tunisi and Via Andrea Doria (closed by 13:30, Monday-Saturday).

Train Connections

Rome to: Amsterdam (2/day, 20 hrs), **Bern** (5/day, 10 hrs), **Brindisi** (2/day, 9 hrs), **Florence** (12/day, 2 hrs), **Frankfurt** (4/day, 14 hrs), **Genova** (7/day, 6 hrs, overnight possible), **Milan** (12/day, 5 hrs, overnight possible), **Munich** (5/day, 12 hrs), **Naples** (12/day, 2-3 hrs), **Nice** (2/day, 10 hrs), **Paris** (5/day, 16 hrs), **Pisa** (8/day, 3-4 hrs), **Venice** (6/day, 5-8 hrs, overnight possible), **Vienna** (3/day, 13-15 hrs). **Città**: Take the Rome-Orvieto train (every 2 hrs, 75 min), catch the bus from Orvieto to Bagnoregio, walk to Città.

Rome and Its Airport

Rome's new rail-air link connects Rome's Leonardo airport with the Termini Station in 30 minutes for L12,000 (non-stop, hourly departures from about 7:00 until 21:00, lobby at track 22). This is far better than the Metro link via Tiburtina. Your hotel can arrange a taxi to the airport at any hour for about L70,000.

Driving in Rome

Greater Rome is circled by the *Grande Raccordo Anulare*. This ring road has spokes that lead you into the center (much like the strings under the skin of a baseball). Entering from the north, take the Via Salaria and work your way doggedly into the Roman thick-of-things (following the black-and-white Rome bull's-eye *centro* signs). Avoid rush hour. Drive defensively: Roman cars stay in their lanes like rocks in an avalanche. Parking in Rome is dangerous. Park near a police station or get advice at your hotel. My favorite hotel is next to the Italian defense ministry—guarded by machine-gunners. You'll pay about L30,000 a day in a garage. In many cases, it's well worth it.

Consider this. Your car is a worthless headache in Rome. Avoid a pile of stress and save money by parking it at the huge, new, easy, and relatively safe lot behind the Orvieto station (drive around about a half-mile south), and catch the train to Rome. The town of Orte, closer to Rome, has easy parking and more frequent trains into Rome (40- to 80-minute rides at least hourly).

FLORENCE

Florence (Firenze), the home of the Renaissance and birthplace of our modern world, is a "supermarket sweep" and the groceries are the best Renaissance art in Europe. Get your bearings with a Renaissance walk. Florentine art goes beyond paintings and statues—there's food, fashion, and handicrafts. You can lick Italy's best gelato while enjoying Europe's best people-watching.

Planning Your Time

If you're in Europe for three weeks, Florence deserves a well-organized day. Siena, an hour away by bus, has none of the awesome sights but is a more enjoyable home base. For a day in Florence, see Michelangelo's *David*, tour the Uffizi gallery (best Italian paintings), tour the underrated Bargello (best statues), and do the Renaissance ramble (explained below). Art lovers will want to chisel another day out of their itinerary for the many other cultural treasures Florence offers. Shoppers and ice-cream lovers may need to do the same. Watch your sightseeing hours. Get an early start. Mondays and afternoons can be sparse.

Orientation (tel. code: 055)

The Florence we're interested in lies mostly on the north bank of the Arno River. Everything is within a 20-minute walk of the train station, cathedral, or Ponte Vecchio (Old Bridge). Just over the bridge is the less awesome but more characteristic Oltrarno (south bank) area. Orient yourself by the huge red-tiled dome of the cathedral (the Duomo) and its tall bell tower (Giotto's Tower). This is the center of historic Florence.

Tourist Information

Normally overcrowded, under-informed, and understaffed, the train station's tourist information office is not worth a stop if you're a good student of this book. If there's no line, pick up a map, a current museum-hours listing, and the periodical entertainment guide or tourist magazine (daily in summer 9:00-21:00, tel. 282893 or 219537). The free monthly

Florence Area

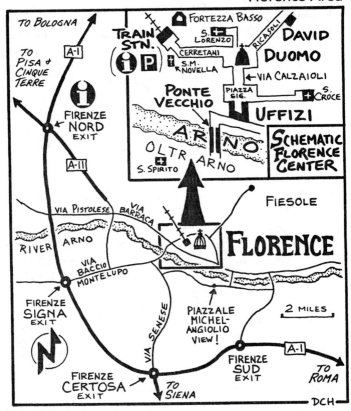

Florence Concierge Information magazine lists the latest museum hours and events. It's stocked by the expensive hotels (pick one up, as if you're staying there).

Getting Around

Taxis are expensive. Buses are cheap. A L1,300 ticket lets you ride anywhere for 60 minutes, L1,800 gives you two hours, and L5,000 gets you 24 hours (tickets not sold on bus, buy in tobacco shop, validate on bus). If you organize your sightseeing with some geographic logic you'll do it all on foot.

Helpful Hints

Museums and Churches: See everyone's essential sight, *David*, right off. In Italy, a masterpiece seen and enjoyed is worth two tomorrow; you never know when a place will unexpectedly close for a holiday, strike, or restoration. Late afternoon is the best time to enjoy the popular Uffizi Gallery without its crowds. Many museums close at 14:00 and stop selling tickets 30 minutes before that. Most close Monday and at 13:00 or 14:00 on Sunday. (The *Concierge Information* magazine thoughtfully lists which sights are open on afternoons, Sundays, and Mondays.) Churches usually close 12:30-15:00 or 16:00. Hours can change radically and no one knows exactly what's going on tomorrow. Local guidebooks are cheap and give you a map and a decent commentary on the sights.

Addresses: Street addresses list businesses in red and residences in black or blue (color coded on the actual street number, and indicated by a letter following the number in printed addresses: n=black, r=red). *Pensioni* are usually black, but can be either.

Theft Alert: Florence has particularly hardworking thief gangs. The cheapest central car park is at Fortezza Basso (clearly sign-posted). Your best bet for free parking is along the river on Lungarno Amerigo Vespucci (leave cookies for the thieves).

Sights—Florence

▲▲▲▲ Florentine Renaissance Walk—For a walk through the core of Renaissance Florence, start at the Accademia (home of Michelangelo's *David*) and cut through the heart of the city to the Ponte Vecchio on the Arno River. (A 10-page, self-guided tour of this walk is outlined in *Mona Winks*.) From the Accademia, walk to the Cathedral (Duomo). Check out the famous doors and the interior of the Baptistery. Consider climbing Giotto's Tower. Continue toward the river on Florence's great pedestrian mall, Via de' Calzaioli (or "Via Calz"), which was part of the original grid plan given the city by the ancient Romans. Down a few blocks, notice the statues on the exterior of the Orsanmichele Church. Via Calz connects the cathedral with the central square (Piazza della Signoria), the city palace (Palazzo Vecchio), and the great Uffizi Gallery.

After you walk past the statues of the great men of the Renaissance in the Uffizi courtyard, you'll reach the Arno River and the Ponte Vecchio. Your introductory walk will be over, and you'll know what sights to concentrate on.

▲▲▲**The Accademia (Galleria dell' Accademia)**—This museum houses Michelangelo's *David* and powerful (unfinished) *Prisoners*. Eavesdrop as tour guides explain these masterpieces. More than any other work of art, when you look into the eyes of *David*, you're looking into the eyes of Renaissance man. This was a radical break with the past. Man was now a confident individual, no longer a plaything of the supernatural. And life was now more than just a preparation for what happens after you die.

The Renaissance was the merging of art and science. In a humanist vein, David is looking at the crude giant of medieval darkness and thinking, "I can take this guy." Back on a religious track (and, speaking of veins), notice how large and overdeveloped David's right hand is. This is symbolic of the hand of God that powered David to slay the giant . . . and, of course, enabled Florence to rise above its crude neighboring city-states.

Beyond the magic marble, there are two floors of interesting pre-Renaissance and Renaissance paintings including a couple of lovely Botticellis (Via Ricasoli 60, L10,000, 9:00-19:00, Sunday 9:00-14:00, closed Monday, may not be open past 14:00, tel. 2388609).

There's a good book-and-poster shop across the street. Behind the Accademia is the Piazza Santissima Annunziata, with its lovely Renaissance harmony, and the Hospital of the Innocents (Spedale degli Innocenti, not worth going inside) by Brunelleschi, with terra-cotta medallions by della Robbia. Built in the 1420s, it is considered the first Renaissance building.

▲▲**Museum of San Marco**—One block north of the Accademia on Piazza San Marco, this museum houses the greatest collection anywhere of dreamy medieval frescoes and paintings by the early Renaissance master, Fra Angelico. You'll see why he thought of painting as a form of prayer and couldn't paint a crucifix without shedding tears. Each of the monks' cells has a Fra Angelico fresco. Don't miss the cell of Savonarola, the charismatic monk who threw out the Medici, turned Florence into a theocracy, sponsored "bonfires of the vanities" (burning books, paintings, and so on), and was finally burned himself when Florence decided to change channels (L6,000, 9:00-14:00, closed Monday).

▲▲**The Duomo**—Florence's mediocre Gothic cathedral has the third-longest nave in Christendom (free, daily, 10:00-17:30, with an occasional lunch break). The church's noisy neo-Gothic facade, from the 1870s, is covered with pink, green, and white Tuscan marble. Since all of its great art is stored in the Museo dell' Opera del Duomo, behind the church, the best thing about the inside is the shade. But it's capped by Brunelleschi's magnificent dome—the first Renaissance dome and the model for domes to follow.

When planning St. Peter's in Rome, Michelangelo said, "I can build a dome bigger, but not more beautiful, than the dome of Florence."

Giotto's Tower—Climbing Giotto's Tower (Campanile, L4,000, daily 9:00-17:30, until 19:30 in summer) beats climbing the neighboring Duomo's dome because it's 50 fewer steps, faster, not so crowded, and offers the same view plus the dome.

▲▲Museo dell' Opera di Santa Maria del Fiore del Duomo—The underrated cathedral museum, behind the church at #9, is great if you like sculpture. It has masterpieces by Donatello (a gruesome wood carving of Mary Magdalene clothed in her matted hair, and the *cantoria*, the delightful choir loft bursting with happy children) and Luca della Robbia (another choir loft, lined with the dreamy faces of musicians praising the Lord), a late Michelangelo Pietà (Nicodemus, on top, is a self-portrait), Brunelleschi's models for his dome, and the original restored panels of Ghiberti's doors to the Baptistery. To get the most out of your sightseeing hours, remember that this is one of the few museums in Florence that stays open late (9:00-17:30, maybe later, closed all Sundays, L4,000, tel. 2302885.)

▲The Baptistery—Michelangelo said its bronze doors were fit to be the gates of Paradise. Check out the gleaming copies of Ghiberti's bronze doors facing the Duomo, and the famous competition doors around to the right. Making a breakthrough in perspective, Ghiberti used mathematical laws to create the illusion of 3-D on a 2-D surface. Go inside Florence's oldest building, and sit and savor the medieval mosaic ceiling. Compare that to the "new, improved" art of the Renaissance (free, 13:00-18:00, Sunday 9:00-13:00, bronze doors always "open"; original panels are in the cathedral museum).

▲Orsanmichele—Mirroring Florentine values, this was a combination church-granary. The best L200 deal in Florence is the machine which lights its glorious tabernacle. Notice the grain spouts on the pillars inside. You can go upstairs through the building behind it and over a sky bridge for the temporary exhibit and a fine city view (free). Also study the sculpture on its outside walls. You can see man stepping out of the literal and figurative shadow of the church in the great

Renaissance sculptor Donatello's *St. George*. (On Via Calzaioli, free, 8:00-12:00, 15:00-18:00.) There are plans for the original Orsanmichele statues to be stationed upstairs. When this happens, it will be one of the great sights of Florence.

▲**Palazzo Vecchio**—The interior of this fortified palace, which was once the home of the Medici family, is worthwhile only if you're a real Florentine art and history fan. (L8,000, 9:00-19:00, Sunday 8:00-13:00, may be closed Saturday or Thursday, handy public WC inside on ground floor.) Until 1873, Michelangelo's *David* stood at the entrance, where the copy is today. The huge statues in the square are important only as the whipping boys of art critics and as pigeon roosts. The important art is in the nearby Loggia dei Lanzi. Notice Cellini's bronze statue of Perseus (with the head of Medusa). The plaque on the pavement in front of the palace marks the spot where Savonarola was burned.

▲▲▲**Uffizi Gallery**—The greatest collection of Italian painting anywhere is a must, with plenty of works by Giotto, Leonardo, Raphael, Caravaggio, Rubens, Titian, and Michelangelo, and a roomful of Botticellis, including his *Birth of Venus*. There are no official tours, so buy a book on the street before entering (or follow *Mona Winks*). The museum is nowhere near as big as it is great: few tourists spend more than two hours inside. The paintings are displayed (behind obnoxious reflective glass) on one comfortable floor in chronological order from the 13th through 17th century.

Essential stops are (in this order): the Gothic altarpieces by Giotto and Cimabue (narrative, pre-realism, no real concern for believable depth); Uccello's *Battle of San Romano*, an early study in perspective; Fra Lippi's cuddly Madonnas; the Botticelli room, filled with masterpieces including the small *La Calumnia*, showing the glasnost of Renaissance free-thinking being clubbed back into the darker age of Savonarola; two minor works by Leonardo; the octagonal classical sculpture room with Praxiteles' *Venus de Medici*, considered the epitome of beauty in Elizabethan Europe; a view of the Arno through two dirty panes of glass; Michelangelo's only surviving easel painting, the round Holy Family; Raphael's *Madonna of the Goldfinch*; Titian's *Venus of Urbino*; and an interesting view of the palace and cathedral from the terrace at the end (L10,000, 9:00-19:00, Sunday 9:00-14:00, closed

Monday, last ticket sold 45 minutes before closing, go very late to avoid the crowds and heat).

Enjoy the Uffizi square, full of artists and souvenir stalls. The surrounding statues honor the earthshaking Florentines of 500 years ago. You'll see all the great artists, plus philosophers (Machiavelli), scientists (Galileo), writers (Dante), explorers (Amerigo Vespucci), and the great patron of so much Renaissance thinking, Lorenzo (the Magnificent) de Medici. The Florentine Renaissance involved more than just the visual arts.

▲▲▲**Bargello (Museo Nazionale)**—The city's underrated museum of sculpture is behind the Palazzo Vecchio (4 blocks from the Uffizi) in a former prison that looks like a mini-Palazzo Vecchio. It has Donatello's *David* (the very-influential first male nude to be sculpted in a thousand years), works by Michelangelo, and much more (Via del Proconsolo 4; L6,000, 9:00-14:00, closed Monday). Dante's house, across the street and around the corner, is interesting only to his Italian-speaking fans.

▲**Medici Chapel (Cappelle dei Medici)**—This chapel, containing two Medici tombs, is drenched in incredibly lavish High Renaissance architecture and sculpture by Michelangelo (L8,000, 9:00-14:00, closed Monday). Behind San Lorenzo on Piazza Madonna, it's surrounded by a lively market scene that, for some reason, I find more interesting.

Museo di Storia della Scienza (Science Museum)—This is a fascinating collection of Renaissance and later clocks, telescopes, maps, and ingenious gadgets. A highlight for many is Galileo's finger in a little shrine-like bottle. English guide-booklets are available. It's friendly, comfortably cool, never crowded, and just downstream from the Uffizi (L10,000, Monday, Wednesday, and Friday 9:30-13:00, 14:00-17:00, Tuesday and Thursday 9:30-13:00, closed Sunday, Piazza dei Giudici 1).

▲**Michelangelo's Home, Casa Buonarroti**—Fans enjoy Michelangelo's house at Via Ghibellina 70 (L8,000, 9:30-13:30, closed Tuesday).

▲**The Pitti Palace**—Across the river, it has the giant Galleria Palatina collection with works of the masters (especially Raphael), plus the enjoyable Galleria d'Arte Moderna (upstairs) and the huge semi-landscaped Boboli Gardens—a cool refuge from the city heat (L8,000, five museums, 9:00-14:00, closed Monday).

▲**Brancacci Chapel**—For the best look at the early Renaissance master Masaccio, see his newly restored frescoes here (L5,000, 10:00-17:00, holidays 10:00-13:00, closed Tuesday, across the Ponte Vecchio and turn left a few blocks to Piazza del Carmine).

▲**Piazzale Michelangelo**—Across the river overlooking the city (look for the huge statue of David), this square is worth the half-hour hike or the drive for the view. After dark it's packed with local school kids sharing slices of watermelon with their dates. Just beyond it is the strikingly beautiful, crowd-free, Romanesque San Miniato church. (Bus #13 from the train station.)

Scenic City Bus Ride—For a candid peek at a Florentine suburb, ride bus #7 (from near the station) for about 20 minutes through neighborhood gardens, vineyards, orchards, and large villas. It ends at a plaza with small eateries and good views of Florence and the nearby hills.

▲▲**Gelato**—Gelato is a great Florentine edible art form. Italy's best ice cream is in Florence. Every year I repeat my taste test. And every year Vivoli's (on Via Stinche, see map, closed Mondays and the last three weeks in August) wins. Festival del Gelato and Perche Non!, just off Via Calz, are also good. That's one souvenir that can't break and won't clutter your luggage. Get a free sample (*"un assagio?"*) of Vivoli's *riso* (rice, my favorite) before ordering.

Siena Evening Side Trip—Connoisseurs of peace and small towns, who aren't into art or shopping (and who won't be seeing Siena otherwise), should consider riding the bus to Siena for the evening. Florence has no after-dark magic. Siena is after-dark magic.

Shopping—Florence is a great shopping town. Busy street scenes and markets abound, especially near San Lorenzo (closed Sunday and Monday), on the Ponte Vecchio, and near Santa Croce. Leather, gold, silver, art prints, and tacky plaster "mini-*Davids*" are most popular.

Sleeping in Florence
(L1,600 = about $1, tel. code: 055)
While Florence is generally crowded and overpriced, the

hotel scene isn't bad. With good information and a phone call ahead, you can find a simple, cheery, and comfortable double for L60,000, with a private shower for L80,000. You get roof-garden elegance for L110,000. Do not use the Tourist Information room-finding service. The prices listed here are guaranteed through 1995 only if you call direct. Involving the tourist office costs your host and jacks up the price. Also, since credit cards cost your host about 5 percent, many of these prices are for cash only. Except for Easter and Christmas, there are plenty of rooms in Florence and budget travelers can call around and find soft prices. If your limit is L55,000 for a double, call four places and stick to it. If you're staying for three or more nights, ask for a discount. The technically optional and overpriced breakfast can be used as a bargaining chip. Call ahead. I repeat, call ahead. Places will happily hold a room until early afternoon. If they say they're full, mention you're using this book. Accept only the prices I've listed through 1995.

Sleep code: **S**=Single, **D**=Double/Twin, **T**=Triple, **Q**=Quad, **B**=Bath/Shower, **WC**=Toilet, **CC**=Credit Card (**V**isa, **M**astercard, **A**mex). English is generally spoken.

Sleeping East of the Train Station

Casa Rabatti (D-L55,000, DB-L60,000-L70,000, L25,000 per bed in shared quad or quint, no breakfast, 6 blocks from station, Via San Zanobi 48 black, doorbell left of door, 50129 Florence, tel. 212393) is the ultimate if you always wanted to be a part of a Florentine family. Simple, clean, friendly, and run by Marcella and Celestino (who don't speak English), this is my best rock-bottom listing.

Hotel Enza (S-L50,000, SB-L60,000, D-L70,000, DB-L85,000, ask about a discount for three nights, no breakfast, 6 blocks from station, Via San Zanobi 45 black, 50129 Florence, tel. 490990) has 16 clean and cheery rooms, run by English-speaking Eugenia who clearly enjoys her work.

Sra. Piera Grossi rents five clean and homey rooms one block from the station (D-L60,000, no breakfast, corner of Via Nationale and Via Fiume, at Via Fiume 1, up lots of stairs, away from the traffic noise, tel. 293040).

Soggiorno Magliani (S-L39,000, D-L54,000, no breakfast, first floor up, 4 blocks from the station on the corner of

Via Guelfa and Via S. Reparata, at Via S. Reparata 1, tel. 287378, little English spoken) is a well-located, untouristy, very simple, local-style inn.

Other guidebooks rave about the same places 2 blocks from the station on Via Faenza. The street is filled with English-speaking tourists and sleepable L60,000 doubles. No. 56 is an English-speaking slumber mill: **Albergo Azzi** (L60,000 doubles, L30,000 per bed in shared quads and quints, L5,000 for breakfast, Via Faenza 56, tel. 213806). Not quite as good are **Merlini** (tel. 212848), **Paola** (tel. 213682), and **Armonia** (tel. 211146).

Hotel Loggiato dei Serviti (L235,000 doubles with everything, Piazza SS. Annunziata 3, Firenze, tel. 289592, fax 289595) has about the most prestigious address in Florence, on the most Renaissance (traffic-free) square in town. It gives you Renaissance romance with a place to plug in your hair dryer. Stone stairways lead you under open beam ceilings through this 16th-century monastery's elegantly appointed public rooms. The cells, with air-conditioning, TVs, mini-bars, and telephones, wouldn't be recognized by their original inhabitants.

Sleeping South of the Station
near Piazza Santa Maria Novella

From the station, follow the underground tunnel to Piazza Santa Maria Novella, a pleasant square by day that's filled with drunks and police after dark. It's handy: 3 blocks from the cathedral, near a good laundromat (La Serena, 8:30-20:00, closed Sunday, Via della Scala 30 red, fast, L18,000 for 11 pounds), cheap restaurants (on Via della Scala and via Palazzuolo, see below), the bus and train station, and with a great Massaccio fresco (*The Trinity*) in the church on the square (free).

Hotel Universo (D-L80,000, DB-L100,000, including breakfast, these discounted prices promised with this book through 1995, CC:VM, elevator, English spoken, right on Piazza S. M. Novella at #20, 50123 Florence, tel. 281951, fax 292335), a big group-friendly hotel with stark concrete hallways but fine rooms, is warmly run by a group of gentle men.

Hotel Visconti (D-L56,000, DB-L70,000, optional L12,000 breakfast, elevator, TV room, peaceful and sunny roof garden, 20 meters off the square opposite the church at Piazza Degli Ottaviani 1, tel. 213877) artfully decorated by English-speaking and very mellow Manara, is like living in a relaxing blue-and-white cameo. In the same building, up one floor, the simple, threadbare, a little bit musty but tidy **Pensione Ottaviani** rattles in its spaciousness (D-L60,000, DB-L75,000 including breakfast, tel. 2396223, fax 293355, English spoken).

Hotel Pensione Elite (SB-L60,000, SBWC-L65,000, DB-L80,000, DBWC-L95,000, optional L10,000 breakfast, at end of square with back to church, go right to Via della Scala 12, second floor, tel. 215395) has eight comfortable rooms. With none of the backpacking flavor of Via Faenze, it's a good basic value; run warmly by Maurizio and Nadia.

Pensione Sole (S-L43,000, D-L64,000, DB-L75,000-L80,000, TB-L105,000, no breakfast, lots of stairs, Via del Sole 8, third floor, no lift, tel. 2396094, Anna speaks no English), a clean, cozy, family-run place with seven bright rooms, is well located just off S.M. Novella toward the river.

Pensione Centrale (D-L105,000, DBWC-L125,000 with breakfast, near the Duomo at Via dei Conti 3, 50123 Florence, tel. 215216) is run by Marie Therese Blot, who is a wealth of information and makes you feel right at home.

Sleeping on the River Arno
Pensione Bretagna (S-L50,000, SB-L65,000, D-L95,000, DB-L105,000, including breakfast, west of the Ponte Vecchio, just past Ponte San Trinita, at Lungarno Corsini 6, 50123 Firenze, tel. 289618, fax 289619), a classy, Old World elegant place with thoughtfully appointed rooms, is run by English-speaking Antonio. Imagine breakfast under a painted, chandeliered ceiling over-looking the Arno river.

Sleeping in Oltrarno, South of the River
Across the river in the Oltrarno area, between the Pitti Palace and the Ponte Vecchio, you'll still find small traditional crafts shops; neighborly piazzas hiding a few offbeat art treasures; family eateries; two distinctive, moderately priced hotels; two student dorms; and a youth hostel. Each of these places is only a few minutes' walk from the Ponte Vecchio.

Hotel La Scaletta (D-L100,000, DB-L135,000, T-L140,000, TB-L170,000, breakfast included, 8% discount for cash, 10% for cash and flowers, elevator, English spoken, Via Guicciardini 13 black, 50125 Firenze, straight up the street from the Ponte Vecchio, next to the AmExCo, tel. 283028, fax 289562, easy telephone reservations, call first) is elegant, friendly, clean, with a dark, cool, labyrinthine floor plan and lots of Old World lounges. Owner Barbara and her children, Manfredo, Bianca, and Diana, elevate this well-worn place with brute charm. Your journal becomes poetry when written on the highest terrace of La Scaletta's panoramic roof garden (cheap drinks). If Manfredo is cooking dinner, eat here.

Pensione Sorelle Bandini (D-L100,000, DB-L125,000, including breakfast, Piazza Santo Spirito 9, 50125 Firenze, tel. 215308, fax 282761) is a ramshackle 500-year-old palace on a perfectly Florentine square, with cavernous rooms, museum warehouse interiors, a musty youthfulness, a balcony lounge-loggia with a view, and an ambience that, for romantic bohemians, can be a highlight of Florence. Mimmo or Sr. Romeo will hold a room until 16:00 with a phone call.

Institute Gould (D-L50,000, DB-L54,000, L21,000 beds in shared doubles and quads, 49 Via dei Serragli, tel. 212576, office open Monday-Friday 9:00-13:00, 15:00-19:00, Saturday 9:00-12:00) is a Protestant Church-run place with 72 beds in 27 rooms and clean, modern facilities. Since you must arrive during their office hours, you can't check in on Sunday.

The Catholic-run **Pensionato Pio X-Artigianelli** (L18,000 beds in doubles and quads, L3,000 extra if you want a single or a private shower, Via dei Serragli 106, tel. 225044) is more free-wheeling and ramshackle, with 44 beds in 20 rooms.

Ostello Santa Monaca (L18,000 beds with sheets, membership required, no breakfast, 6 Via Santa Monaca, a few blocks past Ponte Alla Carraia, tel. 268338, fax 280185), with 146 beds in crowded 8- to 20-bed dorms, takes no reservations. Sign up for available beds from 9:30-13:00 or when the hostel reopens after 16:00. You can leave bags (without valuables) there until it opens after siesta. This and the classy **Villa Camerata IYHF hostel** (tel. 6014151), on the outskirts of Florence, should be last alternatives.

Eating in Florence

Eating South of the River

There are several good and colorful restaurants in Oltrarno near Piazza Santo Spirito. **Trattoria Casalinga** (from Pitti Palace follow via Michelozzi to Santo Spirito, just off Piazza Santo Spirito at 9 Via dei Michelozzi, tel. 218624, closed Sunday) is an inexpensive and popular standby, famous for its home cooking. Good values but more expensive are **Trattoria Sabitino** on Borgo S. Frediano and **Osteria del Cinghiale Bianco** at Borgo S. Jacopo 43 (closed Tuesday and Wednesday). **Trattoria Oreste** (on Piazza S. Spirito at #16), with a renowned cook and on-the-piazza ambience, may have the best L35,000 dinner in the area. The **Ricchi** bar on the same square has some of the best homemade gelati in Firenze and a particularly pleasant interior. The best places change, so I'd just wander in a colorful neighborhood and eat where I see locals eating.

Eating near Santa Maria Novella

Trattoria il Contadino (Via Palazzuolo 69 red, a few blocks south of the train station, 12:00-14:30, 18:00-21:30, closed Sunday, tel. 2382673) and **Trattoria da Giorgio** (Via Palazzuolo 100 red, 12:00-15:00, 18:30-22:00, closed Sunday) each offer a L14,000 hearty family-style, fixed-price menu with a bustling working-class/budget-Yankee-traveler atmosphere. Get there early or be ready to wait. **La Grotta di Leo** (Via della Scala 41 red, tel. 219265, closed Wednesday) has a cheap, straightforward menu and decent food.

A Quick Lunch near the Sights

I keep lunch in Florence fast and simple, eating in one of countless self-service places, Pizza Rusticas (holes-in-walls selling cheap, delicious pizza by weight), or just picnicking (juice, yogurt, cheese, roll: L8,000). For mountains of picnic produce or just a cheap sandwich and piles of people-watching, visit the huge multi-storied **Mercato Centrale** (7:00-14:00, closed Sunday) in the middle of the San Lorenzo street market. Behind the Duomo, **Snack** (15 Pronconsolo) serves decent cheap lunches. For a reasonably priced pizza with a Medici-style view, try one of the pizzerias on Piazza della Signori.

Train Connections

Florence to: Assisi (6/day, 2½ to 3 hrs), **Brindisi** (3/day, 11 hrs with change in Bologna), **Frankfurt** (3/day, 12 hrs), **La Spezia** (for the Cinque Terre, 2/day direct, 2 hrs, or change in Pisa), **Milan** (12/day, 3 hrs), **Naples** (5/day, 5 hrs, possible overnight), **Orvieto** (6/day, 2 hrs), Paris (1/day, 12 hrs overnight), **Pisa** (2/hr, 1 hr), **Rome** (12/day, 2 hrs), **Venice** (7/day, 3 hrs), **Vienna** (4/day, 9-10 hrs). **Siena:** SITA buses go from near the Florence train station nearly hourly (L18,000 round-trip, 75 minutes each way, much better than the train, bus info tel. 483651, the schedule's in Florence's Concierge magazine).

Italy

VENICE

Soak all day in this puddle of elegant decay. Venice (Venezia) is Europe's best-preserved big city, a car-free urban wonderland of 100 islands, laced together by 400 bridges and 2,000 alleys.

Born in a lagoon 1,500 years ago as a refuge from barbarians, Venice is overloaded with tourists and slowly sinking (unrelated facts). In the Middle Ages, after the Venetians created a great trading empire, they smuggled in the bones of St. Mark (San Marco), and Venice gained religious importance as well.

Today, Venice is home to about 75,000 people in its old city, down from a peak population of around 200,000. While there are about 500,000 in greater Venice (counting the mainland, not counting tourists), the old town has a small-town feel. To see small-town Venice through the touristic flak, explore the back streets and try a Stand-Up-Progressive-Venetian-Pub-Crawl-Dinner.

Planning Your Time

Venice is worth at least a day on even the speediest tour. Train travelers can be most efficient by taking the night train in and/or out. Sleep in the old center to experience Venice at its best: early and late. For a one-day visit: cruise the Grand Canal, do the major San Marco sights (square, palace, church), see the Church of the Frari for art, and wander the back streets on a pub crawl. Venice's greatest sight is the city itself. Make time to simply wander. While doable in a day, Venice is worth two. It's a medieval cookie jar, and nobody's looking.

Orientation (tel. code: 041)

The island city of Venice is shaped like a fish. Its major thoroughfares are canals. The Grand Canal snakes through the middle of the fish, starting at the mouth where all the people and food enter, passing under the Rialto Bridge, and ending at St. Mark's Square (San Marco). Park your 20th-century perspective at the mouth, and let Venice swallow you whole.

Venice is a car-less kaleidoscope of people, bridges, and odorless canals. The city has no real streets, and addresses are hopelessly confusing. There are six districts, each with about 6,000 address numbers. Luckily, it's easy to find your way, since many street corners have a sign pointing you to the nearest major landmark (such as San Marco, Accademia, and Rialto). To find your way, navigate by landmarks, not streets. Obedient visitors stick to the main thoroughfares as directed by these signs and miss the charm of back-street Venice.

Parking in Venice

At Venice, the freeway ends like Medusa's head. Follow the green lights directing you to a parking lot with space. The standard place is Tronchetto (across the causeway and on the right) with a huge new multi-storied garage (L36,000 per day, half off with a discount coupon from your hotel; Hotel Guerrato has them). From there you'll find travel agencies masquerading as TIs and *vaporetto* docks for the boat connection (#82) to the town center.

Tourist Information

The best tourist information office (TI) is on St. Mark's Square (tel. 5226356, open maybe 8:30-19:00, closed Sunday). Pick up a city map, public transit map, the latest museum hours, and confirm your sightseeing plans. Drop into any fancy hotel (as if you're sleeping there) and pick up the free periodical entertainment guide, *Un Ospite de Venezia* (a handy listing of events and the latest museum hours). The cheap Venice map on sale at postcard racks has much more detail than the TI map. Also consider the little sold-with-the-postcards guidebook with a city map and explanations of the major sights.

Trains and Buses

A long causeway connects Venice to the mainland. Venice's Santa Lucia train station plops you right into the old town on the Grand Canal, an easy *vaporetto* ride or fascinating 40-minute walk from San Marco. Mestre is the sprawling mainland industrial base of Venice. While there are fewer crowds and cheaper hotels and parking lots here, Mestre has no charm. Don't stop here. The Santa Lucia station is a thriving center of information, but I'd go directly to the center.

Venice

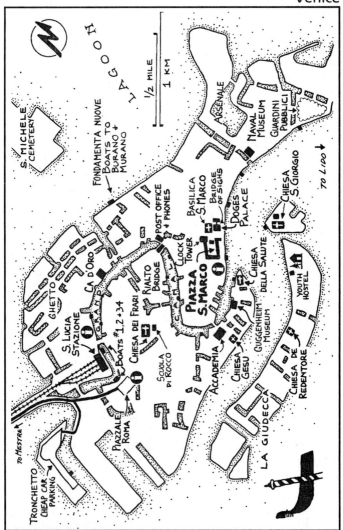

Getting Around Venice

The public transit system is a fleet of bus-boats called *vaporetti*. They work like city buses except that they never get a flat, the stops are docks, and if you get off between stops you may drown. While route numbers seem to change every year, for now only three lines matter: #1 is the slow boat, taking 45 minutes to make every stop along the entire length of the Grand Canal (tickets L2,500), #82 is the fast boat down the Grand Canal, stopping only at the car park, train station, Rialto, and San Marco, making the trip in 20 minutes (tickets L3,500), and #52 gives you an interesting circular tour of the island city (L3,500). Buy tickets before boarding or for an extra fee from a conductor on board. There are one-day and three-day passes, but I've never sailed enough to merit purchasing one.

Only three bridges cross the Grand Canal, but seven *traghetti* (little L500 ferry gondolas, marked on better maps) shuttle locals and in-the-know tourists across the canal, where necessary. Take advantage of these time savers.

Good city maps show boat stops, routes, and *traghetti* crossings. The TI, boat information office at Piazzale Roma, and some hotels can give you the free ACTV Venice public transportation map (which has a good city map on the back).

Helpful Hints

The Venice fly-trap lures us in and takes our money, any way it can. Expect to be shortchanged by any ticket-taker. Wait through the delayed-payment-of-change trick. Count your change carefully. Accept the fact that Venice was a tourist town 400 years ago. It was, is, and always will be crowded. Eighty percent of Venice is actually an untouristy place; 80% percent of the tourists never notice. Hit the back streets.

Get Lost: Venice is the ideal town to explore on foot. Walk and walk to the far reaches of the town. Don't worry about getting lost. Get as lost as possible. Keep reminding yourself, "I'm on an island and I can't get off." When it comes time to find your way, just follow the directional arrows on building corners, or simply ask a local, "*Dové* (DOH-vay) *San Marco?*" ("Where is St. Mark's?") People in the tourist business (that's most Venetians) speak some English.

Money: Bank rates vary. I like the Banco di Sicilia a block towards San Marco from Campo San Bartolomio. AmExCo has bad rates. Non-bank exchange bureaus will cost you $10 more than a bank for a $200 exchange. There's a 24-hour cash machine near the Rialto *vaporetto* stop that exchanges U.S. dollars and other currencies into lire at a fair rate.

The "Rolling Venice" Youth Discount Pass: This gives anyone under 30 discounts on sights, transportation, information on cheap eating and sleeping, and a handy guide-booklet to the city—but for L5,000, it's barely worthwhile (behind the AmExCo at Corte Contarina 1529, Monday-Saturday 9:30-13:00).

Water: Venetians pride themselves on having pure, safe, and tasty tap water, which is piped in from the foothills of the Alps (which you can actually see from Venice on a crisp winter day).

Pigeon Poop: If bombed by a pigeon, resist the initial response to wipe it off immediately—it'll just smear into your hair. Wait until it dries and flake it off cleanly.

Laundry: A handy *lavanderia* (laundromat) near St. Mark's and most of my hotel listings is the full-service Laundry Gabriella (Monday-Friday 8:00-19:00, Rio Terra Colonne, one bridge off the Merceria near San Zulian church, tel. 5221758). There, you can get nine pounds of laundry washed and dried for L15,000. Near the Rialto: Lavanderia SS. Apostoli (8:30-12:00, 15:00-19:00, closed Saturday, tel. 26650, on Campo SS. Apostoli). At either place you can drop it by in the morning, pick it up that afternoon.

Sights—Venice

▲▲▲**Grand Canal Tour**—Grab a front seat on boat #82 (fast, 20 minutes) or #1 (slow, 45 minutes) to cruise the entire Canale Grande from the car park (*Tronchetto*) or train station (*Ferrovia*) to San Marco. While Venice is a barrage on the senses that hardly needs a narration, these notes give the cruise a little meaning and help orient you to this great city. Some city maps (on sale at postcard racks) have a handy Grand Canal map on the back side.

Venice, built in a lagoon, sits on pilings—pine trees driven 15 feet into the mud. Over 100 canals, about 25 miles in length, drain the city, dumping like streams into the Grand Canal.

Venice is a city of palaces. The most lavish were built fronting this canal. This cruise is the only way to really appreciate the front doors of this unique and historic chorus line of mansions from the days when Venice was the world's richest city. Strict laws prohibit any changes in these buildings,

Downtown Venice

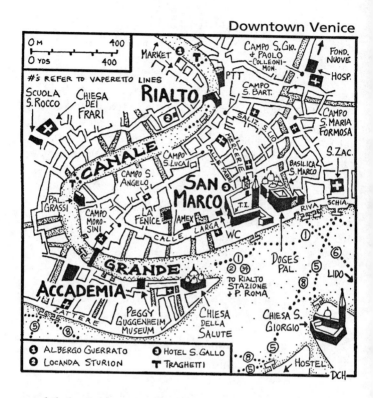

O M 400
O YDS 400

#'s REFER TO VAPORETTO LINES

SCUOLA S.ROCCO
CHIESA DEI FRARI
RIALTO
MARKET
CAMPO S. GIO. & PAOLO - COLLEONI-MON.
FOND. NUOVE
HOSP.
PTT
CAMPO S. BART.
CAMPO S. MARIA FORMOSA
CANALE
CAMPO S.LUCA
SALIZ. S. LIO
MERCERIE
CALLE FABRI
S. ZAC.
BASILICA S.MARCO
CAMPO S. ANGELO
SAN MARCO
T.I.
PAL. GRASSI
CAMPO MOROSINI
LA FENICE
AMEX
CALLE LARGA
WC
RIVA
SCHIA
DOGE'S PAL.
GRANDE
TO RIALTO STAZIONE ↓ P. ROMA
LIDO
ACCADEMIA
ZATTERE
PEGGY GUGGENHEIM MUSEUM
CHIESA DELLA SALUTE
CHIESA S. GIORGIO
HOSTEL
DCH

❶ ALBERGO GUERRATO   ❸ HOTEL S. GALLO
❷ LOCANDA STURION   T TRAGHETTI

so while landowners gnash their teeth, we can enjoy Europe's best-preserved medieval city—slowly rotting. Many of the grand buildings are now vacant. Others harbor chandeliered elegance above mossy basements.

Start at Tronchetto (the bus and car park) or the train station. FS stands for "Ferrovie dello Stato," the Italian state railway system. The bridge at the station is one of only three that cross the Canale Grande.

Vaporetto stop #4 (San Marcuola-Ghetto) is near the world's original ghetto. When this area was set aside as the local Jewish quarter in 1516, it was a kind of urban island which developed into one of the most closely knit business and cultural quarters of any Jewish community in Italy.

As you cruise, notice the traffic signs. Venice's main thoroughfare is busy with traffic. You'll see all kinds of boats: taxis, police boats, garbage, even brown-and-white UPS boats.

Venice's 500 sleek, black, graceful gondolas are a symbol of the city. They cost about $35,000 apiece and are built with a slight curve so that one oar propels them in a straight line.

At the Ca d'Oro stop, notice the palace of the same name. For years it's been under a wooden case of scaffolding for reconstruction. Named the "House of Gold," and considered the most elegant Venetian Gothic palace on the canal, today it's an art gallery with a few important paintings. Unfortunately its interior shows nothing of its palatial origins.

Just before the Rialto Bridge, on the right, the outdoor produce market bustles with people in the morning, but is quiet with only a few grazing pigeons the rest of the day. Can you see the *traghetto* gondola ferrying shoppers back and forth? The huge post office, usually with a postal boat moored at its blue posts, is on the left.

A symbol of Venice, the Rialto Bridge, is lined with shops and tourists. Built in 1592, with a span of 42 meters, it was an impressive engineering feat in its day. Locals call the summit of this bridge the "icebox of Venice" for its cool breeze.

The Rialto, a separate town in the early days of Venice, has always been the commercial district, while San Marco was the religious and governmental center. Today a street called the Merceria connects the two, providing travelers with a gauntlet of shopping temptations.

Take a deep whiff of Venice. What's all this nonsense about stinky canals? All I smell is my shirt. By the way, how's your captain? Smooth dockings? To get to know him, stand up in the bow and block his view.

Notice how the rich marble facades are just a veneer covering no-nonsense brick buildings. And notice the characteristic chimneys.

After passing the British consulate, you'll see the wooden Accademia Bridge, leading to the Accademia Gallery, filled with the best Venetian paintings. The bridge was put up in 1932 as a temporary fix for the original iron one. Locals liked it and it became permanent.

Cruising under the bridge, you'll get a classic view of the Salute Church, built as a thanks to God when the devastating plague of 1630 passed. It's claimed that over a million trees were used for the foundation alone. Much of the surrounding countryside was deforested by Venice. Trees were needed both to fuel the furnaces of its booming glass industry and to prop up this city in the mud.

The low white building on the right (before the church) is the Peggy Guggenheim Gallery. She willed the city a fine collection of modern art.

The building on the right with the golden dome is the Dogana da Mar, a 16th-century customs house. Its two bronze Atlases hold a statue of Fortune riding the dome.

As you prepare to de-boat at stop #15—San Marco—look from left to right out over the lagoon. A wide harbor-front walk leads past the town's most elegant hotels to the green area in the distance. This is the public gardens, the only sizable park in town. Farther out is the Lido, tempting with its beaches and casinos. The dreamy church that seems to float is the architect Palladio's San Giorgio (interesting visit, fine Tintoretto paintings, great view from its bell tower, L2,000, 9:30-12:30, 14:00-18:00 daily). And farther to the right is a residential chunk of Venice called the Guidecca.

For more *vaporetto* fun, ride boat #52 around the city. Plenty of boats leave from San Marco for the beach (Lido), as well as speedboat tours of Burano (a quiet, picturesque fishing and lace town), Murano (the glassblowing island), and Torcello (has the oldest churches and mosaics, but is an otherwise dull and desolate island). Boat #12 takes you to these remote points slower and cheaper.

▲▲▲**St. Mark's Square (Piazza San Marco)**—Surrounded by splashy and historic buildings, Piazza San Marco is filled with music, lovers, pigeons, and tourists from around the world by day and is your private rendezvous with the Middle Ages late at night. Europe's greatest dance floor is the romantic place to be. This is the first place to flood, has Venice's best tourist information office (rear corner), and fine public rest rooms (Albergo Diorno, WC, shower, L3,000 baggage check, behind the TI).

With your back to the church, survey one of Europe's great urban spaces and the only square in Venice to merit the title "Piazza." Nearly two football fields long, it's surrounded by the offices of the republic. On the right are the "old offices," (16th century, Renaissance). On the left are the "new offices" (17th century, Baroque style). Napoleon enclosed the square

St. Mark's Square

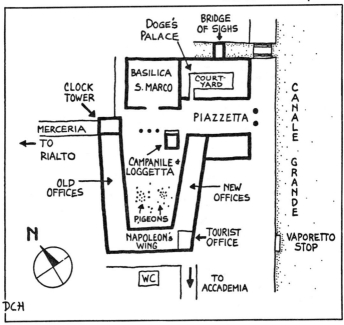

with the more simple and austere Neoclassical wing across the far end and called this "the most beautiful drawing room in Europe."

For a slow and pricey thrill, invest L8,000 in a beer or coffee in one of the elegant cafés with the dueling orchestras. If you're going to sit awhile and savor the scene, it's worth the splurge. Caution: ask if there's an extra music fee. For the most thrills L1,500 can get you in Venice, buy a bag of pigeon seed and become very popular in a flurry.

▲▲**Doge's Palace (Palazzo Ducale)**—The seat of the Venetian government and home of its ruling duke or "doge," this was the most powerful half acre in Europe for 400 years. It was built to show off the power and wealth of the republic and remind all visitors that Venice was number one. Built in Venetian Gothic style, the bottom has pointy arches and the top has an eastern or Islamic flavor. Its columns sat on pedestals, but in the thousand years since they were erected the palace has settled into the mud and they have vanished.

Entering the palace (before the ticket booth) notice a grand staircase (with nearly naked Moses and Paul Newman at the top). Even the most powerful visitors climbed this to meet the doge. This was the beginning of an architectural power trip. The doge, the elected king of this "dictatorial republic," lived on the first floor (now used for special exhibits). You'll tour the public rooms of the top floor. The place is wallpapered with masterpieces by Veronese and Tintoretto. Don't worry much about the great art. Enjoy the building.

In room 12, the Senate Room, the 200 senators met, debated, and passed laws. From the center of the ceiling, Tintoretto's Triumph of Venice shows the city in all her glory. Lady Venice, in heaven with the Greek Gods, stands high above the lesser nations who swirl respectfully at her feet with gifts.

The Armory shows the military might of the empire which was employed to keep the east-west trade lines open (and the local economy booming). Squint out the window at the far end for a fine view of Palladio's San Georgio church and the Lido in the distance.

After the huge old globes, you'll enter the giant Hall of the Grand Council (180 feet long, capacity 2,000) where the entire nobility met to elect the senate and doge. Ringing the room are portraits of 76 doges (in chronological order). One, who opposed the will of the Grand Council, is blacked out. Behind the doge's throne, you can't miss Tintoretto's monsterpiece, *Paradise*. At 1,700 square feet, this is the world's largest oil painting. Christ and Mary are surrounded by 500 saints.

Walking over the Bridge of Sighs, you'll enter the prisons. The doges could sentence, torture, and jail their opponents secretly and in the privacy of their own homes. As you walk back over the bridge, wave to the gang of tourists gawking at you. (L10,000, 9:00-19:00, last entry at 18:00, good WC near exit.)

▲▲**St. Mark's Basilica**—For well over a thousand years, it has housed the saint's bones. The mosaic above the door at the far left of the church shows two guys carrying Mark's coffin into the church. Mark looks pretty grumpy after the long voyage from Egypt. The church has 4,000 square meters of Byzantine mosaics. The best and oldest are in the atrium (turn right as you enter and stop under the last dome). Face the piazza, gape up (it's okay, no pigeons), and study the story of Noah, the Ark, and the flood (two by two, the wicked drowning, Noah sending out the dove, happy rainbow, sacrifice of thanks). Now face the church and read clockwise the story of Adam and Eve that rings the bottom of the dome. Step inside the church (stairs on right lead to horses) and notice the rolling mosaic marble floor. Stop under the central dome and look up for the ascension. (Modest dress, no shorts or bare shoulders, free, 9:00-17:00, Sunday 14:00-17:00, tel. 5225205, see the schedule board in the atrium listing free English guided tours of the church, beautifully lit at the 18:45 mass on Saturday and 14:00-17:00 Sunday.)

Upstairs you can see an up-close mosaic exhibition, a fine view of the church interior, a view of the square from the horse balcony, and the newly restored original bronze horses (L3,000, 9:45-17:00). These horses, made during the days of Alexander the Great (4th century B.C.), were taken to Rome by Nero, to Constantinople by Constantine, to Venice by crusaders, to Paris by Napoleon, back "home" to Venice when Napoleon fell, and finally indoors out of the acidic air.

The treasures of the church (requiring two more L3,000 admissions) give you the best chance outside of Istanbul or Ravenna to see the glories of Byzantium. Venetian crusaders looted the Christian city of Constantinople and brought home piles of lavish loot (until the advent of TV evangelism, perhaps the lowest point in Christian history). Much of this plunder is stored in the treasury of San Marco (*tesaro*). As you view these treasures, remember most were made in A.D. 500, while western Europe was still rooting in the mud. Behind the high altar lies the body of St. Mark ("Marxus") and the Pala d'Oro, a golden altarpiece made (A.D. 1000-1300) with 80 Byzantine enamels. Each shows a religious scene set in gold and precious stones. Both of these sights are interesting and historic, but neither are as much fun as two bags of pigeon seed.

▲**Campanile di San Marco**—Ride the elevator 300 feet to the top of the bell tower for the best view in Venice. Photos on the wall inside show how this bell tower crumbled into a pile of bricks in 1902, one thousand years after it was built. For an ear-shattering experience, be on top when the bells ring (L4,000, 9:30-19:00). The golden angel at its top always faces into the wind.

Clock Tower—From Piazza San Marco you can see the bronze men (Moors) swing their huge clappers at the top of each hour. Notice the world's first "digital" clock on the tower facing the square (flips dramatically every 5 minutes).

▲▲**Galleria dell' Accademia**—Venice's top art museum is packed with the painted highlights of the Venetian Renaissance (Bellini, Giorgione, Veronese, Tiepolo, and Canaletto). It's just over the wooden Accademia Bridge (L10,000, 9:00-14:00, Sunday 9:00-13:00; expect delays, as they allow only 180 visitors at a time, tel. 5222247).

▲**Museo Civico Correr**—The interesting city history museum offers dusty bits of Venice's glory days and fine views of Piazza San Marco. Entry is on the square opposite the church (L5,000, 10:00-17:00, closed Tuesday).

▲▲▲**Chiesa dei Frari**—This great Gothic Franciscan church, an artistic highlight of Venice featuring three great masters, offers more art per lira than any other Venetian sight. Freeload on English-language tours to get the most out of the Titian Assumption above the high altar. Then move one chapel to the right to see Donatello's wood carving of St. John the Baptist almost live. And for the climax, continue right into the sacristy to sit before Bellini's *Madonna and the Saints*. Perhaps the greatest Venetian painter, Bellini's genius is obvious in the pristine clarity, believable depth, and reassuring calm of this three-paneled altarpiece. Notice the rich colors of Mary's clothing and how good it is to see a painting in its intended setting. For many, these three pieces of art make a visit to the Accademia Gallery unnecessary. Before leaving, check out the Neoclassical pyramid-shaped tomb of Canova and (opposite) the grandiose tomb of Titian, the Venetian. Compare the carved marble Assumption behind his tombstone portrait with the painted original above the high altar (L1,000, 9:00-12:00, 14:30-18:00, Sunday 15:00-18:00).

▲**Scuola di San Rocco**—Next to the Frari church, another lavish building bursts with art, including some 50 Tintorettos. The best paintings are upstairs, especially the *Crucifixion* in the smaller room. View the neck-breakingly splendid ceiling paintings with one of the mirrors (specchio) available at the entrance. (L8,000, 9:00-17:30, last entrance 17:00.)

▲**Peggy Guggenheim Collection**—A popular collection of far-out art, including works by Picasso, Chagall, and Dali, that so many try so hard to understand. (L10,000, 11:00-18:00, closed Tuesday.)

Ca' Rezzonico—This 18th-century Grand Canal palazzo is now open as the Museo del '700 Veneziano, offering the best look in Venice about the life of the rich and famous here 200 years ago. (L5,000, 10:00-16:00, closed Friday, tel. 5224543, at a *vaporetto* stop by the same name).

▲**Gondola Rides**—A traditional must for many but a rip-off for most; gondoliers charge about L70,000 for a 40-minute ride. You can divide the cost—and the romance—by up to six people (some take seven if you beg and they're hungry). For cheap gondola thrills, stick to the L500 1-minute ferry ride on a Grand Canal *traghetti*, or hang out on a bridge along the gondola route and wave at the romantics.

▲**Glassblowing**—It's unnecessary to go all the way to Murano Island to see glassblowing demonstrations. For the best show, wait near one of several glassworks near St. Mark's Square and follow any tour group into the furnace room for a fun and free 10-minute show. You'll usually see a vase and a *"leetle orse"* made from molten glass. The commercial that always follows in the showroom is actually entertaining. Prices around St. Mark's have a sizable tour-guide commission built in. Serious glass-shoppers buy at small shops on Murano Island.

Santa Elena—For a pleasant peek into a completely untouristy residential side of Venice, catch the boat from San Marco to the neighborhood of Santa Elena (at the fish's tail). This 100-year-old suburb lives as if there was no tourism. You'll find a kid-friendly park, a few lazy restaurants, and great sunsets over San Marco.

▲▲**Evening: The Stand-up Progressive Venetian Pub Crawl Dinner**—Venice's residential back streets hide plenty of characteristic bars with countless trays of interesting toothpick munchie food (*cicheti*). Partaking in the *"giro di ombre"* (pub crawl) tradition is a great way to mingle and have fun with the Venetians. Real *cicheti* pubs are getting rare in these fast-food days, but locals can point you in the right direction or you can follow the plan below.

   Italian *cicheti* (hors d'oeuvres) wait under glass in bars; try fried mozzarella cheese, blue cheese, calamari, artichoke hearts, and anything ugly on a toothpick. Ask for a *piatto misto* (mixed plate). Drink the house wines. A small beer (*birrino*) or house wine costs about L1,000, meat and fish munchies are expensive, veggies are around L4,000 for a meal-sized plate. A good last drink is the local sweet red wine called Fragolino. To be safe, you might give each place L20,000 (or whatever) for your group and explain you want to eat and drink until it's *finito*. Bars don't stay open very late, and the *cicheti* selection is best early, so start your evening by 18:30.

First course: Start on Campo San Bartolomeo near the Rialto Bridge. If the statue walked backwards 20 yards, turned left, went under a passageway, over one bridge to Campo San Lio, took a left past Hotel Canada and over another bridge, he'd hit Alberto's Osteria, called simply Osteria on Calle Malvasia. This fine local-style bar has plenty of snacks and *cicheti*, available cheap from the bar. Say "hi" to Alberto, order with your best Italian (and by pointing), then sit or stand for same price (17:30-21:00, closed Sunday, tel. 5229038).

Second course: Leaving Alberto's, turn left on Calle Malvasia and go basically straight with a jog to the left through a couple of squares to Campo Santa Maria di Formosa. (Ask *"Dové Santa Maria di Formosa?"*) You could split a pizza with wine on the square (Piero's Bar all' Orologio, opposite the canal, has the worst pizza with the best setting.) *Capricioso* means the house specialty. You can get "pizza to go" on the square from Cip Ciap Pizza Rustica (over the bridge behind the SMF gelateria on Calle del Mondo Novo, open until 21:00, closed Tuesday).

Third course: Fresh fruit and vegetables from the stand on the square next to the water fountain (open until about 20:00).

Fourth course: *Cicheti* and wine. From Bar all' Orologio (on Campo S.M. di Formosa), with your back to the church (follow yellow sign to SS Giov e Paolo) head down the street to Osteria Mascaron (Gigi's bar, best selection by 19:30, closes at 23:00 and on Sunday).

Fifth course: More *cicheti* and wine. Go down the alley across from Gigi's bar (Calle Trevisana o Cicogua, yellow sign to SS G. e P.), over the great gondola voyeurism bridge (pause, sigh *"amoré"*), down Calle Bressana to Campo S. Giovanni e Paolo. Pass the church-looking hospital (notice the illusions painted on its facade, maybe with a drink under the statue at Sergio's Cafe Bar Cavallo). Go over the bridge to the left of the hospital to Calle Larga Gallina, and take the first right to Antiche Cantine Ardenghi de Lucia and Michael at #6369 under the red telephone (no sign for tax reasons, open until 21:00, closed Sunday, tel. 5237691). This *cicheteria* (munchie bar supreme) also serves good sit-down meals.

Sixth course: Gelati. The unfriendly but delicious gelateria on Campo di Formosa closes at about 20:00 and on Thursday. (The owner, Mario, promised me that even if you buy a cone for the L1,000 take-away price, you can sit on his chairs for 5 minutes.) Or head toward San Marco where the gelaterias stay open later (the best is opposite the Doge's Palace, by the two columns, on the bay). There's also a good late-hours gelateria (L1,000 small cones) a block in front of the Rialto Bridge.

You're not a tourist, you're a living part of a soft Venetian night . . . an alley cat with money. Streetlamp halos, live music, floodlit history, and a ceiling of stars make St. Mark's magic at midnight. Shine with the old lanterns on the gondola piers where the sloppy Grand Canal splashes at the Doge's Palace. Comfort the four frightened tetrarchs (ancient Byzantine emperors) under the moon near the Doge's Palace entrance. Cuddle history.

There are also a lot of *cicheta* bars around the Rialto market (between the bridge, Campo San Polo, Chiesa di San Cassiano and recommended hotel Guerrato). You could track down: Do Mori, Cantina Do Spade, Vini da Pinto, All' Arco, Ostaria Antico Dolo, and Osteria Enoteca Vivaldi (most closed on Sunday). You'll notice the same local crowd popping up at each of these characteristic places for *chicheti* and *bon vin*.

Sights—Venice's Lagoon
Several interesting islands hide out in the Venice Lagoon. **Burano**, famous for its lace-making, is a sleepy island with a sleepy community—village Venice without the glitz. Lace fans enjoy Burano's Scuola di Merletti (L3,000, 9:00-18:00, Sunday 10:00-16:00, closed Monday, tel. 730034). **Torcello**, another lagoon island, is dead except for its church, which claims to be the oldest in Venice (L3,000, 10:00-12:30,

Venice Lagoon

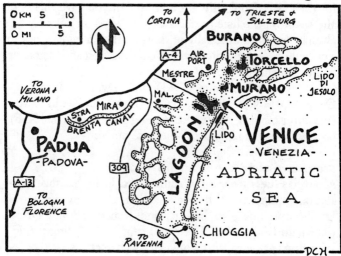

14:00-16:00, closed Monday, tel. 730084). It's impressive for its mosaics but not worth a look on a short visit unless you really have your heart set on Ravenna, but aren't able to make it there. The island of **Murano**, famous for its glass factories, has the Museo Vetrario, which displays the very best of 700 years of Venetian glassmaking (L5,000, 10:00-16:00, closed Wednesday, tel. 739586). The islands are reached easily but slowly by *vaporetto* (catch at Fondamente Nove). Four-hour speedboat tours of these three lagoon destinations leave twice a day from the dock near the Doge's Palace.

Sleeping in Venice
(L1,600 = about $1, tel. code: 041)
Finding a room in Venice is easy. Simply call one of my recommendations a few days in advance, reconfirm by telephone the morning of your arrival day, and arrive by mid-afternoon. While many stay in a nearby less-crowded place and side-trip to Venice, I can't imagine not sleeping downtown. If you arrive on an overnight train, your room may not be ready. Drop your bag at the hotel and dive right into Venice.

Baths (*bagno*) are substantially more expensive than showers (*doccia*). A toilet in the room knocks the price up. Don't book through the tourist office (which pockets a

L15,000 per person "deposit"). The prices I've listed here are for those who book direct (mention that you have this book and insist on the listed price through 1995). Prices may be cheaper (or soft), especially off-season. If on a budget, ask for a cheaper room or a discount. I've let location and character be my priorities.

Sleep code: **S**=Single, **D**=Double/Twin, **T**=Triple, **Q**=Quad, **B**=Bath/Shower, **WC**=Toilet, **CC**=Credit Card (**V**isa, **M**astercard, **A**mex), **SE**=Speaks English (graded **A-F**), breakfast is included unless otherwise noted.

Sleeping near the Rialto Bridge

Albergo Guerrato, near a handy and colorful produce market, one minute from the Rialto action, is warmly run by English-speaking Biba, her husband, Roberto (Bobby Drinkwater), and dog, Lord. Their 800-year-old building is Old World simple, airy, and wonderfully characteristic (D-L70,000, DB-L80,000, DBWC-L95,000, T-L92,000, TB-L103,000, TBWC-L120,000, QB-L120,000, QBWC-L160,000, including a big breakfast and city map, CC:VM, walk over the Rialto away from San Marco, go straight about 3 blocks, turn right on Calle drio la Scimia and you'll see the red sign, Calle drio la Scimia 240a, Rialto, tel. and fax 5227131 or 5285927).

Locanda Sturion (DB-L180,000, QB-L300,000 with canal view, CC:VM, miles of stairs, S. Polo, Rialto, Calle Sturion 679, 30125 Venezia, tel. 5236243, fax 5228378, SE-A), with all the comforts, overlooks the Canal. Helen, Flavia, and Nicolette hold a room until 16:00 with no deposit; 100 yards from the Rialto Bridge (opposite *vaporetto* dock).

Hotel Canada (two D with adjacent bath-L125,000, DB-L160,000, CC:VM, Castello San Lio 5659, 30122 Venezia, tel. 5229912, fax 5235852, SE-B) has 25 rooms, all with private showers, WC, and phones. In a "typical noble Venetian home," it's ideally located on a quiet square, between the Rialto and San Marco. (See directions to Alberto's under Pub Crawl Evening, above.)

Sleeping near St. Mark's Square

Hotel Riva (two 4th-floor view D with adjacent showers-L85,000, DB-L110,000, Ponte dell' Angelo, 5310, Venezia, tel. 5227034), with gleaming marble hallways and bright modern rooms, is romantically situated on a canal along the gondola serenade route. You could actually dunk your breakfast rolls in the canal (but don't). Sandro will hold a corner (*angolo*) room if you ask. It's behind San Marco where the canals Rio di San Zulian and Rio del Mondo Nouvo hit Rio Canonica o Palazzo.

Hotel San Gallo (S-L40,000, SB-L60,000, D-L90,000, DB-L140,000, T-L125,000, TB-L170,000, CC:VM, San Marco 1093/A, 30124 Venice, tel. 5227311 or 5289877, fax 5225702, SE-A, Luca and Franco promise these prices to those with this book) is about 100 yards off Piazza San Marco (with back to the church, take the second-to-last archway right off St. Mark's Square). Breakfast is on a chirpy, breezy roof garden.

Albergo Doni (D-L80,000, Riva Schiavoni, San Zaccaria N. #4656 Calle del Vin, tel. 5224267, SE-B) is a dark, woody, clean, and quiet place with 12 classy rooms run by a likable smart-aleck named Gina, who promises my readers one free down-the-hall shower each. It's two bridges behind the San Marco, or walk east along the San Marco waterfront (Riva Degli Schiavoni), over two bridges, take the first left (Calle del Vin), and follow the signs.

Albergo Corona is a squeaky-clean, Old World gem with nine rooms. (S-L38,000, D-L55,000, breakfast L8,000 extra, showers L3,000, find Campo SS Filippo e Giacomo behind San Marco, go down Calle Sacristia, go left on Calle Corona to #4464, tel. 5229174, lots of stairs, SE-F.)

Locanda Piave, with 12 fine rooms above a bright and classy lobby is a rare value (S-L55,000, D-L82,000, T-120,000, CC:VMA; from Campo Santa Maria Formosa go behind the church, over a bridge and down Parrocchia di San Zaccaria to the first corner, Ruga Giuffa 4838/40, 30122 Venezia, tel. 5285174, fax 5238512, SE-D).

Alloggi Masetto, incredibly well-located with four dirt-cheap rooms, is a homey place filled with birds, goldfish, and stacks of magazines, and run by Irvana Artico, a crusty landlady who surprises you with pretty good English (D-L40,000, DB-L45,000, TB-60,000, no breakfast, just off San Marco, from AmExCo head toward San Marco, first left, first left again through tunnel following yellow sign to

Commmune di Venezia, jog left again and see her sign,
Sotoportego Ramo Contarina, Frezzeria, San Marco 1520
A, tel. 5230505).

Locanda Casa Petrarca, wicker-cozy and bubbling
jazz, hangs like an ivy-framed painting over a dead-end alley.
Nelli is a friend as well as a host. (D-L80,000, DB-L100,000,
Calle Schiavone #4386. With your back to St. Mark's, take
last right off square. From Campo San Luco, go down Calle
dei Fuseri, take left before red "ristorante" sign, look right,
tel. 5200430, SE-A.)

Locanda Gambero, with 30 rooms, is the biggest one-
star hotel in the San Marco area. (S-L50,000, D-L80,000,
DB-L100,000, T-L110,000, TB-L130,000, CC:VM, run by
English-speaking Sandro and Sergio, a straight shot down
Calle dei Fabbri from the Rialto *vaporetto* #1 dock, from
Piazza San Marco walk down Calle dei Fabbri, over one bridge
to #4685, tel. 5224384, fax 5200431, smoke-free rooms upon
request). Gambero runs "La Bistro," a user-friendly French/
Italian eatery with a pleasant art-deco ambiance and good
L7,000 pasta specials with no extra charges.

Sleeping in Other Parts of Venice
Hotel Marin is 3 minutes from the train station but
completely out of the touristic bustle of the Lista di Spagna
(S-L47,000, D-L74,000, DB-L100,000, T-L95,000,
TB-L130,000, Q-L120,000, QB-L160,000, prices include
breakfast and receive a 10% discount with this book,
promised through 1995, CC:VMA, from the train station,
cross the bridge and go behind the big green domed church.
From the bridge go right, left, right, and right to San Croce
670b, tel. and fax 718022). Cozy, plain, and cheery, it will
seem like a 19-bedroom home the moment you cross the
threshold. It's family-run by helpful, English-speaking
Bruno, Nadia, and son Samuel (they have city maps).

Foresteria della Chiesa Valdese is warmly run by a
Protestant church offering dorm beds at youth-hostel prices
in a handier location (halfway between San Marco and Rialto)
in a rundown but charming old palace with elegant paintings
on the ceilings (L22,000 dorm beds or L50,000 doubles with
sheets and breakfast, more expensive for one-night stays,
with some larger "apartments" for small groups; from Campo

Santa Maria Formosa walk past the Orologio bar to the end
of Calle Lungo and cross the bridge, Castello 5170, tel.
5286797, closed 13:30-18:00).

The **Venice youth hostel** (L22,000 beds with sheets
and breakfast in 10- to 18-bed rooms, membership required;
on Giudecca Island, tel. 5238211, boat #1 or #82 from station or San Marco to Zittele) is crowded, cheap, and newly
remodeled (desk open 7:00-13:00, 14:00-22:00). Their budget
cafeteria welcomes non-hostelers.

Eating in Venice

For low-stress, but not necessarily low-price, meals, you'll
find plenty of self-service restaurants (*self-service* in Italian).
One is right at the Rialto Bridge. Pizzerias are cheap and easy.
Those that sell take-out by the slice or gram are cheapest.
Menus should clearly explain the *coperto* (cover charge) and
servicio (service charge).

Any place serving food on the Grand Canal, on St.
Mark's, or along the main road connecting the two, may
have a pleasant setting but is not a good value.

A key to cheap eating in Venice is bar snacks, especially
stand-up mini-meals in out-of-the-way bars. Order by
pointing. *Panini* (sandwiches) are sold fast and cheap at bars
everywhere. My favorite Venetian dinner is the pub crawl
(described above under Sights). Any of the listed bars would
make a fine one-stop, sit-down dinner.

The produce market that sprawls for a few blocks just
past the Rialto Bridge (best 8:00-13:00) is a great place to
assemble a picnic. The nearby street, Ruga Vecchia, has good
bakeries and cheese shops. Side lanes in this area are speckled
with fine little hole-in-the-wall munchie bars.

The Mensa DLF (to the right of the train station as you
face the tracks, 12:30-13:30, 18:00-21:00, closed Saturday,
Sunday, and during lunch on Tuesday and Thursday, tel.
716242), the public transportation workers' cafeteria, is
cheap and open to the public.

Eating near Campo San Bartolomeo

While these places aren't worth hiking to, they're handy,
near the central Campo San Bartolomeo (a block toward San

Marco from the Rialto Bridge). Directions start from the statue in this square's center.

The very local, hustling **Rosticceria San Bartolomeo/ Gislon** (Calle della Bissa 5424, 20 yards behind the statue to its left, under a passageway, tel. 5223569, 9:30-14:30, 17:00-21:00, closed Monday) is a cheap—if confusing—self-service restaurant on the ground floor (L5,000 pasta, prices listed at door, stools along the window). Good but pricier meals are served at the full-service restaurant upstairs. Get a take-out meal to eat on a nearby bridge or campo.

If the statue on the square were to jump off his pedestal, walk ahead 50 yards, and go down a narrow alley to the left, he'd find the **Devil's Forest Pub**, with English decor and self-service Italian food (L7,000 pasta, no cover, open late, closed Monday).

Ristorante Pizzeria da Nane Mora (behind the statue, past PTT, over the bridge, and right at the red Santuario Madonna della Grazie church, on a tiny triangular square, open at 19:00, closed Wednesdays) has good pizza and indoor/ outdoor seating.

Train Connections

Venice to: Bern (4/day, change in Milan, 8 hrs), **Brindisi** (3/day, 11 hrs), **Milan** (12/day, 3-4 hrs), **Munich** (5/day, 8 hrs), **Naples** (2/day, 6 hrs), **Paris** (3/day, 11 hrs), **Rome** (5/day, 4-7 hrs, over night possible), **Verona** (12/day, 1½ hrs), **Vienna** (4/day, 9 hrs). **To the Dolomites**: train from Venice to Bolzano (8/day, 4 hrs with one change) and catch a bus into the mountains from there. Train and couchette reservations (L24,000) are easily made at the AmExCo office near San Marco. Venice train info: tel. 041/715555.

HILL TOWNS OF CENTRAL ITALY

Break out of the Venice-Florence-Rome syndrome. There's more to Italy! Experience the slumber of Umbria, the texture of Tuscany, and the lazy towns of Lazio.

For starters, here are a few of my favorites.

Siena seems to be every Italy connoisseur's pet town. In my office whenever Siena is mentioned, someone moans, "Siena? I luuuv Siena!" San Gimignano is the quintessential hill town, with Italy's best surviving medieval skyline. Popular-but-still-powerful Assisi is known for its hometown boy, St. Francis, who made very good. Orvieto, one of the most famous hill towns, is best used as a springboard for trip to tiny Civitá. Stranded alone on its pinnacle in a vast canyon, Civitá's the most lovable.

Planning Your Time

The hill towns are itinerary wreckers. Don't mess with the mediocre towns. Streamline. By train, keep things simple if you're short on time. By car, this is one of the most charming areas of Italy. If you're traveling with a rail/drive pass, this is definitely a place for cashing in a car day or two and exploring.

Siena, the must-see town, has the easiest train and bus connections. With three weeks for Italy, I'd spend three nights in Siena (with a whole-day side trip into Florence and a day to relax and enjoy Siena). Whatever you do, enjoy a sleepy medieval evening in Siena. After an evening in Siena, its major sights can be seen in half a day.

Civitá di Bagnoregio is the awesome pinnacle town. A night in Bagnoregio (via Orvieto bus) with time to hike to the town and spend three hours makes the visit worthwhile. Two nights and an entire day is a good way to keep your pain/pleasure ratio in order.

Assisi is the third most visit-worthy town. It has half a day of sightseeing and another half a day of wonder. While a zoo by day, it's magic at night.

Siena

Seven hundred years ago, Siena was a major military power
in a class with Florence, Venice, and Genoa. The town was
weakened by a disastrous plague in 1348. In the 1550s her
bitter rival Florence really salted her, making Siena forever a
non-threatening backwater. Siena's loss became our sightseeing gain, as its political and economic irrelevance pickled it
purely Gothic.

Siena is the hill-town equivalent of Venice. Traffic-free
red-brick lanes cascade every which way. Siena's thriving historic center offers Italy's best Gothic city experience. While
most people do Siena, just 30 miles south of Florence, as a
day trip, it's best experienced after dark. In fact, it makes more
sense to do Florence as a day trip from Siena. While Florence
has the blockbuster museums, Siena has an easy-to-enjoy
soul. You'll feel like old friends as soon as you're introduced.

For those who dream of a Fiat-free Italy, this is it. Sit at
a café on the red-bricked main square. Take time to savor the
first European city to eliminate automobile traffic (1966), and
then, just to be silly, wonder what would happen if they did
it in your city.

Hill Towns of Central Italy

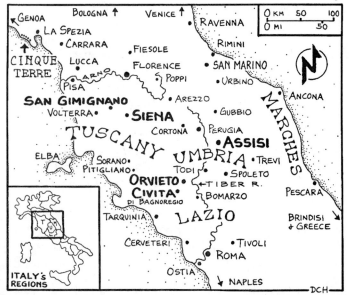

Orientation (tel code: 0577)

Siena lounges atop a hill, stretching its three legs out from Il Campo. This main square is the historic meeting point of Siena's neighborhoods. The entire center is pedestrians-only, no buses and no cars. Everything I mention is within a 15-minute walk of the square. Navigate by landmarks, following the excellent system of signs on every street corner. Landmarks are clearly signposted. The average visitor sticks to the San Domenico–Il Campo axis. There's a handy public WC just off Il Campo at Via Citta (see map).

Tourist Information

Use the main TI on Il Campo (#56, look for the yellow Change sign, 8:30-19:30, less off season, closed Sunday, tel. 280551, get the excellent and free topographical town map). The small hotel information office at San Domenico is in cahoots with local hotels and charges for maps.

Getting Around

From Siena's train station, buy a bus ticket from the yellow machine near the exit, cross the street, and board any orange city bus heading for Piazza Gramsci or via Tozzi. Your hotel is probably within a 5-minute walk of Piazza Gramsci. If you arrive in Siena by intercity bus, you'll be dropped off at Siena's San Domenico church, a 10-minute walk from the center square (go left of the church following yellow signs to Il Campo).

Sights—Siena

Siena is one big sight. Its essential individual sights come in two little clusters: the square, with the museum in the city hall and its tower; and the cathedral, its baptistery, and the cathedral's museum with its surprise viewpoint. Check these sights off, and you're free to wander.

▲▲▲**Il Campo**—Siena's great central piazza is urban harmony at its best. Like a stage set, its gently tilted floor fans out from the tower and city hall backdrop. Notice how beautiful the square is in spite of the complete absence of landscaping. It's the perfect invitation to loiter. Built in 1347, Il Campo was located at the historic junction of Siena's various competing districts, or *contrada*, on the old marketplace. The

Siena

PINACOTECA -PICTURE GALL.-

PIAZZA MERCATO MARKET

PALAZZO PUBLICCO -CITY HALL-

TORRE MANGIA -TOWER- CLIMB FOR A GREAT VIEW!

CAMPO

CASATO DI SOTTO

CITTA

V. S. PIETRO

STALLOREGGI

OPERA METRO- POLITANA -CATHEDRAL MUSEUM-

PIAZZA DUOMO

DUOMO

BAPTISTRY

PIAZZA TOLOMEI

PIAZZA SALIMBENI

PIAZZA MATTEOTTI

*MOST CITY-ORANGE BUSES STOP HERE

PIAZZA GRAMSCI

100 YDS.

V. ROSSI

BANCHI

DI SOPRA

TERMINI

TERME

VIA GALLUZZA

DIACCETO

VIA PELL.

WC

CASTORO

CAPITANO

SANCT. S. CAT.

ESTERNA FONT.

VIA D. CAMPOREGIO

VIA D. SAPIENZA

VIA PARADISO

VIA CURTATONE

VIALE TOZZI

POST

STADIO P

SAN DOMENICO

WC

SITA BUSES TO FLORENCE & REST OF TUSCANY

TO PARKING & AUTOSTRADA

LA LIZZA

VIALE MACCARI

VIALE FRANCHI

VIALE DEI MILLE

25 APRILE

VIALE

FORTEZZA ENOTECA ITALIA

TO TRAIN STATION & CAMPING

❶ LOCANDA GARIBALDI
❷ PICCOLO HOTEL ETRURIA
❸ PENSIONE LA PERLA
❹ HOTEL DUOMO
❺ HOTEL CANNON
❼ PENSION BERNINI
❽ ALMA DOMUS
❾ ❿ LEA & LIBERTY

DCH

brick surface is divided into nine sections, representing the council of nine merchants and city bigwigs who ruled medieval Siena. Don't miss the Fountain of Joy at the square's high point, with its pigeons gingerly tightroping down slippery snouts to slurp a drink. At the base of the tower, the Piazza's chapel was built in 1348 as a thanks to God for ending the Black Plague (after it killed over a third of the population).

▲**Museo Civico**—The Palazzo *Pubblico* (City Hall at the base of the tower) has a fine and manageable museum housing a good sample of Sienese art. You'll see, in the following order, the Sala Risorgimento with dramatic scenes of Victor Emmanuel's unification of Italy, the chapel with impressive inlaid wood chairs in the choir, and the Sala del Mappamondo with Simone Martini's *Maesta* (Enthroned Virgin) facing the faded Guidoriccio da Fogliano (a mercenary providing a more concrete form of protection). Next is the Sala della Pace, which has two interesting frescoes showing "The Effects of Good and Bad Government." Notice the whistle-while-you-work happiness of the utopian community ruled by the utopian government (in the best-preserved fresco) and the fate of a community ruled by politicians with more typical values (in a terrible state of repair). Later you'll see the gruesome *Slaughter of the Innocents* (L6,000, daily 9:00-19:00, winter closing at 13:45, tel. 292111).

▲**Torre del Mangia (the city tower)**—Siena gathers around its city hall, not its church. It was a proud republic and its "declaration of independence" is the tallest secular medieval tower in Italy, the tall-as-a-football-field Torre del Mangia (named after a watchman who did more eating than watching; his statue is in the courtyard, to the left as you enter). Its 300 steps get pretty skinny at the top, but the reward is one of Italy's best views (L4,000, 10:00-18:00 or 19:00, limit of 30 towerists at a time, go early or late to minimize your time in line).

The Palio—The feisty spirit of each of Siena's 17 *contrada*, or districts, lives on. These neighborhoods celebrate, worship, and compete together. Each even has its own historical museum. Contrada pride is evident any time of year in the colorful neighborhood banners, but most evident twice a year (around July 2 and August 16) when they have their world-famous Palio di Siena. Ten of the seventeen neighborhoods compete (chosen by lot), hurling themselves with medieval abandon into several days of trial races and traditional revelry. On the big day, Il Campo is stuffed to the brim with locals and tourists as the horses charge wildly around the square in this literally no-holds-barred race. Of course, the winning neighborhood is the scene of grand celebrations afterward. The grand prize: simply proving your *contrada* is numero uno. You'll see sketches and posters all over town depicting the Palio. The TI has a free scrapbook-quality Palio brochure with English explanations.

▲▲**The Duomo**—Siena's cathedral is as Baroque as Gothic gets. The striped facade is piled with statues and ornamentation, and the interior is decorated from top to bottom. Even the floors are covered with fine inlaid art. In this *panforte* of Italian churches, your special treats are a Donatello statue of St. John the Baptist (in a chapel on the left side) and a couple of Michelangelo statues (on each side of the Piccolomini altar). Above it all peer the heads of 172 popes. This is one busy interior, the antithesis of San Domenico. The artistic highlight is Pisano's pulpit. The library (L2,000) has a Roman copy of the Greek *Three Graces* statue, fine frescoes, and illustrated medieval books (free, 7:30-19:30, until 18:30 off-season, modest dress required).

▲**Baptistery**—Siena is so hilly that there wasn't enough flat ground to build a big church on. What to do? Build a big church and prop up the overhanging edge with the baptistery. This dark and quietly tucked away cave of art is worth a look (and L2,000) for the bronze carvings of Donatello and Ghiberti on the baptismal font (Della Quercia, pay to light it) and for its cool tranquility.

▲▲**The Opera Metropolitana (cathedral museum)**—Siena's most enjoyable museum, on the Campo side of the church (look for the yellow signs), was built to house the cathedral's art. The ground floor is filled with the cathedral's original Gothic sculpture by Pisano. Upstairs to the left awaits a private audience with Duccio's *Maesta* (Enthroned Virgin). Pull up a chair and study this medieval masterpiece. Opposite is what was the flip side of the *Maesta*, with 26 panels, the medieval equivalent of pages, showing scenes from the passion of Christ. After more art, you'll find a little sign directing you to the "panorama." It's a long spiral climb. From the first landing, take the skinnier second spiral for Siena's surprise view. Look back over the Duomo, then consider this: when rival republic Florence began its grand cathedral, Siena decided to outdo it by building a church that would be the biggest in all Christendom. The existing cathedral would be used as a transept. You're atop what would have been the entry. The wall below you that connects the Duomo with the museum of the cathedral was as far as Siena got before the terrible plague killed the city's ability to finish the project. Were it completed, you'd be looking straight down the nave. (L5,000, 9:00-19:30, closing at 18:30 in shoulder months, and 13:30 off-season, tel. 283048.)

Church of San Domenico—This huge brick church, a landmark for those arriving by bus, is worth a quick look. The simple, bland interior fits the austere philosophy of the Dominicans. Walk up the steps in the rear of the church for a look at various paintings from the life of Saint Catherine, patron saint of Siena and, since 1939, of all Italy. Halfway up the church on the right, you'll find her head. (Free, 7:00-13:00, 15:00-17:30, less in winter.)

Sanctuary of Saint Catherine—A few downhill blocks toward the center from San Domenico you'll see signs to the Santuario di Santa Caterina. Step into this cool and peaceful place, the site of Catherine's home. Siena remembers its favorite hometown girl, a simple, unschooled, but almost mystically devout girl who, in the mid-1300s, helped get the pope to return from France to Rome. Pilgrims have come here since 1464. Wander around to enjoy art depicting scenes from her life. Her room is downstairs. (Free, 9:00-12:30, 15:30-18:00.)

▲The Pinacoteca (National Picture Gallery)—Siena was a power in Gothic art. But the average tourist, wrapped up in a love affair with the Renaissance, hardly notices. This museum takes you on a walk through Siena's art, chronologically from the 12th through 15th centuries. For the casual sightseer, the Sienese art in the city hall and cathedral museums is adequate. But art fans enjoy this opportunity to trace the evolution of Siena's delicate and elegant art. (From the Campo, walk out the Via Citta to the Piazza di Postieria and make a left on San Pietro, L8,000, 8:30-19:00 June-September, closes at 14:00 on Monday, 13:00 on Sunday, 13:45 off-season; tel. 281161.)

Sleeping in Siena
(L1,600 = about $1, tel code: 0577, zip code: 53100)
Since most visitors day-trip in from Florence, finding a room is not tough (unless you arrive during Easter or for the Palio

in early July and mid-August). While tour groups turn the town into a Gothic amusement park in midsummer, Siena is basically yours in the evenings and off-season, with your pick of the following hotels.

Nearly all listed hotels lie between Il Campo and the church of San Domenico (the intercity bus stop) and Piazza Gramsci (where the bus from the train station drops you). Call ahead, as it seems Siena's few budget places are listed in all the budget guidebooks. Most places serve no breakfast and are accustomed to holding telephone reservations until 17:00, if you can get the message across in Italian.

Sleep code: **S**=Single, **D**=Double/Twin, **T**=Triple, **Q**=Quad, **B**=Bath/Shower, **WC**=Toilet, **CC**=Credit Card (**V**isa, **M**astercard, **A**mex), **SE**=Speaks English (graded **A-F**).

Sleeping near Il Campo

Each of these first listings is just a horse wreck away from one of Italy's most wonderful civic spaces.

Locanda Garibaldi (D-L60,000-L65,000, half a block downhill off the square to the right of the tower at Via Giovanni Dupre 18, tel. 284204, fax . . . what's that? SE-D) is a dying breed. In this modest, very Sienese restaurant-*albergo*, Marcello wears two hats, running a busy restaurant with seven doubles upstairs. This is a fine place for dinner.

Piccolo Hotel Etruria (SB-L58,000, DB-L85,000, TB-L115,000, QB-L144,000, breakfast L5,000, CC:VMA; with back to the tower, leave Il Campo to the right, Via Donzelle 1-3, tel. and fax 288088, SE-D) is a good bet for a real hotel with all the comforts just off the square. Cheaper rooms (DB-L65,000, QB-L111,000) are in an annex (*dependenza*) across the street.

Albergo Tre Donzelle (S-L32,000, D-L53,000, DB-L67,000, no breakfast, Via Donzelle 5, tel. 280358, SE-F) is a plain, institutional, but decent place next door that makes sense only if you think of Il Campo as your terrace.

Pension La Perla (D-L63,000, DB-L78,000, no breakfast, tiny box showers in the DB rooms, a block off the square opposite the tower on Piazza Independenza at Via della Terme 25, tel. 47114) is a funky, jumbled place with a narrow maze of hallways, forgettable rooms, and a laissez-faire environment, run by English-speaking Paolo.

Hotel Duomo (DB-L150,000, TB-L195,000, including breakfast; CC:VMA; facing the tower, trot right from Il Campo, follow Via Citta, which becomes Via Stalloreggi, to #34 Via Stalloreggi; tel. 289088, fax 43043, SE-B) is the best-in-the-old-town splurge, a truly classy place with spacious, elegant rooms. Don't ask for room #62.

A few blocks up Via Banchi di Sopra, a block off Piazza Matteotti, is the spacious, group-friendly **Hotel Cannon d'Oro** (about SB-L65,000, D-L73,000, DB-L95,000, skip the L9,000 breakfast, CC:VM, Via Montanini 28, tel. 44321, fax 280868, SE-B).

Sleeping Closer to the Bus Stop and San Domenico Church

These hotels are still only a 10-minute walk from Il Campo, but ideal for those arriving by car or wanting to minimize luggage-lugging. Most enjoy fine views of the old town and cathedral (which sits floodlit before me as I type).

Pension Bernini (S-L60,000, D-L60,000-L80,000, L7,500 breakfast on the terrace, from San Domenico follow signs to Il Campo, you'll pass Via Sapienza 15, tel. 289047, SE-F) is the place to stay if you want to join a Sienese family in a modest, clean home with a few immaculate and comfortable rooms. The bathrooms are down the hall, the upholstery is lively, and the welcome is warm. Even if you normally require private plumbing, the spectacular view from the garden terrace and the friendly owner, Nadia, will make the inconvenience seem petty. Picnic on the terrace for dinner.

Alma Domus (S-L34,000, SB-L47,000, DB-L68,000, TB-L90,000, QB-L114,000, from San Domenico, walk downhill toward the view, turn left down Via Camporegio; make a U-turn at the little chapel down the brick steps and you'll see the sign, Via Camporegio 37, tel. 44177, fax 47601, SE-F) is ideal, unless nuns make you nervous or you plan on staying out past the 23:00 curfew. This quasi-hotel (not a convent) is run with firm but angelic smiles by sisters who offer clean, quiet, rooms for a steal and save the best views for the foreigners. Bright lamps, quaint balconies, fine views, grand public rooms, top security, and a friendly atmosphere make this the best deal in town for the lire. The checkout time is a strict 10:00, but they have a *deposito* for luggage.

For a Sienese villa experience in a classy residential neighborhood a few blocks away from the center (past San Domenico), with easy parking on the street, consider **Albergo Lea** (D-L80,000, DB-L95,000 with breakfast, CC:VMA, Viale XXIV Maggio 10, tel. and fax 283207, SE-C), **Hotel Chiusarelli** (S-L46,000, SB-L68,000, DB-L105,000 without breakfast, across from the stadium at Viale Curtone 9, tel. 280562, SE-C), and if you're traveling with rich relatives who want sterility near the action, the **Hotel Villa Liberty** (DB-L180,000 with breakfast, CC:VMA, facing the fortress at Viale V. Veneto 11, tel. 44966, fax 44770, SE-B).

The tourist office has a list of private homes that rent rooms for around L25,000 per person. Many are filled with long-term students, and others require a stay of several days, but some are central and a fine value. Siena's **Guidoriccio Youth Hostel** (L19,000 beds in doubles or triples with breakfast, cheap meals, bus #15 or #10 from Piazza Gramsci or the train station to Via Fiorentina 89 in the Stellino neighborhood, open 7:00-9:00, 15:00-23:30, tel. 52212, SE-B) has 120 cheap beds, but given the hassle of the bus ride and the charm of downtown Siena at night, I'd skip it.

Eating in Siena

Restaurants are reasonable by Florentine and Venetian standards. Don't hesitate to pay a bit more to eat pizza on Il Campo (**Pizzeria Spadaforte**, tel. 281123, mediocre pizza, great setting, the tables are steeper than the price). The ambience is a classic European experience. For authentic Sienese dining at a fair price, eat at the **Locanda Garibaldi** (down Via Giovanni Dupre a few steps from the square [see Sleeping, above], closed Saturday, open at 19:00, arrive early to get a table, L22,000 menu). For a peasant's dessert, take your last glass of Chianti (borrow the *bicchiere for dieci minuti*) with a chunk of bread to the square, lean against a pillar, and sip Siena Classico. Picnics any time of day are royal on the Campo.

Trattoria Tellina (52 via della Terme) is a cozy and reasonable place to eat. **Osteria della Artista** (1 via Stalloreggi) is popular with locals for a cheap meal. **Rosticceria 4 Cantoni** (near Hotel Duomo at Piazza di Postierla 5, tel. 281067, closed Wednesday) is cheap, easy, and away from the tourism.

And **Pizza Rustica** places, scattered throughout Siena, serve up cheap pizza sold by the gram to go.

For a chance to enjoy a snack on a balcony overlooking the Campo, stop by the Gelateria Artigiana or the Bar Barbero (*panforte* and cappuccino), each just off the square at via di Citta.

Siena's claim to caloric fame is its *panforte*, a rich, chewy concoction of nuts, honey, and candied fruits that impresses even fruitcake-haters (although locals I met prefer a white cookie called *Ricciarelli*). All over town *Prodotti Tipici* shops sell Sienese specialties. A handy one is on Il Campo (right of tower). Don't miss the evening *passagiata* (peak time is 19:00) along Via Banchi di Sopra with gelato in hand (**Nannini's** at Piazza Salimbeni has fine gelato).

Transportation Connections
Sienna to Florence: While most trains take longer and require a change (in Empoli), rapido SITA buses go regularly between downtown Florence and Siena's San Domenico church, nonstop by autostrada (L8,300, 70 minutes, info tel. 221221, buy ticket before boarding at the *biglietteria* or ticket office). **Rome trains:** 8/day, 3½ hrs including 20-minute connection in Chiusi.

Arriving by car: Follow the Centro, then Stadio, signs (stadium, soccer ball). The soccer-ball signs take you to the tour-bus lot. Park at any white-striped car stall on the nearby streets or pay L15,000 a day to park down in the stadium, just across from the huge brick San Domenico church.

San Gimignano
The epitome of a Tuscan hill town with 14 medieval towers still standing (out of an original 72!), San Gimignano is a perfectly preserved tourist trap so easy to visit and visually pleasing that it's a good stop. Remember, in the 13th century, back in the days of Romeo and Juliet, towns were run by feuding noble families. And they'd periodically battle things out from the protective bases of their respective family towers. Skylines like San Gimignano's were the norm in medieval Tuscany, and Florence had literally hundreds of towers.

Tourist Information: Get a map at the Tourist Information office in the old center on the Piazza Duomo (daily, 9:30-12:30, 15:00-19:00 tel. 940008).

Sights: While the basic three-star sight here is the town itself, the **Collegiata** (on Piazza del Duomo), a Romanesque church filled with fine Renaissance frescoes, and the **Rocco** (castle, free entry, a short climb behind the church, with a fine view and a great picnic perch, especially at sunset) are important stops. You can also climb San Gimignano's tallest tower, the 180-foot-tall **Torre Grossa** above the Palazzo del Popolo. Market day is Thursday (8:00-13:00), but for local merchants, every day is a sales frenzy. Minimize the rusticated-shopping-mall feeling of downtown San Gimignano by walking around the outside of the wall and nipping in through the wall at various points.

San Gimignano streets are clogged mainly by day-trippers, but its hotels are expensive. The tourist office has a list of private homes that rent rooms. The Convento di Sant' Agostino (S-L25,000, D-L35,000, Piazza Sant' Agostino, tel. 940383) has good cheap beds.

Transportation Connections
San Gimignano to Florence: From Florence, take a bus to San Gimignano (regular departures, 75 min, change in Poggibonsi) or catch the train to Poggibonsi, where buses make the frequent 20-minute ride into San Gimignano. Buses also connect San Gimignano with **Siena** and **Volterra**.

You can't drive within the walled town of San Gimignano, but a car park awaits just a few steps from the town gate which leads straight up the traffic-free town's cobbled main drag to the Piazza del Cisterna (with its 13th-century well) and the Piazza del Duomo.

Assisi
Around the year 1200, a simple monk from Assisi challenged the decadence of church government and society in general with a powerful message of nonmaterialism, simplicity, and a "slow down and smell God's roses" lifestyle. Like Jesus, Francis taught by example. A huge monastic order grew out of his teachings, which were gradually embraced (some would say co-opted) by the church. Catholicism's purest

example of Christ-like simplicity is now glorified in beautiful churches. In 1939, Italy made Francis its patron saint.

Any pilgrimage site will be commercialized, and the legacy of St. Francis is Assisi's basic industry. In summer, the town bursts with splash-in-the-pan Francis fans and Franciscan knickknacks. Those able to see past the tacky monk mementos can actually have a "travel on purpose" experience. Francis's message of love and simplicity and sensitivity to the environment has a broad appeal. Assisi recently hosted an ecumenical summit attended by leaders of nearly every major religion on earth.

Orientation (tel code: 075)
Assisi, crowned by a ruined castle, is beautifully preserved and has a basilica nearly wallpapered by Giotto. Most visitors are day-trippers. Assisi after dark is closer to a place Francis could call home.

Tourist Information
On Piazza della Comune (open 8:00-14:00, 15:30-18:30, Saturday 9:00-13:00, 15:30-18:30, Sunday 9:00-13:00, tel. 812534). Buses connect Assisi's train station with the old town center (2/hr, 5 km).

Sights—Assisi
▲▲**The Basilica of St. Francis**—At Francis's request, he was buried outside of his town with the sinners on the "hill of the damned." This once-humble place is now one of the artistic highlights of medieval Europe. The basilica is actually two churches built over the tomb of St. Francis. Start at the beginning and the bottom by hiking down into the crypt (enter halfway down the nave of the lower church). The lower church is more appropriately Franciscan, subdued and Romanesque, offering a great look at Romanesque painting or fresco. Most important is the Cappella di San Martino (first chapel on the left as you enter the lower nave), which was designed and decorated completely by the Sienese master Simone Martini. Also important are the Madonna, Child, angels, and St. Francis by Cimabue in the south transept.

The upper church, Gothic and therefore lighter, is designed to glorify the saint. It's basically a gallery of frescoes by Giotto and his assistants showing 28 scenes from the life of St. Francis. Follow the great events of Francis's life, starting at the altar and working around clockwise. The cycle culminates in the scene of St. Francis receiving the stigmata (the wounds of the Crucifixion, awarded to only the most pious). Giotto was considered the first modern painter. Note the realism and depth for which he strives as Italy is about to bring Europe out of the Dark Ages. Don't miss Cimabue's powerful *Crucifixion* in the north transept of the upper church. (The church is free, open 7:00-19:00, sometimes closed for lunch or mass, strictly enforced modest dress code; call 813491 and ask for an English tour or to join a scheduled English tour, or tag quietly along with an English-speaking pilgrimage group, which will invariably have an English-speaking Franciscan explaining the basilica.)

Visit the bookshop in the courtyard. A short biography of St. Francis makes a walk through the back streets of Assisi, up to the ruined castle, or through the nearby countryside more of a walk with the saint.

Piazza della Comune—This square is the center of town. You'll find a Roman forum, the temple of Minerva, a Romanesque tower, banks, the post office, the Pinacoteca (art gallery), and the tourist information office. (The square is straight up Via San Francesco from the basilica.)

Views—The Rocca Maggiore (big castle) offers a good look at a 14th-century fortification and a fine view of Assisi and the Umbrian countryside. For a picnic with the same birds and views that inspired St. Francis, leave all the tourists and hike to the smaller castle above St. Clare's church. (The Church of St. Clare, or Basilica de Santa Chiara, is interesting mostly for pilgrims, but her tomb, downstairs, impresses all.)

Santa Maria degli Angeli—Towering above the buildings below Assisi, near the train station, is this huge Baroque church, St. Mary of the Angels. It was built around the tiny chapel, Porziuncola. As you enter, notice the sketch on the door showing the original little chapel with the monk huts around it, and Assisi before it had its huge basilica. Francis lived here after he founded the Franciscan Order in 1208. And this was where he consecrated St. Clare as the Bride of Christ. Clare, St. Francis's partner in poverty, founded the Order of the Poor Clares.

Sleeping in Assisi

(L1,600 = about $1, tel code: 075, zip code: 06081)
The town accommodates large numbers of pilgrims on religious holidays. Finding a room any other time should be easy.

Albergo Italia (D-L42,000, DBWC-L65,000, just off the Piazza del Comune's fountain at Vicolo della Fortezza, tel. 812625) is clean and simple with great beds. Some of its 13 rooms overlook the town square.

Hotel Belvedere (D-L60,000, DBWC-L90,000, 2 blocks from Piazza Santa Chiara and St. Clare's church at Via Borgo Aretino 13, tel. 812460, fax 816812) offers comfortable rooms, good views, and a friendly, English-speaking management.

St. Anthony's Guest House (S-L32,000, SBWC-L38,000, DBWC-L68,000, TBWC-L96,000, with breakfast, two night minimum, between San Rufino and Saint Clare's church, at 10 Via Galeazzo, tel. and fax 812542), run by Franciscan Sisters of the Atonement from New York, offers reasonable beds, easy communications, and a fine view.

Francis probably would have bunked with the peasants in Assisi's **Ostello della Pace** (L17,000 beds with breakfast, in 4- to 6-bed rooms, a 15-minute walk below town at via di Valethye, at the San Pietro stop on the station-town bus, tel. 816767).

Train Connections

Assisi to: Rome (7/day, 2½ hrs with a change in Foligno), **Florence** (6/day, 2½ hrs, sometimes changing at Terontola-Cortona).

Orvieto

Umbria's grand hill town is no secret but still worth a quick look. Just off the freeway, with three popular gimmicks (its ceramics, cathedral, and Classico wine), it's loaded with tourists by day—quiet by night. The TI has a good free map (#24 Piazza Duomo, tel. 0763/41772, 8:00-14:00, 16:00-19:00).

Orientation

Check your bag and your connection at the train station, then hop on the funicular (4/hr, L1,400 ticket includes connecting Piazza Cahen-Piazza Duomo mini-bus transfer, where you'll find the TI and everything that matters). If you have a car, don't drive it up. Park it at the huge, safe, and cheap parking lot behind the Orvieto train station. Take the pedestrian tunnel under the train tracks to the funicular that zips you to the old town.

Sights

The Orvieto Duomo (cathedral) has Italy's most striking facade. Grab a gelato from the gelateria to the left of the church and study this fascinating mass of mosaics and sculpture. In a chapel to the right of the altar, you'll find some great Signorelli frescoes (7:00-13:00, 15:00-20:00, earlier off-season).

Surrounding the striped cathedral are a fine **Etruscan Museum** (L3,000, 9:00-13:30, 15:00-19:00, Sunday 9:00-13:00), a great gelati shop, and unusually clean public toilets (down the stairs). Drinking a shot of wine in a ceramic cup as you gaze up at the cathedral lets you experience all of Orvieto's claims to fame at once.

Orvieto Area

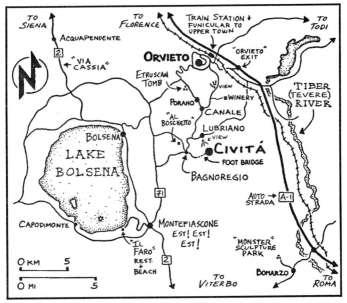

Ask at the TI about English walking tours (L10,000, most days at 10:00). Ride the back streets into the Middle Ages. The town sits majestically on tufa rock. Streets lined with buildings made of the dark volcanic stuff seem to grumble Dark Ages. Piazza Cahen is only a transportation hub at the entry to the hilltop town. It has a ruined fortress with a garden, a commanding view, and a popular well which is an impressive (but overpriced) double helix carved into tufa rock.

Sleeping in Orvieto
(L1,600 = about $1, tel. code: 0763, zip code: 05018)
Here are four places in the old town and one in a more modern neighborhood near the station.

Hotel Corso (DBWC-L80,000, on the main street up from the funicular toward the Duomo at Via Cavour 343, tel. 42020) is small, clean, and friendly, with comfy modern rooms.

Hotel Duomo (D-L48,000, DBWC-L76,000, from the Duomo, turn left past the Gelati to Via di Maurizio 7, tel. 41887) is a funky, brightly colored, Old World place with simple, ugly rooms and a great location.

Albergo Posta (D-L55,000, DBWC-L75,000, Via Luca Signorelli 18, tel. 41909) is in the center of the hill town, a 2-minute walk from the cathedral. It's a big, old, formerly elegant, but well-cared-for-in-its-decline building with a breezy garden, a grand old lobby, and spacious, clean, plain rooms.

Bar Ricci (D-L40,000, via Magalotti 22, tel. 41119) serves up cheap rooms as well as cheap tasty pasta.

Albergo Picchio (D-L40,000, DBWC-L60,000, Via G. Salvatori 17, 05019 Orvieto Scalo, tel. 90246) is a shiny, modern, concrete-and-marble place, more comfortable and family run, but with less character. It's in the lower, ugly part of town, 300 yards from the train station. They have a cheaper annex across the street.

Train Connections
Orvieto to: Rome (8/day, 70 min, take only trains going to Rome's Termini Station where the subway takes day-trippers conveniently to the major sights; consider leaving your car at the large car park behind the Orvieto station), **Siena** (5/day,

2-3 hrs, with change in Chiusi), **Bagnoregio** is a cheap 40-minute bus ride (6:25, 7:50, 9:10, 12:40, 13:55, 14:30, 15:45, and 18:35 from Orvieto's Piazza Cahen and from its train station daily except Sunday, buy tickets on the bus, get return times from the conductor).

Cività di Bagnoregio

Perched on a pinnacle in a grand canyon, this is Italy's ultimate hill town. Immerse yourself in the traffic-free village of Cività. Curl your toes around its Etruscan roots.

Cività is terminally ill. Only 15 residents remain, as bit by bit it's being purchased by rich big-city Italians who will escape to their villas here. Apart from its permanent (and aging) residents and those who have weekend villas here, there is a group of Americans (mostly Seattle-ites), introduced to the town through a small University of Washington architecture program, who have bought into the rare magic of Cività. When the program is in session, 15 students live with residents and study Italian culture and architecture.

Cività is connected to the world and the town of Bagnoregio by a long donkey path. While Bagnoregio lacks the pinnacle-town romance of Cività, it rings true as a pure bit of small-town Italy. It's actually a healthy, vibrant community (unlike Cività, the suburb it calls "the dead city"). Get

a haircut, sip a coffee on the square, walk down to the old laundry (ask, *Dové la lavandaria vecchia?*). From Bagnoregio, yellow signs direct you along its long and skinny spine to its older neighbor, Cività. Enjoy the view as you head up the long donkey (and now, Vespa) path to Cività and its main (and only) square. A shuttle bus runs from Cività to Bagnoregio to Al Boschetto about hourly in season (L800).

Al Forno (green door on main square, open daily, June-October only, tel. 0761/793586), run by the Paolucci family, is the only restaurant in town and serves up a good reasonable pasta and wine lunch or dinner.

At the church on the main square, Anna will give you a tour (tip her and buy your postcards from her). Around the corner, on the main street, is a cool and friendly wine cellar with a dirt floor and stump chairs, where Domenica serves local wine—L1,000 a glass and worth it, if only for the atmosphere. Step down into her cellar and note the traditional wine-making gear and the provisions for rolling huge kegs up the stairs. Tap on the kegs in the cool bottom level to see which are full. Most village houses are connected to cellars like this which often date from Etruscan times.

Down the street is Victoria's **Antico Mulino** (L1,000), an atmospheric room of old olive-presses. Just down the way, Maria (for a tip) will show you through her garden with a fine view (**Maria's Giardino**). Continuing through the town, the main drag peters out and a trail leads you down and around to the right to a tunnel that has cut through the hill under the town since Etruscan times. Slowly the town is being bought up by wealthy, big-city Italians. The "Marchesa," who married into the Fiat family, owns the house at the town gate—complete with Cività's only (for now) hot-tub.

Evenings on the town square are a bite of Italy. The same people sit on the same church steps under the same moon, night after night, year after year. I love my cool late evenings in Cività. Listen to the midnight sounds of the valley from the donkey path.

Whenever you visit, stop halfway up the donkey path and listen to the sounds of rural Italy. Reach out and touch one of the monopoly houses. If you know how to turn the volume up on the crickets, do so. If you visit in the cool of the early morning, have cappuccino and rolls at the small café on the town square.

Sleeping and Eating near Città
(L1,600 = about $1, tel. code: 0761)
When you leave the tourist crush, life as a traveler in Italy becomes easy and prices tumble. Room-finding is easy in small-town Italy.

Just outside Bagnoregio is **Al Boschetto.** The Catarcia family speaks no English; they don't need to. Have an English-speaking Italian call for you from Venice or Florence (D-L60,000, DB-L70,000, breakfast L5,000, Strada Monter-ado, Bagnoregio [Viterbo], Italy, tel. 792369, walking and driving instructions below). Most rooms have private show-ers (no curtains; slippery floors, be careful not to flood the place; sing in search of your shower's resonant frequency).

The Catarcia family (Angelino, his wife Perina, sons Gianfranco and Dominico, daughter-in-law Giuseppina, and the grandchildren) is wonderful, and if you so desire, the boys will take you down deep into the gooey, fragrant bowels of the cantina. Music and vino melt the language barrier in the wine cellar. Maybe Angelino or his sons will teach you their theme song, "Trinka, Trinka, Trinka." The lyrics are easy (see previous sentence). Warning: Angelino is Bacchus squared, and he's taught his boys well. Descend at your own risk. There are no rules unless the female participants set them. (For every three happy reports I get, I receive one angry postcard requesting I drop these guys from my book.) If you are lucky enough to eat dinner at Al Boschetto (L30,000, bunny is the house specialty), ask to try the *dolce* (sweet) dessert wine. Everything at Angelino's is deliciously home-grown—figs, fruit, wine, rabbit, pasta. This is traditional rural Italian cuisine at its best. If you're interested in savoring small-town Italy, it doesn't get any better than Bagnoregio, Città, and Al Boschetto.

The Orvieto bus drops you at the town gate. From there, walk out of town past the old arch (follow Viterbo signs), turn left at the pyramid monument and right at the first fork (follow Montefiascone sign) to get to hotel Al Boschetto. Città is a pleasant 45-minute walk (back through Bagnoregio) from Al Boschetto. If you plan to leave Al Boschetto early in the morning, get them to leave the *chiave* (kee-ah-vee) in the front door or you're locked in.

Hotel Fidanza (DB-L78,000, Via Fidanza 25, Bagnoregio [Viterbo], tel. and fax 793444), comfortable, normal, and right in Bagnoregio town, is the only other hotel in town. Rooms 206 and 207 have views of Civitá.

Transportation Connections

Civitá is a 30-minute walk from **Bagnoregio**. A shuttle bus zips back and forth every hour or so. Public buses connect Bagnoregio to the rest of the world via Orvieto (for connections, see Orvieto, above).

Driving from Orvieto to Bagnoregio: Orvieto overlooks the autostrada (and has its own exit). The shortest way to Civitá from the freeway exit is to turn left (away from Orvieto) and follow signs to Lubriano and Bagnoregio. The more winding and scenic route takes 20 minutes longer: From the freeway, pass under hill-capping Orvieto (on your right, signs to Lago di Bolsena, on Viale I Maggio), take the first left (direction: Bagnoregio), winding up past great Orvieto views, the Orvieto Classico vineyard (see below), through Canale, and through farms and fields of giant shredded wheat to Bagnoregio, where the locals (or rusty old signs) will direct you to Angelino Catarcia's Al Boschetto, just outside town. Either way, just before Bagnoregio, follow the signs left to Lubriano and pull into the first little square by the church on your right for a breathtaking view of Civitá. Then return to the Bagnoregio road. Drive through Bagnoregio (following yellow "Civitá" signs) and park at the base of the steep donkey path up to the traffic-free, 2,500-year-old, canyon-swamped pinnacle town of Civitá di Bagnoregio.

Sights—Near Orvieto, Bagnoregio, and Civitá

If you have a car (and a good local map), it's easy to go to Lake Bolsena for a swim, to Canale for a winery tour, to Porano for a tour of an Etruscan tomb, or to the Bomarzo monster park. None of these places are worth the trouble by public transportation.

▲**Etruscan Tomb**–Driving from Bagnoregio toward Orvieto, stop just past Porano to tour an Etruscan tomb. Follow the yellow road signs, reading *Tomba Etrusca*, to Giuseppe's farm. Walk behind the farm and down into the lantern-lit, 2,500-year-old Hescanos family tomb discovered 100 years ago by Giuseppe's grandfather. New excavations on the site may turn it into the usual turnstile-type visit (open 9:00-12:00, 14:00-17:00, tel. 65242).

Swimming—For a fun and refreshing side trip, take a dip in Lake Bolsena, which is nestled within an extinct volcano, 30 minutes by car from Bagnoregio. Ristorante Il Faro, on the lake below the town of Montefiascone, offers good meals on a leafy terrace overlooking the beach.

Monsters—Nearby Bomarzo has the gimmicky monster park (Parco di Mostri), filled with stone giants and dragons. Built about two centuries ago, it proves that Italy has a long and distinguished tradition of tacky.

Winery—Orvieto Classico wine is justly famous. For a homey peek into a local winery, visit Tanuta Le Velette, where Julia Bottai and her English-speaking son, Corrado, welcome those who'd like a look at their winery and a taste of the final product (daily 8:00-12:00, 14:00-17:00, closed Sunday, tel. 0763/29090 or 29144). You'll see their sign 5 minutes past Orvieto at the top of the switchbacks on the Bagnoregio road.

Still Not Satisfied?

Italy is spiked with hill towns. Perugia is big and reeks with history. Cortona is smaller with a fine youth hostel (tel. 0575/601765). Todi is nearly untouristed. Pienza (Renaissance planned town) and Montepulciano (dramatic setting) are also worth the hill-town lover's energy and time. Sorano and Pitigliano have almost no tourism. Train travelers often use the town of Chuisi as a home base for the hill towns. The region's trains (to Siena, Orvieto, Assisi) go through or change at this hub, and there are several reasonable *pensioni* near the station.

THE CINQUE TERRE

The Cinque Terre, a remote chunk of the Italian Riviera, is the traffic-free, low-brow, underappreciated alternative to the French Riviera. There's not a museum in sight. Just sun, sea, sand (well, pebbles), wine, and pure unadulterated Italy. Give yourself a vacation to enjoy the villages, swimming, hiking, and evening romance of one of God's great gifts to tourism, the Cinque Terre. For a home base, choose among five villages, each filling a ravine with a lazy hive of human activity. Vernazza is my favorite.

Planning Your Time

The Cinque Terre is served by the milk-run train from Genoa and La Spezia. Speed demons arrive in the morning, check their bag in La Spezia, take the 5-hour hike through all five towns, laze away the afternoon on the beach or rock of their choice, and zoom away on the overnight train to somewhere back in the real world. The ideal minimum stay is two nights and a completely uninterrupted day. Each town has its own character, and all are a few minutes apart by an hourly train. There's no checklist of sights or experiences. Just the hike, the towns, and your fondest vacation desires.

For a good Cinque Terre day consider this: Pack your beach and swim gear, wear your walking shoes, and catch the train to Riomaggiore (town #1). Walk the cliff-hanging Via dell' Amore to Manarola (#2) and buy food for a picnic, then hike to Corniglia (#3) for a rocky but pleasant beach. Swim here or in Monterosso (#5). From #5, hike or catch the boat home to Vernazza (#4).

If you're into *la dolce far niente* (the sweetness of doing nada) and don't want to hike, you could enjoy the blast of cool train-tunnel air that announces the arrival of every Cinque Terre train and go directly to Corniglia or Monterosso to maximize beach time.

If you're a hiker, hike from Riomaggiore all the way to Monterosso al Mare, where a sandy "front door"-style beach awaits.

Getting Around

The town of La Spezia is the gateway to the Cinque Terre. In La Spezia's train station, the milk-run Cinque Terre train schedule is posted at window #5. Take the L1,800 half-hour train ride into the Cinque Terre town of your choice.

Cinque Terre Train Schedule: The schedule changes with the seasons. Since the train is the 5-Terre lifeline, any shop or restaurant posts the current schedule (La Spezia train info tel. 0187/714960).

Trains leaving La Spezia for the Cinque Terre villages (last year's June-September schedule): 6:25, 7:14, 8:30, 10:04, 11:00, 12:20, 13:12, 13:47, 14:17, 14:46, 15:22, 16:28, 17:48, 18:17, 19:06, 19:49, 21:10, 22:36, and 23:55.

Within the Cinque Terre: While you can hike or catch the irregular boats, the easy way to zip from town to town is by train. These *locale* trains (that's Italian for "milk-run") are so tiny they don't even register on the Thomas Cook train timetable. But they go nearly hourly and are cheap. To orient yourself, remember that directions are "*per* (to) *Genoa*" or "*per La Spezia,*" and virtually any train that stops at one of the five villages will stop at all five. The five towns are just minutes apart by train. Know your stop. After leaving the town before your destination, move down to the door. Since the stations are small and the trains are long, you may need to get off the train deep in a tunnel and you may need to open the door yourself.

Helpful Hints

Taking Trains: Since a one-town hop costs the same as a five-town hop (L1,500), and every ticket is good all day with stopovers, save money by exploring the region in one direction on one ticket.

Hiking and Swimming: Wear your walking shoes and pack your swim gear. Each beach has showers that may work better than your hotel's. (Bring soap and shampoo.)

Wine: If you like sweet, sherry-like wine, the local *Sciachetra* (shock-ee-TRA) wine is expensive, but delicious. While ten kilos of grapes will give you seven liters of local wine, it yields only 1.5 liters of *Sciachetra*. The local white wine flows cheap and easy throughout the region. In the cool, calm evening, sit on the Vernazza breakwater with a glass of wine, and get mushy.

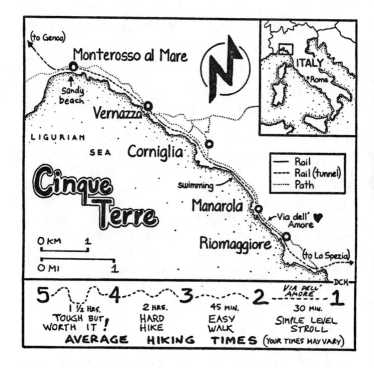

Sights—Cinque Terre

The best way to see the area is to hike from one end to the other. After fifteen years of visits, I still get the names confused. But it's easy to think of the towns by number. Here's a rundown on towns one through five.

Riomaggiore–town #1: The most substantial non-resort town of the group, Riomaggiore is a disappointment from the train station. But walk through the tunnel next to the train tracks (or take the high road, straight up and to the right), and you land in a fascinating tangle of pastel homes leaning on each other as if someone stole their crutches. There is homemade gelati at the Bar Central.

From the Riomaggiore station, the Via del' Amore affords a film-gobbling 15-minute promenade (wide enough for baby strollers) down the coast to Manarola. While there's no beach here, a stairway leads the way for sunbathing on the rocks.

Manarola–town #2: Like town #1, #2 is attached to its station by a 200-yard-long tunnel. Manarola is tiny and rugged, a tumble of buildings bunny-hopping down its ravine to the tiny harbor. This is a good place to buy your picnic (stores close from 13:00-17:00) before walking to the beaches of town #3, Corniglia. To reach town #3 (from the waterfront), it's easiest to take the high trail out of town. The broad and scenic low trail ends with steep stairs leading to the high road. The walk from #2 to #3 is a little longer, and a little more rugged, than from #1 to #2. If it's closed (as it has been for several years) you can climb around one fence, take the narrow trail across a washed-out section, and climb over the other fence. Any cat burglar can handle it. If you're concerned, ask other travelers about its current status.

Corniglia–town #3: A zigzag series of stairs that looks worse than it is leads up to the only town of the five not on the water. Remote and rarely visited, Corniglia has a windy belvedere, a few restaurants, and a handful of often-empty private rooms for rent. (Ask for Sra. Silvani.) Villa Ceccio serves a great and filling L8,000 pasta, and has a house Tiramasu as impressive as its view.

I do my 5-Terre swimming on the pathetic but peaceful manmade beach below the Corniglia station. Unfortunately, much of it has washed away and it's almost nonexistent when the surf's up. It has a couple of buoys to swim to, and is clean and less crowded than the beach at town #5. The beach bar has showers, drinks, and snacks. Between the station and the beach you'll pass "Albergo Europa," a bungalow village filled with Italians doing the Cinque Terre in 14 days.

Vernazza–town #4: With the closest thing to a natural harbor, overseen by a ruined castle and an old church, and only the occasional noisy slurping up of the train by the mountain to remind you these are the 1990s, Vernazza is my 5-Terre home base.

The action is at the harbor, where you'll find a kids' beach, plenty of sunning rocks, outdoor restaurants, a bar hanging on the edge of the castle (great for evening drinks), the tiny town soccer field, the busiest *foosball* game in Italy, and fresh fish filling wheelbarrows each morning.

The hike from #3 to #4 is rewarding, the wildest and greenest of the coast (with the nude Guvano beach about 30 minutes out of Vernazza). The trail from Vernazza to #5 is a scenic, up-and-down-a-lot 90 minutes. Trails are rough, but

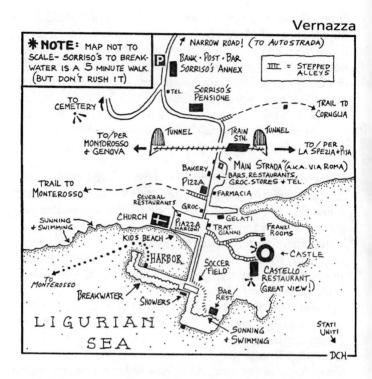

these are the best hikes of the 5-Terre. An hourly boat service connects #4 and #5 (L4,000 one way, L6,000 round-trip). A 5-minute hike in either direction from Vernazza gives you a classic village photo stop. There's a bar with a panoramic terrace at the tower on the trail towards Corniglia.

In the evening, stroll Vernazza's main (and only) street to the harbor to join the visiting Italians in a sing-along. Have a gelato, cappuccino, or glass of the local Cinque Terre wine at a waterfront café or on the bar's patio that overlooks the breakwater (follow the rope railing above the tiny soccer field, notice the photo of rough seas just above the door inside).

Vernazza restaurants are good but expensive. The Castello (Castle) restaurant serves good food just under the castle. Trattoria Franzi (on the waterfront) and Trattoria da Sandro (often with an entertaining musical flair) are better values. The town's only gelateria is good, and most harbor-side bars will let you take your glass on a breakwater stroll. You can get good pizza by the L3,500 slice on the main

street. Grocery store hours are 7:30-13:00, 17:00-19:30.
Monterosso al Mare–town #5: This is a resort with cars, hotels, rentable beach umbrellas, and crowds. Still, if you walk east of the station through the tunnel, you'll find some charm. If you want a sandy beach, this is it. Adventurers may want to rent a rowboat or paddleboat and find their own private cove. There are several coves between #4 and #5, one with its own little waterfall. (Tourist office, 10:00-12:00, 17:00-20:00, closed Sunday afternoon, tel. 817506.)

Sleeping and Eating in the Cinque Terre
(L1,600 = about $1, zip code: 19018, tel. code: 0187)
While the Cinque Terre is too rugged for the mobs that ravage the Spanish and French coasts, it's popular with Italians. Room-finding can be tricky. Easter, July, August, and summer Fridays and Saturdays are tight. August weekends are miserable. If you're trying to avoid my readers, stay away from Vernazza and Mama Rosa's.

Real hotels, which enjoy a demand that exceeds the local supply, are expensive, lazy, and require dinner in the summer. The budget alternative, a room in a private home, often gets you a more comfortable room for about half the price. With any luck, you'll get a smashing view to boot. Any bar has a line on local rooms for rent. If you arrive without a room, ask on the street or in the local bars for *affitta camere* (rooms in private homes). Going direct cuts out a middleman and softens prices. Off season there are plenty of rooms.

Sleep code: **S**=Single, **D**=Double/Twin, **T**=Triple, **Q**=Quad, **B**=Bath/Shower, **WC**=Toilet, **CC**=Credit Card (**V**isa, **M**astercard, **A**mex), **SE**=Speaks English (graded **A-F**), breakfast is included only in real hotels.

Sleeping in Vernazza
Vernazza, the essence of the Cinque Terre, is my favorite town. (Have I mentioned that before?) There is just one real pension, but two restaurants have about a dozen simple rooms each, and a gaggle of locals rent extra rooms. Anywhere you stay here will require some climbing.

Trattoria Gianni (S-L50,000, D-L75,000, DB-L85,000, TB-L110,000, no breakfast, CC: VMA, Piazza Marconi 5, 19018 Vernazza, tel. and fax 812228, tel. 821003, closed

January 6-March 6, SE-D) is the best value in town. They have 14 small, simple, comfortable doubles, artfully decorated à la shipwreck, up lots of tight, winding, spiral stairs near the castle, where the views are Mediterranean blue and the only sounds you'll hear are the surf and the hourly ringing of the church bells (through the night). The restaurant/reception is right on the harbor square. The Franzi family (Dea, Marisa, and Gianni) run their pension simply, but with a smile.

Pension Sorriso is the only real pension in town, and Sr. Sorriso knows it. Don't expect an exuberant welcome. Sr. Sorriso and his nephew, Giovanni, will hold a room for you without a deposit (D-L80,000, DB-L90,000, including breakfast, summertime dinner is required and a room with dinner and breakfast costs L65,000 per person; CC: VM; 19018 Vernazza, Cinque Terre, La Spezia, 50 yards up the street from the train station, tel. 812224; while train sounds rumble through the front rooms of the main building, the annex up the street is quieter; closed January and February, SE-C). Call well in advance and reconfirm a few days before your arrival with another call. If you like sweet wine, you'll love his *Sciachetra*. Sciache-price (after much negotiation, with this book only), L3,000.

Locanda Barbara is run spittoon-style by Giacomo at the Taverna da Capitano (tiny loft D-L65,000, bigger D-L70,000, no breakfast, Piazza Marconi 20, tel. 812201, closed December-January, SE-F). On the harbor square, many of his nine quiet, basic doubles (in the top floors of what seems like a vacant city hall) have harbor views.

Affitta Camere: Vernazza is honeycombed with private rooms and apartments for rent. No English is spoken at these places, and each offers 6 or 8 cheap rooms year-round. **Affitta Camere da Nicolina** (3 apartments with kitchens and 3 rooms, L30,000 per person, great views, right over the harbor but close to the noisy church bell tower, ask at the Vulnetia restaurant/pizzeria, tel. 821193). **Affitta Camere da Filippo** (8 rooms, D-L60,000, T-L70,000, Q-L80,000, no views, less noise, ask at Trattoria da Sandro, tel. 812244). **Affitta Camere da Franco** (4 quiet rooms, D-L55,000, DB with view-L60,000, going down the main street, turn right at the pharmacy, climb via Carattino to #64, tel. 821082, Franco runs the "Bar la Torre" at the top of via Carattino at the ivy-covered tower. Franco speaks German; his wife, Anna Maria, speaks a little English; his cigar-chomping cousin Mike lived in New York and rents an apartment next door (tel. 812374). **Affitta Camere da Giuseppina Villa** (3 rooms including a gorgeous 5-bed apartment with kitchen, D-L60,000, TB-L80,000, QB-L100,000, QuintB-L120,000, Via S. Giovanni Battista 5, tel. 812026, SE-F).

Sleeping in Riomaggiore

Youth Hostel Mama Rosa is run with a splash of John Belushi and a pinch of Mother Theresa by Rosa Ricci (an almost-too-effervescent and friendly character who welcomes backpackers at the train station), her husband, Carmine, and their English-speaking son Silvio. This informal hostel is a chaotic but manageable jumble with the ambiance of a YMCA locker room (with a cat-pee aroma and nearly outdoor toilets and showers behind scanty curtains) filled with bunk beds. (L20,000 beds, price guaranteed through 1995, Piazza Unita 2, 20 yards in front of the station on the right past the "sporting club" in an unmarked building; tel. 920173, rarely answered, most just show up without a reservation, no curfew.) It's the only cheap dorm on the Cinque Terre. The 10 co-ed rooms, with 4-10 beds each, are plain and basic with only roof vents. But a family atmosphere rages with a popular self-serve kitchen, free laundry facilities, showers, and Silvio's five unnamed cats (available as bed partners upon request). This is one of those rare places where perfect strangers become good friends with the slurp of a spaghetti, and wine supersedes the concept of ownership. The Mama Rosa spaghetti-and-wine festa gives you all you can eat for L10,000. Mama Rosa also rents five doubles (*affitta camere*) in nearby homes for L50,000 each. You can eat reasonably next door at the **Vecchio Rio** restaurant (tel. 920173, closed Wednesday except in summer). While the station and hostel are in a bland, concrete part of Riomaggiore, a short walk through the tunnel puts you into its colorful center. For *affitta camere* in Riomaggiore try Michielini Anna (5 D-L60,000 with kitchens, via Colombo 65, tel 920411) and Soggiorno Alle Cinque Terre (Luciano Fazioli, near the castle on the top of the town, Via de Gasperi 1, tel. 920587).

Sleeping in Manarola

Marina Piccola has decent rooms right on the water, so they figure a personal touch is unnecessary (DB-L95,000, breakfast-L8,000, dinner never required, tel. 920103, fax 920966).

Just up the hill, **Albergo ca' d'Andrean** (DB-L91,000, breakfast-L8,000, Via A. Discovolo 25, tel. 920040, fax 920452, closed November) is quiet, comfortable, modern, and very hotel-esque, with ten rooms and a cool garden complete with orange trees.

Farther up the street, **Casa Capellini** (D-L50,000, the *alta camera*, on the top with a kitchen, private terrace and a knockout view-L60,000, no breakfast; take a hard right just off the church square, then two doors down the hill on your right, Via Antonio Discovolo 6, tel. 920823, run by an elderly couple who speak no English) is a private home renting four rooms.

Eating in Manarola

Il Porticiolo (closed Wednesday) near the water on the main street, or **Trattoria da Billy**, with the best view in town up in the residential area, are both reasonable for the over-priced area.

Sleeping Elsewhere in or near the Cinque Terre

Some enjoy staying in Monterosso al Mare, the most beach-resorty and least friendly of the five Cinque Terre towns. There are plenty of hotels, rentable beach umbrellas, shops, and cars. **Albergo Marina** (D-L75,000, DB-L85,000, Via Buranco 40, tel. and fax 817242 or 817613, open March-October); the big, fancy, and a little more expensive **Albergo degli Amici** (next door at via Buranco 36, tel./ fax 817544 or 817424); and **Pensione al Carugio** (D-L80,000, DB-L90,000, tel. 817453) all require dinner in the summer.

Nearby Lerici is a pleasant town with several reasonable harborside hotels and a daily boat connection to Vernazza. The **youth hostel** in Finale Ligure (L16,000 per bed with sheets and breakfast, members only, 019/690515), down the coast a ways, is a friendly, deluxe castle.

When all else fails, you can stay in a noisy bigger town like La Spezia: **Hotel Terminus** (D-L55,000, DB-L65,000, no breakfast, Via Paleocapa 21, just down from the station, tel. 37204) has filthy rooms with worn-out carpets, yellow walls, and old plumbing. **Albergo Parma** (D-L56,000, DB-L66,000, no breakfast, Via Fiume 143, 19100 La Spezia, tel. 743010) brighter but without the character, is located just below the station, down the stairs.

The nearby town of Santa Margherita Ligure (a short train-ride south of the Cinque Terre) offers a nice base for those who want to drive right to their hotel's doorstep and not suffer too much Riviera glitz. The friendly Sabini family runs the stately old **Hotel Nuova Riviera** (D-L75,000, DB-L75,000-L85,000 with a big breakfast, 16038 S. Margherita Ligure, tel. 0185/287403).

Train Connections

The five towns of the Cinque Terre are on a milk-run train line so small it doesn't even register on the Cooks Train Timetable. Hourly trains connect each town with the others, La Spezia and Genova. About ten little beach towns (including the 5-Terre) lie on the line from La Spezia to Genova (a trip which takes about two hours). While a few of the milk-run trains go to more distant points (Milan or Pisa), it's faster to change in La Spezia to a bigger train. **From La Spezia trains go to: Rome** (10/day, 4 hrs), **Pisa** (hrly, 60 min), **Florence** (hrly, 2½ hrs, change at Viareggio), **Milan** (hrly, 3 hrs., change in Genova).

Route Tips for Drivers

Milan to the Cinque Terre (130 miles): Drivers will speed south by autostrada from Milan, skirt Genoa, and drive along some of Italy's most scenic and impressive freeway toward the port of La Spezia. The road via Parma is faster but less scenic.

It's now possible to snake your car down the treacherous little road into the Cinque Terre and park above the town. This is risky in August and on Saturday or Sunday, when Italian day-trippers clog and jam the region. Vernazza has several parking lots above the town. To drive into the Cinque Terre, leave the autostrada at Uscita Brugnato just west of La Spezia.

AMSTERDAM AND HAARLEM

Amsterdam is a progressive way of life housed in Europe's most 17th-century city. It's a city built on good living, cozy cafés, great art, street-corner jazz, stately history, and a spirit of live and let live. It has 800,000 people and as many bikes, with more canals than Venice—and as many tourists. While Amsterdam has grown a bit seedy for many people's taste, this great, historic city is an experiment in freedom and a spice you must try.

Planning Your Time

While I'd sleep in nearby Haarlem, Amsterdam is worth a full day of sightseeing on even the busiest itinerary. While the city has a couple of must-see museums, its best sight is its own breezy ambience. And the best way to experience that is Dutch-style: on two wheels.

Consider this plan for Amsterdam in a day:

Rent a bike at the station. Head west down Haarlemmerstraat, working your wide-eyed way through the Prinsengracht (along the canal) and gentrified Jordan area to Westerkerk, with the tallest spire in the city. Tour Anne Frank's House.

Pedal past the palace, through the Dam Square, down Kalverstraat (the city's bustling pedestrian mall), and poke into the sleepy Begijnhof. Roll down tacky Leidsestraat. Lunch at the Atrium (Spui) or a salad bar in the American Hotel (Leidseplein).

Tour the Rijksmuseum and the Van Gogh museum. Bike Spiegelstraat to Muntplein. Catch the hour-long canal boat tour at Spui.

Pedal back down Damrak to the station. For a detour through seedy, sexy, pot-smoking Amsterdam, roll down Damstraat, then down Oudezijds Voorburgwal through the land of Rastafarian "coffee shops," red lights over black tights, and sailors lost without the sea. Train back to Haarlem for an Indonesian feast.

With two days in Holland I'd sidetrip by bike, bus, or train to an open-air folk museum, Edam, Haarlem, or the "historic triangle." For a third day, I'd do the other great Amsterdam museums. With four days, I'd visit the Hague.

Amsterdam

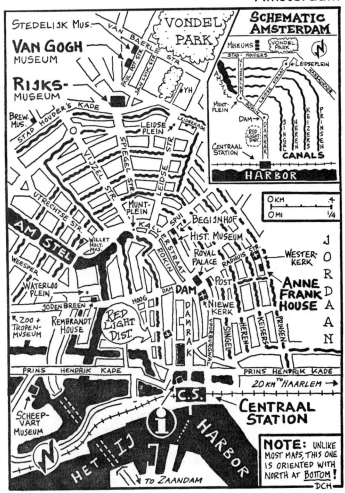

Orientation (tel. code: 020)

The central train station is your starting point (tourist information, bike rental, and trolleys and buses fanning out to all points). Damrak is the main street axis connecting the station with Dam Square (people-watching and hangout center) and the Royal Palace. From this spine, the city spreads out like a fan, with ninety islands, hundreds of bridges, and a series of concentric canals laid out in the 17th century, Holland's

Golden Age. The city's major sights are within walking distance of Dam Square. Tourists are considered green and rich, and the city is a hive of hungry thieves.

Tourist Information

Try to avoid Amsterdam's inefficient VVV office across from the train station. (VVV is Dutch for tourist information office, open daily 9:00-23:00, until 21:00 off-season). Most people wait 30 minutes just to pick up the information brochures and get a room. Avoid this line by going straight to the cash window (where everyone ends up anyway since any information of substance will cost you). Ask for the free city map. Consider buying: the f3 historic downtown walk-ing tour brochure, and *What's On* (f3.50, bimonthly enter-tainment calendar listing all the museum hours and much more). *Use It*, Amsterdam's free youth tourist magazine, has a map and lists museum hours. It's more helpful than the f6 Amsterdam brochure that the TI would rather sell.

The TI on Leidsestraat is much less crowded. But for 50 cents a minute, you can save yourself a trip by calling the tourist information toll line at 06-3403-4066 (Monday-Saturday, 9:00-17:00). The Haarlem TI (see Haarlem) can answer all your questions, provide you with the brochures, and has a toll-free phone number.

You don't need the TI to book you a room. The phone system is easy, everyone speaks English, and the listings in this chapter are a better value than the potluck booking the TI will charge you for.

Trains

Amsterdam swings, and the hinge that connects it to the world is its perfectly central Central Station. Its information center also requires a long wait. Save lots of time by getting train tickets and information in a small-town station or travel agency. For phone information call 06-9292 for local trains, 06-9296 for international (6:00-22:00 daily).

Getting Around Amsterdam

The uncrowded and helpful transit information office (GVB) is next to the TI (in front of the station). Its free multilingual Tourist Guide to Public Transport includes a transit map, and

explains ticket options and tram connections to all the sights.
By Bus and Tram: Individual tickets cost f3 (pay as you
board) and give you an hour on the system. "Strip cards"
are cheaper. Any downtown ride costs two strips (good for
an hour of transfers). A card with 15 strips costs f11 at the
GVB, train stations, post offices, or tobacco shops throughout
the country. These strips are good on buses all over Holland
(e.g., 6 strips for Haarlem to the airport), and you can share
them with your partner. For f12, a Day Card gives you
unlimited transportation for a 24-hour period from 06:00-
06:00. If you get lost, ten of the city's 17 trams take you back
to the central train station.
By Foot: The longest walk a tourist would take is 45 minutes
from the station to the Rijksmuseum. Watch out for silent,
but potentially painful, bikes and trams.
By Bike: One-speed bikes with brrrringing bells and two
locks rent for f8 per day (with a f200 or $100 cash deposit)
at the central train station (8:00-22:00 daily, entrance to the
left down the ramp as you leave the station, tel. 624 8391).
The f1 flier shows a fun countryside bike ride starting with
the free shuttle ferry behind the station. To take advantage
of their (unadvertised) 4 hours for f4.25 rate, have the time
of your checkout noted on the receipt.
By Boat: While the city is great on foot or bike, there is a
"Canal Bus," also called the Museum Boat, with an all-day
ticket that shuttles tourists from sight to sight (every 30 minutes). Tickets cost f19 (with discounts that'll save you about
f5 on admissions) or f35 (with free entry to any 3 sights, a
saving of as much as f27). A sales booth is in front of the
central train station, with handy free brochures with museum
times and admission prices. The narrated ride takes 80 minutes if you don't get off.

Helpful Hints

Many Amsterdam museums are closed on Monday and
many shops are open only in the afternoon. Handy telephone cards (f5, f10, or f25) are sold at the TI, GVB,
tobacco shops, post office, and train stations. A plein is a
square, gracht means canal, and most canals are lined by
streets with the same name.

Sights—Amsterdam

▲▲▲**Rent a Bike**—A day enjoying the bridges, bike lanes, and sleepy off-the-beaten-path canals on your own one-speed is the essential Amsterdam experience. The real joys of Europe's best preserved 17th-century city are the countless intimate glimpses it offers: the laid-back locals sunning on their porches under elegant gables, rusted bikes that look as if they've been lashed to the same lamp post since the '60s, and wasted hedonists planted on canalside benches. To escape to the countryside, hop on the free ferry that departs from behind the Amsterdam station across the canal. In 5 minutes, Amsterdam will be gone, and you'll be rolling through your very own Dutch painting. (To do Amsterdam in a day by bike, see above for renting a bike and a suggested schedule.)

▲▲▲**Rijksmuseum**—Focus on the Dutch masters: Rembrandt, Hals, Vermeer, and Steen. Pick up the museum map and plan your attack (or follow the self-guided tour, one of twenty, in my *Mona Winks* guidebook).

Follow the museum's chronological layout to see painting evolve from narrative religious art, to religious art starring the Dutch love of good living and eating, to the Golden Age when secular art dominates. With no local church or royalty to commission big canvases in the post-1648 Protestant Dutch republic, artists specialized in portraits of the wealthy city class (Hals), pretty still lifes (Claesz), and non-preachy slice-of-life art (Steen). The museum has four quietly wonderful Vermeers. And, of course, a thoughtful brown soup of Rembrandt. Study the Night Watch history room before you see the real thing. Other works by Rembrandt show his excellence as a portraitist for hire (De Staalmeesters) and offer some powerful psychological studies (St. Peter's Denial—with Jesus in the murky background).

The bookshop has good posters, prints, slides, and handy theme charts to the museum, if you always wondered about the role of cats, for example, in Dutch art (f12.50, open daily 10:00-17:00; decent cafeteria, tram 2 or 5 from the station, tel. 673 2121).

▲▲▲**Van Gogh Museum**—Next to the Rijksmuseum, this outstanding, and user-friendly museum is a stroll through a beautifully displayed garden of van Gogh's work and life. (f10, open daily 10:00-17:00. Poster collectors, buy your cardboard tube here, or get one free with a poster purchase at the Rijksmuseum, tel. 570 5200.)

Stedelijk Modern Art Museum—Next to the Van Gogh Museum, this place is fun, far-out, and refreshing, with mostly post-1945 art, but a permanent collection of Monet, Van Gogh, Cezanne, Picasso, and Chagall (f8, open daily 11:00-17:00, tel. 573-2911).

Vondelpark—Amsterdam's huge and lively city park gives the best look at today's Dutch youth, especially on a sunny summer weekend.

▲▲Anne Frank House—A fascinating look at the hideaway where young Anne hid when the Nazis occupied the Netherlands. Pick up the English pamphlet at the door, and don't miss the thought-provoking neo-Nazi exhibit in the last room. Fascism smolders on. (f7, open Monday-Saturday 9:00-17:00; Sunday 10:00-17:00, summer until 19:00, tel. 556 7100, 263 Prinsengracht.) For an entertaining glimpse of Holland under the Nazis, rent the powerful movie *Soldier of Orange* before you leave home.

Westerkerk—Near Anne Frank's house, this landmark church, with a barren interior and Amsterdam's tallest steeple, is worth climbing for the view. (Ascend only with a guide, departures on the hour, April-September, 10:00-16:00, closed Sunday.)

Royal Palace Interior—It's right on Dam Square, built when Amsterdam was feeling its global oats, and worth a look (sometimes open 12:30-16:00).

▲▲Canal Boat Tour—These long, low, tourist-laden boats leave continually from several docks around the town for a good, if uninspiring, 60-minute quad-lingual introduction to the city (f10). The only one with a live guide is very central at the corner of Spui and Rokin, about 5 minutes from Dam Square (tel. 623-3810). No fishing allowed, but bring your camera for this relaxing orientation. If you get seasick, consider a bike or walking tour by the Yellow Bike Tour company (by bike: 3 hrs, f29, on foot: 2 hrs, f15, tel. 620/6940).

▲Begijnhof—Step into this tiny, idyllic courtyard in the city center to escape the crazy 1990s and feel the charm of old Amsterdam. Notice house 34, a 500-year-old wooden structure (rare since repeated fires taught city fathers a trick called brick). Peek into the hidden Catholic church opposite the English Reformed church, where the pilgrims worshiped while waiting for their voyage to the New World (marked by a plaque near door). Be considerate of the people who live here (free, on Begijnensteeg Lane, just off Kalverstraat between 130 and 132, pick up English info flier at office near entrance).

Amsterdam History Museum—The fine Amsterdam historical museum (with a good-value restaurant) offers the town's best look into the age of the Dutch masters. It's next to the Begijnhof at 92 Kalverstraat (f6.5, open 10:00-17:00; Saturday and Sunday 11:00-17:00). Its free pedestrian corridor is a powerful teaser.

Rembrandt's House—Interesting only to his fans, with 250 etchings. (f5, 15-minute English A-V presentation upon request, Jodenbreestraat 4, open Monday-Saturday 10:00-17:00; Sunday 13:00-17:00.)

▲Tropenmuseum (Tropical Museum)—As close to the Third World as you'll get without lots of vaccinations, this imaginative museum offers wonderful re-creations of tropical life scenes and explanations of Third World problems. (f8, open Monday-Friday 10:00-17:00; Saturday and Sunday 12:00-17:00, 2 Linnaeusstrasse, tram 9.)

Netherlands Maritime (Scheepvaart) Museum—This is fascinating if you're into Henry Hudson or scheepvaarts. (f10, open daily 10:00-17:00; Sunday 12:00-17:00, closed Monday, English explanations, 1 Kattenburgerplein, bus #22 or #28.)

▲Herrengracht Canal Mansion, the Willet Holthuysen Museum—This 1687 patrician house offers a fine look at the old rich of Amsterdam, with a good 15-minute English introduction film and a 17th-century garden in back. (f5, open weekdays 10:00-17:00; Saturday and Sunday 11:00-17:00, Herrengracht 605, tram 4 or 9.)

Our Lord in the Attic—Near the station, in the red-light district, you'll find a 17th-century merchant's house-turned-museum (Amstelkring museum) with a fascinating hidden church. This dates from 1661, when post-Reformation Dutch Catholics were not allowed to worship in public. The church fills the attics of several homes (f4.50, open 10:00-17:00; Sunday 13:00-17:00, O.Z. Voorburgwal 40).

▲**Red-Light District**—Europe's most high-profile ladies
of the night shiver and shimmy in display case windows
between the station and the Oudekerk along Voorburgwal.
It's dangerous late at night, but a fascinating walk any other
time after noon.

According to CNN, over 60 percent of Amsterdam's
prostitutes are HIV-positive (but a naive tourist might see
them as just hard-working girls from Latin America or Africa
trying their best to build up a bank account—f35 at a time).

Only Amsterdam has two sex museums—one in the
red-light district (lousy) and one on Damrak (at #17, it's
cheaper and better). Both are open late, graphic, with something to offend almost everyone—but heck, it's historic (and
safe), and there are descriptions in English (erotic hours).
Shopping—Amsterdam brings out the browser even in those
who were not born to shop. Ten general markets, open 6
days a week, keep those who brake for garage sales pulling
U-ies. Shopping highlights include Waterlooplein (flea market),
the huge Albert Cuyp street market, various flower markets
(along Singel Canal near the mint tower, or Munttoren),
diamond dealers (free cutting and polishing demos at
shops behind the Rijksmuseum and on Dam Square), and
Kalverstraat, Amsterdam's teeming walking/shopping
street (parallel to Damrak).

Sleeping in Amsterdam
(f1 = about 60 cents, tel. code: 020)
While I prefer sleeping in cozy Haarlem (see below), those
more into urban charms will find that Amsterdam has plenty
of beds. For a f5 fee, the VVV (tourist office) can find you a
room in the price range of your choice.

Sleep code: **S**=Single, **D**=Double/Twin, **T**=Triple,
Q=Quad, **B**=Bath or Shower usually with a private toilet,
CC=Credit Card (**V**isa, **M**astercard, **A**mex), everyone speaks
English in the Netherlands, prices include breakfast unless
noted.

Sleeping near the Station
Amstel Botel is the city's first and only legal "boat hotel"
is a shipshape, bright, and clean floating hotel with all the
comforts in 175 rooms (DB-f136, TB-f180, CC:VMA, f25

parking pass for a 3-day stay, tel. 626 4247, fax 639 1952, 400 yards from the station, on your left as you leave, Oosterdokskade 2-4, 1011 AE Amsterdam).

Sleeping Between Dam Square and Anne Frank's House

Hotel Toren is a chandeliered historic mansion in a pleasant, canalside setting in downtown Amsterdam. This splurge is classy, quiet, and two blocks from Anne Frank's (DB-f165, ask about Monday-Friday discounts if you're staying several nights, CC:VMA, 164 Keizersgracht, tel. 622 6352, fax 626 9705).

Several cheap hotels line the noisy main drag between the town hall and Anne Frank's House. These are all up a long, steep, and depressing stairway, with quieter rooms in the back. None serves breakfast. **Hotel Pax** is the cheapest and best (D-f70-f80, T-f105, Raadhuisstraat 37, tel. 624 9735), with the largest plain but airy and pleasant rooms, showers down the hall, all carefully managed by Mrs. Veldhuiezen. **Hotel Galery** (S-f40, D-f80, DB-f90, CC:VM, Raadhuisstrasse 43, tel. 624 8851), and **Hotel Aspen** (D-f80, DB-f100, CC:VMA, Raadhuisstrasse 31, tel. 626 6714) are also sleepable.

Sleeping in the Leidseplein Area

The area around Amsterdam's museum square (Museumplein) and the rip-roaring nightlife center (Leidseplein) is colorful, comfortable, convenient, and affordable. These two hotels are on a quiet street, easy to reach from the central station (tram 1, 2, or 5 to Leidseplein, walk to canal and turn right) and within easy walking distance of the Rijksmuseum. **Kooyk Hotel** is a homey place with 19 bright and cheery rooms, 4 on the ground floor. Each room is simply but thoughtfully appointed (S-f75, D-f105, T-f140, Q-f175, Quint-f200, CC:VM, Leidsekade 82, 1017 PM Amsterdam, tel. 623 0295, fax 638 8337). **Hotel Maas,** with an elevator and phone, TV, and coffeepot in every room, is a big, well-run, classy, quiet, and hotelesque place (S-f95, one D-f125, DB-f185, CC:VMA, Leidsekade 91, tel. 623 3868, fax 622 2613).

Hotel De Leydsche Hof is in a fine canalside locale with simple, quiet rooms. Its peaceful and friendly demeanor help you overlook the dirty old carpets and flimsy cots. (D-f85,

DB-f95, TB-f130, QB-f170, no breakfast, Mr. Piller, 14 Leidsegracht, tel. 623 2148).

Hotel Keizershof is a wonderfully Dutch place with 6 bright and airy rooms in a 17th-century canal house. You'll climb a steep spiral staircase to rooms named after old-time Hollywood stars. The friendly De Vries family makes this a treat. (D-f110, DB-f120, with a classy breakfast, CC:VMA, tel. 622 2855, fax 624 8412, where Keizers canal crosses Spiegelstraat at Keizersgracht 618, 1017 ER Amsterdam).

Youth Hostels

The Christian Youth Hostel Eben Haezer (f15 per bed with sheets and breakfast, maximum age 35, near Anne Frank's house, Bloemstrasse 179, tel. 624 4717) is scruffy with 20-bed women's dorms and a 40-bed men's dorm. It's friendly, well run, in a great neighborhood, and has Amsterdam's best rock-bottom budget beds. It serves cheap, hot meals, runs a snack bar, offers lockers to all, leads nightly Bible studies, and closes the dorms from 10:00-14:00. The hostel will happily hold a room for a phone call (ideally 3-7 days in advance). Its sister Christian hostel, **The Shelter** (in the red-light district, open to any traveler, tel. 625 3230), is similar, but definitely not preaching to the choir.

Amsterdam's two IYHF youth hostels are **Vondelpark** (Amsterdam's top hostel, lots of school groups, 6-22 beds per dorm, right on the park at Zandpad 5, f24 with breakfast, f6 sheets, f5 extra for non-members, tel. 683 1744, fax 616 6591) and **Stadsdoelen YH** (just past Dam Square, at Kloveniersburgwal 97, f22 with breakfast, tel. 624 6832, March-October).

Eating in Amsterdam

Dutch food is basic and hearty. Picnics are cheap and easy. Eetcafes are local cafés serving cheap broodjes, soup, eggs, and so on. Cafeterias, sandwich shops (Broodje), and automatic food shops are also good bets for budget eaters.

Eating in the Station

A surprisingly classy budget self-service cafeteria is on platform 1.

Eating near Spui in the Center

The city university's Atrium is a great, cheery budget cafeteria (f8 meals Monday-Friday, 12:00-14:00, 17:00-19:00, from Spui, walk west down Grimburgwal past the canalside Cafe Gasthuys three blocks to Spui Oude Zijds Achterburgwal 237, tel. 525-3999). Keuken van 1870 has been cooking very simple meals in a simple setting since 1870 (cheap self-service, 4 Spuistr, tel. 624 8965).

Eating near Anne Frank's House

For pancakes in a smoky but family atmosphere, try the Pancake Bakery (f13 pancakes, even an Indonesian pancake for those who want two experiences in one, Prinsengracht 191, tel. 625 1333).

Eating near the Rijksmuseum, on Leidseplein

The art deco American Hotel dining room serves an elegant salad bar. For f9, you get the small salad bar (with bread, fruit, and nobody caring if you get refills).

Eating at Any Bar

Try a jenever (Dutch gin), the closest thing to an atomic bomb in a shot glass. While cheese gets harder and sharper with age, jenever grows smooth and soft. Old jenever is best.

Drugs

Amsterdam is Europe's counterculture mecca. While hard drugs are definitely out, marijuana causes about as much excitement as a bottle of beer. A "pot man" with a worldly menu of f25 baggies is a fixture in many bars (walk east from Dam Square on Damstraat for a few blocks, then down to Nieumarket). While several touristy **Bulldog** cafés are very popular with tourists, less glitzy smaller places farther from the tourists offer a better value and a more comfortable atmosphere. For a complete rundown on this side of the town, buy a copy of the "Mellow Pages."

Transportation Connections

Amsterdam to: Schiphol Airport (4/hr, 20 min, f5), **Haarlem** (4/hr, 15 min, f9.50 R/T), **Bern** (8/day, 9 hrs, change in Basel), **Bonn** (10/day, 3 hrs), **Brussels** (hrly, 3 hrs), **The Hague** (2/hr, 45 min), **Frankfurt** (10/day, 5 hrs), **Copenhagen** (5/day, 11 hrs), **London** (6/day, 8 hrs), **Munich** (8/day, 8 hrs, change in Mannheim), **Oostende** (hrly, 4 hrs, change in Roosendaal), **Paris** (6/day, 6 hrs), **Rotterdam** (2/hr, 60 min).

   Amsterdam's Schiphol Airport is, like most of Holland, English-speaking, user-friendly, and below sea-level. Its bank (daily 6:00-24:00) offers fair rates. Schiphol Airport has easy bus and train connections (7 miles) into Amsterdam or Haarlem. The airport also has a train station of its own. (You can validate your Eurailpass and hit the rails immediately or, to stretch your train pass, buy the short ticket today and start the pass later.) Schiphol flight information, tel. 06-350 340 50, can give you flight times and your airline's Amsterdam number for reconfirmation before going home (50 cents a minute to climb through its phone tree).

Haarlem

Cute, cozy yet real, handy to the airport, and just 15 minutes by train from downtown Amsterdam, Haarlem is a fine home base, giving you small-town, overnight warmth with easy access to wild and crazy Amsterdam.

   Haarlem is a busy Dutch market town buzzing with shoppers biking home with fresh bouquets. Enjoy Saturday and Monday market days when the square bustles like a Brueghel painting with cheese, fish, flowers, and families. You'll feel comfortable here. Buy some flowers to brighten your hotel room.

Tourist Information

Haarlem's VVV, at the train station, is friendlier, more help-ful, and less crowded than Amsterdam's. Ask your questions here. Use this for Amsterdam information.

Getting Around Haarlem

By Bike: The train station rents bikes cheap and easy (f5/4 hrs, f8/day, f100 deposit, daily 6:00-24:00).
Parking: The cheapest garage is near the station (f5/day). You can ignore many of the parking meters from 18:00-9:00

(21:00 on Thursday). The VVV and local hotels have a helpful parking brochure.

Sights—Haarlem

▲▲Frans Hals Museum—Haarlem is the hometown of Frans Hals, and this excellent museum displays several of his greatest paintings in a glorious old building (f6.25, open Monday-Saturday 11:00-17:00; Sunday 13:00-17:00). The museum across the street features the architecture of old Haarlem.

Corrie Ten Boom House—As many Americans (but few Dutch) know, Haarlem is also home to Corrie Ten Boom (popularized by *The Hiding Place*, an inspirational book and movie about the Ten Boom family's experience hiding Jews from the Nazis). The Ten Boom House, at 19 Barteljorisstraat, is open for English tours (open Tuesday-Saturday 10:00-15:30, donation requested).

Grote Kerk (church)—You'll see (and maybe hear) Holland's greatest pipe organ (regular free concerts, summer Tuesdays at 20:15, some Thursdays at 15:00, TI office has schedule). The church is open and worth a look if only to see its Oz-like organ (Monday-Saturday 10:00-16:00).

Haarlem

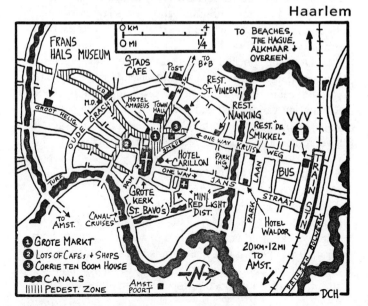

▲**Teylers Museum**, famous as the oldest museum in Holland, is interesting as a look at a 200-year-old museum. The dusty exhibits are diverse but nothing earth-shaking (f6.50, open Tuesday-Saturday 10:00-17:00; Sunday 13:00-17:00).
Red Lights—For a little red-light district cute as a Barbie shop, wander around the church in Haarlem's cutest Begijnhof (two blocks northeast of the church, off Lange Begijnestraat, f50, no senior or student discounts). Don't miss the mall marked by the red neon sign, *t'Steegje*.

Nightlife in Haarlem
Haarlem's evening scene is great. The bars around the Grote Kerk and Lange Veerstraat are colorful, lively, and full of music. The **Studio** (next to the Hotel Carillon), jammed with Haarlem's thirty-something crowd, has a pleasant ambience. **Café Brinkman**, on the square, is a good people-watching perch. **Café 1900** (across from the Corrie Ten Boom House) is classy by day and draws a young crowd with live music on Sunday nights. Lange Veerstraat behind the church is probably the best bar street in town. The **Crack** (32 Lange Veerstraat) is the wild and leathery place to go for loud music and smoking. Pot's for sale across the street at **High Times**. The **Imperial Café and Bar** (next to the Crack) has live jazz on Sunday and Thursday. For live jazz Thursday-Sunday, visit the **Haarlem Jazz Club** near the Frans Hals Museum.

Don't be shocked if locals drop into a bar, plunk down f25 for a baggie of marijuana, and casually roll a joint. (If you don't like the smell of pot, avoid "coffee shops" sporting Rastafarian yellow, red and green colors, wildly painted walls, or plants in the windows.) Holland is an easygoing, love-yourself-as-you-love-*jenever* kind of place.

Sleeping in Haarlem
(f1 = about 60 cents, tel. code: 023)
The helpful Haarlem tourist office ("VVV" at the train station, Monday-Saturday, 9:00-17:30, tel. 023/319059) can nearly always find you a f28 bed in a nearby private home for a f9 per person fee. Haarlem is most crowded in April, on Easter weekend, May, and August, but if you phone ahead, my recommended hotels will happily hold a room

without a deposit (but may ask for a credit card number). Nearly every Dutch person you'll encounter speaks English. Prices include breakfast unless otherwise noted. To avoid this town's louder than normal street noises, forgo views for a room in the back.

Hotel Amadeus has 15 small, bright rooms, all with simple modern furnishings, TV, private shower, and toilet. Some have views of the square. This hotel, ideally located above an Italian restaurant in a characteristic building on the market square, is relatively quiet and has an elevator. The lush old lobby is on the second floor in a "pianola bar" (SB-f85, DB-f110, TB-f150, CC:VMA, seconds-on-everything-welcome buffet breakfast, kid-friendly, a 10-minutes walk from train station, brothers Dave and Mike run the place for their family, Grote Markt 10, 2011 RD Haarlem, tel. 32 45 30, fax 32 23 28, use credit card to secure reservations).

Hotel Carillon, also right on the town square, has ste-e-e-p stairs. Frans will take a phone reservation with no deposit required. (If you don't show up, he'll bill me.) Hotel Carillon's location is ideal, but its well-worn rooms are a cut below the competition. Front rooms come with great town square views and lots of street noise (22 rooms, tiny loft singles-f50, D-f85, DB-f110, T-f125, TB-f160, CC:VMA, no elevator, 10-minute walk from train station, Grote Markt 27, Haarlem, tel. 31 05 91, fax 31 49 09).

The rollicking **Stads Café** has big, bright, and cheery rooms, most with TV and solid modern wood furniture. Its restaurant hops at night (see Eating below), but most of its rooms are in the back and quiet (13 rooms, S-f50, D-f75, DB-f100, TB-f130, breakfast f9, CC:VMA, Zijlstraat 56-58, two blocks off the marketplace, tel. 32 52 02, fax 32 05 04).

Hotel Joops is an innovative concept. A well-organized central office just behind the church in the town center administers a corral of apartments and rooms (all within two blocks of the church). They have bright and spacious rooms (S-f37.50, D-f75, T-110) and elegant full-furnished apartments with kitchen facilities and the lived-in works (Q-f165-f190, 6-bed apartments-f235, rates are 30% cheaper mid-September to March, tel. 322008, fax 329549, office at Oude Groenmarkt 12).

Bed and Breakfast Haus de Kiefte, your cozy, get-into-a-local home budget option, epitomizes the goodness of B&Bs. Marjet and Hans, a young couple, rent 4 bright and cheery no-smoking rooms (with a hearty breakfast and plenty of travel advice) in their 100-year-old home on a quiet neighborhood street (5-minute walk from the center, minimum 2 nights, S-f35, SB-f55, DB-f70, family loft sleeps up to 5, very steep stairs, kid-friendly, easy parking, 15-minute walk or f10 taxi from train station, from Market Square walk straight out Zijlstraat, past Stads Café, over bridge, fourth street on left, Coornhertstraat 3, 2013 Ev Haarlem, tel. 32 29 80).

Hotel Waldor, a creaky, musty old building, has sleepable rooms (D-f75, DB-f120, CC:VMA, 2-minute walk from train station and a big cheap car park, Jansweg 40 Hoek Parklaan, tel. 31 26 22, fax 32 22 79).

The 300-room, modern **Motel Haarlem Zuid** is sterile, but a good value for those interested only in sleeping and eating (DB-f95, f11 for breakfast, CC:VMA, elevator, easy parking, inexpensive hotel restaurant, 20-minute walk from the center on the road to the airport at Toekenweg 2, 2035 LC Haarlem, tel. 36 75 00, fax 36 79 80).

Eating in Haarlem

All restaurants listed are a few blocks of the Market Square. Enjoy a memorable Indonesian rijsttafel feast at the **Nanking Chinese-Indonesian Restaurant** (Kruisstraat 16, tel. 32 07 06). Couples eat plenty, hearty, and more cheaply by splitting a f22 Indonesian rice table for one. (Each eater should order a drink.) Say "hi" to gracious Ai Ping and her daughter, Fan. Don't let them railroad you into a Chinese (their heritage) dinner. They also do cheap and tasty take-out. For more expensive and impressive meals, try **Mooi Java** (they don't mind diners splitting a *rijsttafel*, across from the station. tel. 323121) or **De Lachende Javaan** ("The Laughing Javanese") at Frankestraat 25.

Going Dutch? How about pancakes for dinner at **Pannekoekhuis "De Smikkel"** (tel. 320631, Kruisweg 57, two blocks in front of station, open until 20:00). Dinner and dessert pancakes cost f10 each (f2.50 cover charge, so splitting pancakes is okay).

For a "bread line" experience with basic/bland food, well-worn company, and the cheapest price in town (f8), eat at **Eethuis St. Vincent** (22 Nieuwe Groenmarket, Monday-Friday 12:00-13:30, 17:00-19:00).

For good food, classy atmosphere, and f30 dinners, try the Bastiaan (Lange Veerstrasse 8). **La Plume** is a less expensive steak house (Lange Veerstrasse). For a candle-lit dinner of cheese and wine consider **In't Doede Uur** (Korte Houtstraat 1), or eat well and reasonably, surrounded by trains, in a classy Old World restaurant between tracks 5 and 6 in the Netherlands' oldest train station.

Eko Eet Café (f16 menu, Zijlstraat 39, near the Nieuwe Greenmarket, 17:30-21:30) is great for a cheery, tasty vegetarian meal in Haarlem.

The **Stads Café** (Zijlstraat 56-58, tel. 32 52 02) a three-ring circus of reasonable food (f20 cheese or meat fondue buffets, salad bar, or "meat on a hot rock sizzling at your table") with stained glass, candle-lit, honky-tonk atmosphere, and piano music (Thursday-Sunday), has fun being a restaurant. For a healthy budget lunch with Haarlem's best view, eat on the top floor or roof garden of the **Vroom Dreesman** department store (9:30-18:00; Thursday until 21:00, closed Sunday, on Grote Houtstraat). For a f2 cone of old-fashioned local french fries, drop by the **Vlaams Friethuis** on Warmoesstraat just behind the church.

Transportation Connections

Haarlem and Schiphol Airport: Connected by **train**, twice hourly, in both directions (f8, 40 min, transfer at suburban Amsterdam-Sloterdijk). The express bus #236 is faster (30 min, 2 rides/hr, f8.5). By taxi, it's a f65 ride.

Haarlem and Amsterdam: The train is fastest and easiest (departures every 10 min, 15-minute ride, f10 round-trip). Major trains depart to all points from Amsterdam.

Easy Day-Trips from Haarlem and Amsterdam

▲▲Zaanse Schans is a 17th-century Dutch village turned open-air folk museum where you can see and learn about everything Dutch, from cheese making to wooden shoe carving. Take an inspiring climb to the top of a whirring windmill (get a group of people together and ask for a tour), or you can buy a small jar of fresh, windmill-ground mustard for your next picnic. In the town of Zaandijk, this is your easiest one-stop look at traditional Dutch culture and the Netherlands' best collection of windmills (free, March-October, Tuesday-Saturday 10:00-17:00; winter weekends only 10:00-17:00, 15 minutes by train north of Amsterdam: take the Alkmaar-bound train to Station Koog-Zaandijk and walk—past a fragrant chocolate factory—for 10 minutes, tel. 075/16 22 21).

▲▲**Aalsmeer Flower Auction**—This is your best look at the huge Dutch flower industry. About half of all the flowers exported from Holland are auctioned off here in six huge auditoriums. Visitors are welcome to wander on elevated walkways, through what is claimed to be the biggest building on Earth, over literally trainloads of fresh-cut flowers. (Monday-Friday, 7:30-11:00, it's pretty dead after 9:30 and on Thursday, f4, tel. 02977-32185, bus #172 from Amsterdam's station to Hortensieplein in Aalsmeer, then bus #140 to "bloemveiling" then a 5-minute walk. From Haarlem, take bus #191 at 7:02.) Aalsmeer is close to the airport, and a handy last fling before catching a morning flight.

▲▲▲**Keukenhof**—The greatest bulb flower garden on earth, each spring 6 million flowers conspire to make even a total garden-hater enjoy them. This 70-acre park is packed with tour groups daily (8:00-19:30, last tickets sold at 18:00, about March 23-May 23, f15, bus from Haarlem via Lisse, tel. 02521/19144). Go very late in the day for the best light and the fewest groups.

Zandvoort—For a quick and easy look at a dike and a shell-lover's Shangri-la, visit the beach resort of Zandvoort, a breezy bike ride, or 10 minutes by car or train west of Haarlem (from Haarlem, follow signs to Bloomendal). Caution: between posts 68 and 70, beach bathers work on all-around tans.

Volendam, Marken, and Monnikendam—These famous towns are too touristy.

LISBON

Lisbon (Lisboa) is a wonderful mix of now and then. Old wooden trolleys shiver up and down its hills, bird-stained statues mark grand squares, taxis rattle and screech through cobbled lanes, and well-worn people sip coffee in Art Nouveau cafés.

Present-day Lisbon is revealed by its past. While its history goes back to the Romans and the Moors, the glory days were the 15th and 16th centuries when explorers like Vasco da Gama opened new trade routes around Africa to India, making Lisbon one of Europe's richest cities. The economic boom fueled the flamboyant art boom called the Manueline period, named after Portugal's King Manuel I. Later, in the early 18th century, the gold and diamonds of Brazil, one of Portugal's colonies, made Lisbon even wealthier.

Then, on All Saints' Day in 1755, while most of the population was in church, the city was hit by a tremendous earthquake. Candles quivered as far away as Ireland. Lisbon was dead center. Two-thirds of the city was leveled. Fires, started by the many church candles, raged throughout the city, and a huge tidal wave blasted the waterfront. Forty thousand of Lisbon's 270,000 people were killed.

Under the energetic and eventually dictatorial leadership of Prime Minister Marquis Pombal, Lisbon was rebuilt in a progressive grid plan with broad boulevards and square squares. The charm of pre-earthquake Lisbon survives only in Belém, the Alfama, and the Baírro Alto district.

Portugal's vast colonial empire is now gone. The last bits were let go with the 1974 revolution that delivered her from the right-wing Salazar dictatorship. Emigrants from former colonies such as Mozambique and Angola have added diversity and flavor to the city, making it more likely that you'll hear African music than Portuguese fado these days.

But Lisbon's heritage survives. The city seems better organized, cleaner, and more prosperous and people-friendly now than in the 1980s. Square and elegant outdoor cafés, exciting art, entertaining museums, a hill-capping castle, the saltiest sailors' quarter in Europe, and much more, all at bargain basement prices, make Lisbon a world-class city.

Planning Your Time

With three weeks in Iberia, Lisbon is worth two days.

Day 1: Start by touring the castle Sao Jorge and survey the city from its viewpoint. After a coffee break at the café next to Miradour de Santa Luzia, descend into the Alfama. Explore. Back in the Baixa (lower city), walk to the funicular near Praça dos Restauradores. Start the described walk through the Baírro Alto with a ride up the funicular. This afternoon might be a good time to joyride on trolley #28. If it's not later than 15:00, art lovers can taxi out to the Gulbenkian Museum. After a break at the hotel, have dinner at Cervejaria da Trinidade. Finish off with a fado dinner show in the Baírro Alto.

Day 2: Trolley to Belém, tour the tower, monastery, and coach museum. Lunch in Belem. Catch the bus or drive to Sintra to tour the Pena Palace, explore the ruined Moorish castle. If you have a car, drive out to Cabo da Roca. Spend the evening in the resort of Estoril or Cascais or back in Lisbon. If you're itchy for the beach, you could drive 5 hours from Sintra to the Algarve.

A third day could be easily spent at the museum of ancient art and browsing through the Rossio, Barrío Alto, and Alfama.

The Gulbenkian Museum and the side trip to Sintra/Cabo da Roca are time consuming and rush Lisbon. If you'd appreciate more time to absorb the general ambience of the city, spend a full two days in Lisbon and do the museum (the Gulbenkian is mediocre by Paris or Madrid standards) and side trip only if you have a third day. Most museums are closed Monday. Bullfights are on Thursday and Sunday. Tuesday and Saturday are flea market days in the Alfama.

In general, Portugal is underrated. The country seems somewhere just beyond Europe. The pace of life is noticeably slower than in Spain. Roads are rutted. Prices are cheaper. Ramshackle Lisbon feels almost like some grand Third World capital. The economy (stronger than Albania's) is based on fishing, cork, wine, and manufacturing. Be sure to balance your look at Iberia with enough Portugal.

Lisbon

Map legend:

1. Albergaria Residencial Insulana
2. Hotel Duas Nações
3. Hotel Suisso Atlantico
4. Residencial Nova Silva
5. Residencial Camões
6. Pensão Duque
7. Hotel Borges / Cafe A Brasileira
8. Santa Justa Elevator
9. Largo Portas do Sol
10. Belvedere Santa Luzia – Great View!

Orientation (tel. code: 01)

Lisbon's center is a series of parks, boulevards, and squares bunny-hopping between two hills down to the waterfront. The main boulevard, Avenida da Liberdade, goes from the high-rent district downhill ending at the Praça dos Restauradores (obelisk celebrating the restoration of

Portuguese independence from Spain, TI, Rossio train station). The monumental Rossio and Figueira squares (with plenty of buses, subways, cheap taxis, and pigeons leaving in all directions) are just beyond that. Between the Rossio and the harbor is the flat lower city, the Baixa (bai-shah), with its checkerboard street plan, elegant architecture, bustling shops, and many cafés. Most of Lisbon's prime attractions are within walking distance of the Rossio.

Three characteristic neighborhoods line the downtown harborfront: Baixa (gridplan business district in middle), the Chiado/Baírro Alto (Lisbon's "Latin Quarter" on a hill to the west), and the tangled medieval Alfama (under the castle on a hill to the east).

Avenida da Liberdade is the tree-lined "Champs Elysées" of Lisbon, connecting the Rossio with the newer upper town (airport, bullring, popular fairgrounds, Edward VII Park, and breezy botanical gardens).

Tourist Information

The main tourist information office (TI) at the lower end of Avenida da Liberdade in the Palacio da Foz at Praça dos Restauradores, 3 blocks north of Rossio (daily 9:00-20:00, tel. 346 3643), gives out a map and a monthly "Cultural Agenda" publication. While the general map is not particularly good, its "Old Lisbon" inset is very useful. A periodical entertainment guide, Se7e, is sold at newsstands.

Flights

Lisbon's airport (tel. 80 20 60 general information, TAP Portuguese airlines tel. 386 1020), just 5 miles northeast of downtown, has good bus connections to town (#44, #45, #83, and #91, 140$), reasonable taxis (1,000$ to center), a 24-hour bank, and a tourist office.

Banking

Traveler's checks cost a small fortune to cash (the average fee is about $8 no matter how much you cash), so shop around and try to cash in all your checks at one bank. Automatic bill-changing machines are plentiful and seductive. But they also charge a fee.

Communication

The Portuguese language sounds like a French person speaking Spanish on a pogo stick. In big cities and along the Algarve you can usually find someone who speaks English. Spanish, French, and sign language are helpful. My Spanish and Portuguese phrase book will help you hurdle the language barrier. A few useful words: *bom dia* (hello), *obrigado*(a) (thank you), and *adeus* (goodbye).

Trains

Lisbon has four train stations. Rossio station is the most central and handles most trains from Óbidos, Sintra, Coimbra, Nazaré and the north. There's a handy train information office on the ground floor of the station (daily 9:00-20:00, tel. 888 4025). Lisbon's Santa Apolonia station handles Madrid and international trains and trains that go to north and east Portugal. It's just past the Alfama, with good bus connections to the town center (buses #9 or #46 go from the station through the center and up Avenida da Liberdade), foreign currency change machines, and other services. A taxi from Santa Apolonia to any hotel I recommend should cost no more than 600$ (including the luggage supplement). If there's a long taxi stand line-up, walk a block away and hail one off the street. Barreiro station, a 30-minute ferry ride (free with train pass or ticket) across the Tagus River (Rio Tejo) from Praça do Comércio, is for trains to the Algarve and points south. Caís do Sodré station handles the 30-minute rides to Cascais and Estoril. Train information: 01/888 4025 or 888 5092.

Getting Around

Lisbon's simple, fast, and cheap subway runs only north of Praça Rossio (Rossio Square) into the new town. You'll only need it for the Gulbenkian and a bullfight. The bus system is extensive.

For more fun and practical public transport, use the trolley system, the funicular, and the Eiffel-esque elevator (tickets at the door, going every few minutes) to connect the lower and upper towns. One ride costs 140$. (The 400$-day pass and the 850$ 3-day pass cover all public transport except the metro.) Lisbon taxis are abundant and use their meters. Rides start at 250$ and you can go anywhere in the center for under 400$. Especially if there are two of you, Lisbon cabs are a great and cheap time-saver.

Helpful Hints
Banks, the post office, airlines, and travel agents line the Avenida da Liberdade. American Express is in the Top Tours office at Avenida Duque de Loule 108, tel. 315 5885, weekdays 9:00-13:00 and 14:30-18:30. The telephone center on Rossio Square is open daily until 23:00.

Sights—Lisbon
▲▲**Rossio and Baixa**—In the town center, rebuilt after the earthquake on a grid plan with uniform five-story buildings, several streets have recently been turned into charming pedestrian zones, making this area more enjoyable than ever. The mosaic-decorated Rua Augusta is every bit as delightful as Barcelona's Ramblas for strolling.

Sè (Cathedral)—Just a few blocks east of Praça do Comércio, it's not much on the inside, but its fortress-like exterior is a textbook example of a stark and powerful Romanesque fortress of God. Started in 1150, after the Christians reconquered Lisbon from the Islamic Moors, its crenelated towers made a powerful statement: the Reconquista was here to stay.

▲▲**Ride a Trolley**—Lisbon's vintage trolleys, most from the 1920s, shake and shiver all over town, somehow safely weaving within inches of parked cars, climbing steep hills, and offering sightseers breezy wide-open-window views of the city. Line #28 is a rice-a-roni Lisbon joyride. Starting at the Estrela basilica and park, it runs through the Chiado, Baixa, and Alfama to Santa Clara church near the flea market. Stops from west to east include top of Bica funicular, Chiado square, top of Rua Victor Cordon, in Baixa on Rua da Conceicao between Augusta and Prata, at the cathedral (Sè), at the Alfama viewpoint (Santa Luzia Belvedere, at Portas do Sol and at the Santa Clara church). Just pay the conductor as you board, sit down, and catch the pensioners as they lurch at each stop.

▲▲**The Baírro Alto and Chiado stroll**—This colorful upper city walk starts at the funicular and ends with the elevator (each a funky 140$ experience in itself). Leave the

lower town on the funicular (Elevator da Gloria) near the
obelisk at Praça dos Restauradores. Leaving the funicular on
top, turn right to enjoy the city view from the San Pedro
Park belvedere.

If you're into port (the fortified wine that takes its name
from the city of Oporto), you'll find the world's greatest
selection across the street from the lift at **Solar do Vinho do
Porto** (run by the Port Wine Institute, Rua São Pedro de
Alcantara 45, 10:00-23:45, closed Sunday). In a stuffy '60s-
decor living-room atmosphere you can, for 150-2000 per
glass poured by an English-speaking bartender, taste any of
250 different ports, though you may want to try only 125 or
so and save the rest for the next night. Fans of port describe
it as "a liquid symphony playing on the palate."

Follow the big street (Rua da Misericordia) downhill a
block. São Roque Church is around the corner on Largo
Trinidade Coelho. It looks like just another church, but
wander slowly under its flat painted ceiling and notice the
rich side chapels. The highlight is the Chapel of St. John the
Baptist (left of altar, gold and blue) which looks like it came
right out of the Vatican. It did. Made at the Vatican out of
the most precious materials, it was the site of one papal mass;
then it was taken down and shipped to Lisbon—probably the
most costly chapel per square inch ever constructed. Notice
the beautiful mosaic floor and the three paintings that are
actually intricate mosaics, a Vatican specialty. The São
Roque Museum (150$, 10:00-17:00, closed Monday) has
some impressive old paintings and church riches.

After a visit with the poor pigeon-drenched man in the
square, continue downhill along Rua da Misercordia into the
Chiado (SHEE-ah-doe). Shoppers check out the chic Centro
Commercial Espaco at #14 (with chic public-enough toilets
and classy bars) to Praça Luis de Camões.

A left takes you onto a pleasant square (Largo Chiado)
past **A Brasiliera** café and to the classy Rua Garrett.
Coffeehouse aficionados enjoy this grand old café, reeking
with smoke and the 1930s. After two downhill blocks on Rua
Garrett, take a left uphill along Calle Sacramento, which
leads to another pleasant square, Largo dos Carmo, with the
ruins of the Convento do Carmo (peek in to see the elegant,
earthquake-ruined, Gothic arches for free, or pay 300$ to

get all the way in and see the museum, 10:00-18:00, closed Sunday). From the side of the church, follow the trolley tracks to the Santa Justa elevator. Climb the spiral stairs one floor to the observatory or to the top of this Eiffelian pimple for a great view café (daily, English spoken, reasonable coffee, expensive eats). The elevator takes you back into the Baixa.

▲▲▲**Alfama**—Europe's most colorful sailors' quarter goes back to Visigothic days. It was a rich district during the Arabic period and finally the home of Lisbon's fisherfolk (and of the poet who wrote "our lips meet easily high across the narrow street"). One of the few areas to survive the 1755 earthquake, the Alfama is a cobbled playground of Old World color. A visit is best during the busy midmorning market time or in the late afternoon/early evening when the streets teem with locals.

Wander deep. This urban jungle's roads are squeezed into tangled and confusing alleys; bent houses comfort each other in their romantic shabbiness; and the air drips with laundry and the smell of clams and raw fish. Get lost. Poke aimlessly, sample ample grapes, avoid rabid-looking dogs, peek through windows. Don't miss Rua de São Pedro, the liveliest street around.

Trolley #28 stops at the top of the Alfama. On Tuesday and Saturday mornings, the fun Feira da Ladra flea market rages on the nearby Campo de Santa Clara. To start or finish your Alfama adventure at the top: use the Beco Santa Helena, a stairway that connects the maze with the Largo das Portas do Sol and the Santa Luzia belvedere (or viewpoint). Probably the most scenic cup of coffee in town is enjoyed from the Cerca Moura bar/café terrace (Largo das Portas do Sol 4, top of the stairs).

Castelo São Jorge—The city castle, with a history going back to Roman days, caps the highest hill above the Alfama and offers a pleasant garden and Lisbon's top viewpoint but nothing in the way of an interior. Orient yourself from this perch (daily until sunset, bus #37 from Figueira Square).

▲**Fado**—Mournfully beautiful, haunting ballads about lost sailors, broken hearts, and sad romance are one of Lisbon's favorite late-night tourist traps. Be careful, this is one of those cultural clichés that all too often become rip-offs. The

Alfama has many touristy fado bars, but the Baírro Alto (plenty of joints around Rua Diario de Noticias, Rua das Gaveas, and Rua Norte) is your best bet. Things don't start until 22:00 and then take an hour or two to warm up. A fado performance isn't cheap (expect a 2,000$-3,000$ cover), and many fado joints require dinner. Get advice from your hotel or the Fado listings in *Se7e*.

▲▲**Gulbenkian Museum**—This is the best of Lisbon's 40 museums. Gulbenkian, an Armenian oil tycoon, gave his art collection (or "harem," as he called it) to Portugal in gratitude for the hospitable asylum granted him there during WWII. Now this great collection, spanning 2,000 years, is displayed in a classy and comfortable modern building. Ask for the excellent English text explaining the collection.

You'll stroll chronologically through the ages past the great Egyptian, Greek, and Middle Eastern sections. There are masterpieces by Rembrandt, Rubens, Renoir, Rodin, and artists whose names start with other letters (pleasant gardens, good, air-conditioned cafeteria, bus #46 from downtown or metro from Rossio to Sao Sebastiao, open Tuesday, Thursday, Friday, and Sunday 10:00-17:00, Wednesday and Saturday 14:00-19:30 in summer, closed Monday, tel. 795 0236).

▲▲**Museu Nacional de Arte Antigua**—Lisbon's museum of ancient art is the country's best for Portuguese paintings from her glory days, the 15th and 16th centuries. You'll also find the great European masters (such as Bosch, Jan van Eyck, and Raphael) and rich furniture, all in a grand palace (tram #15 from Praca do Comércio or Figueira, Rua das Janeles Verdes 9, 10:00-17:00, closed Monday, tel. 397 6002, 500$).

▲**Museu Nacional do Azulejo**—This museum, filling the Convento da Madre de Deus, features piles of tiles which, as you've probably noticed, is an art form in Portugal (10 minutes on bus #59 from Figueira, 10:00-18:00, Tuesday 14:00-18:00, closed Monday).

▲▲▲**Portuguese Bullfight**—If you always felt sorry for the bull, this is Toro's Revenge; in a Portuguese bullfight, the matador is brutalized. Unlike the Spanish *corrida*, the bull is not killed in the Portuguese *tourada*. After an exciting equestrian prelude when the horseman *(cavaleiro)* skillfully plants barbs in the bull's back while trying to avoid the padded horns, a colorfully clad, eight-man team (suicide squad) enters the ring and lines up single file facing the bull. The leader prompts the bull to charge, then braces himself for a collision that can be heard all the way up in the cheap seats. As he hangs onto the bull's head, his buddies then pile on, trying to wrestle the bull to a standstill. Finally, one guy hangs onto *el toro's* tail and "water-skis" behind him.

You're most likely to see a bullfight in Lisbon, Estoril, or on the Algarve. Get schedules in the tourist office; fights start late in the evening. In Lisbon, there are fights at Capo Pequeno Thursday nights only from mid-June through September at 22:00, tickets from 2,000$. Nearby arenas advertise fights on Sundays. The season lasts from Easter through October. Tickets are available at the door or at the green ABEP kiosk across the square from Lisbon's central tourist office.

▲**Feira Popular (The People's Fair)**—Consider spending a low-brow evening at Lisbon's Feira Popular, which bustles with Portuguese families at play. Pay the tiny entry fee, then enjoy rides, munchies, great people-watching, entertainment, music—basic Portuguese fun. Have dinner among the chattering families, with endless food and wine paraded frantically in every direction. Food stalls dispense wine from the udders of porcelain cows. Fried ducks drip, barbecues spit, and dogs squirt the legs of chairs while, somehow, local lovers ignore everything but each other's eyes. (Nightly, May 1-September 30, 19:00-midnight, Saturday and Sunday 15:00-midnight. Located on Avenida da República at the "Entre-Campos" metro stop.)

Cristo Rei—A huge statue of Christ (à la Rio de Janeiro) overlooks Lisbon from across the Tagus River. While it's designed to be seen from a distance, a lift takes visitors to the top for a great view. For an interesting circular excursion consider catching the ferry (they leave from downtown for Cacilhas constantly) and a bus (buses leave from the ferry dock to the statue every 15 minutes). Return by taxi (he'll charge you round-trip) to ride over Lisbon's great bridge. (Statue lift runs 10:00-18:00 daily.)

▲**The 25th of April Bridge**—A mile long, this is the third-longest suspension bridge in the world. Built in 1966, it was originally named for the dictator Salazar but renamed for the date of Portugal's revolution and freedom.

Belém

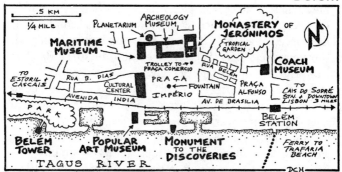

Sights—Lisbon's Belém District

Three miles from downtown Lisbon, the Belém District is a pincushion of important sights from Portugal's Golden Age, when Vasco da Gama and company made it Europe's richest power. This is the best look possible at the grandeur of pre-earthquake Lisbon. While the monastery is great, its many museums are somewhere between good and mediocre, depending upon your interests. You can get there by taxi or bus, but I'd ride trolley #15 from Praça do Comércio or Figueira.

▲**The Belém Tower**—The only purely Manueline building in Portugal (built in 1515), this tower protected Lisbon's harbor and today symbolizes the voyages that made it powerful. This was the last sight sailors saw as they left and the first when they returned loaded with gold, diamonds, spices, and social diseases. Its collection of 15th- and 16th-century armaments is barely worth the admission, but if you do go in, climb up for the view (500$, 10:00-17:00, closed Monday, tel. 362 0034).

▲**Monument to the Discoveries**—This giant monument was built in 1960 to honor Prince Henry the Navigator on the 500th anniversary of his death. Huge statues of Henry and Portugal's leading explorers line the giant concrete prow. Note the marble map chronicling Portugal's empire building on the ground in front. Inside you can ride a lift to a fine view (300$).

▲▲**Monastery of Jerónimos**—This is, for me, Portugal's most exciting building. The giant church and its cloisters were built as a thanks for the discoveries. Vasco da Gama is buried here. Notice how nicely the Manueline style combines Gothic and Renaissance features with motifs from the sea, the source of wealth that made this art possible. Don't miss the elegant cloisters (500$, 10:00-13:00, 14:30-17:00, closed Monday). Go upstairs for a better view.

▲▲Museu dos Coches (Coach Museum)—Claiming be to the most visited sight in Portugal, it's most impressive with over 70 dazzling carriages from the 18th century (400$, 10:00-18:00, closed Monday, tel. 363 8022).

Popular Art Museum—This museum takes you one province at a time through Portugal's folk art (300$, 10:00-12:30, 14:00-17:00, closed Monday).

Maritime Museum—A cut above the average European maritime museum. Sailors love it (250$, 10:00-17:00, closed Monday).

Belém Cultural Center—This modern expansive center (on the west side of the big square between the monastery and the water), filled with galleries, cafés, and concert halls, is worth a wander while you're in Belém. Check its concert schedule.

Shopping

Lisbon is Europe's bargain basement. You'll find decaying but still elegant department stores, teeming flea markets, classy specialty shops, and one of Europe's largest modern shopping centers. The Mercado Ribeira open-air market, next to the Caís do Sodre market, bustles every morning except Sunday—great for picnic stuff and local sweaters. Look for shoes, bags, and leather goods on Rua Garrett and Rua Carmo and gold and silver on the Rua do Ouro (Gold Street). And for the gleaming modern side of things, taxi to Amoreiras Shopping Center de Lisboa (Ave. da Duarte Pacheco, you can see its pink and blue towers from a distance, open daily 10:00-24:00, bus #11 from Rossio) for its more than 350 shops, piles of eateries, and theaters.

Lisbon at Night

From the Baixa, nighttime Lisbon seems dead. But head up into the Baírro Alto and you'll find lots of action. The

Jardim do São Pedro is normally festive and the Rua Diario de Noticias is lined with bars. Fado folk singing is described above. For entertainment specifics, pick up a copy of the periodical *Se7e*. (*Sete* means 7.)

Lisbon reels with theaters, and unlike in Spain, most films are in the original language with subtitles. Many of Lisbon's more than 90 theaters are classy, complete with assigned seats and ushers, and the normally cheap tickets go for half price on Monday.

Sleeping in Lisbon (tel. code: 01, 150$=US$1)

Lisbon has plenty of cheap and handy rooms. Physically, Lisbon is a tired and well-worn city. Rooms in the center feel the same way. To sleep in a well-located place with local character you'll be climbing dark stairways into a world of cracked plaster, taped hand-written signs, dingy carpets, cramped and confusing floor plans, and ramshackle plumbing. If you're on a tight budget, arrive without a reservation and bargain. If you have a room reserved, taxi there from the station. While old Lisbon seems a little sleazy at night, with normal discretion, my listings are safe.

Singles cost nearly the same as doubles. Baths often cost more than showers. Addresses like 26-3 stand for street #26, third floor (which is fourth floor in American terms). Never judge a place by its entryway.

Sleep code: **S**=Single, **D**=Double/Twin, **T**=Triple, **Q**=Quad, **B**=Bath/Shower, **WC**=Toilet, **CC**=Credit Card (**V**isa, **M**astercard, **A**mex), **SE**=Speaks English (graded **A** through **F**).

Sleeping Downtown in Baixa
(postal code: 1100)

Central as can be, this area bustles with lots of shops, traffic, people, buskers, pedestrian areas, and urban intensity. I've listed places that are in relatively quiet areas or on pedestrian streets.

Albergaria Residencial Insulana (DBWC-8,000$ with breakfast, TBWC-10,000$, CC:VMA, elevator, all with air-conditioning, Rua da Assuncao 52, tel. 342 3131, SE-A) is very professional with 32 quiet and comfortable (if a bit smoky) rooms.

Residencial Duas Nações (DBWC-8,000$ with

breakfast, Rua Augusta e Rua da Vitoria 41, elevator, tel. 346 2082, fax 347 0206, SE-C) is a tired old hotel in the heart of Rossio on a classy pedestrian street.

Pensao Aljubarrata (D-3,000$, T-4,500$, Rua da Assuncao 53-4, tel. 346 0112, SE-F) is a family-run sleepable bargain bet if you can handle the long climb up four floors and the bubbly black vinyl flooring. Once on top you'll have cute tiny balconies from which to survey the Rua Augusta scene.

Sleeping Farther Uptown Along Avenida da Liberdade (postal code: 1200)

Hotel Suisso Atlantico (SBWC-7,500$, DBWC-9,500$, TBWC-11,200$ including breakfast, CC:VMA, parking available, Rua da Gloria 3-19, behind the funicular station, around the corner from the tourist office on a quiet street 1 block off Praça dos Restauradores, tel. 346 1713, fax 346 9013, SE-A) is formal, hotelish, and a bit stuffy, with lots of tour groups and dingy carpets throughout, but it has decent rooms and a TV lounge. If you want a functional hotel and practical location, it's a good value.

Residencial Florescente (S or D without windows-2,000$, D-4,000$, DBWC-6,000$, CC:VM, Rua Portas S. Antao 99, tel. 346 3517, fax 342 7733, SE-C) is a slumber mill with 100 rooms on a busy pedestrian street a block off Praça dos Restauradores. It's clean but pretty depressing, with weird squat showers and rooms that vary wildly in quality. Rather than reserving this place, drop in to survey the available rooms and prices.

Albergaria Metro Avenida (D-5,200$, DBWC-6,200$, air-con basement DBWC-10,000$, extra person-2,000$, CC:VMA, parking 1,300$, Av. da Liberdade 140, tel. 346 7367, fax 342 3124, SE-B) is a tired and smoky, recently modern, 32-room place with bleak carpets but a safe, pre-dictable, and reasonably comfortable feel in a great location. The air-con rooms are worst.

Pensao Residencial 13 da Sorte (S-4,000$, DBWC-6,000$, elevator, Rua do Salitre 13, tel. 353 9746, fax 395 6946, SE-B), the cheeriest of all places I found, has big full bathrooms in each of its 24 thoughtfully appointed rooms and bright, small-town tiles throughout. It's just a short walk up Avenida da Liberdade, around the corner from Hotel Plaza and Jardím, a half block off the boulevard on the left. Back rooms are quieter.

Sleeping in Bairro Alto (postal code: 1200)

Just west of downtown, this area is more colorful with less traffic. It's a bit seedy but full of ambience, good bars, local fado clubs, music, and markets. The area may not feel comfortable for women alone at night, but the hotels themselves are safe.

Residencial Nova Silva (S-4,000$, SB-4,500$, D-4,500$, DB-5,000$, DBWC-5,500$, TB-6,000$, QB-6,500$, breakfast 400$, prices vary a little with the room, length of stay, and season, no elevator, Rua Victor Cordón 11, tel. 342 4371, fax 342 7770, SE-B) is a quiet, ramshackle place with a fine location on the crest of the Baírro Alto overlooking the river. Worth requesting are five rooms with grand little river-view balconies, giving you bird noises rather than traffic noises (priority for longer stays). Shamina, Fatima, and Prakash all speak English and are helpful. Call well in advance and reconfirm two days early. Three blocks from the heart of Chiado on the scenic #28 tram line with the easiest street parking of all my listings.

Residencial Camões (S-2,500$, D-5,000$, DBWC-6,000$, T-6,000$, TBWC-7,000$ including breakfast, Trav. Poco da Cidade 38, 1 block in front of São Roque Church and to the right, you'll see the sign, tel. 346 7510, fax 346 4048, SE-B) lies right in the seedy thick of the Baírro Alto but offers fine rooms with a friendly atmosphere and safe feeling.

Pensão Duque (S-1,900$, D-3,000$, T-4,000$, also cheaper no-window rooms, Calçada do Duque 53, tel. 346 3444, SE-B) has a great location on the pedestrian stairway street just off Largo Trinidade at the edge of Baírro Alto, up from Rossio Square, and a friendly staff (ask for Lew-weez). This place, with steep stairways, tacky vinyl floors, yellow paint, and dim lights, is too seedy for most, but the price, location, hard beds, and saggy, ancient atmosphere make it a prize for some.

Hotel Borges (DBWC-9,000$ with breakfast, CC:VMA, Rua Garrett 108, on the shopping street next to A Brasiliera café, tel. 346 1951, fax 342 6617, SE-A) is a big, dark, tired, smoky, formerly regal place with one of the old town's best addresses.

Eating in Lisbon

Eating in the Alfama
This gritty chunk of pre-earthquake Lisbon is full of interesting eateries, especially along the Rua San Pedro (the main drag) and on Largo de São Miguel. For a seafood feast (2,600$ menu) after your Alfama exploration, eat at the gleaming blue-tiled **Farol de Santa Lucia** restaurant (across from the patio viewpoint overlooking the Alfama, no sign, at #5, tel. 863884). For the real thing, cheap (700$ meals) and colorful, walk behind the Santa Luzia belvedere past Portas do Sol (dip into a dark bar for a damp appetizer) to a square called Largo Rodrigues Freitas, where **Nossa Churrasqueira** is busy feeding happy locals on rickety tables and meager budgets. If that's too touristy, walk from there down the steepest lane, Rua do Salvador, to #81. This road continues downhill into the less touristed fringe of the Alfama. While in the Alfama, brighten a few dark bars. Have an aperitif, taste the *branco seco* (local dry white wine). Make a friend, pet a chicken, read the graffiti, pick at the humanity ground between the cobbles.

Eating in Baírro Alto
Lisbon's "high town" is full of small, fun, and cheap places. Fishermen's bars abound. On the stairway next to recommended Pensão Duque, try the very simple and cheap **Casa Trans-Montanta.** Deeper into the Baírro Alto, past Rua de Misericordia, you'll find the area's best meals. The **Cervejareía da Trinidade** at Rua Nova da Trinidade 20C (daily, tel. 342 3506, CC:VMA), a Portuguese-style beer hall covered with historic tiles and full of fish and locals, serves memorable meals.

Eating in Rossio and Baixa (Downtown)
The "eating lane" (opposite the Rossio station, just off Praça dos Restauradores down Rua do Jardim do Regedor and Rua das Portas de Santo Antão) is a galloping gourmet's heaven, a galaxy of eateries with small zoos hanging from their windows

to choose from. The seafood is some of Lisbon's best. The **Express Supermarket** on the Rua Regedor is open until 22:00 and on Sunday. For cod and vegetables faster than a Big Mac and served with more energy than a soccer team, stand or sit at the **Restaurant/Cervejaría Beira-Gare** (a greasy spoon in front of the Rossio station at the end of Rua 1 de Dezembro).

The Rossio is lined with local eateries (like **Restaurant X** at Rua dos Correiros #116, look for the red X). The snack bar at Rua dos Fanqueiros 161 is fun and friendly.

In the suburb of Belém, you'll find several good restaurants along Rua de Belém between the coach museum and the monastery.

Finally, don't miss a chance to go purely local with hundreds of Portuguese families having salad, fries, chicken, and wine at the Feira Popular.

Transportation Connections
Lisbon to: Madrid (2/day, 10-12 hrs, ideal overnight), **Faro** (4/day, 5 hrs), **Paris** (1/day, 26 hrs), **Porto** (12/day, 3½ hrs), **Evora** (5/day, 3 hrs), **Lagos** (5/day, 5 hrs, overnight possible), **Coimbra** (17/day, 2½ hrs), **Nazare Velado** (4/day, 2½ hrs), **Sintra** and **Cascais** (4/hr, 45 min). **Salema:** I like the (23:00-6:45) night train, even with the early morning change of trains, because it allows you to enjoy the entire day on the Algarve. If you insist on daytime travel, both bus and train take about 5 hours to Lagos. Trains from Lisbon to the **south coast** leave from the Barreiro station across the Tagus from downtown. Boats shuttle train travelers from Praça do Comércio to the Barreiro station with several departures each hour (free with Eurailpass, 30-minute ride, note that schedule times listed are often when the boat sails, not when train departs). Many prefer the Rodoviaria express buses to the train (must be booked ahead, get details at the tourist office, 4/day, 5 hrs, depart from Casal Ribiero 18, metro: Saldanha, tel. 54 54 39).

COPENHAGEN

Copenhagen (Kobenhavn) is Scandinavia's largest city. With around a million people, it's home to more than a quarter of all Danes. A busy day cruising the canals, wandering through its palace, taking a historic walk, and strolling the Stroget (Europe's greatest pedestrian shopping mall), will get you oriented and you'll feel right at home. Copenhagen is Scandinavia's cheapest and most fun-loving capital, so live it up.

Denmark

Orientation

Nearly all of your sightseeing is in Copenhagen's compact old town. By doing things on foot you'll stumble into some surprisingly cozy corners, one of the charms of Copenhagen that many miss. Study the map. The medieval walls are now roads that define the center: Vestervoldgade (literally, western wall street), Norrevoldgade, and Ostervoldgade. The fourth side is the harbor and the island of Slotsholmen where *Koben havn* (merchants' harbor) was born in 1167. The next of the city's islands is Amager, where you'll find the local "Little Amsterdam" district of Christianshavn. What was Copenhagen's moat is now a string of pleasant lakes and parks, including Tivoli Gardens. To the north is the old "new town" where the Amalienborg Palace is surrounded by streets on a grid plan and the Little Mermaid poses relentlessly, waiting for her sailor to return and the tourists to leave.

The core of the town, as far as most visitors are concerned, is the axis formed by the train station, Tivoli Gardens, the Radhus (city hall) square, and the Stroget pedestrian street. It's a great walking town, bubbling with street life and colorful pedestrian zones.

Planning Your Time

A decent first visit needs two days.

Day 1: Get set up around 9:00. If staying there, browse Christianshavn, Copenhagen's "little Amsterdam." At 10:00 explore the subterranean Christiansborg Castle ruins under today's palace. At 11:00 take the 50-minute guided tour of Denmark's royal Christiansborg Palace. At 12:00 catch the harbor tour boat for a relaxing cruise out to the mermaid. 13:30 have a buffet lunch at Riz-Raz. Visit the Use-It information center. Tour the Rosenborg Castle and crown jewels. Siesta in the park. Take the "Heart and Soul" walk described below as you shop and stroll the Stroget pedestrian mall. Evening at Tivoli Gardens (or tomorrow evening, if killing time before catching a night train out).

Day 2: Catch the 10:30 city walking tour or tour the Ny Carlsberg Glyptotek art gallery. Smorrebrod lunch. Trace Denmark's cultural roots in the National Museum. The afternoon is free with many options, including a brewery tour, Nazi Resistance museum (free tour often at 14:00), Thorvaldsen's Museum, or the Amalienborg Palace square,

With three days, side trip out to Roskilde and Fredericksborg. Remember the efficiency of sleeping in-and-out by train. If flying in, most flights from the states arrive in the morning. After that, head for Stockholm and Oslo. Kamikaze sightseers see Copenhagen as a Scandinavian bottle-neck. They sleep in-and-out heading north and in-and-out heading south with two days in, and no nights in the city. Considering the joy of Oslo and Stockholm, this isn't that crazy if you have limited time. You can check your bag at the station and take a 10-kr shower in the Interail Center.

You could set yourself up in my best rooms for your entire Scandinavian tour with a quick trip to the Telecom center in the train station.

Tourist Information

The tourist office (across from the train station on the corner of Vesterbrogade and Bernstorffsgade, next to the Tivoli entrance, tel. 33 11 13 25, daily June-mid-September 9:00-20:00; mid-September-May 9:00-16:00, Saturday 9:00-14:00, closed Sunday) is now run by a for-profit consortium called "Wonderful Copenhagen." This colors the advice and information it provides. Still, it's worth a quick stop for the top-notch freebies it provides (city map and *Copenhagen This Week*). Corporate dictates prohibit them from freely offering other brochures, but ask and you shall receive (walking tour schedules and brochures on any sights of special interest). Thinking ahead, get information and ferry schedules for your entire trip in Denmark (for instance, Frederiksborg Castle, Louisiana Museum, Kronborg Castle, Roskilde, Odense, Aero, Arhus, and Legoland).

Copenhagen This Week, a free, handy, and misnamed monthly guide to the city, is worth reading for its good maps, museum hours with telephone numbers, sightseeing tour ideas, shopping ideas, and calendar of events (free English tours and concerts). The TI's room-finding service charges you and the hotel a fee and cannot give hard opinions. Do not use it. Get on the phone and call direct (everyone speaks English).

Use It is a better information service. This "branch" of Huset, a hip, city government-sponsored, student-run cluster of cafés, theaters, and galleries, caters to Copenhagen's young, but welcomes travelers of any age. It's a friendly, driven-to-help, and energetic no-nonsense source of budget travel information, with a free room-finding service, ride-finding board, cheap transportation deals, free luggage storage, pen-pals-wanted scrapbook, free condoms, lockers, and Copenhagen's best free city maps. Their free *Playtime* publication is full of Back-Door-style travel articles on Copenhagen and the Danish culture,special budget tips, and events. They have brochures onjust about everything, including self-guided tours for bikers, walkers, and those riding scenic bus #6. They have a list of private rooms (200 kr doubles without breakfast). Open daily 9:00-19:00 mid-June-mid-September; Monday-Friday 10:00-16:00 the rest of the year. Use It is a 10-minute walk from the station, down Stroget, right on Radhustraede for 3 blocks to #13, tel. 33 15 65 18. After hours, their night board lists the cheapest rooms available in town.

The **Copenhagen Card** covers the public transportation system and admissions to nearly all the sights in greater Copenhagen, which stretches from Helsingor to Roskilde. It covers virtually all the city sights, Tivoli, and the bus in from the airport. Available at any tourist office (including the airport's) and the central station: 1 day, 140 kr; 2 days, 230 kr; 3 days, 295 kr. The sights you're likely to see are included: Christiansborg Palace (30 kr), Palace Ruins (15 kr), National Museum (30 kr), Ny Carlsberg Glyptotek (15 kr), Rosenborg Castle (35 kr), Tivoli (38 kr), Frederiksborg Castle (30 kr), and Roskilde Viking Ships (30 kr). Plus round-trip train rides to Roskilde (70 kr) and Frederiksborg Castle (70 kr). It's hard to break even, unless you're planing to side-trip on the included (and otherwise expensive) rail service. It comes with a handy book explaining the 57 included sights.

Getting Into and Around Copenhagen

Arriving by Train
Most travelers arrive in Copenhagen after an overnight train ride. The station has two long-hours money exchange desks. Den Dansk Bank (7:00-22:00 daily) is fair (charging the standard 40 kr minimum or 20 kr per check fee for travelers checks). ForEx (8:00-21:00 daily), with a worse rate but charging only 10 kr per travelers check with no minimum, is better

Copenhagen

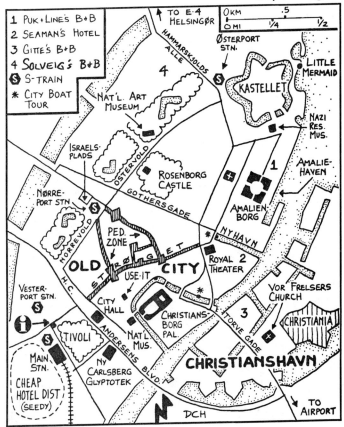

1 PUK + LINE'S B+B
2 SEAMAN'S HOTEL
3 GITTE'S B+B
4 SOLVEIG'S B+B
S S-TRAIN
* CITY BOAT TOUR

TO E·4 HELSINGØR
0 KM · .5
0 MI ¼ ½

ØSTERPORT STN.
LITTLE MERMAID
KASTELLET
HAMMARSKJOLDS ALLE
NAT'L. ART MUSEUM
NAZI RES. MUS.
ISRAELS-PLADS
AMALIE-HAVEN
OSTERVOLD
ROSENBORG CASTLE
GOTHERSGADE
NØRRE-PORT STN.
AMALIEN-BORG
PED. ZONE
NYHAVN
NØRREVOLD
OLD CITY
STRØGET
ROYAL THEATER
USE·IT
H.C.
VESTER-PORT STN.
VOR FRELSERS CHURCH
TORVE GADE
CITY HALL
CHRISTIANS-BORG PAL.
CHRISTIANIA
ANDERSENS BLVD.
NAT'L MUS.
TIVOLI
MAIN STN.
NY CARLSBERG GLYPTOTEK
CHRISTIANSHAVN
CHEAP HOTEL DIST (SEEDY)
DCH
TO AIRPORT

for small exchanges. On $100 exchange, I saved 22 kr at ForEx. While you're in the station, reserve your overnight train seat or couchette out (at *rejsebureau*). Long rides require reservations. Between the escalators to tracks 6 and 7 are great charts of the station. These show you exactly where to catch which buses. Bus #8 (in front of the station on the station side of Bernstorffsgade) goes to Christianshavn B&Bs. Note the time the bus departs. The TI is across the street on the left.

Flights

Copenhagen's International Airport is a traveler's dream, with a tourist office, bank (standard rates), post office, tele-phone center, shopping mall, grocery store, bakery, and rest cabins. You can use American cash at the airport and get change back in kroner. (Airport info tel. 31 54 17 01, flight info tel. 31 54 17 01, SAS tel. 32 00, British Air tel. 31 51 30 17.)

Getting from Airport to Downtown

Taxis are fast and easy, and at about 140 kr to the town center, a good deal for foursomes. The SAS **shuttle bus** will zip you to the central train station in 20 minutes for 28 kr. **City bus #32** gets you downtown (city hall square, TI) in 40 minutes for 15 kr (4/hr, across the street and to the right as you exit the airport). If you're going to the recommended rooms in Christianshavn, ride #9 just past Christianshavn Torv to the last stop before Knippels bridge.

If you need to kill a night at the airport, try the fetal rest cabins (SBWC-250 kr, DBWC-375 kr, rented by the 8-hour period, CC:VMA, reservations same day only, tel. 32 50 93 33, extension 2455; reception open 6:00-22:30).

Trains

Hovedbanegarden, the main train station (learn that word— you'll need to recognize it), is a temple of travel and a hive of travel-related activity. You'll find lockers (20 kr/day), a *"garderobe"* (35 kr per day per rucksack), a post office, a modern telecommunication center (above the post office, daily 8:00-22:00, Saturday and Sunday 9:00-21:00; easy, fair long-distance phone booths and rentable office services), a grocery store (daily 8:00-24:00), 24-hour thievery, bike rentals, and the Interail Center. The Interail Center, a service the station offers to mostly young travelers (but anyone with a Eurailpass, Scanrail, student BIGE or Transalpino ticket, or Interail pass is welcome) is a very pleasant lounge with 10 kr showers, free (if risky) luggage storage, city maps, snacks, information, and other young travelers (June-September 6:30-24:00). If you just need the map and "Play Time," a visit here is quicker than the TI. Train info tel. 33 14 17 01.

Public Buses and Subways

Take advantage of the fine bus (tel. 36 45) and subway system called S-tog (Eurail valid on S-tog, tel. 33 14 17 01). A joint fare covers greater Copenhagen. You pay 10 kr as you board for an hour's travel within two zones, or buy a blue two-zone *klipkort* from the driver (70 kr for 10 1-hr "rides"). A 24-hour pass costs 65 kr. Don't worry much about "zones." Assume you'll be within the middle two zones. Board at the front, tell the driver where you're going, and he'll sell you the appropriate ticket. Drivers are patient, have change, and speak English. City maps list bus and subway routes. Locals are friendly and helpful.

HT Sightseeing Bus

This bus makes a circular route stopping at nine top Copenhagen sights (2/hr, 10:00-16:30, mid-June-August, 20 kr for 24-hour ticket). Scenic bus #6 (10 kr for an hour of stop and go) starts at the Carlsberg Brewery and stops at Tivoli, the town hall, the national museum, palace, Nyhavn, Amalienborg castle, the Kastellet, and the Little Mermaid—all described in a free, easy-to-follow Use It brochure.

Taxis

Taxis are plentiful and easy to flag down (15 kr drop charge, then 7 kr per km). For a short ride, four people can travel cheaper by taxi than by bus (e.g., 40 kr from train station to Christianshavn B&Bs).

Bike Rental

Copenhagen is a joy on a rental bike. Use It has a great biking guide brochure and information about city bike tours (2 hrs, 50 kr including bike, grunge-approach). You can rent bikes at Central Station's Cykelcenter (open 7:00-19:00, Saturday 9:00-15:00, closed Sunday, tel. 33 14 07 17) and Dan Wheel (2 blocks from the station at 3 Colbjornsensgade, on the corner of Vesterbrogade, open 8:00-18:30, Saturday and Sunday 8:00-14:00, 40 kr/day, 60 kr/2 days, tel. 31 21 22 27).

Helpful Hints

Ferries: Book any ferries you plan to use in Scandinavia now. Any travel agent can book the boat rides you plan to take later on your trip, such as the Denmark-Norway ferry (ask for special discounts on this crossing) or the Stockholm-Helsinki-Stockholm cruise (the Silja Line office is directly

across from the station at Vesterbrogade 6D, open Monday-Friday 9:00-16:30, tel. 33 14 40 80). Drivers heading to Sweden via Helsingor should get a reservation for the ferry (tel. 33 14 88 80, and wait through the Danish recording).
Festivals: Expect extra fun and crowds in Copenhagen during its festival times—Carnival in late May, the Roskilde Rock Festival in early July, and the Copenhagen Jazz Festival for ten days starting the first Friday in July.
Telephones: Use the telephone liberally. Phone booths are everywhere, calls are 1 kr, everyone speaks English, and *This Week* and this book list phone numbers for everything you'll be doing. All telephone calls in Denmark, even local ones, must include eight digits. There are no area codes. Calls anywhere in Denmark are cheap. Calls to Norway and Sweden cost 6 kr per minute from a booth (half that from a home). Since coin-operated phone booths are so rare, get a phone card (starting at 20 kr from newsstands).
Traveler's Checks: The American Express Company (Stroget at Amagertorv 18, Monday-Friday 9:00-17:00, Saturday 9:00-12:00, tel. 33 12 23 01) does not charge the 40 kr fees on their checks (or sometimes on any checks).

Sights—Copenhagen
Orientation Walk: "Copenhagen's Heart and Soul"—
Start from Radhuspladsen (City Hall Square), the bustling heart of Copenhagen, dominated by the City Hall spire. This used to be the fortified west end of town. The king cleverly quelled a French revolutionary-type thirst for democracy by giving his people Europe's first great public amusement park. Tivoli was built just outside the city walls in 1843. When the train lines came, the station was placed just beyond Tivoli. The golden girls high up on the building opposite the square tell the weather: on a bike or with an umbrella.

Old Hans Christian Andersen sits to the right of the city hall almost begging to be in another photo (as he did in real life). On a pedestal left of the City Hall, note the Lur-Blowers sculpture. The *lur* is a horn that was used 3,500 years ago. The ancient originals (which still play) are displayed in the National Museum and depicted on most tiny butter tubs.

From the less ancient Burger King stretches Copenhagen's main—and Europe's first—pedestrian street, Stroget.

Stroget (stroy-et) is actually a series of colorful streets and lively squares that bunny-hop through the old town, connecting the City Hall Square with Kongens Nytorv (The King's New Square, a 15-minute walk away)

The most historic bits and pieces of old Copenhagen are just off this commercial can-can. At the end of the first segment, Frederiksberggade, you'll hit Gammel Torv and Nytorv (old and new square). This was the old town center. The Oriental-looking kiosk was one of the city's first community telephone centers before phones were privately owned. The very old fountain was so offensive to people from the Victorian age that the pedestal was added, raising it—hopefully—out of view. The brick church at the start of Amager Torv is the oldest building you'll see here.

The final stretch of Stroget leads past the American Express office and major department stores, to the king's new square (Kongens Nytorv) where you'll find the Royal Theater and Nyhavn, a recently gentrified sailors' quarter. This formerly sleazy harbor is an interesting mix of tattoo parlors, taverns, and trendy (mostly expensive) cafés lining a canal filled with glamorous old sailboats of all sizes. Any historic sloop is welcome to moor here in Copenhagen's ever-changing boat museum. Hans Christian Andersen lived here and wrote his first stories here.

Continuing north, along the harborside, you'll pass a huge ship that sails to Oslo every evening. Follow the water to the modern fountain of Amaliehaven Park. The nearby Amalienborg Palace and Square is a good example of orderly baroque planning. Queen Margrethe II and her family live in the palace to your immediate left as you enter the square from the harbor side. Her son and heir to the throne, Frederik, recently moved into the palace directly opposite his mother's. While the guards change with royal fanfare at noon only when the queen is in residence, they shower every morning.

Leave the square on Amaliegade, heading north to Kastellet (Citadel) Park and a small museum about Denmark's World War II resistance efforts. A short stroll, past the Gefion fountain (showing the mythological story of the carving of Denmark out of Sweden) and a church made of flint and along the water, brings you to the overrated and over-photographed symbol of Copenhagen—the Little Mermaid.

Central Copenhagen

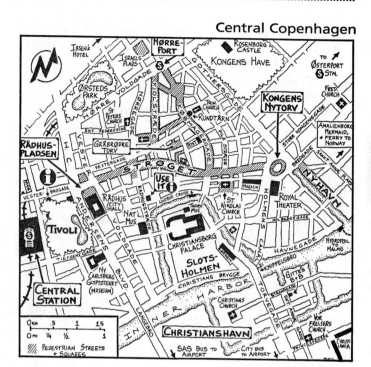

You can get back downtown on foot, by taxi, or on bus #1, #6 or #9 from Store Kongensgade on the other side of Kastellet Park (a special bus may run from the Mermaid in summer).

▲**Copenhagen's Town Hall (Radhus)**—This city landmark, between the station/Tivoli/TI and Stroget pedestrian mall, offers private tours and trips up its 350-foot-high tower. The city hall is open to the public (free, Monday-Friday, 10:00-15:00). Tours are given in English and get you into otherwise-closed rooms (20 kr, 45 minutes, daily 15:00, Saturday 10:00). Tourists are allowed to romp up the tower's 300 steps for the best aerial view of Copenhagen (10 kr, Monday-Friday 10:00, 12:00, and 14:00; Saturday 12:00; off-season 12:00, tel. 33 66 25 82).

▲**Christiansborg Palace**—This modern *slot*, or palace, built on the ruins of the original 12th-century palace, houses the parliament, supreme court, prime minister's headquarters, and royal reception rooms. Guided 40-minute English tours of the Queen's reception rooms (27 kr, May-September, Tuesday-Sunday at 11:00, 13:00, 15:00; off-season Tuesday, Thursday, and Sunday 11:00 and 15:00; tel. 33 92 64 92) let you slip-slide on protect-the-floor slippers through 22 rooms and gain a good feel for Danish history, royalty, and politics in this 100-year-old, still-functioning palace. For a rundown on contemporary government, you can also tour the parliament building. From the equestrian statue in front, go through the wooden door, past the entrance to the Christianborg Castle ruins, into the courtyard, and up the stairs on the right.

▲**Christiansborg Castle Ruins**—An exhibit in the scant remains of the first castle built by Bishop Absalon—the 12th-century founder of Copenhagen—lies under the palace. (15 kr, daily 9:30-15:30, closed off-season Monday and Saturday, good 1 kr guide.) Early birds note that this sight opens 30 minutes before other nearby sights.

▲▲▲**National Museum**—Focus on the excellent and curiously enjoyable Danish collection, which traces this civilization from its ancient beginnings, laid out on the ground floor chronologically starting with the "prehistory" section. Very good English explanations make highlights such as the passage graves, mummified Viking bodies with their armor and weapons, the 2,000-year-old Gunderstrup Caldron, original ancient *lur* horns, Viking gear, mead drinking horns, medieval church art, and domestic furniture particularly interesting. (30 kr, enter from Ny Vestergade, open 10:00-17:00, closed Monday, tel. 33 13 44 11, extension 460; occasional free English tours in the summer, call first.)

▲**Ny Carlsberg Glyptotek**—Scandinavia's top art gallery, with an especially intoxicating Egyptian, Greek, and Etruscan collection, the best of Danish Golden Age (early 19th-century) painting, and a heady, if small, exhibit of 19th-century French paintings (Gericault, Delacroix, Manet, impressionists, Gauguin before and after Tahiti) is an impressive example of what beer money can do. Linger under the palm leaves and glass dome of the very soothing conservatory. One of the original Rodin *Thinker*s can be seen for free (wondering how to scale the Tivoli fence?) in the museum's backyard. (15 kr, free on Wednesday and Sunday, behind Tivoli, open Tuesday-Sunday 10:00-16:00, off-season

12:00-15:00; occasional free English tours, tel. 33 41 81 41.)
This is particularly important if you've not seen the great
galleries of central Europe.

▲▲▲**Tivoli Gardens**—The world's most famous amusement park is 150 years old. It is 20 acres, 110,000 lanterns,
and countless ice cream cones of fun. You pay one 38 kr
admission price and find yourself lost in a Hans Christian
Andersen wonderland of rides, restaurants, games, marching
bands, roulette wheels, and funny mirrors. Tivoli is wonderfully Danish. It doesn't try to be Disney. (Open 10:00-24:00,
late April-mid-September, closed off-season, 27 kr entry until
13:00, all children's amusements in full swing 11:30-22:00; all
amusements open 13:30; events on the half hour 18:30-23:00;
concert in the concert hall at 19:30 for 40 kr-140 kr, tel. 33
15 10 01.) Go in with a full stomach or a discreet picnic (the
food inside is costly). If you must eat inside, there are cheap
Polser stands. **Faergekroen** is a good lakeside place for a
beer or some typical Danish food. The Yugoslavian restaurant, **Hercegovina**, is a decent value (110 kr buffet). For a
reasonable cake and coffee try the **Viften** café.

Pick up a map and schedule as you enter and locate a
billboard schedule of events (British flag for English). Free
concerts, mime, ballet, acrobats, puppets, and other shows
pop up all over the park, and a well-organized visitor can
enjoy an exciting evening of entertainment without spending
a single krone (though occasionally the schedule is a bit
sparse). If the Tivoli Symphony is playing, it's worth paying
for. Rides are reasonable, but the all-day pass for 160 kr is
probably best for those who may have been whirling der-
vishes in a previous life. On Wednesday, Friday, and Saturday the place closes down (at 23:45) with a fireworks show.
If you're taking an overnight train out of Copenhagen,
Tivoli (just across from the station) is the place to spend
your last Copenhagen hours.

▲▲**Rosenborg Castle**—This impressively furnished
Renaissance-style castle houses the Danish crown jewels and
500 years of royal knickknacks. It's musty with history. Pick
up and follow the 1 kr guide page. The castle is surrounded
by the royal gardens, a rare plant collection, and on sunny
days, a minefield of sunbathing Danish beauties. (35 kr, daily
June-August 10:00-16:00; May, September, and October

11:00-15:00; off-season Tuesday, Friday, and Sunday 11:00-14:00; there's no electricity inside so visit at a bright time, tel. 33 15 32 86, S-train: Norreport.) There is a daily changing of the guard mini-parade from Rosenborg Castle (at 11:30) to Amalienborg Castle (at 12:00).

▲**Denmark's Fight for Freedom Museum (Frihedsmuseet)**—The fascinating story of a heroic Nazi resistance struggle is well explained in English. (free, between the Queen's Palace and the Mermaid, daily May to mid-September 10:00-16:00, closed Mondays; off-season 11:00-15:00, tel. 33 13 77 14, bus #1, #6, or #9.)

▲▲▲**Stroget**—Copenhagen's 25-year-old experimental, tremendously successful, and most copied pedestrian shopping mall is a string of serendipitous streets and lovely squares from the city hall to Nyhavn. Spend some time browsing, people-watching, and exploring both here and along adjacent pedestrian-only streets. The commercial focus of an historic street like Stroget drives up the land value, which generally tears down the old buildings. While Stroget has become quite hamburgerized, charm lurks in many adjacent areas, such as nearby Grabrodtorv (Grey Brothers' Square). Straedet ("the street") is Copenhagen's newly pedestrianized street running parallel to Stroget on the water side. (For more on Stroget, see the Orientation Walk above.) Stroget is not an actual street but the popular name for a series of individually named streets. Many of the best night spots are just off Stroget. The best department stores (Illum's and Magazin, see below) are on Stroget.

▲**Copenhagen Walking Tour**—Once upon a time, American Richard Karpen visited Copenhagen and fell in love with the city (and one of its women). He gives daily 2-hour walking tours of his adopted home town covering its people, history, and the contemporary scene. His entertaining one-language walks (there are three covering different parts of the city center) leave daily (May-September) from in front of the TI (30 kr, pick up schedule at the TI or Use It, tel. 32 97 14 40). Richard and the local historian Helge Jacobsen (tel. 31 51 25 90) give reasonably priced private walks and tours.

▲▲**Harbor Cruise and Canal Tours**—Two companies offer basically the same live, four-language, 60-minute tours

through the city canals (2/hr, 10:00-17:00, later in July, May
to mid-September). They cruise around the palace and
Christianshavn area, into the wide open harbor, and out to
the Mermaid. Both leave from near Christiansborg Palace.
It's a pleasant way to see the Mermaid and take a load off
those weary sightseeing feet. Dress warm; boats are open-top.
    The low-overhead 15 kr Netto-Badene Tour boats (tel.
31 54 41 02) leave from Holmens Kirke across from the
Borsen (stock exchange) just over Knippels bridge. The competition, a 36 kr harbor tour with a cheaper unguided ride,
leaves from Gammel Strand near Christiansborg Palace and
National Museum, tel. 33 13 31 05. Don't be confused.
There's no reason to pay double for their tour. Boats can
also be boarded at Nyhavn.

▲**Vor Frelsers (Our Savior's) Church**—The church's bright
baroque interior is worth a look (free, daily June-August 9:00-
16:30, Sunday 13:00-16:30; closes an hour early in spring and
fall; off-season 10:00-13:30, tel. 31 57 27 98, bus #8). The
unique spiral spire that you'll admire from afar can be climbed
for a great city view and a good aerial view of the Christiania
commune below. It's 311 feet high, claims to have 400 steps,
costs 10 kr, and is closed through 1996 for restoration.

Christiania—This is a unique on-again, off-again social
experiment, a counterculture utopia attempt that is, to many,
disillusioning. An ultra-human mishmash of 1,000 idealists,
anarchists, hippies, dope fiends, non-materialists, and people
who dream only of being a Danish bicycle seat has established squatters' rights in a former military barracks (follow
the beer bottles and guitars down Prinsessegade behind Vor
Frelsers' spiral church spire in Christianshavn). This communal cornucopia of dogs, dirt, drugs, and dazed people—
or haven of peace, freedom, and no taxes, depending on your
perspective—is a political hot potato. No one in the establishment wants it—or has the nerve to mash it. While hard
drugs are out, hash and pot are sold openly (with senior discounts) and smoked happily.
    Past the souvenir and hash-vendor entry you'll find a
fascinating ramshackle world of moats and ramparts, alternative housing, unappetizing falafel stands, crispy hash browns,
a good restaurant (Spiseloppen), handicraft shops, and filth.
If you visit, make a point to get off the main "pusher street."

Christiania's most motley inhabitants are low-life vagabonds from other countries who hang out here in the summer. Now that Christiania is no longer a teenager, it's making an effort to connect better with the rest of society. The community is paying its utilities and even offering daily walking tours. Its free English/Dansk visitor's magazine, *Nitten* (available at Use It), is good reading, offering a serious explanation about how this unique community works/survives. It suggests several do-it-yourself walking tours.

Carlsberg Brewery Tour—Denmark's two beloved sources of legal intoxicants, Carlsberg and Tuborg, offer free 1-hour brewery tours followed by 30-minute "tasting sessions." Carlsberg tour: Monday-Friday 11:00 and 14:00 (bus #6 to 140 Ny Carlsberg Vej, tel. 33 27 13 14, ext. 1312). Tuborg tour: Monday-Friday 10:00, 12:30, and 14:30 (bus #6 to Strandvejen 54, Hellerup, tel. 33 27 22 12).

Museum of Erotica—This museum offers a chance to visit a porno shop and call it a museum. It took some digging, but they have documented a history of sex from Pompeii to present day. Visitors get a peep into the world of 19th-century Copenhagen prostitutes, a chance to read up on the sex lives of Martin Luther, Queen Elizabeth, Charlie Chaplin, Casanova (and others), and the arguably artistic experience of watching the "electric tabernakel," (12 busy but silent screens of porn to the accompaniment of classical music). Not worth the 45 kr entry fee but better than the Amsterdam equivalents, just past Tivoli at Vesterbrogade 31, daily 10:00-23:00 May-September; 12:00-18:00 the rest of the year, tel. 33 12 03 11). For the real thing—and free—wander Copenhagen's dreary little red-light district along Istedgade behind the train station.

Hovedbanegarden—The great Copenhagen train station is a fascinating mesh of Scandimanity and transportation efficiency. Even if you're not a train traveler, check it out (fuller description in Orientation, above).

Other Sights to Consider

Torvaldsens Museum (free, next to Christiansborg Palace, 10:00-17:00, closed Monday) features the early 18th-century work of Denmark's greatest sculptor. The noontime **changing of the guard** at the Amalienborg Palace is boring:

except for a parade, all they change is places. **Nyhavn**, with its fine old ships, tattoo shops (pop into Tattoo Ole at #17—fun photos, very traditional), and jazz clubs, is a wonderful place to hang out. Copenhagen's **Open Air Folk Museum** is a park filled with traditional Danish architecture and folk culture (30 kr, S-train to Sorgenfri, open April-October 10:00-17:00, closed Monday; shorter hours off-season, tel. 42 85 02 92). Organized **bus tours** of the city leave from the Town Hall Square (1½-3 hrs, 110 kr-160 kr). The Danes gather at Copenhagen's other great amusement park, **Bakken** (free, daily April-August 14:00-24:00, 30-minutes by S-train to Klampenborg, tel. 31 63 73 00).

If you don't have time to get to the idyllic island of Aero (covered in my Scandinavia guidebook), consider a trip to the tiny fishing village of **Dragor** (30 minutes on bus #30 or #33 from Copenhagen's City Hall Square).

Nightlife

For the latest on Copenhagen's hopping jazz scene, pick up the *Copenhagen Jazz Guide* at the TI or the more "alternative" *Playtime* magazine at Use It.

Shopping

Copenhagen's colorful **flea market** (summer Saturdays 8:00-14:00 at Israels Plads) is small but feisty and surprisingly cheap. An antique market enlivens Nybrogade (near the palace) every Friday and Saturday. Other flea markets are listed in *Copenhagen This Week*. The city's top department stores (Illum at 52 Ostergade, tel. 33 14 40 02, and Magasin at 13 Kongens Nytorv, tel. 33 11 44 33) offer a good, if expensive, look at today's Denmark. Both are on Stroget and have fine cafeterias on their top floors.

Danes shop cheaper at Daell's Varehus (corner of Krystalgade and Fiolstraede). At UFF on Kultorvet you can buy newly new clothes for peanuts and support charity. Just across Vesterbrogade from Tivoli, Scala is a new glitzy mishmash of 45 shops, lots of eateries, and entertainment. Survey Scala from its bubble elevator. Shops are open Monday-Friday 9:30/10:00-18:00/19:00; Saturday 9:00-14:00.

The department stores and the Politiken Bookstore on the Radhus Square have a good selection of maps and

English travel guides. If you buy over 600 kr ($100) worth of stuff, you can get the 25 percent VAT (MOMS in Danish) tax back (if you buy from a shop displaying the Danish Tax-Free Shopping emblem). If you have your purchase mailed, the tax can be deducted from your bill. Call 32 52 55 66, see the shopping-oriented *Copenhagen This Week*, or ask a merchant for specifics.

Sleeping in Copenhagen
(7 kr = about $1)

I've listed the best budget hotels in the center (with doubles for 400 kr-600 kr with breakfast), rooms in private homes an easy bus ride or 15-minute walk from the station (around 330 kr per double with breakfast), and the dormitory options (100 kr per person with breakfast). Unless noted, breakfast is included in the price.

Sleep code: **S**=Single, **D**=Double/Twin, **T**=Triple, **Q**=Quad, **B**=Bath/Shower, **WC**=Toilet, **CC**=Credit Card (**V**isa, **M**astercard, **A**mex).

Hotel Sankt Jorgen has big, friendly-feeling rooms with plain old wood furnishings. Brigitte and Susan offer a warm welcome and a great value (S-300 kr-350 kr, D-400 kr-450 kr, 3rd person 100 kr-125 kr extra, prices flex with the demand; breakfast served in your room, elevator, a 12-minute walk from the station or catch bus #13 to the first stop after the lake; Julius Thomsensgade 22, DK-1632 Copenhagen V, tel. 35 37 15 11, fax 35 37 11 97).

Ibsen's Hotel is a rare simple bath-down-the-hall, cheery, and central budget hotel, run by three women (there's really only two) who treat you like you're paying top dollar. (S-420 kr, D-600 kr, 3rd person-150 kr, CC: VMA, no elevator, lots of stairs; Vendersgade 23, DK 1363, tel. 33 13 19 13, fax 33 13 19 16, bus #16 or S-train: Norreport.)

Hotel KFUM Soldaterhjem, originally for soldiers, is on the fifth floor with no elevators (S-195 kr, D-310 kr without breakfast; Gothersgade 115, Copenhagen K, tel. 33 15 40 44). The reception is on the first floor up (open 8:30-23:00, weekends 15:00-23:00) next to a budget cafeteria.

Cab-Inn Copenhagen (S-395 kr, D-480 kr, T-565 kr, Q-650 kr, Danasvej 32-34, 1910 Frederiksberg C, tel.

31 21 04 00, fax 31 21 74 09, 5 minutes on bus #29 to center) is a radical innovation: 86 identical tiny but luxurious cruise ship-type staterooms, all bright and shiny with TV, video player, coffee pot, shower, and toilet. Each room has a single bed that expands into a comfortable double with 1 or 2 fold-down bunks on the walls. Breakfast, 35 kr; easy parking, 30 kr. The staff will hardly give you the time of day, but it's hard to argue with this efficiency. **Cab-Inn Scandinavia** is its twin, 400 meters away (tel. 35 36 11 11).

Hotel 9 Sma Hjem (DBWC-450 kr, CC:VMA, Classensgade 40, DK-2100 Copenhagen O, tel. 35 26 16 47, fax 35 43 17 84, 12 minutes on bus #40 from the station) is also good.

The Excelsior Hotel (DBWC-650 kr-865 kr in July and August, 4 Colbjornsensgade, DK-1652, tel. 31 24 50 85, fax 31 24 50 87) is a big, mod, tour group hotel a block behind the station. Some people like it.

Sleeping in Rooms in Private Homes

Here are a few leads for Copenhagen's best accommodation values. While each TI has its own list of B&Bs, by booking direct, you'll save yourself and your host the tourist office fee. Always call ahead. Each family speaks English.

Sleeping in Rooms in Private Homes in Christianshavn

This area is a never-a-dull-moment hodgepodge of the chic, artistic, hippie, and hobo, with beer-drinking Greenlanders littering streets in the shadow of fancy government ministries. It's handy with lots of shops, cafés, and canals, a 10-minute walk to the center, and good bus connections to the airport and downtown.

Annette and Rudy Hollender enjoy sharing their 300-year-old home with my readers. Even with sinkless rooms and three rooms sharing one toilet/shower, it's a comfortable and cheery place to call home (S-210 kr, D-270 kr, T-400 kr, breakfast-40 kr, Wildersgade 19, 1408 Copenhagen K, tel. 31 95 96 22, fax 31 57 24 86, after June 1995 tel. 32 95 96 22, fax 32 57 24 86). Take bus #9 from the airport, bus #8 from the station, or bus #2 from the City Hall. From downtown, push the button immediately after crossing Knippels Bridge, and turn left off Torvegade down Wildersgade. If Annette's place is full, she runs a network of about 20 rooms, all at the same price in this charming locale. If you have any personality quirks, she loves to play match-maker.

Morten Frederiksen, a laid-back, ponytailed sort of guy, runs a mod-funky-pleasant loft. It's a clean, comfy, good look at today's hip Danish lifestyle and has a great location right on Christianshavn's main drag (D-250 kr, 2 minutes from Annette's, Torvegade 36, tel. 31 95 32 73, after June 1995 tel. 32 95 32 73).

Solveig Diderichsen rents three rooms (D-270 kr, 3rd person-100 kr) from her comfortable home. She serves no breakfast, but offers kitchen facilities and a good bakery around the corner. Her high-ceilinged, ground-floor apartment is in a quiet embassy neighborhood behind the Oster Anlaeg park (three stops on the subway from the central station, to Osterport, then a 3-minute walk, or bus #6 or #1 from Vesterbrogade near the station, or bus #9 direct from the airport, Upsalagade 26, DK-2100, tel. 35 43 22 70 or 31 38 39 58).

Annette Haugballe rents four modern, comfortable rooms in the quiet, green, and residential Frederiksberg area (S-160 kr, D-250 kr, easy parking, Hoffmeyersvej 33, 2000 Frederiksberg, Copenhagen, tel. 31 74 87 87, on bus line #1 from station or city hall square, and near Peter Bangsvej S subway station). She also has friends who rent rooms.

Sleeping near the Amalienborg Palace

This is a stately embassy neighborhood—no stress but a bit bland. It's very safe, and you can look out your window to see the queen's place (and the guards changing), which is a 10-minute walk north of Nyhavn and Stroget. **Puk De La Cour** (D-250 kr with no breakfast but tea, coffee and a kitchen, family room available, Amaliegade 34, fourth floor, tel. 33 12 04 68) rents two rooms in her mod, bright, and easygoing house. Puk (pook)'s friend, **Line Voutsinos** (Amaliegade 34, 3rd floor, tel. 33 14 71 42), offers a similar deal.

Sleeping in Flats for Hire

Many Copenhagen residents head for their country bungalows in the summer and hire an agency to rent out their homes for a minimum of three nights. These places are mostly in the center of town, completely furnished with a kitchen and the lived-in works (TV, stereo, washer and dryer, and so on) and are a particularly good deal for families or small groups who would trade away the B&B friendliness for the privacy of this less personal alternative. **H.A.Y.4U** (near Stroget at Kronprinsensgade 10, 114 Copenhagen K, tel. 33 33 08 05, fax 33 32 08 04) takes drop-ins, but recommends that you reserve a month in advance. Rates vary from 300 kr a day for 1-bedroom places to 500 kr per day for four-person places.

Sleeping in Youth Hostels

Copenhagen energetically accommodates the young vagabond on a shoestring. The Use It office is your best source of information. Each of these places charges about 100 kr per person for bed and breakfast. Some don't allow sleeping bags, and if you don't have your own hostel bedsheet, you'll normally have to rent one for around 25 kr. IYHF hostels require a membership card, but will normally sell you a "guest pass" for 22 kr.

The modern **Copenhagen Hostel** (IYHF) is huge, with fifty 170-kr doubles and 85 5-bed dorms, no curfew, excellent facilities, cheap meals, and a self-serve laundry. Unfortunately, it's on the edge of town, bus #16 from the station to Mozartplads, then #37 or #38 (200 Vejlands Alle/Sjaellandsbroen 55, 2300 Copenhagen S, tel. 32 52 29 08).

The grungy **City Public Hostel** with 200 beds in one big room and open to all from mid-May to August (8 Absalonsgade, tel. 31 31 20 70) has only one advantage: it's a short walk from the station.

KFUK/KFUM (Danish YMCA/YWCA) has a great location in the pedestrian center with 4- to 6-bed rooms partitioned out of a big hall (July to mid-August only, closed 12:00-14:30, and at 24:00; Kannikestraede 19, behind Grabrodretorv just off Stroget, tel. 33 11 30 31,). There's a similar Y at Valdemarsgade 15 (tel. 31 31 15 74).

The Sleep-In is popular with the desperate or adventurous (July-August, 4-bed cubicles in a huge 452-bed coed room, no curfew, pretty wild, lockers, always has room; Per Henrik Lings Alle 6, tel. 35 26 50 59, S-train A, B, or C to Nordhavn near the Mermaid). Sleeping bag required. No curfew. Free rubbers. In the summer, **Jorgensens Hotel** rents beds to backpackers in small dorms (near Norreport, Romersgade 11, tel. 33 13 81 86, fax 33 15 51 05.)

Eating in Copenhagen

Copenhagen's many good restaurants are well listed by category in *Copenhagen This Week*. Since restaurant prices include 25 percent tax plus a 15 percent tip, your budget may require alternatives. These survival ideas for the hungry budget traveler in Copenhagen will save lots of money.

Picnics

Irma (in arcade next to Tivoli) and **Brugsen** are the two largest supermarket chains. **Netto** and **Aldi** are cut-rate outfits with the cheapest prices. The little grocery store in the central station (daily 8:00-24:00) is picnic-friendly.

Viktualiehandler (small delis) and bakeries, found on nearly every corner, sell fresh bread, tasty pastries (a *wienerbrod* is what we call a "Danish"), juice, milk, cheese, and yogurt (tall liter boxes, drinkable). Liver paste (*postej*) is cheap and a little better than it sounds.

Smorrebrod

Denmark's famous open-face sandwiches cost a fortune in restaurants, but the many smorrebrod shops sell them for 8 kr-26 kr. Drop into one of these often no-name, family-run budget savers, and get several elegant OFSs to go. The tradition calls for three sandwich courses: herring first, then meat, then cheese. It makes for a classy—and cheap—picnic. Downtown you'll find these handy local alternatives to Yankee fast food chains: **Centrum** (6 C. Vesterbrogade, 24 hours a day, across from station and Tivoli), **City Smorrebrod** (12 Gronnegade, open 8:00-14:00, closed Saturday and Sunday, near Kongens Nytorv), **Domhusets Smorrebrod** (18 Kattesundet, Monday-Friday 7:00-14:30), **Sorgenfri** (just off the Stroget, 8 Brolaeggerstraede, Monday-Friday 11:00-14:00), one in a basement 30 meters from Riz Raz, and one at the corner of Magstraede and Radhusstraede

(Monday-Friday, 7:00-14:30, next to Huset/Use It). There is one in Nyhavn, on the corner of Holbergsgade and Peder Skram Gade.

The Polse
The famous Danish hot dog, sold in *polsevogn* (sausage wagons) throughout the city, is one of the few typically Danish institutions to resist the onslaught of our global fast-food culture. They are fast, cheap, tasty, easy to order ("hot dog" is a Danish word for weenie, study the photo menu for variations), and almost worthless nutritionally. Still the local "dead man's finger" is the dog kids love to bite.

By hanging around a *polsevognen* you can study this institution. It's a form of social care: only difficult-to-employ people, such as the handicapped, are licensed to run these wienermobiles. As they gain seniority they are promoted to more central locations. Danes gather here for munchies and *polsesnak* (sausage talk), the local slang for empty chatter.

Inexpensive Restaurants
Riz-Raz (around the corner from Use It at 20 Kompagnistraede) serves a healthy all-you-can eat Mediterranean buffet, 40 kr lunch (daily 11:00-17:00), and an even bigger 60 kr dinner buffet (until 23:00), which has got to be the best deal in town. And they're happy to serve free water with your meal. Department stores (especially the top floor of **Illums**, an elegant circus of reasonable food under a glass dome, **Magasin**, or **Daell's Varehus** at Norregade 12) serve cheery, reasonable meals.

Fast food joints are everywhere. Look for all-you-can-eat pizza and salad bars. **Alexander's Pizza Bar** serves all the pizza and salad you can stand for 40 kr, but they charge 8 kr for a glass of tap water (just off Stroget, between the Frue Church and the Round Tower at Lille Kannikestr 5, daily 12:00-22:30, avoid the late crowds, tel. 33 12 55 36). **Det Lille Apotek** (across the street from Alexander's) is a reasonable, candle-lit place popular with local students. Nearby on Larsbjornsstrade (a hip and colorful, trendy street), **Istanbul Pizza** sells delicious 10 kr/slice pizza.

Koldt Bord

For a fun, affordable way to explore your way through a world of traditional Danish food, try a Danish smorgasbord (an all-you-can-eat buffet). The handiest is the famous Koldt Bord at the central station's **Bistro Restaurant** (130 kr dinner, served daily 11:30-21:30, tel. 33 14 12 32). As their ad brags, "There are more specialties than you can overcome." Use a new plate with each course. The food is laid out chronologically. Start opposite the desserts and work your way through pickled herring, cold cuts, soup, hot meat and vegetables, cheese, and dessert. They also offer a special daily dinner plate for 50 kr-60 kr and happily serve free tap water.

Good Eating in Christianshavn

Cafe Wilder (corner of Wildersgade and Skt Annae Gade, a block off Torvegade) serves creative and hearty dinner salads by candle light to a trendy local clientele. To avoid having to choose just one of their interesting salads, try their three salads plate (55 kr with bread). They also feature a budget dinner plate for around 60 kr and are happy to serve free water. Across the street, the **Luna Cafe** is also good.

Locals like the **La Novo** Italian restaurant (Torvegade 49), where the 50 kr lasagna is a meal in itself. The **Cibi E Vini** take-out deli (Torvegade 28, near the bridge, daily 10:00-18:00, Saturday 10:00-14:00) serves take-out sandwiches and pastas. Right on the community square, you'll find a huge grocery store, fruit stands under the Greenlanders monument, and a great bakery (at the bus stop, Torvegade 45). The **Ravelin Restaurant** (Torvegade 79) serves good traditional Danish-style food at reasonable prices to happy local crowds on a lovely lakeside terrace (only on sunny days).

Eating Downtown

Parnas (live piano sing-song almost every night at 21:30, Lille Kongensgade 4, tel. 33 12 12 24) and **Skindbuksen** (Lille Kongensgade 4, tel. 33 12 90 37) are both cozy, atmospheric, dark, reasonable, popular with locals, and just off Stroget. **Vin and Olgod** (Skindergade 45, 19:00-02:00, closed Sunday and Monday, tel. 33 13 26 25) is the place to go for old-time sing, dance, eat, and drink rowdiness. For an idyllic wooded break from the city, in the city, find **Rob-erta's Cafe** for hearty pita salads (in the northeast corner of Orsteds Park).

Transportation Connections

Copenhagen to: Hillerod/Frederiksborg (40/day, 30 min), **Louisiana** (Helsinger train to Humlebaek, 40/day, 30 min), **Roskilde** (16/day, 30 min), **Odense** (16/day, 3 hrs), **Helsingor** (ferry to Sweden, 40/day, 30 min), **Stockholm** (8/day, 8 hrs), **Oslo** (4/day, 10 hrs), **Vaxjo** (via Alvesta, 6/day, 5 hrs), **Kalmar** (6/day, via Alvesta and Vaxjo, 7 hrs), **Berlin** (via Gedser, 2/day, 9 hrs), **Amsterdam** (2/day, 11 hrs), **Frankfurt/Rhine** (4/day, 10 hrs).

Cheaper **bus trips** are listed at Use It. All Norway and Sweden trains go right onto the Helsingor-Helsingborg ferry. The crossing and reservation are included on any train ticket. There are convenient overnight trains from Copenhagen directly to Stockholm, Oslo, Berlin, Amsterdam, and Frankfurt.

A quickie cruise from Copenhagen to Oslo:
A luxurious cruise ship leaves daily from Copenhagen (departs 17:00, returns 9:15 two days later; 16 hours sailing each way and 7 hours in Norway's capital). Special packages give you a bed in a double cabin, a fine dinner, and two smorgasbord breakfasts for around $200 in summer. Cheaper on Sunday-Thursday departures and after August 22. Call DFDS Scandinavian Seaways (tel. 33 15 76 96). It's easy to make a reservation in the U.S.A. (tel. 800/5DF-DS56).

STOCKHOLM

If I had to call one European city home, it would be Stockholm. Surrounded by water and woods, bubbling with energy and history, Sweden's stunning capital is green, clean, and underrated.

Crawl through Europe's best-preserved old warship and relax on a canal boat tour. Browse the cobbles and antique shops of the lantern-lit old town and take a spin through Skansen, Europe's first and best open-air folk museum. Marvel at Stockholm's glittering city hall, modern department stores, art museums, and futuristic suburbs.

While progressive and sleek, Stockholm respects its heritage. Throughout the summer, mounted bands parade each noontime through the heart of town from Nybroplan to the royal palace, announcing the changing of the guard and turning even the most dignified tourist into a scampering kid. The Gamla Stan (Old Town) celebrates the Midsummer festivities (late June) with the down-home vigor of a rural village, forgetting that it's the core of a gleaming 20th-century metropolis. Stockholm also goes wild during its "Water Festival" (10 days in early August).

Planning Your Time

On a 2- to 3-week trip through Scandinavia, Stockholm is worth 2 days. Efficient train travelers sleep in and out for 2 days in the city with only one night in a hotel. (Copenhagen and Oslo trains arrive at about 8:00 and depart at about 23:00.) To be even more cheap and efficient, you could use the luxury Stockholm-Helsinki as your hotel for two nights (spending a day in Helsinki) and have 2 days in Stockholm without a hotel (e.g. Copenhagen; night train Stockholm, day in Stockholm; night boat Helsinki, day in Helsinki; night boat Stockholm, day in Stockholm; night train Oslo). That may sound crazy, but it gives you 3 interesting and inexpensive days of travel fun. Spend 2 days in Stockholm this way:
Day 1: Arrive by train (or the night before by car), do station chores (reserve next ride, change money, pick up map, "This Week," and a Stockholm Card at the Hotellcentralens TI), check into hotel. At 9:30 catch 1-hour English tour on

Sweden

the Tourist Line bus; 11:00 tour Wasa warship, picnic;
13:00 tour Nordic Museum; 15:00 Skansen; catch 16:00
open-air folk museum tour; 19:00 folk dancing, possible
smorgasbord and evening popular dancing. Or wander
Gamla Stan in the evening.
Day 2: Do the 10:00 city hall tour, climb the city hall tower
for a fine view; 12:00 catch the changing of the guard at the
palace, tour royal palace or explore Gamla Stan, picnic on
1-hour city boat tour; 16:00 browse the modern city center
around Kungstradgarden, Sergels Torg, Hotorget market
and indoor food hall, and Drottninggatan area.

Orientation (tel. code: 08)
Greater Stockholm's 1.4 million residents live on 14 islands,
which are woven together by fifty bridges. Visitors need only
concern themselves with five islands: **Norrmalm** (downtown,

with most hotels, shopping areas, and the train station),
Gamla Stan (the old city of winding lantern-lit streets,
antique shops, and classy glassy cafés clustered around the
royal palace), **Sodermalm** (aptly called Stockholm's
Brooklyn, residential and untouristy), **Skeppsholmen** (the
small, very central traffic-free park island with the Modern
Art Museum and two fine youth hostels), and **Djurgarden**
(literally "deer garden," Stockholm's wonderful green playground, with many of the city's top sights).

Tourist Information
Hotellcentralen is primarily a room-finding service (in the
central train station), but its friendly staff adequately handles
all your sightseeing and transportation questions. This is the
place for anyone arriving by train to arrange accommodations, buy the Tourist Card, and pick up free brochures, city
map, *Stockholm This Week* (which lists opening hours and
directions to all the sights and special events), and brochures
on whatever else you need (city walks, parking, jazz boats,
excursions, bus routes, shopping, etc.). While *This Week* has
a decent map, the 14 kr map covers more area and bus

Greater Stockholm

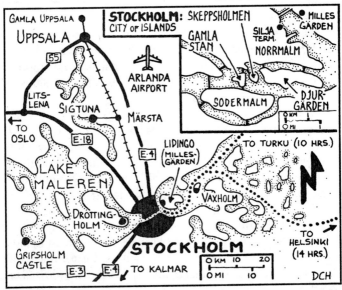

routes. It's worth the extra money if you'll be using the buses. (Open daily June-August 7:00-21:00; May and September 8:00-19:00, shorter hours off-season; tel. 08/240880, fax 791-8666.)

Sweden House (*Sverige Huset*), Stockholm's official tourist information office (a short walk from the station on Kungstradgarden), is very good but usually more crowded than the Hotellcentralen. They've got pamphlets on everything; an "excursion shop" for transportation, day trip and bus tour information, and tickets; and an English library and reading room upstairs with racks of 1 kr information on various aspects of Swedish culture and one state's attempt at cradle-to-grave happiness. (Open June-August, 8:00-18:00, Saturday-Sunday 9:00-17:00; off-season 9:00-18:00, Saturday-Sunday 9:00-15:00; Hamngatan 27, tel. 08/789-2490 for info, 789-2415 for tickets; T-bana: Kungstradgarden.)

Getting Into and Around Stockholm

Arriving at the Train Station
Stockholm's central train station (information tel. toll free in Sweden 020/757575 for trains within Sweden, 227940 for international train info) is a wonderland of services, shops, and people going places. The Interrail Center kiosk in the center is for general help (especially for young travelers). The Hotellcentralen TI is as good as the city TI nearby. There is a Viking Line office if you're sailing to Finland. The ForEx long-hours exchange counter changes traveler's checks for only a 15 kr fee. The Tourist Line bus stops immediately in front of the station.

Parking in Stockholm
Only a Swedish meatball would drive his car in Stockholm. Park it and use the public transit. But parking is confusing, a major hassle, and expensive. Unguarded lots generally aren't safe. Take everything into your hotel, or hostel or pay for a garage. The tourist office has a "Parking in Stockholm" brochure. Those hosteling on Skeppsholmen feel privileged with their 25 kr-a-day island parking passes. Those with the Stockholm Card can park free in a big central garage or at any meter for the duration of the ticket.

Ask for your parking card and specifics when you get your Stockholm Card. There's a safe and reasonable (10 kr per day) garage at Ropsten—the last subway station (near the Silja line terminal). Those sailing to Finland can solve all parking worries by long-term parking on arrival in Stockholm at either terminal's safe and reasonable parking lot (60 kr per day).

Public Transportation

The complete hostess, Stockholm complements her many sightseeing charms with great information services, a fine bus and subway system, and special passes to take the bite out of the city's cost (or at least limit it to one vicious budgetary gash).

Buses and the subway system work on the same tickets. Ignore the zones since everything I mention (except Drottningholm and Carl Millesgarden) are in zone one. Each 13 kr ticket is valid for 1 hour (10-packs cost 85 kr). The subway, called T-bana or tunnelbana, gets you where you want to go very quickly. Ride it just for the futuristic drama of being a human mole (transit info tel. 600-1000). The *"Tourist Card"* (free run of all public transport; 24 hrs/60 kr, 72 hrs/115 kr, sold at TIs and newsstands) is not necessary if you're getting the Stockholm card (see below). The 72-hour pass includes the harbor ferry and admission to Skansen, Grona Lund, and the Kaknas Tower.

The handy **Tourist Line Bus Route** runs mid-June to mid-August, and does a figure-eight, stopping at each of Stockholm's 15 major sights (Swedish-language departures every 15 minutes, English-language tours hourly, schedule in Stockholm Card booklet). You can get off and on as you please to "do the circuit" at your leisure. It's free with the Stockholm Card (40 kr without). Do the entire 50-minute circuit in English for a cheap, easy overview.

It seems too good to be true, but each year I pinch myself and the **Stockholm Card** is still there. This 24-hour 175 kr pass (sold at TIs and ship terminals) gives you free run of all public transit, free use of the Tourist Line Bus, free entry to virtually every sight (71 places), free 1-hour city boat tours, free parking, a handy sightseeing handbook, and the substantial pleasure of doing everything without considering the cost (many of Stockholm's sights are worth the time but not the steep individual ticket costs). This pays for itself if you do Skansen, the Wasa, and the short boat tour. If you enter Skansen on your 24th hour (and head right for the 30 kr aquarium) you get a few extra hours. (Parents get an added bonus: two children under 18, go along for free with each adult pass.)

Harbor Shuttle Ferries

Throughout the summer, ferries connect Stockholm's two most interesting sightseeing districts. They sail from Nybroplan and Slussen to Djurgarden, landing next to the Vasa and Skansen (15 kr, every 20 min).

Stockholm Center

Sights—Downtown Stockholm

▲**Kungstradgarden**—The King's Garden square is the downtown people-watching center. Watch the life-sized game of chess and enjoy the free concerts at the bandstand. Surrounded by the Sweden House, the NK department store, the harborfront, and tour boats, it's the place to feel Stockholm's pulse (with discretion).

▲▲**Sergels Torg**—The heart of modern Stockholm, between Kungstradgarden and the station, is worth a wander. Enjoy the colorful and bustling underground mall and dip into the Gallerien mall. Visit the Kulturhuset, a center for reading, relaxing, and socializing designed for normal people (but welcoming tourists) with music, exhibits, hands-on fun, and an insight into contemporary Sweden. (Free, daily 11:00-17:00, often later, tel. 700-0100.) From Sergels Torg walk up the pedestrian mall, Drottninggatan to Hotorget (see Eating).

▲▲**City Hall**—The Stadshuset is an impressive mix of 8 million bricks, 19 million chips of gilt mosaic, and lots of Stockholm pride. One of Europe's most impressive modern (1923) buildings and site of the Nobel Prize banquet, it's particularly enjoyable and worthwhile for its entertaining tours (30 kr, daily June-August at 10:00, 11:00, 12:00, and 14:00; off season at 10:00 and 12:00, tel. 785-9074, just behind the station, bus #48 or #62). Climb the 350-foot tower for the best possible city view (10:00-16:30, May-September only, 10 kr or free with City Hall ticket). The City Hall also has a TI and a good cafeteria with 55 kr lunches.

▲**Orientation Views**—Try to get a bird's-eye perspective on this wonderful urban mix of water, parks, concrete, and people from the City Hall tower (see above), the Kaknäs Tower (at 500 feet, the tallest building in Scandinavia, 20 kr, May-August 9:00-22:00, tel. 667-8030, bus #69 from Nybroplan or Sergels Torg), the observatory in Skansen, or the top of the Katarina elevator (5 kr, near Slussen subway stop, then walk behind Katarinavagen through classy homes and grand views).

▲**Mini-Orientation Bus Tour**—For a quick big-bus orientation tour, consider those that leave from the Royal Opera House (75 kr, 50 min, 10:00, 11:00, 12:00, 14:00, 15:00, mid-June to late-August, tel. 411 70 23). They also organize 75-minute old town walks (75 kr). For a free self-guided tour, follow the walk laid out in the Stockholm *This Week* publication.

▲**City Boat Tour**—For a good floating look at Stockholm, and a pleasant break, consider a sightseeing cruise. Tour boats leave regularly from in front of the Grand Hotel (tel. 23 33 75). The Historical Stockholm tour (70 kr, 1 hr, departing on the hour 10:00-16:00, late June to mid-August) offers the best informative introduction. The "Under the Bridges" tour (120 kr, 2 hrs, May-September) is basically the first tour with an hour of extra territory. The "Royal Canal" tour (70 kr, 1 hr, mid-May to mid-September) is a scenic joyride through lots of greenery. Their 1-hour tours are free with the Stockholm Card.

▲**National Museum**—It's mediocre by European standards, but small, central, uncrowded, and very user-friendly. The highlights are several Rembrandts, Rubens, a fine group of impressionists, works by the popular and good-to-get-to-know local artists Carl Larsson and Anders Zorn, and some Russian icons. (40 kr, free on Friday, open 11:00-17:00, Tuesday 11:00-20:00, closed Monday; August some Tuesdays until 18:00 because of special concerts, tel. 666-4250).

Museum of Modern Art—This bright and cheery gallery is as far out as can be, with Picasso, Braque, and lots of goofy dada art (such as the *Urinal* and the *Goat with Tire*). It's in a pleasant park on Skeppsholmen. (30 kr, free Thursday, open Tuesday-Friday 11:00-21:00, Saturday-Sunday 11:00-17:00, closed Monday).

Sights—Stockholm's Gamla Stan (Old Town)

▲▲**Gamla Stan**—Stockholm's old island core is charming, fit for a film, and full of antique shops, street lanterns, painted ceilings, and surprises. Spend some time here, browse, enjoy a café, or get to know a shopkeeper. At the tip of the island is Slussen (Swedish for "locks"), where the salty Baltic meets the 1½-foot-higher Lake Malaren (with water so fresh that local politicians brush their teeth with it).

Military Parade—Starting at the Army Museum (daily at 12:00, Sunday at 13:00), the parade culminates at the Royal Palace for the changing of the guard.

▲▲**Royal Palace**—The stately exterior encloses 608 rooms (locals brag that's one more than Britain's Buckingham Palace) of glittering baroque and rococo decor. There are eight different sights with separate admissions here. Most important are the apartments (30 kr, Tuesday-Saturday 10:00-15:00, Sunday and Monday 12:00-15:00; May-August 12:00-15:00, closed Monday the rest of the year). The Royal

Treasury is another ticket (25 kr, similar hours, no samples, tel. 789-8500).

Riksdag—You can tour Sweden's parliament buildings if you'd like a firsthand look at its government. (Free hourly tours in English throughout the summer, usually Monday-Friday at 12:30 and 14:00; off-season at 13:30, but call 786-4000 to confirm).

Museum of Medieval Stockholm (30 kr, July-August 11:00-16:00, Tuesday, Wednesday, Thursday until 18:00; September-June 11:00-16:00, closed Monday; the 5 kr English guide flier is not necessary since the exhibits are well-described in English, enter from the park in front of the Parliament), while grade-schoolish, gives you the best look at medieval Stockholm. The Stromparterren park, with its Carl Milles statue of the "Sun Singer" greeting the day is a pleasant place for a sightseeing break (but an expensive place for a potty break—use the free WC in the museum).

Riddarholm Church—This final resting place for about 600 years of Sweden's royalty is pretty lifeless (10 kr, May-August 10:00-15:00, Sunday 12:00-15:00, less in September, tel. 789-8500).

Sights—Stockholm's Djurgarden

▲▲▲**Skansen**—Europe's original and best open-air folk museum, Skansen is a huge park gathering over 150 historic buildings (homes, churches, schoolhouses, etc.) transplanted from all corners of Sweden. Tourists can explore this Swedish culture on a lazy Susan, seeing folk crafts in action and wonderfully furnished old interiors. In the town quarter (top of the escalator), potters, glassblowers (especially important if you'll be missing Sweden's glass country to the south), and other craftspeople are busy doing their traditional thing in a re-created Old World Stockholm.

Spreading out from there, the sprawling park is designed to show northern Swedish culture and architecture in its north (top of the park map) and southern Sweden in the south. Excellent, free 1-hour guided walks (from Bollnastorget info stand at top of escalator) paint a fine picture of old Swedish lifestyles (usually daily at 13:00 and 16:00 June-August). There's folk dancing daily in summer at 19:00, Sunday at 14:30 and 16:00, and public dancing to live bands nightly (20:30-23:30, call for evening theme—jazz, folk, rock, or disco). The Aquarium (50 kr, 10:00-20:00) is the only admission not covered on your entry ticket.

Kids love Skansen, especially its zoo (ride a life-size wooden Dala-horse and stare down a hedgehog) and Lill' Skansen (Punch 'n' Judy, mini-train, and pony ride fun daily from 10:30 till at least 16:00). There are lots of special events and several restaurants. The main restaurant serves a grand smorgasbord (135 kr). The Ekorren café offers the least-expensive self-service lunches with a view, but the Stora Gun-gan Krog (country inn) at the top of the escalator has better food (60 kr indoor or outdoor lunches with a salad bar).

Skansen is great for people-watching and picnicking, with open and covered benches all over (especially at Torslunden and Bollnastorget, where peacenik local toddlers don't bump on the bumper cars). Consider the 5 kr map or the 30 kr mus-eum guidebook which has the same map, and check the live crafts schedule (*"Oppet I Hus Och Garder,"* strangely in Swedish only) at the information stand at the top of the escalator or at Bollnastorget to confirm your Skansen plans.

Depart by the west entrance (Hazeliusporten) if you're heading for the Nordic Museum. Open May-August 9:00-22:00 (buildings 11:00-17:00); winter 9:00-17:00 (buildings 11:00-15:00). 50 kr entry, 30 kr in winter. (Bus #44, #47, or the Tourist Line, tel. 442-8250 for recorded schedule in Swedish, or 442-8000 for the day's tour, music, and dance schedule.) You can miss Grona Lund, the second-rate amusement park across the street.

▲▲▲Vasa—Stockholm turned a titanic flop into one of Scandinavia's great sightseeing attractions. This glamorous but unseaworthy warship sank 20 minutes into her 1628 maiden voyage. Top-heavy with a tacked on extra cannon deck, a breeze caught the sails and blew it over in the Stockholm harbor. After 333 years, it rose again from the deep (with the help of marine archaeologists), and today is the best-preserved ship of its kind anywhere, housed in a state-of-the-art museum. The masts on the roof are placed to show the actual size of the ship.

Catch the 25-minute English-subtitled movie (at the top of each hour, dubbed versions often play at 11:30 and 13:30), and for more information, take the free 25-minute

English tours (at the bottom of each hour from 10:30, every other hour off-season) to best enjoy and understand the ship. Learn about ship's rules (bread can't be older than 8 years), why it sank (heavy bread?), how it's preserved, and so on. Private tours are easy to freeload on, but the displays are so well described that a tour is hardly necessary. (45 kr, open daily mid-June to mid-August 9:30-19:00; off-season 10:00-17:00, winter on Wednesday until 20:00, tel. 666-4800). Take bus #44 or #47 just past the big brick Nordic Museum and catch the boat or walk from Skansen.

▲▲**Nordic Museum**—This museum, built to look like a Danish palace, offers a look at how Sweden lived over the last 500 years. Highlights include the Food and Drink section with its stunning china and crystal table settings, the Nordic folk art (second and third floors), the huge statue of Gustav Wasa, father of modern Sweden, by Carl Milles (top of second flight of stairs), and the Sami (Lapp) exhibit in the basement. (Open 11:00-17:00, Thursday until 20:00, closed Monday, tel. 666-4600). Worth your time if you have the Stockholm card, but it's over-priced at 50 kr admission. The 30 kr guidebook isn't necessary, but pick up the English brochure at the entrance.

▲**Thielska Galleriet**—If you liked the Larsson and Zorn art in the National Gallery and/or if you're a Munch fan, this charming mansion on the water at the far end of the Djurgarden park is worth the trip. (40 kr, Monday-Saturday 12:00-16:00, Sunday 13:00-16:00, tel. 662-5884, bus #69 from Karlaplan or boat from center).

▲**Sauna**—Sometime while you're in Sweden or Finland you'll have to treat yourself to Scandinavia's answer to support hose and a face lift. (A sauna is actually more Finnish than Swedish.) Simmer down with the local students, retired folks, and busy executives. Try to cook as calmly as the Swedes. Just before bursting, go into the shower room. There's no luke-cold, and the trickle down theory doesn't apply—only one button, bringing a Niagara of liquid ice. Suddenly your shower stall becomes a Cape Canaveral launch pad as your body scatters to every corner of the universe. A moment later you're back together. Rejoin the Swedes in the cooker, this time with their relaxed confidence; you now know that exhilaration is just around the corner. Only very rarely will you feel so good.

Any tourist office can point you toward the nearest birch twigs. Good opportunities include a Stockholm-Helsinki cruise, any major hotel you stay in (Hotel Karelia's is open to the public, 60 kr), some hostels, or least expensively, a public swimming pool. In Stockholm, consider the Eriksdalsbadet (Hammarby Slussvag 8, near Skanstull T-bana). Use of its 50-meter pool and first-rate sauna costs 30 kr.

The newly refurbished Centralbadet lets you enjoy an extensive gym, "bubblepool," sauna, steam room, and an elegant "art nouveau" pool from 1904 (70 kr, long hours, Drottningsgatan 88, 5 minutes up from Sergels Torg, tel. 24 24 03). Bring your towel into the sauna; the steam room is mixed, the sauna is not. Massage and solarium cost extra, and pool is more for floating than jumping and splashing. The leafy courtyard is an appropriately relaxing place to enjoy their restaurant (reasonable and healthy light meals).

Sights—Outer Stockholm

▲▲**Carl Milles Garden**—Here is the home housing the major work of Sweden's greatest sculptor, situated on a cliff overlooking Stockholm. Milles' entertaining, unique, and provocative art was influenced by Rodin. There's a classy café and a great picnic spot. T-bana to Ropsten, then take any bus to the first stop (Torsvik). It's a 5-minute walk from there (follow the signs). (40 kr, open daily 10:00-17:00, May-September; off-season Tuesday-Sunday 11:00-16:00, tel. 731-5060.)

▲**Drottningholm**—The queen's 17th-century summer castle and present royal residence has been called, not surprisingly, Sweden's Versailles. It's great, but if you've seen Denmark's Frederiksborg Palace, skip it. The adjacent, uncannily well-preserved, baroque theater is the real highlight here, especially with its guided tours (30 kr, English theater tours twice an hour, May-September 12:00-16:30; in September 12:00-15:30). Get there by a pleasant, but overpriced, boat ride (55 kr round-trip, 2 hrs) or take the subway to Brommaplan and bus #301 or #323 to Drottningholm. (Palace and Theater open daily 11:00-16:30 May-August; in September daily 13:00-15:30, Saturday and Sunday 12:00-15:30, tel. 759-0310 for palace tours in English schedule often at 11:00, 30 kr.)

The 17th-century Drottningholm court theater performs perfectly authentic operas (about 30 performances each summer). Tickets to these very popular and unique shows go on sale each March. Prices for this time tunnel musical and theatrical experience are 60 kr-400 kr. For information, write (in February) to Drottningholm's Theater Museum, Box 27050, 10251 Stockholm, or phone 08/660-8281.

▲▲**Archipelago**—The world's most scenic islands (24,000 of them!) surround Stockholm. Europeans who spend entire vacations in and around Stockholm rave about them. If you cruise to Finland, you'll get a good 3-hour dose of this island beauty. Otherwise, consider the pleasant hour-long cruise (40 kr each way) from the Grand Hotel downtown to the quiet town of Vaxholm. The Tourist Office has a free Archipelago guide booklet.

Shopping

Modern design, glass, clogs, and wood goods are popular targets for shoppers. Browsing is a free, delightful way to enjoy Sweden's brisk pulse. Cop a feel at the Nordiska Kompaniet (NK, also meaning "no Kroner left") just across from the Sweden House or in the nearby Gallerian mall. The nearby Ahlens is less expensive. Swedish stores are open 9:30-18:00, until 14:00 on Saturday, and closed Sunday. Some of the bigger stores are open later on Saturday and on Sunday afternoon.

For fleas, visit the Loppmarknaden (northern Europe's biggest flea market) at the planned suburb of Skarholmen (10 kr, Monday-Friday 11:00-18:00, Saturday 9:00-15:00, Sunday 10:00-15:00, busiest on weekends, tel. 710-0060).

Sleeping in Stockholm
(7 kr = about $1, tel. code: 08)

Stockholm has plenty of money-saving deals for the savvy visitor. Its youth hostels are among Europe's best ($15 a bed) and plenty of people offer private accommodations ($50 doubles). Peak season for Stockholm's expensive hotels is business time—workdays outside of summer. Rates drop by 30 to 50 percent in the summer or on weekends, and, if business is slow, occasionally any night if you ask). To sort through all of this, the city has helpful, English-speaking room-finding services with handy locations and long hours. (See Hotell-centralen and Sweden House, above.)

The **Stockholm Package** offers business-class doubles with buffet breakfasts for 700 kr, includes two free Stockholm cards, and lets children up to 18 years old sleep for free. This is limited to mid-June to mid-August, and Friday and Saturday throughout the year. Assuming you'll be getting two Stockholm cards anyway (350 kr), this gives you a $200 hotel room for about $50. This is for real (summertime is that dead for business hotels). The procedure (through either tourist office) is easy: a 100 kr advance booking fee (you can arrange by fax, pay when you arrive) or a 40 kr in-person booking fee if you just drop in. Arriving without reservations in July is never a problem. It gets tight during the Water Festival (ten days in early August) and during a convention stretch for a few days in late June.

My listings are only a good value outside of Stockholm Package time, or if the 700 kr for a double and two cards is out of your range and you're hosteling. Every place listed here has staff who speak English and will explain their special deals to you on the phone. If money is limited, ask if they have cheaper rooms. It's not often that a hotel will push their odd misfit room that's 100 kr below all the others. And at any time of year, prices can be soft.

Sleep code: **S**=Single, **D**=Double/Twin, **T**=Triple, **Q**=Quad, **B**=Bath/Shower, **WC**=Toilet, **CC**=Credit Card (**V**isa, **M**astercard, **A**mex). "Summer rates" means mid-June to mid-August, and Friday and Saturday (sometimes Sunday) the rest of the year. Prices include breakfast unless otherwise noted.

Sleeping in Hotels

Queen's Hotel is cheery, clean, and just a 10-minute walk from the station, in a great pedestrian area across the street from the Centralbadet (city baths, listed on all maps). With a fine TV and piano lounge, coffee in the evenings, and a staff that enjoys its guests, this is probably the best cheap hotel in town (summer rates: D-435 kr, DB500 kr, DBWC-585 kr, 640 kr-845 kr in winter, CC:VMA, Drottninggatan 71A, tel. 24 94 60, fax 21 76 20).

Bentley's Hotel is an interesting option with an old English flair (summer rates include winter Sundays: small

DBWC-500 kr, DBWC-600 kr, suite DBWC-700 kr, CC:VMA, a block up the street from Queen's at Drottninggatan 77, 11160 Stockholm, tel. 14 13 95, fax 21 24 92) and a pile of decent but simple rooms with no sinks, plumbing, or breakfast (S-200 kr, D-400 kr). Klas and Agi Kallstrom are attempting to mix elegance, comfort, and simplicity into an affordable package. Each room is tastefully decorated with antique furniture, but has a modern full bathroom. Some rooms are no-smoking rooms.

Hotel Bema, also near the station, is modern, clean, and friendly. Ask for their weekend rate (even on a weekday) and eat pizza next door to save some money (DBWC-480 kr-727 kr depending on the season and day, CC:VMA, Upplandsgatan 13, S-11123 Stockholm, tel. 23 26 75, fax 20 53 38).

Hotel Karelia, a stately old Finnish-run hotel, is centrally located and a good value for a "normal" hotel (summer rates: small DBWC-670 kr, big DBWC-750 kr, but soft if they're really slow; winter rates: DBWC-1,100 kr, CC:VMA, swimming pool and sauna, 35 Birger Jarlsgatan, tel. 24 76 60, fax 24 15 11). They have 15 "cabin" rooms in the basement with no windows. These dark, elegantly wooden bunkbed doubles with modern full bathrooms are rented for 400 kr including their normal buffet breakfast (throughout the year except for a few convention weeks). For the right vagabond, traveling in "high" season, these are a great deal.

Hotel Ostermalm (summer rates: no sink D-290 kr, DBWC-340 kr-460 kr, DBWC suite/family room-490 kr, 120 kr-150 kr for extra beds, 60 kr per double, less without breakfast, pricing here seems arbitrary and banana-firm, elevator, Karlavagen 57, tel. 660-6996, tel./fax 661-0471) is in a simple stately building a block from the T-bahn: Stadion. Narrow, yellow halls connect its generally huge (formerly elegant but now a tad musty) rooms. A funkiness rare in Stockholm, and for the right traveler a ripe deal. Nearby, the proud little **Stureparkens Gastvaning** (summer rates: no sink D-450 kr; high season: no sink D-600 kr, 2-night minimum, CC:VM, elevator, Sturegatan 58, tel. 662-7230, fax 661-5713) is a carefully run, traditional-feeling place with lots of class and ten tastefully decorated rooms. It's a better value during the high season.

Hotel Anno 1647, a typical old Swedish hotel with a few showerless rooms, just off the Old Town near Slussen (under the Katarina elevator), is a good splurge (summer rates, including Sunday through the year: D-500 kr, DBWC-750 kr; high season: D-650 kr, CC:VMA, Mariagrand 3, tel. 644-0480, fax 643-3700).

Sleeping in Rooms in Private Homes

Stockholm's centrally-located private rooms are as expensive as cheap hotels—a deal only in the high season. More reasonable rooms are a few T-bana minutes from the center. Stockholm's tourist offices refer those in search of a room in a private house to Hoteljanst (near the station, at Vasagatan 15, tel. 10 44 67, fax 21 37 16). They can set you up for about 330 kr per double, minimum two nights. Go direct—you'll save your host the listing service's fee. Be sure to get the front door security code when you call, as there's no intercom connection with front doors.

Mrs. Lindstrom rents out three doubles in her comfortable home (D-300 kr with access to a kitchenette, Danavagen 39, tel. 37 16 08, in the Bromma district near the Drottningholm Palace, a 7-minute walk from T-bana: Islandstorget).

Else Mari Sundin (D-400 kr with breakfast, bus #47 or #69 to Torstenssonsgatan 7, go through courtyard to "garden house" and up to second floor, tel. 665-3348, or at her country home, 036/45151) is an effervescent retired actress who rents two rooms in her very homey place, beautifully located just two blocks from the bridge to Djurgarden.

Mrs. Lichtsteiner (DBWC-400 kr without breakfast but with kitchenette, also a family room with a loft, a block from T-bahn: Radhuset, exit T-bahn direction Polisehusit, at Bergsgatan 45, inside go through door on left and up elevator to second floor, tel. 746-9166) will have you singing, "We represent the Lollipop Guild."

Sleeping in Youth Hostels

Stockholm has Europe's best selection of hostels offering good beds in simple but interesting places for 90 kr. If your budget is tight, these are right. Each has a helpful English-speaking staff, pleasant family rooms, good facilities, and good leads on budget survival in Stockholm. All will hold rooms for a phone call. Hosteling is cheap only if you're a member (guest membership: 35 kr a night necessary only in IYHF places), bring your own sheet (paper sheets rent for 30 kr), and picnic for breakfast (breakfasts cost 40 kr). Several of the hostels are often booked up well in advance, but hold a few beds for those who are left in the lurch.

Af Chapman (IYHF)—Europe's most famous youth hostel is the permanently moored cutter ship *Af Chapman*. Just a 5-minute walk from downtown, this floating hostel has 140 beds—2-8 per stateroom. A popular but compassionate place, it's often booked far in advance, but saves some beds each morning for unreserved arrivals. If you call at breakfast time and show up before 12:00, you may land a bed, even in summer. A warm, youthful atmosphere prevails. Study the warden's personal scrapbook of budget Stockholm information (April to mid-December, 7:00-12:00, 15:00-02:00, sleeping bags allowed, with a lounge and cafeteria that welcomes non-hostelers, 12:00-18:00, STF Vandrarhem *Af Chapman*, Skeppsholmen, 11149 Stockholm, tel. 679-5015).

Skeppsholmen Hostel (IYHF)—Just ashore from the *Af Chapman*, this hostel is open all year. It has better facilities and smaller rooms (90 kr per bed in doubles, triples, and quads, only 60 kr in dorms, tel. 679-5017), but it isn't as romantic as its sea-going sister. If you're staying in a hostel on Skeppsholmen island, the neighboring Sommar Café has a laundromat.

Zinken Hostel (IYHF)—This is a big, basic hostel in a busy suburb (T-bana: Zinkensdamm) with plenty of doubles, a launderette, and the best hostel kitchen facilities in town. (STF Vandrarhem Zinken, Zinkens Vag 20, tel. 668-5786, open 24 hours, all year.) If you want a 180 kr double (extra for sheets and non-members), sleep here. A great no-nonsense user-friendly value.

Vandrarhemmet Brygghuset—This former brewery near Odenplan (open June-August 7:00-12:00, 15:00-23:00, no curfew, Norrtullsgatan 12 N, tel. 312424) is small (57 beds in 12 rooms), spacious, bright and clean, quiet, with a laundromat and a kitchen. Since this is a private hostel, its 2- to 6-bed rooms are open to all for 110 kr per bed (no sleeping bags allowed, sheets rent for 30 kr). Doubles are 300 kr.

Café Bed and Breakfast, is Stockholm's newest cozy hostel with only 30 beds (110 kr per bed in 8- to 12-bed rooms, 30 kr for breakfast, 30 kr for sheets, near Radmansgatan T-bana stop, Rehnsgatan 21, tel. 15 28 38). They have three 300 kr doubles. Note: used sheets are rented for 10 kr ("locals don't mind").

Camping—Stockholm has seven campgrounds (located south of town) that are a wonderful solution to your parking and budget problems. The TI's "Camping Stockholm" brochure has specifics.

Eating in Stockholm

Stockholm's elegant department stores (notably NK and Ahlens near Sergelstorg) have cafeterias for the kroner-pinching local shopper. Look for the 50 kr "rodent of the day" (*Dagens ratt*) specials. Most museums have handy cafés. The café at the **Af Chapman youth hostel** (open to the public daily 12:00-18:00) serves a good salad/roll/coffee lunch in an unbeatable deck-of-a-ship atmosphere (if the weather's good).

In the Old Town (Gamla Stan), don't miss the wonderfully atmospheric **Kristina Restaurang** (Vesterlanggatan 68, Gamla Stan, tel. 200529). In this 1632 building, under a leather ceiling steeped in a turn-of-the-century interior, you'll find good dinners from 110 kr, including a salad and cracker bar. (The delicious Swedish meatballs with lingonberries is one of the least expensive meals.) They serve a great 50 kr lunch (11:00-15:30)—entrée, salad bar, bread, and drink. The place is best Wednesday-Saturday 20:00-23:00, when live jazz accompanies your meal (silent in July). You can enjoy the music over just a beer or coffee, too.

Picnics

With higher taxes almost every year, Sweden's restaurant industry is suffering. You'll notice many fine places almost empty. Swedes joke that the local cuisine is now Chinese, Italian, and hamburgers. Here more than anywhere, budget travelers should picnic.

Stockholm's major department stores (and the many small corner groceries) are fine places to assemble a picnic. Ahlens department store (near Sergels Torg, open until

21:00) has a great food section. The late-hours supermarket downstairs in the central train station (Monday-Friday 7:00-23:00, Saturday and Sunday 9:00-23:00) is picnic-friendly with fresh ready-made sandwiches.

The market at **Hotorget** is a fun place to picnic shop, especially in the indoor, exotic ethnic Hotorgshallen. The outdoor market closes at 18:00, and many merchants put their unsold produce on the push list (earlier closing and more desperate merchants on Saturday).

For a classy vegetarian buffet lunch (65 kr, Monday-Friday until 17:00) or dinner (75 kr, evenings and weekends) often with a lunchtime piano serenade, eat at **Ortagarden** (literally "the herb garden," Nybrogatan 31, tel. 662-1728), above the colorful old Ostermalms food market at Ostermalmstorg.

Transportation Connections
Stockholm to: Copenhagen (6/day, 8 hrs), **Oslo** (3/day, 7 hrs), **Kalmar** (6/day 8 hrs), **Uppsala** (30/day, 45 min), **Helsinki** (daily/nightly boats, 14 hrs, for detailed info, see Helsinki chapter), **Turku** (daily/nightly boats, 10 hrs). Estline runs a regular ferry from Stockholm to **Tallinn, Estonia** (every other night at 17:30, arriving at 9:00 the next morning, 385 kr each way). They offer a 36-hour tour (no visa necessary, round-trip, simple 2-bed cabins, two breakfasts, two dinners) for 1,170 kr per person (tel. 08/667-0001).

OSLO

Oslo is the smallest and least earthshaking of the Nordic capitals, but this brisk little city offers more sightseeing thrills than you might expect. Sights of the Viking spirit—past and present—tell an exciting story.
Prowl through the remains of ancient Viking ships and marvel at more peaceful but equally gutsy modern boats like the *Kon Tiki*, *Ra*, and *Fram*. Dive into the country's folk culture at the Norwegian Open Air Folk Museum and get stirred up by the country's heroic spirit at the Norwegian Resistance Museum.

For a look at modern Oslo, browse through the new yuppie-style harbor shopping complex, tour the recently avant garde city hall, take a peek at sculptor Vigeland's people pillars, and climb the towering, knee-shaking Holmenkollen ski jump.

Situated at the head of a 60-mile-long fjord, surrounded by forests, and 500,000 people, small Oslo is Norway's cultural hub and an all-you-can-see smorgasbord of historic sights, trees, art, and Nordic fun.

Planning Your Time

Oslo offers an exciting two-day slate of sightseeing thrills. Ideally, sleep on the train in from Stockholm, spend two days, and leave on the night train to Copenhagen, or on the scenic train to Bergen the third morning. Spend the two days like this:

Day 1: Set up. Tour the Akershus Castle and Nazi Resistance museum. Take a picnic on the ferry to Bygdoy and enjoy a view of the city harbor. Tour the Fram, Kon Tiki, and Viking Ships. Finish the afternoon at the Norwegian Open Air Folk museum. Boat home. For evening culture consider the Norwegian Masters performance (18:00) and the Folk music and dance show (21:00 Monday and Thursday).

Day 2: At 10:00 catch the City Hall tour, then browse through the National museum. Spend the afternoon at Vigeland Park, and at the Holmenkollen ski jump and museum. Browse Karl Johans Gate (all the way to the station)

Norway

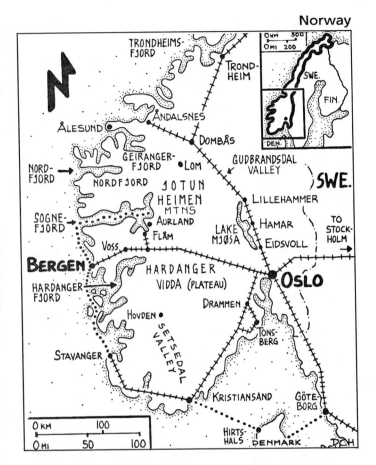

and Aker Brygge harbor in the early evening for the Norwegian paseo. Consider munching a fast food dinner on the mini-harbor cruise.

Orientation

Oslo is easy to manage, with nearly all its sights clustered around the central "barbell" (Karl Johans Street with the Royal Palace on one end and the train station on the other), or in the Bygdoy district, a 10-minute ferry ride across the harbor.

Tourist Information

The **Norwegian Information Center** (on the waterfront next to the city hall, daily 9:00-20:00, shorter hours off season, tel. 22 83 00 50) displays Norway as if it was a giant booth at a trade show. Stock up on brochures for Oslo and all of your Norwegian destinations, especially the Bergen guide. Pick up the free Oslo map, Sporveiskart transit map, *What's on in Oslo* monthly (for the most accurate listing of museum hours and special events), *Streetwise* magazine (hip and fun to read, telling you how to definitely not be one of those tourists), the free annual Oslo Guide, and consider buying the Oslo Card (see below). They have a rack of free pages on contemporary Norwegian issues and life (near the door), a 30-minute "multi-vision" show taking you around Norway (free, top of the hour, in a theater in the back), and rooms showcasing various crafts and ways you can spend your money here. The tourist information window in the central station (daily 8:00-23:00, less off-season, tel. 22 17 11 24) is much simpler, but can handle all of your needs just as well.

Use It is a hardworking youth information center, providing lots of solid money-saving, experience-enhancing information to young, student, and vagabond travelers (summer only 7:30-18:00, Saturday 9:00-14:00, closed Sunday, Mollergata 3, tel. 22 41 51 32). Read their free *Streetwise* magazine for ideas on eating and sleeping cheap, good night spots, best beaches, and so on.

The **Oslo Card** (24 hours–110 kr, 48 hours–190 kr, or 72 hours–240 kr) gives you free use of all city public transit, boats, free entry to all sights, a free harbor "mini cruise" tour, free parking, many more discounts, and a handy handbook. As admissions go up, this card becomes an increasingly better deal. Almost any 2-day visit to Oslo will be cheaper with the Oslo Card (which costs less than three Bygdoy museum admissions, the Ski Jump, and one city bus ride). The TI's special Oslo Package hotel deal (described under Sleeping, below) includes this card with your discounted hotel room.

Because of Norway's passion for minor differences in opening times from month to month, I've generally listed only the peak season hours. Assume opening hours shorten as the days do. The high season in Oslo is mid-June to August. (I'll call that "summer" in this chapter.)

Getting Into and Around Oslo

Trains
The central train station is slick and helpful, with a late-hours TI, room-finding service, late-hours bank (fair rates, normal fee), supermarket (daily 7:00-23:00), and an **Interrail Center** (open 7:00-23:00, mid-June to September, offering any traveler with a train pass, 10 kr showers, free rucksack storage racks, a bright and clean lounge, cheap snacks, a bulletin board for cheap sleeping deals, and an information center; train info tel 22 17 14 00, 7:00-23:00).

Public Transportation
Oslo's public transit system is made up of buses, trams, ferries, and a subway. Tickets cost 16 kr and are good for 1 hour of use on any combination of the above. (Flexi-cards give 10 for 130 kr, buy tickets as you board, bus info tel. 177.) The **Trafikanten**, the public transit information center, is under the ugly tower immediately in front of the station. Their free Sporveiskart transit map is the best city map around and makes the transit system quite inviting. Use it. The *"Tourist Ticket"* is a 35 kr 24-hour transit pass that pays for itself on the third ride. The Oslo Card (see Tourist Information, above) gives you free run of the entire transit system. Note how gracefully the subway lines fan out after huddling at Stortinget. Take advantage of the way they run like clockwork with schedules clearly posted and followed.

Bike Rental
Oslo is a good biking town, especially if you'd like to get out into the woods or ride a tram uphill out of town and coast for miles back. Den Rustne Eike ("the rusty spoke" on the harbor next to the Norway Information Center, daily May-September 10:00-18:30, tel. 22 83 72 31) rents bikes (3 hrs/60 kr, 6 hrs/80 kr) and organizes tours.

Sights—Downtown Oslo
▲▲**City Hall**—Construction on Oslo's richly decorated Radhuset began in 1931. It was finished in 1950 to celebrate the city's 900th birthday. Norway's leading artists all

Oslo Center

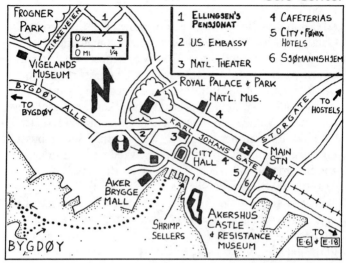

FROGNER PARK

KIRKEVEIEN

1

0 KM 5
0 MI ¼

VIGELANDS MUSEUM

BYGDØY ALLE

← TO BYGDØY

1	ELLINGSEN'S PENSJONAT	4	CAFETERIAS
2	U.S. EMBASSY	5	CITY • FØNIX HOTELS
3	NAT'L THEATER	6	SJØMANNSHJEM

ROYAL PALACE • PARK
NAT'L. MUS.

KARL JOHANS GATE

STORGATE

TO HOSTELS →

2   3

CITY HALL

MAIN STN

5

6

AKER BRYGGE MALL

SHRIMP. SELLERS

AKERSHUS CASTLE • RESISTANCE MUSEUM

BYGDØY

TO E·6 • E·18 →

contributed to what was an avant garde thrill in its day. The interior's 2,000 square yards of bold and colorful murals (which take you on a voyage through the collective psyche of Norway, from its simple rural beginnings through the scar tissue of the Nazi occupation and beyond) are meaningful only with the excellent, free guided tours (15 kr, 10:00, 12:00 and 14:00 Monday-Friday, entry on the Karl Johans side; open 9:00-15:30, Sunday 12:00-15:00, tel. 22 86 16 00).

▲**Akershus Castle**—One of the oldest buildings in town, this castle overlooking Oslo's harbor is mediocre by European standards, but worth a look if you're there for the tour. Its grounds make a pleasant park with grassy ramparts, pigeon-roost cannons, and great picnic spots with city views (English tours, free, daily summer at 11:00, 13:00 and 15:00, Sunday 13:00 and 15:00 only; 50 minutes long, open daily 10:00-16:00, Sunday 12:30-16:00; May to mid-September, closed in winter, 15 kr, tel. 22 41 25 21).

▲▲**Norwegian Resistance Museum (Norges Hjemmefront-museum)**—A stirring story about the Nazi invasion and occupation is told with wonderful English descriptions. This is the best look in Europe at how national spirit can endure total German occupation (in the Akershus

Castle, 15 kr, daily summer 10:00-17:00, Sunday 11:00-17:00, closes 1 hour earlier off-season).

▲**National Gallery**—Located downtown (13 Universitets Gata), this easy-to-handle museum gives you an effortless tour back in time and through Norway's most beautiful valleys, mountains, and villages with the help of its romantic painters (especially Dahl). It also has a noteworthy impressionist collection, some Vigeland statues, and a representative roomful of Munch paintings, including one of two *Screams*. The Munch paintings here make a trip to the Munch museum unnecessary for most (free, Monday, Wednesday, Friday, and Saturday 10:00-16:00; Thursday 10:00-20:00; Sunday 11:00-15:00, closed Tuesday, tel. 22 20 04 04).

▲▲**Browsing**—Oslo's pulse is best felt along and near the central Karl Johans Gate (from station to palace) and in the trendy new harborside Aker Brygge Festival Market Mall (a glass-and-chrome collection of sharp cafés and polished produce stalls just west of the city hall). The buskers are among the best in Europe.

▲▲▲**Vigeland Sculptures in Frogner Park and the Vigeland Museum**—The 75-acre park contains a lifetime of work by Norway's greatest sculptor, Gustav Vigeland. From 1906 through 1942, he sculpted 175 bronze and granite statues. The statues—all nude and each unique—surround Vigeland's 60-foot-high tangled tower of 121 bodies called "the monolith of life." Pick up the free map from the box on the kiosk wall as you enter. The park is more than great art. It's a city at play. Enjoy its urban Norwegian ambience. Then visit the Vigeland Museum to see the models for the statues and more in the artist's studio. Don't miss the photos on the wall showing the construction of the monolith (museum open 10:00-18:00, Sunday 12:00-19:00, closed Monday, 20 kr, open 12:00-16:00 and free off-season, tel. 22 44 11 36). The park is always open and free. Take T-banen #2 or bus #72, #73, or #20 to Frogner Plass.

Oslo City Museum—Located in the Frogner Manor farm in the Frogner park, this museum tells the story of Oslo since 1909. A helpful free English brochure guides you through the exhibits (20 kr, open 10:00-18:00, Saturday and Sunday 11:00-17:00, closed Monday; shorter hours off-season, tel. 22 43 06 45).

▲▲**Edvard Munch Museum**—The only Norwegian painter to have a serious impact on European art, Munch (monk) is a surprise to many who visit this fine museum. The emotional, disturbing, and powerfully expressionist work of this strange and perplexing man is arranged chronologically. You'll see paintings, drawings, lithographs, and photographs. Don't miss *The Scream*, which captures the fright many feel as the human "race" does just that (50 kr, 10:00-18:00, Sunday 12:00-18:00, off-season closed at 16:00 and all day Monday, tel. 22 67 37 74). If the price or location is a problem, you can see a roomful of Munch in the free National Gallery downtown.

Sights—Oslo's Bygdoy Neighborhood

▲▲▲**Bygdoy**—This exciting cluster of sights is on a park-like peninsula just across the harbor from downtown (reached by bus #30 from the Station and National Theater or by ferry, departing from City Hall three times an hour, 8:30-21:00, 16 kr, free with transit pass or Oslo card). The Folk Museum and Viking ships are near the first stop, Dronningen. The other museums are at the second stop, Bygdoynes. (See inset on the Greater Oslo map.) Otherwise, all Bygdoy sights are within a 15-minute walk of each other.

▲▲**Norwegian Folk Museum**—Brought from all corners of Norway, 140 buildings are reassembled on these 35 acres. While Stockholm's Skansen claims to be the first (and was the first to open to the public), this museum is a bit older, starting in 1885 as the king's private collection. You'll find craftspeople doing their traditional things, security guards disguised in cute, colorful, and traditional local costumes, endless creative ways to make do in a primitive log-cabin-and-goats-on-the-roof age, a 12th-century stave church, and a museum filled with toys and fine folk costumes. The place hops in the summer but is dead off-season. Catch the free 1-hour guided walks (call for schedule). Otherwise, glean information from the 20 kr guidebook and the informative guards who look like Rebecca Boone's Norwegian pen-pals (50 kr, daily June-August 10:00-18:00; off-season 11:00-17:00). For folk-dance performances, tour, and crafts demonstration schedules, call 22 43 70 20.

▲▲**Viking Ships**—Three great ninth-century Viking ships are surrounded by artifacts from the days of rape, pillage,

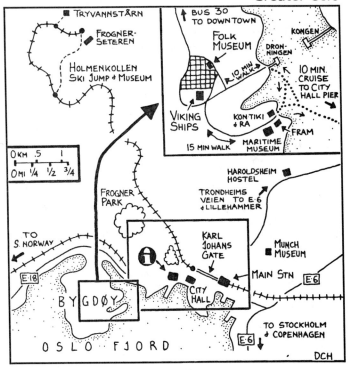

and—ya sure ya betcha—plunder. Don't miss the old cloth and embroidery in the dark room you light by entering. There are no museum tours, but everything is well described in English, and it's hard not to hear the English-speaking bus tour guides. There was a time when much of a frightened Europe closed every prayer with "and deliver us from the Vikings, Amen." Gazing up at the prow of one of these sleek time-stained vessels, you can almost hear the screams and smell the armpits of those redheads on the rampage (20 kr, daily summer 9:00-18:00, less in off-season).

▲▲**The *Fram***—This great ship took modern-day Vikings Amundsen and Nansen deep into the Arctic and Antarctic, farther north and south than any ship before. For three years the *Fram* was part of an arctic ice drift. The exhibit is fascinating. Read the ground floor displays, then explore the boat (20 kr, daily summer 9:00-17:45, shorter hours off-season). You can step into the lobby and see the ship's hull for free. Dry-docked by the waterfront is the boat Amundsen used to "discover" the northwest passage (Fram ticket gets you aboard).

▲▲The *Kon Tiki* **Museum**—Next to the *Fram* are the *Kon Tiki* and the *Ra II*, the boats Thor Heyerdahl built and sailed 4,000 and 3,000 miles, respectively, to prove that early South Americans could have sailed to Polynesia and Africans could have populated Barbados. He made enough money from his adventures to also prove that rich Norwegians can stay that way only by moving to low-tax Monaco (25 kr, daily 9:00-18:00, off-season 10:30-17:00).

▲**Norwegian Maritime Museum**—If you like the sea, this museum is a saltlick, providing a fine look at Norway's maritime heritage (20 kr, daily 10:00-19:00, off-season 10:30-16:00).

Other Oslo Sights and Activities

▲**Henie-Onstad Art Center** Norway's best private modern art collection, donated by the famous Norwegian Olympic skater/movie star, Sonja Henie (and her husband), combines modern art, a stunning building, a beautiful fjord-side setting, and a great café/restaurant. Don't miss Sonja Henie's glittering trophy room near the entrance. (30 kr, Monday, Saturday, and Sunday 11:00-17:00; Tuesday-Friday 9:00-21:00; in Hovikodden, tel. 67 54 30 50, 8 miles SW of Oslo, bus #151, #153, #161, #162, #251, or #261 from the main station.)

▲▲**Holmenkollen Ski Jump and Ski Museum**— Overlooking Oslo is a tremendous ski jump with a unique museum of skiing. The T-bane gets you out of the city and into the hills and forests that surround Oslo. After touring the history of skiing in the museum, ride the elevator and climb the 100-step stairway to the thrilling top of the jump for the best possible view of Oslo—and a chance to look down the long and frightening ramp that has sent so many tumbling into the agony of defeat. The ski museum is a must for skiers—tracing the evolution of the sport from 4,000-year-old rock paintings to crude 1,500-year-old skis to the slick and quickly evolving skis of our century. (Ski Jump and Museum open daily 9:00/10:00-22:00 in July; till 20:00 June and August; closes earlier off-season, 50 kr.)

For a special thrill, step into the **Simulator** and fly down the French Alps in a Disneyland-style downhill ski race simulator. My legs were exhausted after the 4-minute terror. This stimulator, parked in front of the ski museum, costs 35 kr. (Japanese tourists, who wig out over this one, are usually given a free ride after paying for four.)

To get to the ski jump, ride the T-bana (tram 15) to the Holmenkollen stop and hike up. For a longer but easier walk, ride to the end of the line and walk down past the Frognerseteren Hovedrestaurant. This classy, traditional old place, with a terrace that offers a commanding view of the city, is a popular stop for apple cake and coffee or a splurge dinner (open until 22:00, tel. 22 14 37 36).

The nearby Tryvannstarnet observatory tower offers a lofty 360-degree view with Oslo in the distance, the fjord and endless forests, lakes, and soft hills. It's impressive, but not necessary if you climbed the ski jump, which gives you a much better view of Oslo.

Forests, Lakes, and Beaches—Oslo is surrounded by a vast forest dotted with idyllic little lakes, huts, joggers, bikers, and sun-worshippers. Mountain bike riding possibilities are endless (as you'll discover if you go exploring without a guide or good map). For a quick ride, you can take the T-banen (with your bike, it needs a ticket too) to the end of line #15 (Frognerseteren, 30 minutes from Nationaltheatret, gaining you the most altitude possible) and follow the gravelly roads (mostly downhill but with some climbing) past several dreamy lakes to Sognsvann at the end of T-banen line #4 (a 1-hr ride, not counting time lost). Farther east, from Maridalsvannet, a bike path follows the Aker River all the way back into town. For plenty of trees and none of the exercise, ride the T-banen to Sognsvann (with a beach towel rather than a bike) and join in the lake-side scene. Other popular beaches (like those on islands in the harbor) are described in Use It's *Streetwise* magazine.

Harbor and Fjord Tours—Several tour boats leave regularly from Pier 3 in front of the city hall. A relaxing and scenic 50-minute mini-cruise with a boring three-language commentary departs hourly and costs only 60 kr (or free with Oslo Card, daily 10:00-20:00, tel. 22 20 07 15). They won't scream if you bring something to Munch. The cheapest way to enjoy the scenic Oslo fjord is to simply ride the ferries which regularly connect the nearby islands with downtown (free with the city transport pass).

▲▲▲**Folk Entertainment**—A group of amateur musicians and dancers (Leikarringen, Bondeungdomslaget) gives a short, sweet, caring, and vibrant 1-hour show at the Oslo Concert Hall (100 kr, 60 kr for students, Monday and Thursday in July and August at 21:00; tel. 22 83 32 00, look for the big brown glassy overpass on Munkedamsveien, the recommended Vegata Vertshus restaurant is just up the street). For their off-season concert schedule (different locales, usually once a week), call 22 41 40 70.

▲**Grieg, Ibsen, and Munch: Norwegian Masters**—For an evening of Norwegian classical music (Grieg), poetry (Ibsen), and art (Munch) in the elegant 150-year-old Gamle Logen concert hall, consider this concert. A cast of four including a pianist, violinist and soprano explore how the collage of nature and life unique to Norway inspired the masters. This is accomplished by weaving their words, music, and paintings into a 70-minute drama (160 kr, almost nightly in summer at 18:00, Kirkegaten behind the Akershus Fort, all in English, tel. 22 43 43 70). Get there early enough to prepare for the performance by reading the program. (This is heavy-duty culture—husbands should down a Coke or coffee beforehand.) For 70 minutes, it's a bit pricey. But from cow-calls to Trollhaugen to the *Scream*, (other than reading the rest of my books) this is your most accessible opportunity to gain an appreciation of the creative Norwegian mind.

Parks, Pools, and Wet Fun—The Tusenfryd Amusement Park offers over fifty rides, plenty of entertainment, family fun, and restaurants. A free, hourly coach shuttles fun-seekers 20 minutes to the park from the Oslo City Hall (50 kr, 60 kr in July, free with Oslo Card, open 10:30-20:00, 22:00 in July).

Oslo offers lots of water fun for about 35 kr. In Frogner Park, the Frognerbadet (mid-May to August, Middelthuns-gate 28, tel. 22 44 74 29, free with Oslo card) has a sauna, outdoor pools, lots of young families, a cafeteria, and high dives. Toyenbadet is a modern indoor pool complex with mini golf and a 100-yard-long water slide (free with Oslo Card, open at odd hours throughout the year, Helgengate 90, a 10-minute walk from Munch Museum, tel. 22 67 18 89). Oslo's botanical gardens (free) are nearby. (For more ideas on swimming, see *Streetwise*.)

Nightlife—They used to tell people who asked about nightlife in Oslo that Copenhagen was only an hour away by airplane. Now Oslo has sprouted a nightlife of its own. The scene is always changing. The tourist office has information on Oslo's many cafés, discos, and jazz clubs. Use It is the best source of information for local hot spots.

Shopping—For a great selection (but high prices) in sweaters and other Norwegian crafts, shop at Husfliden (daily 9:00-17:00, Saturday until 14:00, Den Norske Husflidsforening, 4 Mollergate behind the cathedral, tel. 22 42 10 75), the retail center for the Norwegian Association of Home Arts and Crafts. Shops are generally open 10:00-18:00. Many stay open until 20:00 on Thursday and close early on Saturday and all day Sunday.

Sleeping in Oslo
(7 kr = about $1)

Yes, Oslo is expensive. In Oslo, the season dictates the best deals. In low season (July to mid-August, and Friday, Saturday and Sunday the rest of the year) fancy hotels are the best value for softies with 600 kr for a double with breakfast. In high season (business days outside of summer), your affordable choices are dumpy-for-Scandinavia (but still nice by European standards) hotel doubles (300 kr-400 kr) and 270 kr doubles in private homes. For experience and economy (but not convenience), go for a private home. Oslo's two hostels are far from the center, expensive (160 kr per bed), and usually full. Summer vagabonds sleep cheap (100 kr) at the downtown sleep-in.

Like its sister Scandinavian capitals, Oslo's hotels are designed for business travelers. Expensive in high season, empty otherwise. Only the TI can sort through all the confusing hotel "specials" and get you the best deal possible on a fancy hotel—push-list rooms at about half price. Half price is still 500 kr-600 kr, but that includes breakfast and a lot of extra comfort for a few extra kroner over the cost of a cheap hotel. Cheap hotels, whose rates are the same throughout the year, are a bad value in summer, but offer a real savings in low season. The TI's "Experience Oslo" package advertises 600 kr doubles in business-class (1,200 kr) rooms and includes a free Oslo Card (worth 100 kr/day).

Only use the TI for these push-list deals, not for cheap hotels or private homes. Many of the cheapest hotels (my listings) tell the TI (which gets a 10% fee) they're full when they're not. Go direct. A hotel getting 100 percent of your payment is more likely to have a room. July and early August are easy, but early June and September can be tight.

Sleep code: **S**=Single, **D**=Double/Twin, **T**=Triple, **Q**=Quad, **B**=Bath/Shower, **WC**=Toilet, **CC**=Credit Card (**V**isa, **M**astercard, **A**mex).

Sleeping in Hotels near the Train Station

Each of these places is within a 2-minute walk of the station, in a neighborhood your mom probably wouldn't want you hanging around in at night. The hotels themselves, however, are secure and comfortable. Leave nothing in your car. The Paleet parking garage is handy but not cheap—120 kr per 24 hours.

Sjomannshjem (S-250 kr-300 kr, simple seventh-floor D-300 kr, sixth-floor D/DWCB-400 kr with newer furniture, no breakfast, elevator; enter on Fred Olsengate, Tollbugt 4, 0152 Oslo, tel. 22 41 20 05) is a "retired seaman's hotel." But since most Norwegian captains are commanding Third World sailors these days, the seaman's union welcomes tourists in their underused Oslo hotel. One of Oslo's great bargains, it's plain, clean, simple (e.g., one towel for your entire stay), and shipshape.

City Hotel, clean, basic, very homey, and with a wonderful lounge, originated 100 years ago as a cheap place for Norwegians to sleep while they waited to sail to their new homes in America. It now serves the opposite purpose. (DBWC-500 kr-800 kr depending on season, with breakfast, CC:VMA, Skippergatan 19, tel. 22 41 36 10, fax 22 42 24 29.)

Rainbow Hotel Astoria (SWCB-375 kr-585 kr, TwinWCB-500 kr-685 kr, DWCB-600 kr-785 kr, with buffet breakfast, rates vary with season, CC:VMA, 3 blocks in front of the station, 50 yards off Karl Johans Gate, Dronningensgate 21, 0154 Oslo, tel. 22 42 00 10, fax 22 42 57 65) is a comfortable, modern place, part of the quickly growing "Rainbow Hotels" chain which understands what comforts are worth paying for. There are smoke-free floors, an included buffet breakfast, televisions, telephones, full modern bathrooms in each room. Ice machines! Most "twins" are actually "combi" rooms with a regular bed and a fold down sofa bed.

The newest Oslo Rainbow hotel is **Rainbow Hotel Spectrum** ("combi" TwinBWC-500 kr-685 kr, full doubles 100 kr more, no smoking rooms available, 3 blocks to the right as you leave the station on Lilletorget, Brugata 7, 0186 Oslo, tel. 22 17 60 30, fax 22 17 60 80) is also well located and a good value.

Sleeping in the West End

Ellingsen's Pensjonat, run by a friendly woman whose name is Mrs. Wecking (Viking), is a textbook example of a good accommodations value with no lounge or breakfasts, dreary halls but fine rooms, fluffy down comforters, and a great residential location 4 blocks behind the Royal Palace (a lot of S-190 kr, 3 D-300 kr, call well in advance for doubles, Holtegt 25, 0355, Oslo 3, on the corner of Uranienborg veien and Holtegatan, near the Uranienborg church, it's the #25 on the east side of the street, T-banen #1 from the station, tel. 22 60 03 59, fax 22 60 99 21).

Cochs Pensjonat (D-380 kr, DBWC-490 kr, no breakfast, CC:VM, tram #11 to Parkveien 25, tel. 22 60 48 36, fax 22 46 54 02) has plain rooms and a stale wet-noodle atmosphere, but is right behind the palace.

Lindes Pensionat is a great deal with kitchenette and refrigerator (D-270 kr for 2 or more nights, no breakfast, near Frogner park, train #2 to Frogner Plass, 41 Thomas Heftyes Gate, tel. 22 55 37 82).

Sleeping in Private Homes

The Caspari family rents three comfortable rooms in their home (S-150 kr, D-270 kr without breakfast, price with book if you go direct, one shared bathroom, extra cots available for 100 kr, 60 kr extra for 1-night stay, a 15-minute walk from the center, behind Frogner park, immediately across the street from the Heggeli T-bana stop at Heggeliveien 55, same side you exit train on, tel. 22 14 57 70). This woodsy, peaceful suburb is a place you'd like to raise your kids in—or call home for a couple of days in Oslo. And it couldn't be handier by T-banen, literally a few steps and 7 minutes from the center.

Mr. Naess (S-125 kr, D-250 kr, T-375 kr, 40 kr extra for one night, no breakfast, walk 20 minutes from the station or take bus #27 or #56 from tower in front of station 5 stops to Olaf Ryes Place, facing a park at Toftestrasse 45, tel. 22 37 58 94) offers big, homey old rooms overlooking a park and the use of a fully-loaded kitchen. More urban, this place is a flat in a big old building with plenty of work-a-day shops and eateries nearby.

Sleeping in Youth Hostels
Haraldsheim Youth Hostel (IYHF), a huge, modern hostel, is open all year, situated far from the center on a hill with a grand view, laundry, and self-service kitchen. Its 270 beds (4 per room) are often completely booked. Beds in the new fancy quads with private showers and toilets are 165 kr per person with buffet breakfast. (Simpler beds cost 145 kr, with breakfast, sheets 35 kr, guest membership 25 kr, 4 Heraldsheimveien, tram #1 or #7 from station to Sinsen, 4 km out of town, 5-minute uphill hike.) Eurailers can train (2/hr, to Gressen) to the hostel for free (tel. 22 15 50 43).

Holtekilen Sommerhotel is a comfortable university dorm a bit out of town (June to mid-August, D-390 kr with breakfast, 145 kr dorm beds with breakfast, sheets 35 kr, non-members 25 kr extra, Michelets vei 55, Stabekk/Oslo 1320, train to Stabbek and walk 10 minutes, or bus #151 or #251 and walk 3 minutes, ideal for drivers, go west 9 km from center, exit E-18 at Strand, tel. 67 53 38 53).

YMCA Sleep-In Oslo—Located near the station, this sleep-in offers the cheapest mattresses in town in three large unisex rooms with 30 mattresses each, left luggage room, piano lounge, kitchen, and ear plugs for sale. It's as pleasant as a sleep-in can be (100 kr, no bedding provided, you must bring a sleeping bag, open 8:00-11:00, 17:00-24:00 July to mid-August, Mollergata 1, entry from Grubbegata, one block beyond the cathedral, tel. 22 20 83 97). They take no reservations, but call to see if there's a place.

Sleeping on the Train
Norway's trains offer 100 kr beds in triple compartments. Eurailers who sleep well to the rhythm of the rails have several very scenic overnight trips to choose from (it's light until midnight at Oslo's latitude for much of the early summer).

Eating in Oslo

The thought of a simple open-face sandwich (which looks and tastes like half of something I can make, with an inedible garnish added) for $5, and a beer for nearly as much, ruins my appetite. Nevertheless, one can't continue to sightsee on postcards and train tickets alone.

My strategy is to splurge for a hotel that includes breakfast. A 50 kr Norwegian breakfast is fit for a Viking. Have a picnic for lunch or dinner. There are plenty of grocery stores. Big department stores have huge first-class supermarkets in their basements with lots of picnic dinner-quality alternatives to sandwiches. Most of the little yogurt tubs with cereal come with a collapsible spoon. The train station has a late hours grocery.

Since Norwegians eat early, between 16:00-19:00, the cheapest places close by 19:00. Later dinners are elegant dining and normally quite expensive. Pizzerias and salad bars are the trend. Ask your receptionist for advice. Many pizzerias have all-you-can-eat specials. Chinese and ethnic places are everywhere and reasonably priced.

The **Aker Brygge** (harborfront mall) development isn't cheap, but it has some cheery cafés, classy delis, open-till-22:00 restaurants, and markets. The **Cruise Café** has reasonable light meals.

Oslo's several **Kaffistova** cafeterias are alcohol-free, clean (check out the revolving toilet seats), and serve simple, hearty, and typically Norwegian (read "bland") meals for the best price around. At 8 Rosenkrantzgate, you'll get your choice of an entrée and all the salad, cooked vegetables, and "flat bread" you want (or at least need) for around 80 kr. It's open 12:00-21:00 (17:00 Saturday, 18:00 Sunday) in summer and closes earlier off-season. The **Norrona Cafeteria** is another traditional budget-saver (65 kr *dagens ratt*, central at 19 Grensen, closes at 17:00, 19:00 off-season). Other cafeterias are found in department stores.

Vegeta Vertshus, which has been keeping Oslo vegetarians fat, happy, and low on the food chain for fifty years, serves a huge selection of hearty vegetarian food that would satisfy even a Republican president. Fill your plate once (medium plate/65 kr, large plate/75 kr) or eternally for 98 kr. How's your balance? One plate did me fine (daily 10:00-

23:00, no smoking, no alcohol, no meat, Munkedamsveien 3B, near top of Stortingsgata between palace and city hall, tel. 22 83 42 32).

Transportation Connections

Oslo to Bergen: These cities are linked by a spectacularly scenic 7-hour train ride. Reservations are required. Departures are at about 7:30, 10:30, 15:30, 15:40, and 23:00 daily in both directions (480 kr, or 380 kr if you buy a day early and don't travel on Friday or Sunday). For more info, see my *Best of Scandinavia* guidebook.

Oslo to Copenhagen: Consider the cheap quickie cruise that leaves daily from Copenhagen (departs 17:00, returns 9:15 2 days later; 16 hrs sailing each way and 7 hrs in Norway's capital). See Copenhagen chapter for specifics.

Scandinavia

BARCELONA

Barcelona is (at least) Spain's second city and the capital of the proud and distinct region of Catalunya (Catalonia). With Franco's fascism now history, Catalunya flags wave once again. The local language and culture are on a roll in Spain's most cosmopolitan and European corner.

Still enjoying the momentum of the 1992 Olympics, Barcelona bubbles with life in the narrow alleys of the old Gothic Quarter, along the grand boulevards, and throughout the chic grid-planned new town. While Barcelona had an exciting past as a Roman colony, Visigothic capital, 14th-century maritime power, and, in more modern times, a top Mediterranean trading and manufacturing center, it's most enjoyable to throw out the history books and just drift through the city. If you're in the mood to surrender to a city's charms, let it be in Barcelona.

Planning Your Time

Most important, sandwich Barcelona between flights or overnight train rides. There's not much of earth-shaking importance within 8 hours by train. It's as easy to fly into Barcelona as into Madrid, Lisbon, or Paris for most travelers from the U.S.A. Even if you're renting a car, plan on starting your Iberian vacation here, sleeping on the train to Madrid, and picking up your car after seeing Madrid.

Barcelona is worth at least two nights. On the shortest visit it's worth one night, one day, and an overnight train out. The Ramblas is two different streets by day and night. Stroll it from top to bottom at night and again the next morning, grabbing breakfast on a stool in a café in the market. Wander the Gothic Quarter, see the cathedral and have lunch in Eixample. The three top sights in town, Gaudí's Sacred Family Church, the Picasso Museum, and the Catalonian Art Museum (in that order), are usually open until about 20:00. The illuminated fountains are a good finale for your day.

Of course Barcelona in a day is a dash. To better appreciate the city's ample charm spread your visit over two days.

Orientation (tel. code: 93)

Locate these orientation essentials on the map in this book: *Barri Gotic/Ramblas* (old town), *Eixample* (fashionable modern town), *Montjuic* (hill covered with sights and parks), *Sants Station* (train to Madrid). The soul of Barcelona is in its compact core—the *Barri Gòtic* (Gothic Quarter) and the *Ramblas* (main boulevard). This is your strolling, shopping, and people-watching nucleus. The city's sights are widely scattered, but with a basic map and a willingness to figure out the sleek subway system, all is manageable.

Tourist Information

The best TI is 3 blocks from Plaça de Catalunya at Gran Vía 658 (Monday-Friday 9:00-19:00, Saturday 9:00-14:00, tel. 301 7443). Other TIs are at the airport, the Franca Station, and Sants-Central station (8:00-20:00, Saturday and Sunday 8:00-14:00, tel. 491 4431). Wherever you go for information, get the large city map, general city information, and brochures listing historic walks, Gaudí sights, Miró sights, and the monthly music and cultural activities. For the latest TI, you can call 010.

Trains

Although many international trains use the Franca Station, all domestic trains use the Sants-Central Station. Train information: 490 0202. Both stations have subway stations (Franca's is Barceloneta). Sants-Central station has plenty of expensive baggage lockers (600 ptas/day), a good TI, a world of handy shops and eateries (including a juice shop behind the TI with a fascinating orange juicer), and a classy "Club Intercity" lounge for anyone with a first-class pass or ticket (quiet, plush, TV, shower, study tables, coffee bar—have a hot milk with sugar). There is nothing you want within easy walking distance from the train station. Catch the subway or a taxi.

Getting Around

Barcelona's subway, which may be Europe's best if not biggest, can be faster than a taxi and connects just about every place you'll visit. It has four color-coded lines (L1 is red, L3 is green, L4 is yellow, L5 is blue, L2 is missing). Rides cost 120 ptas each, but a T1 pack gives you 10 tickets for 600 ptas and a T2 pack is a better deal, giving you 10 tickets good for the bus or metro (subway) for only 625 ptas. Pick up a guide to public transport at the TI.

The Tourist Bus 100 (Transports Turistics) shuttles tourists on a 15-stop circuit (covering the must-sees, the funicular, and the teleféric) from mid-June through mid-October. The 1,000 ptas one-day ticket (or half day or two-day version) includes some serious discounts to the city's

Barcelona

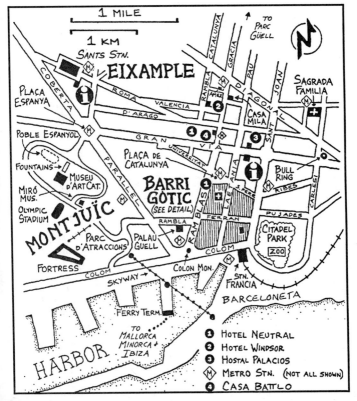

major sights. Buses run every 20 minutes and take 2 hours to do the entire circuit.

Taxis are plentiful, honest, and don't charge extra for evening rides. Rides start at 260 ptas. You can go from the Ramblas to the Sants Station for 500 ptas.

Helpful Hints

Theft Alert: Be on guard. Barcelona's thieves thrive on unwary tourists. While the city is better lit and better policed than ever, more bags and wallets seem to be stolen here than anywhere.

Language: Although Spanish is understood here (and the basic survival words are the same), Barcelona speaks a different language—Catalán. (Most place names in this chapter are listed in Catalán.)

American Express company (metro: Diagonal, at Rossello 259, tel. 217 0070).

Sights—The Ramblas

(Walking from Plaça de Catalunya downhill to the harbor.) More than a Champs-Elysées, this grand boulevard takes you from rich at the top to rough at the port, a 20-minute walk. You'll find the grand opera house, ornate churches, prostitutes, pickpockets, con men, artists, an outdoor bird market, elegant cafés, great shopping, and people willing to charge more for a shoeshine than you paid for the shoes. When Hans Christian Andersen saw this street over 100 years ago, he wrote that there could be no doubt that Barcelona was a great city.

Rambla means stream in Arabic. The Ramblas was a drainage ditch along the medieval wall that used to define what is now called the Gothic Quarter. It has five separately named segments, but addresses treat it as 1-mile-long boulevard.

Highlights include (from top to bottom of the Ramblas):

▲**Plaça de Catalunya**—This is the city's vast central square, metro, bus, and airport shuttle hub, and divider of old and new. The huge El Corte Inglés department store (10:00-21:00, closed Sunday, supermarket in basement, ninth-floor terrace cafeteria with city view, tel. 302 1212), offering everything from a travel agency and haircuts to cheap souvenirs, overlooks the square. Four great boulevards start here—the Ramblas, the fashionable Passeig de Gracia, the cosier but still fashionable parallel Rambla Catalunya, and the stubby, shopping pedestrian-only Portal de L'Angel.

▲▲**Mercat de Sant Josep**—This lively produce market (8:00-15:00, 18:00-20:00, closed Sunday) is an explosion of chicken legs, bags of live snails, stiff fish, delicious oranges, sleeping dogs, and great bars for a cheap breakfast (try a *tortilla española* and *café con leche*).

Gran Teatre del Liceu—Spain's only real opera house, it's luscious but closed for a few years because of a fire (tourable when it reopens).

Plaça Reial—This elegant, neoclassical square comes complete with old-fashioned taverns, a Sunday coin and stamp market (10:00-14:00), and characters who don't need the palm trees to be shady. Escudellers, a street one block toward the water from the square, is lined with bars whose counters are strewn with vampy ladies. The area is well policed, but if you tried, you could get into trouble.

▲▲**Palau Güell**—This offers the only look at a Gaudí art nouveau interior, and for me, the most enjoyable look at Barcelona's organic architect (the exterior is a theater museum, 300 ptas, usually open Tuesday-Saturday, 11:00-14:00, 17:00-20:00).

Barri Xines (Chinatown)—Farther downhill, on the right-hand side, is the world's only Chinatown with nothing even remotely Chinese in or near it—a dingy, dangerous-after-dark nightclub district with lots of street girls and a monument to Dr. Fuller, the Canadian who discovered penicillin. Don't venture in.

Monument a Colon (Columbus Monument)—At the end of the Ramblas, at the harbor, this monument offers an elevator-assisted view from its top (225 ptas, daily 9:00-21:00, off-season 10:00-14:00, 15:30-18:30, closed Monday). It's interesting that Barcelona would so honor the man whose discoveries ultimately led to its downfall as a great trading power.

Museu Maritim (Maritime Museum)—For a look at Barcelona's sea power, before Columbus' discoveries shifted the world's focus west (fleets of seemingly unimportant replicas of old boats explained in Catalán and Spanish), check out this museum in the impressive old Drassanes (Royal Ship-

Barcelona's Gothic Quarter

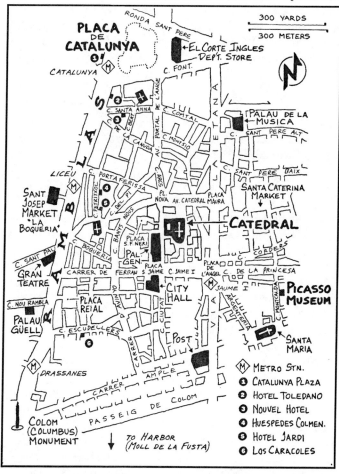

yards, across the street, 300 ptas, 9:30-13:00, 16:00-19:00, Sunday 10:00-14:00, closed Monday).

Golondrinas—Little tourist boats make a half-hour tour of the harbor on the half hour from 11:00-18:00 (at the foot of the Columbus Monument, 355 ptas). Consider this ride or the harbor steps here for a picnic.

Sights—Barri Gòtic (Gothic Quarter)

The Barri Gòtic is a bustling world of shops, bars, and nightlife packed between hard-to-be-thrilled-about 14th-

and 15th-century buildings. Except for the part closest to the port, the area now feels safe, thanks to police and countless quaint but very bright streetlights. There is a tangled grabbag of undiscovered squares, grand squares, schoolyard plazas, Art Nouveau storefronts, baby flea markets, musty antique shops, classy antique shops, and balconies with jungles behind wrought-iron bars. Go on a cultural scavenger hunt. Write a poem.

▲▲**Cathedral**—The colossal cathedral, a fine example of Catalán Gothic, was started about 1300 and wasn't completed for 600 years. Like the Gothic churches of Italy, rather than stretching toward heaven, it makes a point to be simply massive. The heavy choir (coro) in the middle confuses the dark and muddled interior. Admission fee to enter the coro from the back, but you can see everything for free from the front. Don't miss the cloister with its wispy garden and worthwhile little museum (cathedral open daily 7:30-13:30, 16:00-19:30).

Museo del Calzado—Shoe lovers can find this two-room shoe museum (with a we-try-harder attendant) on Plaça Sant Felip Neri, about a block beyond the outside door of the cloister (150 ptas, 11:00-14:00, closed Monday). It stinks so bad, it's fun.

Palau Reial (Royal Palace)—The royal palace contains museums showing off Barcelona's Roman and medieval history, and the Arxiu de la Corona d'Aragon (Archives of the Kingdom of Aragon) with piles of medieval documents.

▲▲**The Picasso Museum**—Far and away the best collection of Picasso's (1881-1973) work in Spain, this is a great chance to see his earliest sketches and paintings and better understand his genius (metro: Jaume, 500 ptas, 10:00-20:00, Sunday 10:00-15:00, closed Monday).

Sights—Gaudí's Architecture
Barcelona is an architectural scrapbook of the galloping gables and organic curves of hometown boy Antoni Gaudí. Gaudí gave Art Nouveau a Catalonian twist and they called it modernisme. For more information on Gaudí, pick up a brochure at the tourist office.

▲▲▲**Sagrada Familia (Sacred Family) Church**—Gaudí's most famous and persistent work is this unfinished landmark (metro: Sagrada Familia, 500 ptas, daily 9:00-21:00, off-season 9:00-18:00, tel. 455 0247). From 1891 to 1925, Gaudí worked on this monumental church of eight 100-meter spires that will someday dance around a 160-meter granddaddy spire. With the cranes, rusty forests of rebar, and scaffolding requiring a powerful faith, it offers a fun look at a living, growing, bigger-than-life building. Take the lift or the stairs up to the dizzy lookout bridging two spires for a great city view and a gargoyle's-eye perspective of the loopy church. If there's any building on earth I'd like to see, it's the Sagrada Familia—finished. Judge for yourself how the controversial current work fits in with the old.

▲▲**Palau Güell**—This is the best chance to enjoy a Gaudí interior (see above under Ramblas). Curvy.

Casa Mila—This house and nearby Casa Battlo have Gaudí exteriors that laugh down on the crowds that fill Passeig de Gràcia. Casa Mila, also called La Pedrera, or "the Quarry," has a much-photographed roller-coaster of melting ice cream eaves (Pg. del Garcia #92, metro: Diagonal, roof tours are given at 10:00, 11:00, 12:00, and 13:00, tel. 487 3613).

Casa Battlo—Four blocks from Casa Mila (Pg. de Gràcia #43, metro: Passeig de Gràcia), this house's roof has a cresting wave of tiles (or is it a dragon's back?). Check out the geometric facade of the house next door by the architect Puig i Cadafalch. This Barcelonian version of keeping up with the Joneses led to the Passeig de Gràcia's local nickname "the street of discord." If you're tempted to frame your photo from the middle of the street, be careful— Gaudí died under a streetcar!

Parc Güell—Gaudí fans enjoy this fanciful park (free, daily 10:00-20:00). A small **Gaudí Museum** is also here (150 ptas, museum open 10:00-14:00, 16:00-19:00, closed Saturday, metro: Vallarca, but easier by bus #24 from Pl. de Catalunya, 1,000 ptas by taxi). Even after reminding myself that Gaudí's work is a very careful rhythm of color, shapes, and space, I was disappointed in the park.

Sights—Barcelona's Montjuïc

The Montjuïc (Mount of the Jews) overlooking Barcelona's hazy port has always been a show-off. Ages ago it had the impressive fortress. In 1929, it hosted an International Fair, from which most of today's sights originated. And in 1992, the Summer Olympics directed the world's attention to this pincushion of sightseeing attractions.

Skyway Ride—Barcelona's skyway (Transbordador Aeri) is a temptation when you see it gliding fitfully across the harbor from a distance. It's an expensive (950 ptas one way, 1,100 ptas round-trip) and time-consuming headache but offers exceptional views of the normally smoggy city. Open whenever you see the two little red cars dangling, it's a handy way to glide between the attractions of Montjuïc and the fine fish restaurants or sandy beaches of Barceloneta.

Parc d'Atraccions de Montjuïc (Amusement Park)—This is your best chance to eat, whirl, and hurl with local families (free, daily in summers until late, access from metro: Parallel, from where you can walk or ride the Montjuïc teleférico, which stops here on its way up to the fortress, and by the skyway).

Fortress—This offers great city views and an impressive military museum (150 ptas, 9:30-14:00, 15:30-20:00, closed Monday).

▲**Fonts Lluminoses (Fountains)**—Music, colored lights, and impressive amounts of water make an artistic and coordinated splash on summer Thursday, Friday, and Saturday nights (30-minute shows start on the half hour, 21:30-24:00, walk toward huge towering National Palace from the metro: Pl. Espanya).

Poble Espanyol (Spanish Village)—This tacky 5-acre model village uses fake traditional architecture from all over Spain as a shell to contain gift shops. Crafts people do their clichétic thing only in the morning. (9:00-19:30 but dead after 13:00, not worth the time or the 650 ptas.) After hours it becomes a popular local night spot.

▲▲**Museu d'Art de Catalunya (Catalonian Art Museum)**— Often called "the Prado of Romanesque art," this is a rare and world-class collection of Romanesque frescoes, statues, and paintings, much of it from remote Catalán village churches in the Pyrenees. Also see Gothic work and paintings by the great Spanish masters (after years of remodeling, it should reopen in 1995, 600 ptas, former hours: Wednesday-Monday, 9:00-21:00).

▲**Fundació Joan Miró**—For something a bit more up-to-date, this museum showcases the modern art talents of yet another Catalonian artist (500 ptas, 11:00-19:00, Sunday 10:30-14:30, Thursday until 21:30, closed Monday).

More Sights—Barcelona

Eixample—Uptown Barcelona is a unique variation on the grid-planned cities you find all over. Barcelona snipped off the building corners to create light and spacious eight-sided squares at every intersection (and difficulty in finding signs of cross roads). Wide sidewalks, hardy trees offering shade, chic shops, and plenty of Art Nouveau (Gaudí and company) fun make the Eixample (ay-sham-pla) a refreshing break from the old town. For the best Eixample example, ramble Rambla Catalunya (unrelated to the more famous Ramblas) and pass through Passeig de Gràcia (metro: Passeig de Gràcia).

Sleeping in Barcelona
(tel. code: 93, 125 ptas=$1)

Barcelona is Spain's most expensive city. Still, it has reasonable rooms, so your big decision is which neighborhood. A few places raise their rates for "high season," which, for business hotels, is outside of summer, weekdays, and during conventions. Since dumpy cheap hotels cater only to tourists, their high season is summer. Most prices listed include the 6 percent for tax and not the optional breakfast.

Sleep code: **S**=Single, **D**=Double/Twin, **T**=Triple, **Q**=Quad, **B**=Bath/Shower, **WC**=Toilet, **CC**=Credit Card (Visa, Mastercard, Amex), **SE**=Speaks English (graded **A** through **F**).

Sleeping near the Ramblas and in the Gothic Quarter (postal code: 08002)

(These accommodations are listed in geographical order from Plaça de Catalunya down.) **Catalunya Plaza** (DBWC-14,000 ptas, CC:VMA, on the plaza at Pl. Catalunya 7, tel. 317 7171, fax 317 7855, SE-A) is a business hotel with all the air-con, mini-bar comforts. When it drops its rates (usually DBWC-10,000 ptas in June and September, 9,000 ptas in July and August) it's a great value for those needing all the sterile comforts in an elegant old building. **Hotel Barcelona** (DBWC-15,000 ptas, with a sun roof terrace, a block away at Caspe 1-13, tel. 302 5858, fax 301 8674) is another big American-style hotel with soft prices.

Hotel Toledano's elevator takes you high above the noise and into the zona bella vista. Request a view balcony to overlook the Ramblas. It's small and folksy and owner Juan Sanz speaks English (SB-3,400 ptas, SBWC-3,800 ptas, DBWC-6,200 ptas, TBWC-8,000 ptas, QBWC-9,000 ptas, about 400 ptas more per person in July, August, and September, CC:VMA, Rambla de Canaletas 138, tel. 301 0872, fax 412 3142). Juan runs **Hostal Residencia Capitol** one floor above, which is cheaper and appropriate for backpackers (D-4,000 ptas, DB-4,500 ptas, up to six in a room gets down to youth hostel prices).

The **Hotel Lloret** is a big, old world, well-worn, and airy place right on the Ramblas (DBWC-6,000 ptas, request Ramblas balcony or *tranquilo*, CC:VMA, elevator dominates the stairwell, Rambla de Canaletas 125, tel. 317 3366, fax 301 9283, SE-B). If you want to immerse yourself in the Ramblas, do it here.

Huéspedes Santa Ana, nearby on Calle Santa Ana, a wonderful pedestrian street one block down the Ramblas, has plain, clean, quiet, dumpy rooms (S-2,000 ptas, D-3,000 ptas, DBWC-4,000 ptas, T-3,500 ptas, C. Santa Ana 23, tel. 301 2246, SE-F).

Nouvel Hotel, an elegant Victorian-style building on the same great street, ran out of renovation steam so is actually two hotels in one: a classy place and a cheap one with one classy lounge and management. Prices vary widely between the "old" rooms (D-6,400 ptas, DBWC-8,600 ptas) and the "new" rooms (SBWC-9,000 ptas, DBWC-11,000 ptas, or huge DBWC-15,000 ptas, air-con and royal, CC: VMA, C. Santa Ana 18, tel. 301 8274, fax 301 8370, SE-A). Sister hotels (DBWC-7,500 ptas) straddling the same street and run by one company, with shiny, modern bathrooms and all the comforts but in a building that feels more concrete than Victorian, are **Hotel Cataluna** (C. Santa Ana 24, tel. 301 9120, fax 302 7870, elevator) and **Hotel Cortes** (C. Santa Ana 25, tel. 317 9112, fax 302 7870, no elevator but feels better). **Hostal Campi** (DBWC-4,200 ptas, around the corner at Canuda 4, no elevator, tel. 301 3545), big, old, and ramshackle, is a few doors off the Ramblas.

Huéspedes Colmenero (S-2,000 ptas, D-3,000 ptas, DBWC-4,000 ptas, 1,000 ptas more if staying only one night, two streets toward the cathedral from the Ramblas at Petritxol 12, tel. 302 6634, fax: what's that) is very clean and family run on a great, safe, and quiet street, with cute rooms and tiny balconies. Rosa speaks French but no English and offers the best cheap rooms in the old town.

Hotel Jardi is a hard-working, plain place on the happiest little square in the Gothic Quarter (SBWC-3,800 ptas, DBWC-5,000 ptas-7,000 ptas, depending on newness and view balconies, TBWC-5,600 ptas-8,5000 ptas, CC:VMA, no elevator, halfway between the Ramblas and the cathedral on Plaça Sant Josep Oriol #1, tel. 301 5900, fax 318 3664). Bathrooms are modern; except for smudged white walls, it's clean; and rooms with balconies enjoy a classic plaza setting.

To sleep safe and quiet but deeper in the Gothic Quarter, these two new, modern neighbors keep businessmen happy with TV, telephone, and air con: **Hotel Adagio** (SBWC-5,500 ptas, DBWC-7,000 ptas, TBWC-8,000 ptas, CC:VMA, elevator, Fernando 21, tel. and fax 318 3724). **Hotel California** (SBWC-5,000 ptas, DBWC-7,600 ptas, TBWC-9,500 ptas, including breakfast, CC:VMA, Raurich 14, tel. 317 7766, fax 317 5474). The California lacks an elevator but has bigger and brighter halls and bathrooms.

Sleeping in Eixample (postal code: 08008)

For a more elegant and boulevardian neighborhood, sleep north of Gran Vía Cortes Catalanes in Eixample, a 10-minute walk from the Ramblas action.

There's nothing noncommital about Hotel Residencia Neutral (tiny SB-2,500 ptas, big SB-3,000 ptas, DB-4,000 ptas, DBWC-5,035 ptas, TB-5,000 ptas, TBWC-6,300 ptas, elegantly located two blocks north of Gran Vía at Rambla Cataluña 42, 08007 Barcelona, tel/fax 487 6390, SE-B). With 35 cheery rooms, classy public rooms, mosaic floors, high ceilings, and a passion for cleanliness, it's the best Eixample value.

Hostal Residencia Windsor has musty carpets but is peaceful and a decent value (DB-5,500 ptas, DBWC-6,000 ptas, elevator, Rambla Cataluña 84, tel. 215 1198).

Pensión Fani is a rare budget find for women only (as Aussies already may have guessed). Clean, dark, quiet, and with a whiff of mystery to a male researcher (1,500 ptas per person in 1- or 2-bed rooms, Valencia 278, second floor, elevator, tel. 215 3645 and 215 3044).

Hostal Palacios, on Gran Vía across from the tourist info (S-2,300 ptas, SB-3,300 ptas, SBWC-3,700 ptas, DB-4,100 ptas, DBWC-4,500 ptas, more roommates-1,200 ptas each, CC:VMA, elevator, Gran Vía Cortes Catalanas #629, tel. 301 3792, SE-C), was classy but is now just tired and well-worn.

Youth Hostels
Hostal de Joves (1,000 ptas per person, Pg. de Pujades 29, next to Parc de la Ciutadella and metro: Marina, tel. 300 3104, open 7:00-10:00 and 15:00-24:00) is clean and well-run. The **Hostal Mare de Deu de Montserrat** (1,300 ptas bed and breakfast, 1,700 ptas with dinner, 600 ptas more if you're over 25, sheets 350 ptas, must be a member, Pg. Mare de Deu del Coll 41, near Parc Güell, bus #28 from Pl. Catalunya (also near Parc Güell) or metro: Vallcarca, tel. 210 5151) is open all day, much cheerier than Hostal de Joves, and worth the extra commute time. **Hostal Pere Tarres** (C. Numancia 149, near the Sants-Central station and metro: Les Corts, tel. 410 2309) is also good and accepts nonmembers willing to pay a bit more.

Eating in Barcelona
Barcelona, the capital of Catalonian cuisine, offers a tremendous variety of colorful places to eat. The harbor area, especially Barceloneta, is famous for fish. The best tapa bars are in the Barri Gòtic and around the Picasso Museum. **Los Caracoles** at Escudelleros 14 (a block off the Plaça Reial in red-light bar country, open 13:00-24:00 daily) is a sort of Spanish beer hall—huge and always packed. My favorite place for local-style food in a local-style setting is **Restaurant Agut** (C. Gignas 16, tel. 315 1709, huge servings, inexpensive, closed in July). **El Portalon at Calle Banys Nous 20** in the bowels of the Gothic Quarter (between Ramblas and cathedral) drips with atmosphere and offers good food and drink. For fewer tourists, less color, and more class, you can find good reasonable meals in the Gràcia and Eixample districts.

Self Naturista (near several recommended hotels, just off the top of Ramblas at 13 Carrer di Santa Ana, 11:30-

22:00, closed Sunday) is a bright and cheery buffet that will make vegetarians and health food lovers feel right at home. Others may find a few unidentifiable plates and drinks.

Transportation Connections
Barcelona to Lisbon: (2/day, 20 hrs with change in Madrid), **Madrid** (7/day, 7-9 hrs, $50 with a couchette), **Paris** (3/day, 11-15 hrs), **Sevilla** (4/day, 10-14 hrs). **By bus: Madrid** (6/day, 8 hrs, half the price of a train ticket).
Barcelona's El Prat Airport is 12 km out of town and connected cheap, fast, and easy by Aerobus (immediately in front of arrivals lobby, 4/hr, 20 min to Pl. de Catalunya, buy 400-ptas ticket from driver) or by RENFE train (walk the tunnel overpass from airport to station, 2/hr, 20 min, 250 ptas, to Sants Station and Pl. de Catalunya). Airport information: tel. 478 5000.

Spain and Portugal

MADRID

Today's Madrid is upbeat and vibrant, enjoying a kind of post-Franco renaissance. You'll feel it. Even the statue-maker beggars have pride.

Madrid is the hub of Spain. This modern capital, Europe's highest at over 2,000 feet, has a population of more than 4 million. It's young by European standards. Only 400 years ago, King Philip II decided to move the capital of his empire from Toledo to Madrid. One hundred years ago, Madrid had only 400,000 people, so nine-tenths of the city is modern sprawl, surrounding an intact, easy to navigate historic center.

Dive headlong into the grandeur and intimate charms of Madrid. The lavish Royal Palace, with its gilded rooms and frescoed ceilings, rivals Versailles. The Prado has Europe's top collection of paintings. The city's huge Retiro Park invites you for a shady siesta and a hopscotch through a mosaic of lovers, families, skateboarders, pets walking their masters, and old-time bench-sitters. Make time for Madrid's elegant shops and people-friendly pedestrian zones. On Sundays, cheer for the bull at a bullfight or bargain like mad at a mega-flea market. Lively Madrid has enough street-singing, bar-hopping, and people-watching vitality to give any visitor a boost of youth.

Planning Your Time

Madrid's top two sights, the Prado and the palace, are worth a day. If you hit the city on a Sunday, allot another day for the flea market and a bullfight.

Ideally, give Madrid two days (outside of Sunday events) and spend them this way:

Day 1: Breakfast of *churros* as recommended below before a brisk, good morning Madrid walk for 20 minutes from Puerto del Sol to the Prado. 9:00 to noon in the Prado. Lunch at La Plaza. Afternoon siesta in the Retiro Park or lapping up the modern art at Reina Sofia *(Guernica)* and/or the Thyssen-Bornemisza Museum. Early evening paseo, tapas for dinner around Plaza Santa Ana.

Day 2: Breakfast and browse through San Miguel market,

tour Royal Palace, lunch near Plaza Mayor, afternoon free
for other sights, shopping, or side trip to El Escorial (open
until 19:00). Note that the Prado, the T-B Museum, and El
Escorial are closed on Monday.

Madrid

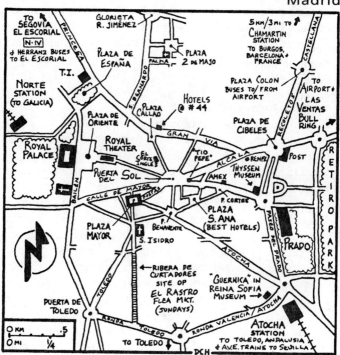

Orientation (tel. code: 91)

The historic center can be covered easily on foot. No major
sight is more than a 15-minute walk from the Puerta del Sol,
Madrid's central square. Your time will be divided between
the city's two major sights—the palace and the Prado—and its
bar-hopping, car-honking, sky-scraping contemporary scene.

The Puerta del Sol is at the dead center of Madrid and
of Spain itself; notice the kilometer zero marker, from which
all of Spain is surveyed, at the police station (southwest corner). The Royal Palace to the west and the Prado Museum
and Retiro Park to the east frame Madrid's historic center.

Southwest of Puerta del Sol is a 17th-century district

with the slow-down-and-smell-the-cobbles Plaza Mayor and plenty of relics from pre-industrial Spain.

North of Puerta del Sol runs the Gran Vía. Between the Gran Vía and the Puerta del Sol are lively pedestrian shopping streets. The Gran Vía, bubbling with business, expensive shops, and cinemas, leads down to the impressively modern Plaza de España. North of the Gran Vía is the gritty Malasana quarter with its colorful small houses, shoemakers' shops, sleazy-looking *hombres*, milk vendors, bars, and hip night scene.

Tourist Information

Madrid's main Turismo is on the ground floor of the Torre de Madrid (the only skyscraper in town, on Plaza de España, open 9:00-19:00, Saturday 9:30-13:30, closed Sunday, tel. 541 2325). There is another office 2 blocks toward the center from the Prado (Duque de Medinaceli 2, tel. 429 4951, same hours) and smaller offices at the airport and train stations. Confirm your sightseeing plans and pick up the free monthly city guide with a map. Ask about bullfights and Zarzuela if interested. If you're heading to other destinations in Spain, (cover your head and) ask for the free brochures titled *Toledo, Salamanca, Madrid and Its Surroundings, Segovia, Cuidad Real, Sevilla, Granada, Pueblos Blancos of Andalucia, Costa de la Luz* (for Tarifa), *Costa del Sol* (for Nerja), and the amazingly informative *Mapa de Comunicaciones España*, listing all the Turismos, paradores, RENFE train information telephone numbers, and highway SOS numbers with a road map of Spain. Many small town Turismos keep erratic hours and run out of these pamphlets, so get what you can here. Madrid's easy-to-decipher periodical entertainment guide, *Guía del Ocio*, is on sale at streetside newsstands.

Arriving by Air

Madrid's Barajas Airport, 10 miles east of downtown, comes well equipped to help new arrivals: Airport info tel. 329 1212, 24-hour bank with fair rates, TI (8:00-20:00, Saturday 9:00-13:00, closed Sunday, tel. 305 8656, see list of what to get under Tourist Info above), a telephone office where you can buy a phone card, a RENFE desk for rail information, a pharmacy, on-the-spot car rental agencies, and easy public transportation into town. Use your phone card and call to confirm your hotel and the price, then take the yellow bus into Madrid (to Plaza Colón, 4/hr, 30 min, 325 ptas). From Plaza Colón, take the subway to your hotel. To find the nearest subway stop, walk past the modern sculpture on Plaza Colón and cross the street. (If you taxi, insist on the meter.)

Trains

The two main rail stations, Atocha and Chamartin, are both on subway lines and easily accessible from anywhere in the city. Note that there are two Atocha metro stations. The train station's metro station is called Atocha RENFE. Each station has all the services. Train information: 563 0202. Remember, in Spain, train rides longer than about 3 hours require reservations, even if you have a Eurailpass. To avoid needless running around, arrange your departure upon arrival.

Buses

The two key bus stations are both on metro lines as well: Estacion La Sepulvedana at Paseo de la Florida, metro Norte (service to Segovia); and Estacion Herranz, on Calle Fernandez de los Rios metro Moncloa (service to El Escorial).

Getting Around Madrid

By Subway: Madrid's subway is cheap (125 ptas/ride, buy the 10-ride ticket for 600 ptas), speedy (you'll go about seven stops in 10 minutes) and simple. The city's broad streets can be hot and exhausting. A subway trip of even a stop or two can save time and energy. Pick up a free map (Plano del Metro) at any station. Navigate by subway stops (shown on maps). To transfer, follow signs to the next subway line (numbered and color-coded). As in Paris, end stops are used to indicate directions. Insert your ticket in the turnstile and retrieve it as you pass through. Green *Salida* signs point to the exit. Since most stations have several exits, choosing the correct exit (streets marked) can avoid needless walking. City buses, while not so cheap or easy, can be helpful (details and schedules at booth on Puerta del Sol).

By Taxi: Taxis are reasonable but for long rides (e.g., to Chamartin station) you'll go faster and cheaper by subway.

Helpful Hints

The American Express office at Plaza Cortes 2 is a handy place to cash travelers' checks and buy AVE train tickets (tel. 322 5500). The U.S. Embassy is at Serrano 75 (tel. 577 4000) and the Canadian Embassy is at Nuñez de Balboa 35 (tel. 431 4300). The grand department store, El Corte Inglés (just off Puerto del Sol, 10:00-21:00 Monday-Saturday) has a travel agency and gives free Madrid maps (an enlarged original of the one the TI gives). The telephone office, centrally located at Gran Vía 30, (daily 9:30-23:30), accepts credit cards.

Sights—Madrid

▲▲▲**Prado Museum**—The Prado is my favorite collection of paintings, anywhere. With over 3,000 paintings, including entire rooms of masterpieces by Velázquez, Goya, El Greco, and Bosch, it's overwhelming. Take a tour or buy a guidebook (or bring me along by ripping out and packing the Prado chapter from *Mona Winks*). Focus on the Flemish and northern art (Bosch, Dürer, Rubens), the Italian collection (Fra Angelico, Raphael, Botticelli, Titian), and the Spanish art (El Greco, Velázquez, Goya).

Follow Goya through his cheery (*The Parasol*), political (*The Third of May*), and dark (*Saturn Devouring His Children*) stages. In each stage, Goya asserted his independence from artistic conventions. Even the standard court portraits of his "first" stage reflect his politically liberal viewpoint, subtly showing the vanity and stupidity of his subjects by the look in their goony eyes. His political stage, with paintings like *The Third of May*, depicting a massacre of Spaniards by Napoleon's troops, makes him one of the first artists with a social conscience. Finally, in his gloomy "dark stage," Goya probed the inner world of fears and nightmares, anticipating the 20th-century preoccupation with dreams. Also, don't miss Bosch's Garden of Delights. Most art is grouped by painters and any guard can point you in the right direction if you say "*¿Donde está . . . ?*" and the painter's name as Españoled as you can (e.g., Titian is "*Ticiano*" and Bosch is "*El Bosco*"). The Prado (400 ptas, 9:00-19:00, Sunday 9:00-14:00, closed Monday, tel. 420 2836) is quietest at lunchtime, from 14:00-16:00.

The Prado has a fine cafeteria with tables in an outdoor courtyard upstairs. But wait, if Madrid's museum trio has you exhausted and hungry, pamper yourself in the healthy, air-con garden world of **La Plaza**, a bright and breezy cafeteria in the Galeria del Prado on the ground floor of the Palace Hotel across the street from the Prado where San Jeronimo hits Plaza Canovas del Castillo (piled high salad plate, 450 ptas).

▲▲**Picasso's Guernica**—Located in the Centro de Arte Reina Sofia, three blocks south of the Prado across from the Atocha train station, this famous painting showing the horror of modern war deserves much study. The death of Franco ended the work's exile in America, and now it reigns as Spain's national piece of art—behind bulletproof glass. (400 ptas, students free, 10:00-21:00, Sunday 10:00-14:30, closed Tuesday, Santa Isabel 52, tel. 467 5062.)

▲▲**Thyssen-Bornemisza Museum**—This stunning new museum displays the impressive collection of Baron Thyssen, a wealthy German married to a former Miss Spain. Art lovers appreciate how the good baron's art complements the Prado's collection. For a fine walk through art history, start on the top floor and do the rooms in numerical order. While it's basically minor works by major artists and major works by minor artists (the real big guns are over at the Prado), the Thyssen is stronger in Impressionism and 20th-century art. Located across from the Prado at Paseo del Prado 8 in the Palacio de Villahermosa (600 ptas, 10:00-19:00, closed Monday, tel. 369 0151).

▲▲**Plaza Mayor and Medieval Madrid**—The Plaza Mayor, a vast, cobbled, traffic-free chunk of 17th-century Spain, is just a short walk from the Puerta del Sol. Each side of the square is uniform, as if a grand palace were turned inside out. Throughout Spain, lesser *plaza mayors* provide peaceful pools for the river of Spanish life. A stamp and coin market bustles here on Sunday mornings, and any day it's a colorful (and affordable) place to enjoy a cup of coffee.

Medieval Madrid is now a rather sterile tangle of narrow streets bounded by the Royal Palace, Plaza Mayor, Teatro Real, and Plaza Puerta de Moros. The uninviting old Plaza de la Villa was the center of Madrid before Madrid was the center of Spain. The most enjoyable action in this area is contained in a glass and iron cage called the Mercado de San Miguel (produce market) next to the Plaza Mayor. Drop by for the morning flurry. Pull up a stool for breakfast.

▲▲▲**Palacio Real (Royal Palace)**—Europe's third-greatest palace (after Versailles and Vienna) is packed with tourists and royal antiques. You can wander on your own through its clock-filled, lavish interior, or join an English tour (free with admission, going whenever a group of 10 to 20 gather, if you just missed one try to catch up with it, 800 ptas, daily 9:00-18:00, Sunday 9:00-15:00, tel. 542 0059, very crowded in summer, arrive early or late). Your ticket includes the impressive armory and the pharmacy, both on the courtyard. The nearby Museo de Carruajes Reales has an excellent collection of royal carriages (closed, probably through 1995). The newly consecrated Cathedral de la Almudena (free, 10:00-13:00, 18:00-20:00) facing the palace where you enter is refreshingly clean, modern, and utilitarian.

▲▲**Zarzuela**—For a delightful look at Spanish light opera that even English-speakers can enjoy, try an evening of Zarzuela. Guitar-strumming Napoleons in red capes, buxom women with masks and fans, castanets and stomping feet, aficionados singing along from the cheap seats where the acoustics are best, Spanish-speaking pharaohs, melodramatic spotlights, bullfight music with legions of glittering matadors—that's Zarzuela. The TI's monthly guide has a special Zarzuela listing. Don't mess with flamenco in Madrid. Save it for Sevilla.

▲▲**El Rastro**—Europe's biggest flea market is a field day for people watchers (Sunday 9:00-12:00, best early). Thousands of stalls titillate over a million browsers. If you brake for garage sales, you'll pull a U-turn for El Rastro. You can buy or sell nearly anything here. Start at the Plaza Mayor and head south, or take the subway to Tirso de Molina. Hang onto your wallet. Munch on a *pepito* (sweet pudding-filled pastry) or a *relleno*. Europe's biggest stamp market thrives simultaneously on the Plaza Mayor.

Chapel San Antonio de la Florida—Goya's tomb stares up at a splendid cupola filled with his own frescoes (free, 10:00-14:00 and 16:00-20:00, Saturday and Sunday 10:00-14:00, closed Monday, Po. de la Florida 5, metro: Norte, tel. 547 0722).

▲▲**Retiro Park**—Siesta in this 350-acre green and breezy escape from the city. Rent a rowboat, have a picnic. These peaceful gardens offer great people-watching. The Botanical Garden (Jardín Botánico) nearby is a pleasant extension of Retiro Park to the southwest. Ride the metro to Retiro, walk to the big lake (El Estanque) where you can rent a rowboat, or wander through the Palacio de Crystal. A grand boulevard of statues leads to the Prado.

▲▲▲**Bullfight**—Madrid's Plaza de Toros hosts Spain's top bullfights on most Sundays and holidays from Easter through October and nearly every day mid-May through early June. Top fights sell out in advance. Fights usually start at 19:00 and are a rare example of Spanish punctuality. Tickets range from 1,000 ptas-6,000 ptas. There are no bad seats; paying more gets you in the shade and/or closer to the gore (filas 8, 9, and 10 tend to be closest to the action). Bookings offices (C. de la Victoria 3, tel. 521 1213, or Pl. del Carmen 1, tel. 431 2732) add 20 percent and don't sell the cheap seats. To save money, buy your ticket at the bull-ring. Ten percent of the seats are kept available to be sold 2 hours before the fight. The bullfighting museum (Museo Taurino) is next to the bullring (free, daily 9:00-14:00, metro: Ventas).

▲**Real Fabrica de Tapices (Royal Tapestry Factory)**—Have a look at the traditional making of tapestries (cheap tours in Spanish only, 50 ptas, Monday-Friday 9:00-12:30, closed August, metro: Menendez Pelayo, tel. 551 3400).

▲**Paseo**—The people of Madrid (*Madrileños*) siesta because so much goes on in the evening. The nightly paseo is Madrid on parade. Young and old, everyone's outside taking a stroll, "cruising" without cars, seeing and being seen. Gran Vía and the Paseo del Prado are particularly active scenes.

Parque de Atracciones—For a colorful amusement park scene, complete with Venetian canals, dancing, eating, games, free shows, and top-notch people-watching, try Parque de Atracciones (open most afternoons and evenings until around midnight, only Saturday and Sunday in off-season, tel. 463 2900 for exact times, metro: Batan). This fun fair and Spain's best zoo (open 10:00-21:00) are both in the vast Casa del Campo Park just west of the Royal Palace.

Heart of Madrid

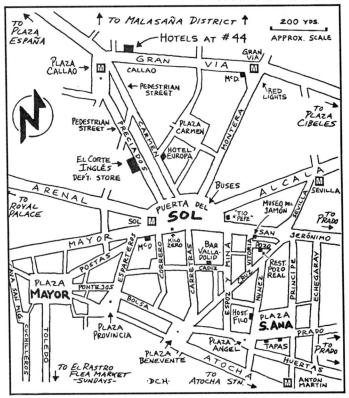

Shopping—Shoppers can focus on the colorful pedestrian area between Gran Vía and Puerta del Sol. The giant queen of Spanish department stores, El Corte Inglés (10:00-21:00, closed Sunday, free maps, supermarket in basement), is a block off Puerta del Sol and a handy place to pick up just about anything you may need.

Sleeping in Madrid (tel. code: 91, 125 ptas=$1)
Madrid has plenty of centrally located budget hotels and pensions. You'll have no trouble finding a decent double for $25-$50. Madrid is most crowded in July and August, but prices are the same throughout the year, and it's almost always easy to find a place. The places I've listed are all within a few minutes' walk of Puerta del Sol.

Competition is stiff. Those on a budget can bargain. Nighttime Madrid's economy is brisk. Even decent areas are littered with shady-looking people after dark. Just don't invite them in.

Sleep code: **S**=Single, **D**=Double/Twin, **T**=Triple, **Q**=Quad, **B**=Bath/Shower, **WC**=Toilet, **CC**=Credit Card (**V**isa, **M**astercard, **A**mex), **SE**=Speaks English (graded **A** through **F**).

Sleeping on Plaza Santa Ana
(postal code: 28012)
The Plaza Santa Ana area has plenty of small, pleasant, and cheap places. It's my favorite Madrid locale for its almost Parisian ambience, colorful bars, and very central location— 3 minutes past the Puerta del Sol's "Tío Pepe" sign, walk down Calle San Jeronimo and make a right on Principe. Metro: Sol.

In the beautifully tiled Plaza Santa Ana 15 building, on the corner of the square closest to Puerta del Sol and all the good tapas bars, and up a dark wooden staircase are three of my favorites: **Hostal Filo** is squeaky clean with a nervous but helpful management and 20 rooms hiding in a confusing floor plan (S-2,000 ptas, D-3,500 ptas, DB-4,500 ptas, T-4,000 ptas, TB-4,900 ptas, second floor, tel. 522 4056, closed August). **Hostal Delvi**, upstairs on the third floor, is smaller and cozier with nine bright and clean rooms (S-1,800 ptas, D-3,000 ptas, T-4,500 ptas, tel. 522 5998, no English spoken). Marie promises these "special" prices to those with this book. The best value, if you don't mind climbing the stairs may be **Hostal la Rosa**, also on the third floor, with shiny wood floors and charming rooms (S-1,800 ptas, small D-2,200 ptas, D-3,000 ptas, DB-4,000 ptas, TB-5,200 ptas, QB-6,000 ptas, 5B-6,500 ptas, tel. 532 5805). Encarnita speaks no English, but for 800 ptas you can use her washing machine.

Across the street, **Hostal Lucense** offers basic rooms and hard-working English-speaking managers, Sr. and Sra. Muñoz (S-1,200 ptas, D-2,000 ptas, DB-2,600 ptas, T-3,000 ptas, 150 ptas per shower, Nuñez de Arce 15, tel. 522 4888). They also run the neighboring and similar **Casa Huéspedes Poza** (same prices, Nuñez de Arce 9, tel. 222 4871). Easy-to-please vagabonds might enjoy playing corkscrew up the rickety cut-glass elevator to **Pensión La Valenciana** with old and funky rooms, springy beds, three rooms with great balconies over the square (D-3,000 ptas, Principe 27, fourth floor, right on Plaza Santa Ana next to the theater, tel. 429 6317, SE-F). Because of these three places I list no Madrid youth hostels.

To be on the same square and spend in a day what others spend in a week, luxuriate in the **Hotel Victoria** (DBWC-20,000 ptas, tel. 531 4500, fax 522 0307, SE-A). For a royal, air-conditioned breather and some cheap entertainment, spit out your gum, step into its lobby, grab a sofa, and watch the bellboys push the beggars back out the revolving doors.

Hostal Montalvo is sprawling, dark, and comfortable, and just 85 cobbles off the elegant Plaza Mayor on a quiet, traffic-free street (DBWC-4,800 ptas, TBWC-7,000 ptas, Zaragoza 6, third floor, tel. 365 5910).

Sleeping at Gran Vía #44 (postal code: 28013)

The pulse (and noise) of today's Madrid is best felt along the Gran Vía. This main drag in the heart of the city stays alight all night. Despite the dreary pile of prostitutes just a block north, there's a certain urban decency about it. My choices (all at Gran Vía #44, entrance between the Lladro shop and the Loteria) are across from Plaza del Callão, a colorful 4 blocks of pedestrian malls up from the Puerta del Sol. Although many rooms are high above the traffic noise, I'd request *tranquilo* for a brick-wall view on the back side. The fancy old Café Fuyma next door provides a classy way to breakfast, and there are a couple of good delis around the corner, half a block up Calle de Miguel Moya. The Callão metro stop is at your doorstep and the handy Gran Vía stop (direct to Atocha) is 2 blocks away.

Hostal Residencia Miami is clean, quiet, and cheery, with lovely, well-lit rooms, padded doors, and plastic flower decor throughout. It's like staying at your eccentric aunt's in Miami Beach. The bubbly landlady, Sra. Sanz, and her too careful husband, who dresses up each day for work here, speak no English (S-2,800 ptas, D-3,800 ptas, DBWC-4,000 ptas, eighth floor, tel. 521 1464, closed August).

Across the hall, **Hostal Alibel**, like Miami with more smiles and less sugar, rents eight big, airy, and quiet rooms (D-3,000 ptas, DB-4,000 ptas, DBWC-4,300, tel. 521 0051, SE-D). Downstairs, **Hostal Josefina** smells like fish, has creaky vinyl floors and junkyard doors but strong beds in museum-warehouse rooms (S-1,800 ptas, SB-2,000 ptas, DB-3,000 ptas, seventh floor, tel. 521 8131 and 531 0466, SE-F).

Hostal Residencia Valencia is bright, cheery, and much more professional than the others. The friendly manager, Antonio Ramirez, speaks English (SBWC-3,700 ptas, big SBWC-4,200 ptas, DB-5,000 ptas, DBWC-5,500 ptas, CC:VM, fifth floor, tel. 522 1115, fax 522 1113). Also friendly and a good value but with less character is **Hostal Residencia Continental** (SB-3,600 ptas, DBWC-4,700 ptas, CC:VMA, fourth floor, tel. 521 4640, fax 521 4649).

Sleeping in the Pedestrian Zone Between Puerta del Sol and Gran Vía (postal code: 28013)

I've listed these places for my softer and more well-heeled readers. Away from the seediness and totally predictable, these are good values for those wanting to spend a little more. Especially for these hotels, call first to see if the price is firm. Their formal prices may be inflated. Metro: Sol or Callao.

Hotel Europa (SBWC-5,500 ptas, DBWC-7,500 ptas, TBWC-9,500 ptas, no CC, C. del Carmen 4, tel. 521 2900, fax 521 4696, SE-A, easy telephone reservations with no deposit) has red carpet charm. A quiet courtyard, a royal salon, plush halls, squeaky clean rooms with balconies over the pedestrian zone or over a peaceful inner courtyard, polished wood floors, and all rooms with TVs and big modern bathrooms. They have a 750-ptas a day parking deal. **Hotel Londres** (DBWC-9,400 with air-con, 8,400 ptas without air-con, CC:VM, Galdo 2, tel. 531 4105, fax 531 4101, SE-B) is a business-class hotel: dark, stark, a bit smoky, but well run and with all the comforts. Thirty of its rooms are air-conditioned. **Hotel Euromadrid** (DBWC-7,500 ptas, Mesonero Romanos 7, tel. 521 7200, fax 521 4582, SE-B) is bright, modern, with a concrete character rather than charm. It's all air-con with modern full baths, flimsy beds, TVs, and an elevator.

Eating in Madrid

In Spain, only Barcelona rivals Madrid for taste bud thrills. You have two basic dining choices: an atmospheric sit-down meal in a well-chosen restaurant or making a meal of tapas (appetizers) in a bar—or series of bars.

Restaurants

I can't begin to know Madrid's best restaurants. But for an inexpensive, local-style dinner within 2 blocks of the Puerta del Sol consider the **Restaurant Pozo Real** (C. Del Pozo 6, tel. 521 7951, friendly, popular with locals, quiet tables in back, Madrid's best pastry shop is next door), or **Restaurante Rodriguez** (850-ptas menu, 15 San Cristobal, one block toward Sol from Plaza Mayor, tel. 231 1136) where the TV's on and the locals know each other. Most Americans are drawn to Hemingway's favorite, **Sobrinos del Botín** (Cuchilleros 17 in old town, tel. 266 4217). Frighteningly touristy, it's the last place he'd go now.

Tapas: For maximum fun, people, and atmosphere, go mobile and do the "tapa tango"—a local tradition of going from one bar to the next, munching, drinking, and socializing. Tapas are toothpick appetizers, salads, and deep-fried foods served in most bars. Madrid is Spain's tapa capital. Grab a toothpick and stab something strange. Establish prices first. Some items are very pricey and bartenders push larger r*acions* rather than smaller tapas. *Un pincho* is a bite-sized serving, *una tapa* is a bit more, and *una racion* is a half a meal. Say *"un bocadillo"* and it comes on bread as a sandwich. *Caña* is a glass of draft beer.

For a central, good tapas district, prowl the area between Puerta del Sol and Plaza Santa Ana. There's no ideal route, but the little streets (listed in this book's map) between Puerta del Sol, San Jeronimo, and Plaza Santa Ana hold some tasty surprises. From Puerta del Sol, head east to Carrera de San Jeronimo 6 for your first stop: the **Museo del Jamón** (Museum of Ham)—tastefully decorated unless you happen to be a pig). This frenetic, cheap, stand-up bar is an assembly line of fast and deliciously simple *bocadillos* and *raciones*. Options are shown in photographs with prices. Just point and eat. Shrimp lovers, head up the street to tiny **La Casa del Abuelo** (at Victoria 12), where sizzling *gambas*

go down great with the house wine. From there fan out
walking each little street within a hundred yards. Finish by
following Nuñez de Arce up to Plaza Santa Ana where (on
the far side) several upscale *cervecerias* spill onto the sidewalk. A relaxing and classy spot for your last tapa.

Picnics: The department store El Corte Inglés has a
well-stocked deli, but its produce is sold only in large quantities. A perfect place to assemble a cheap picnic is downtown
Madrid's neighborhood market, Mercado de San Miguel
(from the Plaza Mayor, face the colorful building and exit
from the upper left-hand corner). How about breakfast in
the market's café/bar surrounded by early morning shoppers,
with a couple of delicious oranges to go?

Churros con chocolate for breakfast: If you like hash
browns and eggs in American greasy spoon joints, you must
try the Spanish equivalent: greasy, cigar-shaped fritters
dipped in pudding-like chocolate at **Bar Vallodolid** (two
blocks off the Tío Pepe end of Puerta del Sol, up Espoz y
Mina, turn right on C. de Cadiz). It's the changing of the
guard, as workers of the night finish their day by downing
a cognac and workers of the day start theirs by dipping *churros*
into chocolate. With luck, the *churros* machine in the back will
be cooking. Throw your napkin on the floor like you own the
place. For something with less grease and more substance, ask
for a *tortilla española* (potato omelet) and *café con leche*.

Transportation Connections
Madrid to: Barcelona (7/day, 8-9 hrs), **Granada** (3/day, 6-9
hrs), **Sevilla** (12/day, 9 hrs or 2½ by AVE), **Lisbon** (2/day, 8-
10 hrs), **Paris** (5/day, 12-16 hrs), **Toledo** (10/day, 1 hr),
Segovia (10/day, 2 hrs), **Salamanca** (3/day, 3 hrs).

Spain's new AVE (ah-vay) bullet train opens up some
good itinerary options. Pick up the brochure at the station.
Prices vary with times and class. The basic Madrid-Sevilla fare
is 8,400 ptas. AVE is now 85 percent covered by Eurail (so the
Madrid-Sevilla-Madrid trip costs Eurailers about $20). So far
AVE only covers Madrid-Córdoba-Sevilla. Consider this
exciting day trip from Madrid: 8:00 depart, 9:40-12:40 in
Cordoba, 13:30-21:00 in Sevilla, 23:30 back in Madrid.

THE BERNER OBERLAND

Frolic and hike high above the stress and clouds of the real world. Take a vacation from your busy vacation. Recharge your touristic batteries up here in the Alps where distant avalanches, cowbells, the fluff of a down comforter, and the crunchy footsteps of happy hikers are the dominant sounds. If the weather's good, ride a gondola from the traffic-free village of Gimmelwald to a hearty breakfast at Schilthorn's 10,000-foot revolving Piz Gloria restaurant. Linger among Alpine whitecaps before riding, hiking, or hang gliding down (5,000 feet) to Mürren and home to Gimmelwald.

Your gateway to the wonderfully mountainous Berner Oberland is the grand old resort town of Interlaken. Near Interlaken is Switzerland's greatest open-air folk museum, Ballenberg, where you climb through traditional houses from every corner of this diverse country.

Ah, but the weather's fine and the Alps beckon. Head deep into the heart of the Alps and ride the gondola to the stop just this side of heaven—Gimmelwald.

Planning Your Time

Rather than tackling a checklist of famous Swiss mountains and resorts, choose one area to savor. That area is the Berner Oberland. Interlaken is the administrative headquarters (fine transportation hub, banking, post office, laundry, shopping). Use it for that business and as a springboard for Alpine thrills. With decent weather, explore the two areas (south of Interlaken) which tower above either side of the Lauterbrunnen Valley: Kleine Scheidegg/Jungfrau and the Schilthorn/Mürren. Ideally, homebase three nights in the village of Gimmelwald and spend a day in each area. If on a speedy train trip, you can overnight into and out of Interlaken. For the speediest look, consider a night in Gimmelwald, breakfast at the Schilthorn, an afternoon doing the Mannlichen-to-Wengen hike, and an evening or night train out. Not spending the night is Alpus-interruptus.

Getting Around the Berner Oberland

For over a hundred years this has been the target of nature-worshipping pilgrims. And the Swiss have made the most exciting Alpine perches accessible by lift or train. Part of the fun (and most of the expense) of the area is riding the many lifts. Generally, scenic trains and lifts are not covered on train passes. There are several discount plans for early-birds, families, seniors, groups, and those staying a while. Get a list of discounts and the free fare and time schedule at any station or in Interlaken. Study the "Alpine Lifts in the Jungfrau Region" chart on page 508. Lifts generally go at least twice an hour 7:00-20:00 but you can take advantage of the time schedule to plan efficiently.

Interlaken

When the 19th-century Romantics redefined mountains as something more than cold and troublesome obstacles, Interlaken became the original Alpine resort. Ever since then, tourists have flocked to the Alps "because they're

Interlaken

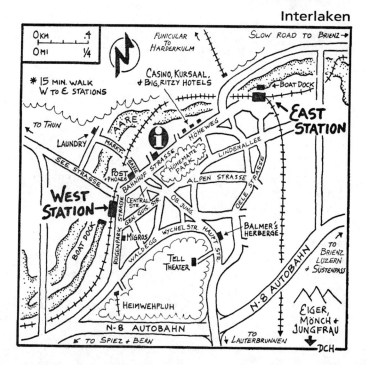

there." Interlaken's glory days are long gone, its elegant old hotels eclipsed by the new, more jet-setty Alpine resorts. Today, its shops are filled with chocolate bars, Swiss Army knives, and sunburned backpackers. Efficient Interlaken is a good administrative and shopping center. Take care of business, give the town a quick look, view the live TV coverage of the Jungfrau and Schilthorn weather in the window of the Schilthornbahn office on the main street (Höheweg), and head for the hills.

Orientation (tel. code: 036)

Tourist Information
The tourist office (on the main street, a 5-minute walk from the West Station, daily 8:00-12:00, 14:00-18:00, less on weekends and off-season; tel. 036/222121) has good information for the whole region and advice on Alpine lift discounts. Pick up a Bern map; while the Jungfrau region map costs 1.50 SF, a perfectly good version of it is in the free Jungfrau region train timetable.

Trains
Interlaken has two train stations. Most major trains stop at the Interlaken-West station. The station's train information desk has some tourist info and an exchange desk with fair rates (daily until 19:00, Sunday until 18:00). An open-late Migros supermarket is across the street. From the Interlaken-East station, private trains (not covered by Eurailpass) take you deep into the mountainous Jungfrau region. Ask at the station about discount passes, special fares, and schedules for the scenic (and non-Eurail) mountain trains (tel. 036/264233). It's a pleasant 15-minute walk between the East and West stations.

Helpful Hints
Telephone: In the center of town, next to the handy post office, you'll find a late-hours long-distance phone booth (daily 7:30-12:00, 13:45-18:30).
Laundry: Helen Schmocker's Wascherei Laundry has a change machine, soap, English instructions, and a pleasant riverside place to hang out (from the post office, follow

Marktgasse over two bridges to Beatenbergstrasse, open daily
7:00-22:00 for self-service, 8 SF to wash and dry 10 pounds;
Monday-Friday 8:00-12:00 and 13:30-18:00 for full service:
drop off 10 pounds and 12 SF in the morning and pick up
clean clothes that afternoon; tel. 221566).

Gimmelwald

Saved from developers by its "avalanche zone" classification,
Gimmelwald is one of the poorest places in Switzerland. Its
economy is stuck in the hay and many of the farmers, unable
to make it in their disadvantaged trade, are subsidized by the
Swiss government. For some travelers, there's little to see in
the village. Others enjoy a fascinating day sitting on a bench
and learning why they say, "If Heaven isn't what it's cracked
up to be, send me back to Gimmelwald."

Take a walk through the town. Notice the traditional
log-cabin architecture and blond-braided children. The
numbers on the buildings are not addresses, but fire insurance numbers. The cute little hut near the station is for stor-
ing and aging cheese, not youth hostelers. Do not confuse
obscure Gimmelwald with touristy and commercialized
Grindelwald just over the Kleine Scheidegg ridge.

Gimmelwald Side of Lauterbrunnen Valley

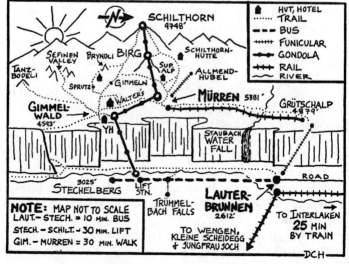

Evening fun in Gimmelwald is found at the youth hostel (lots of young Alp-aholics and a good chance to share information on the surrounding mountains) and up at Walter's Hotel Mittaghorn (see Sleeping, below). Walter's bar is a local farmer's hangout. When they've made their hay, they come here to play. They look like what we'd call "hicks" (former city-slicker Walter still isn't fully accepted by the gang), but they speak some English and can be fun to get to know. Walter knows how many beers they've had according to whether they're talking, singing, fighting, or snoring. For less smoke and some powerful solitude, sit outside (benches just below the rails, 100 yards down the lane from Walter's) and watch the sun tuck the mountaintops into bed as the moon rises over the Jungfrau.

Sights—Alpine Hikes from Gimmelwald

There are days of possible hikes from Gimmelwald. Many are a fun combination of trails, mountain trains, and gondola rides.

▲▲▲**Hike 1: The Schilthorn: Hikes, Lifts, and a 10,000-foot Breakfast**—If the weather's good, have breakfast atop the Schilthorn, in the slowly revolving, mountain-capping restaurant (of James Bond movie fame). The early-bird special gondola tickets (rides before 9:00) take you from Gimmelwald to the Schilthorn and back with a great continental breakfast on top for 55 SF—cheaper than the normal round-trip without breakfast. (Buy tickets from Walter or at the gondola station.) Bear with the slow service, and ask for more hot drinks if necessary. If you're not revolving, ask them to turn it on.

The Gimmelwald–Schilthorn hike is free, if you don't mind a 5,000-foot altitude gain. You can ride up and hike down, or for a less scary hike, go halfway down by cable car and walk down from the Birg station. Lifts go twice an hour, and the ride (including two transfers) takes 30 minutes. Watch the altitude meter in the gondola. Buy the round-trip excursion early-bird fare (cheaper than the Gimmelwald-Schilthorn-Birg ticket) and decide at Birg if you want to hike or ride down.

Linger on top. Piz Gloria has been newly renovated. There's a souvenir shop, the rocks of the region on the

restaurant wall, telescopes, a "touristorama" film room showing explosive highlights from the James Bond thriller that
featured the Schilthorn, and a multi-screen slide show. (It's
free and self-serve. Push the button for slides or, after a long
pause for the projector to rewind, push for 007.)

Watch hang gliders set up, psych up, and take off, flying 30 minutes with the birds to distant Interlaken. Walk
along the ridge out back to the "No High Heels" signpost.
This is a great place for a photo of the "mountain-climber
you." For another cheap thrill, ask the gondola attendant to
crank down the window, stick your head out, and pretend
you're hang gliding, ideally, over the bump going down from
Gimmelwald. (For an expensive thrill, you can bungee-jump
from the Stechelberg-Mürren service gondola.)

Think twice before hiking down from the Schilthorn
(weather can change, have good shoes). Hiking down from
Birg is easier but still very steep and gravelly. Just below Birg
is the Schilthorn-Hutte. Drop in for soup, cocoa, or a coffee
schnapps. You can spend the night in the hut's loft (40
mattresses, open July-September, tel. 551167 or 552512).
Youth hostelers scream down the ice fields on plastic-bag
sleds from the Schilthorn. (English-speaking doctor in
Mürren.)

The most interesting trail from Birg (or Mürren) to
Gimmelwald is the high one via Suppenalp, Schiltalp,
Gimmeln, and the Sprütz waterfall. Mürren has plenty of
shops, bakeries, banks, a TI, a modern sports complex for
rainy days, and accommodations (see Sleeping, below). Ask
at the Schilthorn station in Mürren for a gondola souvenir
pin or sticker.

▲▲▲**Hike 2: The Männlichen-Kleine Scheidegg Hike—**
This is my favorite easy Alpine hike, entertaining you all the
way with glorious Jungfrau, Eiger, and Mönch views. (That's
the Young Maiden being protected from the Ogre by the
Monk.)

If the weather's good, descend from Gimmelwald bright
and early. Catch the post bus to the Lauterbrunnen train station (or drive, parking at the large multi-storied pay lot
behind the station). Buy a ticket to Männlichen and catch the
train. Ride past great valley views to Wengen, where you'll
walk across town (buy a picnic, but don't waste time here if

Berner Oberland

NOTE: THIS BIRD'S EYE VIEW LOOKS SOUTH...

EIGER 13026'   MONCH 13449'   JUNGFRAU 13642'   SCHILT-HORN 9748'

JUNG-FRAU-JOCH

TUNNEL

KLEINE SCHEIDEGG 6762'

GIMMEL-WALD 4593'

BIRG 8784'

HIKE #1

GRINDEL-WALD 3393'

HIKE #2

MÄNN-LICHEN 7317'

W. ALP

STECHEL-BERG 3025'

MÜRREN 5381'

← NICE WALK

GRUND

GRÜTSCHALP 4879'

TO FIRST

WENGEN 4180'

LAUTERBRUNNEN 2612'

HIKE #3

SCHYNIGE PLATTE 6454'

ISELT-WALD

WILDERSWIL 1916'

TO LUZERN

SPIEZ

LAKE BRIENZ

E.   W.

LAKE   THUN

TO BERN

BRIENZ

BALLENBERG

INTER-LAKEN 1860'

⊢⊣ PRIVATE RAIL - EURAIL NOT VALID
⊢⊣ OTHER RAIL - EURAIL VALID
o—o MTN. LIFTS
- - - BUS
•••• TRAIL

NOT TO SCALE!

DCH

it's sunny), and catch the Männlichen lift (departing every 15 minutes) to the top of the ridge high above you.

From the tip of the Männlichen lift, hike (20 minutes north) to the little peak for that king- or queen-of-the-mountain feeling. It's an easy hour's walk from there to Kleine Scheidegg for a picnic or restaurant lunch. (For accommodations, see Sleeping, below.) If you've got an extra 90 SF and the weather's perfect, ride the train from Kleine Scheidegg through the Eiger to the towering Jungfraujoch and back. Check for discount trips up to Jungfraujoch; three trips a day (early or late, tel. 264111, weather info: tel. 551022). Jungfraujoch crowds can be frightening. The price has been jacked up to reduce the mobs, but sunny days are still a mess.

From Kleine Scheidegg, enjoy the ever-changing Alpine panorama of the North Face of the Eiger, Jungfrau, and Mönch, probably accompanied by the valley-filling mellow sound of Alp horns and distant avalanches, as you ride the

Alpine Lifts in the Berner Oberland

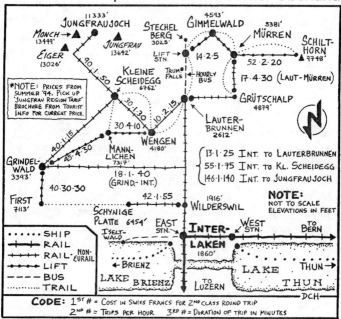

train or hike downhill (30 gorgeous minutes to Wengeralp,
90 more steep minutes from there into the town of Wengen).
If the weather turns bad, or you run out of steam, catch the
train early at the little Wengeralp station along the way.
After Wengeralp, the trail to Wengen is steep and, while not
dangerous, requires a good set of knees. Wengen is a fine
shopping town. (For accommodations, see Sleeping, below.)
The boring final descent from Wengen to Lauterbrunnen is
knee-killer steep, so catch the train. Trails may be snow-
bound into early summer. Ask about conditions at lift stations. If the Männlichen lift is closed, take the train straight
from Lauterbrunnen to Kleine Scheidegg. Many take
the risk of slipping and enjoy the Kleine Scheidegg to
Wengeralp hike even with a little snow.

▲▲**Hike 3: Schynige Platte to First**—The best day I've
had hiking in the Berner Oberland is the demanding 6-hour
ridge walk high above Lake Brienz on one side and all that
Jungfrau beauty on the other. Start at Wilderswil (just above
Interlaken) where you catch the little train up to Schynige

Platte (2,000 meters). Walk through the Alpine flower display garden and into the wild Alpine yonder. The high point is Faulhorn (2,680 meters, with its famous mountain-top hotel). Hike to a chairlift called First (2,168 meters), where you descend to Grindelwald and catch a train back to your starting point, Wilderswil (or, if you have a regional train pass or no car but endless money, return to Gimmel-wald via Lauterbrunnen from Grindelwald over Kleine Scheidegg).

▲**Other Hikes near Gimmelwald**—For a not-too-tough 3-hour walk (there's a scary 20-minute stretch that comes with ropes) with great Jungfrau views and some mountain farm action, ride the funicular from Mürren to Allmend-hübel (1,934 meters), and walk to Marchegg, Saustal, and Grütschalp (a drop of about 500 meters), where you catch the panorama train back to Mürren. An easier version is the lower "Bergweg" from Allmenhübel to Grütschalp via Winteregg. For an easy family stoll with grand views, walk from Mürren just above the train tracks to either Winteregg (40 min, restaurant, playground, train station) or Grütschalp (60 min, train station) and catch the panorama train back to Mürren. An easy, go-as-far-as-you-like trail from Gimmel-wald is up the Sefinen Valley. Or, you can wind from Gimmelwald down to Stechelberg (1 hour).

You can get specifics at the Mürren TI. The TI, Hotel Belmont, and Hotel Mittaghorn each have a "Hiking Possibilities: Schilthorn—Panoramaland" flier that describes 12 recommended hikes. For a more extensive rundown on the area (hikes, flora, fauna, culture, travel tips) get Don Chmura's fine 5-SF Gimmelwald guidebook (available at Hotel Mittaghorn).

Rainy Day Options

If clouds roll in, don't despair. They can roll out just as quickly and there are some good bad-weather options. There are easy trails and pleasant walks along the floor of the Lau-terbrunnen Valley. If all the waterfalls have you intrigued, sneak a behind-the-scenes look at the valley's most powerful one, Trümmelbach Falls (8 SF, on the Lauterbrunnen-Stechelberg road, daily April-October 9:00-18:00). You'll ride an elevator up through the mountain and climb through several caves to see the melt from the Eiger, Mönch, and Jungfrau grinding like God's bandsaw through the mountain at the rate of up to 20,000 liters a second (nearly double the beer consumption at Oktoberfest). The upper area, "chutes 6 to 10," are the best, so if your legs ache you can skip the lower ones and ride the lift down. Lauterbrunnen's Heimatmuseum (3 SF, mid-June through September, Tuesday, Thursday, Saturday, and Sunday 14:00-17:30, just over the bridge) shows off the local folk culture.

Mürren's slick Sports Center (pool open only mid-June through October) offers a world of indoor activities (7 SF for use of the swimming pool and whirlpool).

Boat Trips from Interlaken—From Interlaken there are regular boat trips on Lake Thun and Lake Brienz. The super-cute and quiet village of Iseltwald is just a bus or boat ride from Interlaken. On Lake Thun, both Spiez and Thun are visit-worthy towns.

▲▲**Ballenberg**—Near Interlaken, the Ballenberg Open-Air Museum is a rich collection of traditional and historic farmhouses from every region of the country. Each house is carefully furnished, and many feature traditional crafts-people at work. The sprawling 50-acre park, laid out roughly as a huge Swiss map, is a natural preserve providing a won-derful setting for this culture-on-a-lazy-Susan look at Switzerland.

The Thurgau house (#621) has an interesting wattle-and-daub (half-timbered construction) display and house #331 has a fun bread museum. Use the 2-SF map/guide. The more expensive picture book is a better souvenir than guide. Open daily April-October 10:00 to 17:00; 12-SF entry, half-price after 16:00 (houses close at 17:00, park stays open later); craft demonstration schedules are listed just inside the entry; tel. 036/511123. There's a reasonable outdoor cafete-ria inside the west entrance, and fresh-baked bread, sausage, and mountain cheese, or other cooked goodies are on sale in several houses. Picnic tables and grills with free firewood are scattered throughout the park. The little wooden village of Brienzwiller (near the east entrance) is a museum in itself with a lovely little church. Trains go regularly from Inter-laken to Brienzwiller, an easy walk from the museum.

Sleeping in the Alps
(1.4 SF = about $1, tel. code: 036)

To inhale the Alps and really hold it in, sleep high in Gimmelwald.

Sleep code: **S**=Single, **D**=Double/Twin, **T**=Triple, **Q**=Quad, **B**=Bath/Shower, **WC**=Toilet, **CC**=Credit Card (**V**isa, **M**astercard, **A**mex), **SE**=Speaks English (graded **A** through **F**).

Sleeping and Eating in Gimmelwald
(4,500 feet, zip code: 3826)

Poor, happily stuck in the past, avalanche-zone Gimmelwald has a happy youth hostel, a cranky pension, and a creaky hotel. The only bad news is that the lift costs 7 SF each way.

The **Mountain Hostel** (9 SF per bed in 2- to 15-bed rooms, 2 SF for sheets, closed mid-December through February; 50 yards from the lift station, tel. 551704, SE-B) is goat-simple, as clean as its guests, cheap, and very friendly. Its 45 beds are often taken in July and August, so call ahead to Lena, the elderly woman who runs the place. The hostel has low ceilings, a self-serve kitchen (pack in groceries, 20- and 50-cent coins for the stove), coed washrooms, and enough hot water for ten (1 SF, 5 minutes) hot showers a day (or you can drop by the Mürren Sports Center with a towel and 3 SF).

This relaxed hostel is struggling to survive. Please read the signs, respect its rules, and leave it cleaner than you found it. Treat it and Lena with loving care. Without Lena, there's no hostel in Gimmelwald. The place, because of the spirit of its rugged but sensitive visitors and the help of Marc (a local Englishman), almost runs itself. It's one of those rare places where a family atmosphere spontaneously combusts and spaghetti becomes communal as it softens.

The **Pension Gimmelwald** (20-SF dorm beds on its top floor without breakfast, D-90 SF, DB-110 SF, two-night minimum, open mid-June through October, tel. 551730), next door, serves meals.

Hotel Mittaghorn, the treasure of Gimmelwald, is run by Walter Mittler, a perfect Swiss gentleman (D-60 SF, T-85 SF, Q-105 SF, loft beds-25 SF, all with breakfast, family discounts; CH-3826 Gimmelwald/Bern, tel. 551658; SE-A;

reserve by telephone only and then you must reconfirm by telephone the day before your arrival, at this time you can order dinner, a deal at 15 SF if Walter's cooking; don't show up without a reservation; closed for a week in early May and mid-November through March).

Hotel Mittaghorn is a classic, creaky, Alpine-style place with memorable beds, ancient down comforters (short and fat, wear socks and drape the blanket over your feet), and a million-dollar view of the Jungfrau Alps. The hotel has two rooms with private showers and one shower for everyone else (1 SF for 5 minutes). Walter is careful not to get too hectic or big and enjoys sensitive Back Door travelers. He runs the hotel with the help of Don von Gimmelwald (actually Don Chmura, "von" Winnipeg), keeping it simple but with class. This is a good place to receive mail from home (mail barrel in entry hall).

To some, Hotel Mittaghorn is a fire just waiting to happen, with a kitchen that would never pass code, lumpy beds, teeny towels, and nowhere near enough plumbing, run by an eccentric grouch. These people enjoy Interlaken, Wengen, or Mürren, and that's where they should sleep. Be warned, you may meet more of my readers than you hoped for, but it's a fun crowd, an extended family.

Gimmelwald feeds its goats better than its people. The hostel has a decent members' kitchen but serves no food. There are no groceries in town. The wise and frugal buy food from the Co-ops in Mürren or Lauterbrunnen and pack it in. Walter, at Hotel Mittaghorn, is Gimmelwald's best cook (not saying much, but he is good). His salad is best eaten one leaf at a time with your fingers. There's no menu, and dinner's served at 19:30 sharp. When Walter's in the mood, his place is the best bar in town: good cheap beer, strong *kaffee fertigs* (coffee with schnapps), and Heidi cocoa (cocoa *mit schnapps*) or Virgin Heidis.

Meals (including hamburgers I'll never forget) are also served at Pension Gimmelwald next to the hostel. For a rare bit of ruggedness and the best budget food in the center of Mürren, eat at the Stägerstübli. Brian's sandwich bar at the Hotel Belmont across from the Mürren train station is ideal for those who blew their budget on Alpine lifts.

Sleeping in Mürren (5,500 feet, zip code: 3825)

Mürren is as pleasant as an Alpine resort can be. It's traffic-free, filled with bakeries, cafés, souvenirs, old-timers with walking sticks, GE employees enjoying incentive trips, and Japanese making movies of each other with a Fujichrome backdrop. Its chalets are prefab-rustic. Sitting on a ledge 2,000 feet above the Lauterbrunnen valley, surrounded by a fortissimo chorus of mountains, it has all the comforts of home and then some, with Alp-high prices. Mürren's Tourist Office can find you a room, give hiking advice, and change money (in the Sporthaus, mountain bikes for rent, open daily 9:00-12:00, 13:00-18:30, less off-season, tel. 551616).

Hotel Belmont (D-100 SF, DB-130 SF, with breakfast, discounts for rooms without views, CC:VM; across from the train station, tel. 553535, fax 553531, SE-A) offers Mürren's best budget rooms. Andreas and Anne Marie Goetschi, former travelers with a great "back door" travel perspective, make this a friendly home away from home in Mürren. Their restaurant is economical and the attached "Brian's sandwich bar" is a fun hangout. **Hotel Alpenblick** (tel. 551327, fax 551391, closed off-season), next door, and **Hotel Alpina** (tel. 551361) also have affordable rooms.

Chalet Fontana (35 SF-45 SF per person in doubles or triples with breakfast and kitchenette, tel. 552686; across the street from the Stägerstübli in the town center, mid-June through September), run by Denise Fussel, is well-worn and basic but a rare budget option in Mürren. Off-season you can rent a room here cheaper through the Ed Abegglen shop next door (tel. 551245).

Sleeping in Wengen (4,200 feet)

Wengen is a fancy Mürren on the other side of the valley. It's traffic-free and an easy lift ride above Lauterbrunnen. Wengen is halfway up to Kleine Scheidegg and Männlichen. It has more tennis courts than budget beds. **Hotel Berner-hof** (D-80 SF, DB-120 SF with breakfast, more during peak times and for one night, tel. 552721 or 553358) has dorm beds (20 SF, no sheets). The **Chalet Bergheim,** open June through mid-October, has reasonable doubles, and six 20-SF dorm beds (plus 6 SF for sheets and

11 SF for breakfast, tel. 552755). The **Chalet Schweizerheim Garni** (D-100 SF, tel. 551581, summer only) is the cheapest hotel in Wengen.

Sleeping in Kleine Scheidegg (6,762 feet)

For 30-SF dorm beds with breakfast high in the mountains, you can sleep at Kleine Scheidegg's **Bahnhof Buffet** (tel. 551151) or at **Restaurant Grindelwaldblick** (12-bed dorm rooms, no sheets, tel. 533043, open June-October).

Sleeping below Gimmelwald, near the Stechelberg Lift (2,800 feet)

The local **Naturfreundehaus Alpenhof** (60 coed beds, 4-8 per room, 16 SF per bed, 7-SF breakfast, 13-SF dinner, no sheets; Stechelberg, tel. 551202; closed November; near Stechelberg bus stop) is a rugged Alpine lodge for local hikers at the far end of Lauterbrunnen Valley. The neighboring **Hotel Stechelberg** (D-78 SF, DB-98 SF and 118 SF including breakfast, tel. 552921, SE-B) has 13 clean and quiet rooms. **Klara von Allmen** (D-50 SF, minimum two nights; just over the river from the Stechelberg post office at big "*Zimmer*" sign, Pfang, 3824 Stechelberg, tel. 552554, SE-F) rents out three rooms in a quiet, scenic, and folky setting.

Sleeping in Lauterbrunnen (2,600 feet)

Masenlager Stocki (12 SF a night with sheets in an easy-going little 30-bed coed dorm with a kitchen; tel. 551754; across the river, take the first left; closed November through mid-December) is a great value. Two campgrounds just south of town work very hard to provide 15- to 25-SF beds. They each have dorms, 2-, 4-, and 6-bed bungalows, no sheets, kitchen facilities, and big English-speaking tour groups. **Camping Jungfrau** (tel. 552010), romantically situated just beyond the stones hurled by Staubbach Falls, is huge and well organized, with a Heidi Shop and clocks showing the time in Sydney and Vancouver. It also has fancier cabins and trailers for the classier camper. **Schützenbach Campground** (tel. 551268), on the left just past Lauterbrunnen toward Stechelberg, is simpler.

Sleeping in Interlaken
(1.4 SF = about $1, tel. code: 036)

I'd head for Gimmelwald. Interlaken is not the Alps.
But if you must stay, here are two good choices: **Hotel
Lotschberg** (DBWC-100 SF-180 SF, CC:VMA, 2-minute
walk from the West Station, look for the wall painting, at
General Guesan Strasse 31, 3800 Interlaken, tel. 036/
222545), with easy parking and a sun terrace, is run by
English-speaking Susie and Fritz. And backpackers enjoy
Balmer's Herberge (17-SF dorm beds, 28 SF per person in
simple doubles, and 12 SF in overflow on-the-floor accommodations, all with breakfast; Haupstrasse 23, in Matten, a
15-minute walk from either Interlaken station, tel. 221961).
This Interlaken institution is run by a creative tornado of
entrepreneurial energy, Eric Balmer. With movies, ping-
pong, laundromat, a secondhand English book-swapping
library, rafting excursions, plenty of tips on budget eating
and hiking, and a friendly, hardworking, mostly American
staff, this little Nebraska is home for those who miss their
fraternity (but not their parents).

Train Connections

Interlaken to: Bern (hrly, 60 min), **Spiez** (2/hr, 15 min),
Brienz (hrly, 20 min). While there are a few long trains
from Interlaken, you'll generally connect from Bern where
trains go to **Frankfurt** (4½ hrs), **Munich** (4/day, 5½ hrs),
Lausanne (hrly, 70 min), **Paris** (4/day, 4½ hrs), and **Zurich**
(hrly, 75 min).

Interlaken and Gimmelwald: Take the train from the
Interlaken-East station to Lauterbrunnen, then cross the
street to catch the funicular to Mürren. You'll ride up to
Grütschalp where a special scenic train (*panorama fahrt*
in German) rolls you along the cliff into Mürren. From
there, either walk an easy, paved 30 minutes downhill to
Gimmelwald or walk 10 minutes across Mürren to catch the
gondola (7 SF and a 5-minute steep uphill backtrack) to
Gimmelwald. A good bad-weather option (or vice versa) is
to ride the post bus from Lauterbrunnen (leaves at 5 minutes past the hour) to Stechelberg and the base of the
Schilthornbahn (a big, gray gondola station, tel. 036/231444
or 552141).

By car, it's a 30-minute drive from Interlaken to Stechelberg. The parking lot at the gondola station is safe and free. Gimmelwald is the first stop above Stechelberg on the Schilthorn gondola (7 SF, 2 trips/hr at :25 and :55; get off at first stop, walk into the village, hard right at PTT, signs direct you up the path on a steep 300-yard climb to the chalet marked simply "Hotel"). This is my home in Switzerland, Walter's Hotel Mittaghorn. Note that for a week in early May and from mid-November through early December, the Schilthornbahn is closed for servicing.

Switzerland

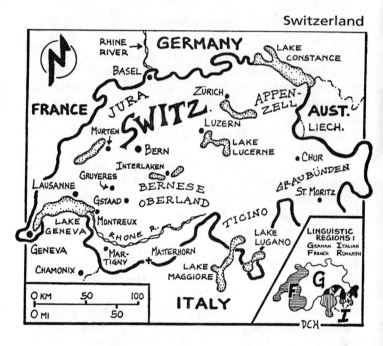

APPENDIX

European National Tourist Offices

Before your trip, send a letter to each country's National Tourist Office (listed below) telling them of your general plans and asking for information. They'll send you the basic information packet, and if you ask for specifics (calendars of local events, city maps, good hikes around Füssen, castle hotels along the Rhine, the wines of Austria), you'll get an impressive amount of help.

Austrian National Tourist Office, P.O. Box 491938, Los Angeles, CA 90049, 310/477-3332, fax 310/477-5141; Box 1142 Times Square, New York, NY 10108-1142, 212/944-6880, fax 212/730-4568. Ask for their "Vacation Kit" map.

Belgian National Tourist Office, 780 3rd Ave., New York, NY 10017, 212/758-8130, fax 212/355-7675, elaborate phone tree.

British Tourist Authority, 551 5th Ave., 7th Floor, New York, NY 10176, 212/986-2200, fax 212/986-1188 (free maps of London and Britain which otherwise cost).

Bulgaria—Balkan Holidays, 41 E. 42nd St., New York, NY 10017, 212/573-5536, fax 212/573-5538. Scanty information but friendly advice over the phone.

Denmark *See Scandinavia.*

Finland *See Scandinavia.*

French Tourist Office, 610 Fifth Ave., #222, New York, NY 10020-2452, may move in 1995; 9454 Wilshire Blvd., #303, Beverly Hills, CA 90212-2967. Rather than mess with their flakey 900 number, write a card with your requests.

German National Tourist Office, 122 E. 42nd St., 52nd Floor, New York, NY 10168, 212/661-7200, fax 212/661-7174; 11766 Wilshire Blvd., Suite 750, Los Angeles, CA 90025, 310/575-9799, fax 310/575-1565 (Germany map, Romantic Road map, city maps, Rhine schedules, events, very helpful).

Greek National Tourist Organization, 645 Fifth Ave., 5th floor, New York, NY 10022, 212/421-5777, fax 212/826-6940; 168 N Michigan Ave., Chicago, IL 60601, tel. 312/782-1084, fax 312/782-1091; 611 West 6th St., #2198, Los Angeles, CA 90017, 213/626-6696, fax 213/489-9744

(general how to booklet, map of Athens, plenty on the islands and ferries.)

Hungarian Tourist Board, 1 Parker Plaza, #1104, Fort Lee, NJ 07024, 201/592-8585, fax 201/592-8736.

Irish Tourist Board, 345 Park Ave., 17th floor, New York, NY 10154, 1-800-223-6470, 212/418-0800, fax 212/371-9052.

Italian Government Travel Office, 630 Fifth Ave., #1565, New York, NY 10111, 212/245-4822, fax 212/586-9249; 12400 Wilshire Blvd., #550, Los Angeles, CA 90025, 310/820-0098, 310/820-6357. Ask for their great art book and city maps.

Luxembourg National Tourist Office, 17 Beekman Place, New York, NY 10022, 212/935-8888, fax 212/935-5896.

Netherlands National Tourist Office, 225 North Michigan Ave., #326, Chicago, IL 60601, tel. 312/819-0300, fax 312/819-1636.

Norway *See Scandinavia.*

Polish Tourist Office, 275 Madison Ave., #1711, New York, NY 10016, 212/338-9412, fax 212/338-9283, regional and city maps.

Portuguese National Tourist Office, 590 Fifth Ave., New York, NY 10036, 212/354-4403.

Scandinavian National Tourist Office, 655 3rd Ave., 18th Floor, New York, NY 10017, 212/949-2333, fax 212/983-5260 (Offers a good general book on all five countries, but be sure to ask for city maps and specifics).

Spanish National Tourist Office, 665 Fifth Ave., New York, NY 10022, 212/759-8822, fax 212/980 1053; 845 N Michigan Ave., Chicago Il 60611, tel. 312/642 1992, fax 312/642-9817; 8383 Wilshire Blvd., Suite 960, Beverly Hills, CA 90211, 213/658-7188, fax 213/658-2061.

Sweden *See Scandinavia.*

Swiss National Tourist Office, 608 Fifth Ave., New York, NY 10020, 212/757-5944, fax 212/262-6116; 150 North Michigan Ave., #2930, Chicago, IL 60601, tel. 312/630-5840, fax 312/630-5848; 222 North Sepulveda Blvd., #1570, El Segundo, CA 90245, tel. 310/335-5980, fax 310/335-5982. Great maps and service.

Turkish Tourism Office, 821 United Nations Plaza, New York, NY 10017, 212/687-2194, fax 212/599-7568.

Telephone Directory

Smart travelers use the telephone every day. The key to dialing long distance is understanding area codes and having a local phone card. Hotel room phones are reasonable for local calls, but a rip-off for long distance calls. Never call home from your hotel room (unless you are putting the call on your credit card).

For calls to other European countries, dial the international access code, followed by the country code, followed by the area code without its leading zero, and finally the local number (four to seven digits). When dialing long distance within a country, start with the area code (including its leading zero), then the local number. France, Denmark, and Norway have no area codes (see text for long-distance instructions).

All countries now have phone cards (worth $4-$10; buy at post offices, TIs, and tobacco shops), which are much easier than coins for long-distance calls. Buy one on your first day in each country to force yourself to find smart reasons to use the local phones. Blow the last of your card with a call home before leaving each country.

Telephoning the United States from a pay phone is easy if you have a local phone card or an AT&T or MCI credit card or can call with a coin ($1 for 20 seconds) to have the other person call you back at a specified time at your hotel. From the United States, they'd dial 011-country code-area code (without zero)-local number. Europe-to-United States calls are twice as expensive as direct calls from the United States. Midnight in California is breakfast time in Europe.

If you plan to call home often, get an international AT&T, MCI, or SPRINT card. Each card company has a toll-free number in each European country that puts you in touch with an American operator who takes your card number and the number you want to call, puts you through, and bills your home telephone number for the call (at the cheap U.S.A. rate of about a dollar a minute plus a $3 service charge). If you talk for 3 minutes, you save more than enough in the rates to cover the service charge. Some MCI, AT&T, and SPRINT numbers are listed below.

Appendix**521**

International Access Codes

Austria: 00
Belgium: 32
France: 19
Germany: 00
Great Britain: 010

Italy: 00
Netherlands: 09
Switzerland: 00
United States: 011

Country Prefix Codes

Austria: 43
Belgium: 32
Canada: 1
Denmark: 45
England: 44
France: 33
Germany: 49
Greece: 30

Italy: 39
Netherlands: 31
Norway: 47
Portugal: 351
Spain: 34
Sweden: 46
Switzerland: 41
United States: 1

USA Direct Toll-free Credit Card Operators

Country	AT&T	MCI	SPRINT
Austria	022-903-011	022-903-012	022-903-014
France	19-tone-00-11	19-tone-00-19	91-tone-00-87
Germany	0130-0010	0130-0012	0130-0013
Italy	172-1011	172-1022	172-1877
Netherlands	06-tone-022-9111	06-tone-022-9122	06-tone-0229119
Switzerland	046-05-011	155-02-22	155-9777

Exchange Rates

As of December 1994

Country–Currency	$1 = approximately
Austria–*schilling*	10
Belgium–*franc*	30
Britain–*pound*	.60
Denmark–*krone*	4.6
Finland–*mark*	4.8
France–*franc*	5.0
Germany–*Deutsche mark*	1.5
Greece–*drachma*	230
Ireland–*punt*	.60
Italy–*lira*	1500
Netherlands–*guilder*	1.65
Portugal–*escudo*	150

Spain–*peseta*	120
Sweden–*krona*	7
Switzerland–*franc*	1.25

Metric Conversions
(approximate)

1 inch = 25 millimeters	1 quart = 0.95 liter
1 foot = 0.3 meter	1 ounce = 28 grams
32 degrees F = 0 degrees C	82 degrees F = about 28 degrees C
1 yard = 0.9 meter	1 meter = 39.4 inches
1 mile = 1.6 kilometers	1 kilogram = 2.2 pounds
1 square yard = 0.8 square meter	1 kilometer = .62 mile
1 acre = 0.4 hectare	1 centimeter = 0.4 inch

Weather Chart

Here is a list of average temperatures and days of no rain. This can be helpful in planning your itinerary, but I have never found European weather to be particularly predictable, and these charts ignore humidity.

(1st line, avg. daily low; 2nd line, avg. daily high; 3rd line, days of no rain)

	J	F	M	A	M	J	J	A	S	O	N	D
France	32°	34°	36°	41°	47°	52°	55°	55°	50°	44°	38°	33°
Paris	42°	45°	52°	60°	67°	73°	76°	75°	69°	59°	49°	43°
	16	15	16	16	18	19	19	19	19	17	15	14
Germany	29°	31°	35°	41°	48°	53°	56°	55°	51°	43°	36°	31°
Frankfurt	37°	42°	49°	58°	67°	72°	75°	74°	67°	56°	45°	39°
	22	19	22	21	22	21	21	21	21	22	21	20°
Great Britain	35°	35°	37°	40°	45°	51°	55°	54°	51°	44°	39°	36°
London	44°	45°	51°	56°	63°	69°	73°	72°	67°	58°	49°	45°
	14	15	20	16	18	19	18	18	17	17	14	15
Italy	39°	39°	42°	46°	55°	60°	64°	64°	61°	53°	46°	41°
Rome	54°	56°	62°	68°	74°	82°	88°	88°	83°	73°	63°	56°
	23	17	26	24	25	28	29	28	24	22	22	22
Netherlands	34°	34°	37°	43°	50°	55°	59°	59°	56°	48°	41°	35°
Amsterdam	40°	41°	46°	52°	60°	65°	69°	68°	64°	56°	47°	41°
	12	13	18	16	19	18	17	17	15	13	11	12
Switzerland	29°	30°	35°	41°	48°	55°	58°	57°	52°	44°	37°	31°
Geneva	39°	43°	51°	58°	66°	73°	77°	76°	69°	58°	47°	40°
	20	19	21	19	19	19	22	21	20	20	19	21

Sample European Regional Itineraries

The destinations proposed in each of these "Best 22 Days" itineraries are featured in the Rick Steves' Country Guide for that area.

22 Days in Europe

Each of the following destinations is covered in this book.

Day 1 - Depart U.S. for Amsterdam
Day 2 - Arrive in Amsterdam
Day 3 - Amsterdam
Day 4 - From Holland to the Rhine
Day 5 - The Rhine to Rothenburg
Day 6 - Rothenburg ob der Tauber
Day 7 - Romantic Road, Dachau, Tirol
Day 8 - Bavaria and Castle Day
Day 9 - Over Alps to Venice
Day 10 - Venice
Day 11 - Florence
Day 12 - Rome
Day 13 - Rome
Day 14 - Italian hill towns
Day 15 - Drive the Italian Riviera
Day 16 - Free on Cinque Terre beach
Day 17 - Drive to the Alps
Day 18 - Alps hike day, Gimmelwald
Day 19 - Free in Alps; evening to France
Day 20 - Colmar, Alsatian villages, wine
Day 21 - On to Paris, stop at Reims
Day 22 - Paris

22 Days in France

Day 1 - Arrive in Paris
Day 2 - Paris
Day 3 - Paris
Day 4 - Paris
Day 5 - Into Normandy via Rouen
Day 6 - Bayeux, D-Day beaches
Day 7 - Mont St. Michel, Brittany, and to the Loire Valley
Day 8 - Loire Chateau hopping
Day 9 - Sarlat, the Dordogne Valley
Day 10 - Dordogne Valley
Day 11 - Sarlat, Albi, and Carcassonne
Day 12 - From Carcassonne to Arles

Day 13 - La Crême de Provence
Day 14 - From the Rhone to the Riviera
Day 15 - Beaches on the Côte d'Azur
Day 16 - From Riviera to Alps
Day 17 - Alps Admiration
Day 18 - From Chamonix to Chardonnay
Day 19 - A Taste of Burgundy
Day 20 - From Burgundy to Alsace—Beaune to Colmar via Dijon
Day 21 - Colmar and the Route du Vin
Day 22 - Back to Paris, Verdun, and Reims
For all the specifics, see *Rick Steves' Best of France, Belgium, and the Netherlands*

22 Days in Germany, Austria, and Switzerland
Day 1 - Arrive Frankfurt, to Rothenburg
Day 2 - Rothenburg
Day 3 - Romantic Road to Tirol
Day 4 - Bavarian highlights, castle day
Day 5 - Bavaria to Munich
Day 6 - Munich, capital of Bavaria
Day 7 - Munich to Salzburg
Day 8 - Salzburg, Lakes District
Day 9 - Hallstatt to Vienna
Day 10 - Vienna, Paris's eastern rival
Day 11 - Vienna to Hall in Tirol
Day 12 - Innsbruck and into Switzerland
Day 13 - Interlaken and up into the Alps
Day 14 - Alps hike day, Gimmelwald
Day 15 - Free time in Alps, French Switzerland
Day 16 - Cheese and chocolate, Mürten
Day 17 - Bern, drive into Germany
Day 18 - Black Forest
Day 19 - Baden-Baden to the Rhineland
Day 20 - The Rhine and its Castles
Day 21 - Mosel Valley, Köln, Bonn
Day 22 - Berlin
For all the specifics, see *Rick Steves' Best of Germany, Austria, and Switzerland*

22 Days in Great Britain
Day 1 - Arrive and set up in London
Day 2 - London
Day 3 - London

Day   4 - Salisbury, Stonehenge, Bath
Day   5 - Bath
Day   6 - Side trip to Glastonbury, Wells
Day   7 - South Wales, Folk Museum
Day   8 - Cotswold villages, Blenheim
Day   9 - Stratford, Warwick Castle, Coventry Cathedral
Day 10 - Industrial Revolution Museum
Day 11 - North Wales, Snowdon National Park, Caenarfon Castle, Medieval Banquet
Day 12 - Blackpool
Day 13 - Windermere Lake District
Day 14 - Hike and explore Lake District
Day 15 - Loch Lomond, Scottish West Coast
Day 16 - Scottish Highlands, Loch Ness
Day 17 - Edinburgh
Day 18 - Edinburgh
Day 19 - Hadrian's Wall, Durham Cathedral, Beamish Folk Museum
Day 20 - North York Moors, York
Day 21 - York
Day 22 - Cambridge, evening to London
For all the specifics, see *Rick Steves' Best of Great Britain*

22 Days in Italy

Day   1 - Arrive in Milan
Day   2 - Sightsee Milan
Day   3 - Train to Riviera
Day   4 - All Day in Cinque Terre
Day   5 - Pisa, Florence
Day   6 - Florence
Day   7 - Florence, Siena
Day   8 - Siena
Day   9 - Orvieto, Città
Day 10 - Hill Towns to Rome
Day 11 - Rome
Day 12 - Rome
Day 13 - Rome
Day 14 - Rome, Naples, Sorrento
Day 15 - Amalfi, Paestum, night train
Day 16 - Venice
Day 17 - Venice, Side-Trips
Day 18 - Dolomites
Day 19 - Dolomites
Day 20 - Dolomites to the Lakes

Day 21 - Lake Como, Varenna
Day 22 - Return to Milan, Trip Over
For all the specifics, see *Rick Steves' Best of Italy*

22 Days in Scandinavia
Day 1 - Arrive in Copenhagen
Day 2 - Sightsee in Copenhagen
Day 3 - Sightsee in Copenhagen
Day 4 - Frederiksborg Castle, N. Zealand
Day 5 - Vaxjo, Kalmar, glass country
Day 6 - Pass Gota Canal to Stockholm
Day 7 - Sightsee in Stockholm
Day 8 - Sightsee in Stockholm, evening cruise
Day 9 - Helsinki, Finland
Day 10 - Stockholm, Uppsala, to Oslo
Day 11 - Sightsee Oslo
Day 12 - Sightsee Oslo
Day 13 - Gudbrandsdalen, Peer Gynt country
Day 14 - Glacier hike, Sognefjord
Day 15 - Fjord cruise to Gudvangen—"Norway in a Nutshell"
Day 16 - Sightsee in Bergen
Day 17 - Drive from Bergen to Setesdal
Day 18 - Traditional Setesdal Valley, evening sail to Denmark
Day 19 - Jutland, Arhus
Day 20 - Aero Island
Day 21 - Aero, Odense, Roskilde, Copenhagen
Day 22 - Fly home from Copenhagen
For all the specifics, see *Rick Steves' Best of Scandinavia*

22 Days in Spain and Portugal
Day 1 - Arrive and set up in Madrid
Day 2 - Madrid
Day 3 - Madrid
Day 4 - Segovia
Day 5 - Salamanca to Coimbra, Portugal
Day 6 - Nazaré
Day 7 - Nazaré, beach day
Day 8 - Obidos and on to Lisbon
Day 9 - Lisbon
Day 10 - Lisbon and nearby beach towns
Day 11 - Salema
Day 12 - Salema and nearby beaches
Day 13 - Seville

Day 14 -Seville
Day 15 - Arcos de la Frontera, Tarifa
Day 16 - Tarifa
Day 17 - Morocco
Day 18 - Gibraltar
Day 19 - Costa del Sol and Granada
Day 20 - Granada and Moorish Alhambra
Day 21 - Toledo
Day 22 - Madrid
For all the specifics, see *Rick Steves' Best of Spain and Portugal*

The Rick Steves Travel Library

This book gives you the nitty-gritty necessary to navigate
smoothly through Europe's greatest destinations. Rick's
other books compliment this book, covering travel skills, art
appreciation, and hurdling the language barrier. If you like
this book, consider rounding out your trip library with these
other Rick Steves books.

For Skills: *Rick Steves' Europe Through the Back Door*
Now in its 13th edition, Rick's most important book is considered a classic by most travel bookstores. Packed with
lessons gleaned from 20 years of budget travel, *Europe
Through the Back Door* answers all your questions. In 450
pages Rick covers all the necessary skills from sleeping and
eating cheap and packing light to recognizing rip-offs and
changing money smartly.

For the Love of Art: *Europe 101* and *Mona Winks*
Read *Europe 101* before your trip to bring your sightseeing
to life. It's a fun-to-read and practical crash course in the
story of Europe designed for smart people who were sleeping
in their history and art classes before they knew they were
Europe-bound. With four pages of information on Gothic,
you'll step into the Notre Dame, nudge your partner, and
marvel "Isn't this a great improvement over Romanesque!"

Pack *Mona Winks* with you for a take-you-by-the-hand
two-hour tour of each of Europe's 20 most exhausting and
overwhelming museums. This covers the biggies in London,
Amsterdam, Paris, Venice, Florence, Rome, Madrid, and
more with easy to follow self-guided walks. The Vatican,

Prado, Louvre, and National Gallery museums should be a joy. With *Mona's* help they are.

Hurdling the Language Barrier: Rick Steves' Phrase Books for French, Italian, German, and Spanish/Portuguese

After 20 years of struggling with Berlitz, Rick knows what's needed and what's not for the monolingual American budget traveler to handle (and even enjoy) the language barrier. Berlitz knew the languages. But he never slept in a hotel where you needed to ask, "At what time is the water hot?" Each pocket-sized volume is packed with practical words and phrases, and peppered with tongue twisters and language fun to make meeting the locals easy.

For other Rick Steves' titles, see the John Muir Publications catalog, to follow.

Faxing Your Hotel Reservation

Most hotel managers know basic "hotel English." Faxing is the preferred method for reserving a room. It's more accurate and cheaper than telephoning and much faster than writing a letter. Use this handy form for your fax. Photocopy and fax away.

One-Page Fax

To: _____ @ _____
    hotel   *fax*

From: _____ @ _____
      name   *fax*

Today's date: ___ /____ /___
              day *month* *year*

Dear Hotel _____,

Please make this reservation for me:

Name: _____

Total # of people: _____   # of rooms: _____   # of nights: _____

Arriving: ___ /____ /___   My time of arrival (24-hr clock): _____
          day *month* *year*   (I will telephone if I will be late)

Departing: ___ /_____ /___
           day *month* *year*

Room(s):   Single___   Double___   Twin___   Triple___   Quad___

With: Toilet___   Shower___   Bath___   Sink only___

Special needs: View___   Quiet___   Cheapest Room___

Credit card: Visa___   MasterCard___   American Express___

Card #: _____

Name on card: _____

You may charge me for the first night as a deposit. Please fax or mail me confirmation of my reservation, along with the type of room reserved, the price, and whether the price includes breakfast. Thank you.

_____
Signature

_____
Name

_____
Address

_____
City   *State*   *Zip Code*   *Country*

INDEX

Page numbers in bold type indicate maps.

Other Books from John Muir Publications

2 to 22 Days in Asia, 192 pp. $10.95

2 to 22 Days in Australia, 192 pp. $10.95

2 to 22 Days in California, 1995 ed., 192 pp. $11.95

2 to 22 Days in Eastern Canada, 1995 ed., 240 pp $11.95

2 to 22 Days in Florida, 1995 ed., 192 pp. $11.95

2 to 22 Days Around the Great Lakes, 1995 ed., 192 pp. $11.95

2 to 22 Days in Hawaii, 1995 ed., 192 pp. $11.95

2 to 22 Days in New England, 1995 ed., 192 pp. $11.95

2 to 22 Days in New Zealand, 192 pp. $10.95

2 to 22 Days in the Pacific Northwest, 1995 ed., 192 pp. $11.95

2 to 22 Days in the Rockies, 1995 ed., 192 pp. $11.95

2 to 22 Days in Texas, 1995 ed., 192 pp. $11.95

2 to 22 Days in Thailand, 192 pp. $10.95

22 Days Around the World, 264 pp. $13.95

Other Terrific Travel Titles

The 100 Best Small Art Towns in America, 224 pp. $12.95

Elderhostels: The Students' Choice, 2nd ed., 304 pp. $15.95

Environmental Vacations: Volunteer Projects to Save the Planet, 2nd ed., 248 pp. $16.95

A Foreign Visitor's Guide to America, 224 pp. $12.95

Great Cities of Eastern Europe, 256 pp. $16.95

Indian America: A Traveler's Companion, 3rd ed., 432 pp. $18.95

Interior Furnishings Southwest, 256 pp. $19.95

Opera! The Guide to Western Europe's Great Houses, 296 pp. $18.95

Paintbrushes and Pistols:

How the Taos Artists Sold the West, 288 pp. $17.95

The People's Guide to Mexico, 9th ed., 608 pp. $18.95

Ranch Vacations: The Complete Guide to Guest and Resort, Fly-Fishing, and Cross-Country Skiing Ranches, 3rd ed., 512 pp. $19.95

The Shopper's Guide to Art and Crafts in the Hawaiian Islands, 272 pp. $13.95

The Shopper's Guide to Mexico, 224 pp. $9.95

Understanding Europeans, 272 pp. $14.95

A Viewer's Guide to Art: A Glossary of Gods, People, and Creatures, 144 pp. $10.95

Watch It Made in the U.S.A.: A Visitor's Guide to the Companies that Make Your Favorite Products, 272 pp. $16.95

Parenting Titles

Being a Father: Family, Work, and Self, 176 pp. $12.95

Preconception: A Woman's Guide to Preparing for Pregnancy and Parenthood, 232 pp. $14.95

Schooling at Home: Parents, Kids, and Learning, 264 pp., $14.95

Teens: A Fresh Look, 240 pp. $14.95

Automotive Titles

The Greaseless Guide to Car Care Confidence, 224 pp. $14.95

How to Keep Your Datsun/Nissan Alive, 544 pp. $21.95

How to Keep Your Subaru Alive, 480 pp. $21.95

How to Keep Your Toyota Pickup Alive, 392 pp. $21.95

How to Keep Your VW Alive, 25th Anniversary ed., 464 pp. spiral bound $25

TITLES FOR YOUNG READERS AGES 8 AND UP

American Origins Series
Each is 48 pages and $12.95 hardcover.
Tracing Our English Roots
Tracing Our French Roots
Tracing Our German Roots
Tracing Our Irish Roots
Tracing Our Italian Roots
Tracing Our Japanese Roots
Tracing Our Jewish Roots
Tracing Our Polish Roots

Bizarre & Beautiful Series
Each is 48 pages, $9.95 paperback, and $14.95 hardcover.
Bizarre & Beautiful Ears
Bizarre & Beautiful Eyes
Bizarre & Beautiful Feelers
Bizarre & Beautiful Noses
Bizarre & Beautiful Tongues

Environmental Titles
Habitats: Where the Wild Things Live, 48 pp. $9.95
The Indian Way: Learning to Communicate with Mother Earth, 114 pp. $9.95
Rads, Ergs, and Cheeseburgers: The Kids' Guide to Energy and the Environment, 108 pp. $13.95
The Kids' Environment Book: What's Awry and Why, 192 pp. $13.95

Extremely Weird Series
Each is 48 pages, $9.95 paperback, and $14.95 hardcover.
Extremely Weird Bats
Extremely Weird Birds
Extremely Weird Endangered Species
Extremely Weird Fishes
Extremely Weird Frogs
Extremely Weird Insects
Extremely Weird Mammals
Extremely Weird Micro Monsters
Extremely Weird Primates
Extremely Weird Reptiles
Extremely Weird Sea Creatures
Extremely Weird Snakes
Extremely Weird Spiders

Kidding Around Travel Series
All are 64 pages and $9.95 paperback, except for *Kidding Around Spain* and *Kidding Around the National Parks of the Southwest*, which are 108 pages and $12.95 paperback.
Kidding Around Atlanta
Kidding Around Boston, 2nd ed.
Kidding Around Chicago, 2nd ed.
Kidding Around the Hawaiian Islands
Kidding Around London
Kidding Around Los Angeles
Kidding Around the National Parks of the Southwest
Kidding Around New York City, 2nd ed.
Kidding Around Paris
Kidding Around Philadelphia
Kidding Around San Diego
Kidding Around San Francisco
Kidding Around Santa Fe
Kidding Around Seattle
Kidding Around Spain
Kidding Around Washington, D.C., 2nd ed.

Kids Explore Series
Written by kids for kids, all are $9.95 paperback.
Kids Explore America's African American Heritage, 128 pp.
Kids Explore the Gifts of Children with Special Needs, 128 pp.
Kids Explore America's Hispanic Heritage, 112 pp.
Kids Explore America's Japanese American Heritage, 144 pp.

Masters of Motion Series
Each is 48 pages and $9.95 paperback.
How to Drive an Indy Race Car
How to Fly a 747
How to Fly the Space Shuttle

Rainbow Warrior Artists Series
Each is 48 pages and $14.95 hardcover.
Native Artists of Africa
Native Artists of Europe
Native Artists of North America

Rough and Ready Series
Each is 48 pages and $12.95 hardcover.
Rough and Ready Cowboys
Rough and Ready Homesteaders
Rough and Ready Loggers
Rough and Ready Outlaws and Lawmen
Rough and Ready Prospectors
Rough and Ready Railroaders

X-ray Vision Series
Each is 48 pages and $9.95 paperback.
Looking Inside the Brain
Looking Inside Cartoon Animation
Looking Inside Caves and Caverns
Looking Inside Sports Aerodynamics
Looking Inside Sunken Treasures
Looking Inside Telescopes and the Night Sky

Ordering Information
Please check your local bookstore for our books, or call **1-800-888-7504** to order direct. All orders are shipped via UPS; see chart below to calculate your shipping charge for U.S. destinations. **No post office boxes please; we must have a street address to ensure delivery**. If the book you request is not available, we will hold your check until we can ship it. Foreign orders will be shipped surface rate unless otherwise requested; please enclose $3 for the first item and $1 for each additional item.

For U.S. Orders

Totaling	Add
Up to $15.00	$4.25
$15.01 to $45.00	$5.25
$45.01 to $75.00	$6.25
$75.01 or more	$7.25

Methods of Payment
Check, money order, American Express, MasterCard, or Visa. We cannot be responsible for cash sent through the mail. For credit card orders, include your card number, expiration date, and your signature, or call **1-800-888-7504**. American Express card orders can only be shipped to billing address of cardholder. Sorry, no C.O.D.'s. Residents of sunny New Mexico, add 6.25% tax to total.

Address all orders and inquiries to:
John Muir Publications
P.O. Box 613
Santa Fe, NM 87504
(505) 982-4078
(800) 888-7504